Computers

Understanding Technology

Sixth Edition

Floyd Fuller   Brian Larson   Lisa A. Bucki   Faithe Wempen

PARADIGM
EDUCATION SOLUTIONS

St. Paul

Senior Vice President: Linda Hein
Editor in Chief: Christine Hurney
Senior Editor: Cheryl Drivdahl
Assistant Developmental Editors: Mamie Clark, Katie Werdick
Contributing Writers: Janet Blum, Jan Marrelli, Brienna R. McWade, and Nancy Muir
Director of Production: Timothy W. Larson
Production Editor: Shannon Kottke
Cover Designer: Dasha Wagner
Text Designer and Senior Design and Production Specialist: Valerie King
Art Manager, Researcher, and Illustrator: Hespenheide Design
Copy Editors and Proofreaders: Susan Freese, Communicáto, Ltd.; Sara Dovre Wudali, Buuji, Inc.; and Joanna Grote
Testers: Pat Jarvis, Jeff Johnson, and Ann E. Mills
Technical Reviewer: Brian Larson
Indexer: Teresa A. Casey
Vice President Sales and Marketing: Scott Burns
Director of Marketing: Lara Weber McLellan
Vice President of Information Technology: Chuck Bratton
Digital Projects Manager: Tom Modl
Digital Development Manager: Troy Weets
Digital Production Manager: Aaron Esnough
Senior Digital Production Specialist: Julie Johnston
Web Developer: Blue Earth Interactive
Video Producers: Braahmam Net Solutions, Dizilu Animation, Linnihan Foy Advertising, and Softcrylic, LLC
Audio Producer: Paul Kelly Audio
Interactive Practice Developer: Interactive Works

ISBN 978-0-76386-856-7 (print)
ISBN 978-0-76386-858-1 (digital)

875 Montreal Way
St. Paul, MN 55102
Email: educate@emcp.com
Website: ParadigmCollege.com

Brief Contents

Contents

Chapter 4

Using Applications
to Tackle Tasks 137

Chapter 5

Plugging In to the Internet and All Its Resources 183

Chapter 6

Networking and Communicating with Computers and Other Devices 239

Chapter 7

Taking Advantage of the Cloud: Teamwork, Apps, and Storage........285

Chapter 8

Maintaining and Managing
Your Devices 325

Chapter 9

Understanding Your Role
as a Digital Citizen:
Security, Privacy, and Ethics..........361

Chapter 10

Leveraging Technology
in Business..................................429

Chapter 11

Using Programming Concepts and Languages 491

Chapter 12

Changing Everything
with Big Data 531

Preface

For billions of people worldwide, the computer, handheld devices such as mobile phones and tablets, and the Internet help perform integral and essential life activities. In the home, we use computers to communicate quickly with family and friends, manage our finances, control appliances, enjoy music and games, shop for products and services, and much more. In the workplace, computers enable us to become more efficient, productive, and creative employees, and make it possible for companies to connect almost instantly with suppliers and partners everywhere, including the other side of the world. Mobile devices help keep us engaged and productive wherever we are, providing essential features such as messaging and navigation, productivity software, and even games and online media for entertainment on the go.

Computers: Understanding Technology, Sixth Edition, will help prepare you for the modern workplace, in which most careers require basic computer skills. Many jobs require more advanced skills with a variety of software and hardware, giving employees with the desired skills and knowledge an advantage. This book will help you start developing the tech skills you need for job survival and career growth, as well as introduce you to a wide variety of technology career possibilities.

Textbook Overview

Computers: Understanding Technology introduces basic concepts in computer and information technology. Instructors and experts participating in surveys, reviews, and focus groups have contributed to ongoing improvements that have emerged in the various editions of this book. Throughout the various editions, we have incorporated their feedback to create an innovative, effective computer concepts program intended to meet and exceed your needs and expectations. In this newest edition, we updated figures, references, and examples in the textbook and other program resources to align with the latest versions of Microsoft and Apple operating systems (Windows 10 and Mac OS X El Capitan) and Microsoft Office 2016. We also updated facts and figures throughout to represent the most current information available.

This textbook is offered in two versions to match the needs of the most common computer concepts courses. The brief version consists of five chapters covering the digital world, hardware, software, the Internet, and computer applications. The comprehensive version consists of 13 chapters, beginning with the identical five chapters and adding eight chapters covering networking and communication, the cloud, maintaining and managing devices, security and ethics, technology in business, programming, big data, and the future of computing.

Program Methodology and Structure

Computers: Understanding Technology, Sixth Edition, is a competency-based, objective-driven program that provides concept-level feedback. The textbook is divided into chapters, each focusing on a single goal. Each chapter is divided into learning objectives, and each learning objective covers a number of key concepts. The learning objectives are numbered for easy reference, and the key concepts (also called *key terms*) are boldfaced.

This structure allows you and your instructor to customize learning for your own particular situation. Before starting each learning objective (that is, each numbered section in the textbook), you can go to your SNAP Assignments page to take an interactive Precheck quiz. You will receive immediate feedback, including a Study Plan indicating which key concepts require further study and identifying the chapter resources you can use to master those concepts. At any point during or after your study of a particular objective, you may take the Recheck quiz to assess your progress.

Chapter Features

The following visual guide shows how you can use this program's interactive and enriching features to reinforce and expand on the concepts presented in the main body of the text.

Goals and Objectives

Chapter Goal provides a concise statement of the objectives covered in the chapter.

> **Chapter Goal**
>
> To learn about the types of applications available and be able to select an appropriate application for the task you need to complete

Learning Objectives are numbered and align with the major sections of the chapter.

> **Learning Objectives**
>
> **4.1** Explain the ways in which application software is classified, sold, and licensed.
>
> **4.2** Differentiate between types of business productivity software and select the right tool for a task.

Numbered section headings divide a chapter into major sections that align with the chapter learning objectives.

> **4.1 Distinguishing between Types of Application Software**
>
> **Application software** enables users to do useful and fun things with a Applications are available for almost every computing need you can ima

Interactive Quizzes and Activities

SNAP icons (🅢) indicate interactive resources that are available in SNAP. Go to your SNAP Assignments page to complete these quizzes and activities.

Precheck quizzes test your knowledge of the learning objectives before you study the material. Use the results to help focus your study on the concepts you need to learn.

> 🅢 Precheck **4.1**
>
> Check your understanding of the concepts covered by this objective.

Video Activities highlight interesting tech topics, directly related to material that is covered in the textbook. Each tutorial ends with five Checkpoint review questions.

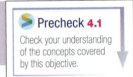

> 🅢 Activity **4.1.2**
>
> Video
> **Installing Applications**

Practice Activities engage you in drag-and-drop interactions to reinforce and test your knowledge and understanding of key figures.

> 🅢 Activity **4.1.1**
>
> Practice
> **Software Distribution Types**

Article Activities expand chapter content with relevant and interesting topics. Each article ends with five Checkpoint review questions.

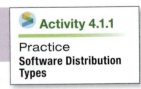

> 🅢 Activity **4.1.4**
>
> Article
> **Software Licensing Arrangements**

Recheck quizzes at the end of each section enable you to recheck your understanding of the key concepts covered in the section. You may recheck your understanding at any time and as many times as you wish.

> 🅢 Recheck **4.1**
>
> Recheck your understanding of the concepts covered by this objective.

Tracking Down Tech features challenge you to get off the computer and out of the study lab—to explore on campus and beyond to learn about technology while completing a scavenger hunt.

Tracking Down Tech ⟩⟩⟩⟩⟩

Everyday Applications

Many people use computer applications on a daily basis to accomplish their work, keep their homes and families organized, and entertain themselves. By seeing what applications other people have found useful, you can get ideas for how you might use a computer yourself. Complete this scavenger hunt to discover what applications your friends, coworkers, classmates, and family members use in their daily activities.

Tech Career Explorer features help you explore a wide variety of tech career options and opportunities. Activities range from completing interactive tutorials to researching and writing.

Tech Career Explorer 🌐 🌐

Microsoft Certifications

If you like working with applications and helping other people figure them out, look into certification as a Microsoft Office Specialist (MOS) or a Microsoft Certified Trainer (MCT). Becoming a MOS involves testing your ability to use Office applications. To learn more, complete this exercise.

Hands On features provide step-by-step instructions for specific tech tasks that are directly related to the concept material you are studying.

Hands On 👆👆👆👆👆👆

Using a Word Template to Create a Flyer

Using the templates in Microsoft Word to create documents is very easy. Follow the steps in this resource to create a flyer in Word 2016.

Textbook Elements and Online Connections

Rich graphics and textbook features explore related and relevant topics. Bold blue links (e.g., http://CUT6.emcp.net/WindowsPhone) connect you to websites with relevant information. Open the links menu in your ebook to access live versions of these links.

Infographics, figures, tables, and photos add interesting facts and visual emphasis to support your understanding of important concepts.

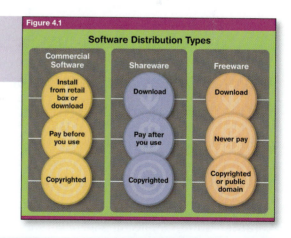

Figure 4.1

Practical Tech features provide real-world examples and advice about the best technologies or methods you can use to accomplish tasks or achieve objectives.

Practical TECH ⚙⚙⚙⚙⚙⚙⚙

Syncing between Phones and Computers

Many smartphones have calendar, email, contacts, and to-do list utilities. If your phone and your computer run operating systems by the same company (for example, if they are both Apple or both Microsoft) and the PIM application on your computer is also by that manufacturer, then you should have no trouble setting up the application to synchronize PIM data between the two devices without any special setup.

If your phone and computer have different platforms (such as an iPhone and a Windows desktop or a Windows phone and an Apple Macintosh notebook), then synchronization may be more difficult. If you have a Windows phone and a Mac computer, download the Windows Phone for Mac application from Microsoft (available at http://CUT6.emcp.net/WindowsPhone). If you have an iPhone and a Windows computer, you can use the iTunes application to synchronize your phone and Microsoft Outlook, as described at http://CUT6.emcp.net/SyncingMSContacts.

Hotspot features focus on wireless technology and its interesting twists, perspectives, and uses related to communications and community-building issues.

Hotspot

The App-ification of the Software Industry

As more and more people switch to mobile devices as their primary computing tools, apps are becoming an increasingly larger share of the software market. The Apple Store has over 1.5 million apps for the iPhone and iPad, and more are being added every day. App developers have earned more than $25 billion from Apple Store sales.

A key characteristic of most apps is their specialization: each app performs one task, or a narrow range of tasks. Rather than purchase a large suite of applications, as for a desktop, a mobile user can select a customized combination of apps that accomplish the specific tasks he or she needs to perform, such as playing music clips, browsing a certain social networking site, or checking stock prices. Apps are typically very inexpensive ($5 or less), so consumers can afford to take chances on new apps that promise new capabilities.

This trend toward specialized apps has affected the software industry overall. As consumers become accustomed to using a different app for each task they perform, they start looking at desktop software in new ways. In the future, you may see desktop software become more compact, more specialized, and simpler to install and remove. App popularity is also encouraging programmers to work independently to develop and sell their own apps, rather than work with large software development teams on large desktop applications.

Cutting Edge features showcase hot new technologies.

Cutting Edge

Gaming-Optimized PCs

People who are serious about game playing are often people who don't mind spending more money on a computer to ensure the best possible gaming experience. A whole subclass of desktop computers (and some notebook computers) has been designed with game playing in mind. These computers have the very best of all the components that a game relies on, including CPU, RAM, display adapter, monitor, and sound.

But a gaming computer doesn't stop at having high-quality basic components. Gaming computers are often flashy models designed to express the personalities of their owners, with colored lights, colored components, nontraditional cooling systems (for example, water cooling instead of traditional air cooling), semitransparent or unusually shaped cases, and elaborate logos. One popular line of gaming computers is Alienware, a division of Dell Computers. (Visit http://CUT6.emcp.net/Alienware to see their latest offerings and price out your ideal system.)

Tech Ethics features highlight ethical issues and situations in IT. Throughout the book, these features provide an ongoing discussion of ethics in the profession.

Tech Ethics

Paying for Shareware

Some shareware is distributed through an honor system. The developer makes available to the public a full-featured version of the program with no time limits and asks people to send in money if they like and continue to use the product. This distribution method worked well in the early days of the Internet. At that time, most of the people who downloaded shareware were tech enthusiasts—among them, many programmers who understood the time and effort put into developing shareware. But today, shareware developers who don't demand payment by limiting the program's features or usage time seldom get paid.

Suppose you download a shareware application for free and digitally sign a license agreement in which you promise to pay for the software if you continue to use it after 14 days. Will you make that payment if you use the software beyond the 14-day limit? Why or why not? Does it matter how much the payment is or what payment methods are available?

Chapter Review and Reinforcement

A variety of study aids and exercises offer ample opportunities to check your understanding of the chapter content. Green go-online icons () indicate interactive study resources that are available in your ebook.

SNAP icons (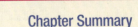) indicate interactive exercises that are available in SNAP; go to your SNAP Assignments page to complete these exercises.

Chapter Summary features highlight the most important concepts for each major section of the chapter. Interactive **Chapter Summaries**, **Study Notes** documents, and **Slide Presentations** with audio support are accessed from the links menu in your ebook.

174   Chapter 4 Using Applications to Tackle Tasks

Chapter Summary

An interactive Chapter Summary, Study Notes, and a Slide Presentation with audio are available from the links menu on this page in your ebook.

4.1 Distinguishing between Types of Application Software

Application software can be categorized as **individual application software**, **collaboration software**, or **vertical application software** based on the number of people it serves at once. Application software can also be divided into **desktop applications** versus **apps**.

In addition, software can be categorized by how it's developed and sold: as **commercial software**, **shareware**, or **freeware**. Commercial software may have **software piracy** features, such as a **registra-** calculating them are called **formulas**. Formulas can contain **functions**, which are named instructions for performing a calculation (such as COUNT and AVERAGE). A spreadsheet consists of **cells** arranged in a grid of rows and columns; each cell can be formatted separately. You can make **charts** based on the values in cells and record **macros** (sets of memorized steps) to save time in performing commonly repeated tasks.

A database is a collection of data organized into one or more data tables. Each table contains records, which are collections of data about specific instances. The parts of a record are called *fields*

Key Terms features list the key concepts you should know after completing each major section of the chapter. An interactive **Glossary** provides additional study opportunities and is accessed from the links menu in your ebook.

Chapter Exercises features offer opportunities to check your knowledge through the following categories of questions and prompts. Interactive **Flash Cards** and **Games** offer more options for self-assessment and are accessed from the links menu in your ebook.

- Terms Check: Matching
- Knowledge Check: Multiple-Choice
- Key Principles: Completion
- Tech Illustrated: Figure Labeling
- Tech to Come: Brainstorming
- Tech Literacy: Internet Research and Writing
- Tech Issues: Team Problem-Solving
- Tech Timeline: Predicting Next Steps
- Ethical Dilemmas: Group Discussion and Debate

Interactive versions of the **Terms Check**, **Knowledge Check**, **Key Principles**, and **Tech Illustrated** exercises are available in SNAP. Go to your SNAP Assignments page to complete these exercises.

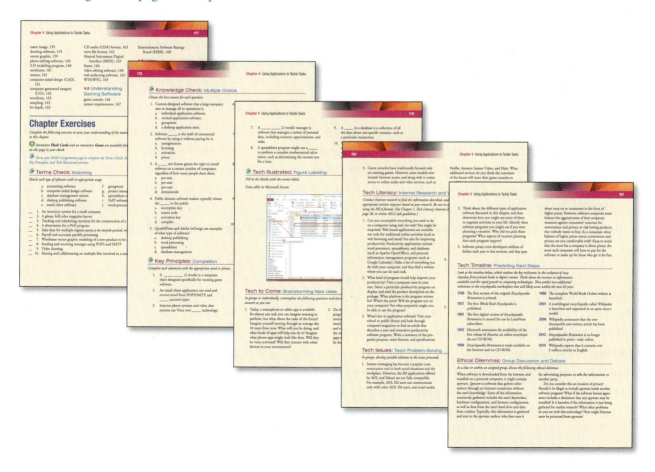

Course Components

The *Computers: Understanding Technology*, Sixth Edition, textbook contains all the content you will need to master the introductory concepts covered in the quizzes and exams that are provided with this program. Additional resources offered by the following digital components can enhance and reinforce the learning experience.

SNAP Web-Based Training and Assessment for Microsoft® Office 2016

SNAP is a web-based training and assessment program and learning management system (LMS) for computer technology courses and Microsoft Office 2016. SNAP offers rich content, a sophisticated grade book, and robust scheduling and analytics tools. SNAP courseware supports the *Computers: Understanding Technology* content and delivers easy access to all course materials.

The SNAP course includes a Precheck quiz and Recheck quiz for each major section in the book, and an exam for each chapter. It also provides a concept exam item bank for each chapter, which can be used to create custom exams. Each quiz and exam item is aligned to a key concept (boldfaced key term) and a learning objective. This pairing allows students to check their understanding of each key concept through a self-administered quiz, and instructors to test understanding of the same concept through an assigned exam.

SNAP provides automatic scoring and detailed feedback on the program's many objective exercises and assessments to help identify areas where additional support is needed, evaluating student performance at both the individual level and the course level. The SNAP Study Planner charts student performance on Precheck and Recheck quizzes and on instructor-scheduled exams. Each assessment question is keyed to a learning objective. When a student takes an assessment, SNAP generates a Study Planner report showing how the student did on each objective covered. The report can be filtered by objectives mastered, objectives still to be learned, and objectives not yet assessed. The Study Planner can generate this report for a given assessment, for a chapter, or for the whole course. For each learning objective still to be learned, the Study Planner provides quick access to the specific ebook content covering that objective, allowing students to focus their review and maximize their study time.

The *Computers: Understanding Technology* SNAP course content is also available to export into any LMS system that supports LTI tools. Paradigm Education Solutions provides technical support for SNAP through 24-7 chat at ParadigmCollege.com. In addition, an online user guide and other training tools for SNAP are available.

Student eBook

The student ebook provides access to the *Computers: Understanding Technology* text and study resources from any type of computing device (desktop, tablet, or smartphone), anywhere, through a live Internet connection. The versatile ebook platform features dynamic navigation tools including a linked table of contents and the ability to jump to specific pages, search for terms, bookmark, highlight, and take notes. The student ebook is accessed through SNAP.

Instructor eResources

All instructor resources are available digitally through a web-based ebook online at Paradigm.bookshelf.emcp.com. The materials are organized by type and can be previewed from the ebook or downloaded. The instructor materials include the following items:

- Open-ended, optional Bonus Exercises for selected article activities
- Answer keys, model answers, and rubrics for evaluating responses to chapter activities and exercises

- Lesson blueprints with teaching hints, lecture tips, and discussion questions
- Syllabus suggestions and course planning resources
- PowerPoint presentations with lecture notes
- Quiz and exam item banks

  Instructors can use the banks of over 2,000 multiple-choice and true/false items to create customized tests. The banks are organized by learning objective and divided into quiz banks and exam banks. Each key concept in the textbook has a related quiz item and exam item—so the quizzes can be used for formative assessment and the exams for summative assessment. Approximately 10 percent of the questions include graphics based on key figures and tables from the textbook.

Acknowledgments

Creating and publishing a book requires the dedicated efforts of many people. Throughout this project, we authors have had the pleasure and privilege of working closely with the highly skilled and quality-focused professionals at Paradigm Education Solutions, a division of New Mountain Learning.

We offer our sincere appreciation to Senior Vice President Linda Hein and Director of Editorial Christine Hurney for their continued support of this program. Both Senior Editor Cheryl Drivdahl and Digital Projects Manager Tom Modl deserve special recognition for the long hours they dedicated to helping us refine the content of the textbook and enhance the interactive and online components of this total learning package. Working closely with these professionals has been a privilege and a pleasure. To the entire team of editors, designers, programmers, proofreaders, testers, and others who worked on this program, we extend our thanks and gratitude.

Consultants and Reviewers

We thank the instructors and other professionals who provided valuable feedback about the enhancements made for this edition. As instructors who teach introductory computer courses, and as practicing professionals who are knowledgeable about the latest computer technologies, they brought a real-world perspective to the project.

Gilbert Armour
Virginia Western Community College
Roanoke, Virginia

Debbie J. Ball
Tennessee College of Applied
    Technology—Murfreesboro
Murfreesboro, Tennessee

Susan Healey
Senior Systems Engineer at Earthsoft
Northfield, Minnesota

Paul Koester
Tarrant County College
Fort Worth, Texas

Thomas P. Martin, Ed.D.
Shasta College
Redding, California

Pat McKeown
Independent IT Consultant
    and Business Analyst
Plymouth, Minnesota

Lisa M. Moeller
Chatfield College
St. Martin, Ohio

Jeffrey Spector
Middlesex County College
Edison, New Jersey

Chapter 1

Touring Our Digital World

Chapter Goal

To explore the expanding computer and technology field and learn how computers work and impact our lives

Learning Objectives

1.1 Give examples of digital technologies.

1.2 Discuss the advantages of using computers.

1.3 Briefly explain how computing works.

1.4 Differentiate between computers and computer systems.

1.5 Identify the hardware and software that make up a computer system.

1.6 Describe the categories of computers.

Green go-online icons indicate resources that are accessed from the links menu in your ebook.

SNAP icons indicate interactive resources that are available in SNAP. Go to your SNAP Assignments page to complete these quizzes, activities, and exercises.

1.1 Being Immersed in Digital Technology

Computers and other "smart" digital devices permeate our daily lives. High-definition TVs (HDTVs) display amazingly clear, colorful images of sports events, reality shows, and other popular programs. Smart TVs can connect to the Internet, enabling you to download movies and other content on demand. Smartphones and tablets equipped with a plethora of useful apps simplify and speed up your daily routines. Appliances with smart technology built in help you make coffee at a set time, control home heating and cooling costs, manage home lighting, and more. Your car is likely run by an onboard computer and may include such features as global positioning system (GPS) navigation, hands-free calling via your smartphone and Bluetooth, hard disk storage for digital music, and even streaming digital music from another device or playing music from satellite radio stations.

Manufacturers increasingly use computerized robots to build products and manage shipping. Businesses increasingly rely on electronic mail (email) to communicate internally and externally, as well as a growing number of other information

 Precheck 1.1

Check your understanding of the concepts covered by this objective.

 Activity 1.1.1

Video
A Digital Lifestyle

Many appliances now include digital technology that enables you to use your smartphone to control them when you are away. For example, you can use the 6th Sense Live technology from Whirlpool to start and pause this washer and dryer remotely.

Smartphones have become so common in everyday life that most people would be lost without them.

Tracking Down Tech »»»»»

Watching Technology Add Up in Your Life

The world isn't yet paperless, but it's swiftly embracing technology that's leading us in that direction. Computers and other types of devices that you will learn about in this chapter are being used increasingly for education, business, and personal planning and tracking. You can see this change in your own daily activities, such as visiting your local coffee shop or other hangout to chat with friends, plan your week, and study. To start observing how technological changes have driven new habits and behaviors and how these changes impact your life, complete this scavenger hunt in which you identify computing devices in action on campus and beyond.

technology tools. **Information technology (IT)** is the use of computer, electronics, and telecommunications equipment and technologies to gather, process, store, and transfer data. For example, even a small business such as your dentist or hair stylist likely tracks appointments using a computerized system that may also include the capability to send you an appointment reminder via text message. The next several years could see the rapid growth of technology in the medical field, as providers

Figure 1.1

Source: Gartner, Inc., 2015

Figure 1.2

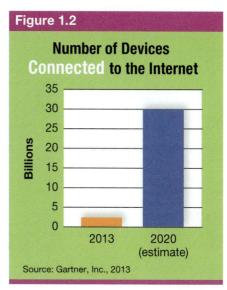

Source: Gartner, Inc., 2013

strive to make medical care easier to deliver and more cost effective. Around the world, we spend trillions of dollars on all kinds of information technology every year (see Figure 1.1).

In 2015, approximately 84 percent of US residents used the Internet from home, school, or another location, according to the Pew Research Center—and the number of devices connected to the Internet is expected to increase twelvefold by 2020 (see Figure 1.2). In today's world, very few people go even a single day without interacting with some type of digital technology. What about you? How digital is your life?

Like most people, you probably realize that you interact with electronic devices every day. Nevertheless, if you completed the Tracking Down Tech activity for this chapter, you might have been surprised by the large number of your digital experiences. The extent to which computers and digital technology drive daily life has led historians to characterize today's world as a "digital world." You likely know that the term *digital* has something to do with computers. Here's a closer look at what the term really means and why it's important.

Digital Information

The term **digital** describes an electronic signal that's processed, sent, and stored in discrete (separate) parts called *bits*. In contrast, an analog electronic signal is continuous, but the voltage, frequency, and current vary to represent information in a wave form. Other forms of analog signals include sound waves, light waves (which produce variations in intensity and color), and more. For example, the continuous sweep of the second hand on an old clock face provides an analog representation of time passing, while the numbers on a digital clock face present discrete, digital indications of the time.

"On" and "off" electrical states represent the discrete parts (bits) of a digital signal. Those states correspond to the digits 1 (on) and 0 (off). In a computer or digital device, this system of 1s and 0s corresponding to on and off electrical currents represents all information. Thus, computers use digital information, and computer technology in general is considered digital technology. You will learn more about this fundamental IT concept in later chapters, but for now, remember that *digital* refers to information represented by numbers.

Activity 1.1.2

Video
Analog versus Digital

Activity 1.1.3

Video
Digitizing Information

The WeMo Insight Switch, one of Belkin's home automation products, lets you use your smartphone or tablet to control any appliance you plug into the switch.

Computerized Devices versus Computers

Digital processing occurs within miniature electrical transistors etched onto a tiny square of silicon or another material called a *chip*, a *microprocessor*, or an *integrated circuit* (*IC*). Digital cameras, basic-feature mobile phones and smartphones, electronic appliances, and computers all contain electronic chips. However, the chips within computerized devices differ considerably depending on the purpose or functionality of the device. Generally, computers require more from chips in terms of power and capability, a distinction that separates electronic devices into two broad groups: special-purpose or embedded computers and general-purpose computers (also simply called *computers*).

The chip comprising a special-purpose or **embedded computer** (or *embedded system*) performs just a few specific actions. For example, the embedded chip in a digital camera automatically controls the speed of the lens, so that the right amount of light enters through the lens. The embedded chip in a bar code scanner reads the bar code on a clothing tag, converts it to digital information, and sends it to the computer or system that uses the digital information to identify the item and its price. The tiny chip in a digital thermometer helps determine the body temperature of a patient at a medical clinic. Embedded chips in home appliances enable you to program the appliances for a delayed start and other automatic operations, or you can set up home automation via smart switches that enable you to control appliances and lighting.

The microprocessor chips in a **general-purpose computer**, on the other hand, provide numerous powerful capabilities and work with programs that enable the system to perform a range of complex processes and calculations. For example, you can use a computer with a word-processing program installed to create, edit, print, and save various kinds of documents, including letters, memos, reports, and brochures. A **computer**, therefore, is defined as an electronic device that
- has one or more chips, memory, and storage that together enable it to operate under the control of a set of instructions called a **program**;
- accepts data that a user supplies;
- manipulates the data according to the programmed instructions;
- produces the results (information) from the data manipulation; and
- stores the results for future use.

Hands On

Finding Out What Processor Your Computer Has

Follow the steps in this resource to find out what processor your computer system has.

Numerous companies design and/or manufacture micropro-cessors. Some, such as longtime chip pioneer Intel, make multiple types of processors for all types of computers, includ-ing desktop and larger comput-ers, mobile notebook computers and tablets, smartphones, and embedded systems. Others focus on particular types of proces-sors. For example, Qualcomm designs and licenses processing technology primarily for mobile and wireless devices, and has been moving into embedded technologies for markets such as automotive and consumer elec-tronics, as well as releasing its own smartwatch. Still other chip companies excel in a particular niche or two, such as the graphics processors pioneered by NVIDIA and NVIDIA's mobile processors.

Computer processors, such as the Intel Core i7, may have multiple processing cores and enable both desktop and mobile computers to handle powerful business and creative activities while conserving power.

Recheck 1.1
Recheck your under-standing of the concepts covered by this objective.

1.2 Discovering the Computer Advantage

Precheck 1.2
Check your understanding of the concepts covered by this objective.

Before the early 1980s, the average person had never seen a computer, let alone used one. The limited number of computers that existed were relatively large, bulky systems confined to secure computer centers in corporate and government facilities. Referred to as *mainframes*, these computers required intense maintenance, including special climate-controlled conditions and several full-time operators for each machine. Because of the expense and difficulty involved in operating early mainframes, most

Early mainframe computers like this one were large, bulky, and difficult to operate. Many of them used large reels of magnetic tape for storage.

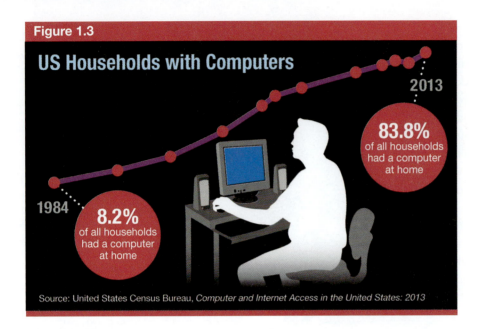

Figure 1.3

US Households with Computers

2013

83.8%
of all households
had a computer
at home

1984

8.2%
of all households
had a computer
at home

Source: United States Census Bureau, *Computer and Internet Access in the United States: 2013*

were used only by computer programmers and scientists for complex operations, such as handling large amounts of business data and compiling and analyzing study data. Other than a few researchers and technicians who had security clearances, most employees were prohibited from entering the areas housing these computers.

Beginning in the early 1980s, the computer world changed dramatically with the introduction of the **microcomputer**. This new type of computer was also called the *personal computer* (or *PC*), because it was designed for easy operation by an individual user. Compared to mainframes, personal computers were more affordable, significantly smaller, and much easier to use. Within a few years, many workplaces relied on PCs for handling a variety of tasks. Today, you can find personal computers alongside standard appliances in homes and schools (see Figure 1.3).

Today's computers come in a variety of shapes and sizes and differ significantly in computing capability, speed, and price. For example, a powerful corporate computer capable of processing millions of customer records in a few minutes may cost millions of dollars, while a small office desktop computer used for creating correspondence and budget forecasts typically costs less than $1,000. Whatever the size, power, or cost, all computers offer advantages over manual technologies in the following areas:

- Speed
- Accuracy
- Versatility
- Storage capabilities
- Communications capabilities

Speed

Today's computers operate with lightning-like speed, and processing speeds will continue to increase as computer manufacturers introduce new and improved models. Contemporary PCs can execute billions of program instructions in one second. Some of the most powerful computers (such as supercomputers) can execute quadrillions of instructions per second. A rate this fast is needed to process the huge amounts of data involved in forecasting weather, mapping how blood flows through the human body, constructing scientific models that re-create the Big Bang, conducting national cybersecurity operations to thwart cyberattacks, and more.

 **Activity 1.2.1**

Video
Computer History I

 **Activity 1.2.2**

Video
Computer History II

 **Activity 1.2.3**

Video
Computer History III

 **Activity 1.2.4**

Video
Computer History IV

Accuracy

People sometimes blame human errors and mistakes on a computer. In truth, computers offer extreme accuracy when they are equipped with error-free programs and are processing accurate user-entered data. Computer professionals like to use the phrase **garbage in, garbage out (GIGO)**, which means that if a program has logical or other errors and/or the data entered for processing has errors, then the resulting output can only be inaccurate.

Let's say you're shopping and the store owner uses a computer and program to track the sale, calculate the sales tax due, and print your receipt. If the program has an error, such as the wrong sales tax rate, or the store owner types the wrong price, the receipt will show the wrong amount due. Using high-quality, error-free computer programs and double-checking the accuracy of the data you enter will help ensure you won't get garbage out.

Computers, such as those found on communications, imaging, and weather satellites, can process information with speed and accuracy. For example, both the National Aeronautics and Space Administration (NASA) and Google Earth rely on satellites to take digital images of the Earth and then organize and beam that information back for analysis and mapping.

Practical TECH

Tapping the Crowd's Opinion

You don't always need to pay high prices for computer programs. You can often find good free or low-cost programs and apps for your computer or mobile device at a variety of online stores and download websites. However, a free or low-cost program isn't a bargain if it doesn't work as expected, has errors, is difficult to use, or otherwise wastes your time. Fortunately, most online stores and websites ask users to rate how well programs performed and then display the results. Some also offer a "Comments" feature that lets users explain their ratings. Before you download a program, check out the ratings and comments from other users. These will give you a sense of how well the program works and whether it will perform as advertised.

Versatility

Computers and mobile devices provide amazing versatility. With the right programs or apps installed, a computer or device can perform a variety of personal, business, and scientific applications. Families use computers for entertainment, communications, budgeting, online shopping, completing homework assignments, playing games, and listening to music. Banks use computers to conduct money transfers and account withdrawals. Retailers use computers to process sales transactions and check on product availability. Manufacturers can manage entire production, warehousing, and selling processes with computerized systems and smart devices. Schools use computers for keeping records, conducting distance-learning courses, scheduling events, and analyzing budgets. Universities, government agencies, hospitals, and scientific organizations conduct life-enhancing research using computers.

Members of a family may use computers for a variety of purposes: budgeting and paying bills, corresponding with friends and relatives, shopping online, completing homework assignments, viewing and printing photos, playing games, and listening to music.

Perhaps the most ambitious computer-based scientific research of all time was the Human Genome Project (HGP), completed in April 2003, more than two years ahead of schedule and at a cost considerably lower than originally forecast. This project represented an international effort to sequence the 3 billion DNA (deoxyribonucleic acid) letters in the human genome, which is the collection of gene types that makes up every person. Scientists from all over the world can now access the genome database and use the information to research ways of improving human health and fighting disease. They can also share that information with others, as the US government's National Human Genome Research Institute does in its website (see Figure 1.4).

Figure 1.4

The National Human Genome Research Institute (NHGRI) funds genetic and genomic research, studies the related ethics, and provides educational resources to the public and to health professionals. The NHGRI uses computers to gather and process the data from its various research projects, as well as to present that information in a variety of digital formats that members of the public can access via computer.

Storage

Program and data storage revolutionized early computing by making computers incredibly flexible. Once you have installed a program, it's stored in the computer. This means that you and other users can access it again and again to process different data. For example, you can install the spreadsheet program Microsoft Excel and then access it repeatedly to track budget items and to explore possible outcomes if income and expenses change.

A flash drive can hold a large amount of data in a small physical space. It is also highly portable, allowing you to move information easily from one computer to another.

Computers can store huge amounts of data in comparably tiny physical spaces. For example, one compact disc (CD) can store about 109,000 pages of magazine text. Internal storage devices and many external storage devices offer capacities many times larger than a CD.

Communications

Most modern computers and devices contain equipment and programs that enable them to communicate with other computers through cable connections, fiber-optic cables, satellites, and wireless connections. Connecting these devices allows users to share programs, data, information, messages, and equipment (such as printers). The structure in which computers are linked using special programs and equipment is called a *network* (see Figure 1.5). Wireless networks enable users to communicate and share data over wireless connections by connecting devices such as tablets, smart-phones, and wireless-capable printers.

A network can be relatively small or quite large. A local area network (LAN) operates within a relatively small geographical area, such as a home, office building,

---

Figure 1.5

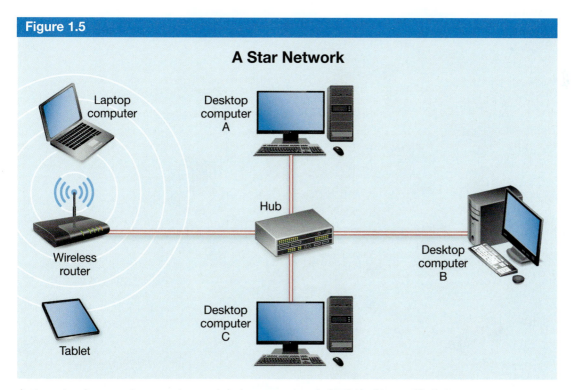

A star network connects computers and devices over a central hub. In this modified star network, the wireless router that's connected to the hub enables computers and devices to connect to the network wirelessly.

factory, or school campus. A wide area network (WAN) links many LANs and might connect a company's manufacturing plants located throughout the United States.

Constant, quick connections, along with other computer technologies, have helped boost productivity for many manufacturers. For example, some manufacturers reduce production time by networking production equipment to share information with other planning and production systems in the organization.

The Internet: A Super Network The network you are most likely familiar with is the Internet, which is the world's largest network. The **Internet** (also called the *net*) is a worldwide network made up of large and small networks linked by communications hardware, software, telephone, cable, fiber-optic, wireless, and satellite systems for the purposes of communicating and sharing information (see Figure 1.6). Network service providers (NSPs) provide access to Internet service providers (ISPs), who sell various types of Internet access to consumers. The ISPs use different connection types to deliver the access.

Figure 1.6

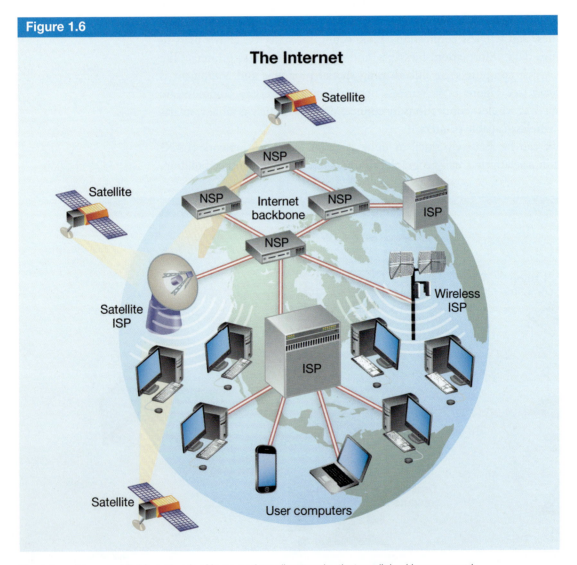

The Internet is a worldwide network of large and small networks that are linked by communications hardware and software for the purposes of communicating and sharing information.

Figure 1.7

An ISP such as att.net offers users Internet access, daily weather reports, news stories, and other types of information.

As of 2015, more than 3.2 billion people worldwide used the Internet for various purposes:

- Sending and receiving email
- Finding information, such as weather forecasts, maps, stock quotes, news reports, airline schedules, and newspaper and magazine articles
- Buying and selling products and services
- Taking online courses
- Using social media
- Accessing entertainment, such as online games and music

Many Internet service providers (ISPs) offer Internet access and provide a portal that displays daily weather reports, stock quotes, news, and other types of information (see Figure 1.7, for example). Users can leave the ISP's portal to access other websites of interest.

The World Wide Web A widely used part of the Internet is the World Wide Web (WWW or web), a global system within the Internet that enables users to move from one linked website or web page to another. A website is a collection of web pages stored on a web server. A web page is an electronic document that may contain text, images, sound, video, and links to other web pages and websites. Some websites and web pages have interactive features, such as online shopping carts, pop-up descriptions, and self-guided slide shows. Other websites offer cloud-based services, such as online file storage, that you'll learn more about in Chapter 7.

When using the web, you can navigate directly to a particular page or browse to a location by following hyperlinks. When you aren't sure where to find the information you need, you can use a search engine,

Tech Career Explorer

Taking a Look at Web Jobs

Chapter 5 provides more details about the Internet, the web, and the growing number of things you can do and find online. If you are curious about what kinds of web-related careers await you, complete this exercise for an overview of the possibilities.

Figure 1.8

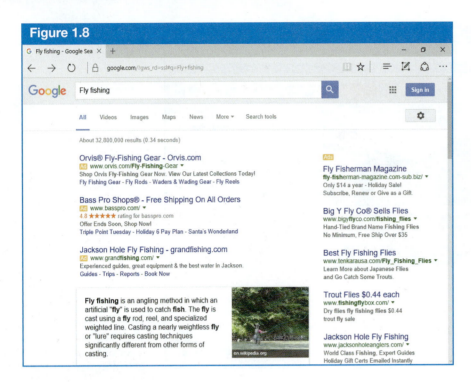

A search engine such as Google enables the user to search for, locate, and retrieve information available on the World Wide Web.

which is a website or service that enables you to enter search terms in a search box. The search engine uses those terms to locate and retrieve a list of websites and web pages that might contain the requested information. For example, if you type "Fly fishing" into a search box, the search engine will display a list of links to web sources that contain information about those terms, as shown in Figure 1.8.

 **Recheck 1.2**

Recheck your understanding of the concepts covered by this objective.

1.3 Understanding How Computers Work

 **Precheck 1.3**

Check your understanding of the concepts covered by this objective.

Understanding the broad steps involved in information processing is key to recognizing the significance of computer technology. A computer accepts the data a user enters, processes the data according to instructions provided by the program, and then outputs the data in a useful form: information. Read on to learn about how the recurring series of events that make up the *information processing cycle* change data into information.

Data and Information

Data consists of raw, unorganized facts and figures. By itself, a piece of data may be meaningless. For example, the fact that an employee has worked 40 hours in one week doesn't provide enough meaning to enable the payroll department staff to calculate his or her total pay and issue a paycheck. Entering additional data—such as the employee's pay rate, number of exemptions, and number of deductions—and then processing the data enables payroll staff to generate useful information, including paychecks, earnings statements, and payroll reports.

Data that's been processed (organized, arranged, or calculated) in a way that converts it into a useful form is called **information**. Once a computer has created information, it can display the information on screen or print it on paper. The computer also can store information for future use, such as processing monthly or quarterly payroll reports.

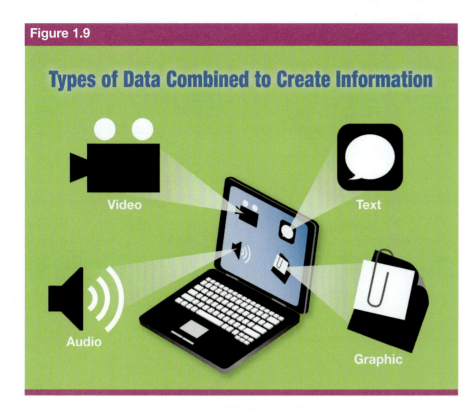

Figure 1.9

Types of Data Combined to Create Information

Video

Text

Audio

Graphic

Text, graphic, audio, and video data can all be combined to create a compelling message or presentation.

Activity 1.3.1

Practice
Types of Data Combined to Create Information

Data that's been entered into a computer can be of one or more of the following types (see Figure 1.9):

- **Text data** consists of alphabetic letters, numbers, and special characters. It might also consist of the formulas you enter in a spreadsheet program. These data typically enable the computer to produce output such as letters, email messages, reports, and sales and profit projections.
- **Graphic data** consists of still images, including photographs, charts, and drawings. Graphic data may also include various types of maps and mapped data, such as an online road map, a topographical map, a property survey map, or maps with various types of weather data.
- **Audio data** refers to sound, such as voice and music. For example, you can use a microphone to record the narration for an onscreen presentation, which the computer stores in digitized form. Or you can download music from an online service and play it back through your computer's speakers or transfer it to another playback device.
- **Video data** refers to moving pictures and images, such as webcam data from a videoconference, a video clip, or a full-length movie. For example, you might use a video camera, smartphone, or tablet to record video of a new product demonstration (demo). After transferring the video to your computer, you could play it back onscreen, share it with potential customers, or include it in a larger project for promoting the new product.

The Information Processing Cycle

Information processing (also called *data processing*) means using a computer to convert data into useful information. Processing data into information involves four basic functions: input, processing, output, and storage. During processing, the computer may perform these four functions sequentially but not always.

Figure 1.10

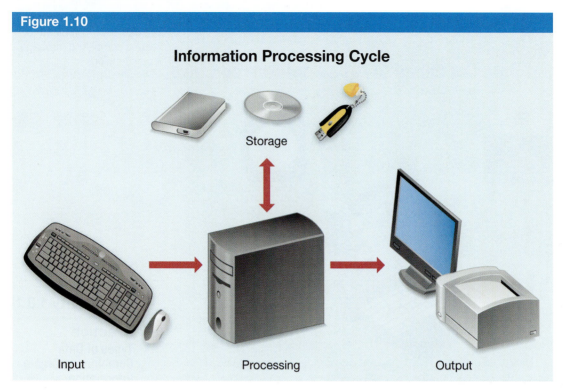

Information Processing Cycle

Storage

Input   Processing   Output

During the information processing cycle, data is entered into a computer, processed, sent as output, and then stored (if required for future use).

Figure 1.10 illustrates how these four functions form the **information processing cycle**.

The term used to identify the first step in the information processing cycle—**input**—is also used to describe physically entering data into a computer or device. After you enter data using an input device such as a keyboard, mouse, or touchscreen, the computer handles the data according to the programmed instructions. (Keep in mind that your inputs will likely also include selecting commands and options in the program being used.) **Processing** occurs in the computer's electrical circuits and creates information called **output**. Next, the computer sends the output to one or more output devices, such as a monitor or printer. Usually, you will also direct the computer to send the information to **storage** (such as a hard disk, flash drive, external hard disk, or cloud storage area) for future use. The information a computer processes can be output in a variety of forms:

- Written or textual form, such as research reports and letters
- Numerical form, such as a spreadsheet analysis of a company's finances
- Verbal or audio form, such as recorded voice and music
- Visual form, such as digital photos, drawings, and videos

1.4 Differentiating between Computers and Computer Systems

Technically, the term *computer* identifies only the system unit: the part of a desktop computer system that processes data and stores information. A **computer system**, however, includes the system unit along with input devices, output devices, and external storage devices.

Recheck 1.3
Recheck your understanding of the concepts covered by this objective.

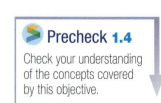

Precheck 1.4
Check your understanding of the concepts covered by this objective.

The user's individual needs and preferences will determine which additional devices he or she needs. For example, an engineer in a structural design firm will need a powerful system unit that's capable of running sophisticated design software, along with one or more large monitors, a plotter, and a multifunction device that provides printing, scanning, copying, and faxing capabilities. Most mobile computers and devices already include the built-in input and output devices that most users are likely to want, such as speakers, cameras, and touchscreens. But if you are shopping for your first desktop PC, you will probably purchase an entire system, including the system unit, keyboard, mouse, monitor, external storage devices, and perhaps a printer. Figure 1.11 shows a variety of input, processing, output, and storage devices that may be included in a PC system.

The rest of this book uses the term *computer* or *PC* to refer to a computer system that includes all of the devices necessary to input programs and data, process the data, output the results, and store the results for future use. Chapter 2 goes into detail about computer system components, including input, output, and storage devices.

You also can think about a computer system in terms of how many people can use it simultaneously. A **single-user computer system**, as the name implies, can accommodate one user at a time. This term applies to PC systems found in homes and small businesses and organizations. A **multiuser computer system** can accommodate many users at a time. Large businesses and organizations typically use such systems to enable several managers and employees to simultaneously access, use, and update information stored in a central storage location. For example, a payroll clerk can access and view an employee's payroll record from one computer connected to the system while a shipping clerk tracks a customer's shipment from a computer in the warehouse. In addition, the users can interact with each other easily and quickly.

Activity 1.4.1

Article
Major Advances in the History of Computing

Activity 1.4.2

Practice
Computer System Components

Figure 1.11

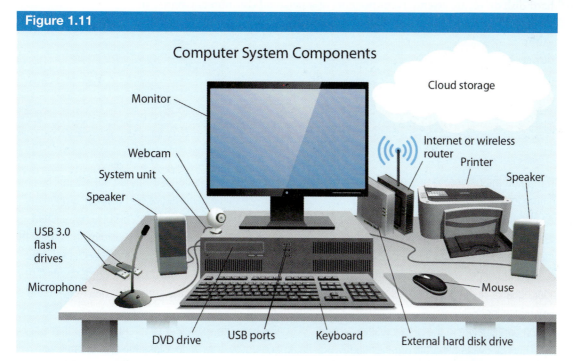

At a minimum, a desktop computer system consists of more than just the system unit, which contains the hard disk drive, video processor, central processing unit, motherboard, and power supply. It also includes a monitor, keyboard, and mouse. Users can add a variety of other input, output, and storage devices.

This book provides a lot of discussion about general-purpose, single-user computers—personal computers—that enable users to complete a variety of computing tasks. These are the computers you will most likely work with in your home, in your school's computer lab, and on the job. However, this book also covers large-scale, multiuser systems and their applications; reading about these computers will give you a sense of the scope of computing and how it affects many aspects of society.

Recheck 1.4

Recheck your understanding of the concepts covered by this objective.

Precheck 1.5

Check your understanding of the concepts covered by this objective.

1.5 Understanding Hardware and Software

A computer system includes both hardware and software. The combination of the two that makes up a particular computer system depends on the user's requirements. Given the number of hardware devices and software programs available in the marketplace, you can customize a system for nearly any purpose—from typical business use, to graphic design, to home media and entertainment, to gaming. Manufacturers typically offer a system unit, monitor, and mouse and keyboard package; the choice of the printer and other hardware devices is left up to the buyer. The majority of desktop and notebook computers come with the operating system software preinstalled, plus some basic software such as a word-processing program.

Hardware Overview

Hardware includes all the physical components that make up the system unit plus the other devices connected to it, such as a keyboard or monitor, as discussed earlier in this chapter. You can also call a connected device a **peripheral device**, because in many cases it is outside of (or peripheral to) the computer. Examples include a keyboard, mouse, webcam, and printer. Some peripheral devices, such as a monitor and internal hard disk drive, are essential components of a personal computer system. Hardware devices can be grouped into the following categories:

- System unit
- Input devices
- Output devices

Tech Ethics

Close the Gap

The year 2000 marked the beginning of the new millennium—a good time to set resolutions for the future. In that spirit, the United Nations (UN) established a set of goals to improve the lives of people around the globe. The Millennium Development Goals focused on causes that included diminishing poverty and hunger, reducing child mortality, promoting gender equality, fighting disease, and achieving universal primary education.

One organization participating in the UN's initiative is Close the Gap. This worldwide nonprofit organization aims to improve access to computers and communication technology in developing countries to help them improve educational and economic performance. The word *gap* in the organization's name refers to what's called the *digital divide*: the gap in opportunities between people who have

access to technology and those who do not. By 2013, Close the Gap had established 2,500 projects around the world and delivered more than 250,000 refurbished computers (donated by its corporate partners in Europe) to educational, medical, entrepreneurial, and social projects in developing countries. Close the Gap even recycles the donated computers once the equipment has reached the end of its life.

Considering the volume of electronics waste that's being generated worldwide, Close the Gap creates win–win outcomes. Corporations have a place to send their old equipment, and recipients receive assistance in bridging the digital divide. Has your family ever donated an old computer or mobile phone to a charity or needy person?

- Storage devices
- Communications devices

(Chapters 2 and 3 go into detail about the system unit, input devices, output devices, and storage devices, and Chapters 5 and 6 discuss communications and networking hardware and setup.)

The System Unit The system unit is a relatively small, metal and plastic cabinet that houses the electronic components involved in processing data. The cabinet holds the main circuit board (called the *motherboard*), which includes slots and sockets for installing and connecting other electronic components (see Figure 1.12). Once installed on the motherboard, the components can communicate with each other to change data into information.

The main components of the motherboard are the central processing unit (CPU) (also called the *microprocessor* or *processor*) and internal memory. The CPU consists of one or more electronic chips that read, interpret, and execute the instructions that operate the computer and perform specific computing tasks. When executing a program, the processor temporarily stores in the computer's memory the program's instructions and the data needed by the instructions. **Main memory** (also called *primary storage* or *random access memory* [*RAM*]) consists of banks of electronic chips that provide temporary storage for instructions and data during processing.

Input Devices An input device is a form of hardware that enables the user to enter program instructions, data, and commands when using a program on the computer. The program or application determines the type of input device needed. Common input devices are the keyboard, mouse, microphone, graphics tablet, and touchscreen.

Output Devices An output device is a form of hardware that makes information available to the user. Popular output devices include display screens (monitors),

Activity 1.5.1

Article
The Continuing Evolution of Personal Computing Technology

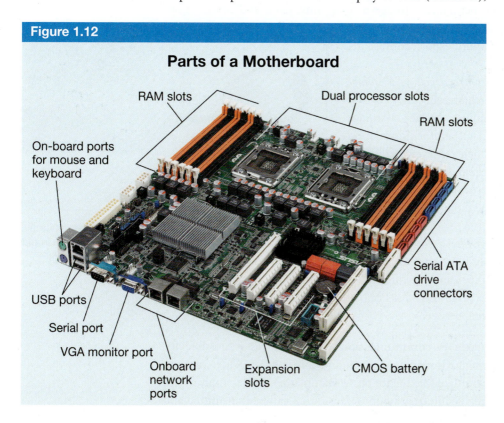

Figure 1.12

Parts of a Motherboard

RAM slots

Dual processor slots

RAM slots

On-board ports for mouse and keyboard

Serial ATA drive connectors

USB ports

Serial port

VGA monitor port

Onboard network ports

Expansion slots

CMOS battery

This empty motherboard is ready for chips and cards to be placed in the open slots.

Just for the fun of it, try naming all the devices you see in this image, and categorizing each one as an input device or an output device. Compare results with a classmate to see how well you know your devices.

printers, TV screens, and speakers. Some types of output devices (such as printers) produce output in **hard copy** (tangible) form, such as on paper or plastic. Other output devices (such as monitors) produce output in **soft copy** (intangible) form, which can be viewed but not physically handled.

Storage Devices In contrast to memory, which stores instructions and data temporarily during processing, a **storage device** (often called a *storage medium* or *secondary storage*) provides more permanent storage of programs, data, and information. After you have stored data and information, you can retrieve, modify, display, import, export, copy, share, or print it.

Although the terms *storage device* and *storage medium* are often used interchangeably, they actually have slightly different meanings. In fact, a storage device records programs, data, and/or information to a storage medium and then retrieves them from the storage medium. For example, a DVD-R drive (optical storage device) writes data to a DVD-R disc (storage medium), and the drive can also later retrieve data from the disc.

Connecting an external hard drive will add large amounts of storage to your system.

External hard drives provide a cost-effective way to expand storage beyond the internal storage in the system unit. These drives provide as much space as or more than some internal hard disks; they can plug directly into a USB port on the system and require little setup. Some external hard disks can also connect to your home or small network to enable easy sharing between users.

Communications Devices A **communications device** makes it possible for multiple computers to exchange instructions, data, and information. One common communications device is a **modem** (*mo*dulator plus *dem*odulator): an electronic device that converts computer-readable information into a form that can be transmitted and

Communications devices for wireless networking enable users to exchange information between computers.

received over a communications system. In the early days of the Internet (and even before that), many modems enabled communications through standard telephone landlines. Today, most modems enable connections to newer and faster Internet infrastructures (which you will learn about in Chapter 5). In addition, many computer systems include devices for connecting to a wired or wireless network and for transferring information over short distances using radio waves.

Software Overview

Software (also called *programs*) consists of the instructions that direct operation of the computer system and enable users to perform specific tasks, such as word processing. The two main types of software are system software and application software. Chapters 3 and 4 provide a more in-depth look at each of these types of software beyond the brief introduction you'll read next.

System Software System software tells the computer how to function and includes operating system software and utility software. The operating system contains instructions for starting the computer and coordinates the activities of all hardware devices and other software. Most PCs use a version of the Microsoft Windows operating system (see Figure 1.13). Apple computers use the Mac OS X operating system (shown

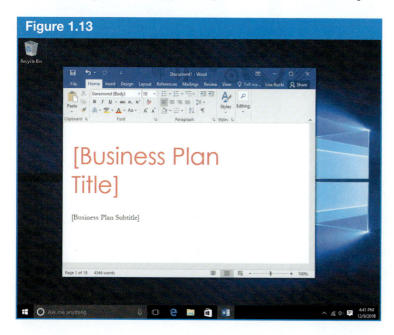

Figure 1.13

The Windows operating system runs computers from a wide variety of manufacturers.

Figure 1.14

Apple's computers are powered by the Mac OS X operating system.

in Figure 1.14), although they can also be set up to run Windows. Other power users may prefer the open source Linux operating system, available in various versions called *distributions*. Both Mac OS X and Linux share origins from the Unix operating system, originally developed decades ago. Utility software consists of programs that perform administrative tasks, such as checking the computer's components to determine whether each is working properly, managing disk drives and printers, and looking for computer viruses.

Most new mobile devices are effectively small computers, and they also have operating systems. The latest mobile operating systems include iOS for Apple iPhones and iPads (see Figure 1.15), and Windows and Android (Droid) for devices from other manufacturers. Although Droid was released by Google, it's considered open source; this means that hardware manufacturers are free to tailor it to the capabilities of specific devices. For that reason, Droid is used to run everything from smartphones to the Kindle Fire ebook reader. Google's Chrome OS open source operating system entered the market more recently. Developed to provide a platform for basic web browsing on inexpensive lightweight notebooks called *Chromebooks*, Chrome may soon feature a wider variety of applications.

Figure 1.15

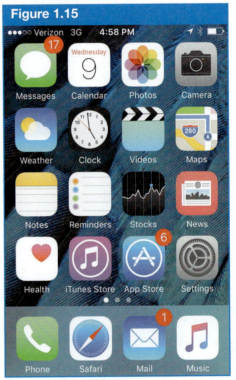

iPhones and iPads run iOS, Apple's operating system for its mobile devices.

Application Software Application software, also called *programs*, runs along with the operating system to perform specific tasks, such as creating word-processing documents, preparing spreadsheets, searching databases and developing reports, and presenting slide shows. You can find an application for doing nearly any personal, school, or business task. On mobile devices, applications are known as *apps* because they are often streamlined and have focused capabilities. The programs installed on the Windows Start screen or Start menu are known as *Apps*.

 **Recheck 1.5**

Recheck your understanding of the concepts covered by this objective.

1.6 Identifying Categories of Computers

Rapid advances in computer technology often blur the differences among types of computers, and industry professionals sometimes disagree on how computers should be categorized. Typically, the categories are based on differences in usage, size, speed, processing capabilities, and price, but there's a lot of overlap even among very different types of computers. You can think of computers as falling into the categories listed here and described in more detail in the following sections:

- Smart devices (embedded computers)
- Wearable devices
- Smartphones, tablets, and other mobile devices
- Personal computers and workstations (desktops, notebooks, laptops, and convertibles)
- Midrange servers and minicomputers
- Large servers and mainframe computers
- Supercomputers

Table 1.1 summarizes the basic differences among these categories of computers.

Precheck 1.6
Check your understanding of the concepts covered by this objective.

Activity 1.6.1

Article
Enterprise versus Personal Computing

Table 1.1 Categories of Computers

Category	Size	Number of Users Accommodated	Approximate Price Range
Smart devices (embedded computers)	Generally small, contained within another product	As many as are using the host appliance or item	$ Often included as part of the price of the appliance, vehicle, or other item in which the device is embedded; otherwise, about $50 to hundreds of dollars
Wearable devices	Fit on the wrist, head, or elsewhere	A single user, although these devices can often share information with other devices	$ $100 to $1,500 or more
Smartphones, tablets, and other mobile devices	Fit in the hand(s) and/ or a pocket	A single user or as part of a network	$ $100 to several hundred dollars
Personal computers and workstations (desktops, notebooks, laptops, and convertibles)	Fit on a desk, in a briefcase, on a lap, or on another workspace	A single user or as part of a network	$$ A few hundred to thousands of dollars
Servers (midrange servers and minicomputers)	Fit into a large cabinet or small room	Hundreds of users concurrently	$$$ $5,000 to hundreds of thousands of dollars
Mainframe computers	With needed equipment, occupy part of a room or a full room	Hundreds or thousands of users concurrently	$$$$ Several thousand to millions of dollars
Supercomputers	With needed equipment, occupy a full room	Thousands of users concurrently	$$$$$ Several million to nearly $100,000,000

Smart Devices (Embedded Computers)

Technology seems to be entering a new era of convergence, in which different technologies are combined into a single package. The result is a product that features all the benefits of the individual technologies plus additional benefits derived from merging the component technologies. Perfect examples of this convergence are found in embedded computers, which are used to make other consumer products "smart."

Previously, the term **smart device** referred strictly to a smartphone. Today, however, the term refers more broadly to any type of appliance or device that has embedded technology. Even cars and trucks now feature central computers (as shown in Figure 1.16). In addition, numerous sensors within vehicles provide data on the performance and status of various systems. For instance, sensors might report the air pressure from your tires to the computer, which turns on a tire pressure warning light when the pressure gets low. In-dash systems provide GPS navigation and location information for your travel needs, such as listings of nearby restaurants, gas stations, and attractions. You may also be able to connect a music player such as an iPod using a USB cable and control playback from the car's audio system. If the system includes a hard disk drive, you can copy digital music files to it from a USB flash drive and play it back through the system. Some in-dash computers can connect or pair with your smartphone wirelessly over a standard called *Bluetooth*; this feature enables you to make hands-free calls or stream music from a service such as Rhapsody.

Like the smart washer and dryer pictured earlier in the chapter, many smart devices bring additional convenience, capabilities, and energy savings to appliances and other tools in the home or office.

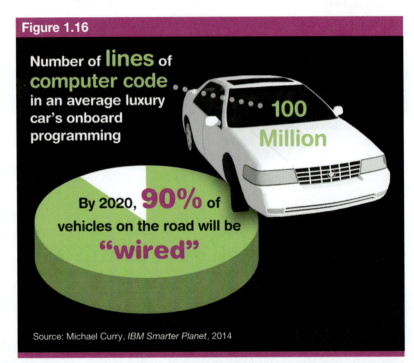

Figure 1.16

Number of **lines** of **computer code** in an average luxury car's onboard programming

100 Million

By 2020, **90%** of vehicles on the road will be **"wired"**

Source: Michael Curry, *IBM Smarter Planet*, 2014

Cutting Edge

Previewing the Latest at CES

Every January, the Consumer Electronics Show (CES) takes place in Las Vegas, Nevada. Technology companies and other types of businesses converge there to introduce new products and emerging technologies. Some of the products that are listed in Table 1.2 were introduced at the CES event.

Companies also use CES to introduce concepts for products that might be developed in the future. For example, at the 2014 CES, Whirlpool introduced its concept for an interactive cooktop. The cooktop would be a sleek, flat surface without separate burners; you could put a pot or pan anywhere on it to cook. The cooktop would use touch controls on the surface, rather than knobs or buttons. Finally, the cooktop would include Internet connectivity, so you could not only control it with a smartphone but also download and view recipes right on the cooktop.

Table 1.2 lists a sampling of the types of smart devices that have brought technology to products that had changed little for decades. You can control many of these

Table 1.2 Examples of Smart Devices

	Categories	Example Products	Example Functions
	Locks	Goji Smart Lock Kwikset Kevo Bluetooth Deadbolt Schlage Camelot Touchscreen Deadbolt Yale Real Living Touchscreen Deadbolt	Enable using methods other than a key to open the door. For example, the lock might detect your smartphone or a key fob as you approach, so you finish unlocking by touching the lock or entering a code on a touchscreen. Some enable creating multiple unique codes to allow access by multiple users; others have an alarm that will signal potentially illegal entry attempts.
	Large appliances	Samsung Smart Home LG HomeChat Whirlpool 6th Sense Live	Allow control of large appliances (such as washers and dryers) remotely; also perform other functions.
	Small appliances	Belkin Crock-Pot Smart Slow Cooker (enabled by WeMo)	Can calculate cooking time and process and send reminders. Enable you to turn the appliance on and off, change the temperature, and change time settings from anywhere.
	Security and smoke detectors	iSmartAlarm Oplink Security Nest Protect Smoke Detector	Include motion sensors, contact sensors for doors and windows, and alarms; also provide the ability to arm, disarm, and monitor security devices from a remote location, often without a monthly service fee.
	Thermostats	Nest Learning Thermostat Honeywell Wi-Fi Smart Thermostat	Learn the home's heating and cooling habits to program themselves; may include extra devices, such as a humidity sensor.
	Lighting and smart outlets and switches	Belkin WeMo Light Switch Connected by TCP Wireless LED Lighting System Insteon LED Bulbs	Enable remote control of lighting and plugged-in devices, such as turning on/off, dimming, and changing LED lighting colors.
	Garage door controllers and other devices	Garageio (garage door app) Hiku (shopping app) Samsung Smart TV	Allow performing a wide variety of functions, including using your smartphone to control your garage door and to create a shopping list (by voice or barcode scanning). Also allow Internet access through your TV for streaming video from services such as Hulu and YouTube.

devices with your smartphone (using either an app or text messaging); doing so allows you to monitor their operation, turn them on and off, and perform other tasks either locally or from a remote location. These emerging technologies form the basis for a concept called the **connected home**, where numerous networked home devices provide specific, usually automated functions, and share data and media.

Wearable Devices

Wearable computers continue to emerge and specialize to serve specific functions beyond what's offered by a simple pair of eyeglasses or wristwatch. As the name implies, a **wearable computer** is a computer device that's worn somewhere on the body—most often, on the head or wrist.

Wrist-based smartbands typically gather data about your physical activities. Examples include the Jawbone UP, FitBit Flex and Force bands, Nike+ Fuelband, and Nike+ SportWatch GPS. You can then transfer the data to a smartphone or computer over a wireless, USB, or other direct connection. Using an app or website, you can review metrics such as steps taken, miles run, route followed, level of activity, and more. The use of these self-tracking tools and the personal data they provide is part of a movement called the *Quantified Self*.

A smartwatch provides you with access to mobile computing capabilities and information through an Internet connection or a wireless connection to a smartphone. Products include the Apple Watch, Fitbit Surge, Samsung Galaxy Gear, and Pebble.

A smartwatch, such as this Apple Watch, typically interfaces with your smartphone. By wearing this device, you can manage calls, text messages, and reminders such as appointment alerts from your wrist.

Practical TECH

Creating Your Own Automation

A hot technology called *Arduino* enables you to create your own smart automation projects. According to Adruino's creators, it is intended for use by "artists, designers, hobbyists and anyone interested in creating interactive objects or environments." The Arduino microcontroller board can receive input from sensors and other means, and it can send output to control lights, motors, and actuators (devices that run mechanisms or systems). The Arduino platform includes a programming language and a programming (development) environment, and it's open source, which means anyone can freely modify the source code. To get started with Arduino, you buy the board and accessories or a kit, download and install the free software, review the generous quantity of examples at the company's website

(available at **http://CUT6.emcp.net/Arduino**), and then start coding and building. You can also incorporate Arduino-compatible components from other sources. For example, as of this writing, a new company called *Printoo* was developing Arduino-compatible flexible printed circuit boards and offering other types of modules.

The avid Arduino community has developed projects ranging from an aquarium control system to interactive visual art installations consisting of LED lights that respond to viewers' movements. You can join other enthusiasts and learn more at Arduino workshops and events held all over the world. For instance, an annual Arduino Day features 24 hours of official and unofficial events in locations worldwide. What objects or systems would you like to automate at home?

Wrist-based devices are growing in popularity. Canalys, a research and analysis company, predicted that sales of smartbands would reach 17 million in 2014 and then jump to 45 million in 2017. Vandrico, a wearable technology experts firm, has established a Wearable Technology Database to track and analyze the growing number of wearable devices that are available (see Figure 1.17). You can visit the firm's website at http://CUT6.emcp.net/Vandrico to see the latest data, such as the number of devices available, as well as average costs, typical uses, and number of devices worn at particular locations.

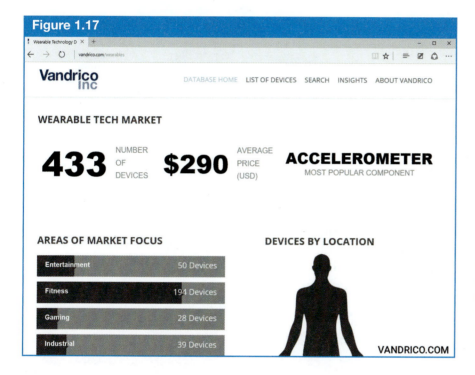

Figure 1.17

Vandrico's Wearable Technology Database tracks the number of available wearable devices and provides information about average cost, range of purposes, and where devices are worn.

Cutting Edge

A Computer in Your Eye

Have you ever thought about what kind of superpower you would want to have, if such a thing were possible? If bionic eyesight tops your list, then you will be glad to know that engineers at the University of Washington (UW) in Seattle are working on it. A research team at the university is developing an electronic contact lens that could have a major impact on both the medical and computer industries.

The lens is still in its early stages, but the UW team has developed a prototype with an electronic circuit and red light-emitting diodes (LEDs). Although the prototype isn't yet functional, its creation represents a breakthrough for the engineers. They hope to eventually outfit each lens with several types of circuits and antennas, hundreds of LEDs, and a wireless signal. Lens wearers would use it like a regular computer, but the images would appear in front of the eye, rather than on a traditional screen.

What about the lens's medical capabilities? The lens would use the biomarkers present on the surface of the eye to monitor how the body's systems are functioning and then transmit that information directly to doctors. This technology could lead to making quicker and more accurate diagnoses and greatly reduce the need to take blood samples.

Verily, a division of Alphabet (the parent holding company that evolved from and owns Google) is working on a similar contact lens that's designed specifically to monitor blood glucose. Wearing this lens would eliminate the need for diabetics to prick their fingers to test blood glucose levels.

While the design of the bionic lens is far from completion, UW researchers are moving forward. They are currently studying how to power and mass produce the device.

Smartphones, Tablets, and Other Mobile Devices

The term *handheld computer* used to refer to dedicated small computers, such as the Pocket PC and Apple Newton. The user typically operated these devices by tapping on the screen with a stylus. These types of devices have mostly become obsolete. Today, a **handheld computer** comes in one of two general forms: smartphones and tablets. (Some other smart devices—including advanced portable music players, such as the iPod Touch, and some mobile gaming devices—may also be thought of as computers.) You can hold one of these devices in your hands and use it for almost the same functions as a full-featured computer.

A handheld computer is small enough to fit in the palm of a user's hand.

A **smartphone** is a cell phone that can make and receive calls and text messages on a cellular network; it can also connect to the Internet via the cellular network or a wireless network and perform numerous computing functions. Smartphones measure up to 6 inches or so diagonally and can fit in your hand or pocket. A **tablet** (sometimes called a *tablet computer* or *tablet PC*) is larger than a smartphone and generally used on your lap or on a table. Tablets can also connect wirelessly to the Internet and perform computing activities. Only some models of tablets can connect to the cellular network, and to do so, they must be covered by a data plan from a cell phone carrier.

You operate a smartphone or tablet primarily through its touchscreen by using a variety of gestures, such as tapping and swiping. These devices also typically include a microphone and a combination still/video camera. Smartphones and tablets use a special class of mobile processor (or mobile CPU) that's typically designed to save power and facilitate longer battery life. Some include additional chips that provide location services (via GPS) and other capabilities. These devices also come with a special mobile operating system installed.

Hands On

Checking Out Your Mobile OS

Most smartphones and tablet devices use a mobile operating system (OS). Follow steps like the ones listed in this resource to find out which OS your mobile device uses.

Hotspot

An Inside Look at Your Small Intestine

While the medical community has been using endoscopy to diagnose and treat problems in the esophagus and stomach, and colonoscopy to see the large intestine, the small intestine has remained out of view until recently. Feeding patients barium and then making X-rays of the small intestine has provided only limited diagnostic and treatment value. Now, physicians can use *capsule endoscopy* to get a direct view of the small intestine. A patient swallows a capsule containing up to two video camera chips, as well as a light, battery, and radio transmitter. Over the course of about eight hours, the capsule takes images as it passes through the esophagus, stomach, and small intestine, transmitting the images to a receiver worn by the patient. The physician later transfers the images from the receiver for review and diagnosis. Capsule endoscopy now provides a more patient-friendly way of diagnosing problems such as gastrointestinal bleeding and Chrohn's disease.

A smartphone with a diagonal screen measurement greater than 5.25 inches, sometimes called a *phablet*, combines mobile calling with easier web browsing and multimedia viewing made possible on larger tablet screens.

To add functions to mobile devices, you can download and install apps that perform specific activities—for instance, sending and receiving email, taking and editing photos and videos, using social media sites (such as Facebook and Twitter), video chatting, online banking, and gaming (see Figure 1.18). These devices use flash storage (the same type of storage found in portable USB flash drives) rather than a hard disk drive. The amount of storage determines how many apps you can install, how many photos you can take, and so on. You may need or want to synchronize (sync) your mobile device with your main computer from time to time to perform updates, back up content, organize contact lists, and so on. For some tablet models, you can get an add-on keyboard, which enables you to use the tablet more like a notebook computer. Other popular hardware add-ons you may use with a smartphone or tablet include speaker docks, external battery chargers, and enhanced cameras.

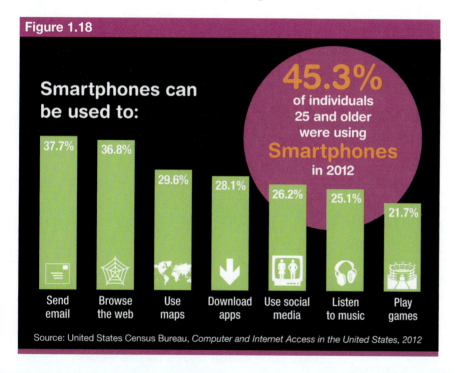

Figure 1.18

Smartphones can be used to:

45.3% of individuals 25 and older were using **Smartphones** in 2012

- 37.7% Send email
- 36.8% Browse the web
- 29.6% Use maps
- 28.1% Download apps
- 26.2% Use social media
- 25.1% Listen to music
- 21.7% Play games

Source: United States Census Bureau, *Computer and Internet Access in the United States, 2012*

Practical TECH

Dealing with Older Devices

Small mobile devices evolve so quickly that some users upgrade them as quickly as they can afford to. Most major data services carriers, such as Verizon and AT&T, provide trade-in and recycle programs. These programs may save you money on a new phone and ensure that your device won't wind up in a landfill when you leave it behind. If your carrier doesn't offer such a program or you would like to find out what your phone is worth, you can check prices at a general auction website, such as

eBay. Better yet, you can go to a specialized website such as Gazelle (available at **http://CUT6.emcp.net/Gazelle**), which purchases and resells used iPods, iPhones, and iPads. Other websites offer the opportunity to donate an older phone or recycle a very old device that no longer has any value. No matter how you decide to dispose of your outdated device, be sure to first wipe it clean of your personal data.

As the name suggests, a desktop computer fits on top of a work area. A tower-type system unit, like the one shown here, can be placed on the floor.

Personal Computers and Workstations

A **personal computer (PC)**—often referred to as simply a *computer*—is a self-contained computer that can perform input, processing, output, and storage functions. A PC must have at least one input device, one storage device, and one output device, as well as a processor and memory. Smartphone and tablet devices technically meet these criteria. However, PCs are generally larger, use a keyboard and mouse or a touchpad for input, and can run full-blown applications for business and other purposes. PCs might have multiple processors or microprocessors or CPUs. (Think of the CPU as the "brain" of the computer.) The three major groups of PCs are desktop computers, portable (mobile) computers, and workstations.

Desktop Computers A **desktop computer** is a PC that's designed to allow the system unit, input devices, output devices, and other connected devices to fit on top of, beside, or under a desk or table. This type of computer may be used in a home, a home office, a library, or a corporate setting. The monitor and speakers may have wired connections to the main system unit. Peripheral devices such as a mouse, keyboard, and printer may have wired or wireless connections. Desktop computers may have a wired or wireless connection to the local network and/or the Internet.

Desktop computers offer greater expansion and upgrade capabilities than mobile computers (described next). Desktop computers are made so that you can "crack the case" (open the CPU) and add or replace internal hardware on your own. They include expansion slots that enable upgrading the RAM and adding features such as a graphics card for a second monitor.

Portable (Mobile) Computers The mobility of today's workforce and the need for Internet access anytime, anywhere have increased the demand for mobile computers. A **portable computer** (sometimes called a *mobile computer*) is a PC that's small enough to be moved around easily.

A notebook computer is a PC designed for people who frequently move about in their work.

There are several types of portable computers. As its name suggests, a **laptop computer** can fit comfortably on your lap. As this type of computer decreased in size, many users began using a new term for it: **notebook computer**. Another type of portable computer, called a *netbook*, emerged as a low-cost alternative to a full notebook computer. A **netbook** is usually smaller and less powerful than a notebook; it's intended primarily for web browsing and emailing over the Internet. Each of these types of portable computers has a flat screen, and the screen and keyboard fold together like a clamshell for easy transport.

Because many people are more comfortable entering data on an external keyboard than a touchscreen, convertible models attempt to bridge the gap between a tablet and a notebook. A convertible computer has a touchscreen like a tablet, but it also has a keyboard that either attaches and detaches (as on the Microsoft Surface) or swivels and snaps in behind the screen (both Dell and Lenovo offer this type of system). This feature lets you use either the keyboard or the touchscreen.

A new high-performance class of small notebook computer called an *ultrabook* emerged in 2012. Intel set the standard for this new class of portable computers. An **ultrabook** must use low-power Intel Core processors, has solid-state drives for storage (rather than a hard disk drive), and features a unibody chassis for durability. While this lightweight machine tends to have a long battery life, it also may lack features present in other types of notebooks, such as a DVD-R drive and certain ports.

Workstations Workstations resemble desktop PCs but provide more processing power and capabilities. A **workstation** is a high-performance, single-user computer with advanced input, output, and storage components. A workstation can be networked with other workstations and with larger computers.

Tech Career Explorer

Step Up to the Service Side of Tech

If you were the sort of kid who took apart your toys and then reassembled them or spent hours troubleshooting and fixing a broken bike, then you can transfer interests like those to a variety of careers in tech. Technical service jobs involve setting up technology for customers, while technical support jobs typically find you diagnosing and fixing hardware and software problems. If roll-up-your-sleeves tech jobs like these appeal to you, complete this exercise to learn more.

Workstations provide the enhanced power and graphics capabilities required for some applications such as programming, computer-aided design, and desktop publishing and graphics.

Previously, workstations used a specific operating system and different hardware than a standard desktop computer. But today, workstations generally use a standard Windows or Mac operating system and have more powerful hardware.

Workstations are typically used by companies for complex applications that require considerable computing power and high-quality graphics resolution. Examples of these applications include computer-aided design (CAD), computer-aided manufacturing (CAM), desktop publishing, and software development. Workstations generally come with large, high-resolution graphics displays and/or multiple displays, built-in network capability, and high-density storage devices. Like PCs, workstations can serve as single-user computers but more often connect to a network and have access to larger computers (often, servers and mainframes).

Servers (Midrange Servers and Minicomputers)

In a large organization, networked computers typically connect to a larger and more powerful computer called a *server* (sometimes referred to as the *host computer*). Although the size and capacity of network servers vary considerably, most are midrange rather than large main-frame computers (discussed later). Sun Microsystems, Dell, and Hewlett-Packard are the leading manufacturers of servers.

A **server** (formerly known as a *midrange server* or *minicomputer*) is a powerful computer that's capable of accommodating numerous client computers at the same time. Midrange servers are widely used in networks to provide users with computing capability and resources available through the network. Those resources gener-ally include Internet content and software that's critical to business operations, such as an accounting system, manufacturing planning software, customer relationship management (CRM) software, and

A server is a powerful computer that can accommodate (serve) multiple users in a network. Many servers use hardware that's configured in a rack like this—a setup known as a *rack server*.

more. Because servers must respond to the needs of many users, system reliability and access have become key considerations in planning and maintaining these computers.

In terms of physical hardware, a modern server often consists of multiple different server and storage units in storage racks. These so-called rack servers consume a lot of power and generate a lot of heat; to ensure optimum operation, they are often located in a separate room with enhanced power and cooling capabilities. Blade servers also mount in racks, but they require less space and use less power.

Mainframe Computers

In a small business environment, a personal computer can be used as a server. Large businesses, which need more powerful servers, may use mainframe computers. Bigger, more powerful, and more expensive than a midrange server, a **mainframe computer** can accommodate hundreds or thousands of network users performing different computing tasks. A mainframe's internal storage can handle hundreds of millions of characters. Mainframe applications are often large and complex. These computers are useful for

Activity 1.6.2

Article
Enterprise Computing Trends

Activity 1.6.3

Article
A History of Computers Timeline

A mainframe computer, such as this IBM zEnterprise, is a large, powerful, expensive computer system that can accommodate multiple users at the same time. The tremendous processing capability of mainframes differentiates them from server systems.

Supercomputers are among the world's fastest, most powerful, and most expensive computers. They are capable of processing huge amounts of data quickly and accommodating thousands of users at the same time. The Titan supercomputer at Oak Ridge National Labs in Tennessee is the most powerful supercomputer in the United States.

dealing with large, ever-changing collections of data that can be accessed by many users simultaneously. A mainframe computer can also function as a network server.

Government agencies, banks, universities, and insurance companies use mainframes to handle millions of transactions each day. The latest generation of mainframe computers from IBM is called *zEnterprise* and operates on the System z platform.

Supercomputers

Supercomputers are the current "Goliaths" of the computer industry. A **supercomputer** is an extremely fast, powerful, and expensive computer. Many supercomputers are capable of performing quadrillions of calculations in a single second. Performing the same number of calculations on a handheld calculator would take 2 million years!

Supercomputer designers achieve stunning calculation speeds by joining thousands of separate microprocessors. Many supercomputers provide enough disk storage capacity for dozens of petabytes of data. (One **petabyte** is the equivalent of 1 quadrillion alphabet letters, numbers, or special characters.)

In a move to expand supercomputing into the realm of the unimaginable, Oak Ridge National Labs has developed Titan, the most powerful supercomputer in the United States. With 18,688 CPUs and 18,688 GPUs (graphics processing units), Titan can process data at a peak speed of 17.59 petaflops, with a theoretical peak of 20-plus petaflops. (A **petaflop** is equivalent to 1 quadrillion calculations per second.) Titan will be used for high-end scientific projects, such as gathering and tracking statistics about fluctuations in nanoscale materials and systems (nanotechnology experiments). Titan cost more than $97 million to develop and was the leading supercomputer in the world until 2013, according to a TOP500 survey of supercomputer sites (available at **http://CUT6 .emcp.net/TOP500**). That year, it was surpassed by the Chinese Tianhe-2 system.

Recheck 1.6

Recheck your understanding of the concepts covered by this objective.

Cutting Edge

Beyond Super

Quantum computers exceed the capabilities of supercomputers. So far, though, they haven't been used much for practical applications because of their high cost and the difficulties of operating them. Quantum computers will be used to perform computations beyond what supercomputers can currently tackle, for example, evaluating trillions of amino acid combinations to find a particular protein for diagnosis and drug development. Chapter 13 introduces this exciting and emerging generation of computers.

Chapter Summary

*An interactive **Chapter Summary**, **Study Notes**, and a **Slide Presentation** with audio are available from the links menu on this page in your ebook.*

1.1 Being Immersed in Digital Technology

We live in a **digital** world, in which computer technology increasingly powers the devices that are part our daily lives. Those devices include smart TVs and appliances, smartphones, and **embedded computers** in everything from wearable devices to automobiles. Technologies such as embedded chips, computers, networks, and the Internet and World Wide Web enable us to communicate globally. No digital device has had a greater impact on our lives than the computer. A **computer** is an electronic device that operates under the control of programmed instructions stored in its memory.

1.2 Discovering the Computer Advantage

Computers offer advantages in the areas of speed, accuracy, versatility, storage, and communications. As a result, they are widely used in homes, schools, businesses, and other organizations for communicating, managing finances, analyzing data, planning, researching, and hundreds of other purposes. The **Internet** and the World Wide Web, in which networks of computers around the world are linked, continue to serve an important function in all areas of human activity.

1.3 Understanding How Computers Work

Data is raw, unorganized content, such as facts and figures. Data entered into a computer consists of one or more of the following types: **text data**, **graphic data**, **audio data**, and **video data**. **Information** is data that's been processed (manipulated, organized, or arranged) in a way that's converted it into a useful form. Using a computer to convert data into useful information is called **information processing** (or *data processing*). The **information processing cycle** involves four stages: **input**, **processing**, **output**, and **storage**. It accepts data (input) that's manipulated (processed) according to the instructions and

output as information, which may be placed in storage for future use.

1.4 Differentiating between Computers and Computer Systems

The term *computer* identifies only the system unit—the part of a desktop computer system that processes data into information. A **computer system** includes the system unit along with input, output, storage, and communications devices.

1.5 Understanding Hardware and Software

There are two general types of computer system components: hardware and software. **Hardware** includes all of the physical components of the computer and the **peripheral devices** connected to it. The main hardware components are the system unit, input devices, output devices, **storage devices**, and **communications devices**.

Software consists of the programs that contain instructions that direct the operation of the computer system and programs that enable users to perform specific applications. There are two main types of software: system software, consisting of the operating system and utility software, and application software, or apps on a mobile device. Mobile devices also use separate mobile operating systems.

1.6 Identifying Categories of Computers

A **smart device** is an everyday appliance or piece of equipment that has capabilities provided by an embedded computer; examples include the computing technologies being introduced in vehicles and home appliances. Similarly, a **wearable computer**, which is typically worn on the wrist, performs specific computing functions; examples include tracking the number of steps taken or miles run and helping the user respond to alerts and messages from a smartphone. **Tablets** and **smartphones** are really

handheld computers; these Internet-connected devices are operated via a built-in touchscreen. A **personal computer (PC)** is a self-contained computer capable of input, processing, output, and storage; types of PCs are **desktop computers**, **portable computers** (which are also called *mobile computers* and include **laptop computers** and **notebook computers**), and **workstations**.

A **server** can accommodate hundreds of client computers or terminals (users) at the same time. A **mainframe computer** is capable of accommodating hundreds to thousands of network users performing different tasks. A **supercomputer** exceeds the power and capabilities of a mainframe; the fastest supercomputer in the United States is capable of processing quadrillions of calculations per second.

Key Terms

Numbers indicate the pages where terms are first cited with their full definition in the chapter. An alphabetized list of key terms with definitions is included in the end-of-book glossary.

➡ *An interactive **Glossary** is available from the links menu on this page in your ebook.*

Chapter Exercises

Complete the following exercises to assess your understanding of the material covered in this chapter.

Interactive **Flash Cards** and an interactive **Game** are available from the links menu on this page in your ebook.

Go to your SNAP Assignments page to complete the Terms Check, Knowledge Check, Key Principles, and Tech Illustrated exercises.

Terms Check: Matching

Match each term with its definition.

a.	digital	f.	personal computer
b.	smart device	g.	information
c.	Internet	h.	computer
d.	data	i.	peripheral device
e.	software	j.	hardware

___ 1. A collection of raw, unorganized content in the form of words, numbers, sounds, or images.

___ 2. A worldwide network of computers that are linked using communications software and media for the purpose of sharing information.

___ 3. Data that has been organized to be meaningful and potentially useful.

___ 4. A piece of hardware connected to a computer, such as a keyboard or monitor.

___ 5. An everyday device or item that has new capabilities provided by an embedded computer.

___ 6. A computer designed for use by a single individual and capable of performing its own input, processing, output, and storage.

___ 7. Programs containing instructions that direct the operation of the computer system.

___ 8. A computer's physical components and devices.

___ 9. An electronic device that accepts input (data), processes the data into information using programs, delivers output (information) to users, and stores data and information for later use.

___ 10. An electronic signal that's processed, sent, and stored in discrete parts called bits.

Knowledge Check: Multiple Choice

Choose the best answer for each question.

1. A small, electronic chip that a manufacturer develops for use in another product (such as a digital camera or microwave oven) is called a(n)
   a. programmed chip.
   b. embedded chip.
   c. component chip.
   d. storage chip.

2. Computers are incredibly useful because of their speed, accuracy, versatility, reliability, storage, and
   a. communications capabilities.
   b. peripheral components.

   c. decreasing prices.
   d. hard shell.

3. A setup that consists of two or more computers or devices and software connected by one or more communications media (such as wireless) is called a(n)
   a. computer.
   b. communication.
   c. information processing cycle.
   d. network.

4. A self-contained computer capable of performing its own input, processing, output, and storage is called a
   a. hard disk drive.
   b. digital chip.
   c. dual-purpose processor.
   d. personal computer.

5. A computer component that's contained on a single chip (a thin piece of silicon containing electrical circuitry) and often serves as the computer's central processing unit (CPU) is called a(n)
   a. wired component.
   b. GPU.
   c. microprocessor.
   d. expansion slot.

6. Titan at Oak Ridge National Labs is an example of a
   a. personal computer.
   b. supercomputer.
   c. mainframe computer.
   d. server.

7. Data that has been processed into a useful form is called
   a. digital data.
   b. input.
   c. information.
   d. output.

8. A powerful computer capable of accommodating numerous client computers at the same time is called a(n)
   a. personal computer.
   b. embedded computer.
   c. netcomputer.
   d. server.

9. The main circuit board inside the cabinet of a PC that allows other electronic components to be installed and connected is the
   a. modem.
   b. secondary circuit board.
   c. motherboard.
   d. attachment board.

10. The software that contains instructions for starting the computer and coordinates the activities of all hardware devices and other software is the
    a. operating system.
    b. application software.
    c. utility software.
    d. communications software.

Key Principles: Completion

Complete each statement with the appropriate word or phrase.

1. The term _____ refers to information represented by the numbers 1 (on) and 0 (off).

2. In a personal computer, the term *computer* identifies only the _____, which is the part of a desktop computer system that processes data into information.

3. A(n) _____, which is also called a *host computer*, is the computer to which other computers are connected and on which programs, data, and information are stored on a network.

4. Main memory, which is also called _____, consists of banks of electronic chips that provide temporary storage for instructions and data during processing.

5. Software that tells the computer how to function is called _____.

6. A monitor produces output in _____ form; this type of output can be viewed but not physically handled.

7. Software that performs administrative tasks—such as checking the computer's components to determine whether they are working properly—is called _____.

8. A(n) _____ operating system such as iOS or Droid runs many smartphones or handheld devices

9. The processor and memory chips are the main components found on a computer's _____.

10. USB flash drives and hard disk drives are examples of _____ devices.

Tech Illustrated: Figure Labeling

Fill in the blanks with the correct labels.

1. Star network

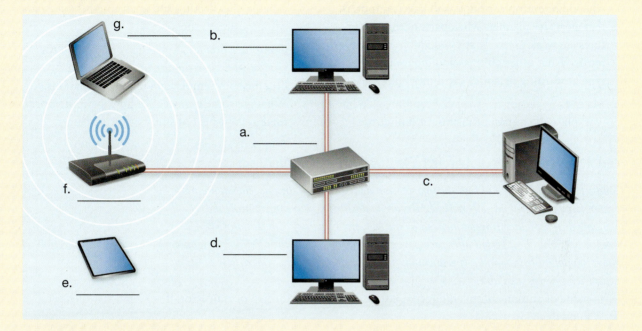

g. _____
b. _____
a. _____
c. _____
f. _____
d. _____
e. _____

2. Information processing cycle

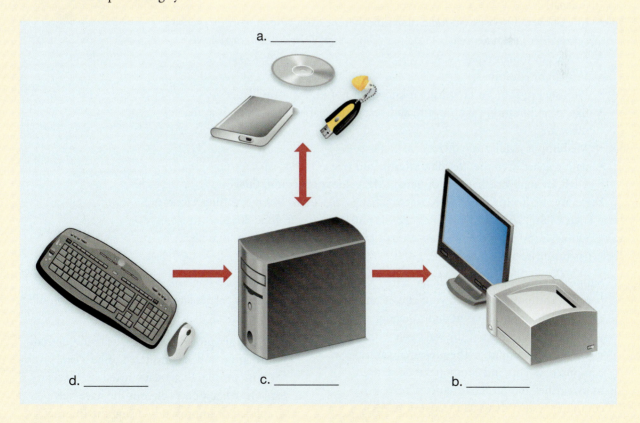

a. _____
d. _____
c. _____
b. _____

Tech to Come: Brainstorming New Uses

In groups or individually, contemplate the following questions and develop as many answers as you can.

1. Futurists predict that computers will be everywhere. For example, bridges will have computers that alert city planners when parts of these structures are weak or overly stressed and in need of repair. What other objects should have the same type of warning or notice capability built into it?

2. Many of us already use wearable computers. What workplace dilemmas, problems, or limitations might be solved if we wore computers that are capable of collecting and analyzing personal data while we are on the job?

3. Computer literacy is extremely important for workers, because the use of computers has become commonplace in many occupations. What are some examples of how computers are used in your field of study or future career?

Tech Literacy: Internet Research and Writing

Conduct Internet research to find the information described, and then develop appropriate written responses based on your research. Be sure to document your sources using the following format, which is recommended by the Modern Language Association (MLA), Seventh Edition. Use a period after each part of the citation except the publisher or sponsor, which is followed by a comma. If you cannot find some of the information described below, include whatever is available.

- name of author, compiler, director, editor, narrator, performer, or translator, if known
- title of work (in italic type if work is independent; in roman type and enclosed in quotation marks if work is part of larger work, such as an article within a journal)
- title of overall website (in italic font), if different from title of work (if website is not titled, use a genre label, such as *Home Page, Introduction,* or *Online posting,* in roman type)
- Version or edition
- Publisher or sponsor of website if known; if not known, use *N.p.*
- date of publication (day, month, and year, as available); if nothing is available, use *n.d.*
- Medium of publication (*Web.*)
- date you accessed the site (day, month, and year)
- URL, in angle brackets <> (optional; MLA does not require this)

For example: Justin Gillis and Kenneth Chang. "Scientists Warn of Rising Oceans from Polar Melt." *The New York Times.* 12 May 2014. Web. 26 June 2016. <http://www.nytimes.com/2014/05/13/science/earth/collapse-of-parts-of-west-antarctica-ice-sheet-has-begun-scientists-say.html?_r=0>.

1. Suppose that you have been offered a free personal computer system of your choice and can select the input, output, and storage devices you want. Create a list of the ways you will use your new computer. Then research various computer systems and components advertised in magazines and on the Internet. Create a computer system that will meet your needs, and write a paragraph explaining why you selected a particular system or combination of components.

2. The Internet provides easy access to a wealth of information and is considered to be a timesaver for busy people. Prepare a written report that explains what aspects of your life have been simplified or improved by using the Internet.

Include predictions for additional Internet capabilities you expect to use in the next five years.

3. Many projects are under way to expand the use of wearable computers in the workplace, in military applications, and for personal use. Using your school library and other sources of information, research the uses of wearable computers. Based on your findings, write an article that describes ways in which wearable computers can enhance our daily lives.

4. Two websites gather stats for people browsing the web. Go to http://CUT6.emcp.net/StatCounter and http://CUT6.emcp.net/NetMarketShare, and use the tools provided to find statistics on what operating systems are installed for users browsing the web. Write a brief article summarizing your findings, including one or more charts, if possible.

Tech Issues: Team Problem-Solving

In groups, develop possible solutions to the issues presented.

1. The students in today's classrooms are more diverse and have a wider range of abilities than students from previous decades. In fact, some experts claim that the learning rate in classrooms today is twice as fast that of years past. Imagine how computers will help instructors teach so many different types of students. Consider both traditional and distance learning courses and programs.

2. Artificially intelligent robots are likely to have many uses in the future. What new applications of this technology seem possible in the areas of manufacturing, health care, and home maintenance?

3. Since computers were first introduced, there has been considerable debate about their effects on employment. For example, some people argue that computers have replaced many workers and are therefore harmful to society. Others argue that computers increase productivity and that the computer industry has created many new high-paying jobs. In your group, discuss both sides of this issue: Overall, have computers had a good effect or a bad effect on employment?

Tech Timeline: Predicting Next Steps

Look at the timeline below outlining the major benchmarks in the development of computing. Research this topic and fill in as many steps as you can. What do you think the next steps will be? Complete the timeline through the year 2030.

1941 Konrad Zuse completes work on the world's first electronic computer, called the Z3.

1942 Dr. John Atanasoff and Clifford Berry complete work on the *Atanasoff–Berry Computer* (or *ABC*), a forerunner of today's modern computers.

1958 Jack Kilby, an engineer at Texas Instruments, and Robert Noyce, an electrical engineer at Fairchild Semiconductor, simultaneously and independently invent the integrated circuit, thereby laying the foundation for fast computers and large-capacity memory.

1981 IBM enters the personal computer field by introducing the IBM PC.

1993 World Wide Web technology and programming is officially proclaimed "public domain"

and thus available to everyone.

2004 Wireless computer devices—including keyboards, mice, and wireless home networks—become widely accepted among users.

2006 Five million subscribers connect to BlackBerry Internet Service (BIS) for work and personal communications.

2007 The first iPhone is released by Apple.

2010 The first iPad is released by Apple.

2013 The Titan supercomputer becomes available for use by researchers.

2014 Apple introduces the Apple Watch, calling it a "comprehensive health and fitness device."

Ethical Dilemmas: Group Discussion and Debate

As a class or within an assigned group, discuss the following ethical dilemma.

The term *plagiarism* refers to the unauthorized and illegal use of another person's writing or creative work. For example, a student may copy text from a magazine article or web page and submit the report without crediting the author of the material.

In your group, discuss the issue of plagiarism for class assignments and reports. What types of plagiarism are you aware of? Are there tools that instructors can use to detect and protect against plagiarism?

Chapter 2

Sizing Up Computer and Device Hardware

Chapter Goal

To understand and identify computer input, processing, and output devices

Learning Objectives

2.1 Identify types of input devices.

2.2 Explain how computers represent and process data with bits and bytes.

2.3 Describe the components of a system unit.

2.4 Explain how a CPU functions.

2.5 Differentiate between types of memory.

2.6 Differentiate between types of display technologies and understand digital audio.

2.7 Describe several printer technologies and their advantages and disadvantages.

2.8 Identify ergonomic practices that make computing safer and more comfortable.

 Green go-online icons indicate resources that are accessed from the links menu in your ebook.

 SNAP icons indicate interactive resources that are available in SNAP. Go to your SNAP Assignments page to complete these quizzes, activities, and exercises.

2.1 Working with Input Technology

 Precheck **2.1**

Check your understanding of the concepts covered by this objective.

As you learned in Chapter 1, the four steps of the information processing cycle are input, processing, output, and storage. We will begin this chapter by looking at the first step in that process: input.

Input is any data or instruction entered into a computer. You can enter input in a variety of ways, such as typing on a keyboard, clicking with a mouse, dragging and tapping on a touchscreen, and speaking into a microphone.

An **input device** is any hardware component that enables you to perform one or more input operations. What types of input devices are available depends on the type of computer. For a desktop personal computer (PC), for example, the most common input devices are a keyboard and a mouse. For a notebook PC, a touchpad is the most common pointing device, replacing the mouse. On a tablet PC, the screen is touch sensitive and functions as an input device. Figure 2.1 shows a variety of common input devices.

Keyboards

The most common input device is the **keyboard**, which is used to enter text characters (letters, numbers, and symbols). Some computers, such as notebooks, have the keyboard built in; other computers accept a keyboard as an external device. An external keyboard can be plugged into the computer or connected wirelessly through a radio frequency (RF) technology such as Bluetooth.

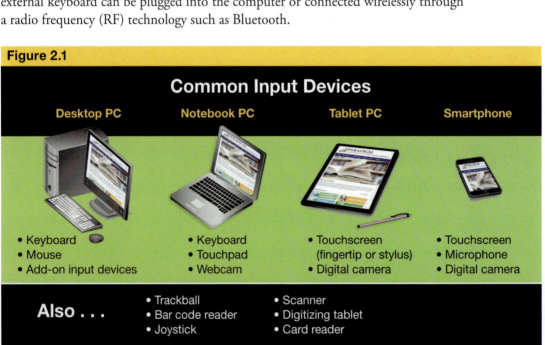

Figure 2.1

Common Input Devices

Desktop PC	Notebook PC	Tablet PC	Smartphone
• Keyboard • Mouse • Add-on input devices	• Keyboard • Touchpad • Webcam	• Touchscreen (fingertip or stylus) • Digital camera	• Touchscreen • Microphone • Digital camera

Also . . .
- Trackball
- Bar code reader
- Joystick
- Scanner
- Digitizing tablet
- Card reader

Tracking Down Tech ❯❯❯❯❯

Identifying Input and Output Devices

Input and output devices come in many different forms, from traditional keyboards and monitors to more contemporary touchscreens and biometric devices.

Complete this scavenger hunt to discover examples of input and output devices on campus and beyond.

The most common keyboard is alphanumeric and has a QWERTY layout. The term **alphanumeric keyboard** means that the keyboard has both letters (*alpha-*) and numbers (*-numeric*), and the term **QWERTY layout** refers to the first six letters in the top row of letters on the keyboard. Figure 2.2 shows a typical external keyboard with a QWERTY layout. Notice that in addition to the letters and numbers, there are several other types of keys. Function keys (F1 through F12) run across the top of the keyboard; these keys are assigned specific purposes in different operating systems and applications. Other special-purpose keys, such as Ctrl and Alt, are located to the right and left of the space bar. To the immediate right of those keys are cursor control keys (arrow keys), which control the movement of the cursor. Along the right side is a numeric keypad. The positions of some of the additional keys may vary between keyboards made by different manufacturers, and not all keyboards have all of these keys.

Not all computers require having a full alphanumeric keyboard; some work most efficiently with a special-function keyboard. For example, at a fast-food restaurant, employees take customers' orders by pressing keys on a customized grid that has a separate key for each item on the menu. Computerized voting booths also use a special-function

Activity 2.1.1

Video
Keyboard Layout

Figure 2.2

An Alphanumeric Computer Keyboard

Function keys, labeled F1, F2, F3, and so on, allow a user to quickly access commands and functions

The numeric keypad, which performs the same functions as a calculator, is used for entering numbers quickly

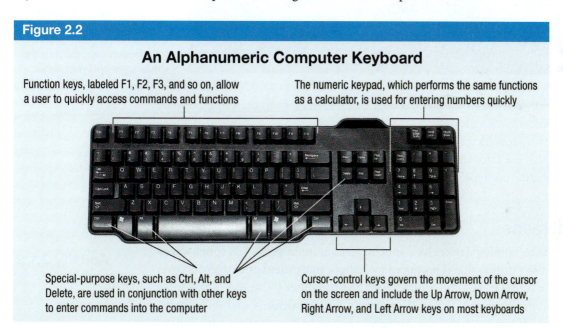

Special-purpose keys, such as Ctrl, Alt, and Delete, are used in conjunction with other keys to enter commands into the computer

Cursor-control keys govern the movement of the cursor on the screen and include the Up Arrow, Down Arrow, Right Arrow, and Left Arrow keys on most keyboards

An alphanumeric computer keyboard is organized into several groups of related keys.

Practical TECH

Are Some of Your Keys Not Working?

A keyboard is a grid of uncompleted circuits. When you press a key, a connection is made inside the keyboard, completing the circuit and sending an electrical pulse to the computer. The computer interprets the electrical pulse and inputs the corresponding character in the software you are using.

A keyboard gets dirty through normal use, and various types of debris collect under some of the keys. The debris prevents the circuit from being completed, which can cause the keys not to work. You can clean underneath the keys using compressed air or by turning the keyboard upside down and shaking it. To clean the surface of the keys, use a paper towel or soft cloth and a small amount of an all-purpose household cleaning product. Don't spray or pour the cleaning liquid directly onto the keyboard, because moisture can cause the electronics to short-circuit. Instead, spray or pour the liquid onto the cloth and wipe the cloth across the keyboard.

Figure 2.3

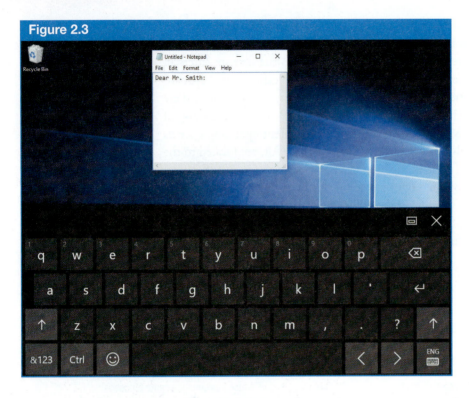

A virtual keyboard enables you to type without having a physical keyboard. You can use a pointing device (such as a mouse) to click the keys on the screen, or on a touchscreen, you can tap the virtual keys with your finger.

keyboard; in this case, the layout that has been customized for both the voting software and the candidates running for office.

A device with a touchscreen, such as a tablet PC or smartphone, may have a **virtual keyboard**, which is a software-generated, simulated keyboard (see Figure 2.3). To use a virtual keyboard, you "type" by clicking the buttons of the keyboard that appears on the screen.

Touchscreens

Many portable computing devices have touchscreens as input devices. A **touchscreen** is a touch-sensitive display that is produced by laying a transparent grid of sensors over the screen of a monitor. You can interact with the computer by tapping and sliding your fingers across the screen. Tablet PCs typically use touchscreens, and so do smartphones. Many self-service kiosks also use touchscreens, such as shopping mall directories, bridal registries at department stores, and check-in stations at airline terminals.

Activity 2.1.2

Video
Touchscreens

A touchscreen enables the user to interact with the computer by tapping and sliding his or her fingers across the surface.

Mice and Other Pointing Devices

Most operating systems represent program features and commands visually on the screen by incorporating a graphical user interface (GUI, pronounced "gooey"), which contains buttons, drop-down menus, and icons. The easiest way to interact with a GUI is with a **pointing device**—that is, an input device that moves an onscreen pointer (usually, an arrow). Pointing devices typically include buttons for making selections. The left button is usually the primary button, and the right button is generally assigned to special functions, such as displaying a pop-up menu of choices.

The most common type of pointing device is a **mouse**, a handheld device that you move across a flat surface (like a desk) to move the onscreen pointer. An alternative is a **trackball**, which is a stationary device with a ball that you roll with your fingers to move the pointer. Like a keyboard, a mouse or trackball connects to your computer using either a cord or wireless technology such as Bluetooth.

Both a mouse (top) and a trackball (bottom) connect to your computer and allow you to control an onscreen pointer.

Practical TECH

Touchscreen Gestures

Touchscreens are different from other types of input devices, and you will need some special skills to use this form of device. Here are a few important terms you should know:

- **Tap (or touch).** Tap the screen with your finger, pressing and quickly releasing on the same spot. You tap to make a selection or issue a command.

- **Pinch.** Touch two fingers to the screen in different spots and then drag the fingers together. You pinch to zoom out (and display a larger area).

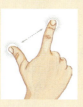

- **Stretch (or unpinch).** Touch two fingers to the screen in adjacent spots and then drag the fingers farther apart. You stretch to zoom in (and display a smaller area).

- **Drag (or slide or swipe).** Touch one finger to the screen and then slide it along the surface. You drag to perform a variety of functions, depending on the software and context. For example, dragging can open menu bars, exit applications, scroll the display, or move items around on the screen.

- **Rotate.** Touch two fingers on the desired object or area and then drag them in a circular motion.

Sliding your finger across the touchpad on a notebook computer is like moving a mouse across your desk. In this photo, below the touchpad are two buttons that function like left and right mouse buttons.

Engineers, drafters, and artists use a graphics tablet to create precise, detailed drawings.

A **touchpad** (also called a *track pad*) is a small, rectangular pad that's sensitive to pressure and motion. Many portable computers have built-in touchpads. The onscreen pointer moves as you slide your finger across the surface of the touchpad. Tapping the pad is the equivalent of pressing the primary button on a mouse. Most touchpads also have nearby buttons that work like the buttons on a mouse.

Graphics Tablets and Styluses

Artists, engineers, and others who need precise control over input can use a graphics tablet to simulate drawing on paper. A **graphics tablet** is a flat grid of intersecting wires that form uncompleted digital circuits. Each two-wire intersection has a unique numeric value. When you touch a stylus to a spot on the surface of the tablet, the circuit is completed and the computer receives a digital code that corresponds to the location of the circuit on the grid. A **stylus** resembles an inkless pen, and is used much like a normal pen, except instead of leaving ink marks directly on the tablet, it causes marks to be made in the computer software.

Tech Career Explorer

Computer-Aided Design Drafter

Before a product is manufactured, someone must first create a technical drawing defining its specifications. A computer-aided design (CAD) drafter is the person who creates this drawing, basing it on specifications from a design engineer. If you like both drawing and computers, a career in CAD might be a good fit for you. Complete this exercise to learn about a career as a CAD drafter.

Practical TECH

Pointing Device Actions

Moving the onscreen pointer is likely the action you perform most often with a pointing device. But after you have positioned the pointer at the item you want to work with, you must take one of these actions:

- **Click.** Press and release the left mouse button once without moving the pointer. You usually click to select something; for example, clicking may open a menu or select an icon.
- **Double-click.** Press and release the left mouse button twice in quick succession without moving the mouse

pointer. You usually double-click to activate something; for example, if you double-click the icon for a document, the document will open.

- **Right-click.** Press and release the right mouse button once without moving the pointer. You usually right-click to open a shortcut menu, from which you can select a command (by left-clicking it).
- **Drag.** Press and hold the left mouse button and then move the mouse. You usually drag to move whatever you have selected from one place to another onscreen.

Scanners

A **scanner** is a light-sensing device that detects and captures text and images from a printed page. It works by shining a bright light on the page and measuring the amount of light that bounces back from each spot. Lighter areas reflect the light and darker areas absorb the light—so the darker the area, the less the amount of light that bounced back. The strength of the captured light is digitized (converted to digits) and the **digitized information** is sent to the computer for recording. Figure 2.4 outlines the scanning process. Color scanners measure the amounts of red, green, and blue individually. The sensor that records the light strength is a **charge-coupled device (CCD)**.

The scanned material is stored as a **bitmap**, which is a matrix of rows and columns of pixels. A **pixel** is the smallest picture element that a monitor can display (an individual dot on the screen) and is represented by one or more bits of binary data. The more bits that are used to represent each pixel, the more different colors that can be recorded. The measurement of bits used to store information about a pixel is known as *color depth*. (This term will be discussed more later in this chapter.) For example, a

Activity 2.1.3

Practice
The Scanning Process

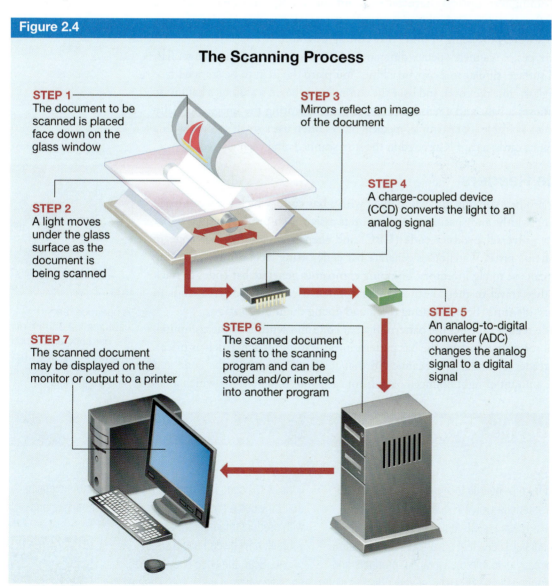

Figure 2.4

The Scanning Process

STEP 1
The document to be scanned is placed face down on the glass window

STEP 2
A light moves under the glass surface as the document is being scanned

STEP 3
Mirrors reflect an image of the document

STEP 4
A charge-coupled device (CCD) converts the light to an analog signal

STEP 5
An analog-to-digital converter (ADC) changes the analog signal to a digital signal

STEP 6
The scanned document is sent to the scanning program and can be stored and/or inserted into another program

STEP 7
The scanned document may be displayed on the monitor or output to a printer

A scanner captures text and graphic images and converts them into a format the computer can understand and display.

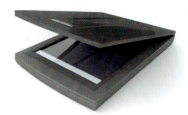

1-bit image shows each pixel as black (represented by a 1) or white (represented by a 0). A 4-bit image differentiates among 16 shades of gray, because there are 16 possible combinations of 1 and 0 in a four-digit string (0000 through 1111). A color scanner splits the number of bits among the three colors; for example, a scan with a 24-bit color depth uses 8 bits for red, 8 for green, and 8 for blue. Modern scanners typically use 30 to 48 bits per pixel. Most of those bits describe the pixel's color and shade, but some are used for error correction.

A flat-bed scanner is used to scan flat items, such as pages of a document and printed photos.

Resolution is the number of pixels captured per inch of the original page; this value is measured in **dots per inch (dpi)**. A scanner with 1,200 dpi resolution can capture 1,200 pixels per inch in each direction (horizontally and vertically). Scanners capture images at higher resolutions than most people need for displaying them, as computer screens typically display only 96 dpi. When scanning materials for use in a printout, though, you need higher resolutions and must pay more attention to dpi. The drawback of scanning at a high resolution is that the resulting image file is many times larger than that of scan at a lower resolution.

When scanning text, **optical character recognition (OCR)** software is used. This specialized software converts the bitmap images of text to actual text that you can work with in a word-processing or other text-editing program.

Different types of scanners operate differently. A **flat-bed scanner** has a large, flat, glass-covered surface, similar to a copy machine. You place the item to be scanned face down on the glass, close the cover, and issue the command to begin scanning; a bar inside the scanner moves a light and a sensor across the glass, capturing the image. Specialty scanners are also available. For example, medical offices often use a small scanner with a slot for insurance cards; a card is inserted in the slot, scanned, and then ejected.

Bar Code Readers

Nearly every product you buy today is marked with a **bar code**, which is a set of black bars of varying widths and spacing. Manufacturers assign each product a unique bar code called a **universal product code (UPC)** and then stores use the bar code to look up the item's price. Warehouses generate bar codes using label printers, creating stickers they can use to tag inventory. Shipping companies generate bar codes to track packages as they travel to their destinations. Hospitals use bar-coded wristbands to verify patients' identities before treating them and giving them medication.

A **bar code reader** captures the pattern in a bar code and sends it to the computer, where special software translates the bar pattern into meaningful data (such as price). A bar code reader is similar to a scanner in that it shines a light on the code and measures the amount of light bounced back from each spot to determine which areas

A bar code reader captures the pattern of the bar code and sends it to the computer, which translates the pattern into meaningful data.

Hotspot

QR Codes

On everything from billboards to store windows, you are likely to see mysterious-looking squares of black-and-white splotches. These are QR (quick response) codes—two-dimensional bar codes that advertisers and organizations use to direct you to information about products and services. Smartphones use QR code reader software, along with a built-in digital camera, to read a QR code and direct the device's browser to a website that is linked to that code. A QR code in a product ad might link to a website that provides a coupon or other sales promotion, along with product information. Try it for yourself now if you have a smartphone. Scan the code shown here, and see where it takes you. Then do a web search for QR code generators, and make your own QR code.

are light and which are dark. Unlike a scanner, though, a bar code reader is designed to read codes on three-dimensional (3-D) objects, not just flat pieces of paper. Bar code readers are also not nearly as technologically sophisticated as scanners. They typically record only 1 bit (black or white) for each pixel that's scanned.

Digital Cameras and Video Devices

A **digital camera** captures images in a digital format that a computer can use and display. Technologically, a digital camera is similar to a scanner: it captures the image with a charge-coupled device and uses multiple bits to describe each pixel of the image in terms of its red, green, and blue values. The main difference between the devices is that a digital camera takes pictures of 3-D objects, not just flat pieces of paper. Digital cameras are built into almost all cell phones sold today and can also be purchased as standalone devices. Figure 2.5 shows the process of capturing an image with a standalone digital camera and then transferring the image to a computer.

Activity 2.1.4

Practice
Capturing an Image with a Digital Camera

Figure 2.5

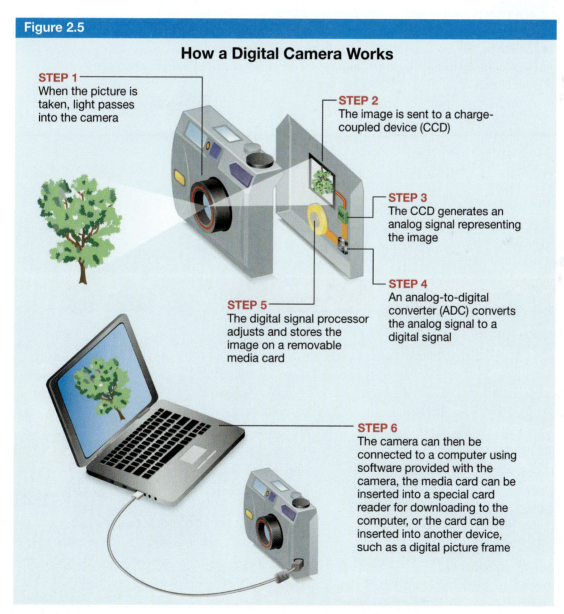

How a Digital Camera Works

STEP 1
When the picture is taken, light passes into the camera

STEP 2
The image is sent to a charge-coupled device (CCD)

STEP 3
The CCD generates an analog signal representing the image

STEP 4
An analog-to-digital converter (ADC) converts the analog signal to a digital signal

STEP 5
The digital signal processor adjusts and stores the image on a removable media card

STEP 6
The camera can then be connected to a computer using software provided with the camera, the media card can be inserted into a special card reader for downloading to the computer, or the card can be inserted into another device, such as a digital picture frame

A digital camera captures images and stores them in the camera. You can connect the camera to a computer to transfer the images to it.

From left to right: a digital camera, a digital video camera, and a webcam.

Like a scanned image, a digital photo is represented by pixels, and its color depth is measured as the number of bits used per pixel (for example, 24 bits). The resolution of the camera is the number of pixels in the highest resolution it's capable of producing; for example, a camera might have a maximum resolution of 4,096 horizontal pixels and 4,096 vertical pixels. Digital camera resolution is described in megapixels (a **megapixel** is 1 million pixels). To determine the number of megapixels, multiply the camera's vertical resolution by its horizontal resolution. For example, a 4,096 × 4,096 resolution has a total of 16,777,216 pixels (16.7 megapixels).

Some digital cameras can capture both video and still images, but a **digital video camera** is designed primarily for capturing video. A digital video camera may be portable, like a regular camera, or it may be tethered to a computer (either by a cable or wirelessly). A digital video camera that must be connected to a computer to take pictures is called a **webcam**, because it's commonly used to capture live video that's streamed to the public via a website.

Digital cameras have other uses too. In some newer cars, the rear-view camera is a digital camera. Likewise, the active parking assistance feature in some cars relies on input from a video camera to gauge how close the car is to surrounding vehicles.

Hotspot

Photo Storage in the Cloud

Transferring pictures from a smartphone's digital camera is a snap. Many smartphones can be set up to automatically upload the photos you take to your own private storage area online, in the cloud. (You'll learn more about the cloud in Chapter 7.) For example, you can set up a Windows Phone to send your pictures to your OneDrive (for more information, go to http://CUT6.emcp.net/OneDrive), or set up an iPhone to upload your pictures to iCloud (http://CUT6.emcp.net/iCloud). You can then easily retrieve your pictures from any other computing device by logging in to the cloud storage service with your user account for that service.

Many businesses use digital camera and video technology to help make their practices more efficient. For example, many businesses use digital video cameras to record the activities of employees and customers; this is done

not only for security purposes but also to collect data for efficiency studies and audits. Businesses may also use digital cameras to make sure employees are authorized to enter certain restricted areas or access sensitive data on a computer. Some manufacturers use video technology for quality control. For example, a product moving along an assembly line can be photographed and instantly compared with a stored photograph of the perfect product. If a missing or broken part is detected, the product is rejected before it's packaged for shipment.

Audio Input Devices

The speech, music, and sound effects that are entered into a computer are called **audio input**. Nearly all PCs today have sound support that's either built in or provided by an add-on circuit board called a **sound card**. A sound card works by going back and forth between the analog sounds that humans hear and the digital recordings of sound that computers store and play back—translating one into the other. Sound support on a system also typically includes ports for connecting microphones, digital musical instruments, and other sound input devices. There may also be ports for output devices such as speakers and headphones, covered later in this chapter.

A headset that includes both headphones (for output) and a microphone (for input) enables two-way communication with the computer and with other people.

Voice input technologies enable users to enter data by talking to the computer. Some operating systems, including Windows, provide basic software for voice input as part of their accessibility tools. Some application software, such as word-processing programs, also support voice input.

There are two types of voice input programs: voice recognition and speech recognition. A **voice recognition software** doesn't understand or process speech. Instead, it recognizes only preprogrammed words that are stored in a database. This type of program is also speaker independent, which means it doesn't pay attention to a person's vocal tone, pitch, or inflections. For example, a voice-activated automated teller machine (ATM) enables customers to conduct financial transactions by speaking into the machine. Voice recognition programs are also included in Microsoft Windows and Microsoft Office.

Voice recognition software has two main drawbacks: it recognizes only the words in the database, and it may have difficulty understanding individuals with accents or unusual speech inflections. **Speech recognition software** offers an alternative. It's

Cutting Edge

Biometric Security

Authenticating computer users by analyzing their physical characteristics is known as biometric security. All biometric security technologies rely on various types of digital input devices, such as fingerprint readers, cameras and video cameras, and microphones. These devices record input from the person attempting to access the computer, such as his or her fingerprint, face, retina, or voice. That input is then compared against scans, pictures, video clips, and audio clips for allowed users, which are stored in a database. The person is permitted access to the computer only if it finds a match.

Until recently, biometric security was very expensive, because the technology for reliably scanning and analyzing physical characteristics was still new. However, recent technological advances have made this type of security system affordable for almost any business or individual.

New versions of the iPhone, for example, have a fingerprint identity sensor built in, enabling password-free security.

Biometric security is not perfect, however. Hackers have found ways to fool some biometric devices to gain access to computer systems—not just in the movies, but in real life too, as we discovered in 2013 when hackers publicized their success at fooling the iPhone's fingerprint scanner. Occasionally, too, a device will not recognize a legitimate user and will lock him or her out, but workarounds such as alternative authentication methods can allow the user access until a system administrator can correct the problem.

"trained" to understand a specific person's voice by completing a series of practice drills. The speaker reads many paragraphs of text into a microphone, and the software stores his or her voice patterns as examples of what specific words sounds like. This software can also learn new words. Speech recognition software is speaker dependent; it works best when accepting input from a user it has been trained to understand.

Sensory and Location Input Devices

A computer can accept input not only from a human user but also from the environment. For example, some portable Apple devices accept input data from several types of environmental sensors. An **accelerometer** reports how fast an object is moving; a **gyroscope** describes an object's orientation in space; and a **compass** reports the direction of an object's location. Sensors like these can provide data to fitness-tracking applications (apps), as well as apps that need to be aware of the user's activities, such as whether he or she is driving, running, or walking. Some advanced pedometers (which count steps taken) also use sensory input. For example, some models of Fitbits can be worn when sleeping and then connected to a computer to analyze how much the wearer tosses and turns during the night.

Global positioning system (GPS) devices also provide location information. A GPS works by orienting the current location of the device to a signal from an orbiting satellite. Based on this information, the device can report its position on Earth to within about 15 meters (50 feet). In addition to the traditional driving GPS models used in automobiles, there are several specialized models. GPS devices can be attached to children's clothing or pets' collars and used to report their locations.

A global positioning system (GPS) provides a map and/or directions for driving or walking to a particular destination.

Recheck 2.1
Recheck your understanding of the concepts covered by this objective.

Tech Ethics

The Chip Debate

Radio frequency identification (RFID) chips have long been used in labels to track products and packages, and in badges to allow employees into secure areas of a facility. Alzheimer's patients may be fitted with ankle or wrist bracelets containing RFID chips to help care providers locate them if they wander off. People generally accept these uses of RFID. But how would you feel about having such a chip implanted inside your body?

Certain types of RFID chips can be embedded under the skin of living beings. Dog and cat owners already take advantage of this technology, "microchipping" pets to help facilitate their return if they are ever lost. The same technology is used as an alternative to branding on livestock such as cattle. Implanting RFID chips in humans, though, has proved to be controversial.

From 2004 to 2010, PositiveID (formerly VeriChip) marketed a chip that could be implanted in humans and

that seemed poised for wide adoption. This glass-encapsulated RFID chip, about an inch long, could be implanted in a doctor's office under local anesthetic. When read, it generated a 16-digit number that could then be matched with a database entry to identify the person. That ID number, as unique as a person's Social Security number, could potentially match that person up with a variety of databases containing security clearance, medical, and military information.

PositiveID stopped making the chip, amid widespread international debate over its use. One controversial issue was that the chip's number was unencrypted, so anyone with a chip reader could easily identify the person, with or without his or her permission. However, this technology might be revived in the future if someone develops an innovative use that is so valuable that it outweighs most people's privacy concerns.

2.2 Understanding How Computers Process Data

 Precheck **2.2**

Check your understanding of the concepts covered by this objective.

So far in this chapter, you have learned about several ways in which data can enter a computer system. After data is entered, it's temporarily stored in memory until the software asks the central processing unit (CPU) to perform calculations on it. The CPU delivers the calculated data back to the software, and the software uses it to create output. The output is then stored temporarily in memory until the software is ready to deliver the data to an output device or another program.

At a basic level, you can think about data processing by observing how the applications you use manipulate and change the data you enter. For example, a payroll program manipulates data by calculating employees' gross pay, tax withholdings, deductions, and net pay. The results of those calculations can then be used to print employee paychecks and reports. The CPU calculates all of those amounts. (Of course, the CPU also calculates millions of other pieces of data that aren't as readily visible, such as which pixels will light up with a certain color onscreen when you move the mouse pointer or open a window.)

At a technical level, data processing is much more complicated than just described and involves millions of operations per second (MIPS). A computer might have many programs running at once, each sending millions of processing requests to the CPU. All of these requests wait in a queue for their turn to run through the CPU, which performs the actual math operations. When the completed calculations exit the CPU, they are returned to the program from which they were requested.

In addition to the applications you might run, the operating system itself also makes millions of requests of the CPU. These requests are necessary to keep the operating system's user interface up and running.

Bits and Bytes

Computers are electronic devices, which means they operate using electricity. The earliest developers of computer systems used this fact to construct a language for communicating with the CPU. In this language, an electrical charge or pulse is a 1 and a lack of an electrical charge is a 0 (see Figure 2.6). Computers represent all data using binary strings of numbers. (A **binary string** consists of only 1s and 0s.) Each individual 1 or 0 is a **bit**, which is short for *binary digit*.

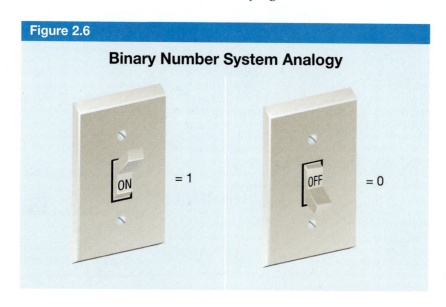

Figure 2.6

Binary Number System Analogy

ON = 1   OFF = 0

Computer circuits are toggled on and off by transistors, which operate like light switches. When current flows through the transistor, it's on, and a 1 value is represented. When current does not flow through the transistor, it's off, and a 0 value is represented.

Table 2.1 Measures of Computer Storage Capacity

Term	Abbreviation	Approximate Number of Bytes	Exact Number of Bytes
Byte		1	1
Kilobyte	KB	1 thousand	1,024
Megabyte	MB	1 million	1,048,576
Gigabyte	GB	1 billion	1,073,741,824
Terabyte	TB	1 trillion	1,099,411,627,776
Petabyte	PB	1 quadrillion	1,125,899,906,842,624
Exabyte	EB	1 quintillion	1,151,921,504,606,846,976
Zettabyte	ZB	1 sextillion	1,180,591,620,717,303,424
Yottabyte	YB	1 septillion	1,208,925,819,614,629,174,706,176

A group of 8 bits is a **byte**. A byte is an 8-digit binary number between 00000000 and 11111111. There are 256 possible combinations of 1s and 0s in a string of 8. Most computer programs work with bytes, rather than bits. Computer memory and disk storage capacity is also measured in bytes. A **kilobyte** is approximately 1 thousand bytes. Today's systems work with bytes by the millions and billions; one **megabyte** is 1 million bytes, and one **gigabyte** is 1 billion bytes. See Table 2.1 for other measures of computer memory.

Encoding Schemes

If all of the data in a computer is binary, how does the computer store and display text that humans can understand? It uses an **encoding scheme**, which is a system of binary codes that represent different letters, numbers, and symbols.

Early personal computers employed an encoding scheme called **American Standard Code for Information Interchange (ASCII)**, which assigned a unique 8-bit binary code to each number and letter in the English

Table 2.2 Examples of Characters Encoded with ASCII

Character	ASCII
A	01000001
B	01000010
C	01000011
1	01100001
2	01100010
$	00100100

language plus many of the most common symbols such as punctuation and currency marks. Table 2.2 shows a few examples of ASCII encoding.

Although ASCII was widely adopted as a standard for PCs, over time it proved too limited. ASCII's main shortcoming was that it couldn't deal with languages such as Chinese, which have a more complicated alphabet than English. To accommodate a larger selection of characters, a system called **Unicode** was developed. Unicode uses 2 bytes (16 bits) per character and can represent up to 65,536 characters. The first 256 codes are the same in both ASCII and Unicode, so existing ASCII-coded data is compatible with modern Unicode-based operating systems, such as Microsoft Windows and Macintosh OS X.

Recheck **2.2**
Recheck your understanding of the concepts covered by this objective.

2.3 Identifying Components in the System Unit

The main part of the computer is the **system unit**; it houses the major components used in processing data. For a desktop PC, the system unit is a large box. A notebook or tablet contains many of the same components, but the system unit is smaller and packed together more tightly. The following sections discuss the components inside a typical system unit, like the one shown in Figure 2.7.

Power Supply

The **power supply** converts the 110-volt or 220-volt alternating current (AC) from your wall outlet to the much lower voltage direct current (DC) that computer components require. In a notebook computer, this function is handled by the power converter block that's built into the power cord. In a desktop PC, the power supply is a large, silver box. A desktop power supply usually contains one or more fans, which cool both the power supply and the entire system unit.

Motherboard

The **motherboard** is the large circuit board that covers almost the entire floor of the system unit (or the side, depending on how the unit is oriented). Like other circuit boards, the motherboard consists of a variety of electronic components (including sockets, chips, and connectors) that are mounted onto a sheet of fiberglass or other material. The electronic components are connected by conductive pathways called **traces**. The motherboard has a controller chip (or set of chips) called a **chipset**, which controls and directs all of the data traffic on the board. The chipset determines the motherboard's capabilities—from the CPUs and RAM types it will support to the speed at which data flows through it.

Precheck 2.3

Check your understanding of the concepts covered by this objective.

Activity 2.3.1

Video
External Parts of a PC

Activity 2.3.2

Video
Internal PC Components

Figure 2.7

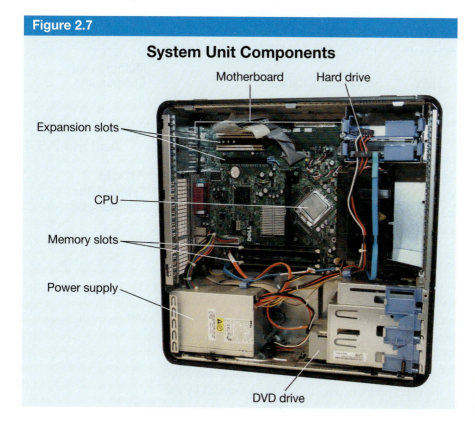

System Unit Components

- Motherboard
- Hard drive
- Expansion slots
- CPU
- Memory slots
- Power supply
- DVD drive

The system unit is the main part of a desktop PC and contains the components necessary for processing data.

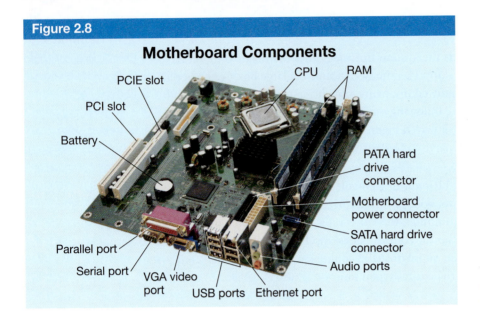

Figure 2.8

Motherboard Components

- PCIE slot
- PCI slot
- Battery
- CPU
- RAM
- PATA hard drive connector
- Motherboard power connector
- SATA hard drive connector
- Audio ports
- Parallel port
- Serial port
- VGA video port
- USB ports
- Ethernet port

The motherboard holds the major processing and memory components.

Other components found on a motherboard include the following:

- The CPU, which processes the data
- A coin-style battery (on older systems) for keeping certain chips powered when the system is off
- Slots for connecting random access memory (RAM) modules, which provide temporary storage for the data applications and operating system to use while running
- Slots for attaching expansion boards, which add various capabilities to the computer (as described in the next section)
- Ports for connecting input devices (such as a keyboard and mouse) and output devices (such as a speaker, monitor, and printer)
- A power connector for accepting the electricity needed to keep each component powered

Figure 2.8 identifies some of the features of a typical motherboard.

 Activity 2.3.3

Video
Motherboard Components

Buses

Data moves from one component to another on the motherboard by means of buses. A **bus** is an electronic path along which data is transmitted. Most buses are embedded into the motherboard.

The size of a bus is referred to as **bus width**; it determines the number of bits the bus can transmit or receive at one time. For example, a 32-bit bus can carry 32 bits at a time, whereas a 64-bit bus can carry 64 bits. The larger the bus width, the more data the bus can carry per second.

 Activity 2.3.4

Article
External Bus Technologies

One way to visualize a bus is to think of it as a highway, with stops along the way (exits) where data is dropped off or picked up. The bus width is like the number of lanes on the highway. The more lanes, the more traffic the highway can handle without delays. Each bus also has a certain speed at which it operates. Think of this as the speed limit on the highway. (On computer buses, however, there are no speeders; all data travels at exactly the speed for which the bus was designed.)

Computers contain two basic bus types: a system bus and an expansion bus. The **system bus** connects the CPU to the main memory, and its speed is governed by the system clock (which you will learn about later in this chapter). An **expansion bus** provides communication between the CPU and a peripheral device, which may be connected through an expansion board or port (covered in the next two sections of this chapter).

Expansion Slots and Expansion Boards

An **expansion slot** is a narrow opening in the motherboard that allows the insertion of an expansion board. An **expansion board** (also called an *expansion card* or *adapter*) adds some specific capability to the system, such as sound, networking, or extra ports for connecting external devices. Even if the motherboard already has built-in support for a particular capability, an expansion board is sometimes needed to provide better quality support or support for additional devices. For example, you might add another display adapter to support having more than one monitor.

An expansion board is manufactured to fit in one type of slot, and slot types correspond to different types of buses. Over the years, computers have had several different slot types for expansion boards. When you purchase an expansion board, make sure you get a model that will fit in one of the empty slots in your motherboard.

The most common type of expansion bus in motherboards today is the **Peripheral Component Interconnect Express (PCIe) bus**. PCIe slots come in different sizes. The most common interface for display adapters is PCIe ×16, which is a high-speed slot with 16 data channels. The most common interface for other expansion boards is PCIe ×1, which uses only 1 data channel. You may also come across a legacy PCI slot, which is an early technology that many motherboards still support.

Portable computers, such as notebooks and tablets, don't have room for traditional expansion slots and boards. However, some of these devices have a PCI Express Mini Card slot, into which you can insert a miniature version of an expansion board. To install or remove a PCI Express Mini Card, you must shut down the computer and remove a panel on the bottom to access the slot.

Some notebook computers also accept ExpressCard expansion cards, although this is becoming less common. An **ExpressCard** is a cartridge about the size of a credit card but thicker that slides into a slot in the side of a computer device. One of the most popular uses for an ExpressCard is to add wireless network functionality to a device that doesn't have it built in. Earlier technologies that looked and acted a lot like ExpressCards were called *CardBus*, *PC Card*, and *PCMCIA*.

ExpressCard cards are used primarily in notebook computers.

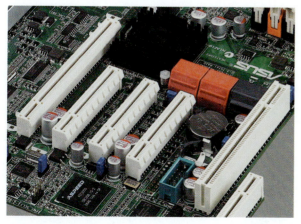

This photo shows four PCIe slots of different sizes: one ×16 (left) and three ×4 (middle). The fifth slot (right) is a traditional 32-bit PCI slot.

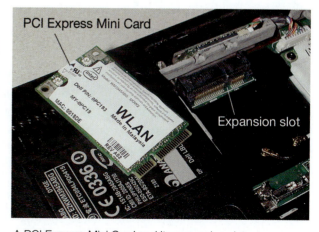

A PCI Express Mini Card and its expansion slot.

Ports

A **port** (sometimes called an *interface*) is an external plug-in socket on a computing device. Ports are used to connect external devices such as printers, modems, and routers to a computer. Some ports are dedicated, or reserved for one specific type of device. Other types of ports are generic and used for a variety of different devices. Table 2.3 shows examples of the types of ports commonly found on personal computers.

Universal Serial Bus (USB) A **universal serial bus (USB) port** is a general-purpose port that's used by many different devices, including input devices (such as keyboards and mice) and external storage devices (such as external hard drives, USB flash drives, and digital cameras). USB technology has many attractive features. For example, you can connect an external hub to a USB port and then connect more than 100 devices to it (in theory, anyway); all of the devices will run off that single USB port in your computer. USB ports are also hot-pluggable, so you can connect and disconnect devices while the computer is running.

Different speeds of USBs have been available over the years. USB 1.1 operates at 1.5 megabits per second (Mbps) and is usually colored white. USB 2.0 (also called *Hi-Speed USB*) operates at up to 480 Mbps and is usually colored black. USB 3.0 (also called *SuperSpeed*) transfers data at up to 4 gigabits per second (Gbps) and is usually colored blue.

IEEE 1394 (FireWire) FireWire is a competitor to USB. A **FireWire port** is more widely known by its standard number: IEEE 1394. (*IEEE* stands for *Institute of Electrical and Electronics Engineers*, an international standards organization.) A FireWire port is a general-purpose port that's often used to connect external drives and video cameras. FireWire 400 (IEEE 1394a) is the port used on most personal computers; it transfers data at up to 400 Mbps. Two different connectors are used for this port: a 6-wire model and a 4-wire model. FireWire 800 (IEEE 1394b) uses a different connector, and is twice as fast (800 Mbps); it is used for connecting high-speed drives.

eSATA eSATA is an external version of the Serial ATA standard that's used for connecting internal hard drives (as you will learn in Chapter 3). (The *e* in *eSATA* stands for *external*.) Most external hard drives connect to a computer via the USB or FireWire port, but some newer models use the **eSATA port** for faster transfer speeds. eSATA can transfer data four times faster than the IEEE 1394a or USB 2.0.

S-Video S-video (also known as *i480*) is a standard for video output for TVs. (The *S* is for *standard*, meaning "not high-definition.") Some computers have an **S-video port** for connecting with a TV and using it as a monitor.

Table 2.3 Common Types of PC Ports

	Universal serial bus (USB)
	FireWire 400 (IEEE 1394a)
	FireWire 800 (IEEE 1394b)
	eSATA
	Digital visual interface (DVI)
	Video graphics adapter (VGA)
	S-video
	High-definition multimedia interface (HDMI)
	Ethernet
	Telephone/Modem
	3.5-millimeter audio
	Serial (COM)
	Parallel (LPT)
	PS/2

High-Definition Multimedia Interface (HDMI) High-definition multimedia interface (HDMI) is the interface for high-definition (HD) TV and home theater equipment. It's a digital format and was designed for interfacing with digital devices. Some computers have a **high-definition multimedia interface (HDMI) port** for connecting to HDMI-capable input and output devices.

Digital Visual Interface (DVI) A **digital visual interface (DVI) port** is the most common type of port for display monitors in modern computer systems. A DVI port is used not only to connect computer monitors but also in consumer electronics devices such as home theater systems, game consoles, and TVs. Unlike HDMI, which is the dominant video standard for HDTV, DVI is backward compatible with VGA, the previous standard for connecting computer monitors. An adapter plug is used to change the connector type for older monitors.

VGA A **video graphics adapter (VGA) port** is an older type of monitor connector that's still used in many systems. On a PC, the VGA is a 15-pin female D-sub connector (often abbreviated as DB15F). A **D-sub connector** is a D-shaped ring with metal pins inside it. D-sub connectors are described based on the number of pins and whether they are male (having pins) or female (having holes).

Ethernet An **Ethernet port** enables a computer to connect to a router, cable modem, or other networking device using a cable. (Wireless Ethernet doesn't require a port.) An Ethernet port and cable resemble those used for a telephone jack but are a little wider. The official name of the Ethernet connector is **RJ-45 port**. (*RJ* stands for *registered jack*.)

Telephone/Modem A **dial-up modem** is a device for connecting to the Internet or a remote network via telephone. Your system has this type of connection if you see two telephone jacks side by side. One jack is for the phone cable from the wall outlet, and the other is for plugging in a telephone; this enables the phone signal to pass through the modem on its way to your telephone handset. With this setup, a modem and a handset can share a single outlet. The official name for the plug that connects a telephone is RJ-11 (for a single-line cable with two wires) or RJ-14 (for a dual-line cable with four wires).

Audio An **audio port** is generally a small, circular hole into which a 3.5-millimeter connector is plugged for analog input devices (such as microphones, analog stereo equipment, and musical instruments) and output devices (such as speakers and headphones). Sometimes these ports are color-coded, as described in Table 2.4.

Table 2.4 Color Coding of Audio Ports

Color	Common Use
Pink or red	Analog microphone input
Light blue	Analog line input (from a cassette tape deck or turntable)
Lime green	Analog output (speakers or headphones)
Black	Analog output (rear speakers in a surround sound system)
Silver	Analog output (side speakers in a surround sound system)
Orange	Analog output (center speaker or subwoofer in a surround sound system)

Legacy Ports In computer terms, *legacy* means older technology that enables backward compatibility. A **legacy port** is a computer port that is still in use but has been largely replaced by a port with more functionality. The following kinds of ports are mostly obsolete, but you may still find them on older systems:

- A **serial port** (also called a *COM port*, which is short for *communications port*) is a 9-pin male D-sub connector on the PC. Serial ports were used to connect a variety of devices a decade or more ago, but today, almost all of these devices use USB.
- A **parallel port** (also called an *LPT port*, which is short for *line printer*) is a 25-pin female D-sub connector on the PC, which matches up with a 25-pin male connector on the cable. This type of port was used to connect printers before USB became popular.
- A **PS/2 port** is a small, round port that used to be the standard for connecting the keyboard and the mouse to the computer. The keyboard port was light green and the mouse port was purple, but physically, the two ports were identical. The term *PS/2* comes from the name of a very old IBM computer that introduced this connector style.

Storage Bays

A **storage bay** (often referred to as a *bay*) is a space in the system unit where a storage device (such as a hard drive or a DVD drive) can be installed. The number of bays in the system unit determines the maximum number of internal storage devices the system can have, so it's an important factor to consider when purchasing a PC. Most portable PCs (that is, notebooks and tablets) don't have any empty storage bays, so bays aren't an issue on them. Figure 2.9 shows an empty desktop case with several storage bays.

Storage bays come in two sizes. Small bays are designed to hold hard drives. (They also hold floppy disk drives, if present, although such drives are now obsolete.) Large bays are designed to hold CD and DVD drives. A case has one or more pop-out panels that you can remove to provide a storage device with outside access. For example, a DVD drive needs outside access so you can insert and eject discs. Storage devices are typically mounted into bays with screws that fit in the holes in the bay housing, but some system units use sliding rails to mount devices.

The case of a typical desktop computer has several storage bays.

Figure 2.9

Desktop Computer Storage Bays

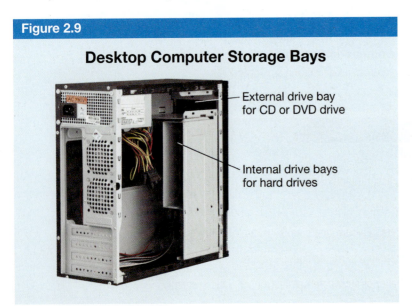

External drive bay for CD or DVD drive

Internal drive bays for hard drives

Recheck 2.3

Recheck your understanding of the concepts covered by this objective.

2.4 Understanding the CPU

 Precheck 2.4

Check your understanding of the concepts covered by this objective.

Every computer contains a **central processing unit (CPU)**, which is also sometimes called a *microprocessor* or *processor*. The CPU is responsible for performing all of the calculations for the system—and just about everything that happens in a computer requires performing millions of calculations. These facts make the CPU the most essential (and also the busiest) component in the system.

Physically, a CPU is a very small wafer of **semiconductor material**; a complex set of tiny transistors and other electronic components are etched into it. The term *semiconductor* is used because this material is neither a good conductor of electricity (like copper would be) nor a good insulator against electricity (like rubber would be). Semiconductor material therefore doesn't interfere with the flow of electricity in a chip's circuits one way or the other. The most commonly used semiconductor material in CPUs is silicon, which is a type of purified glass. This very complex and expensive wafer is mounted on a small circuit board and protected by a ceramic and metal casing.

From the outside, a CPU may look like a metal or ceramic plate with many short pins (metal spikes) or tiny dots of metal on one side. The type of CPU packaging that has pins is called a *pin grid array* (*PGA*). The pins fit into holes in the CPU socket in the motherboard. The type of CPU packaging that has metal dots is called a *land grid array* (*LGA*). The metal dots line up with metal contacts on the CPU socket, making an electrical connection.

 **Activity 2.4.1**

Video
PGA and LGA CPUs

This pin grid array (PGA) chip has a series of pins on its underside. The pins fit into holes in a socket, and each pin transfers a different piece of data into or out of the CPU.

Hotspot

Coming Soon: Transistors on Steroids!

What's in a chip? Millions of microscopic transistors—those tiny pieces of semiconductor material that amplify a signal or open and close a circuit.

What happens when you lace silicon with the chemical element germanium and cool it down to a temperature of absolute zero? You get a supersonic transistor—the building block used to produce supersonic chips. This is what IBM has done. It's created a superfast transistor that will lead to ever-faster computers and wireless networks.

IBM's speedy transistors run 100 times faster than the transistors currently available, reaching speeds of 500 gigahertz (GHz). For comparison, cell phone chips dawdle along at a mere 2 GHz, and digital music player chips at around 5 GHz.

In initial tests, the IBM transistor attained its highest speed at a temperature near absolute zero (which is -451 degrees Fahrenheit). But even at room temperature, the transistor ran at 300 GHz. Although mass-produced transistors probably wouldn't match the racecar speed of the prototype, they would still be much faster than what is available today.

Superfast transistors might make it possible for a wireless network to download a DVD in five seconds and for buildings to be outfitted with 60 GHz wireless connections. Better yet, cars could come equipped with radar that would automatically adjust speed according to traffic or swerve to avoid oncoming vehicles.

Internal Components

Inside a typical CPU, there are three main components: a control unit, an arithmetic logic unit (ALU), and registers (see Figure 2.10).

The CPU's internal components perform four basic operations that are collectively called a **machine cycle**. The machine cycle includes fetching an instruction, decoding the instruction, executing the instruction, and storing the result.

Control Unit The **control unit** directs and coordinates the overall operation of the CPU. It acts as a "traffic officer," signaling to other parts of the computer system what they should do. The control unit interprets instructions and initiates the action needed to carry them out. First it fetches, which means it retrieves an instruction or data from memory. Then it decodes, which means it interprets or translates the instruction into strings of binary digits that the computer understands.

Arithmetic Logic Unit (ALU) As shown in Figure 2.10, the **arithmetic logic unit (ALU)** is the part of the CPU that executes the instruction during the machine cycle. In other words, the ALU carries out the instructions and performs arithmetic and logical operations on the data. The arithmetic operations the ALU can perform are addition, subtraction, multiplication, and division. The ALU can also perform logical operations, such as comparing two data strings and determining whether they are identical.

Registers A **register** functions as a "workbench" inside the CPU, holding the data that the ALU is processing. Placing data into a register is the storing step of the machine cycle. Registers can be accessed much faster than memory locations outside the CPU.

Various types of registers are available in the CPU, and each serves a specific purpose. Once processing begins, an instruction register holds the instructions currently being executed. A data register holds the data items being acted on by the ALU. A storage register holds the immediate and final results of the processing.

Activity 2.4.2

Video
How Data Flows into a PC

Activity 2.4.3

Practice
Looking Inside a CPU

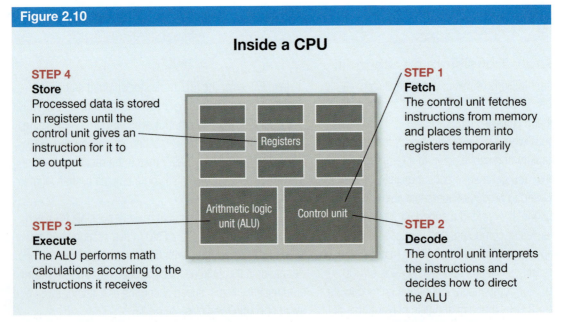

Figure 2.10

Inside a CPU

STEP 4
Store
Processed data is stored in registers until the control unit gives an instruction for it to be output

STEP 1
Fetch
The control unit fetches instructions from memory and places them into registers temporarily

Registers

Arithmetic logic unit (ALU)

Control unit

STEP 3
Execute
The ALU performs math calculations according to the instructions it receives

STEP 2
Decode
The control unit interprets the instructions and decides how to direct the ALU

The CPU contains a control unit, arithmetic logic unit (ALU), and registers. These components interact in a machine cycle to fetch, decode, execute, and store instructions and data.

Caches Because the CPU is so much faster than the computer's other components, it can potentially spend a lot of time idle, waiting for data to be delivered or picked up. The farther the data has to travel to get to the CPU, the longer the delay. To help minimize these delays, modern CPUs have multiple caches. A **cache** (pronounced "cash") is a pool of extremely fast memory that's stored close to the CPU and connected to it by a very fast pathway. Only when the needed data isn't found in any of the caches does the system have to fetch data from storage (for example, the main memory of the PC, or a hard drive).

When the CPU needs some data, it looks first in the L1 (level 1) cache, which is the one closest to the CPU. The L1 cache is an **on die cache**; this means that when the CPU is stamped into the silicon wafer, the L1 cache is stamped into the same piece of silicon at the same time. The L1 cache is quite small, so it can't hold everything the CPU has recently used or may need to use soon.

If the data needed isn't found in the L1 cache, the system looks in the L2 cache. On older systems, the L2 cache was on the motherboard, but on modern systems, it's in the CPU package, next to the silicon chip. If the data isn't in the L2 cache, the system checks the L3 cache, which is larger and slightly farther away from the CPU. On a multicore CPU (discussed on pages 64–65), all of the cores share a common L3 cache.

Speed and Processing Capability

The most obvious quality of a CPU is its speed, which is measured as the number of operations it can perform per second. A CPU's advertised speed is the maximum speed at which it can reliably operate without overheating or malfunctioning. The speed of a CPU is measured in gigahertz (GHz). One hertz is one cycle per second, and one gigahertz is 1 billion hertz.

The CPU's speed rating is just a suggestion. The actual speed at which the system components function is determined by a chip on the motherboard called the **system clock** (or *system crystal*). It's a small oscillator crystal that synchronizes the timing of all operations on the motherboard. The CPU is so much faster than the other components in the system that it typically operates at a multiple of the other components' speeds, performing multiple actions per tick of the clock. For example, the system clock rate might be 300 megahertz (MHz), and the CPU might run at 10 times that speed (3 GHz).

A CPU's performance depends on more than just its maximum speed. The number of transistors inside the CPU is equally important. Modern CPUs have millions or even billions of transistors. For example, the Intel i7-4960X CPU (introduced in 2013) has more than 1.86 billion transistors. In contrast, the Intel 80286 (introduced in 1982) had about 134,000 transistors. More modern and more expensive CPUs tend to have more transistors.

Another factor is a CPU's **word size**. In computer terms, a *word* is a group of bits that a computer can manipulate or process as a unit. If a CPU is 32-bit, it can handle 32-bit blocks of data at a time. Most modern desktop systems have 64-bit CPUs, and 32-bit CPUs are found in many mobile devices. The Microsoft Windows operating system is available in versions for both 32-bit and 64-bit systems.

 **Activity 2.4.4**

Article
Benchmarking a System

 Tech Career Explorer

Programming in Assembly Language

Are you interested in hard-core computer programming at the CPU level? The 1s-and-0s level of programming is called *machine language*. One step up from that is *assembly language*, which uses simple text strings to communicate directly with the CPU, telling it what registers to store each byte of data in and what instructions from its instruction set to load and run. This type of low-level programming proficiency is required if you want to be a computer engineer who designs the next generation of CPUs. If you think you might like to experiment with assembly language, complete this exercise.

The performance of a CPU also depends on a variety of special data-handling procedures that manufacturers have built into CPU designs over the years. Many of these procedures provide different ways to process multiple instructions at a time. Here are some of the key advances to date in CPU design and manufacturing:

- **Better manufacturing.** CPU manufacturing has greatly improved, resulting in smaller and closer circuits. Having smaller circuits means that more transistors can be fit on the same size chip and that the CPU will generate less heat as it operates. Having circuits be closer together means the data and instructions don't have to travel as far, and so they reach their destinations faster. CPU manufacturing has also been improved by the use of better materials; for instance, using copper rather than aluminum allows better conductivity.

- **Pipelining.** In older computers, the CPU had to completely execute one instruction before starting a second instruction. Modern computers can perform multiple instructions at once by using a technique called **pipelining**. This technique enables the CPU to begin executing another instruction as soon as the previous one reaches the next phase of the machine cycle. Figure 2.11 illustrates the difference in productivity that pipelining provides.

- **Parallel processing.** A **thread** is a part of a program that can execute independently of other parts. Early computer systems had only one CPU, and it could process only one thread at a time. **Parallel processing** allows two or more processors (or cores within a single processor) in the same computer to work on different threads simultaneously.

- **Superscalar architecture.** **Superscalar architecture** is a type of CPU design that creates better throughput. Specifically, it enables the operating system to send instructions to multiple components inside the CPU during a single clock cycle. For example, a single clock cycle might deliver instructions to an ALU and store data in a register.

- **Multithreading. Multithreading** enables the operating system to address two or more virtual cores in a single-core CPU and share the workload between them. Intel's version of multithreading is called **hyper-threading**.

- **Multicore processors.** The term **core** refers to the essential processor components (that is, the ALU, registers, and control unit). Most modern computers

 **Activity 2.4.5**

Article
**Advances
in Chip Architecture**

 Activity 2.4.6

Article
**Improvements
in Chip Materials
and Manufacturing
Processes**

 **Activity 2.4.7**

Video
Multicore Processors

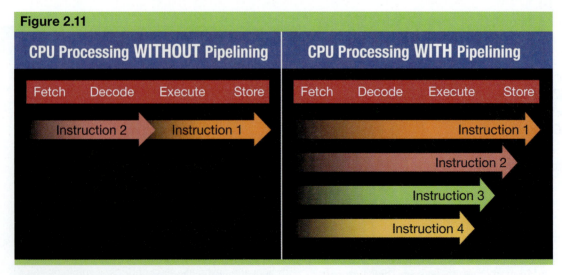

Figure 2.11

Without pipelining, the CPU must complete one instruction before starting a second instruction. With pipelining, the CPU begins executing a new instruction as soon as the previous instruction reaches the next phase of the machine cycle.

have multicore processors. A **multicore processor** enables a computer to process several instructions at once, as if the system physically contains more than one CPU. Each core has its own L1 and L2 cache, and all of the cores share a single L3 cache.

2.5 Understanding Memory

At the most basic level, **memory** is an electronic chip that contains a grid of transistors that can be on (1) or off (0). Memory stores data by holding a 1 or 0 value in each transistor and then reporting it when requested to do so.

There are two types of memory: **read-only memory (ROM)** and **random access memory (RAM)**. ROM chips store the same data permanently, regardless of whether the computer is powered on. ROM can't be rewritten (at least not by the computer in which it's installed). ROM chips are used to store data that never changes. For example, the motherboard may contain a small amount of ROM that provides the startup instructions for the processing component of the system. ROM has the advantage of being very quick to read from, but the fact that it can't be updated easily limits its functionality. In contrast, the values stored on RAM chips can be easily changed as the computer operates, storing first one value and then another as needed. For this reason, RAM is the primary type of memory used in almost all computing devices. When people refer to a computer's "memory," they are usually referring to RAM.

RAM Basics

The most common use for RAM is as temporary storage for data and programs when the computer is in use. When people refer to a computer's "main memory," they generally mean the RAM that's installed on the motherboard and available for use by the operating system.

 Recheck 2.4
Recheck your understanding of the concepts covered by this objective.

 Precheck 2.5
Check your understanding of the concepts covered by this objective.

 Activity 2.5.1
Video
Memory Installation

Cutting Edge

Nanotechnology

A *nanometer* (nm) is one-billionth of a meter. How small is that? It's so small that it's atomic. (Individual atoms range in size from 0.25 to 1.75 nm.) *Nanotechnology* is the engineering field of creating useful materials and even machines out of individual atoms. The general idea is that computers can be built at a microscopic level and programmed to perform specific functions. For example, researchers in the medical field hope to create nanotechnology robots (called *nanobots*) that can be injected into a human body. Inside the body, the nanobots would replicate (or make duplicates of themselves) and then hunt down and kill certain viruses or cancers. The same technology could be used to create nanobots that clean up dangerous environmental spills and perform other tasks that aren't well suited to humans.

Nanotechnology has already been used successfully in several fields. For example, scientists have used this technology to create carbon nanotubes that are 100 times stronger and 100 times lighter than steel. Nanotubes can be used to make many types of objects stronger and lighter—from boats and aircraft to golf clubs and bicycle parts.

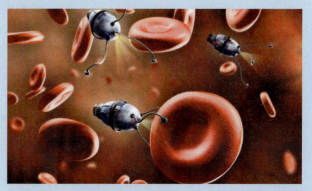

Scientists hope to create nanobots that can be programmed to repair blood cells in a human body.

As your computer starts up, the operating system is loaded into RAM. The RAM functions as a work area. Then, when you use the operating system to start an application, the program files are loaded into RAM. When you create a data file using that application, that file is also placed in RAM. The operating system retrieves data from RAM and sends it to the CPU for processing; after that, the operating system accepts the output from the CPU and places it back into RAM.

RAM is a critical part of a computer's functionality. The more RAM a computer has, the more applications and data files you can have open at once. On some computers, you can install additional RAM if needed.

RAM has three main functions:

1. To accept and hold program instructions and data

2. To supply data to the CPU for processing and then temporarily store the results

3. To hold the final processed information until it can be sent to a more permanent storage location (such as disk drive) or sent to an output device (such as a printer)

The CPU must be able to find programs and data once they have been stored in RAM. To enable retrieval, program instructions and data are placed at specific, named locations in RAM. This storage organization method enables the finding of particular data and instructions no matter which part of the RAM they are physically stored in—hence, the term *random access memory*. Each location in RAM has an individual **memory address** that the operating system can work with directly, rather than having to search from beginning to end (like you would do to find information stored on a cassette or VHS tape).

The content of RAM is easily changed. In fact, it changes almost constantly while the computer is running. Data moves freely from storage devices to RAM, from RAM to the CPU, and from the CPU to RAM. Processed data is then discarded from RAM (if it's no longer needed) or saved to a storage device (if it is needed).

Static versus Dynamic RAM

The RAM that comprises the computer's main memory is **dynamic RAM (DRAM).** This type of RAM requires a constant supply of electricity to keep its contents intact; another term sometimes used for it is *volatile RAM*. If the computer loses power, the content of RAM will be lost because all of the bits will go back to 0. Because of this possibility, you should save your work frequently when working in applications. Doing so will guard against data loss in the event of a power outage or a system error that requires restarting.

In contrast, some RAM is static; it does not lose its data when the power goes off. **Static RAM (SRAM)**, also called **nonvolatile RAM**, is faster than dynamic RAM (DRAM) and much more expensive, so it isn't used as the main memory in PCs. However, many common computing devices use small amounts of static RAM for special purposes.

Practical TECH

Upgrading Your RAM

If your computer's performance is sluggish when you run several programs at once, you would likely benefit from having additional RAM installed. If you aren't very tech savvy, you can have this upgrade done at a PC repair shop or the service department of an electronics store. The staff there will be able to determine whether your RAM can be upgraded and if so, what type of RAM you need to buy and how to install it.

For example, the caches in a CPU are static RAM, and so are the buffers (temporary data-holding areas) in some hard disks, routers, printers, and liquid crystal display (LCD) screens.

The DRAM in a typical PC consists of tiny silicon wafers mounted in ceramic chips. These chips are in turn mounted on one or more small, rectangular circuit boards called **dual inline memory modules (DIMMs)**. The word *dual* indicates that both sides of the circuit board contain memory chips. Each DIMM has a particular capacity (the amount of RAM it holds) and speed (the motherboard bus speed it's rated to keep up with).

RAM Speed and Performance

In early computer systems, dynamic RAM operated at a certain speed that was independent of the system bus. In other words, it was asynchronous dynamic RAM. In modern systems, however, most RAM is **synchronous dynamic RAM (SDRAM)**, which means its operations are synchronized with the system clock.

With **single data rate (SDR) SDRAM**, data moves into or out of RAM at the rate of one word per clock cycle. With **double data rate (DDR) SDRAM**, data transfers twice as fast as with SDR SDRAM, because it reads or writes two words of data per clock cycle. DDR2 doubles that rate (reading or writing four words of data per clock cycle), and DDR3 doubles it again (reading or writing eight words). DDR4 doesn't increase the number of words per clock cycle, but it offers some other technical changes that improve performance.

Another way to describe the speed or efficiency of RAM is as **memory access time**: the time required for the processor to access (read) data and instructions from memory. Access time is usually stated in fractions of a second. For example, a millisecond (abbreviated *ms*) is one-thousandth of a second. See Table 2.5 for a summary of the terms and abbreviations used to describe memory access times.

RAM comes mounted on dual inline memory modules (DIMMs), which fit into memory slots on the motherboard.

Table 2.5 Memory Access Times

Unit of Time	Abbreviation	Speed
Millisecond	ms	One-thousandth of a second
Microsecond	µs	One-millionth of a second
Nanosecond	ns	One-billionth of a second
Picosecond	ps	One-trillionth of a second

RAM Storage Capacity

RAM capacity is measured in bytes, and so is disk storage capacity (covered later in this chapter). Most computers have enough memory to store millions or even billions of bytes. Because of this fact, it's common to refer to storage capacity in terms of megabytes (1 million bytes), gigabytes (1 billion bytes), and terabytes (1 trillion bytes). A typical desktop computer system today might have 4 gigabytes (GB) of RAM, for example.

Table 2.1 (on page 54) lists the names given to various quantities of bytes; these terms are used when describing both RAM and storage capacity. The numbers of bytes given in the table are slightly off, because 1 kilobyte isn't exactly 1,000 bytes but rather 1,024 bytes (2 to the tenth power, or 2^{10}). That means that another 24 bytes should be added to every 1,000. In 1 megabyte, for example, there are 1,048,576 bytes ($1,024 \times 1,024$, or 2^{20}), rather than an even 1 million.

ROM and Flash Memory

A computer's system unit has one or more ROM chips that contain instructions or data permanently placed on them by the manufacturer. A typical PC has ROM chips on which essential startup programs have been stored. These programs are stored on read-only chips because it's critical that they not be erased or corrupted.

One type of startup program on a PC is the basic input/output system (BIOS), which boots (starts) the computer when it's turned on. (On a Mac, there is no BIOS, but there is a system-level utility called *OpenFirmware* that is roughly equivalent.) The BIOS also controls communications with the keyboard, disk drives, and other components. Also stored in ROM and activated with the startup of the computer is the power-on self-test (POST) program. The POST checks the physical components of the system to make sure they are all working properly.

When ROM was originally developed, it was unchangeable—true to its name. Replacing the BIOS in a system required installing a new chip. Because ROM chips were expensive, engineers developed a technology called **erasable programmable ROM (EPROM)** that allowed chips to be erased with a strong flash of ultraviolet light and then reprogrammed. EPROM enabled the reuse of a system chip but required removing the chip from the computer and placing it in a special machine, which wasn't very convenient. The use of ultraviolet light to erase ROM chips was referred to with the phrase "flashing the BIOS." This phrase continues to be tech lingo for updating a computer's BIOS, even though EPROM technology is no longer used.

As computer technology evolved, users wanted to be able to rewrite certain ROM chips on their own. A technology called **electrically erasable programmable ROM (EEPROM)** was developed that allows reprogramming a ROM chip electronically using only the hardware that comes with the computer. EEPROM allows upgrading the computer's BIOS without removing the BIOS chip from the motherboard and placing it in a special machine. A utility program activates the erase function for the ROM chip and then writes new data to it. If you want to

USB flash drives hold flash ROM, which is technically a form of read-only memory but can be written and rewritten.

Cutting Edge

Goodbye to Flash Memory?

For many years, flash memory has been the dominant technology for solid-state storage in everything from cell phones to digital cameras—but that may soon change. A technology called *phase-change RAM (PRAM)* is faster and more efficient than flash and may replace it altogether.

The idea behind PRAM has been around for several decades. The chip contains a chemical compound called *chalcogenide*; heating this compound to a very high temperature changes its physical state. The two states

serve as the 1s and 0s of the binary code used for data storage. The benefit of PRAM technology is that the chip doesn't need to erase a block of cells before writing new data; the bits can be changed individually. Because of this, PRAM chips can read and write data 10 times faster than flash counterparts and use less power in the process. In a cell phone, for example, PRAM memory could increase the battery life by up to 20 percent.

update the BIOS of a modern PC, you can do so in just a few minutes. All you need to do is download and install a BIOS update utility and the latest BIOS software from the PC's manufacturer.

Flash memory is a type of EEPROM. It may seem like RAM, because it's so easily written and erased. But the technology behind it is much more similar to EEPROM than to static RAM. Flash memory is read and written in blocks (or pages), rather than individual bytes (as RAM is). Also, like EEPROM, flash memory can be reprogrammed only a limited number of times: 1 million write operations. Because of this limitation, flash memory is used primarily for storage—not as a substitute for RAM in the main memory of a computer.

Flash memory is used for storage in a variety of devices, including USB flash drives, solid state hard drives, digital cameras, digital audio players, cell phones, and video game systems. A variety of flash memory cards are also available, which plug into slots on devices such as printers, cameras, scanners, and copiers to enable easy data exchange. Types of flash cards include CompactFlash (CF), SmartMedia, Secure Digital (SD), MultiMediaCard (MMC), ×D-Picture, and Memory Stick.

Recheck 2.5
Recheck your understanding of the concepts covered by this objective.

2.6 Exploring Visual and Audio Output

Precheck 2.6
Check your understanding of the concepts covered by this objective.

As you learned in Chapter 1, output is one of the four steps of the information processing cycle. Specifically, output is processed data that exits from the computer. Output can be temporary or permanent. For example, the output that appears on your display screen is temporary, as is the output that you hear through speakers or headphones. Output that still exists after the computer has been turned off is permanent—for example, the printout from a printer (sometimes called a *hard copy*).

An **output device** is any type of hardware that makes information available to a user. Popular output devices for visual and audio output include displays (or monitors), projectors, and speakers and headphones.

Displays

Nearly every computer has some sort of display on which users can view output, such as a stand-alone monitor or built-in screen. Displays are available in a wide variety of shapes, size, costs, and capabilities. The term **screen** refers to the viewable area of any display device. For example, notebooks, tablets, and cell phones all have built-in screens. When the display device is separate from the computer and has its own power supply and plastic housing, it's called a **monitor**.

Display Types The original type of display for a desktop computer was the **cathode ray tube (CRT) monitor**. A CRT monitor uses the same technology as an old TV set and so is usually large, heavy, and bulky. A CRT is essentially a large vacuum tube. At the back of the CRT is a long, narrow neck that contains a cathode, and at the front is a broad, rectangular surface with colored phosphors on it. When the cathode is heated, it emits negatively charged electrons. Those electrons are attracted to the positively charged front of the CRT, where they strike the phosphors and make them light up for a brief time. The phosphors are arranged in clusters of three (one red, one green, and one blue), and each cluster is called a **triad**. Depending on the resolution of the display, different numbers of triads may comprise 1 pixel.

A flat-screen monitor is thin and lightweight compared with a CRT monitor, and it uses less electricity. Flat-screen monitors were very expensive in the past, but recent

CRT monitors are no longer popular, but you may occasionally see one in use with an old computer system.

A flat-screen monitor, such as this LCD model, is lightweight and thin and uses less electricity than a CRT monitor.

improvements in manufacturing technology have made them very affordable. They are so affordable, in fact, that they have almost completely replaced CRT monitors.

Most flat-screen monitors show information onscreen using a **liquid crystal display (LCD)**. Figure 2.12 illustrates how an LCD crystal produces an image on the display. An LCD screen has two polarized filters, and between them are liquid crystals. For light to appear on the display, it must pass through the first filter, then through the crystals, and finally through the second filter. The second filter is at an angle to the

Activity 2.6.1

Practice
How Liquid Crystals Work

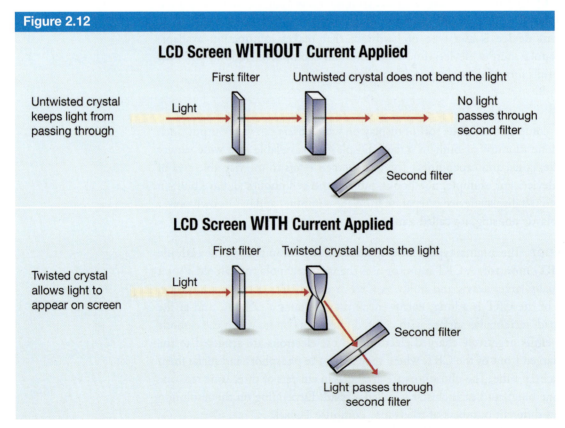

Figure 2.12

LCD Screen WITHOUT Current Applied

First filter   Untwisted crystal does not bend the light

Untwisted crystal keeps light from passing through

Light

No light passes through second filter

Second filter

LCD Screen WITH Current Applied

First filter   Twisted crystal bends the light

Twisted crystal allows light to appear on screen

Light

Second filter

Light passes through second filter

The liquid crystals in an LCD screen twist when an electrical current is applied to them. This changes the angle of the light passing through them, allowing it to reach the second filter and display an image on the screen.

first, so by default, light doesn't reach it after passing through the crystals. However, when current is applied to the crystals, they twist; this makes the light passing through the crystals change angle and point in the direction of the second filter. When the light passes through the second filter, it lights up an area of the display. Color LCD screens use a filter that splits the light into separate cells for red, green, and blue.

Activity 2.6.2

Video
Display Resolution

Display Performance and Quality Factors Both CRT and LCD displays have a **maximum resolution** (sometimes called *native resolution*, especially for LCD monitors), which is the highest display mode they can support. Images are displayed on the monitor screen using pixels (see Figure 2.13). Maximum resolution is expressed as the maximum number of pixels that will display horizontally multiplied by the maximum number of pixels that will display vertically—for example, 1,600 × 900.

On an LCD monitor, images look best at the native resolution, because there is a one-to-one relationship between the monitor's physical pixels and the number of pixels that the operating system's display mode tells the monitor to use. Images are sharp and clear at this resolution but may appear fuzzy at lower resolutions. So, if you prefer a certain resolution, you should use a monitor that has that particular resolution as its maximum. Native resolution isn't a consideration on CRT monitors, because the images they display look sharp and clear at any resolution.

Another important feature of a computer monitor is the **aspect ratio**, which is the ratio of width to height. The traditional aspect ratio of a monitor is 4:3, the same as for an older-model TV. Many newer monitors (especially LCDs) are widescreen models and have an aspect ratio of 16:9, the same as for a widescreen high-definition TV. When selecting a monitor resolution in your operating system, keep in mind the physical dimensions of the screen you are using. For example, the resolution 1,024 × 768 has an aspect ratio of 4:3, and the resolution 1,024 × 600 has an aspect ratio of 16:9. If the resolution you choose has a different aspect ratio than your monitor, images may appear squashed or elongated.

Hands On

Are Your Onscreen Items Tiny?
At your monitor's maximum resolution, the icons and text on your computer screen may be so tiny that they are difficult to see. You can adjust the sizes of these items in your system settings. To do so on a computer running Windows 10, follow the steps in this resource.

Figure 2.13

A **pixel** is the smallest element that displays on a monitor screen

YOUR WORLDWIDE SOURCE

Both CRT and LCD monitors have a **refresh rate**, which is the number of times per second that each pixel is re-energized. Refresh rate is measured in hertz (Hz).

On an LCD monitor, the pixels stay at a consistent brightness all the time without being re-energized. Refreshing involves checking for updates to the pixels' colors. LCD monitors have a refresh rate of about 60 Hz (or 60 times per second), and that's sufficient for most uses.

Display Adapters A display doesn't have much (or any) processing power of its own; it relies on the computer to feed it the information it shows. Providing that information is the purpose of the **display adapter** (sometimes called *video card*, *video adapter*, or *graphics card*). A display adapter is typically added as an expansion board or built into the motherboard. It converts the computer's digital output to instructions and sends them to the display. If the display adapter is a separate board, it has its own RAM, chipset, and data bus (to carry data from place to place on its own circuit board). If it's built into the motherboard, it uses the bus, chipset, and RAM of the motherboard.

A display adapter may connect to the monitor with either a DVI or a VGA connector. A display adapter has its own processor, called a **graphics processing unit (GPU)**; the GPU works in cooperation with the computer's CPU.

The display adapter requires memory, because it must hold all of the data needed to display the contents of the screen. For instance, the display adapter keeps track of what color each individual pixel should show at any given moment and continuously feeds that information to the display. Some older displays show output in only one color; this type of display is called a **monochrome display**. You might occasionally use a monochrome display, such as at an ATM or in the LCD display on a microwave or other appliance. Most computer displays, however, support thousands or even millions of color choices for each pixel.

Each color has a numeric value. The number of binary digits needed to describe a particular color uniquely depends on the color depth of the operating system's display mode. The **color depth** (also called *bit depth*) is the number of bits used in a graphics expansion board to store information about each pixel. The greater the color depth, the more data the operating system must send to the display adapter and the display adapter must send to the monitor every second. For example, in a four-digit binary

This display adapter is an expansion board and thus separate from the motherboard. The model shown here has DVI, S-Video, and VGA ports. The large, circular object is a cooling fan for the adapter's processor.

number, there are 16 possible values. It follows that 4-bit color allows for 16 different colors, 8-bit color allows for 256 colors, and so on. Most displays on modern computers operate at 16-bit (high color) or 32-bit (true color) color depth.

The higher the resolution and the greater the color depth, the more RAM the display adapter requires. However, modern display adapters use RAM for much more than storing the values of individual pixels. Display adapters also use RAM to support the many special features they have for improving display performance. For instance, display adapters have processors that help render the complex 3-D objects that appear in the latest games and drawing software. The exact capabilities of the display adapter are determined by its chipset.

Projectors

A **video projector** (or *screen projector*) is a device that captures the text and images displayed on a computer screen and projects them onto a large screen so an audience can see them clearly. Projectors are often used in classrooms, conference and meetings rooms, and convention halls.

A projector can be connected to a PC through the same port as the monitor (VGA or DVI). Some projectors can also be connected via USB or another port; having this type of connection allows the PC to use a regular monitor and a projector at the same time.

A projector's brightness is measured in **lumens (lm)**. The brighter the projector, the better it will work when projecting a large image in a big, well-lit room. For example, in a small, dark room, 1,500 to 2,500 lm is an adequate brightness, but in a large, well-lit room, more than 4,000 lm is optimal. Most projectors have a replaceable **lamp** (like a lightbulb) inside that generates the brightness. Some projectors use a light-emitting diode (LED), which never needs to be replaced.

Using a projector allows multiple people to view the output from a computer on a large screen at a meeting or conference.

Speakers and Headphones

Most computers provide a means of producing audio output, which can include music playback, system sound effects and game sounds, the narration of a presentation, and the audio part of video chatting. Having audio output can also enable people with visual impairments to control and interact with the computer.

As noted earlier in this chapter, the sound card (or audio adapter) is both an input device and an output device. It translates the digital instructions from the computer into analog output, such as sound waves that a person can hear through a speaker. It also does the reverse, translating analog input (such as the sound waves produced by a person speaking into a microphone) into digital input for an application. Depending on the computer system, the sound card may be built into the motherboard or it may be an actual card (that is, an expansion board).

A sound card typically has a series of color-coded RCA jacks for plugging in different input and output devices. These jacks are called *RCA jacks* because they were invented by the Radio Corporation of America (RCA). The term *jack* is often used to refer to audio connectors because of their origin in home stereo systems, whereas *port* is used for most other computer connectors. Either term can be used for audio connectors on a computer. Refer back to Table 2.4 on page 59 to review the colors and meanings of these different types of connectors.

Sound exits the computer via speakers or headphones. Most computers have separate ports for these two output devices, so you don't have to disconnect one to use the other. When a set of headphones is attached, the system may automatically direct the sound output to that port, muting the sound to the speakers.

When choosing speakers for a computer system, key considerations are as follows:

- **Amplification.** *Amplification* refers to an increase in a physical property. For speakers, **amplification** describes increasing sound volume. Speakers that allow greater amounts of amplification have the capacity to transmit louder sounds.
- **Frequency range.** Frequency involves the number of repeated events per second. For sound, the event is called a *cycle* (1 cycle every second is equivalent to 1 Hz). Many objects, such as the human voice or electronic speakers, emit sound over a range of frequencies. Speakers with a wide **frequency range** reproduce sounds much more accurately than those with a narrow frequency range. Look for a frequency range of at least 50 to 10,000 Hz.
- **Wattage.** The amount of power that a machine has to accomplish a task (such as a speaker discharging sound) is measured in watts. The **wattage** of a speaker is described by three measurements:
    - **Root mean squared (RMS)** is a standard measurement of the wattage that a speaker can handle in a reliable and sustained manner.
    - **RMS maximum** is the maximum wattage that a speaker can handle in short bursts.
    - **Peak momentary performance output (PMPO)** is the absolute maximum wattage that a speaker can handle for a split second before it dies from wattage overload. PMPO isn't a realistic measurement of a speaker's capabilities.
- **Shielding.** Speakers designed for use with computers have **shielding**—a protective barrier that prevents electromagnetic interference. Speakers designed for home stereo systems usually don't have shielding.
- **Number of speakers.** Simple speakers usually come in pairs (left and right, for stereo output). High-end speaker systems have more speakers; for example, the Dolby Digital 5.1 (Surround Sound) system uses five speakers.

Practical TECH

Connecting Speakers to Your Computer

Most speaker systems have multiple speakers, but most computers have only one speaker port. Fortunately, this isn't a problem with the speaker systems designed for use with computers. In a system with two speakers, one speaker connects to the computer and the other speaker connects to the first speaker. If a subwoofer unit is part of the speaker system (as it is for Dolby Digital 2.1 or 5.1), the subwoofer connects to the computer and all the speakers in the system connect to the subwoofer. (A subwoofer is a speaker that produces very low sounds; the term *subwoofer* is also popularly used to refer to the central connecting speaker in a multispeaker system, regardless of the tones it produces.)

Some speaker systems have a subwoofer unit to which individual speakers connect.

Some speaker systems are wireless, which means they can connect to the computer via a wireless technology (such as Bluetooth). Some speakers can also function as docking stations for mobile devices, such as iPods. A **docking station** is like a home base for a portable device and gives it extra capabilities, such as better speakers, more ports, and power recharging.

Recheck 2.6

Recheck your understanding of the concepts covered by this objective.

2.7 Differentiating between Types of Printers

A **printer** is the most common type of device used to produce hard-copy output on paper or another physical medium, such as transparency film. Printers are categorized into two broad groups based on how they affix or attach the print to the medium: nonimpact and impact.

Precheck 2.7

Check your understanding of the concepts covered by this objective.

A **nonimpact printer** forms the characters and images without actually striking the output medium; it creates print using electricity, heat, or photographic techniques. Most printers sold today are nonimpact, including inkjet printers, laser printers, thermal printers, and plotters. All of these printers use ink or toner to create print, whether black or color. The ink or toner cartridge must be replaced or refilled to keep this type of printer operating.

An **impact printer** is a lot like an old-fashioned typewriter; it forms characters and images by physically striking an inked ribbon against the output medium. Impact printers aren't commonly used anymore, but they are still found in some business and factory settings that require the same image to be printed on each page of a multipart form. Impact printers do a good job of printing text on multipart forms, but they don't print graphics very well and they don't print in color. Impact printers are economical to use, however; the ribbons they use don't cost much compared with the ink and toner used by other printers.

Most printers sold today connect to the computer using a USB port, but some older printers may use a legacy parallel port. Some printers can also connect to computers via wireless networking, such as Bluetooth or Wi-Fi.

Hands On

What Printers Are Installed on Your Computer?

Your computer operating system doesn't deal directly with printers. Rather, your computer deals with printer drivers, which are configuration files that tell the system how to talk to particular models of printers. Follow the steps in this resource to see what printer drivers are set up on a system running Windows 10.

Inkjet Printers

An **inkjet printer** is a nonimpact printer. It forms characters and images by spraying thousands of tiny droplets of ink through a set of tiny nozzles and onto a sheet of paper as the sheet passes through it.

Two technologies are used to force the ink through the nozzle: thermal and piezoelectric. A **thermal inkjet printer** heats the ink to about 400 degrees Fahrenheit; doing so creates a vapor bubble that forces the ink out of its cartridge and through a nozzle.

Inkjet printers provide good-quality color output. They are inexpensive to buy, but the per-page cost of operation can be high because of the price of ink cartridges.

A vacuum is created inside the cartridge, which draws more ink into the nozzle. Figure 2.14 illustrates the operation of a thermal inkjet printer.

A **piezoelectric inkjet printer** (or piezo printer) moves the ink with electricity instead of heat. Each nozzle contains piezoelectric crystals, which change their shape when electricity is applied to them and then force out the ink. The electrical process is easier on the printer, because it doesn't require heating the ink. It also produces better output, because the ink used is less prone to smearing.

Inkjet printers vary in the following ways:

- **Ink cartridges.** Most inkjet printers use four cartridges with different colors of ink: black, cyan (blue), magenta (red), and yellow. However, some high-end printers have more than four cartridges. In most cases, the cartridges contain the print heads, which makes them expensive. On a high-end inkjet printer, the print heads may be separate cartridges, which can be replaced less often than ink cartridges. These printers can use a better-quality print head but still be economical because the cost of the ink cartridges is lower.

- **Speed.** Print speed is measured in **pages per minute (ppm)**. The advertised speed of a printer is the speed at which it can print once the print cycle begins. This means that the actual print speed may be slower, because additional time may be needed for a print job to reach the printer and for the printer to warm up so it can print the first page.

- **Resolution.** The number of dots per inch (dpi) determines the printer's resolution. A typical resolution for an inkjet printer is between 600 and 2,400 dpi.

- **Photorealism.** Some inkjet printers can print photo-quality images if special photo paper is used. To produce the best-quality photo printouts, some printers require special photo ink cartridges. Specialty photo printers are available that are designed to print photos on specially sized and treated paper.

- **Interface.** A typical inkjet printer uses a USB connection to the computer; some inkjet printers also have Ethernet (wired network) or Wi-Fi (wireless network) capability.

Most inkjet ink cartridges are more than just ink reservoirs; they also contain the print heads. The dots on the strip at the top of each cartridge function as electrical contacts; they allow the printer to instruct the print head how and when to discharge ink.

 **Activity 2.7.1**

Practice
Thermal Inkjet Printer Operation

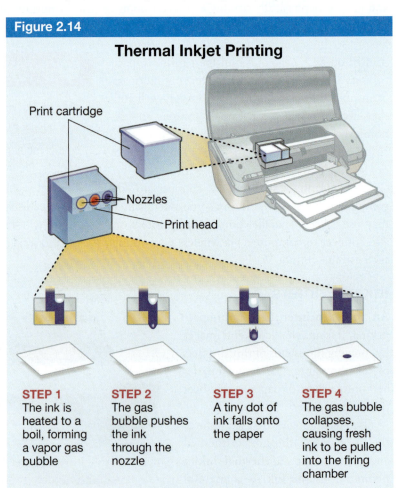

Figure 2.14

Thermal Inkjet Printing

Print cartridge

Nozzles

Print head

STEP 1
The ink is heated to a boil, forming a vapor gas bubble

STEP 2
The gas bubble pushes the ink through the nozzle

STEP 3
A tiny dot of ink falls onto the paper

STEP 4
The gas bubble collapses, causing fresh ink to be pulled into the firing chamber

A thermal inkjet printer produces output by heating the ink until a gas bubble forces it out of the cartridge through the nozzle. Doing this creates a spray of tiny ink droplets that form text and images on a sheet of paper or other medium.

Figure 2.15

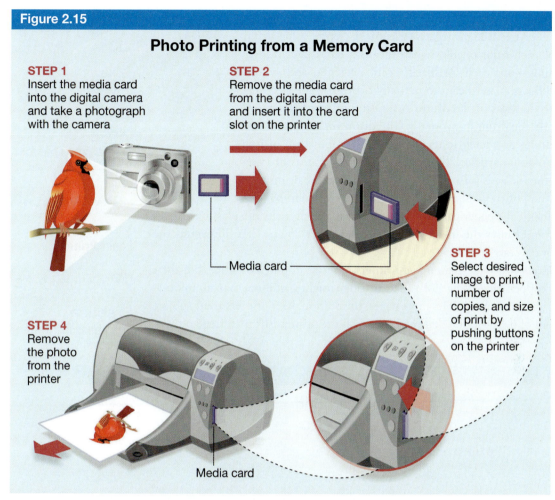

Photo Printing from a Memory Card

STEP 1
Insert the media card into the digital camera and take a photograph with the camera

STEP 2
Remove the media card from the digital camera and insert it into the card slot on the printer

Media card

STEP 3
Select desired image to print, number of copies, and size of print by pushing buttons on the printer

STEP 4
Remove the photo from the printer

Media card

A printer that has a memory card slot can print photographs without a computer. It processes the data directly from the memory card removed from a digital camera.

- **Memory card slots.** Some printers accept flash memory cards, so you can print images from a digital camera or other source without using a computer. Figure 2.15 shows how a printer with a memory card slot can accept pictures from a digital camera.

Inkjet printers are popular for use in homes and small businesses, because they are inexpensive. As mentioned earlier, though, the cost of the replacement ink cartridges is high, so the cost per page with inkjet printers is higher than with laser printers. Another disadvantage is that liquid ink tends to dry out over time, especially if the printer isn't used frequently, and the print heads can get clogged with dried ink. This problem can be solved by running a cleaning cycle, which forces more ink through the heads to break up the clogs. Unfortunately, running a cleaning cycle also wastes some ink, creating further expense. For these reasons, larger businesses often use laser printers.

Laser Printers

A **laser printer** works much like a photocopier. The main difference is that a photocopier scans a document and then prints the scanned copy, whereas a laser printer receives digitized data from a computer and then prints the data. Typically, a laser printer looks like a big, square box with a paper tray inside. Laser printers are used extensively in business and industry because of their durability, speed, and low cost per page.

A laser printer is typically taller than an inkjet printer, because it has to accommodate the drum and one or more toner cartridges inside.

A laser printer contains at least one large cylinder (known as a **drum**) that carries a high negative electrical charge. One drum is needed for each color of ink, which means a color laser printer has four drums—one each for black, cyan, magenta, and yellow. The printer directs a laser beam to partially neutralize the electrical charge in certain areas of the drum. A rotating mirror helps move the laser across the drum horizontally. The drum rotates past a reservoir containing powdered **toner**, which is a combination of iron and colored plastic particles. The toner clings to the areas of lesser charge, and the image is formed on the drum. Next, the drum then rotates past the positively charged paper, and the toner jumps onto the paper. Finally, the paper passes through a **fuser**, which melts the plastic particles in the toner and causes the image to stick to the paper. Figure 2.16 illustrates the laser printing process.

Toner comes in cartridges that fit into the laser printer. A color laser printer has four toner cartridges: black, cyan, magenta, and yellow.

Laser printers cost more than inkjet printers in terms of purchase price, but their operational cost per page is lower. A toner cartridge might cost more than an ink cartridge, but it will print many times more pages. In addition, laser printers aren't subject to the problem of dried-up ink that might occur if the printer isn't used frequently.

Activity 2.7.2

Video
Laser Printer

Activity 2.7.3

Practice
The Laser Printing Process

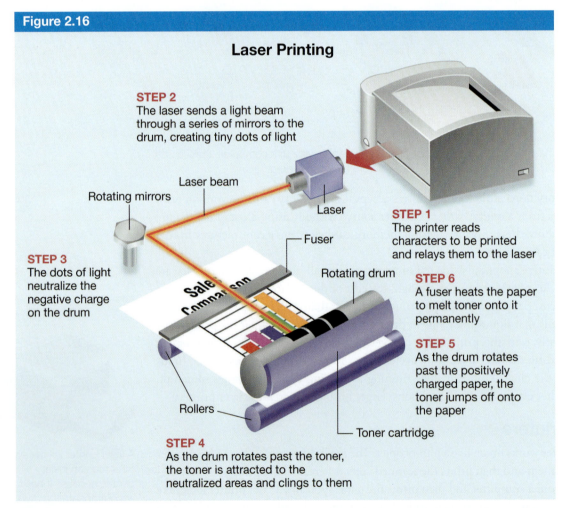

Figure 2.16

Laser Printing

STEP 2
The laser sends a light beam through a series of mirrors to the drum, creating tiny dots of light

Rotating mirrors

Laser beam

Laser

Fuser

STEP 1
The printer reads characters to be printed and relays them to the laser

STEP 3
The dots of light neutralize the negative charge on the drum

Rotating drum

STEP 6
A fuser heats the paper to melt toner onto it permanently

STEP 5
As the drum rotates past the positively charged paper, the toner jumps off onto the paper

Rollers

Toner cartridge

STEP 4
As the drum rotates past the toner, the toner is attracted to the neutralized areas and clings to them

A laser printer produces output by neutralizing the negative electrical charge on certain areas of a rotating drum; the drum then picks up toner in these neutralized areas.

Multifunction Devices and Fax Machines

A **multifunction device (MFD)** is a printer that also functions as a copier and a scanner (and sometimes a fax machine). Because MFDs serve all these purposes, they are also called *all-in-one devices*. They are popular with small businesses, because they provide the key functions needed in a single machine that takes up less space than would be needed for separate machines. Almost all MFDs use inkjet or laser technology.

A **fax machine** can send and receive copies of documents through a telephone line, similar to the way a dial-up modem sends network data. (The word *fax* is short for *facsimile*, which means "exact copy.") A fax machine can be a stand-alone device or part of an MFD.

Microsoft Windows includes a Fax and Scan utility that enables the computer's modem to send and receive faxes. If you have this utility and a dial-up modem that is connected to your telephone line, you don't need a fax machine or MFD to send and receive faxes.

A multifunction device (MFD) typically includes a printer, a copier, and a scanner in one unit. Some models also have fax capabilities.

Thermal Printers

A **thermal printer** uses heat to transfer an impression onto the paper. Thermal printers are not as common as inkjet and laser printers, but they are ideal for certain uses. Three main types of thermal printers are available:

- A **direct thermal printer** prints an image by burning dots into a sheet of coated paper when it passes over a line of heating elements. Early fax machines used direct thermal printing. The quality produced by this type of printer isn't very good, and it can't produce shades of gray or colors—only black and white. Direct thermal printers are used in a variety of places where print quality is less important than inexpensive, high-volume output, such as on cash register receipts, bar code labels, rental car paperwork, and theater tickets.

- A **thermal wax transfer printer** adheres a wax-based ink onto the paper. During the printing process, a thermal print head melts this ink from a ribbon onto the paper. When the wax has cooled down, it is permanently affixed. Images are printed as dots, which means they must be dithered to produce shades of colors. (*Dithering* is a technique that creates the illusions of new colors and shades by using varying patterns of dots. As a result, the quality of images produced by a thermal wax transfer printer can't compete with that of images produced by a modern inkjet or laser printer.)

- A **dye sublimation printer** (also called a *thermal dye transfer printer*) produces an image by heating ribbons containing dye and then dispersing the dyes onto a specially coated paper or transparency. This type of printer is the most expensive and slowest type of thermal printer; it also requires special paper, which is quite expensive. Even so, thermal dye transfer printers produce exceptional high-quality, continuous-tone images that are similar to actual photographs. A new type of thermal dye transfer printer called a *snapshot printer* produces small, photographic snapshots and is much less expensive than a full-size thermal printer.

Plotters

A **plotter** is a type of printer that produces large-size, high-quality precision documents, such as architectural drawings, charts, maps, and diagrams. Plotters are also used to create engineering drawings for machine parts and equipment.

Plotters use a variety of technologies. For example, an electrostatic plotter produces a high-quality image using a series of tiny dots that are tightly packed together. The printing mechanism consists of a row of fine, electrically charged wires. When the wires contact the specially coated paper, an electrostatic pattern is produced that causes the toner to be fused onto the paper. An inkjet plotter (also called a *wide-format inkjet printer*) may be used when large color images need to be produced.

Engineers often use plotters to produce high-quality, large-size prints of plans and designs for buildings, processes, and machines.

Special-Purpose Printers

Some printers are designed for specific tasks, rather than for general use. For example, there are special-purpose printers that print labels, badges, photos, postage, and bar codes. Other printers produce full-color advertisements for mass mailing, and some even print on cardboard boxes or etch images into glass or metal.

A **label printer** is a small device that holds a roll of labels and feeds them continuously past a print head. After the labels have been printed, they are peeled from their backing and pressed on letters, packages, or other items. Label printers can be color or black-and-white, and can use inkjet or thermal technology.

A **postage printer** is similar to a label printer but may include a scale for weighing letters and packages. The postage amount that's printed depends on the weight of the item and its destination, which is typically input using software or a numeric keypad on the printer. To use a postage printer, you must first purchase a specific amount of postage from an authorized service (such as a branch of the US Post Office). Each time you print postage, the amount is subtracted from your account balance.

A label printer is designed specifically to print adhesive labels.

Cutting Edge

Wearable Computers

Will you be wearing your next computer? Wearable computers are popular among people on the go. Headsets, eyeglasses, watches, and other accessories can serve as input and output devices. When combined with a wireless Internet or network connection, such devices enable people to look up information, input new data, issue commands, and communicate with other users wherever they are.

The Apple Watch is a wristwatch computer that has many of the same capabilities as a smartphone, including messaging, fitness tracking, mapping, and calendar management. It also interfaces wirelessly with an iPhone,

so the two devices can work cooperatively. For example, you can set up your iPhone to take a photo, and then trigger the camera from your Apple Watch. The Fitbit is another wrist-worn computer, recording your body's activity and then sending that data to a personal computer.

A **portable printer** is a lightweight, battery-powered printer that can be easily transported. This type of printer can connect to a notebook or tablet computer, as well as a smartphone. Repair and service technicians that travel to remote sites use portable printers to generate invoices and receipts for customers.

3-D printing is an exciting new technology that promises to change the way we think about printing in the next decade. A **3-D printer** uses a special kind of plastic, metal, or other material to create a three-dimensional model of just about any object you can design in a 3-D modeling program on a computer. The possible uses for 3-D printing are many. For example, a company designing a new object can create a working prototype of it on a 3-D printer much more inexpensively than having the object milled or fabricated in a machine shop. 3-D printing could also be used to reproduce parts for old machines for which replacement parts are no longer being manufactured. And, instead of buying a new toy for a child, parents could purchase the design for the toy online and print it on their own 3-D printer.

 Recheck 2.7
Recheck your understanding of the concepts covered by this objective.

2.8 Using Ergonomics to Prevent Injury and Discomfort

 Precheck 2.8
Check your understanding of the concepts covered by this objective.

Ergonomics is the study of the interaction between humans and the equipment they use. Extensive research has shown that people can greatly reduce stress and strain on their bodies while using computers by following ergonomic design principles in their work areas.

For example, someone who uses a computer keyboard for many hours a day can develop carpal tunnel syndrome from holding his or her hands and wrists in a bent position. When you type at your computer keyboard, do your hands extend straight out from your wrists, or do your wrists tilt in toward each other? Ideally, your wrists should be straight. Some keyboards have a split design that slants the keys slightly toward your hands to ensure proper form. Other keyboards can tilt forward and backward to allow you to keep your hands in a more comfortable vertical position. The keyboard and mouse should be placed on a work surface that's positioned so your forearms are parallel to the floor when typing or using the mouse.

Some people develop pain and numbness in the hand they use for operating the mouse. In some cases, replacing the mouse with another pointing device, such as a track-ball, solves the problem.

Tech Career Explorer

Ergonomic Consultant

An ergonomic consultant helps keep workers safe and healthy as they perform their jobs by ensuring that they are sitting, standing, and moving in the best possible ways. Hiring an ergonomic consultant can save a company thousands of dollars in health-related worker absences and Workers' Compensation claims. For a career as an ergonomic consultant, you should have a bachelor of science degree in ergonomics or a related field such as kinesiology; it is also helpful to pursue a Certified Professional Ergonomist (CPE) certificate. You can learn more about the job of ergonomic consultant by completing this exercise.

Using a split keyboard can help you avoid slanting your wrists inward as you type.

Figure 2.17

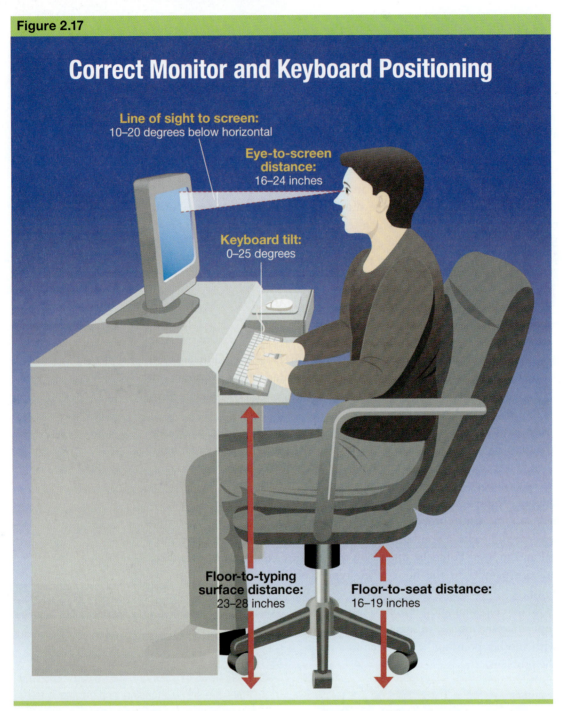

Correct Monitor and Keyboard Positioning

Line of sight to screen:
10–20 degrees below horizontal

Eye-to-screen distance:
16–24 inches

Keyboard tilt:
0–25 degrees

Floor-to-typing surface distance:
23–28 inches

Floor-to-seat distance:
16–19 inches

Correct positioning when using a computer can reduce physical fatigue and discomfort and help prevent stress-related injuries.

Monitor height and body position are also issues. If your monitor is too high or too low, eyestrain and fatigue can result. If your keyboard is too high or too low, your arms can get tired and cramped. The monitor should be 16 to 24 inches away from your eyes and at a 10 to 20 degree angle below your eyes. Figure 2.17 shows the correct positioning for working at a computer at a desk.

 **Recheck 2.8**
Recheck your understanding of the concepts covered by this objective.

Chapter Summary

*An interactive **Chapter Summary**, **Study Notes**, and a **Slide Presentation** with audio are available from the links menu on this page in your ebook.*

2.1 Working with Input Technology

An **input device** is any hardware component that enables users to input information. **Keyboards** are used with almost all desktop and notebook computers; for tablet PCs and smartphones, software-generated **virtual keyboards** substitute for physical keyboards. **Pointing devices** move the onscreen pointer in a graphical user interface (GUI); common pointing devices include **mice**, **trackballs**, **touchpads**, and **touchscreens**. Some other input devices include **graphics tablets**, **scanners**, **digital cameras**, and microphones.

2.2 Understanding How Computers Process Data

Binary strings of data consist of individual **bits** that are either on (1) or off (0), like light switches. A group of 8 bits is a **byte**. One thousand twenty-four bytes (which is 2^{10} bytes) is a **kilobyte**, and 1,024 kilobytes (2^{20}, or approximately 1 million bytes) is a **megabyte**. Larger measurements include a **gigabyte** (2^{30}, or approximately 1 billion bytes) and a terabyte (2^{40}, or approximately 1 trillion bytes). Letters, numbers, and symbols are represented using encoding schemes such as **ASCII** and **Unicode**.

2.3 Identifying Components in the System Unit

The main circuit board is the **motherboard**; all other components connect to it. Data moves around on the motherboard by way of pathways called **buses**. Electricity is provide to each component in the proper voltages through the **power supply**. Add-on capabilities are provided by **expansion boards**, which are inserted into **expansion slots** in the motherboard. The most common type of expansion bus today is the **Peripheral Component Interconnect Express (PCIe) bus**. The computer case may contain one or more **storage bays** for holding disk drives.

The **USB port** is the most popular general-purpose port, and it comes in several speeds. **DVI** is a digital interface for monitors; **VGA** is an analog interface for monitors. Older keyboards and mice use **PS/2** ports. A **legacy port** is a computer port that is still in use but has been largely replaced by a port with more functionality. Older printers use legacy ports, such as a **parallel port** (25-pin D-sub connector). Network cables plug into **RJ-45 ports** (also called **Ethernet ports**). **Dial-up modems** use RJ-11 connectors (telephone cables). **Audio ports** use 3.5-millimeter round plugs.

2.4 Understanding the CPU

A **central processing unit (CPU)** processes data in four steps: fetching an instruction, decoding the instruction, executing the instruction, and storing the result. The **control unit** directs the overall process; it fetches and decodes. The **arithmetic logic unit (ALU)** executes the instruction. **Registers** store the data temporarily until it exits the CPU. To minimize the CPU's idle time waiting for data to be delivered, **caches** are used; they store data temporarily just outside the CPU, where it can be accessed quickly.

A CPU has a maximum speed in GHz for which it's rated, but its actual speed (number of operations per second) is determined by the **system clock** on the motherboard. The amount of data processed per clock cycle depends on the **word size** of the CPU (32-bit or 64-bit). Advanced CPUs have many special features that improve processing efficiency, such as **pipelining**, **parallel processing**, **superscalar architecture**, **multithreading**, and **multicore processors**.

2.5 Understanding Memory

There are two types of **memory: read-only memory (ROM)**, which is unchangeable, and **random access memory (RAM)**, which is changeable. **Static RAM (SRAM)** doesn't require electrical refreshing to hold its contents, but dynamic RAM does. **Dynamic RAM (DRAM)** can be synchronous (operating in time with the system clock) or asynchronous (not dependent on the system clock). **Synchronous dynamic RAM (SDRAM)** can complete one operation (**single data rate**, or **SDR**), two operations (**double data rate**, or **DDR**), or three operations (DDR3 and DDR4) per clock tick. RAM storage capacity is measured in bytes (kilobytes, mega-bytes, gigabytes, and so on). **Flash memory** is a type of **electrically erasable programmable ROM (EEPROM)**, which maintains its data without power but can be easily rewritten.

2.6 Exploring Visual and Audio Output

An **output device** is any type of hardware that makes information available to a user. Some devices, such as notebooks and tablets, have built-in display **screens**. Display screens that are separate from computers are called **monitors**. A **cathode ray tube (CRT) monitor** is an old type of monitor that uses a beam of electrons to light up phosphors on the screen. A flat-screen monitor is a **liquid crystal display (LCD)**; it uses transistors to light up each pixel. A display has a **maximum resolution**, which is the number of pixels it can display; the resolution is expressed as horizontal × vertical pixels (for example, 1,600 × 900). The **color depth** is the number of bits needed to describe the color of each pixel in a particular display mode, such as 16-bit or 32-bit. The number of times per second the display is re-energized is its **refresh rate**. The monitor connects to the computer via a **display adapter** with a DVI or VGA connector. **Video projectors** can serve as monitors too; projector brightness is measured in **lumens**. Audio output goes through the audio adapter to speakers or headphones.

2.7 Differentiating between Types of Printers

Both of the printer types commonly used today are **nonimpact printers**. An **inkjet printer** sprays small dots of liquid ink onto a page. A **laser printer** transfers powdered **toner** to a **drum** and then from the drum to paper, where it's heated and transferred onto the page via a **fuser**. Inkjet printers are inexpensive to purchase, but the ink cartridges are expensive in terms of cost per page. Laser printers are more expensive to purchase, but the toner cartridges last longer than ink cartridges, so the cost per page is lower. Other types of printers include **thermal printers** and **plotters**. **Multifunction devices (MFD)** combine printing functionality with copying, scanning, and sometimes faxing.

2.8 Using Ergonomics to Prevent Injury and Discomfort

Ergonomics is the study of the interactions between humans and equipment. Humans can avoid hand and wrist stress by using ergonomically designed keyboards and by positioning the keyboard and mouse at a height so that the forearms are parallel to the ground. This is usually a height of 23 to 28 inches from the typing surface to the ground. The monitor should be placed so that the eyes are 16 to 24 inches from the screen and the line of sight is 10 to 20 degrees below horizontal.

Key Terms

Numbers indicate the pages where terms are first cited with their full definition in the chapter. An alphabetized list of key terms with definitions is included in the end-of-book glossary.

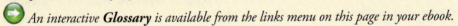 *An interactive **Glossary** is available from the links menu on this page in your ebook.*

Chapter Exercises

Complete the following exercises to assess your understanding of the material covered in this chapter.

 *Interactive **Flash Cards** and an interactive **Game** are available from the links menu on this page in your ebook.*

 Go to your SNAP Assignments page to complete the Terms Check, Knowledge Check, Key Principles, and Tech Illustrated exercises.

Terms Check: Matching

Match each term with its definition.

a.	ALU	f.	lumens
b.	fuser	g.	PCIe
c.	chipset	h.	pixel
d.	DDR	i.	toner
e.	ergonomics	j.	Unicode

___ 1. The unit of measurement for describing projector brightness.

___ 2. An individual dot of color in a display screen.

___ 3. The component in a laser printer that melts the toner so it sticks to the paper.

___ 4. A combination of iron and colored plastic particles that's used to create images with a laser printer.

___ 5. The study of the interaction between humans and the equipment they use.

___ 6. An encoding system that uses binary digits to represent letters, numbers, and symbols.

___ 7. The controller chip on the motherboard that directs the board's data traffic.

___ 8. A type of expansion bus on a motherboard.

___ 9. The part of the CPU that does the actual calculations of data.

___ 10. A type of SDRAM that can read or write two words of data per clock cycle.

Knowledge Check: Multiple Choice

Choose the best answer for each question.

1. Which of these is an input device?
   a. mouse
   b. speaker
   c. CPU
   d. RAM

2. Which of these is a pointing device?
   a. keyboard
   b. trackball
   c. modem
   d. display adapter

3. Which of these contains a charge-coupled device?
   a. CPU
   b. monitor
   c. keyboard
   d. scanner

4. Root mean squared (RMS) is a measurement of what component's performance?
   a. a microphone
   b. a speaker
   c. a sound card
   d. a monitor

5. A _____ is approximately 1 trillion bytes.
   a. gigabyte
   b. terabyte
   c. petabyte
   d. exabyte

6. The conductive pathways in a motherboard are called
   a. chipsets.
   b. registers.
   c. ROM.
   d. traces.

7. What does a VGA connector look like?
   a. a phone connector but wider
   b. a round PS/2 port
   c. a DB15F connector
   d. a USB connector

8. A microphone plugs into what type of connector?
   a. 3.5-millimeter round
   b. PCIe
   c. PS/2
   d. DVI

9. Flash memory is a type of
   a. SDRAM.
   b. EEPROM.
   c. PRAM.
   d. CPU.

10. _____ software can be trained to understand a specific person's speech through a series of practice drills.
    a. Speech recognition
    b. Voice recognition
    c. Word modulating
    d. Accelerometer

Key Principles: Completion

Complete each statement with the appropriate word or phrase.

1. The _____ _____ (2 words) converts the AC wall outlet current to the lower DC current that computer components require.

2. The _____ bus connects the CPU to the main memory; its speed is governed by the system clock.

3. The _____ of speakers, which is measured in watts, determines the maximum volume level.

4. A _____ processor can process several instructions at once, as if the system has more than one CPU.

5. _____ is a type of RAM that loses its data when it's unpowered.

6. The BIOS of a motherboard is an example of _____ memory.

7. A monitor's _____ _____ (2 words) is the ratio of its width to its height—for example, 4:3.

8. Inkjet printers use liquid ink, and laser printers use powdered _____.

9. An engineer or architect might use a _____ to create large-format drawings or maps.

10. The _____ _____ (2 words) is the part of the CPU that directs and coordinates its overall operation and that performs the fetch and decode portions of the machine cycle.

Tech Illustrated: Figure Labeling

Fill in the blanks with the correct labels.

1. System unit

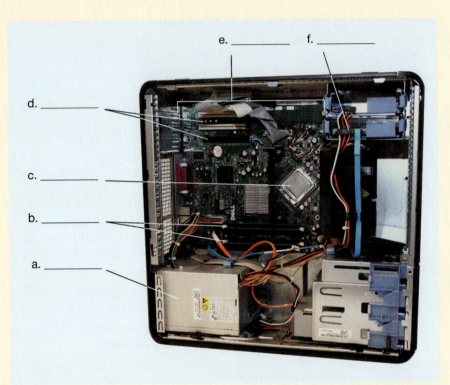

2. Motherboard

Tech to Come: Brainstorming New Uses

In groups or individually, contemplate the following questions and develop as many answers as you can.

1. As touchscreens have become more affordable, more devices have started including them. Touchscreens are even provided with some devices you might not normally think of as computers, such as kitchen appliances and car radios. What devices besides traditional computer systems have you seen—either in person or on the Internet or in print media—that have touchscreens?

2. Bluetooth is a short-range, wireless networking technology that was mentioned several times in this chapter. One of the most common uses for Bluetooth is to connect a cell phone to a wireless headset. What other uses can you think of for Bluetooth technology in your home, school, and workplace? (Keep in mind that Bluetooth has a range limit of about 33 feet.)

Tech Literacy: Internet Research and Writing

Conduct Internet research to find the information described, and then develop appropriate written responses based on your research. Be sure to document your sources using the MLA format. (See Chapter 1, Tech Literacy: Internet Research and Writing, page 38, to review MLA style guidelines.)

1. Suppose you have a friend who has a movement disability that makes it difficult to use a regular mouse; specifically, she can't position the pointer precisely enough. Research the availability of alternative input devices that would provide greater functionality, and write your friend a letter telling her about your findings.

2. What is Moore's law, and how does it affect the PCs that you use and purchase? Write a paragraph that explains the concept and that provides an estimate of CPU speed on a computer purchased three years from now.

3. Conduct Internet research about impact printers. Where are they still available for sale and at what prices? Supply web addresses for at least two online stores that carry them. Who buys them, and what are they used for? After finding out the answers to these questions, write a fictional scenario of a company in which impact printers are important to day-to-day business.

4. Go to the Intel website (http://CUT6.emcp.net /IntelProducts) and locate information about the latest Intel Core CPUs for desktop PCs. Choose one of the CPUs and find the following facts about it:

- Number of cores
- Number of threads
- Clock speed
- Word size (may be labeled as "Instruction Set")

Use the System Information utility in the Microsoft Windows operating system (or an equivalent utility, if using a different operating system) to determine the CPU used in your own computer. Compare its performance stats to those of the Intel CPU you researched.

5. Suppose you need a motherboard that meets the following specifications:
- Will support an Intel Core i7 processor (LGA1155 processor socket)
- Will support at least 32 GB of DDR3 RAM
- Has at least 2 ×16 PCIe slots
- Has at least 3 ×1 PCIe slots
- Has at least 1 PCI slot
- Has built-in sound support
- Has at least 2 USB 2.0 ports and at least 2 USB 3.0 ports

Find at least two motherboards for sale online that meet or exceed these specs. Use a spreadsheet application to compare the two boards.

Tech Issues: Team Problem-Solving

In groups, develop possible solutions to the issues presented.

1. Schools and businesses lose millions of dollars a year because of computer thefts. What are some ways that schools and businesses can prevent desktop computers from being taken from their buildings without authorization?

2. Suppose you have been tasked with choosing new printers for your school's computer lab. Would you buy several of the same kind, or a variety? What type(s) of printers would you get, and why? Consider factors such as initial cost, cost per page, reliability, speed, and compatibility with your computer lab's network. Create a spreadsheet that summarizes your findings.

3. Computers have become so inexpensive that it may cost you more to have your old PC repaired than it does to buy a new one with better features. However, discarding your old computer every few years can be seen as wasteful and environmentally damaging. What could you do to lessen the negative impact on the environment? Suppose you had an old but still repairable computer to get rid of. Use the web to find charities or businesses in your area that will take your old computer and dispose of it responsibly or repair it and find it a new home.

Tech Timeline: Predicting Next Steps

Early computers were huge mainframes in special rooms that couldn't be moved without a forklift. The invention of desktop PCs enabled each user to have a computer on his or her desk, but the user was still tethered to the desk. Notebooks, tablets, and smartphones have taken personal computing to progressively smaller and more portable levels. What do you think is next? Look at the timeline below outlining the major benchmarks in the development of computer portability. Complete the timeline through the year 2030 with your predictions.

Mainframes

1952 IBM introduces the IBM 701 Electronic Data Processing Machine, one of the earliest mainframe computers, which uses vacuum tubes for processing and memory.

1959 IBM introduces the IBM 7090, a mainframe that uses transistors for processing and magnetic core memory.

Desktop and Luggable Computers

1981 IBM introduces the original IBM PC, one of the first commercially successful desktop personal computers.

1984 Apple introduces the Macintosh desktop computer.

Laptop and Notebook Computers

1982 The Kaypro Corporation releases the Kaypro II, one of the first transportable computers; it weighed 26 pounds and was built into an aluminum case.

1984 IBM releases the IBM Portable Personal Computer 5155; it was essentially a PC in a carrying case and weighed 30 pounds.

1986 IBM releases the IBM Convertible Personal Computer 5140; it weighed just 12 pounds and was the first PC to run on batteries.

1988 NEC releases the UltraLite, a true notebook computer; it's just 1.4 inches thick and weighs 4.4 pounds.

PDAs and Tablets

1993 Apple releases the Newton MessagePad, one of the first hand-held personal digital assistants (PDAs).

1996 Palm Computing introduces the Palm Pilot (later called a *Palm*), one of the most successful PDAs ever.

2000 Microsoft launches the Pocket PC, which uses a touch-capable version of Windows called *Windows CE 3.0*.

2010 Apple releases the iPad Version 1 with up to 64 GB of storage, 256 MB of RAM, and a 1 GHz CPU.

Smartphones

1994 IBM and BellSouth release the Simon Personal Communicator, the first smartphone; it could make calls and send and receive faxes and emails.

1999 Research in Motion (RIM) releases the first BlackBerry smartphone, integrating multiple communication types (phone, text, and email) into a single inbox.

2007 Apple releases the iPhone, featuring a phone, a camera, audio and video capabilities, and personal organizer utilities.

2010 Microsoft releases Windows Phone 7, with a tile-based user interface that resembles the Start screen in Windows 8.

Wearable Computers

1972 Hamilton Watch Company introduces the Pulsar, the first digital programmable watch.

1983 Casio releases a line of computer watches that store data, play simple games, and have built-in calculators, alarms, and timers.

2013 Samsung launches the Galaxy Gear Smartwatch, an Android-based watch with gesture-based navigation.

2014 Google makes available for consumer purchase Google Glass, a head-mounted, display-based computer that uses natural language commands to communicate with the Internet. Google suspended the product in 2015, promising to continue to work on the technology.

2015 Apple introduces Apple Watch, a wrist-wearable computer that runs many of the same apps as the iPhone.

Ethical Dilemmas: Group Discussion and Debate

As a class or within an assigned group, discuss the following ethical dilemma.

As computer technology becomes increasingly portable, having a computer with you 24 hours a day is feasible. Many people carry a computer or smartphone with them wherever they go.

Do you think that employers have a right to limit employees' use of personal smartphones or tablet PCs during work hours? If you were an employer, what would your policy be and why? If you were an employee of this employer, how would

you feel about the policy? What sort of compromise policy would be fair to both the employee and the employer?

What about in school? Should school administrators be able to ban or limit students' use of smartphones during classes? What about during free times, such as between classes, during lunch, and during before-school and after-school organized activities and clubs?

Chapter 3

Working with System Software and File Storage

Chapter Goal

To understand how operating systems and data storage devices contribute to computing productivity

Learning Objectives

3.1 Define *software* and identify four types of system software.

3.2 Explain the purpose of the system BIOS.

3.3 Explain the main functions of an operating system.

3.4 Differentiate between types of operating systems.

3.5 Describe the major types of utility programs and their purposes.

3.6 Explain how software is used to create computer programs.

3.7 Explain how file storage works.

3.8 Differentiate between types of storage devices and media.

3.9 Describe the uses and functions of large-scale storage.

Green go-online icons indicate resources that are accessed from the links menu in your ebook.

SNAP icons indicate interactive resources that are available in SNAP. Go to your SNAP Assignments page to complete these quizzes, activities, and exercises.

3.1 Defining System Software

 Precheck 3.1

Check your understanding of the concepts covered by this objective.

As you learned in Chapter 1, a computer system consists of both hardware (the physical parts) and software (the programming instructions). Software gives orders, and hardware carries them out.

Application software helps users perform both useful and fun tasks, such as word processing, accounting, and game playing. You buy application software because you want to do the activities it enables you to do. (Application software is covered in detail in Chapter 4.)

System software, on the other hand, exists as a support platform for running application software. System software starts up the computer, keeps it running smoothly, and translates human-language instructions into computer-language instructions. There are four categories of system software:

- **BIOS programs.** A **basic input/output system (BIOS)** is software on a chip on the motherboard that helps the computer start up. Chip-stored software is sometimes called **firmware** because it is hybrid of hardware and software.
- **Operating systems.** An **operating system (OS)** is software that provides the user interface, manages files, runs applications, and communicates with hardware.
- **Utilities.** A **utility program** is software that performs troubleshooting or maintenance tasks that keep the computer running well and protect the computer from security and privacy violations.
- **Translators.** A **translator** is software that translates programming code into instructions (software) the computer will understand.

Operating systems are found not only in personal computers, but also in automobile dashboard computers and other devices.

ⓢ Tracking Down Tech ⟫⟫⟫⟫⟫

Operating Systems and You

Any time you use any kind of computer, you interact with an operating system. Microsoft Windows and Mac OS X are the most popular operating systems for personal computers (PCs), but computing extends far beyond PCs. For example, your bank's automated teller machine

(ATM) has its own operating system, and so does your cell phone. Complete this scavenger hunt to identify different operating systems in your home, school, work, and social environments.

Figure 3.1

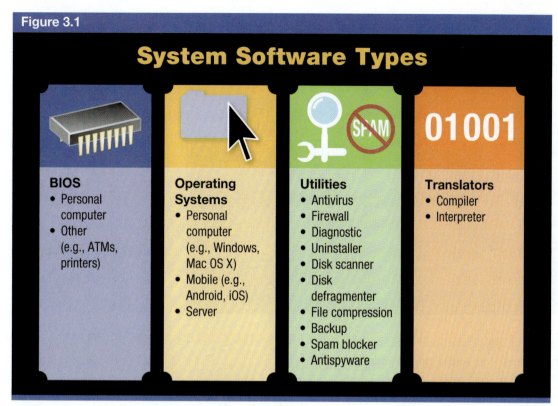

System Software Types

BIOS
- Personal computer
- Other (e.g., ATMs, printers)

Operating Systems
- Personal computer (e.g., Windows, Mac OS X)
- Mobile (e.g., Android, iOS)
- Server

Utilities
- Antivirus
- Firewall
- Diagnostic
- Uninstaller
- Disk scanner
- Disk defragmenter
- File compression
- Backup
- Spam blocker
- Antispyware

Translators
- Compiler
- Interpreter

System software includes these four categories.

See Figure 3.1 for examples of each type of system software. You will learn about each type in the next several sections of this chapter.

3.2 Understanding the System BIOS

The low-level programs that help hardware start up and communicate with other pieces of hardware are stored on read-only memory (ROM) chips on the circuit boards. That way, they can never be accidentally erased or changed. This ROM-stored software is known as the *BIOS*, or sometimes *ROM-BIOS*. The BIOS for the motherboard is the **system BIOS**. Other devices have BIOSs too. For example, a printer has software that starts it and runs a self-test when the power comes on.

The motherboard's BIOS is able to automatically detect some aspects of the system configuration, such as the amount of random-access memory (RAM) installed, the type of central processing unit (CPU), and the capacity of the hard drives. However, since the motherboard manufacturer can't anticipate all the customization that a given user will perform, the user needs to be able to modify the BIOS settings. This modification is performed through the **BIOS Setup utility**. (This is also sometimes called a *CMOS Setup* utility because in older systems, the settings were stored on complementary metal-oxide semiconductor chips.)

The exact procedure for entering the BIOS Setup utility varies depending on the PC. As the PC starts, the screen briefly displays a message telling you what key to press to enter Setup. For example, you might see a message like this: *Press F2 for Setup*. The key that's specified could be F1, F2, Delete, or any other key, depending on the manufacturer and version of the BIOS. If you don't press the specified key, the message will go away after several seconds and the PC will proceed to start up normally. If you press the named key while the message is still on the screen, however, the Setup program

 **Recheck 3.1**
Recheck your understanding of the concepts covered by this objective.

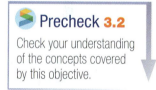 **Precheck 3.2**
Check your understanding of the concepts covered by this objective.

Figure 3.2

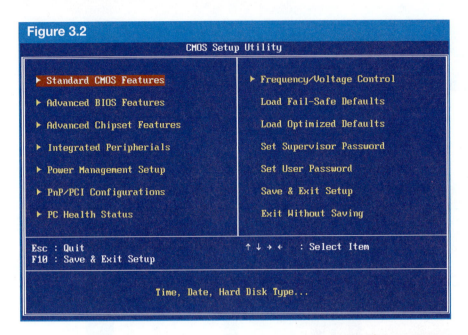

This generic BIOS Setup utility screen is typical of many such screens. It displays instructions that provide shortcut keys and navigation guidance.

that's stored on the BIOS chip will appear. On some newer systems, you might not be able to enter the BIOS Setup program by pressing a key; see the Hands On feature "Checking Out Your BIOS Setup" to learn an alternative method.

Figure 3.2 shows a generic version of a BIOS Setup program. Notice that the program calls itself *CMOS Setup Utility*, which is the same thing. The program you see on your computer may look very different from this, as the look and interface vary greatly across BIOS manufacturers and models.

Why would you want to enter the BIOS Setup utility and make modifications? Here are some of the most common reasons:

- **To check the system specs.** You may want to check the system specs to make sure the BIOS is correctly seeing the hardware you have. If you install some new RAM, for example, BIOS Setup will tell you whether it's working. If you are having a problem with a certain disk drive, BIOS Setup will tell you whether the motherboard sees the drive.

- **To change the boot order.** The boot order is the order in which the computer tries the drives to find one with a valid operating system. If you want to boot from a DVD (for example, to run a diagnostic utility) rather than your hard drive, setting the DVD drive as the first boot device will allow the system to do so.

- **To disable certain built-in components.** You may want to disable certain components on the motherboard that you don't use. Disabling these components will prevent memory and other system resources from being wasted by being assigned to them. For example, if your motherboard has a built-in display adapter but you prefer to use a different display adapter installed in one of the motherboard's expansion slots instead, you can turn off the built-in one.

Hands On

Checking Out Your BIOS Setup

Follow the steps in this resource to check out your computer's BIOS Setup utility.

Tech Career Explorer

Working with BIOS Setup

Computer technicians routinely use the BIOS setup on computer systems to reconfigure them for different hardware and to troubleshoot hardware problems. Complete this exercise to explore BIOS settings using a simulator.

 **Recheck 3.2**
Recheck your understanding of the concepts covered by this objective.

3.3 Understanding What an Operating System Does

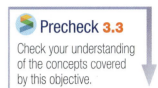 **Precheck 3.3**
Check your understanding of the concepts covered by this objective.

The operating system (OS) is the most important piece of software on a PC. When the computer starts up, the BIOS completes its initial testing and then searches the **boot drive** (a drive that contains a valid operating system). Next, the BIOS passes control to the operating system, which loads itself into memory and completes the startup process. Once loaded, the OS manages the computer and performs a variety of interdependent functions related to input, processing, output, and storage, such as these (see also Figure 3.3):

- Booting (starting up) the computer
- Providing a user interface
- Running programs
- Configuring and controlling devices
- Managing essential file operations, such as saving and opening files

You will learn more about each of these five functions later in this chapter.

Operating systems differ from one another in several important ways. For example, they can be graphics based or text based. They can also support a single user or multiple users at a time, and they can run on different sizes and types of computers.

One defining characteristic of an OS is the hardware it will run on—in other words, its **platform**. The most popular platforms for desktop and notebook PCs are IBM compatible and Macintosh. An **IBM-compatible platform** is based on the same standard as the original IBM PC back in the 1980s, which ran an operating system called *MS-DOS*. The IBM-compatible platform is also called the **Intel platform**. This platform comes in two versions: 32-bit and 64-bit. The 32-bit version is called **x86** (a reference to the numbering system of Intel CPUs that was used in early computers: 286, 386, and 486). The 64-bit version is called **x64**.

Figure 3.3

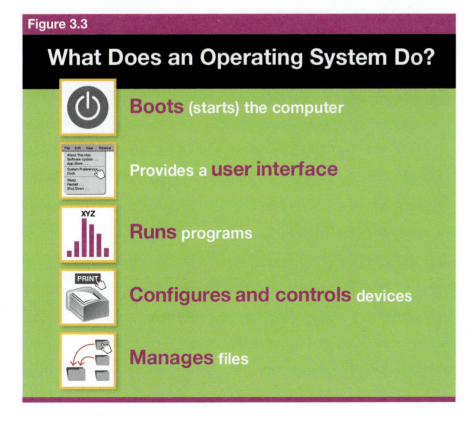

What Does an Operating System Do?

Boots (starts) the computer

Provides a **user interface**

Runs programs

Configures and controls devices

Manages files

Despite the differences across operating systems, they all perform the same five basic functions.

Windows is the most common OS installed on the IBM-compatible platform. Other operating systems, such as Linux and UNIX, also work on the IBM-compatible platform. See section 3.4, "Looking at Operating Systems by Computer Type," on page 102, for more details about operating systems and platforms.

Starting Up the Computer

Booting (or starting) a computer after the power has been turned off is referred to as a **cold boot**. Restarting a computer without powering off is a **warm boot**. When a PC starts up, the BIOS software automatically executes its programming. It completes a **power-on self-test (POST)** that checks the essential hardware devices to make sure they are operational. It also looks for a storage device such as a hard drive that contains a usable operating system. When the BIOS software finds one, it transfers control to that operating system. The operating system loads itself and finishes starting up the computer.

The OS loads into memory the system configuration and other necessary operating system files, such as the kernel. The **kernel** manages computer components, peripheral devices, and memory. It also maintains the system clock and loads other operating system and application programs as they are required. The kernel is a **memory resident** part of the operating system, which means that it remains in memory while the computer is in operation. Other parts of the operating system are nonresident; a **nonresident** part of the operating system remains on the hard disk until it is needed. The loaded (memory resident) portion of the operating system contains the most essential instructions for operating the computer, controlling the monitor display, and managing RAM efficiently to increase the computer's overall performance. The process of starting up a computer is illustrated in Figure 3.4.

 **Activity 3.3.1**

Practice
How a PC Starts Up

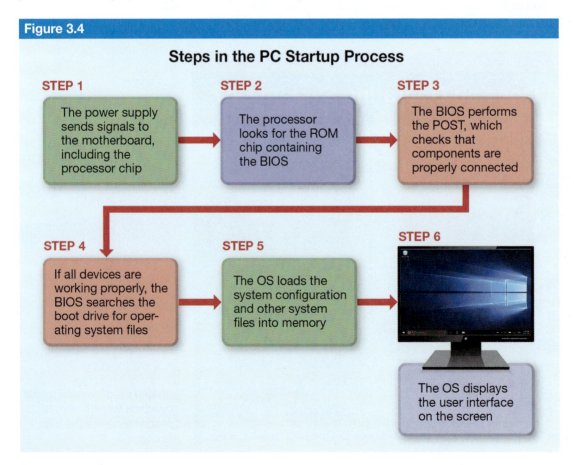

Figure 3.4

Steps in the PC Startup Process

STEP 1
The power supply sends signals to the motherboard, including the processor chip

STEP 2
The processor looks for the ROM chip containing the BIOS

STEP 3
The BIOS performs the POST, which checks that components are properly connected

STEP 4
If all devices are working properly, the BIOS searches the boot drive for operating system files

STEP 5
The OS loads the system configuration and other system files into memory

STEP 6

The OS displays the user interface on the screen

Providing a User Interface

Any type of software, including an operating system, contains a **user interface** that allows communication between the software and the user. Another name for a user interface is a **shell**. The user interface controls how data and commands are entered, as well as how information and processing options are presented as output on the screen. There are two main types of user interfaces: text-based and graphical user interface.

Early personal computers, such as the original IBM PC, used an OS called *MS-DOS*. MS-DOS has a text-based interface, which is also called a **command-line interface**. A command-line interface presents the user with a group of characters called a *command prompt* (for example, C:\>). The command prompt indicates the computer is ready to receive a command. In response to the command prompt, the user types a line of code that tells the computer what to do. For example, the command *copy A:\income.doc C:* instructs the computer to copy a file named income.doc located on drive A to drive C. The command-line interface isn't common anymore, but neither is it obsolete.

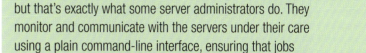

Tech Career Explorer

Working with a Command-Line Interface

Working all day at a command prompt isn't for everyone, but that's exactly what some server administrators do. They monitor and communicate with the servers under their care using a plain command-line interface, ensuring that jobs flow smoothly through the server and there are no security breaches. If you would like to work with a Linux command-line interface, complete this exercise.

Hands On

Comparing GUIs and Command-Line Interfaces

The primary file management interface for Windows 10 is the GUI-based File Explorer. However, you can also display file listings in a command-line interface. Follow the steps in this resource to compare the two interfaces.

It's still the native interface for the UNIX and Linux operating systems, for example, but users can choose a graphical shell if they prefer. Windows users see a graphical interface by default. However, they have the option of opening a command prompt window to interact with the operating system through a command-line interface, as shown in Figure 3.5.

A **graphical user interface (GUI)** enables the user to select commands by pointing and clicking with a mouse or other pointing device or by tapping with a finger. With this type of interface, the keyboard is used primarily for data entry. Microsoft Windows

Figure 3.5

```
C:\>dir /w
 Volume in drive C is OS
 Volume Serial Number is 8043-EB9D

 Directory of C:\

2108FP.TXT              accelmagsetup.log       autoexec.bat
[Books]                 config.sys              [dell]
[Drivers]               [Ebook files]           [EMCP]
[Intel]                 [IUware Online]         mini-agent.log
mini-agent.txt          [Nancy]                 [PerfLogs]
[Program Files]         [Snagit]                [Users]
vcredist_x86.log        [Windows]               [Workgroup Templates]
               7 File(s)      1,593,164 bytes
              14 Dir(s)  273,125,781,504 bytes free

C:\>_
```

A command-line interface for the Windows operating system.

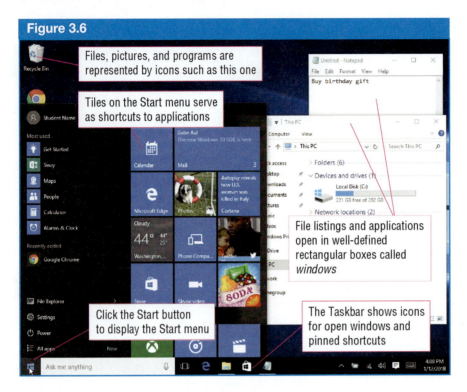

Figure 3.6

Files, pictures, and programs are represented by icons such as this one

Tiles on the Start menu serve as shortcuts to applications

File listings and applications open in well-defined rectangular boxes called *windows*

Click the Start button to display the Start menu

The Taskbar shows icons for open windows and pinned shortcuts

The graphical user interface (GUI) desktop for Windows 10.

and Macintosh OS X are both GUIs. Figure 3.6 shows the Microsoft Windows 10 desktop. The **desktop** is the background for the GUI—the environment in which all the windows and applications open and close. Files, folders, and programs are represented by small pictures called **icons**. File listings and applications open in **windows**, which are well-defined rectangular areas on the computer screen. Most windows are movable, so you can arrange multiple windows side by side to view them simultaneously. On the Start menu, large rectangular **tiles** serve as shortcuts to applications you can run.

Until a few years ago, almost all graphical user interfaces were based on the desktop metaphor. The user used a mouse to select and move objects on the desktop, to run programs, and to manage files. However, many newer portable devices have touch screens, and new operating systems are designed to take advantage of that capability.

Practical TECH

Command Line: What Is It Good For?

Graphical user interfaces are attractive and easy to figure out, but many computer professionals prefer to use command-line interfaces for some tasks. That's why server operating systems such as Linux make the GUI optional. If you know what you want the computer to do, expressing that command in text form can sometimes be the easiest approach. For example, suppose you have 100 files that all start with *BX* (*BX001.doc*, *BX002.doc*, and so on), and you want to rename them so they all begin with *AG* instead (*AG001.doc*, *AG002.doc*, and so on). In a GUI, you will have to rename each file individually by clicking

the name and editing it. But at a command prompt, you can type REN BX*.doc AG*.doc and the files will all be renamed at once, saving you at least 30 minutes of work.

This is just one example. Some network-related commands are also available only at the command prompt. For instance, the command PING checks whether a particular network location is reachable, and TRACERT traces the path between your PC and a network location.

Figure 3.7

Click an icon to run an application

Some icons represent groups of related applications

Apple iOS operating system on an iPhone.

In user interfaces designed primarily for use via a touch screen, the graphics have an entirely different look and feel. They are typically based on pages or menus of icons. The user taps an icon to select it. The user can also drag across the screen with a finger to perform various actions, such as scrolling to different pages of the display and shutting down an application. You learned about these actions in Chapter 2. Figure 3.7 shows the Apple iOS operating system, which is designed for easy use on a touchscreen device such as an iPad tablet or an iPhone.

Running Applications

The main job of any computer is to run applications—that is, programs that perform tasks the user wants to accomplish, whether for work or for entertainment. The user can access applications by browsing the file system for them or by using shortcuts set up on the desktop, on a toolbar, or in the case of Windows, on the Start menu. For example, many of the tiles on the Windows 10 Start menu in Figure 3.6 are shortcuts to applications you can run, such as Calendar, Mail, and Microsoft Edge.

Most operating systems enable you to run multiple applications at a time and switch freely between them. In Windows 10, shown in Figure 3.6 on page 100, you can click an application's button on the Taskbar to switch to that application. In iOS, shown in Figure 3.7, you can press and release the Home button two times quickly to see thumbnails of running applications, and then tap the thumbnail for the application you want.

Hands On

Opening and Closing Applications

Follow the steps in this resource to become familiar with opening and closing applications in Windows 10.

Configuring and Controlling Devices

Configuring and controlling computer components and attached devices is a major function of the OS. Each device speaks its own language, so the OS uses a driver to communicate with each one. A **driver** is a small program that translates commands between the OS and the device. Windows comes with a large collection of drivers for popular device types, such as keyboards, mice, network adapters, and display adapters. Most devices come with their own driver disks as well.

Managing Files

An OS provides an interface that enables users to work with files and folders (see Figure 3.8). File management includes moving, copying, renaming, and deleting files and folders. In addition, it includes formatting and copying disks and viewing file listings in various ways (for example, sorted by a certain property or filtered to show only files of a certain type).

The name of the file management utility is different not only in different operating systems but even in different versions of the same operating system. In Windows 10, the file management utility is called *File Explorer*; in some earlier versions of Windows it was called *Windows Explorer*. In Mac OS X, the file management feature is called *Finder*.

Command-line interfaces (such as UNIX) don't have a separate file management application. The user types file management commands directly into the command prompt.

Hands On

Viewing Devices and Drivers

If you are curious about the devices on a Windows 10 system, follow the steps in this resource to browse them in a utility called *Device Manager*.

Activity 3.3.2

Video
Device Drivers

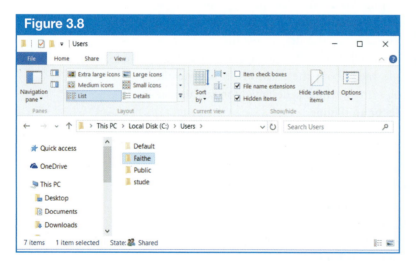

Figure 3.8

The Windows 10 File Explorer displays files and folders in a window. Here you see a list of the operating system's Users folders.

Recheck 3.3

Recheck your understanding of the concepts covered by this objective.

3.4 Looking at Operating Systems by Computer Type

The previous section described how operating systems can be differentiated by the types of functions they perform. Another way to differentiate OSs is by the types of computers they are designed to run. Operating systems are designed for three main types of computers: personal computers, mobile devices, and servers. Each type of computer has its own special needs based on what tasks it performs and who uses it. The following sections look at the most popular OSs for each type of computer.

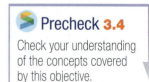

Precheck 3.4

Check your understanding of the concepts covered by this objective.

Personal Computer Operating Systems

A personal computer (PC) is one that's designed to be used by one person at a time, such as a desktop or notebook PC. Smaller mobile devices, such as tablets and phones, also qualify as PCs according to this definition.

Microsoft Windows **Microsoft Windows** is the most popular PC operating system in the world. In 2015, a Net Market Share survey reported that more than 90 percent of all desktop and notebook PCs used some version of Windows. Windows 10 is the most recent version at this writing. Earlier versions include Windows 8.1, Windows 8, Windows 7, Windows Vista, and Windows XP.

Activity 3.4.1

Video
The History of Windows

As you saw in Figure 3.6 on page 100, the Windows 10 desktop provides a user-friendly environment in which to work. The Taskbar provides access to open applications and windows. The Start button opens the Start menu, which provides access to all installed applications.

Windows 8 and 8.1 worked differently in that they had a Start screen that covered the entire screen instead of a Start menu. This Start screen, shown in Figure 3.9, was the default interface in Windows 8, and could be optionally set as the default interface in Windows 8.1. Many tablet users praised the tile-focused Start screen for its ease of use without a keyboard. However, many desktop and notebook PC users missed the familiar desktop, so Microsoft returned to the desktop interface in Windows 10.

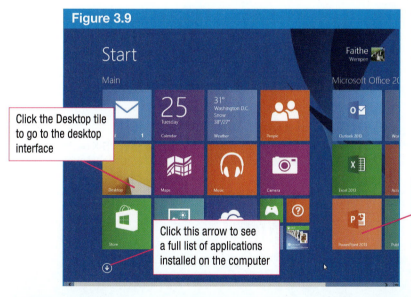

Figure 3.9

Windows 8 and Windows 8.1 (shown here) had a full-screen Start screen rather than a Start menu.

Click the Desktop tile to go to the desktop interface

Click this arrow to see a full list of applications installed on the computer

Click an app tile, such as the PowerPoint tile, to open that program in a new window

Practical TECH

Reinstalling Windows

If your older Windows desktop or notebook PC is running poorly, a clean install of the OS could make it run much faster. By wiping out everything on the hard drive and starting fresh, you get rid of any unwanted software that you may have inadvertently downloaded or imperfectly removed over the years. To do a clean install, boot from the Windows DVD that came with your computer and follow the prompts to reformat the hard drive and reinstall Windows.

If your computer did not come with a Windows DVD, check the computer's documentation to see if your computer has a hidden partition that contains system files, and that you can boot to for reinstallation. If you have Windows 10, you can also refresh or reinstall Windows via the Settings app. Click *Update & security*, click *Recovery* in the Navigation pane, and then click the Get Started button in the *Reset this PC* section.

Mac OS X **Mac OS X** is used on Apple Macintosh computers. Apple assigns names to differentiate versions of its operating system. The current version at this writing is El Capitan; earlier versions included Yosemite, Mavericks, and Lion. Like Windows, Mac OS X uses a desktop metaphor for its user interface. Figure 3.10 shows a Macintosh desktop. Notice the similarities between this desktop and the Windows desktop in Figure 3.6 on page 100. The functionality of the Mac OS X is also similar to that of the Windows operating system, although the features have different names, as noted in Figure 3.11.

Macintosh computers and the Mac OS are popular among graphics professionals. In fact, some of the most powerful software for page layout and graphics editing (such as Adobe Photoshop) was originally designed for the Mac. Today, however, much of the same software is available for both Windows and Mac OS X.

Figure 3.10

The Mac OS X desktop looks similar to the Windows desktop.

Figure 3.11

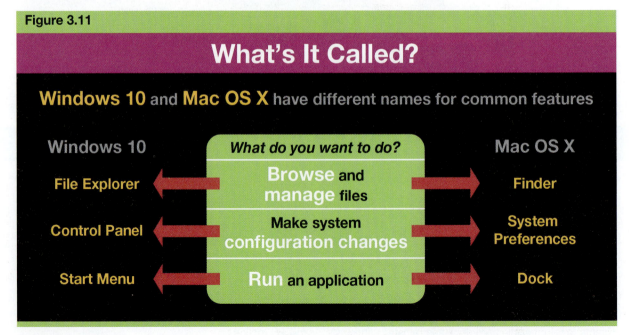

What's It Called?

Windows 10 and **Mac OS X** have different names for common features

Windows 10	What do you want to do?	Mac OS X
File Explorer	Browse and manage files	Finder
Control Panel	Make system configuration changes	System Preferences
Start Menu	Run an application	Dock

Figure 3.12

The popular Ubuntu Linux distribution includes an attractive GUI.

Linux **Linux** (pronounced "LIN-uks") is a UNIX-based operating system that runs on a number of platforms, including Intel-based PCs, servers, and handheld devices. The Linux kernel (that is, the central module) was developed mainly by computer programmer Linus Torvalds, and the name *Linux* is a combination of *Linus* and *UNIX*. UNIX is a command-line operating system for servers that has been popular for many years; you will learn more about it later in this chapter.

Torvalds designed Linux as **open source software**. This means that the developer retains ownership of the original programming code but makes the code available free to the general public. People are encouraged to experiment with the software, make improvements, and share the improvements with the entire user community. Open source software is quite different from **proprietary software**, which is software that an individual or company holds the exclusive rights to develop and sell. Proprietary software uses code and file formats that are designed exclusively for that software; its developers don't standardize it or make its source code available to the general public.

Fans of Linux praise its stability, flexibility, security, and generally low cost. The Linux kernel is free, but vendors usually package it with various tools, utilities, and shells and then charge users for the package. This package is called a **distribution (distro)**. A number of commercially available Linux distros are available for personal and business computers, including Red Hat Linux, Novell Linux Desktop, SUSE Linux, and Ubuntu Linux. One important feature of most distros is a GUI shell that enables the user to interact with the operating system using a graphical desktop. Figure 3.12 shows the shell for Ubuntu Linux, one of the most popular distributions available today.

The popularity of Linux on PCs is growing, especially as the number of software programs available on the Linux platform increases. Word-processing, spreadsheet, and presentation programs are available in an open source format called *Open Office*. Software companies are also developing programs that will allow Windows-based applications to run on Linux-based computers.

Chrome OS *Chrome* is the name of both an operating system and a web browser, and both are produced by Google. Chrome OS is based on Linux. It's a commercial distribution of an open source project called *Chromium OS*.

 **Activity 3.4.2**

Video
Linux Timeline

 **Activity 3.4.3**

Article
Open Source Software

Figure 3.13

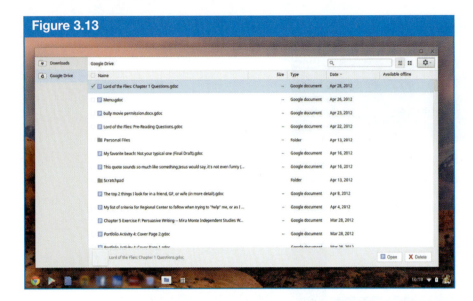

The Chrome OS contains a simple file management utility (shown here), plus the Google Chrome browser, a media player, and a few other simple utilities.

Chrome OS is a simple operating system that was designed primarily for thin clients. A **thin client** is a computer that has only minimal processing capabilities of its own, and is designed primarily to interface with other computers (such as on the Internet). A netbook is a small notebook computer that's equipped as a thin client. The most common way to acquire Chrome is to buy a netbook with Chrome preinstalled as its operating system. This configuration is sometimes called a *Chromebook*.

The Chrome OS was intentionally designed to have few features. It includes the Google Chrome web browser, of course, and a simple file manager (see Figure 3.13) and media player. Having a smaller, leaner operating system on a computer that performs only simple tasks can be an advantage. It can start up, shut down, and respond to commands more quickly than a more full-featured operating system.

Mobile Operating Systems

As computing devices have gotten smaller, what they need in an operating system has changed. As you learned in the previous section about the Chrome OS, some thin clients designed mostly for web use don't need the full-featured power of an operating system such as Microsoft Windows or Mac OS X. In fact, they run better and faster with a smaller, more agile OS.

A mobile device such as a tablet or smartphone typically doesn't include a mechanical hard drive. Instead, it uses solid-state memory (like the memory in a USB flash drive) to store both the operating system and any data files the user might save. Solid-state memory and storage is expensive, so having a smaller operating system means

Hotspot

OS Simulators

Are you interested in trying out some old operating systems without having to download and install them? Here are links to simulators that you can use with a web browser:

- Windows 1.01 (1985)—http://CUT6.emcp.net/Windows1.01
- Mac OS System 7 (1991)—http://CUT6.emcp.net/MacOS7
- Windows 3.1 (1992)—http://CUT6.emcp.net/Windows3.1

For slightly newer versions of Windows and Mac OS, check out http://CUT6.emcp.net/OSsimulators, where you will find simulators for a dozen or so Windows versions (starting with Windows 95) and Mac OS versions (starting with Mac OS 8.6).

Figure 3.14

The Apple iPad and iPhone use the iOS operating system. A number in a small red circle at the upper right corner of an icon alerts you to items that require your attention. In this case, one new email is available for viewing.

more memory will be available for user data; the user won't have to add more memory (and expense) to the device's configuration.

Most mobile devices have a touch-sensitive screen (rather than a keyboard and mouse) as the primary user interface. As a result, the operating system's user interface relies heavily on tapping onscreen icons or tiles and performing various swipes, drags, stretches, and pinches with the fingers.

iOS **iOS** is the operating system used in Apple mobile devices, such as iPhones and iPads. Apple doesn't license this operating system for any third-party devices, so you will find it only on Apple hardware. Figure 3.14 shows an iPad running iOS Version 9. To open an application in this interface, you tap its icon.

One benefit of iOS is that hundreds of thousands of applications (apps) are available for it—some for free and others for small fees. You can extend the basic default capabilities of your Apple device by downloading apps from the Apple Store. Use the App Store icon to access the App Store app, and from there, browse the available apps by category or keyword.

Android **Android** is an open source OS created by Google; it's similar to Google's Chrome OS, discussed on pages 105–106. Android is commonly used on smartphones and tablets, because it's simple and easy to use and a large number of apps are available for it. Because the Android OS is free, devices that run it are often less expensive than Windows- and iOS-based devices. Figure 3.15 shows an Android-based smartphone screen.

Figure 3.15

The Android OS on a smartphone.

Windows Phone The **Windows Phone OS** is a variant of Windows that's designed for the ultraportable platform of a smartphone. Its Start screen consists of a series of rectangular tiles, much like the ones on the Windows Start screen shown in Figure 3.9 on page 103. The tiles are resizable and customizable, and users can "pin" any apps they want to the Start screen (see Figure 3.16). Although reviewers have praised the usability of the Windows Phone operating system, it lags behind iOS and Android operating systems in terms of the number of apps available for it.

Figure 3.16

Windows Phone uses a tile-based interface similar to the Start screen in Windows 8.1 and the Start menu in Windows 10.

Server Operating Systems

Some operating systems are designed specifically for use with network servers. These OSs allow multiple users to connect to the server and share network resources, such as files and printers. A server version of an operating system contains many special features that aren't included in a PC operating system—for example, software for managing connections, authenticating users, prioritizing requests from multiple users, and providing multiuser access to databases. Some servers are specialized and provide a certain type of service on the network, such as database server, file server, mail server, print server, or Internet server.

The three most popular server OSs are UNIX, Linux, and Windows Server. Each has approximately one-third of the market share for web servers, according to a 2014 W3Techs survey. Each of these operating systems actually comes in many variants:

- UNIX servers include BSD, HP-UX, Aix, and Solaris.
- Popular Linux distros designed for server use include Debian, CenOS, and RHEL.
- Windows Server comes in many different versions.

Some server OSs don't have a graphical user interface. Many IT professionals prefer to use a command prompt when managing a server. UNIX and Linux, for example, don't include a GUI as part of the main kernel, although a GUI can be added to Linux if desired. Windows Server, on the other hand, is mainly administered through a GUI, although a command prompt is available when needed.

Of the three main server operating systems, **UNIX** (pronounced "YOO-niks") has been in existence the longest and is the only one that was developed from the ground up for servers. UNIX was created in the 1970s by programmers at Bell Laboratories to run servers and large computer systems. It uses a complex command-line interface and offers some superb capabilities, including allowing simultaneous access by many users to a single powerful computer. From its inception, UNIX has been a **multiuser operating system**: one that allows many people to use one CPU from remote stations. UNIX is also a **cross-platform operating system**: one that runs on computers of all kinds, from PCs to supercomputers. Because UNIX was used on most servers at universities

 **Activity 3.4.4**

Article
Server Operating Systems

Servers like this one use operating systems such as UNIX, Linux, and Windows Server.

and laboratories, most early Internet activities were UNIX-based, and many Internet service providers (ISPs) continue to use UNIX for their servers.

Linux is a variant of UNIX, although it has developed so much on its own that it's now considered a separate operating system. Because Linux is open source, many variants of this OS are available for server use. One of the most popular server configurations is a **solution stack,** which is a set of complementary applications. It's called *LAMP*, which is an acronym of the features it includes: the Linux kernel; a web server such as Apache; a database such as MariaDB, MySQL, or MongoDB; and CGI scripting tools such as Pert, PHP, and/or Python. Most Linux distributions include all these tools and many more like them, so any user with the right knowledge and skills can set up a Linux server without buying any commercial software.

Windows Server is a variant of Microsoft Windows. Microsoft has released many versions of Windows Server since the original Windows NT 3.1 Advanced Server in 1993. Each version has provided a GUI that resembles the equivalent desktop Windows version; the Windows Server 2016 GUI interface closely resembles Windows 10, for example. Windows Server versions are available in several editions. Each targets the needs of a specific size of company, such as Essentials (for small companies), Standard (for medium-sized companies), and Datacenter (for large companies that maintain a lot of data). Windows Server can be configured to run in Server Core mode (command-line interface) or in Server with a GUI mode (GUI interface).

Recheck 3.4
Recheck your understanding of the concepts covered by this objective.

3.5 Exploring Types of Utility Programs

A utility program performs a maintenance or repair task, such as checking for viruses, uninstalling programs, or deleting data that's no longer needed. An operating system typically includes several utility programs that are preinstalled at the factory. Several companies, including Symantec and McAfee, produce software suites that contain a variety of utility programs. Norton 360 (shown in Figure 3.17) is a comprehensive software suite that provides complete security, performance optimization, and data backup and restore functionality. It includes online threat protection and powerful

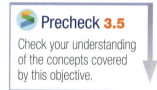

Precheck 3.5
Check your understanding of the concepts covered by this objective.

Figure 3.17

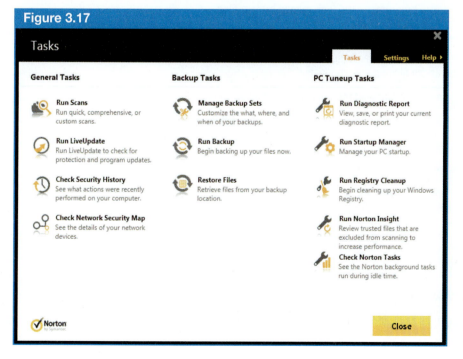

Security suites offer a variety of maintenance utilities to correct and avoid problems and to improve system performance.

features for backing up your data securely as well as continuously fine-tuning your PC for best performance.

Utility programs are useful for avoiding and correcting many of the problems that computer users are likely to encounter. These programs are usually stored on the hard drive along with the basic operating system and activated when needed by the user. Table 3.1 lists popular kinds of utility programs, some of which are described more fully in the following pages.

Antivirus Software

Activity 3.5.1

Video
Antivirus Software

Antivirus software (also called a *virus checker*) is one of the most important types of utility programs. Examples include Norton AntiVirus and McAfee AntiVirus Plus; Windows 7 and higher also includes basic antivirus protection in the Windows Defender utility.

A virus is harm-causing code that's buried within a computer program; it's transferred to a computer system without the user's knowledge when he or she runs the program to which the virus has attached itself. A worm is a variation that doesn't require running an **executable file** (a file that runs a program) to infect; it's spread through networks and email systems or by visiting an infected website.

Virus contamination of a computer system can have consequences that range in severity from being mildly annoying to disastrous. Antivirus utilities search for viruses, worms, and **malware** (malicious software) on a system and delete or quarantine them

Table 3.1 Utility Programs and Their Functions

Utility Program	Function
Antivirus	Protects the computer system from a virus attack
Firewall	Protects a personal computer or network from access by unauthorized users, such as hackers
Diagnostic	Examines the computer system and corrects problems that are identified
Uninstaller	Removes programs, along with related system files
Disk scanner	Identifies and fixes errors in the file storage system
Disk optimizer (defragmenter)	Identifies disk problems (such as separated files) and rearranges files so they run faster
Disk toolkit	Recovers lost files and repairs files that may be damaged
File compression	Reduces the sizes of files so they take up less disk space
Backup	Makes a backup copy of files on a separate disk
Spam blocker	Filters incoming spam messages
Antispyware	Protects the computer system from software that tracks the activities of Internet users
Device driver	Allows hardware devices (such as disk drives and printers) to work with the computer system
Extender	Adds new programs and fonts to the computer system
File viewer	Quickly displays the contents of a file
Screen capture	Captures as a file the content shown on the monitor

when they are found. Antivirus utilities can also monitor system operations for suspicious activities (such as the rewriting of system resource files) and alert users when they are occurring.

Firewalls

A **firewall** is a security system that acts as a boundary to protect a computer or network from unauthorized access (see Figure 3.18). It's designed to work like the firewalls between individual units in an apartment building, whose purpose is to prevent fire from spreading from one apartment to another. A computer firewall may consist of hardware, software, or a combination of the two.

The data traffic between your computer and the Internet may carry information for multiple programs, including web browsers and email programs. Your PC keeps this data organized by assigning different port numbers to different kinds of traffic. For example, port 110 is usually used for incoming mail messages. There are many ports, and most of them are unused most of the time. If an intruder knows that a particular port number is available, he or she might be able to use it to gain access to your computer and steal passwords and personal data. A firewall prevents such intrusions by allowing port access only to the specific users and applications you set up.

A **personal firewall** is a software-based system designed to protect a PC from unauthorized users attempting to access other computers through an Internet connection. Symantec and McAfee both make personal firewall software, both as stand-alone products and as part of security suites. Windows also includes a personal firewall called *Windows Firewall* that's enabled by default and adequate for most PCs.

A **network firewall** typically consists of a combination of hardware and software. In addition to installing firewall software, a company may add a hardware device (such as a dedicated firewall device or **proxy server**) that screens all communications

Activity 3.5.2

Practice
How a Firewall Works

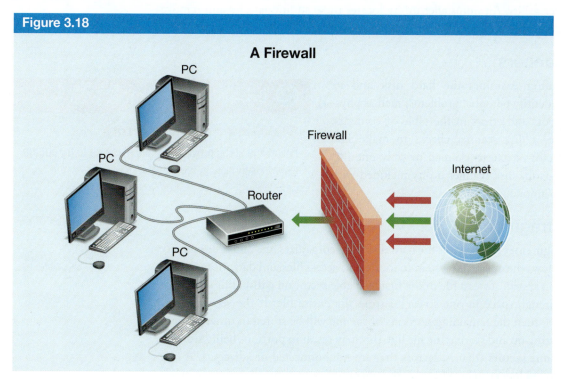

Figure 3.18

A Firewall

PC

PC

Router

Firewall

Internet

PC

A firewall is designed to prevent unauthorized users from accessing a PC or a network connected to the Internet.

entering and leaving networked computers to prevent unauthorized access. For example, the device or server may check an incoming message to determine whether it's from an authorized user. If the message is not from an authorized user, it is blocked from entering the network.

A firewall provides a first line of defense against unauthorized access and intrusion. Although most firewall systems are effective, users should practice other security measures, as well, such as safeguarding passwords.

Hands On

Examining Firewall Settings

The Windows 10 firewall is enabled by default unless you have another firewall application installed. Follow the steps in this resource to check the firewall status on a computer running Windows 10.

Diagnostic Utilities

A **diagnostic utility** analyzes a computer's components and system software programs and creates a report that identifies the problems found. The utility also provides suggestions for correcting these problems, and in some situations, it can repair problems automatically. The Windows operating system contains many different Troubleshooter utilities; you can access them from the Help system or from the Action Center. More advanced diagnostic utility software can be purchased separately from software vendors.

Uninstallers

An **uninstaller** is a utility program for removing (deleting) software programs and associated entries in the system files. When an application program is installed, the operating system stores additional files related to the program. Those files may remain on the hard disk and waste valuable space if you remove a program without using an uninstaller utility. An uninstaller utility locates these additional files and removes them along with the program, freeing up valuable disk space.

Disk Scanners

A **disk scanner** examines the hard disk and its contents to identify potential problems, such as physically bad spots and errors in the table of contents. For example, a disk scanner checks to make sure that each sector of data is claimed by only one file. Check Disk is the disk scanner utility included with Microsoft Windows.

Hands On

Checking a Disk for Errors

Follow the steps provided in this resource to try out the Check Disk utility in Windows 10.

Disk Defragmenters

A **disk defragmenter** utility scans the hard disk and reorganizes files and unused space; doing this allows the operating system to locate and access files and data more quickly. The operating system stores a file in the first available sector on a disk, but sometimes there isn't enough space in one sector to store the entire file. If the sector already contains data, then the remaining portions of the file will be stored in other available sectors. Splitting up and storing the file like this may result in portions being stored in **noncontiguous sectors** (that is, sectors that are not connected or adjacent). A fragmented file takes longer to load because the operating system must locate and retrieve all the various pieces of the file.

This problem can be solved by defragmenting the disk so files are stored in contiguous sectors. Microsoft Windows includes a disk defragmenting utility called *Disk Defragmenter*. If your operating system doesn't come equipped with a disk defragmenter, you can purchase a utilities package that contains one. Defragmenting should be done only on mechanical hard disk drives; solid-state drives don't benefit from it.

File Compression Utilities

A **file compression utility** compresses (or shrinks) the size of a file so it occupies less disk space; some types of this utility also combine multiple files into a single compressed file for easier transfer. Files are compressed by reducing redundancies (that is, instances of repeated bits). For example, suppose that the text in a file has 28 zero (0) bits in a row. Rather than write this sequence as 28 separate digits, a file compression program might rewrite it as 28×0—a space savings of about 85 percent. When the file is decompressed, the long string of 0 bits is restored.

One of the most popular extensions for compressed files is .zip; thus, the term *zip file* has come to mean a compressed archive file. Windows supports the zip file format for compressed archives and can open zip files as if they are folders. Third-party compression utilities are also available with more features, such as WinZip and StuffIt.

Backup Utilities

A **backup utility** allows the user to make copies of the contents of storage media. The utility can be directed to back up the entire contents or only selected files. Some backup utilities compress files so they take up less space than the original files. Because compressed files are unusable until they have been uncompressed, many backup utilities include a restore program for uncompressing files.

Windows 8 and higher don't have a backup utility, but earlier versions of Windows did. However, you don't have to use a backup utility to back up files. You can manually copy them to a backup location using File Explorer or whatever file management utility is provided by your operating system.

Spam Blockers

Unwanted commercial email is known as **spam**, or junk mail. According to Brightmail, a company that blocks spam for some of the United States' top Internet service providers, spam now accounts for nearly 80 percent of all Internet email traffic. A utility program called a **spam blocker** is often used to filter incoming spam messages. Most email programs include a basic spam blocking utility, and third-party programs are also available with more features and more intelligent methods of differentiating spam from legitimate email.

Antispyware

Spyware is a form of malware that tracks the activities of an Internet user for the benefit of a third party. Spyware is secretly downloaded to the user's computer to collect keystrokes or trace website activity for malicious purposes, such as password interception, fraudulent credit card use, and identity theft. One particular type of spyware, called **adware**, is more annoying than harmful. Adware tracks the websites that a user visits to collect information for marketing and advertising companies. Some adware presents users with pop-up advertisements that contain contests, games, or links to unrelated websites.

Not all antivirus software protects Internet users from spyware, so users should consider getting separate antispyware and adware protection software. The utility Windows Defender, which comes with Microsoft Windows, contains both anti-malware and antivirus protection. Third-party products are also available, such as Webroot's SecureAnywhere and Lavasoft's Ad-Aware.

Recheck 3.5
Recheck your understanding of the concepts covered by this objective.

3.6 Programming Translation Software

The final type of system software we will look at falls under the broad heading of *translators*. A translator converts programming code to machine language. Translators are needed because computers can't understand programming code written in a human language, such as English or Spanish. Instead, they can only understand binary code written in zeroes (0s) and ones (1s), which is sometimes called **machine language**. (The concept of binary code was explained in Chapter 2.) Machine language is considered a **low-level language**.

Machine language is difficult to learn, and programmers find that writing machine language programs is boring and time consuming. To get around these problems, application programs are usually written using an English-like programming language called a **high-level language**. Examples of high-level languages are COBOL, Java, and BASIC (which has several versions). Figure 3.19 shows a sample of programming code in DOS BASIC.

Precheck 3.6
Check your understanding of the concepts covered by this objective.

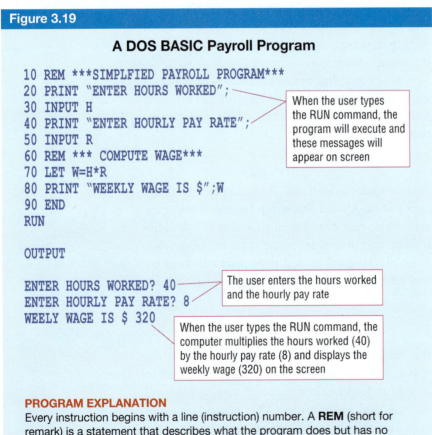

Figure 3.19

A DOS BASIC Payroll Program

```
10 REM ***SIMPLFIED PAYROLL PROGRAM***
20 PRINT "ENTER HOURS WORKED";
30 INPUT H
40 PRINT "ENTER HOURLY PAY RATE";
50 INPUT R
60 REM *** COMPUTE WAGE***
70 LET W=H*R
80 PRINT "WEEKLY WAGE IS $";W
90 END
RUN


OUTPUT


ENTER HOURS WORKED? 40
ENTER HOURLY PAY RATE? 8
WEELY WAGE IS $ 320
```

When the user types the RUN command, the program will execute and these messages will appear on screen

The user enters the hours worked and the hourly pay rate

When the user types the RUN command, the computer multiplies the hours worked (40) by the hourly pay rate (8) and displays the weekly wage (320) on the screen

PROGRAM EXPLANATION
Every instruction begins with a line (instruction) number. A **REM** (short for remark) is a statement that describes what the program does but has no effect on the program itself. A **PRINT** statement displays on the screen the text within quotes. An **INPUT** instruction requires the programmer to enter specific data when prompted. A **LET** statement processes the data according to the formula identified. An **END** statement indicates the end of the program.

This simple payroll program is written in DOS BASIC, a high-level language.

A high-level language must be translated into machine language format before the CPU can execute it. The two major types of language-translating software are interpreters and compilers. Each programming language generates code that needs to be compiled or interpreted for execution.

A **compiler** translates an entire program into machine language once and then saves it in a file that can be reused over and over. Each programming language has its own compiler. After reading and translating the program, the compiler displays a list of errors it encountered in the compiling process. The programmer corrects the errors and recompiles the program until there are no more errors. Compiling it creates an executable file, which usually has a .com or .exe extension. Most programming languages are compiled including C++ and Visual Basic.

Some programming languages are interpreted, not compiled. An **interpreter** reads, translates, and executes one line of instruction at a time, and identifies errors as they are encountered. In this sense, interpreters are somewhat more user friendly than compilers. An interpreted program must be re-interpreted each time it's run; it doesn't become an executable file. Hypertext Markup Language (HTML) and JavaScript are examples of interpreted programming languages. The code exists in the web page file in human-readable form; you can open any HTML file in a text-editing program and see it. The web browser serves as the interpreter.

Compiled programs run faster than interpreted programs, because they don't have to be reprocessed each time they are run. For this reason, most applications are written in compiled languages, not interpreted ones. You will learn much more about programming languages, both compiled and interpreted, in Chapter 11.

Recheck 3.6
Recheck your understanding of the concepts covered by this objective.

Precheck 3.7
Check your understanding of the concepts covered by this objective.

3.7 Working with File Storage Systems

As you learned in Chapter 2, a computer system consists of input, processing, output, and storage devices. Now that you know something about how computers use system software to perform the first three functions, let's take a look at the last function: storage.

How File Storage Works

Information is stored on your computer in files and folders that are saved on a drive—either a disk drive or a solid-state drive. A **disk drive** is a mechanical device that reads data from and writes data to a disk, such as a hard disk or DVD. A **solid-state drive (SSD)** is a device that stores data in nonvolatile memory, which is memory that persists even if the power is turned off. A familiar example of a solid-state drive is a USB flash drive. (Storage devices and media are discussed in more detail in section 3.8, "Understanding File Storage Devices and Media," on page 118.)

Each physical drive has one or more logical volumes. A **volume** is a storage unit with a letter assigned to it, such as *C* or *D*. Some drives are set up to divide the available space into multiple volumes; other drives allow the entire storage area to be addressed as a single volume letter.

Within each volume, the top level of the storage hierarchy is the **root directory**. For example, if you display the contents of drive C: in your file management utility, the files and folders that appear are located in the root directory of the C: drive. The root directory is like the lobby of a building: it provides an entryway to the disk, but you don't want to store much in it because it will get crowded in there (metaphorically, anyway).

Most files are stored in folders. A **folder** is an organizing unit, like a box or a physical file folder. A volume can have hundreds or even thousands of folders. For example, a volume on which Windows is installed may have folders named *Windows*, *Program Files*, and *Users*, among others. A folder that is located within another folder is called a **child folder** (or *subfolder*), and a folder that contains a child folder is called a **parent folder**.

One advantage of a graphical user interface over a command-line interface is that it allows you to see the folder structure more easily. To see this for yourself, compare Figures 3.20 and 3.21. With a graphical user interface, you can browse different folders by clicking or double-clicking their icons onscreen. With a command-line interface, however, you must type a command to display the contents of a particular folder.

The **path** to a file provides the information you need to locate the file in the storage medium. It includes the letter of the volume in which the file is located, the names

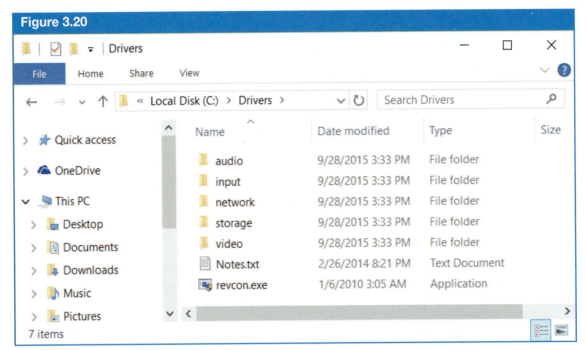

Figure 3.20

This screen capture shows the contents of a folder called Drivers as it appears in a GUI Windows 10. Notice that the Drivers parent folder contains five child folders and two files.

Figure 3.21

```
C:\Drivers>dir
 Volume in drive C has no label.
 Volume Serial Number is 8043-EB9D

 Directory of C:\Drivers

09/28/2015  03:33 PM    <DIR>          .
09/28/2015  03:33 PM    <DIR>          ..
09/28/2015  03:33 PM    <DIR>          audio
09/28/2015  03:33 PM    <DIR>          input
09/28/2015  03:33 PM    <DIR>          network
02/26/2014  09:21 PM                34 Notes.txt
01/06/2010  04:05 AM            82,464 revcon.exe
09/28/2015  03:33 PM    <DIR>          storage
09/28/2015  03:33 PM    <DIR>          video
               2 File(s)         82,498 bytes
               7 Dir(s)  232,689,238,016 bytes free

C:\Drivers>
```

This screen capture shows the same contents displayed in Figure 3.20 but as it appears in a command-line interface.

of the folders to go through to get to the file, and the name of the file. Each location name is followed by a backslash (\). For example, the Notes.txt file shown in Figures 3.20 and 3.21 has a path of C:\Driver\Notes.txt. Figure 3.22 identifies the individual pieces of the path.

Using a **folder tree** is often helpful in understanding the folder structure of a volume. In Windows 10, you can browse a folder tree in the Navigation pane on the left side of the File Explorer window. Figure 3.23 shows the path C:\Drivers\audio\ R283235\W7-32 in a folder tree. Notice that you don't see any files in the folder tree—only folders.

File Types and Extensions

There are hundreds of file types, and operating systems generally handle them differently. How does the OS know what type a file is? It depends on the OS. Some OSs examine a file's content to determine its type, but most rely on the file's extension. A **file extension** is a short code (usually, three or four characters) that appears at the end of the file name, separated from the name by a period. In the file name *Notes.txt*, for example, *Notes* is the file name and *.txt* is the file extension.

Microsoft Windows uses extensions to determine if a file is a system file, an executable file that runs an application, a helper file for an application, or a data file (and if so, what type). Windows maintains an internal database containing the **file association** for each file extension. File association defines a default application and/or action. You can customize the entries in this database, so that a particular type of file opens in a different application than the one assigned by default. Doing this is useful if you have multiple applications that will open a certain file type and you prefer one over the others. For example, suppose both Windows Media Player and Apple iTunes are installed on your computer. Windows Media Player is the default application for mp3 files, but you can change the file association to Apple iTunes. Table 3.2 lists some of the most common file extensions and applications that might be set up to open those files.

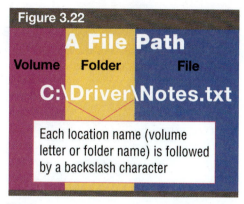

Figure 3.22

A File Path

| Volume | Folder | File |

C:\Driver\Notes.txt

Each location name (volume letter or folder name) is followed by a backslash character

The file path is the same whether you view the file through a GUI or a command-line interface.

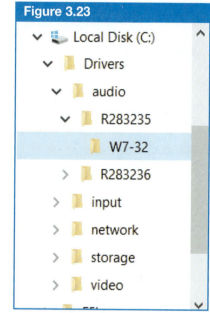

Figure 3.23

- ∨ 💻 Local Disk (C:)
  - ∨ 📁 Drivers
    - ∨ 📁 audio
      - ∨ 📁 R283235
        - 📁 W7-32
      - › 📁 R283236
    - › 📁 input
    - › 📁 network
    - › 📁 storage
    - › 📁 video

Here you see the tree structure in the Navigation pane of the File Explorer in Windows 10.

Table 3.2 Common File Extensions and Associated Applications

File Extension	File Type	Associated Applications
.bat .com .exe	Executable file	
.doc .docm .docx	Word-processing document	Microsoft Word WordPad
.pdf	Portable Document Format	Adobe Acrobat Adobe Reader
.txt	Plain text file	Notepad
.rtf	Rich text format (a generic word-processing format)	Microsoft Word WordPad

continues

Table 3.2 Common File Extensions and Associated Applications—*continued*

File Extension	File Type	Associated Applications
.bmp .gif .jpg .pcx .png .tif	Graphics files	Adobe Photoshop Paint Windows Photo Viewer Photos (Windows app)
.ppt .pptm .pptx	Presentation	Microsoft PowerPoint
.xls .xlsm .xlsx	Spreadsheet	Microsoft Excel
.au .mp3 .wma	Audio clips	Apple iTunes Windows Media Player Groove Music
.m4v .mod .mov .mp4 .qt .wmv	Video clips	Apple QuickTime Windows Media Player Movies & TV (Windows app)
.htm .html .mht	Web pages	Firefox Google Chrome Microsoft Internet Explorer Microsoft Edge
.accdb .mdb	Access database	Microsoft Access

Recheck **3.7**

Recheck your understanding of the concepts covered by this objective.

3.8 Understanding File Storage Devices and Media

Precheck **3.8**

Check your understanding of the concepts covered by this objective.

The computer's RAM is **primary storage**, because it's where the data is placed immediately after it's input or processed. Primary storage is by nature temporary. **Secondary storage**, on the other hand, is permanent. Secondary storage devices include all the devices represented by volume letters in your computer's file storage system: hard drives, removable flash drives, CD and DVD drives, and so on.

There are two types of secondary storage: fixed and removable. **Fixed storage** is mounted inside the computer; to get it out, you would have to open up the computer's case. An internal hard disk drive is an example of fixed storage. **Removable storage** can easily be separated from the computer. CDs, DVDs, external hard drives, and USB flash drives are all examples of removable storage. External storage devices can use a variety of different interfaces. USB is the most common, followed by FireWire (IEEE 1394a) and eSATA (external SATA). (Refer to the "Ports" section in Chapter 2 for more information about these different types of ports.)

Some storage is disk based—that is, the data is stored on disc platters that rotate past a read/write head. Hard disk drives (HDDs), CD drives, and DVD drives are all disk based. Other storage is solid state—that is, the data is stored on nonvolatile memory chips. USB flash drives and solid-state drives (SSDs) are examples.

Finally, some storage media can be separated from its drive and some cannot. For example, in an HDD or SSD, the storage media and the means of reading it are permanently sealed together in a metal cartridge. In contrast, a CD or DVD can be popped out of the drive that reads it.

The following sections examine the technologies behind several storage device types and weigh their pros and cons.

Hard Disk Drives

A **hard disk drive (HDD)** is the traditional type of mechanical hard drive that has dominated the computer market for several decades. Most desktop and notebook computers have at least one HDD.

An HDD consists of one or more rigid metal platters (disks) mounted on a spindle in a metal box with a set of read/write heads—one for each side of each platter. The box is sealed to prevent contamination from dust, moisture, and other airborne particles. Storage capacity ranges from a few hundred gigabytes to more than 2 terabytes.

The drive mechanism is integrated with the platters; you can't physically separate the drive from the platters without destroying the drive. For this reason, the terms *hard disk* and *hard drive* are mostly synonymous; there is little reason to refer to one separately from the other, since they are never apart. But technically, a hard disk is a platter and a hard drive is the device consisting of the mechanical components that spin a set of platters and read from and write to the platters. Figure 3.24 shows the inner workings of a hard drive.

Data is stored along the tracks and sectors of hard disks. A **track** is a numbered, concentric ring or circle on a hard disk. A **sector** is a numbered section of a track. One sector holds 512 bytes of data. Because most files are larger than 512 bytes, a disk is

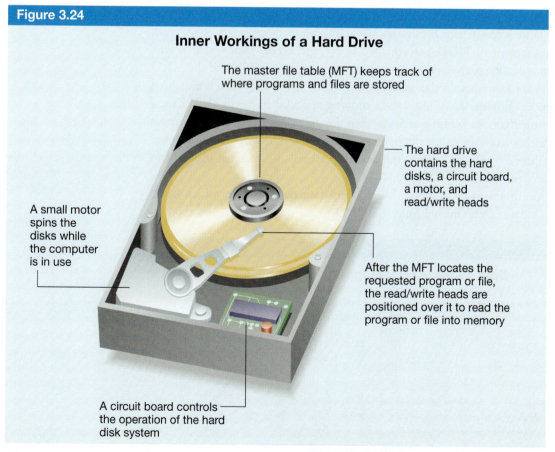

Figure 3.24

Inner Workings of a Hard Drive

The master file table (MFT) keeps track of where programs and files are stored

The hard drive contains the hard disks, a circuit board, a motor, and read/write heads

A small motor spins the disks while the computer is in use

After the MFT locates the requested program or file, the read/write heads are positioned over it to read the program or file into memory

A circuit board controls the operation of the hard disk system

A hard drive contains one or more hard disks on which data is stored. When activated, read/write heads move in and out between the disks to record and/or read data.

organized logically into groups of sectors called **clusters**. The OS addresses clusters, rather than individual sectors, to keep the disk's list of content at a manageable size.

The disk's table of contents is called the **master file table (MFT)** or **file allocation table (FAT)**, depending on the file system in use. The file system used in modern versions of Windows—called the **New Technology File System (NTFS)**—uses a master file table.

As the platters spin, they rotate past the read/write heads. The heads are attached to a metal arm that moves in and out to position the heads so that specific tracks pass underneath them. When the user wants to access a particular file, the computer determines its location on the disk and tells the hard drive to retrieve it.

Data is stored magnetically on the surfaces of the platters. **Magnetic storage** creates transitions by magnetizing areas of the disk with a positive or negative polarity. The transitions between positive and negative areas are read as 1s, and the areas that lack transitions are read as 0s. Although the read/write head is a single unit, it actually performs two different functions: it magnetizes areas of the disk, and it reads changes in polarity and relays them to the drive controller. The drive controller specifies whether the head should read or write at any given moment.

The disk surface is coated with a thin layer of iron oxide particles. The read/write head has a wire coil around it, and electricity passes through the coil. This generates a magnetic field, which polarizes the surface of the disk as positive or negative. The flow of electricity through the wire then reverses, changing the polarization and creating a transition point on the disk, as shown in Figure 3.25. This is known as a **flux transition**.

An HDD spins continuously while the computer is on, whereas a CD or DVD in its drive spins only when data is being stored or accessed. The continuous spinning of a hard disk provides faster access to data, because there's no wait while the drive gets up to speed.

One measurement of HDD performance is **average access time**—that is, the average amount of time between the operating system requesting a file and the HDD delivering it. A key factor involved in access time is rotational speed, which is measured in revolutions per minute (rpm). An HDD running at 7,200 rpm will likely have a faster access time than one running at 5,400 rpm, for example. The faster the platters rotate, the quicker a certain sector can be placed under the read/write head. Another key factor in access time is the speed and accuracy at which the actuator arms can move the read/write heads.

Another measurement of HDD performance is **data transfer rate**, which is the speed at which data can be moved from the HDD to the motherboard and then on

Figure 3.25

Data Storage on a Magnetic Disk

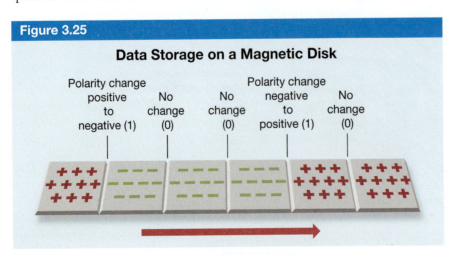

Polarity change positive to negative (1)   No change (0)   No change (0)   Polarity change negative to positive (1)   No change (0)

The transition on a magnetic disk between areas of positive polarity and negative polarity.

to the CPU. Data transfer rate is dependent on the interface used to connect the HDD to the motherboard. The traditional interface for many years was **parallel ATA (PATA)**; it uses a 40-pin ribbon cable between the HDD and the motherboard. This interface has a maximum transfer rate of 133 megabytes per second (MB/s). The modern interface is **serial ATA (SATA)**; it transfers data at up to 308 MB/s. (HDDs are limited to about 158 MB/s, but solid-state drives that use SATA as the interface can achieve higher speeds.)

USB Flash Drives and Solid-State Drives

A solid-state drive (SSD) stores data in a type of electrically erasable programmable ROM (EEPROM). As you may recall from Chapter 2, EEPROM can be erased and written with electricity. EEPROM is a nonvolatile type of memory, which means it retains whatever you put in it—even when the power is off. Thus, in a solid-state drive, electricity controls the on/off state of the transistors within the semiconductor material inside the memory chips. A solid-state drive has no moving parts; the term *drive* is used metaphorically.

USB flash drives use solid-state storage, and so do solid-state hard drives. **Solid-state hard drives (SSHDs)** are solid-state equivalents of HDDs in terms of storage capacity and physical size of the box. SSHDs generally use the SATA interface to the motherboard.

Practical TECH

How Fast Is *Your* SSHD?

How much performance improvement can you expect when moving from HDD to SSHD? Quite a bit. For example, on a system that boots up Windows in 40 seconds from an HDD, a boot time of about 22 seconds can be expected from an SSHD. A large Excel workbook that takes 14 seconds to open from an HDD can open in about 4 seconds from an SSHD. People who work with large files will notice a big difference when moving from HDD to SSHD, and so will people who play graphics-intensive games. People who mostly use computers to check email and surf the Internet won't notice as big a difference, since these activities are not very storage intensive.

Network and Cloud Drives

Not all storage is local—that is, directly connected to your computer. If you are connected to a network or the Internet, you may have other storage options in addition to your own volumes.

A **network share** is a drive or folder that's been made available to users on other computers than the one on which the content actually resides. You can browse the available network locations through the file management utility in your operating system (File Explorer in Windows, for example). You might see a network share as a

Cutting Edge

Hybrid Drives

SSDs are fast and quiet, whereas traditional HDDs are inexpensive and high capacity. So, why not have the best of both! A dual-drive hybrid system combines two separate drives in the same computer: one SSD and one HDD. You can store your most frequently used files (such as operating system files) on the SSD and use the HDD for less frequently accessed files (such as data files). In addition, some operating systems can combine the two drives into a hybrid volume to automatically optimize the computer's usage of each.

An even newer technology is called a *solid-state hybrid drive*. It incorporates solid-state memory into a modified version of a traditional HDD, and the result is a single drive that merges the capabilities of the two types of drives. The most frequently accessed data is stored in the solid-state portion, and the less frequently accessed data is placed on the mechanical hard disk platters. A hybrid drive boosts disk performance without the expense of a full-sized solid state hard drive.

Figure 3.26

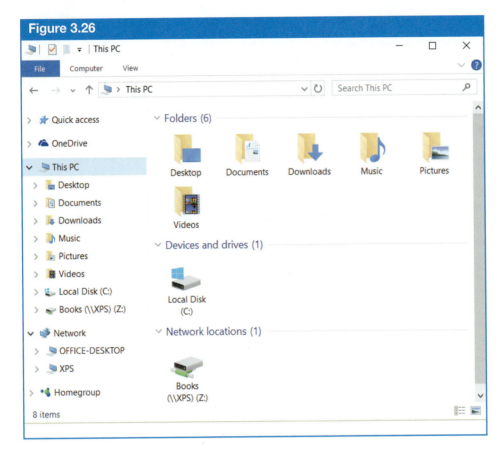

A mapped network drive shows up along with the local drive letters in the This PC window in Windows 10.

volume letter on your computer, even if it's an individual folder and not really a whole volume at its source. Assigning a volume letter to a network folder is called *mapping a network drive*; Figure 3.26 shows a mapped network drive in Windows 10. Some network shares don't allow users access until they have gone through authentication (positive identification), such as by providing a password or a preapproved user ID.

A **cloud drive** isn't technically a drive but rather a secure storage location on an Internet-accessible remote server. For example, Microsoft's OneDrive service provides a free cloud drive to anyone who signs up for a Microsoft account. Similarly, Apple offers iCloud storage to users of iPad, iPhone, and other Apple devices. Storing data files on a cloud drive keeps them safe, because their existence doesn't depend on the health of your computer's own hardware. Cloud drives can also be accessed from multiple devices. You can upload a photo you took with your camera phone to your cloud drive and then print it from your desktop PC.

Optical Storage Devices and Media

CDs and DVDs are optical discs. An **optical disc** stores data in patterns of greater and lesser reflectivity on its surface. They are read and written in **optical drives** that contain a laser that shines light on the surface and a sensor that measures the amount of light that bounces back. On a writeable drive, the laser also can change the surface of the disc, altering its reflectivity in certain areas. CD and DVD technologies were

Hands On

Mapping a Network Drive

Follow the steps provided in this resource to map a network drive so that it shows as a local drive letter in Windows 10.

 **Activity 3.8.1**

Article
DVD Technology

originally developed for music and video storage, but today CDs and DVDs can store music, videos, and computer data. Most optical drives in computers today can accommodate both CDs and DVDs, and some can even read and write to Blu-ray discs as well.

Optical drives are usually backward compatible. For example, a DVD drive can read and write CDs and DVDs, and a Blu-ray drive can read and write Blu-ray discs, DVDs, and CDs.

How Optical Storage Works An optical disc is divided into areas of greater reflectivity (called **lands**) and areas of lesser reflectivity (called **pits**). The drive shines a laser beam onto the disc and then a sensor measures the amount of light that bounces back. From this measurement, the sensor determines whether the area is land or pit. When the sensor detects a change in reflectivity—either from more to less or less to more—it sends a pulse indicating a 1 value. When it doesn't detect a change, it sends a 0 value. See Figure 3.27.

Unlike HDDs, which store data in concentric circles (tracks), optical discs typically store data along a single track that spirals outward from the center of the disc to the outer edge. The data is stored in sectors, similar to the sectors on an HDD (see Figure 3.28).

Figure 3.27

How an Optical Disc Works

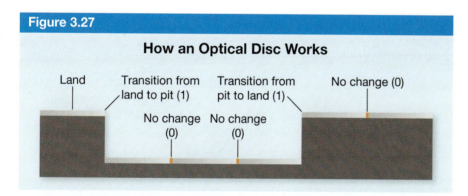

An optical disc stores data by differentiating between areas of greater and lesser reflectivity.

Figure 3.28

An Optical Disc

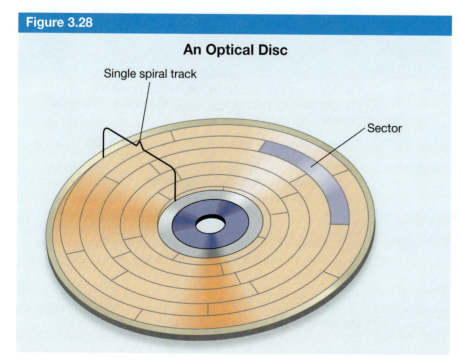

On an optical disc, information is stored in a series of sectors along a single spiral track.

Types of Optical Discs Most optical discs have the same diameter and thickness, but they differ widely in capacity and features, depending on their specifications (see Table 3.3). These are the three most common types of optical discs:

- A **compact disc (CD)** can store up to 900 MB of data. CDs are commonly used for distributing music and small applications and for inexpensively storing and transferring data.
- A **digital versatile disc (DVD)** can store up to 17 gigabytes (GB) of data, although the most common type (single-sided, single layer) stores up to 4.7 GB of data. DVDs are most often used to distribute large applications and standard-definition movies.
- A **Blu-ray disc (BD)** can store up to 128 GB of data in up to four layers. BDs are used to distribute high-definition movies and to store and transfer large amounts of data.

All three types of discs can be read-only (ROM), recordable one time (R), or rewriteable multiple times (RW for CDs and DVDs; RE for Blu-ray). Read-only discs are manufactured with their content built in and can't be modified. Recordable discs can be written once but not changed after that. Rewriteable discs can be rewritten multiple times. There are two competing standards for writeable and rewriteable DVDs, and they are indicated by plus and minus signs like this: DVD+R and DVD-R.

Table 3.3 Types, Storage Capacities, and Features of Optical Discs

Type	Storage Capacity	Features
Compact disc (CD)	**650–900 MB**	
CD-ROM		The data is stamped into the CD at the factory and can't be changed. Used for distributing digital data, such as computer software and copyrighted music.
CD-R		Can be written to only once. Used for creating one-of-a-kind CDs, such as music compilations and presentations for business distribution.
CD-RW		Allows rewriting. Used for backing up important files that change over time.
Digital versatile disc (DVD)	**4.7–17.0 GB (depending on number of sides and layers)**	
DVD-ROM	4.7 GB per side (single layer)	The data is stamped into the DVD at the factory and can't be changed. Used for distributing copyrighted movies and computer software.
DVD-R DVD+R		Can be written to only once. Used to create one-of-a-kind DVDs that won't be changed later.
DVD-RW DVD+RW		Recordable and rewriteable up to 1,000 times. Used for backing up important files that change over time.
Blu-ray disc (BD)	**25–128 GB (depending on number of layers)**	
BD-ROM		The data is stamped into the disc at the factory and can't be changed. Used for distributing high-definition movies.
BD-R		Can be written to only once.
BD-RE		Can be erased and rewritten multiple times.

DVDs can be single sided or double sided. On a double-sided DVD, both sides contain data. Each side of the DVD can be single layer or dual layer in terms of its storage system. A dual-layer model can store twice the data of a single-layer model by using a semitransparent top layer to store data that's read using a laser at a different angle. A Blu-ray disc can contain up to four layers.

Caring for Optical Discs Table 3.4 lists guidelines for the handling and care of optical discs. Dirt and other foreign substances on optical discs can cause read errors and/or prevent the discs from working at all. Even so, optical discs don't require routine cleaning and should be cleaned only when necessary. Using a commercially available cleaning kit is recommended, but other methods can also be used.

Hands On

Cleaning an Optical Disc
Follow the steps provided in this resource to clean an optical disc when it becomes dirty.

Table 3.4 Care Instructions for Optical Discs

Do
Store each disc in a jewel case or disc sleeve when not in use.
Use a felt-tip, permanent marker to write on the nonshiny side of the disc.
Hold the disc only by its edges.
Use the recommended disc cleaning method to remove dirt and other substances.

Don't
Allow anything to touch the shiny (data) side of the disc.
Stack disks that aren't stored in jewel cases or disc sleeves.
Place objects on the disc.
Expose disc to direct sunlight or excessive heat.
Place food or beverages near a disc.

Recheck 3.8
Recheck your understanding of the concepts covered by this objective.

Tech Ethics

The Stored Communications Act

Do you know that different legal standards apply to the privacy of your information stored online versus on your local hard disk drive? Law enforcement authorities require a warrant and probable cause to search your home and your local hard drive. However, they may need only a subpoena or a court order and prior notice to look at your online storage.

The Stored Communications Act (SCA), which was part of the Electronic Communications Privacy Act of 1986, enacted some privacy protections for electronic data held by a third party (such as your online storage provider), but the act goes only so far. The SCA protections for electronic data are similar to the Fourth Amendment protections against unreasonable search and seizure. Legal precedents establishing the limits of the SCA protections are still evolving, and it has even been suggested that the SCA is unconstitutional because it permits a lower standard of privacy than the Fourth Amendment would normally provide.

For a summary of recent legal decisions about this issue, see http://CUT6.emcp.net/SCA. As more people move toward cloud storage and cloud-based applications, protecting the privacy of information held in those services will become increasingly relevant.

3.9 Understanding Large-Scale Storage

Precheck 3.9

Check your understanding of the concepts covered by this objective.

Large businesses must store huge amounts of data—both for internal use (such as personnel records) and customer use (such as product listings). Imagine all the data required for an airline reservation system, for example, or an online merchant such as Amazon.com. And imagine the impact on the company's business if some of that data was lost because of a defective storage device.

Large computer systems, such as mainframe and server systems, typically use the same basic storage technologies as smaller computer systems: HDDs, SSDs, and optical discs. However, because of the large volume of the data and the need to store and back it up safely, extra technologies are employed to work with these basic storage components.

There are two main concerns in large-scale data storage: how quickly data can be stored and retrieved, and how easily and reliably lost data can be restored when hardware failures or other problems occur.

Online retailers and other large businesses maintain entire rooms and even buildings full of servers and related equipment.

Local versus Network Storage

With a personal computer, data is usually stored locally—that is, on the computer itself or on an external device directly plugged into it. Local data storage is known as **direct-attached storage (DAS)**.

In a large company, it isn't practical to have multiple users store their data locally. Data should be stored in a central location, where everyone who needs it can access it, regardless of which PCs are in use. **Network-attached storage (NAS)** is storage that's made available over a network, such as on a centrally accessible file server. The file server holds the files that multiple users need to access, and the users retrieve the data via the company's network or via the Internet.

An ordinary server (running UNIX or Windows Server, for example) can be used as NAS. It's more common, however, to use a **NAS appliance**, which is a specialized computer built specifically for network file storage and retrieval. A NAS appliance connects directly to the network and can be configured and administered through another computer on the network; a NAS appliance doesn't need to have its own keyboard, mouse, and monitor.

When a company has a lot of data, it's typically stored on many different drives and computers, but the users should be shielded from that fact. For example, when you shop at an online retailer like Amazon.com, you shouldn't have to know which of Amazon's file servers stores a particular category of product information. A **storage area network (SAN)** enables users to interact with a large pool of storage (including multiple devices and media) as if it were a single local volume. For large companies, SANs offer many of the advantages of DAS and NAS, including less network traffic, easier disaster recovery, and simpler administration.

NAS drives provide centrally accessible storage space for many computers at once through a network connection.

Activity 3.9.1

Article
Storage Area Networks

RAID

In business storage, both speed and reliability are important. Unfortunately, traditional HDDs have neither of these qualities. When data is stored on a single HDD, the data retrieval speed is limited by the device's access time and interface speed. And if that drive fails, all the data on it will be lost.

A technology called **redundant array of inexpensive disks (RAID)** attempts to correct both of these problems by combining multiple physical HDDs. RAID is a group of related disk management methods, numbered 0 through 6. Each method employs a different combination of data-handling features.

RAID0: Striping **RAID0** addresses the issue of performance speed by **striping** disks (see Figure 3.29). In striping, each write operation is spread over all the physical drives, so the file can be written and read more quickly. For example, suppose you have four drives in your RAID, and each drive can store and retrieve data at about 100 MB/s. If you are writing a 400 MB file, it will take 4 seconds on a single drive, but if you write one-fourth of the file to each of four drives, the write operation will be accomplished in only 1 second. The file is distributed among the drives at an individual bit level: one bit gets written to disk 1, the next bit to disk 2, and so on. RAID0 doesn't have any means of protecting data from loss; it's purely a performance-enhancing tool.

RAID1: Mirroring **RAID1** addresses the issue of data protection by **mirroring** the drive (see Figure 3.30). In RAID1, each HDD has an identical backup (a mirror), and the same data is written to both drives simultaneously. That way, if the main drive fails, the backup drive can supply the data. RAID1 has double the hardware cost, because you pay for twice as many drives as you actually use. Also, it does nothing to enhance performance.

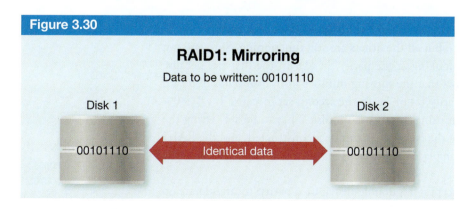

Figure 3.29

RAID0: Striping

Data to be written: 00101110

Disk 1	Disk 2	Disk 3	Disk 4
0	0	1	0
1	1	1	0

RAID0 spreads out data evenly across all the available disks, one bit at a time.

Figure 3.30

RAID1: Mirroring

Data to be written: 00101110

Disk 1	Disk 2
00101110	00101110

← Identical data →

RAID1 mirrors the data on a second drive for data protection in case one drive goes bad.

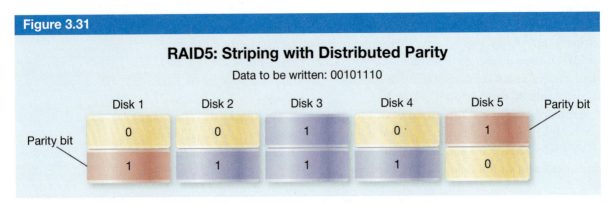

Figure 3.31

RAID5: Striping with Distributed Parity

Data to be written: 00101110

RAID5 stripes the data, like RAID0 does, but it also includes a parity bit for data recovery.

RAID2–RAID6: Striping with Distributed Parity
RAID2, RAID3, and RAID4 were early attempts at combining the benefits offered by both RAID0 (performance) and RAID1 (data protection) in a single method. The attempt that ultimately became popular is RAID5.

RAID5 combines striping (for performance) with distributed parity (for data protection). Here's a very basic explanation of how distributed parity works: Let's say you have five disks in your **disk array** (set of disks). When you write some data to the disks, four of them each receive a bit (either 0 or 1). The fifth drive receives a **parity bit**. The parity bit is determined by the values of the other bits, which are added up. If the result is odd, the parity bit is 1; if the result is even, the parity bit is 0. The parity bit is used to reconstruct data if one of the disks goes bad.

Figure 3.31 shows a simple example of distributed parity using a five-disk array. The data to be written is 00101110. The first four numbers are written to the first four disks, like this:

>   **Disk 1: 0**
>   **Disk 2: 0**
>   **Disk 3: 1**
>   **Disk 4: 0**

These numbers add up to 1, which is an odd number, so the parity bit is 1. It's placed on disk 5.

The disks alternate as to which one contains the parity bit. The next four numbers are written to disks 2 through 5, reserving disk 1 for the parity bit:

>   **Disk 2: 1**
>   **Disk 3: 1**
>   **Disk 4: 1**
>   **Disk 5: 0**

These numbers add up to 3, which is odd, so the parity bit is 1. It's placed on disk 1.

Now, let's say that disk 2 fails, but all the others are still functioning. Software can determine what disk 2 held by looking at the parity bit (1). In the first set, because $0 + 1 + 0 = 1$, the software knows that the missing number from disk 2 has to be a 0 to make the overall sum odd (parity bit of 1). In the second set, because $1 + 1 + 0 = 2$, the software knows that the missing number from disk 2 has to be a 1. Using the parity bits, the entire contents of the failed drive can be reconstructed, and the RAID can continue to function until a replacement drive is installed and populated with the correct bits.

RAID6 is just like RAID5 except it has double-distributed parity; it can tolerate up to two failed drives and still function.

Recheck 3.9
Recheck your understanding of the concepts covered by this objective.

Chapter Summary

*An interactive **Chapter Summary**, **Study Notes**, and a **Slide Presentation** with audio are available from the links menu on this page in your ebook*

3.1 Defining System Software

System software is designed to keep the computer up and running so it can run useful applications. System software includes the **basic input/output system (BIOS)** (which is considered **firmware**), the **operating system (OS)**, **utility programs**, and **translators** (compilers and interpreters).

3.2 Understanding the System BIOS

The BIOS stores low-level programs on a non-volatile memory chip. The **system BIOS** is stored on a chip on the motherboard, and helps start up the computer. You can modify the startup settings for the motherboard by making changes in the **BIOS Setup utility**.

3.3 Understanding What an Operating System Does

An OS boots the computer, provides a user interface, runs programs, configures and controls devices, and manages essential file operations. The OSs a computer will accept depend on its **platform**. The platform of an **IBM-compatible platform** (also called the **Intel platform**) can run **Microsoft Windows**: the 32-bit version (**x86**) or the 64-bit version (**x64**).

Starting from a turned-off condition is a **cold boot**; restarting an already running computer is a **warm boot**. When starting the computer, after the BIOS completes its **power-on self-test (POST),** the operating system loads the **kernel** into memory and the user interface appears. The kernel is **memory resident**; however, some parts of the OS are **nonresident** and loaded only when needed.

The **user interface** (or **shell**) allows communication between the software and the user. The user interface can be a **command-line interface** or a **graphical user interface (GUI)**. Both Microsoft Windows and the Mac OS X use a **desktop** metaphor, with **windows** and **icons**. A tablet operating system uses a touch-driven user interface, with **tiles** or icons you can tap.

The operating system runs applications. Most GUI operating systems work on a desktop metaphor and run applications in **windows**. Windows controls hardware devices by using **drivers** to communicate with them. The OS also provides a file management utility that enables users to work with files and folders.

3.4 Looking at Operating Systems by Computer Type

A personal computer (PC) is a desktop or notebook computer designed for use by one person at a time. Personal computer operating systems include **Microsoft Windows**, **Mac OS X**, **Linux**, and Chrome OS. Linux and Chrome OS are **open source software**; Windows and Mac OS X are **proprietary software**. The Linux kernel is a command-line interface, but there are many **distributions (distros)** that contain attractive graphical shells for the user interface. Chrome OS is a **thin-client** OS designed for netbooks.

Mobile operating systems run on tablets and smartphones. Popular examples include **iOS** for iPad and iPhone, **Android** (a free OS developed by Google), and the **Windows Phone OS** for smartphones.

Server operating systems support multiple simultaneous users and manage many tasks at once. Server operating systems include **Windows Server**, UNIX, and Linux (with an appropriate **solution stack**).

3.5 Exploring Types of Utility Programs

A utility program performs a single maintenance or repair task. **Antivirus software** is one of the most common types of utility programs; these programs detect and eliminate viruses and worms. A **firewall** is a security system that blocks unused ports from being used to gain access to a computer. A **diagnostic utility** analyzes the computer's problems and creates a report about them. An **uninstaller** removes software and updates the system files. A **disk scanner** checks for disk storage errors. A **disk defragmenter** reorganizes files to optimize how they are stored. A **file compression utility** shrinks file sizes and packages multiple files in a single archive. A **backup utility** allows users to make copies of files and folders. A **spam blocker** is a junk email filter. Antispyware software detects and removes **spyware** and **adware**, which are both forms of **malware**.

3.6 Programming Translation Software

A computer programmer uses **high-level language** to write a program, and then he or she uses a **compiler** to turn the program into **machine language**. Compiled code results in an executable file. Some programming languages, such as HTML, are interpreted rather than compiled. Interpreted code is re-interpreted line by line each time the program is run. It doesn't result in an executable file. Web browser software is an example of an **interpreter** utility.

3.7 Working with File Storage Systems

A drive letter is a **volume**, and each volume has a **root directory**. Within the root directory are **folders**. A folder within a folder is a **child folder**; the folder that holds the child folder is its **parent folder**. The **path** to a file is the volume and folders that contain the file. Using a **folder tree** is one way of understanding and browsing a folder structure on a volume.

A **file extension** at the end of a file's name indicates its type, as in myfile.txt. The operating system knows what program to open a file with based on its extension. For example, .txt opens in Notepad in Windows. A file with an .exe, .com, or .bat extension is an executable file that runs a program.

3.8 Understanding File Storage Devices and Media

Primary storage is RAM; **secondary storage** is storage that holds data more permanently. **Fixed storage** is mounted inside a computer, such as a hard drive; **removable storage** can easily be removed, such as a DVD.

A **hard disk drive (HDD)** is a traditional mechanical hard drive. Data stored on a hard disk is organized into concentric rings called **tracks**, and each track is broken up into sections called **sectors** of 512 bytes. Multiple sectors are grouped into **clusters**. The disk's table of contents is the **master file table (MFT)** or **file allocation table (FAT)** depending on the file system. The most common file system used in Windows is **New Technology File System (NTFS).**

Magnetic storage, such as an HDD, stores data in transitions of positive and negative magnetic polarity. A transition between the two is a **flux transition**. Measurements of HDD performance include **average access time** and **data transfer rate**. The two common interfaces for hard disk drives are **parallel ATA (PATA)** and **serial ATA (SATA).**

A solid-state drive stores data in a type of EEPROM. A **solid-state hard drive (SSHD)** is the solid state equivalent of an HDD. A **USB flash drive** is a smaller-capacity, more portable solid-state drive.

A **network share** is a drive or folder that's been made available to users on other computers. Some networks require authentication before granting users access to a network share. A **cloud drive** is not really a drive, but a secure storage location on an Internet-accessible remote server.

An **optical disc** stores data in patterns of reflectivity called **pits** and **lands**. They are read and written by **optical drives** with lasers in them. Types of optical discs include **Blu-ray**, **digital versatile disc (DVD),** and **compact disc (CD).**

3.9 Understanding Large-Scale Storage

Direct-attached storage (DAS) is local storage. **Network attached storage (NAS)** is a folder or volume that is shared on a network. NAS can be a file server or a **NAS appliance**. A **storage area network (SAN)** enables users to interact with a large pool of storage as if it were a single local volume.

A **redundant array of inexpensive disks (RAID)** helps to solve difficulties with data access speed and/or data safety and reliability. **RAID0** increases performance by **striping**. **RAID1** increases data safety by **mirroring**. **RAID5** combines the two by striping multiple disks in a **disk array** and including a **parity bit**.

Key Terms

Numbers indicate the pages where terms are first cited with their full definition in the chapter.
An alphabetized list of key terms with definitions is included in the end-of-book glossary.

*An interactive **Glossary** is available from the links menu on this page in your ebook.*

Chapter Exercises

Complete the following exercises to assess your understanding of the material covered in this chapter.

 *Interactive **Flash Cards** and an interactive **Game** are available from the links menu on this page in your ebook.*

 Go to your SNAP Assignments page to complete the Terms Check, Knowledge Check, Key Principles, and Tech Illustrated exercises.

Terms Check: Matching

Match each term with its definition.

a.	BIOS	f.	optical
b.	compiler	g.	OS
c.	driver	h.	platform
d.	firewall	i.	solid state
e.	GUI	j.	tracks

___ 1. The low-level software on the motherboard that starts up the computer.

___ 2. The software that provides the user interface, runs programs, and communicates with devices.

___ 3. A utility that turns high-level language programming into executable files.

___ 4. Numbered, concentric circles on the surface of a hard disk.

___ 5. The type of hardware for which a particular program or operating system is designed.

___ 6. The type of data storage that has no moving parts.

___ 7. A helper file that enables the operating system to communicate with a hardware device.

___ 8. A graphical environment in which to communicate within the operating system.

___ 9. The type of storage that holds data in patterns of more and less reflective areas.

___ 10. A utility that blocks ports to make a computer more secure.

Knowledge Check: Multiple Choice

Choose the best answer for each question.

1. UNIX is an example of a(n):
   a. compiler.
   b. firewall.
   c. operating system.
   d. BIOS.

2. The _____ is stored on a chip on the motherboard on a desktop PC.
   a. interpreter
   b. HDD
   c. OS
   d. system BIOS.

3. Which of these is NOT one of the functions of the operating system?
   a. to provide a user interface
   b. to run programs
   c. to control devices
   d. to compile applications

4. Which operating system is used on some smartphones?
   a. UNIX
   b. iOS
   c. Windows Server
   d. x86

5. Which of these terms or phrases does NOT describe UNIX?
   a. multiuser
   b. cross-platform
   c. command-line interface
   d. commonly used on thin clients

6. A(n) _____ translates an entire program written in high-level programming code into machine language.
   a. SSD

   b. firewall
   c. compiler
   d. interpreter

7. In the path C:\Household\September\Budget.xls, C: is the
   a. parent folder.
   b. volume.
   c. child folder.
   d. extension.

8. The purpose of a(n) _____ is to tell the operating system how to handle a file, such as what application to use to open it.
   a. extension
   b. compiler
   c. volume
   d. path

9. A(n) _____ is an example of mechanical, magnetic, fixed, secondary storage.
   a. USB flash drive
   b. DVD
   c. solid-state drive (SSD)
   d. hard disk drive (HDD)

10. A _____ can be written to only once and can hold 4.7 GB per side and layer.
    a. CD-RW
    b. DVD+R
    c. BD-R
    d. DVD-RW

Key Principles: Completion

Complete each statement with the appropriate word or phrase.

1. A _____ is a storage unit with a letter assigned to it, such as C: or D:.

2. The _____ is the top level of the storage hierarchy for a volume.

3. The _____ to a file includes the volume letter and the names of the folders to go through to get to it.

4. The file _____ tells the operating system what kind of file it is.

5. Software that consists of programs that perform administrative tasks (such as checking the computer's components to determine whether each is working properly) is called _____.

6. Storage that has no moving parts is known as _____ state.

7. CDs, DVDs, and Blu-ray discs are examples of _____ storage.

8. _____ attached storage is storage made available over a network, such as on a file server.

9. In RAID5, data can be reconstructed if needed, because each write operation striped across the physical disk contains a _____ bit.

10. A _____ interface interacts with the user by accepting typed commands.

Tech Illustrated: Figure Labeling

Fill in the blanks with the correct labels.

1. Operating systems

a. _____   b. _____

c. _____   d. _____   e. _____

2. File path

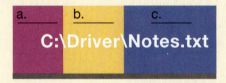

a. _____   b. _____   c. _____

C:\Driver\Notes.txt

Tech to Come: Brainstorming New Uses

In groups or individually, contemplate the following questions and develop as many answers as you can.

1. The 2013 movie *Her* was a fantasy about an operating system with a humanlike personality that the user could interact with as he or she would with a real person. What if having that type of user interface were an option for a personal computer? Would you like such an operating system? Why or why not?

2. Linux, Chrome OS, and other operating systems are free, whereas Microsoft Windows and Mac OS X (the most popular operating systems) are not. What would happen if all operating systems were free? How might the software industry change?

3. In an interpreted program language, the source code is available to anyone who wants it. For example, anyone can look at the source code for an HTML-based web page. Source code for some compiled software is also freely available, such as the Linux kernel. What would happen if all software were open source, so that anyone could go in and change anything in any program (provided he or she had the programming skills to do so)? How might the software industry change?

Tech Literacy: Internet Research and Writing

Conduct Internet research to find the information described, and then develop appropriate written responses based on your research. Be sure to document your sources using the MLA format. (See Chapter 1, Tech Literacy: Internet Research and Writing, page 38, to review MLA style guidelines.)

1. You have been tasked to copy the Birthdays.txt file from a USB flash drive to the Backup folder on the C: volume on a computer that runs UNIX, but you don't know the UNIX command for copying files. How can you find out what command to type? Research UNIX commands online, and write a step-by-step procedure with the exact commands you would use. Assume that the volume letter for the flash drive is F.

2. Suppose you want to try out Linux by installing it on an older computer and using it to browse the web, send and receive email, and run Apache OpenOffice (an open source suite of applications that's similar to Microsoft Office). Which distribution will you get and why? Research the available distributions, determine the best one for your needs, and then write an explanation of your choice. As part of your research, find out whether OpenOffice includes an email program. If it doesn't, identify a free email program that will work with the Linux distribution you have chosen.

3. Suppose you want to put your entire music collection on a NAS device so it's available to every computer in your house all the time. Assume that you have 500 music CDs, each containing about 700 MB of files. Calculate how much storage you will need, and then select a NAS appliance with at least 2.5 times that much storage. Compare prices for the same model across three different online shopping sites, and write a report detailing your findings.

Tech Issues: Team Problem-Solving

In groups, develop possible solutions to the issues presented.

1. Suppose a friend gives you a computer, but when you try to start it, a message appears asking for a BIOS password. You can't contact the friend to find out the password. How should you proceed? Start by using the Internet to determine what other people have done in the same situation.

2. A friend's Windows phone won't start up properly; when she turns it on, all she sees is a graphic of a frowning face. Tech support has recommended a hard reset of the operating system. Write a note to your friend explaining what a hard reset is, how to perform one, and what the results will be. Use the Internet to get the information you need, and document your sources.

3. Suppose you own a small accounting company (20 employees), and so far, you have allowed each employee to choose his or her own operating system. Your technical support staff has run into problems supporting so many different OSs and versions (some of which they aren't very familiar with). You plan to standardize all of the company computers to a single operating system and version. Which one will it be and why? Write a short report that explains the operating systems you considered, announces your decision, and explains the factors that went into making it.

Tech Timeline: Predicting Next Steps

Many improvements have been made to the Windows operating system since Microsoft first introduced it. The timeline below shows a number of versions of Microsoft Windows for the PC and the year each was introduced. Microsoft has stated that Windows 10 will be the final version of Windows, but that doesn't mean the company won't continue adding features to it over the course of many years, much as Apple has done with OS X.

Visit Microsoft's website at http://CUT6.emcp.net/Microsoft along with other sites to learn more about Windows and its features. Prepare a list of features that you believe Microsoft will (or should) add to Windows in the future.

1983	Windows 1.0 (released to the public in 1985)	**2001**	Windows XP
1992	Windows 3.1	**2006**	Windows Vista
1995	Windows 95	**2009**	Windows 7
1998	Windows 98	**2012**	Windows 8
1999	Windows 2000	**2013**	Windows 8.1
2000	Windows Millennium Edition	**2015**	Windows 10

Ethical Dilemmas: Group Discussion and Debate

As a class or within an assigned group, discuss the following ethical dilemma.

When you buy a software product like Microsoft Windows, you aren't buying unlimited use of it; rather, you are buying a license to use it on one computer (or a specific number of computers). Yet each year, thousands of illegal copies of Microsoft Windows are made and distributed. Windows includes a Product Activation feature that's intended to cut down on this activity, but thieves still find ways of circumventing the system and making illegal copies available.

Software publishers lose money when their software is copied, because the individuals who are getting the illegal copies would otherwise have had to pay for legitimate copies. Software publishers pass on the cost of such losses to consumers, and higher software prices are the result.

What's your position on software theft? Can copying copyrighted software be justified in any situation? Why or why not? What are your ethical obligations, if any, concerning this matter? Would you report your employer for copyright violation? Would you accept or use illegally produced copies of software on your own computer?

Chapter 4

Using Applications to Tackle Tasks

Chapter Goal

To learn about the types of applications available and be able to select an appropriate application for the task you need to complete

Learning Objectives

4.1 Explain the ways in which application software is classified, sold, and licensed.

4.2 Differentiate between types of business productivity software and select the right tool for a task.

4.3 Explain how personal productivity and lifestyle software can assist individuals and families.

4.4 Describe and differentiate between the types of graphics and multimedia software available.

4.5 Explain the types of game software available and how to determine a game's age appropriateness.

4.6 Explain the ways that communication software enables people to work together.

 Green go-online icons indicate resources that are accessed from the links menu in your ebook.

 SNAP icons indicate interactive resources that are available in SNAP. Go to your SNAP Assignments page to complete these quizzes, activities, and exercises.

4.1 Distinguishing between Types of Application Software

 Precheck **4.1**

Check your understanding of the concepts covered by this objective.

Application software enables users to do useful and fun things with a computer. Applications are available for almost every computing need you can imagine, and you will learn about many of them in this chapter. You can start to gain a deeper understanding of software by seeing how it's classified according to some basic characteristics, such as the number of intended users, the type of device on which it will function, and how it's sold and licensed.

Individual, Group, or Enterprise Use

One way to categorize applications is according to the numbers of people they serve at once. **Individual application software**—such as a word processor, accounting package, or game—generally serves only one person at a time. Most of the software on a typical home computer falls into this category.

Collaboration software (also called *groupware*) enables people at separate computers to work together on the same document or project. For example, a team of developers might use group management software on their local area network to collaborate on documents, communicate (via messaging, email, and video chat), and share calendars and databases.

Vertical application software is a complete package of programs that work together to perform core business functions for a large organization. For example, a bank might have a mainframe computer at its corporate headquarters. The mainframe is connected to conventional terminals in branch offices, and those terminals are used by managers, tellers, loan officers, and other employees. All financial transactions are fed to the central computer for processing. The system then generates managers' reports, account statements, and other essential documents. This type of software is usually custom built and is frequently found in the banking, insurance, and retail industries.

Desktop Applications versus Mobile Apps

Another way to distinguish applications is to look at what types of devices they are designed to be used on. A **desktop application**, as the name suggests, is designed to be run on full-featured desktop and notebook computers. Desktop applications take up a lot of storage space—sometimes 1 gigabyte (GB) or more—and may include additional software tools that support the main program. In contrast, an application designed for tablets and smartphones—popularly known as an **app**—is designed to be compact and to run quickly and efficiently on minimal hardware. Whereas desktop applications may be installed from a CD or DVD, apps are usually downloaded from

Tracking Down Tech >>>>>>

Everyday Applications

Many people use computer applications on a daily basis to accomplish their work, keep their homes and families organized, and entertain themselves. By seeing what applications other people have found useful, you can get ideas for how you might use a computer yourself. Complete this scavenger hunt to discover what applications your friends, coworkers, classmates, and family members use in their daily activities.

an online store (such as the Apple Store or Windows Store) through a store app that comes with the device.

Software Sales and Licensing

Application software can also be categorized by the way it's developed and sold. The three main types of software distribution are commercial software, shareware, and freeware (see Figure 4.1).

Commercial Software **Commercial software** is created by a company (or an individual, in rare cases) that takes on all the financial risk for its development and distribution upfront. The programmers, testers, DVD copiers, box designers, attorneys,

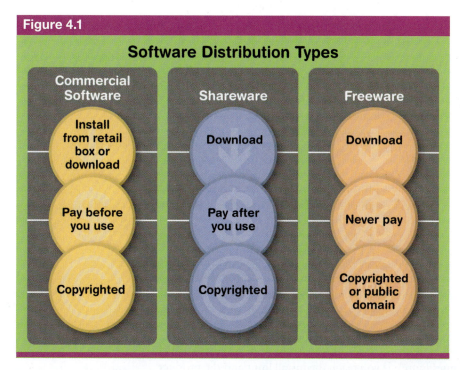

Figure 4.1

Software Distribution Types

Activity 4.1.1

Practice
Software Distribution Types

Hotspot

The App-ification of the Software Industry

As more and more people switch to mobile devices as their primary computing tools, apps are becoming an increasingly larger share of the software market. The Apple Store has over 1.5 million apps for the iPhone and iPad, and more are being added every day. App developers have earned more than $25 billion from Apple Store sales.

A key characteristic of most apps is their specialization: each app performs one task, or a narrow range of tasks. Rather than purchase a large suite of applications, as for a desktop, a mobile user can select a customized combination of apps that accomplish the specific tasks he or she needs to perform, such as playing music clips, browsing a certain social networking site, or checking stock

prices. Apps are typically very inexpensive ($5 or less), so consumers can afford to take chances on new apps that promise new capabilities.

This trend toward specialized apps has affected the software industry overall. As consumers become accustomed to using a different app for each task they perform, they start looking at desktop software in new ways. In the future, you may see desktop software become more compact, more specialized, and simpler to install and remove. App popularity is also encouraging programmers to work independently to develop and sell their own apps, rather than work with large software development teams on large desktop applications.

and others involved in developing, producing, and marketing the software are all paid in advance to create a commercial product that the company then sells to the public. You can purchase commercial software as a boxed product in a retail store or as an online product from the company's website or an online store (see Figure 4.2).

Some software isn't installed on your computer but rather is accessed from the Internet or from a secure cloud. This arrangement is sometimes called *Software as a Service* (*SaaS*). SaaS has several advantages over traditionally installed software. For instance, it requires little or no local storage space, and you never have to worry about downloading updates, fixes, or new editions. Also, your data files can be stored in a secure online location, so you don't have to back them up to ensure their safety. SaaS is typically less expensive than an equivalent retail boxed product too. However, SaaS requires that you be connected to the Internet to use the software, so it isn't suitable for people with slow or unreliable Internet connections. (SaaS is also discussed in Chapter 7.)

Because developing commercial software is a big financial risk, the companies involved in producing it want to make sure that everyone who uses the software pays for it. Stealing commercial software by using it without paying is called **software piracy** and costs companies millions of dollars a year. To cut down on piracy, many companies include various kinds of protective measures in their applications.

The most common antipiracy measure is to write the software's Setup program so that it requires the user to enter a registration key. A **registration key,** sometimes called an *installation key*, is a string of characters that uniquely identifies the user's purchase of the software. On a retail boxed product, the registration key is typically printed on the disk's sleeve or packaging. For an online purchase, the registration key is delivered in an email.

For additional protection, some software requires activation. If you don't activate the software within a certain number of days, it stops working. **Activation** is a process that generates a unique code based on the hardware in your computer and the registration key you used when installing the software. This unique code is sent online to the company's registration database and effectively locks that registration code to your current hardware. If you try to activate another copy of the software on a different computer, the database may not accept it. Most products that require activation allow you to install them on two computers (sometimes more). If you reach the install limit and the product

Activity 4.1.2

Video
Installing Applications

Activity 4.1.3

Video
Applications on the Web

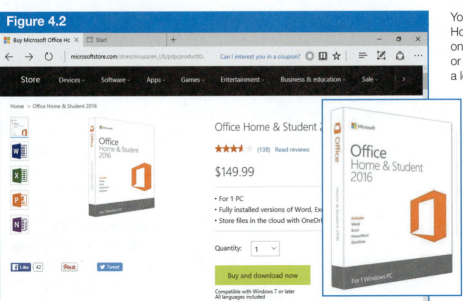

You can purchase Office Home & Student 2016 online at Microsoft.com, or as a boxed product in a local store.

won't activate, you can call the customer support line for the developer and ask for additional activations. These requests are usually granted (within reason).

When you buy commercial software, you aren't really buying the software itself but rather the right to use it in ways that the license agreement permits. The **license agreement** (sometimes called an *End User License Agreement*, or *EULA*) is the legal information that's included in the software packaging or that appears onscreen during setup and asks for your compliance. A license agreement may specify, for instance, the number of computers on which you can legally install the software for your personal use. It may also limit the purposes for which the software may be used. For example, some versions of software are licensed only for use by individuals, students, and nonprofit organizations.

Most PC software is licensed on an individual copy basis, but other license types are also available. For example, Microsoft allows a business to buy a site license for many of its products. A **site license** grants permission to make multiple copies of the software and install it on multiple computers. A site license can allow either per-user or per-seat use. A **per-user site license** grants use by a certain number of users, regardless of the number of computers. A **per-seat site license** grants use for a certain number of computers, regardless of the number of users. See Figure 4.3 for an example showing the difference between the two types of licenses.

Activity 4.1.4

Article
Software Licensing Arrangements

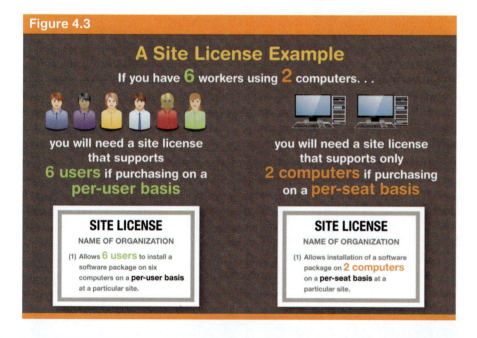

Figure 4.3

A Site License Example

If you have **6** workers using **2** computers. . .

you will need a site license that supports **6 users** if purchasing on a **per-user basis**

you will need a site license that supports only **2 computers** if purchasing on a **per-seat basis**

SITE LICENSE
NAME OF ORGANIZATION
(1) Allows **6 users** to install a software package on six computers on a **per-user basis** at a particular site.

SITE LICENSE
NAME OF ORGANIZATION
(1) Allows installation of a software package on **2 computers** on a **per-seat basis** at a particular site.

Practical TECH

Purchasing and Downloading Software Online

Buying commercial software online and downloading it to your computer is more convenient than purchasing a CD or DVD at a store and taking it home to install it. To purchase the software online, you can use a credit card or an online payment system (such as PayPal). After you do so, you receive a download link on a web page or in an email (or both). You click that link to download an installer file and then run the installer to set up the application. To complete the installation, you might need a code or password; you should receive that from the seller in an email too.

It's important to keep that code somewhere safe, because you will need it if you ever reinstall the software. You might also need it to get the discounted price when buying an upgrade for the software later. You should store the code somewhere other than on your hard drive, such as on a hard copy with your important papers or on a cloud storage drive.

Many large companies have specialized software needs that can't be met by the mainstream commercial software available. Such companies can choose an off-the-shelf application and then hire programmers to write add-ons and customizations for it, or they can hire developers to create custom software. Although developing custom software costs many thousands of dollars upfront, a company can make up that investment over time through increased worker productivity.

Shareware and Freeware Many small software development companies struggle to get the public's attention for their products. One way that many companies have increased their popularity is to offer their software as **shareware**. With a shareware product, you can try it before you buy it. You can download a trial version for free and use it for a specified number of days or use a limited set of features. If you like the program, you can buy a registration key that will unlock the rest of the features or remove the time limit. Most shareware has a time or feature limitation that lasts until you pay for the product.

Software that's made available at no charge is known as **freeware**. Because freeware is often developed by individuals rather than companies, the quality varies and so do the levels of documentation and support available. The developer of freeware may retain its copyright or give up the copyright and make the program available in the public domain. If a program is in the **public domain**, other people can do what they like with it. In addition, the developer usually makes the **source code** available so others can modify and improve the program.

Activity 4.1.5

Video
Shareware and Freeware

Recheck 4.1
Recheck your understanding of the concepts covered by this objective.

Precheck 4.2
Check your understanding of the concepts covered by this objective.

4.2 Using Business Productivity Software

No matter what the business or industry, certain common tasks need to be performed. For example, businesses must do the following:

- Communicate with customers, suppliers, and coworkers
- Store information about customers, products, services, and orders
- Schedule meetings and other activities that involve people, locations, and equipment
- Market the product or service to potential customers
- Make and receive payments and maintain accurate financial records
- Analyze current trends to predict future needs

Tech Ethics

Paying for Shareware

Some shareware is distributed through an honor system. The developer makes available to the public a full-featured version of the program with no time limits and asks people to send in money if they like and continue to use the product. This distribution method worked well in the early days of the Internet. At that time, most of the people who downloaded shareware were tech enthusiasts—among them, many programmers who understood the time and effort put into developing shareware. But today, shareware developers who don't demand payment by limiting the program's features or usage time seldom get paid.

Suppose you download a shareware application for free and digitally sign a license agreement in which you promise to pay for the software if you continue to use it after 14 days. Will you make that payment if you use the software beyond the 14-day limit? Why or why not? Does it matter how much the payment is or what payment methods are available?

Table 4.1 Examples of Business Productivity Software

Category	Example(s)	Common Uses
Word processing	WordPad Microsoft Word Corel WordPerfect	Prepare correspondence (letters, envelopes), labels, reports, and book manuscripts.
Desktop publishing	Microsoft Publisher QuarkXPress Adobe InDesign	Design and produce newsletters, advertisements, brochures, books, and magazines.
Spreadsheet	Microsoft Excel	Record and organize numerical data and prepare summary charts and reports.
Database management	Microsoft Access	Provide structured data storage for customer, order, and product records and prepare reports and charts based on the data.
Presentation graphics	Microsoft PowerPoint	Design and produce text- and graphics-based slides for presentations.
Personal information manager (PIM)	Microsoft Outlook	Schedule appointments and tasks and store contact information; may also send and receive email.
Project management	Microsoft Project	Schedule and track stages and tasks of complex projects that involve people, locations, and equipment.
Accounting	Intuit QuickBooks	Record and analyze financial data, including bank accounts, transactions, inventory, and payroll.

Business productivity software can help with all these activities. You can purchase several applications to perform specific activities, or you can use a suite of related applications to perform multiple tasks. Table 4.1 provides some examples of business productivity software.

Word-Processing Software

Word-processing software can be used to create most kinds of printed documents, including letters, labels, newsletters, brochures, reports, and certificates. Word-processing programs are the most widely used of all software applications in business, because nearly every company needs to generate some type of printed information. Word-processing programs are often available for more than one operating system. For example, versions of Microsoft Word are available for both the Windows

Figure 4.4

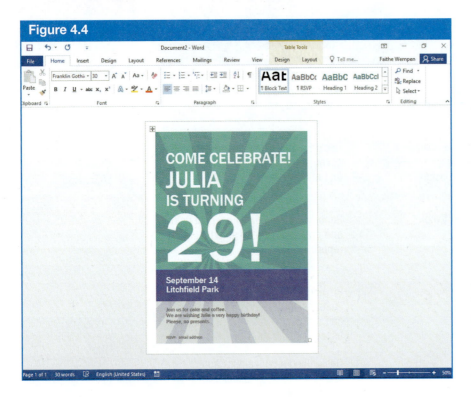

Microsoft Word 2016 offers a comprehensive set of tools for creating and modifying text and images in word-processing documents. The tools are displayed in a ribbon interface and organized in tabs, groups, and buttons for easy access.

operating system and Mac OS X. Figure 4.4 shows the Windows version of Microsoft Word 2016.

You can start a new word-processing document from a blank page, or you can use a previously created and stored model called a **template**. Microsoft Word provides access to a large library of templates that are stored online. Templates are available to help you create newsletters, flyers, reports, greeting cards, certificates, and many more document types.

After creating a document, you can freely type and edit the text by using the keyboard's arrow keys to move the **insertion point** (blinking vertical cursor). You can use the Backspace key to remove text to the left of the insertion point and the Delete key to remove text to the right. To delete an entire block of text, you select the text by dragging across it with the mouse and then press Delete.

Perhaps the most valued editing feature in a word-processing program is the **spelling checker**; it checks each word in a document against a word list or dictionary and identifies possible errors. A spelling checker isn't context sensitive, however. This means that it won't flag words that are spelled correctly but used incorrectly—for example, the use of *their* when *there* is correct.

A **grammar checker** checks a document for common errors in grammar, usage, and mechanics. Using a grammar checker is no substitute for the careful review of a knowledgeable editor, but running a grammar check can be useful for identifying problems such as run-on sentences, sentence fragments, double negatives, and misplaced apostrophes.

Word-processing software allows many different types of formatting—that is, manipulation of the text to change its appearance at the word, paragraph, or document level. **Text formatting** is applied to

Hands On

Using a Word Template to Create a Flyer

Using the templates in Microsoft Word to create documents is very easy. Follow the steps in this resource to create a flyer in Word 2016.

Figure 4.5

In Microsoft Word 2016, the Print Preview feature allows you to see exactly what your document will look like when you print it.

individual characters of text; you can change the font, size, and color of the text. **Paragraph formatting** is applied to entire paragraphs at a time; you can adjust the line spacing, indentation, horizontal alignment between margins, and use of bulleted and numbered lists. **Document formatting** (also called *page formatting* or *section formatting*) is applied to the entire document, page, or section; you can set the paper size, margins, number of columns, and background color. To save time and ensure consistency, you can create and apply styles to a document. A **style** is a named combination of formats; for instance, you can apply a certain font size, font color, and horizontal alignment to all headings in a document.

After creating a document, you can save it for later use and perhaps print a hard copy of it and/or send it to someone by email. In Microsoft Word, when you open the controls for printing, you see a **print preview** of the document. If you see any problems in the document, you can go back and fix them before completing the print command. Figure 4.5 shows the Print controls in Word 2016.

Desktop Publishing Software

Desktop publishing software allows users to create documents with complex page layouts that include text and graphics of various types. At a very basic level, desktop publishing software is similar to word-processing software. Both can be used to combine text and graphics to create many different types of documents. However, desktop publishing software is more sophisticated and more focused on the page layout; it enables many complex layout and typesetting actions. People who design books, magazines, and advertising use desktop publishing software to create professional-quality layouts.

Consumer-level desktop publishing software is available (such as Microsoft Publisher), but most desktop publishing software is oriented toward professionals. Programs such as Adobe InDesign and QuarkXPress are expensive and take a lot of

Figure 4.6

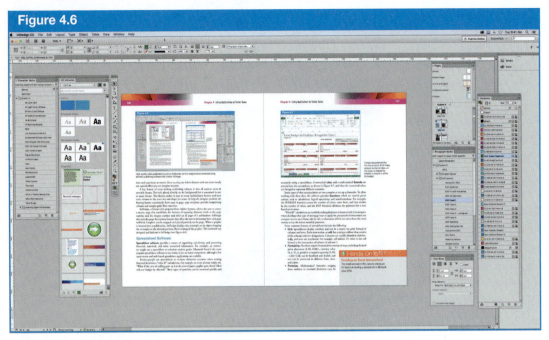

High-quality color publications such as textbooks can be designed and produced using desktop publishing software like Adobe InDesign.

time and experience to master. Even so, they are rich in features and can create nearly any special effect you can imagine in print.

A key feature of most desktop publishing software is that all content exists in movable frames. Text isn't placed directly on the background but is contained in one or more frames. This feature makes it easy to create multicolumn layouts and have each column be the exact size and shape you want. To help the designer position the floating frames consistently from page to page, page templates provide nonprinting column and margin guide lines onscreen.

InDesign, a feature-rich program from Adobe Systems, allows the user to create a master page that establishes the formats of repeating elements (such as the page number and the chapter number and title) on all pages of a publication. InDesign also includes page description features that allow the user to determine how each page will look. Graphics can be cropped and placed precisely on the page. When a graphic is inserted into a publication, InDesign displays tiny rectangles at its edges; dragging the rectangles to the desired position allows resizing of the graphic. This textbook was designed and laid out in InDesign (see Figure 4.6).

Spreadsheet Software

Spreadsheet software provides a means of organizing, calculating, and presenting financial, statistical, and other numerical information. For example, an instructor might use a spreadsheet to calculate student grades. Microsoft Excel is the most popular spreadsheet software in use today; it has no major competitors, although a few open source and web-based spreadsheet applications are available.

Businesspeople use spreadsheets to evaluate alternative scenarios when making financial decisions—"what if?" calculations. For example, an event planner might ask, "What if the cost of staffing goes up but the cost of paper supplies goes down? How will our budget be affected?" These types of questions can be answered quickly and

Figure 4.7

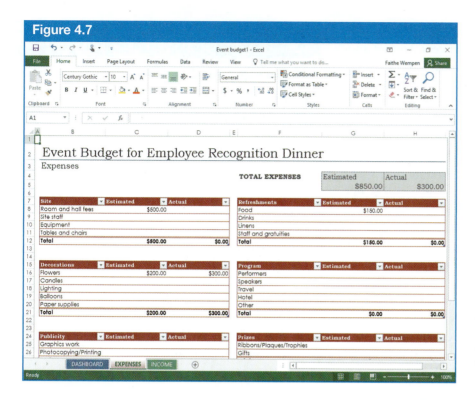

Using a spreadsheet like this one in Excel 2016 helps analyze numerical data—in this case, to determine whether a project is within its budget.

accurately using a spreadsheet. A numerical **value** and a mathematical **formula** are entered into the spreadsheet, as shown in Figure 4.7, and then the numerical values are changed to represent different scenarios.

Some types of data manipulation are too complex to set up as formulas. To allow working with these data, the software provides **functions**, which are named, preset actions, such as calculations, logical operations, and transformations. For example, the AVERAGE function counts the number of values, sums them, and then divides by the number of values, and the PMT function calculates the payments for a loan based on its terms.

"What if?" calculations are useful in making decisions at home as well. For example, when deciding what type of mortgage loan to apply for, prospective homeowners can compare two or more loans side by side to determine which one saves them the most money or has the lowest monthly payment.

Some common features of spreadsheets include the following:

- **Grid.** Spreadsheets display numbers and text in a matrix (or grid) formed of columns and rows. Each intersection, or **cell**, has a unique address that consists of the column and row designations. Columns are usually identified alphabetically, and rows are numbered. For example, cell address A1 refers to the cell located at the intersection of column A and row 1.
- **Formatting.** Numbers may be formatted in a variety of ways, including decimal point placement (1.00, 0.001), currency value ($, £, ¥), or positive or negative quantity (1.00, –1.00). Cells can be bordered and shaded, and text can be presented in different fonts, sizes, and colors.
- **Formulas.** Mathematical formulas—ranging from addition to standard deviation—can be

Hands On 👆👆👆👆👆👆

Creating an Excel Spreadsheet

The simple exercise in this resource shows you the basics of creating a spreadsheet in Microsoft Excel 2016.

entered into cells, and they can process information derived from other cells. Formulas use cell addresses, not cell contents. For example, a formula might direct a program to multiply cell F1 by cell A4, and then it will multiply the numerical contents of the two cells. The use of cell addresses means that a spreadsheet can automatically update the result if the value in a cell changes. A spreadsheet formula always begins with an equal symbol (=), like this: =F1*A4.

Tech Career Explorer

Microsoft Certifications

If you like working with applications and helping other people figure them out, look into certification as a Microsoft Office Specialist (MOS) or a Microsoft Certified Trainer (MCT). Becoming a MOS involves testing your ability to use Office applications. To learn more, complete this exercise.

- **Charting.** A **chart** is a visual representation of data that often makes the data easier to read and understand. Spreadsheet programs allow users to display selected data in line, bar, pie, and other chart forms.

- **Macros.** Most spreadsheets allow the user to create a **macro**, which is a set of commands that automates complex or repetitive actions. For example, a macro can be created to check sales figures to see if they meet quotas and then compile a separate chart for those figures that do not. The macro will automatically perform all the steps required.

Database Management Software

Before computers, employee, voter, and customer records were typically placed in file folders and stored in metal cabinets, along with thousands of other folders. Locating a particular folder could be time consuming and frustrating, even if the records were stored in an organized manner.

Many of these manual storage systems have been replaced with electronic databases, which use software to manage data more efficiently. A database is a collection of data organized in one or more data tables. Each data table contains records. A record is a collection of all the data about one specific instance, such as a person, a business, an item, or a transaction. Each individual piece of data in a record is called a *field*, and each field is filled with data related to its field name. For example, in a database that stores information about customers, *FirstName* is one field name and *LastName* is another field name. Each record in a table uses the same field names, and you can sort and filter the database by one or more of those field names. For example, in the customer database, you can filter it to display only records for which the *City* field shows "Chicago." You can also provide multiple filter criteria, such as only records in which the City is Chicago and the transaction date is less than six months ago.

The software you use to manage a database is called a **database management system (DBMS)**. A large database (sometimes called an **enterprise database**) is stored on a server and managed using professional tools such as Oracle Database and structured query language (SQL). The data can be stored on a local server or on a remote server accessed through a company's data network or a cloud. Multiple users can update and query the database simultaneously using any of a variety of interfaces, both command line and graphical.

Personal DBMS applications (such as Microsoft Access and FileMaker Pro) enable ordinary users to create and manage databases on a small scale. Personal DBMS applications usually have a friendly graphical user interface (GUI) and many tools for easily generating helper objects, such as data entry forms and printable reports. Figure 4.8 shows a data table in Microsoft Access.

Most databases have more than one table, and all the tables are somehow related. Such a database is known as a *relational database*. Figure 4.9 shows a relationships diagram for a database that keeps track of product sales. Notice the tables that have relationships to the Orders table: Customers, Order Details, and Salespeople. When a customer places an order, the salesperson opens an order entry form and chooses his or her own name from the list of salespeople on the form (from the Salespeople table).

Figure 4.8

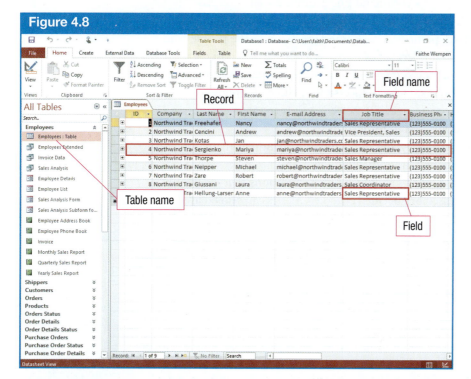

Microsoft Access displays tables in a spreadsheet-like grid for easy browsing.

Activity 4.2.1

Practice
A Relational Database Example

Figure 4.9

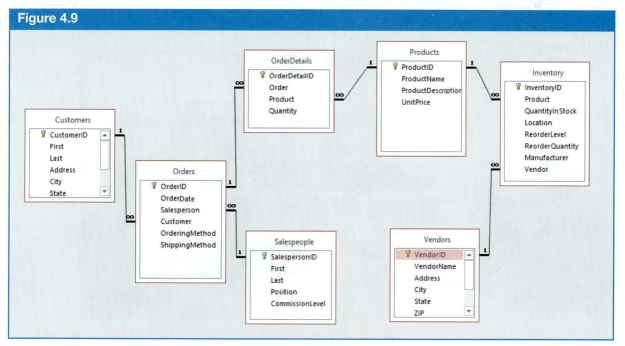

This example shows relationships for a business database that tracks orders.

The salesperson then uses a link to the Customers table to locate the customer's account details and link them to the order. The salesperson selects the items the customer wants from a link from the Products table and specifies a quantity for each product; that data is then added to the Order Details table. As the salesperson adds each item to the order, the database interface checks the inventory level in the Inventory table for each ordered product and alerts the salesperson if any items are out of stock.

Databases are most often created by computer professionals but used by ordinary end users. Whereas the developer who creates a database might interact with the database by typing text commands at a command line prompt on an enterprise-level system, hundreds of clerks and administrative assistants in multiple locations might access the database via a graphical point-and-click interface. Because the people who use the database may not have the same level of expertise as its developer, most database systems enable the developer to create *helper objects* to make the database friendlier and more easily accessed for end-users. Helper objects can include the following:

- **Forms.** A form is an easy-to-navigate, onscreen document that enables end users to enter, edit, delete, and search for records.
- **Reports.** A report is an attractively laid out, printable document that summarizes raw data with subtotals and other calculations.
- **Queries.** A query is a set of saved sort-and-filter specifications that show only certain records and fields based on specified criteria. Queries can also be used to temporarily join records from multiple tables, so the combined data set can be used for a report, form, or other query.
- **Macros.** A macro is a saved group of commands that can be executed with a single command.

Tables, forms, reports, queries, and macros are all **objects** in the database.

Presentation Graphics Software

Anyone who has attended group lectures or presentations knows how boring they can be. One way to make a presentation more interesting is to use presentation graphics software. **Presentation graphics software** allows users to create computerized slide

With presentation graphics software, you can create slide shows that combine text, graphics, audio, and video.

shows that combine text, numbers, animation, and graphics, as well as audio and video. Microsoft PowerPoint is the most popular application in this category.

A **slide** is an individual page or screen that's created in presentation graphics software. A **slide show** may consist of any number of individual slides. For example, a sales representative might use a slide show to promote a product to customers; the electronic format allows featuring key components of the product. An instructor might use a slide show to accompany a lecture and make it more engaging and informative. A businessperson might use a slide show to deliver information and present strategies at a meeting.

Presentation software accepts content in a variety of external formats, such as text, photos, videos, and music. With the software, users can repurpose existing content in new ways to suit different audiences. Users can also incorporate ready-made, royalty-free drawings by using **clip art** from online repositories such as Office.com (for Microsoft products, including PowerPoint). Figure 4.10 shows several examples of the types of content you can create and import in PowerPoint.

A presentation can be delivered by computer in a real-time environment with a live audience—either in person or remotely over the Internet—or it can be recorded

Hands On

Exploring PowerPoint

Follow the steps in this resource to create a PowerPoint presentation that will take you on a tour of the program's basic features.

Figure 4.10

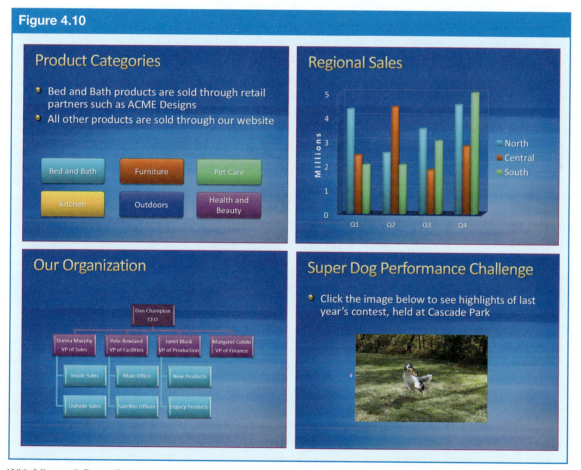

With Microsoft PowerPoint, users can create slides with rich content, including appealing backgrounds, effective titles and subheads, compelling bullet points, colorful charts and graphs, clear flowcharts, interesting photos, and even audio, video, web links, and other media elements.

to a computer file for later playback. In addition to presenting a slide show on a computer, the user can also output the slides in a variety of ways, including DVD videos, still-image graphics (one graphic per slide), portable document format (PDF) files, and hard-copy handouts.

Software Suites

Some software vendors bundle and sell a group of applications as a single package called a **software suite**. Microsoft Office is the best-known software suite; it consists of a word-processing program (Microsoft Word), a spreadsheet program (Microsoft Excel), a presentation application (Microsoft PowerPoint), and an email and personal information manager (Microsoft Outlook). Some versions of Microsoft Office contain other programs too, such as a DBMS (Microsoft Access) and a note-organizing program (Microsoft OneNote).

A software suite is typically less expensive than the combined cost of the applications when purchased separately. Because all the applications are designed with a common interface, the basic features and functions work the same way in every program. This means there's less to learn when you start using an unfamiliar application.

Another advantage of software suites is their ability to share content between applications. For example, both Microsoft Word and Microsoft PowerPoint easily accept charts and spreadsheets from Microsoft Excel. You can freely copy and paste these materials between applications. You can also link or embed content from one application or data file into another. When you **embed** content, the pasted content retains its memory of what application it came from, and if you double-click that embedded content, it reopens in its native application. When you **link** content from one data file to another, the pasted content retains its memory of not only its original application but also its original data file. If the original data file changes, the linked content in another file changes automatically the next time that other file is opened. Embedding and linking are parts of the content-sharing feature in Windows and Office programs known as **object linking and embedding (OLE)**. You don't have to have a software suite to use OLE; it works between any applications that support it (and most do).

Personal Information Management (PIM) Software

Businesspeople need to keep in contact with a wide variety of people such as customers, suppliers, and coworkers, and they need to organize the contact information for

Practical TECH

Syncing between Phones and Computers

Many smartphones have calendar, email, contacts, and to-do list utilities. If your phone and your computer run operating systems by the same company (for example, if they are both Apple or both Microsoft) and the PIM application on your computer is also by that manufacturer, then you should have no trouble setting up the application to synchronize PIM data between the two devices without any special setup.

If your phone and computer have different platforms (such as an iPhone and a Windows desktop or a Windows phone and an Apple Macintosh notebook), then synchronization may be more difficult. If you have a Windows phone and a Mac computer, download the Windows Phone for Mac application from Microsoft (available at **http://CUT6 .emcp.net/WindowsPhone**). If you have an iPhone and a Windows computer, you can use the iTunes application to synchronize your phone and Microsoft Outlook, as described at **http://CUT6.emcp.net/SyncingMSContacts**.

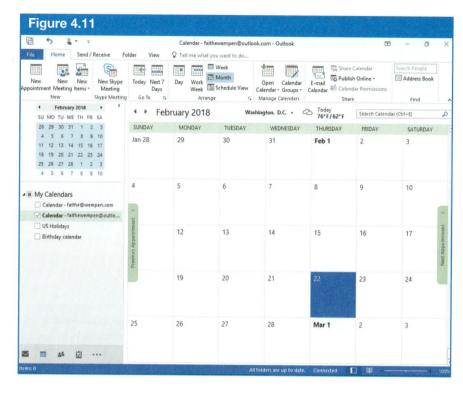

Figure 4.11

Microsoft Outlook includes a full-featured calendar application.

all these individuals, along with their scheduled meetings and phone calls. **Personal information management (PIM) software** fulfills this need by providing an address book, calendar, and to-do list in one convenient interface. Some PIM software also sends and receives email. Microsoft Outlook is best known as an *email application*, but it also offers a full array of PIM components, including Calendar, People, Tasks, and Notes (see Figure 4.11).

Some people choose to use online PIM tools rather than tools that are installed on their individual devices. One popular online PIM tool is Google Calendar, which allows multiple people to share calendars. With an online calendar, contact list, and to-do list, you don't have to worry about the copy on any of your devices ever being out of sync.

Project Management Software

Many businesses regularly engage in planning and designing projects, as well as scheduling and controlling the various activities that occur throughout the term of a project. For example, before a construction firm begins to erect a building, it needs to develop a comprehensive plan for completing the structure. During planning, an architect prepares a detailed building design, or set of blueprints. Schedules are then prepared so that workers, building materials, and other resources are available when needed. Once construction begins, all activities are monitored and controlled to ensure that they are started and completed on schedule.

Before computers were available, projects like this were planned, designed, scheduled, and controlled manually. Today, these tasks are performed electronically using **project management software**. This type of software helps manage complex projects by keeping track of schedules, constraints, and budgets. It can be used for most kinds of projects, including those involving construction, software development,

Activity 4.2.2

Article
Project Management Software

Figure 4.12

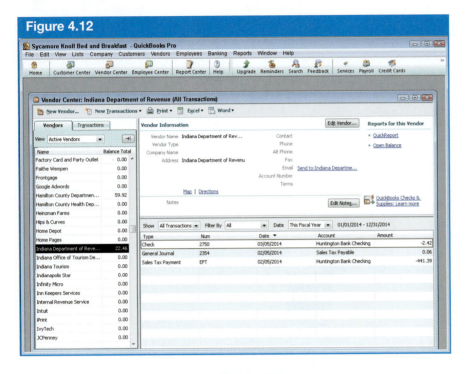

Intuit QuickBooks helps small businesses manage their accounting and finances.

and manufacturing. The most frequently used project management software today is Microsoft Project; it helps users optimize the planning of projects and track schedules and budgets.

Accounting Software

Keeping track of a business's financial affairs can be complicated—much too complicated to manage with a simple spreadsheet. **Accounting software** integrates all the financial activities of a company into a single interface. It can track money coming in and going out; monitor bank account transactions and statements (including connecting online to the bank); create purchase orders, estimates, and invoices; and even process employee time cards and payroll.

Large businesses typically have their own enterprise-level software that multiple users can access simultaneously from different computers. Small businesses might use an off-the-shelf product, such as Intuit QuickBooks (shown in Figure 4.12) or Sage 50 Accounting (formerly Peachtree Accounting). Accounting software can save money for a small business because a full-time accountant is not needed. Office workers can handle the bulk of the accounting throughout the year, with an accountant involved only at tax time.

Note-Taking Software

Gathering information often involves collecting multiple types of input. For example, if you are researching a new product, you might have digital ink sketches made at a planning meeting, handwritten notes, typed notes in several different formats, website addresses, and photos from a digital camera. Microsoft OneNote, which is included in some versions of the Office suite, enables users to collect many types of data in a single place. It integrates with the OneNote app on a Windows phone or tablet, so you can take photos and collect information wherever you are. An alternative to OneNote is Evernote, which has similar features.

Recheck 4.2

Recheck your understanding of the concepts covered by this objective.

4.3 Selecting Personal Productivity and Lifestyle Software

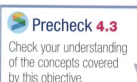

Precheck 4.3

Check your understanding of the concepts covered by this objective.

Personal software is designed for individuals to use for their own enrichment and entertainment. If you want to accomplish a task that isn't related to your work, chances are you can find an application that will help you do it more easily. Popular categories of personal software include lifestyle and hobby, personal finance and tax, legal document preparation, and educational and reference.

Lifestyle and Hobby Software

Lifestyle and hobby applications help you live the way you want to live and make the most of your special interests. Here are just a few examples:

- **Home and garden architecture.** Plan the home you want to build and where to put the furniture. Lay out your garden, specifying the location for each plant.
- **Diet and fitness.** Track your calorie intake, and plan and track your exercise and fitness activities.
- **Home inventory.** Create a database listing everything you own; you can use it to file an insurance claim for a disaster such as a fire.

All the things that these specialized applications do can also be accomplished using general purpose software; you don't necessarily need special programs. For example, you can do home design using a CAD program, track diet and fitness using a spreadsheet, or create a home inventory using a DBMS—if you know how to use these general purpose programs. The specialized programs are designed to be simple, so you can enjoy their benefits without having any previous software experience.

Legal Software

Legal software is designed to help analyze, plan, and prepare a variety of legal documents, including wills and trusts. It can also be used to prepare other legal documents, such as the forms required for real estate purchases and sales, rental contracts, and estate planning. Included in most packages are standard templates for various legal documents, along with suggestions for preparing them.

This type of program begins by asking the user to select the type of document he or she wants to prepare. To complete a document, the user may need to answer a series of questions or enter information into a form. Once that task has been completed, the software adapts the final document to meet the individual's needs. After a document has been prepared, it can be sent to the appropriate department, agency, or court for processing and registration. It's always a good idea to have an attorney review documents to make certain they are correct and legal in the intended state or local jurisdiction.

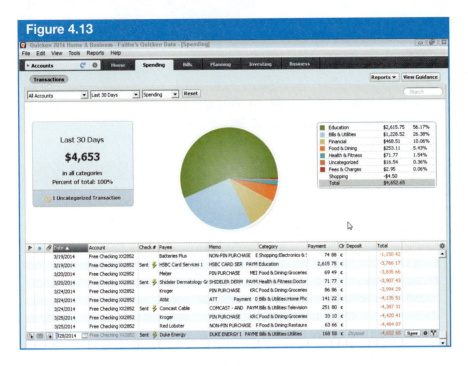

Figure 4.13

Quicken, by Intuit, is a popular application for managing personal finances. It includes easy-to-use tools for paying bills, balancing a checkbook, tracking income and expenses, maintaining investment records, and performing other financial tasks.

Personal Finance and Tax Software

Personal finance software helps users pay bills, balance checkbooks, track income and expenses, maintain investment records, and perform other financial activities. Figure 4.13 shows Intuit Quicken, which is a popular personal finance application. This software also enables users to view reports and charts that show how they are spending their money.

Some personal finance programs provide services on the Internet and web. Users can go online to learn the status of their investments and insurance coverage, for example. They can also conduct normal banking transactions, such as accessing and printing bank statements that show summaries of monthly transactions. These programs can perform most of the financial activities that used to require mail or telephone contact.

Tax preparation software is designed to aid in analyzing federal and state tax status, as well as preparing and filing tax returns. Most tax preparation programs provide tips that can help identify deductions, possibly resulting in great savings. Some programs include actual state and federal tax forms for entering tax data. Programs that don't include these forms provide instructions for downloading them from the software publisher's website. Completed tax returns can be printed for mailing or filed electronically. Because federal and state tax laws change frequently (as do tax forms), users should be sure to use the software version for the appropriate year or period.

Educational and Reference Software

A computer can be an unparalleled learning tool, especially with the wealth of resources available online. Among the free educational and reference materials on websites are online dictionaries and encyclopedias. You can also purchase educational and reference software—either on a CD or DVD for local use on your personal computer or as a subscription to an online learning service. You might even take classes at colleges and universities that are delivered entirely through Internet-accessed software.

Encyclopedias and Dictionaries Almost everyone has used an encyclopedia or dictionary at one time or another. An encyclopedia is a comprehensive reference work that contains articles on a broad range of subjects. Before computers, encyclopedias

Cutting Edge

To Catch a Plagiarist

Think twice about getting a term paper from an essay-writing website or online database. State-of-the-art antiplagiarism software can expose your cheating in a nanosecond.

Plagiarism—the passing off of someone else's writing as your own—has become epidemic on college campuses. According to one study, 36 percent of students admit to having plagiarized a written paper during their college careers. The reasons for the growth of this behavior may be varied. For instance, some college students left high school without being properly educated in citing sources for research papers. Also, today's students, who file-swap music without a care, have a foggier definition of concepts such as copyright. And of course, using the Internet makes finding information and then copying and pasting it into a document all too easy.

To combat the misappropriation of the written word, colleges are turning to software such as Turnitin and SafeAssign. These antiplagiarism programs generate a "digital fingerprint" of a document that has been submitted electronically. The document's verbal patterns are cross-checked against a huge database of Internet, newspaper, and encyclopedia archives, as well as previously submitted student work. Suspicious sentences and paragraphs are highlighted, and source matches are annotated. The thieving writer is busted in seconds.

Students can also use plagiarism-detection programs as self-screening tools to make sure they present and cite information properly. And even for classes whose professors don't use these programs, their very existence discourages students from copycat writing.

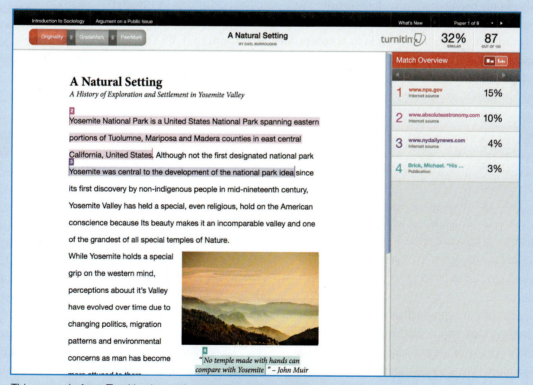

This example from Turnitin shows the overall percentage of nonoriginal work in the submitted paper and identifies specific copied passages and their sources.

Figure 4.14

If you type a word or phrase into the search text box at a dictionary site such as Dictionary.com, a definition will appear. Some online dictionaries include features such as audio pronunciations, images, and example sentences.

and dictionaries were available only in book form. Now, they are available both on the web and on DVDs you can purchase. Figure 4.14 shows a word that's been looked up at Dictionary.com.

Tutorials Many people learn new skills by using computer-driven tutorials. A **tutorial** is a form of instruction in which the student is guided step by step through the learning process. Tutorials are sometimes referred to as **computer-based training (CBT)** or *web-based training (WBT)*.

Tutorials are available for almost all subjects, including how to assemble a bicycle, use a word processor, and write a letter. The student and instructor resources for this

Activity 4.3.1

Article
Computer-Based Learning

Tech Ethics

Should You Cite Wikis in Academic Papers?

Wikipedia is the world's largest and most popular online encyclopedia; it contains entries on millions of topics. The term *wiki* refers to an online application that allows people to collaborate by uploading and editing content. In other words, a wiki is a shared project in which anyone may participate.

Some quality safeguards are in place to prevent obvious untruths from being stated in wikis. But wikis are by nature vulnerable to containing misinformation, whether it's placed there accidentally or intentionally. For example, rival scientists might update the wiki page on their competitors' research to indicate that the research is unsuccessful, or a rival business could edit the language on a competitor's page to make the competitor's products seem unreliable.

This potential for misinformation is an important difference between *Wikipedia* (**http://CUT6.emcp.net /Wikipedia**) and traditional research sources, such as *Encyclopedia Britannica* (**http://CUT6.emcp.net /Britannica**), in which research experts carefully check each article. Many teachers (especially at the college level) don't accept *Wikipedia* as a cited source in academic papers because of its inconsistent quality and accuracy. When you are writing research papers for your own classes, be sure to check with your instructors to find out their policies on citing wikis.

Figure 4.15

Tutorials such as the video activities for this textbook help students understand concepts by providing a combination of text, graphics, animation, and interaction.

book include dozens of tutorials; you may have already been assigned some of them in this class, such as the one in Figure 4.15.

4.4 Exploring Graphics and Multimedia Software

 Recheck 4.3
Recheck your understanding of the concepts covered by this objective.

Graphics and **multimedia software** enable both professional and home users to work with graphics, video, and audio. A variety of applications are focused in this area, including painting and drawing, image editing, video and audio editing, web authoring, and computer-aided design (CAD) software.

Precheck 4.4
Check your understanding of the concepts covered by this objective.

Painting and Drawing Software

Painting and drawing programs are available for both professional and home users. The more expensive professional versions typically include more features and greater capabilities than the less expensive personal versions.

Painting software enables users to create and edit bitmap images. As you learned in Chapter 2 in the section discussing scanners, a *bitmap* is a grid of pixels, or a map of bits (which is where the name comes from), and each pixel has a color assigned to it. A bitmap image can be created from scratch in a painting program, or it can be imported from a digital camera, digitized with a scanner, captured from a computer screen, or acquired as a file. Another name for a bitmap image is a **raster image**.

Adobe Photoshop is a popular and powerful painting program that has many tools for creating new bitmap images and editing photos professionally. Microsoft Windows comes with a very basic painting program called *Paint*.

Drawing software creates and edits images called *vector graphics*. A **vector graphic** is formed using mathematical formulas in the same way that lines and shapes are formed using geometry. Because a particular shape is based on math, it can be resized freely without distorting it. In contrast, a bitmap image can become jagged edged or distorted when resized, especially when it's made larger. Vector graphics also take up much less disk space than bitmap images do, because less data is involved in creating them. The main drawback to vector graphics is that they can't generate photo-realistic images.

Hands On

Trying Out Painting

You can try out painting techniques using basic software that's probably already on your computer. The steps in this resource are for Windows 10 and Office 2016, but other versions of Windows and Office have similar programs and features.

Figure 4.16

Adobe Photoshop Elements is a painting program that's useful for editing digital photos.

Much of the clip art provided on clip art websites is vector based. CorelDRAW Graphics Suite and Adobe Illustrator CC are two full-featured applications that specialize in generating vector graphics.

Microsoft Windows doesn't come with a drawing program, but you can experiment with the drawing tools in Microsoft Office applications such as Word, Excel, and PowerPoint.

Photo-Editing Software

Photo-editing software is designed specifically for manipulating photos and has little or no capability for creating original images. For example, Windows Live Photo Gallery transfers pictures from a digital camera to your computer and then organizes them, applies various types of corrections to them, annotates them, and more; you can download this free application from Microsoft. Apple also offers a free photo editing program called *iPhoto*.

Adobe Photoshop Elements (shown in Figure 4.16) is a basic version of Photoshop that can create new bitmap content, but it's best known for its photo-editing capabilities. Amateur photographers can use this program to fix problems in their photos—for instance, people with red eyes and images that are too dark or too light. Photoshop Elements can also apply interesting special effects to pictures to make them look like watercolor paintings, pencil sketches, photographic negatives, and line drawings.

3-D Modeling and CAD Software

Vector drawing programs can be used to create three-dimensional (3-D) models. A **3-D modeling program** is used to generate the graphics for blueprints and technical drawings for items that will

Tech Career Explorer

CAD Across the Board

Computer-aided design is used in almost every phase of a product's development, whether it's a new automobile or a pop-up toaster. Designers can use CAD tools to experiment with product design, to analyze a design's potential weaknesses before it is manufactured, and to program computerized tools to mold and mill the parts. Complete this exercise to explore some of the jobs available in this broad field.

be built, as well as 3-D representations of people and objects in games. For example, if you have ever played The Sims or Second Life, you have seen humanlike avatars developed using 3-D vector graphics.

Each 3-D vector graphic is first drawn as a **wireframe**, which is a surfaceless outline of an object composed of lines. If you were to bend pieces of wire to create the outline of an object, it might look similar to an onscreen wireframe image. Next, a pattern, or **texture**, is added to the surface of the object to make it look more realistic. Finally, light and shadow are added to complete the effect. Figure 4.17 shows a computer-generated chessboard with one of the pieces shown in wireframe mode so you can see how it's constructed.

Figure 4.17

Vector-based graphics programs store images as a series of geometric shapes.

Technical object modeling with vector graphics is also called **computer-aided design (CAD)**. CAD software enables professionals to create architectural, engineering, product, and scientific designs with a high degree of precision and detail. For example, engineers can use CAD software to design buildings and bridges, and scientists can use it to create graphic designs of plants, animals, and chemical structures. Most CAD software can also create and display designs in 3-D, so they can be viewed from various angles.

Practical TECH

Graphics File Formats

The term *bitmap* provides a general description of a type of file, but it is also a specific file format (BMP) with a .bmp extension. Some other file formats that are also bitmap graphics in the larger sense of the word include portable network graphics (PNG), graphics interchange format (GIF), Joint Photographic Experts Group (JPEG, pronounced "jay-peg"), and tagged image file format (TIFF). Each of these formats has its own benefits and drawbacks.

Some graphics formats support greater color depth than others. For example, a GIF file has a limit of 8 bits per pixel, for a maximum of 256 colors per image. This means that GIF isn't a very good format for photos. The PNG format supports up to 24-bit color. Both GIF and PNG are designed primarily for online use; they don't work well for high-quality print publications, such as magazines.

Both PNG and GIF employ *lossless compression* to make file sizes smaller. In lossless compression, the file loses no quality by being compressed, and when it's decompressed, it retains its original properties. Other graphics formats, however, employ *lossy compression*. When a file is saved in such a format, its quality is permanently reduced to make the file size smaller. JPEG is an example of a format that uses lossy compression. JPEG format's compression is adjustable. The user saving the file can specify an amount of compression and corresponding amount of loss of image quality—whatever is appropriate for the situation at hand. In contrast, the BMP image format does not employ compression of any kind.

TIFF format is designed for high-quality images in print publications. High-quality digital cameras usually save pictures in TIFF format. While TIFF does support some lossless compression, overall its files are larger than the same size images in other formats. TIFF supports not only the red-green-blue (RGB) color model common to most home computer and printer systems but also the cyan-magenta-yellow-black (CMYK) color model used in professional printing.

CAD software helps technical professionals design objects for manufacturing and construction.

Once a design has been created, changes can easily be made to it until it's finalized. For instance, an aircraft engineer designing a new type of aircraft can use CAD software to test many versions of the design before it's approved and the first prototype is built. Using this process can save companies considerable time and money by eliminating defective designs before beginning production.

Full-feature CAD applications, such as AutoCAD, are very expensive. Using them may also require special computer workstations that have more powerful processors and more RAM than standard desktop PCs typically have. Some producers of CAD software offer scaled-down versions of their more expensive software for use by small businesses and for individual and home use.

Animation Software

Film animation used to be a labor-intensive industry, with hundreds of artists drawing cartoon images frame by frame. The same was true of stop-motion photography; to capture live action one frame at a time, an assistant moved a model a fraction of an inch for each new frame. Movie making is changing, however, and more and more films are being made with the aid of **computer-generated imagery (CGI)**. With CGI programs, no pen touches paper to create an animated world. And the quality is so good that the effects created with CGI are more or less indistinguishable from those created using models and other tricks in older movies.

The cost savings in movie making are also significant with CGI. It's far cheaper to use a computer program to draw a dinosaur than it is to create a realistic robotic dinosaur. And instead of building and exploding a model of a spaceship or a building, the same effect can be achieved through computer animation. Even better, the computer animation can be easily manipulated; any image can be redrawn until it's just exactly right.

CGI isn't something that the average user would attempt, because the software is expensive and the learning curve for using it is steep. One popular application that professionals use is Lightwave by NewTek. Many different tools for CGI professionals are also available from Autodesk, a company that's a leader in CAD software.

Audio-Editing Software

Computers can store, edit, copy, and reproduce sounds, as you learned in Chapter 2 when discussing audio adapters. Sound files vary first and foremost depending on their origin: analog or digital. A **waveform** (often abbreviated *wave* or *WAV*) file is a sound file that has an analog origin—that is, an origin outside a computer system. If you sing into a microphone or record an instrument being played, the sound waves coming from it go through a process called **sampling**, in which they are recorded thousands of times per second, creating a digitized version. When the digitized clip is played back, it sounds to a human ear just like the original live version.

The quality of the recording depends in large part on the number of samples taken per second. A human voice can be captured clearly when sampled at about 11 kilohertz (KHz), or 11,000 digital measurements per second. For this reason, voice equipment such as digital cell phones and voice recording devices usually encode sound at or near this rate. Clear, sharp musical reproductions are recorded at 44 KHz—almost four times the rate used for voice recordings. Creating these recorded sounds as stereo (two-channel) music requires twice as many measurements per second. That's the quality level of most music CDs and DVDs.

The number of bits used to describe each sample is known as the **bit depth**. CD-quality music uses 16 bits per sample, resulting in a file that is about 10 megabytes in size per one minute of recording. In fact, one minute of CD-quality stereo music requires about 10 megabytes (MB) of sound data. That means that one CD with a 650 MB capacity holds just over an hour's worth of music. Audio CDs use a special file format called **CD audio (CDA) format** to store music files. The commercial audio CDs you buy store tracks in this format, and so do those you burn yourself using your computer's CD burner.

A **wave file format** is a noncompressed file type identified with a .wav extension, used to produce any kind of sound. Like a graphic file, a wave file can be compressed to make it take up less disk space. The most popular compression format is the MP3 format. This format takes a wave file and reduces its size by about 90 percent, leaving behind a high-quality reproduction. This means that a 30 MB wave file will end up as a 3 MB MP3 file. MP3 uses a data compression system similar to that used in JPEG files. Only a highly sensitive ear can hear any difference in the music quality after compression. This dramatic reduction in size, combined with very little loss in quality, has led to an explosion in the use of the MP3 file format.

The main drawback to using a compressed format is that not all audio music players support it. Older car and home stereo systems may not support MP3 and other compressed formats; they may require CDs in the traditional CDA format. Other wave compression file formats include Windows Media Audio (WMA) format, which was developed by Microsoft, and the Advanced Audio Coding (AAC) format, which was designed to be the successor to MP3.

In contrast to a waveform file, an all-digital music file isn't analog in origin and it's created, not recorded. This type of music clip is known as **Musical Instrument Digital Interface (MIDI)**, and it's created by digitally simulating the sounds of various musical instruments. A digital piano keyboard can be connected to a computer to record MIDI music, and the software that accepts the input can be programmed to make the piano sound like any of dozens of different instruments. A skilled musical composer can build an entire orchestral performance—woodwind, string, brass, and percussion instruments—with a single digital keyboard by allowing the MIDI software to simulate each instrument as its part is performed.

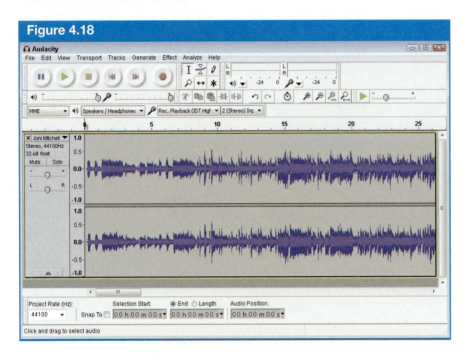

Figure 4.18

Audio-editing programs, such as Audacity, represent sound waves graphically and enable you to crop and adjust them.

An advantage of MIDI files is that they are extremely small and compact compared with wave music files. The main drawback of MIDI is that the output doesn't sound exactly like the instruments it's simulating (although with high-quality software and hardware, it can come close).

You can record and edit audio files with a variety of applications: from free hobbyist-quality programs to those designed for professional audio technicians. Figure 4.18 shows a screenshot of Audacity, a free audio-editing program that supports many formats and capabilities. Consumer-level programs, such as Roxio Creator NXT, offer a variety of applications designed for casual users, including the ability to burn CDs and DVDs and perform basic editing.

Video-Editing Software

Video clips are essentially groups of still images, or **frames**, that are played back in a certain order, at a certain rate (the frame rate), and accompanied by an audio soundtrack stored within the same container file. **Video-editing software** enables you to import digital video clips that you have taken with your own video camera or acquired from another source and then modify them in various ways. For instance, you can combine video with audio, superimpose text over the top of the video clip, edit out certain sections, and much more, depending on the video-editing software you are using.

Video-editing software can also compress video clips. The capacity for data compression with movies is in many ways greater than with music or still images. In a digital video clip, most parts of any given frame are identical to those in the previous one. This means that for each frame, it's necessary to store only the portion of the frame that's changed from the previous frame, rather than every pixel. For this reason, compressed movies maintain good quality despite being dramatically reduced in size.

Video-editing software ranges from simple programs intended for amateurs to the powerful programs used by movie-making professionals. Adobe Premiere Elements is a full-featured tool for building movies out of different types of content, including sounds, still images, and raw video footage. Other programs for video editing include Sony Vegas Pro and CyberLink PowerDirector.

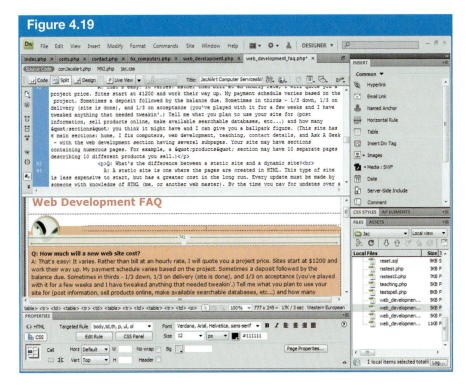

Figure 4.19

Web authoring software enables users to create web pages without having to learn web programming.

Web Authoring Software

Web authoring software (shown in Figure 4.19) helps users develop web pages without having to learn web programming. Software packages such as Adobe DreamWeaver CC and Microsoft Expression Web use a **WYSIWYG** (what you see is what you get) approach to web page development. This means that during the development process, you can see the layout and content of the web page within the authoring software.

Basic web creation software focuses on generating code in Hypertext Markup Language (HTML). However, not all of the content found on web pages today can be generated in HTML. More and more sites are including interactive animation and video effects that are created in other formats and then integrated into the web page.

The most popular of these formats are Adobe Flash and Adobe Shockwave. Adobe Flash is a file format in which you can create multimedia content that includes vector graphics and animations. Flash can even be used to create games and rich Internet applications (RIAs) that can be played back in a web browser that has the Adobe Flash Player plug-in. Flash files are created in a program called *Adobe Flash Professional CC*. Adobe Shockwave is a similar file format but has more capabilities. A browser that has the Shockwave plug-in installed can play Shockwave content, which can include both animation and user interactivity. Shockwave content is created using Adobe Director.

Recheck 4.4
Recheck your understanding of the concepts covered by this objective.

Cutting Edge

HTML5

In HTML4 and earlier versions of HTML, the text and its formatting were implemented in HTML, but many types of graphical and interactive content were handled by external formats such as Adobe Flash. That may change with HTML5, which includes support for new types of content through the use of *<video>*, *<audio>*, and *<canvas>* elements. HTML5 provides scripting APIs (application programming interfaces) that can be used with JavaScript to create active content that doesn't rely on third-party plug-ins and players to deliver active content.

4.5 Understanding Gaming Software

 **Precheck 4.5**

Check your understanding
of the concepts covered
by this objective.

Although many people would have you believe that they keep computers around strictly for serious reasons, the majority of them also play games on their computers. In fact, the Entertainment Software Association estimates that 58 percent of all Americans play video games and that the average age of a game player is 30. (See Figure 4.20 for more interesting statistics on game playing in the United States.)

These figures represents a broad section of the population, but then, gaming is a broad subject, including everything from casual Facebook games to the very latest in shoot-em-up monster action. Computer-based versions have been created of almost every traditional card and board game you can imagine, as well as casino games, fantasy-world exploration games, character-based games, city- and civilization-building games, and of course, the very popular first-person shooter games, in which you see what the character sees as you move through a virtual world.

Types of Gaming Software

Gaming software falls into three broad categories depending on the device used to play the game: dedicated gaming devices, PCs, and mobile devices like smartphones.

Applications for Dedicated Gaming Devices Companies that develop video games usually do so for multiple platforms. As you learned in Chapter 2, a *platform* is a type of hardware. Microsoft Windows is one platform (sometimes referred to as *PC*); Apple Macintosh is another. A **game console** is a platform designed specifically for running game software. A game consoles typically uses a TV as a monitor and hand-held controls such as game pads, steering wheels, and joysticks for input. Motion sensors, cameras, and other physical feedback devices are also available, so your whole body can control input. These devices are also available for PCs, so you can enjoy a full gaming experience with applications developed for delivery on your personal computer.

Game consoles have powerful central processing units (CPUs) and display adapters that are optimized for graphics-intensive games with a lot of motion. Game consoles provide sound support through the TV's speakers, along with support for external speaker systems. Modern game consoles usually have Internet connectivity (wired, wireless, or both), so game players can play some games collaboratively online. Users may also be able to download new games online and to download and install game

Figure 4.20

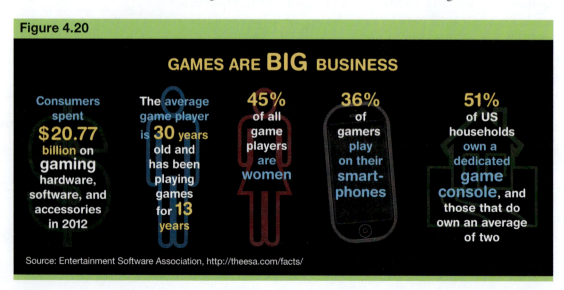

GAMES ARE **BIG** BUSINESS

Consumers spent **$20.77** billion on **gaming** hardware, software, and accessories in 2012

The average game player is **30** years old and has been playing games for **13** years

45% of all game players are women

36% of gamers play on their smart-phones

51% of US households own a dedicated **game console,** and those that do own an average of two

Source: Entertainment Software Association, http://theesa.com/facts/

Game consoles typically come with one or more input devices optimized for game playing, such as the game pad, left, steering wheel, middle, and joystick, right, shown here.

updates. Some of the most popular gaming console systems are Microsoft XBox, Nintendo Wii, and Sony PlayStation.

Versions of games designed for a particular game console have system requirements consistent with that console. For example, if you buy a game designed for the Xbox 360, it will play on any Xbox 360—even the model with the minimum amount of RAM and storage.

Applications for PCs With gaming software developed for installation on PCs, you will need to consult the application's system requirements to determine whether the game will run on your particular computer. **System requirements** include the minimum CPU speed, amount of RAM, and amount of disk space required to install and run the application. The system requirements are printed on the box the game comes in, if you buy it retail, and can also be found on the manufacturer's website.

The system requirements for a game might include a minimum CPU speed, a minimum amount of RAM, a certain brand or model of display adapter, and/or an amount of RAM dedicated to the display adapter. For example, Figure 4.21 shows the system requirements provided on the web page for Diablo III, a popular game that has some strict requirements for the computers on which it will run. If your

Figure 4.21

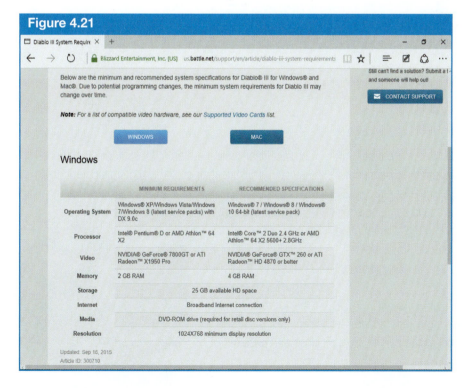

Check a game's system requirements before buying it to make sure your computer will run it well.

computer doesn't meet or exceed the system requirements, the game might not install or run at all, or it might run slowly or with audio or video distortion.

Game Ratings

Not all games are suitable for all users. Young children shouldn't have access to games with violent or sexual themes, for example, or games that include illegal activity or drug use. Because parents can't possibly prescreen every part of every game before their children play it, they rely on game ratings to determine what games are suitable for children of various ages.

The game rating system summarized in Table 4.2 is administered by the **Entertainment Software Ratings Board (ESRB)**. It classifies each game according to the youngest suitable user. For example, games rated *T* for *Teens* are acceptable for

Table 4.2 Entertainment Software Ratings Board (ESRB) Game Ratings

Rating	Description
Early Childhood	Content that may be suitable for persons ages 3 and older. Titles in this category contain no material that parents will find inappropriate.
Everyone	Content that may be suitable for persons ages 6 and older. Titles in this category may contain minimal violence, some comic mischief, and/or mild language.
Everyone 10+	Content that may be suitable for persons ages 10 and older. Titles in this category may contain more cartoon, fantasy, or mild violence, as well as mild language and/or minimal suggestive themes.
Teen	Content that may be suitable for persons ages 13 and older. Titles in this category may contain violent content and/or strong language.
Mature	Content that may be suitable for persons ages 17 and older. Titles in this category may contain mature sexual themes, more intense violence, and/or strong language.
Adults Only	Content suitable only for adults—not intended for persons under the age of 18. Titles in this category may include graphic depictions of sex and/or violence.

Cutting Edge

Gaming-Optimized PCs

People who are serious about game playing are often people who don't mind spending more money on a computer to ensure the best possible gaming experience. A whole subclass of desktop computers (and some notebook computers) has been designed with game playing in mind. These computers have the very best of all the components that a game relies on, including CPU, RAM, display adapter, monitor, and sound.

But a gaming computer doesn't stop at having high-quality basic components. Gaming computers are often flashy models designed to express the personalities of their owners, with colored lights, colored components,

nontraditional cooling systems (for example, water cooling instead of traditional air cooling), semitransparent or unusually shaped cases, and elaborate logos. One popular line of gaming computers is Alienware, a division of Dell Computers. (Visit http://CUT6.emcp .net/Alienware to see their latest offerings and price out your ideal system.)

teenagers (ages 13+) and individuals older than that. The descriptions provided are the same ones that Microsoft provides in Windows in the *Family Safety* feature. (For more information about the ratings system, see **http://CUT6.emcp.net /ESRBratings**.)

Recheck 4.5
Recheck your understanding of the concepts covered by this objective.

4.6 Using Communications Software

One of the major reasons people use computers is to communicate with others. Software that enables communication over the Internet and the web is available for individual, home, and business use. These programs allow users to send and receive email, browse and search the web, engage in group communications and discussions, and participate in web conferencing activities.

Precheck 4.6
Check your understanding of the concepts covered by this objective.

Email Applications

Electronic mail (email) is rapidly becoming the main method of communication for many individual, home, and business users. Email involves the transmission and receipt of private electronic messages over a worldwide system of networks and email servers. Messages are sent and received within seconds or minutes, and transmission costs are minimal. Email is a **store-and-forward system**. Messages are forwarded to a mail server and then stored there until the recipient picks them up using either a web interface or an email application.

There are three main types of email accounts: web-based, POP3 and IMAP. Table 4.3 summarizes key points of comparison among these account types.

Table 4.3 Key Characteristics of Email Account Types

Characteristic	Web-Based	POP3	IMAP
Uses email client?	Depends on compatibility between the service and the email client	Yes	Yes
Web interface available?	Yes	Depends on provider	Depends on provider
Message storage location	Mail server	Local PC	Mail server
Key benefit(s)	Can be accessed via any web browser	Provides access to full features of email client; can view received mail even if no Internet connection is available	Provides access to full features of email client; can send and receive mail from multiple computers
Key drawback(s)	Web browser interface may not be full featured; account may not work with email client software	Email client should be used to access the account from only one PC, or the mail archive will be incomplete	Email client must be set up separately on each PC; no access to stored email if no Internet connection

Web-based email accounts are available through Yahoo! Mail, Gmail (Google Mail), Microsoft Hotmail, and Microsoft Outlook.com. You don't need any special software to read and compose email with one of these accounts; you simply open a web browser and navigate to the page for that email service. Messages remain on the host company's server, and you can access your inbox from any computer. This type of account is suitable for someone who frequently checks his or her email from different computers and devices. The quality and features of the web-based interface vary depending on the provider. Figure 4.22 shows how an Inbox looks in Outlook.com.

A user who sticks with one computer most of the time may prefer a traditional email account, which is sometimes called a *POP* or *POP3* account. (*POP* stands for Post Office Protocol.) This type of email account uses an email client application installed on the user's main PC. An **email client** is an application designed specifically for sending, receiving, storing, and organizing email messages. An email client may have special features that aren't found in a web-based email interface—for instance, linking scheduled meetings to your calendar, flagging messages with high or low importance, and scheduling mail to be delivered after a specified date and time.

After messages are downloaded from the mail server to the email client, they are usually deleted from the mail server and exist only in the local PC's email client. A web-based interface may be available for checking mail while away from the main PC, but mail is organized and stored primarily on that PC. Therefore, this isn't a good type of account for someone who switches between several computers. Although this type of account is commonly known as POP3, POP3 is actually only the protocol for receiving email; there's a separate protocol commonly paired with it for sending email called SMTP (which stands for *Simple Mail Transfer Protocol*).

An alternative for someone who uses several computers but wants to use an email client is IMAP (which stands for *Internet Message Access Protocol*). An IMAP account keeps all the messages on the mail server and provides on-the-spot access to them via an email client when prompted to do so. The email client doesn't maintain local mail

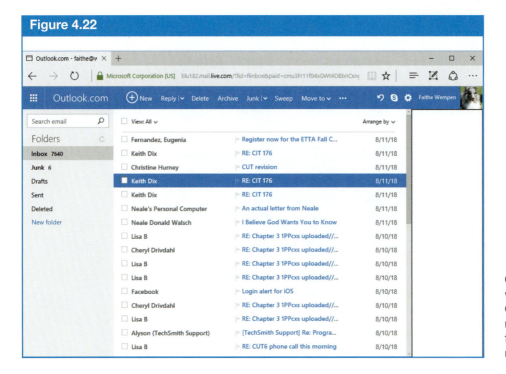

Figure 4.22

Outlook.com provides web-based access to email. Outlook.com's file management tools include options for deleting, archiving, and moving messages.

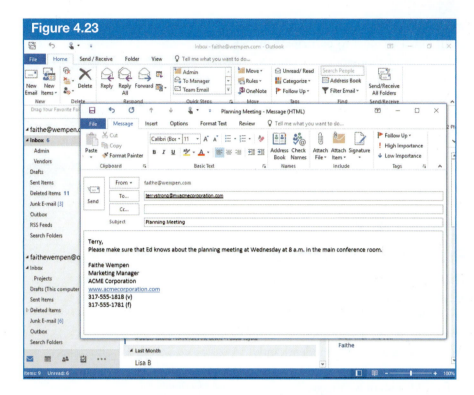

Figure 4.23

Outlook 2016 is a powerful program for working with email. The formatting tools available for messages are similar to those of other Microsoft Office applications, such as Word and PowerPoint.

folders; instead, it queries the server for the folders and their contents when it connects to send and receive mail. You can use the same email client software to work with both POP3 and IMAP accounts. Some email client software also enables you to set up web-based email accounts and work with them as if they were POP3 or IMAP, but the client software may have limitations on which services it supports.

Examples of email clients include Microsoft Outlook, Windows Live Mail, Eudora, and Mozilla Thunderbird. Outlook is more than just an email client; it also stores and organizes personal information, such as contacts, appointments, and tasks. Figure 4.23 shows how an email message looks after being composed in Outlook 2016.

Web Browser Applications

A web browser is an application that enables users to read web-based content and use web-based applications. Microsoft's Internet Explorer comes with Windows, and Windows 10 also includes another browser, Microsoft Edge. Other popular browsers include Google Chrome, Mozilla Firefox, Safari (the default browser in Mac OS X), and Opera. Web browsers are covered in detail in Chapter 5.

Instant Messaging (IM) and Chat Software

Instant messaging (IM) is a technology that enables people to communicate privately with other users over the Internet in real time. Many IM services are available, including Yahoo! Messenger and AOL Instant Messenger (AIM). Each service has its own IM software. Applications are also available that can connect to multiple IM services in a single interface, such as Trillian (created by Cerulean Studios). Instant messaging was originally a text-only medium, but most IM clients now also support sharing of photos, files, sounds, and even videos. Some social networking sites, like Facebook, also offer their own IM services.

In addition to the large commercial IM services, there are Internet chat servers, where you can talk to multiple people in a public forum. You can access most of these servers through an Internet relay chat (IRC) client application. IRC servers have channels, and you can join a channel to participate in the discussion going on there. Hundreds of thousands of channels are available on more than 1,500 IRC servers worldwide.

Instant messaging can be used on all types of devices, including PCs, handheld computers, notebook computers, and web-enabled cell phones and smartphones. PCs, handheld computers, and notebook computers require IM software to be installed, whereas cell phones and smartphones often have built-in messaging capabilities. Subscribers to instant messaging services must have IM software installed on their computers. Figure 4.24 shows an IM client window on a Windows-based PC with Yahoo! Messenger software.

Voice over Internet Protocol (VoIP) Software

Voice over Internet Protocol (VoIP) is the technology that Internet phone services use. Rather than rely on traditional phone lines, this kind of service sends and receives phone calls digitally over your Internet connection. A VoIP system is driven by a VoIP modem that connects to your Internet service box (such as a cable modem) and to a telephone jack in your home or business, serving as a bridge between the two. One example of a VoIP system is Vonage.

VoIP is best known for replacing analog telephone service, but its capabilities are much broader. For example, services like Microsoft Skype enable video chatting by computer using webcams and the computers' microphones and speakers. Apple's Mac OS X and iOS 7 and higher operating systems for mobile devices also include video chat capabilities through the FaceTime application, and many other video chat services are also available. Some IM programs, such as Yahoo! Messenger, also offer video chatting capabilities, blurring the line between IM and VoIP.

Web Conferencing Software

Web conferencing is an enhanced, group participation version of VoIP. Groups of people can have joint conversations online, including video chat, instant messaging, and application sharing. Participants can show one another presentations, diagrams, documents, and spreadsheets within the web conferencing software, as well as draw on a virtual whiteboard and send one another private instant messages as the meeting progresses. For the audio portion of the meeting, users can either use Internet voice capabilities with their computer's microphone or dial in using their telephone.

Because it saves time and travel expenses, many businesses are promoting the use of web conferencing software over face-to-face meetings. Some web conferencing software requires users to download a small application onto their computer—but most is completely web-based, requiring only a browser on each participant's computer. Accusoft Centra, Cisco WebEx, Cisco Unified MeetingPlace, and Citrix GoToMeeting are some examples of web conferencing software.

Groupware

Groupware, which is also called *collaboration software*, allows people to share information and collaborate on a project, such as designing a new product or preparing an employee manual. Groupware can be used over a local area network (LAN), wide area

Figure 4.24

A Yahoo! Messenger IM client window enables you to communicate with people in your *Contacts* list.

network (WAN), or the Internet. All group members must use the same groupware program to collaborate on a project.

Microsoft produces a groupware application called *SharePoint* that enables groups of users to collaborate on documents of all types. SharePoint has robust features for managing the sharing of permission levels and creating clear accountability chains that document who reviewed a document, what changes were made, and who approved them. SharePoint is installed on a company's own servers and creates an intranet environment (or a web browser–based internal network). Microsoft Office 365 offers group management capabilities similar to those provided by SharePoint but for smaller groups. Office 365 also manages and stores the group management software in Microsoft's cloud environment, rather than on the company's own server.

Most groupware applications include an address book of members' contact information and an appointment calendar. One desirable feature is a scheduling calendar that allows each member to track the schedules of the other members. Doing so makes it possible to coordinate activities and arrange meetings to discuss project activities and other matters.

Shared calendaring is also a part of Microsoft Exchange, a mail server technology that some large organizations use to manage their email systems, instead of relying on an Internet service provider (ISP). On an Exchange server, users can not only send and receive email, but also use many features of Microsoft Outlook, such as meeting scheduling, calendar sharing, and global address book management.

Social Media Apps

If you use social media sites, such as Facebook and Pinterest, you probably access them through your web browser on a desktop or notebook PC. When you access these sites on a mobile device, like a tablet or smartphone, using the web-based interface is sometimes awkward, because the sites aren't optimized for small-screen use, slower Internet speed, and data usage limitations. To improve the experience on mobile devices, many social media sites provide customized apps. For example, Facebook provides mobile apps for iPhone, Windows Phone, and Android users. Mobile apps are also available for Snapchat, Instagram, Pinterest, Twitter, and many other sites.

Activity 4.6.1

Article
Collaboration Software Trends

Activity 4.6.2

Video
Mobile Apps

Recheck **4.6**
Recheck your understanding of the concepts covered by this objective.

Hotspot

Can You Meet Me Now?

MoSoSo stands for Mobile Social Software, and it's the logical extension of social networking services, such as Twitter and Facebook. Accessible from either a mobile phone or a laptop, MoSoSo weaves time and location into digital networking to help individuals find people near them with similar interests and current needs. For example, if at 2:00 a.m. you are sleepless in your dorm and wonder if anyone wants to go in with you on a pizza, a MoSoSo might be able to find you a dinner companion.

The challenge to makers of MoSoSo software is adoption. If only a few people use the software, the ones who do will stop checking it because they won't ever have any success with it. Many MoSoSo companies have come and

gone as their founders have attempted to provide social connection services to high school and college students.

One company that has stayed in business (although its focus has changed) is Rave Mobile Safety (formerly Rave Wireless). Rave Mobile Safety provides a MoSoSo suite of applications that some university campuses, 911 centers, and public safety organizations use to connect people who need emergency services with the providers of those services. For example, a college campus might use Rave Mobile Safety software to enable students walking home at night from a class to connect to a companion to walk with or to contact the university police if they are harassed.

Chapter Summary

➲ *An interactive **Chapter Summary**, **Study Notes**, and a **Slide Presentation** with audio are available from the links menu on this page in your ebook.*

4.1 Distinguishing between Types of Application Software

Application software can be categorized as **individual application software**, **collaboration software**, or **vertical application software** based on the number of people it serves at once. Application software can also be divided into **desktop applications** versus **apps**.

In addition, software can be categorized by how it's developed and sold: as **commercial software**, **shareware**, or **freeware**. Commercial software may have **software piracy** features, such as a **registration key** or **activation** requirement. The terms for use of an application are determined by its **license agreement**. Companies that need many copies of an application may choose to buy a **per-user site license** or a **per-seat site license**. Free software that others may modify and redistribute is available in the **public domain**, and the developers make the **source code** available along with the compiled application.

4.2 Using Business Productivity Software

Business productivity software provides tools for people to accomplish business tasks, such as writing, performing calculations, and storing information. **Word-processing software** is used to create many types of text-based documents, either from scratch or using a **template**. You position the **insertion point** in the document and then type the desired text. Most word-processing applications have a **spelling checker** and **grammar checker** and enable **text formatting**, **paragraph formatting**, and **document formatting**, as well as the creation and use of **styles**. A **print preview** feature shows the document as it will look when printed. **Desktop publishing software** enables users to create complex page layouts with text and graphics.

Spreadsheet software enables you to organize, calculate, and present numerical data. Numerical entries are called **values**, and the instructions for calculating them are called **formulas**. Formulas can contain **functions**, which are named instructions for performing a calculation (such as COUNT and AVERAGE). A spreadsheet consists of **cells** arranged in a grid of rows and columns; each cell can be formatted separately. You can make **charts** based on the values in cells and record **macros** (sets of memorized steps) to save time in performing commonly repeated tasks.

A database is a collection of data organized into one or more data tables. Each table contains records, which are collections of data about specific instances. The parts of a record are called *fields* (for example, *FirstName* and *LastName*). Database software is called a **database management system (DBMS)**.

A large database is called an **enterprise database**, and it may be stored and managed using professional tools such as Oracle Database and structured query language (SQL). A smaller database might be created in a personal program such as Microsoft Access and stored on an individual PC or server. Databases that have multiple tables that are connected are known as *relational databases*; most business databases are relational. In addition to tables, a database can also have saved forms, reports, and queries that can be used to view and modify the data.

Presentation graphics software allows users to create computerized slide shows. A **slide** is an individual page or screen in a presentation. A **slide show** may consist of any number of slides. Slides can incorporate many types of content, including text, photos, **clip art**, charts, and tables.

A **software suite** combines multiple applications in a single package. Microsoft Office, for example, combines Word, PowerPoint, Excel, and other applications. The applications within a suite have a common interface style. You can **embed** or **link** content between applications and documents not only in suites but in any applications that support **object linking and embedding (OLE)**.

Personal information management (PIM) software helps organize your schedule and activities by storing contacts, calendars, lists, and notes in one place. A PIM application may also serve as an email application. **Project management software** provides tools for managing the resources, people, and locations involved in a major business initiative, such as constructing a new building or organizing an event. **Accounting software** helps a company track its accounts payable, accounts receivable, payroll, sales, and so on. Note-taking software (such as Microsoft OneNote) helps bring together different types of content for logical sorting and organizing.

4.3 Selecting Personal Productivity and Lifestyle Software

Personal software is designed for individuals to use for their own enrichment and entertainment. Lifestyle and hobby software helps users plan and track their hobbies such as gardening or fitness. **Legal software** helps users plan and prepare legal documents. **Personal finance software** helps users pay bills and track finances. **Tax preparation software** helps them fill out federal and state tax forms. Encyclopedias and dictionaries provide reference sources. **Tutorials** provide step-by-step learning; this is sometimes called **computer-based training**.

4.4 Exploring Graphics and Multimedia Software

Painting and drawing programs both create and modify artwork, but in different formats. **Painting software** works with bitmap images, also called **raster images**. **Drawing software** creates and edits **vector graphics**, which are math-based drawings. **Photo-editing software** is a variant of painting software that is used to correct common problems in photos, such as overexposure and red-eye.

3-D modeling programs and **computer-aided design (CAD)** software also use vector graphics. These programs are used to create sophisticated technical drawings and models in fields such as manufacturing and architecture, and they are also used to create the graphics in many video games. A **wireframe** (outline) is first constructed, and then **texture** and color are applied to the surface. Animation software extends 3-D modeling to create objects that appear to move. Professional animation software is responsible for the **computer-generated imagery (CGI)** in some movies.

Audio-editing software records and modifies **waveform** sounds, which are an analog in origin and **sampled** to create digital versions. Uncompressed waveform recordings, such as the **CD audio (CDA) format**, take up a great deal of disk space. Compressed versions, including MP3, Advanced Audio Coding (AAC), and Windows Media Audio (WMA) formats, are much more compact but require a computer (or compression-aware player) to decompress and play back the clips.

A video clip is a group of still-image **frames** that plays back sequentially along with a digital audio track. Video clips can be edited with **video-editing software**.

Web authoring software enables users to develop web pages without having to learn programming. This software uses a **WYSIWYG** interface to show the page being developed as it will appear in a browser. Web pages are saved in Hypertext Markup Language (HTML), but not all web content is in that format. Animated multimedia content and interactive content are sometimes generated in programs such as Adobe Flash and Adobe Shockwave.

4.5 Understanding Gaming Software

Games are available both for desktop and notebook PCs and for **game consoles**. Game consoles are optimized for game playing; they typically use a TV for output and a game pad, joystick, or steering wheel for input. Each game has **system requirements** that detail the minimum hardware specifications required to play that game on a particular platform.

Games have content ratings that advise consumers about the appropriate minimum age for a player. The most widely used rating system is from the **Entertainment Software Ratings Board (ESRB)** and includes ratings such as *Everyone*, *Teen*, and *Mature*.

4.6 Using Communications Software

Electronic mail (email) involves the transmission and receipt of private electronic messages using a **store-and-forward system**. Types of email accounts include web-based, POP3, and **IMAP**, and each type has both benefits and drawbacks. **Email client** software stores and organizes received and sent messages. A web browser is an application designed to view web pages. Most operating systems include a web browser, and you can also install a third-party web browser.

Instant messaging (IM) enables private, person-to-person conversations in real time. For public chats, Internet Relay Chat (IRC) provides access to IRC servers and channels all over the world. Voice over Internet Protocol (VoIP) is a technology that allows audio and video conversations over the Internet. It's used for Internet phone service and for video chatting via Skype and similar services. Web conferencing extends video chatting to groups of people and often includes application and screen-sharing capabilities.

Groupware, or collaboration software, enables people to share information on various projects. SharePoint is one common groupware product; using it enables companies to create private intranet environments, in which employees can collaborate. Office 365 is a Microsoft service that enables groups to collaborate via Microsoft's software cloud, which eliminates the need for a dedicated server for sharing. For companies that operate their own mail systems, Microsoft Exchange can not only manage a company's email but can also offer shared scheduling features.

Social media started out as a web-based system, but today people access social media on mobile devices using applications written specifically for a particular media site such as Facebook or Twitter.

Key Terms

Numbers indicate the pages where terms are first cited with their full definition in the chapter.
An alphabetized list of key terms with definitions is included in the end-of-book glossary.

 *An interactive **Glossary** is available from the links menu on this page in your ebook.*

Chapter Exercises

Complete the following exercises to assess your understanding of the material covered in this chapter.

*Interactive **Flash Cards** and an interactive **Game** are available from the links menu on this page in your ebook.*

Go to your SNAP Assignments page to complete the Terms Check, Knowledge Check, Key Principles, and Tech Illustrated exercises.

Terms Check: Matching

Match each type of software with its appropriate usage.

a.	accounting software	f	groupware
b.	computer-aided design software	g.	project management software
c.	database management system	h.	spreadsheet software
d.	desktop publishing software	i	VoIP software
e.	email client software	j.	word-processing software

__ 1. An inventory system for a small company

__ 2. A glossy, full-color magazine layout

__ 3. Tracking and scheduling resources for the construction of a building

__ 4. A dissertation for a PhD program

__ 5. Sales data for multiple regions across a six-month period, with charts that summarize the information

__ 6. Payroll and accounts payable processing

__ 7. Wireframe vector graphic modeling of a new product to be manufactured

__ 8. Sending and receiving messages using POP3 and SMTP

__ 9. Video chatting

__ 10. Sharing and collaborating on multiple files involved in a multiperson project

Knowledge Check: Multiple Choice

Choose the best answer for each question.

1. Custom-designed software that a large company uses to manage all its operations is
   a. individual application software.
   b. vertical application software.
   c. groupware.
   d. a desktop application suite.

2. Software _____ is the theft of commercial software by using it without paying for it.
   a. unregistration
   b. licensing
   c. activation
   d. piracy

3. A _____ site license grants the right to install software on a certain number of computers, regardless of how many people share them.
   a. per-seat
   b. per-user
   c. per-case
   d. domainwide

4. Public domain software makers typically release the _____ to the public.
   a. encryption key
   b. source code
   c. activation key
   d. compiler

5. QuarkXPress and Adobe InDesign are examples of what type of software?
   a. desktop publishing
   b. word processing
   c. spreadsheet
   d. database management

6. You might enter =*SUM(B2:B4)* as a formula in what type of software?
   a. database
   b. spreadsheet
   c. word processing
   d. project management

7. Macros, forms, reports, and queries are objects you might find in
   a. a slide show presentation.
   b. groupware.
   c. a spreadsheet.
   d. a database.

8. What is OLE?
   a. A method of sharing content between applications
   b. An animation feature in presentation software
   c. A type of database
   d. A method of automatically creating styles

9. What type of program edits bitmap files?
   a. audio editing
   b. video editing
   c. painting
   d. drawing

10. 3-D modeling is done with what type of image?
    a. GIF
    b. bitmap
    c. vector
    d. raster

 ## Key Principles: Completion

Complete each statement with the appropriate word or phrase.

1. A _____ _____ (2 words) is a computer that's designed specifically for running game software.

2. An email client application can send and receive email from POP3/SMTP and _____ account types.

3. Internet phone systems and video chat systems use Voice over _____ technology.

4. SharePoint is an example of _____ software, which allows people to share information and collaborate on projects.

5. Software accessed from a secure cloud on the Internet is called Software as a _____.

6. Software in the _____ _____ (2 words) can be freely modified by anyone using the source code provided.

7. A _____ _____ (2 words) manager is software that manages a variety of personal data, including contacts, appointments, and tasks.

8. A spreadsheet program might use a _____ to perform a complex mathematical calculation, such as determining the interest rate for a loan.

9. A _____ in a database is a collection of all the data about one specific instance, such as a particular transaction.

10. When you _____ content from one application into another, the pasted content retains its memory of what application it came from.

 ## Tech Illustrated: Figure Labeling

Fill in the blanks with the correct labels.

Data table in Microsoft Access

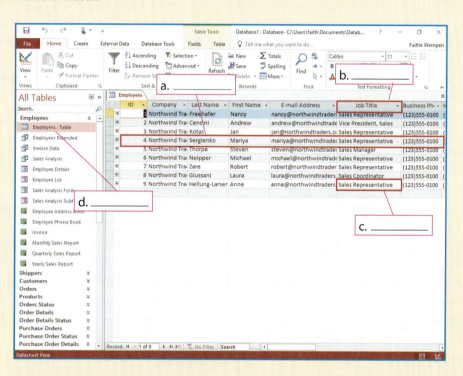

Tech to Come: Brainstorming New Uses

In groups or individually, contemplate the following questions and develop as many answers as you can.

1. Today, a smartphone or tablet app is available for almost any task you can imagine wanting to perform, but what about the tasks of the future? Imagine yourself moving through an average day 10 years from now. What will you be doing, and what kinds of apps will help you do it? Imagine what phone apps might look like then. Will they be voice activated? Will they interact with other devices in your environment?

2. On the desktop platform, multifunction programs like Microsoft Outlook combine several popular activities into a single interface: email, contact management, calendar scheduling, and to-do lists. But on smartphones and tablets, the trend is the opposite; many small, individual apps take care of specific tasks. Which trend will be dominant in the future?

3. Game consoles have traditionally focused only on running games. However, some models now include Internet access, and along with it comes access to online audio and video services, such as Netflix, Amazon Instant Video, and Hulu. What additional services do you think the customers of the future will want their game consoles to provide?

Tech Literacy: Internet Research and Writing

Conduct Internet research to find the information described, and then develop appropriate written responses based on your research. Be sure to document your sources using the MLA format. (See Chapter 1, Tech Literacy: Internet Research and Writing, page 38, to review MLA style guidelines.)

1. Can you accomplish everything you need to do on a computer using only the web? You might be surprised. Web-based applications are available not only for traditional online activities (such as web browsing and email) but also for improving productivity. Productivity applications include word processors, spreadsheets, and databases (such as Apache OpenOffice), and personal information management programs (such as Google Calendar), Make a list of everything you do with your computer, and then find a website where you can do each task.

2. What kind of program would help improve your productivity? Visit a computer store in your area. Select a particular productivity program on display, and read the product description on the package. What platform is the program written for? What's the price? Will the program run on your computer? For what purpose(s) might you be able to use the program?

3. What's hot in application software? Visit your school or public library and look through computer magazines to find an article that describes a new and innovative productivity software program. Write a summary of the program's purpose, main features, and specifications.

Include information about the user interface, amount of internal memory needed to run the program, and amount of disk space required to store the program. Why do you think this program is innovative? What needs does this product fulfill? Are competing products available on the market? Do you think the product will be a commercial success? Why or why not?

4. Is a picture worth a thousand words? Ask your instructor (or another person) for the name of a business or organization in your area that regularly uses presentation graphics software to provide information to clients or to train employees. Find out if you can obtain a copy of a presentation. Watch the slide show, and then write an evaluation of its effectiveness. List the technologies used (hardware and software), and describe the features that impressed you most.

5. The first "killer app" in the history of software development was VisiCalc. This early calculation program is credited with founding the electronic spreadsheet software industry and launching widespread sales of the personal computer. Research the meaning of the term "killer app," and propose some possibilities for the next one. Explain the reasons for your choice.

Tech Issues: Team Problem-Solving

In groups, develop possible solutions to the issues presented.

1. Instant messaging has become a popular communication tool in both social situations and the workplace. However, the IM applications offered by AOL and Yahoo! are not fully compatible. For example, AOL IM users can communicate only with other AOL IM users, and social media sites that have their own chat functions (such as Facebook) are separate as well. What will be the benefits and drawbacks for these companies if they open up their software to allow communication with anyone using any kind of instant messaging? How might this change come about?

2. Think about the different types of application software discussed in this chapter, and then determine how you might use some of them to organize activities in your life. Identify three software programs you might use if you were planning a vacation. Why did you pick these programs? What aspects of vacation planning does each program support?

3. Software piracy costs developers millions of dollars each year in lost revenue, and they pass those costs on to consumers in the form of higher prices. However, software companies must balance the aggressiveness of their antipiracy measures against consumers' concerns for convenience and privacy or risk having products that nobody wants to buy. As a consumer, what balance of higher prices versus convenience and privacy are you comfortable with? Keep in mind that the more lax a company is about piracy, the more each consumer will have to pay for the software to make up for those who get it for free.

Tech Timeline: Predicting Next Steps

Look at the timeline below, which outlines the key milestones in the evolution of encyclopedias from printed books to digital content. Think about the increase in information available and the rapid growth in computing technologies. Then predict two additional milestones in the encyclopedia marketplace that will likely occur within the next 20 years.

1768 The first section of the original *Encyclopaedia Britannica* is printed.

1917 The first *World Book Encyclopedia* is published.

1981 The first digital version of *Encyclopaedia Britannica* is created for use by LexisNexis subscribers.

1993 Microsoft announces the availability of the first release of *Encarta*, an online encyclopedia on CD-ROM.

1994 *Encyclopaedia Britannica* is made available on the Internet and on CD-ROM.

1998 The complete World Book Online website is launched.

2001 A multilingual encyclopedia called *Wikipedia* is launched and supported in an open source model.

2006 Wikipedia announces that the one-thousandth user-written article has been published.

2012 *Encyclopaedia Britannica* is no longer published in print—only online.

2015 Wikipedia reports that it contains over 5 million articles in English.

Ethical Dilemmas: Group Discussion and Debate

As a class or within an assigned group, discuss the following ethical dilemma.

When software is downloaded from the Internet and installed on a personal computer, it might contain spyware. *Spyware* is software that gathers information through an Internet connection without the user's knowledge. Some of the information commonly gathered includes the user's keystrokes, hardware configuration, and Internet configuration, as well as data from the user's hard drive and data from cookies. Typically, this information is gathered and sent to the spyware author, who then uses it for advertising purposes or sells the information to another party.

Do you consider this an invasion of privacy? Should it be illegal to include spyware inside another software program? What if the software license agreement includes a disclaimer that says spyware may be installed? Is it harmless if the information is just being gathered for market research? What other problems do you see with this technology? How might Internet users be protected from spyware?

Chapter 5

Plugging In to the Internet and All Its Resources

Chapter Goal

To learn how the Internet works and how you can use it properly to perform a variety of life-enhancing activities

Learning Objectives

5.1 Describe the overall types of activities made possible by the Internet.

5.2 Explain how to connect to the Internet, including needed hardware and software and different types of connections.

5.3 Discuss how the Internet delivers page information to a web browser from the specified IP address or URL as you navigate the web.

5.4 Describe the language used to create web pages and the basics of publishing to a website.

5.5 Describe how to use basic web browser techniques to view web pages and content.

5.6 Use fundamental search techniques to find information on the web.

5.7 Discuss diverse uses and services on the Internet, including the emergence of social media and services.

5.8 Behave appropriately as a member of the Internet community.

Green go-online icons indicate resources that are accessed from the links menu in your ebook.

SNAP icons indicate interactive resources that are available in SNAP. Go to your SNAP Assignments page to complete these quizzes, activities, and exercises.

5.1 Exploring Our World's Network: The Internet

Precheck 5.1

Check your understanding of the concepts covered by this objective.

The Internet is the largest computer network in the world. Its design closely resembles a client/server model, with network groups acting as clients and Internet service providers (ISPs) acting as servers. (You will learn more about networks and network structures in Chapter 6.) Since the launch of the Internet in the early 1970s, this enormous system has expanded to connect more than 3.2 billion users worldwide (see Figure 5.1).

Many experts within and beyond the information technology (IT) industry consider this vast structure of networked computers and telecommunications systems the most significant technical development of the twentieth century. The Internet has the potential to connect every person on Earth to a vast collection of resources, information, and services.

Individuals, organizations, businesses, and governments use the Internet to accomplish a number of different activities, which can be divided into these general categories:

- Communications
- Telecommuting and collaboration
- Entertainment and social connections
- Electronic commerce
- Research and reference
- Distance learning

This section provides an overview of these categories. See section 5.7, "Using Other Internet Resources and Services," on page 212, for more details on specific tasks you can accomplish on the Internet.

Communications

One of the chief functions of the Internet is to allow people to communicate with one another quickly and easily. Internet users can take advantage of a number of different communications applications, including email, instant messaging,

Figure 5.1

AS OF **2015**, THE **INTERNET** HAD MORE THAN **3.2 BILLION USERS WORLDWIDE**, VERSUS ABOUT **400 MILLION USERS** IN 2000

2015

2000

Source: Data from International Telecommunication Union (ITU)

🔅 Tracking Down Tech »»»»

Observing the Internet in Action

The Internet enables you to interact with people and information sources around the globe. Connecting to the Internet greatly expands what you can do with a computer or mobile device. You can take advantage of what the Internet has to offer nearly any place and any time using a variety of technologies, which you will learn about in this chapter. Complete this scavenger hunt to discover examples of the Internet in action on campus and beyond.

social networking services, video messaging, and more. Also, users are no longer tethered to the computer to use the Internet to communicate. Smartphones and other portable devices can enable you to communicate using various applications (apps) over a wireless connection to the Internet or a mobile network. In the case of a mobile (cellular) network, a device such as a tablet would have to be mobile capable and the user would have to have a mobile data plan for the device. Many restaurants and cafes, including popular chains such as Starbucks and McDonald's, offer free wireless service. Having this service lets users connect to the Internet with a laptop or other portable, mobile-capable device.

Telecommuting and Collaboration

Millions of workers now perform their work activities at home using a computer and Internet connection (see Figure 5.2). This activity is known as **telecommuting** (also called *teleworking*). Some employers have discovered that allowing employees to telecommute offers important advantages—for example, increased worker productivity, savings on travel costs to and from the workplace, and an opportunity to employ individuals who are highly productive but have physical limitations.

Activity 5.1.1

Video
Real-Time Meetings

Several types of telecommuting arrangements are possible. In some cases, the employer provides the employee with a computer and pays for some or all of the employee's cell phone and Internet service. In other cases, the employee supplies his or her own computer equipment and pays for necessary phone and Internet service plans. Generally, the employer identifies much of the software the employee will use, such as a particular email program or online (over the Internet) collaborative platform (which you will learn about in Chapter 7). Many telecommuting employees sign in to the company's email system and

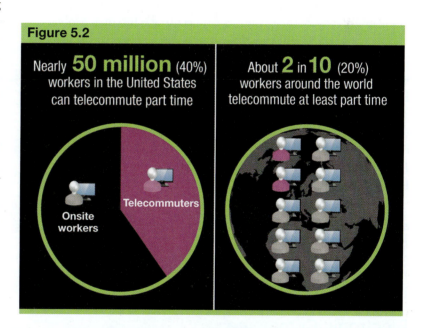

Figure 5.2

Nearly **50 million** (40%) workers in the United States can telecommute part time

Onsite workers

Telecommuters

About **2** in **10** (20%) workers around the world telecommute at least part time

Practical TECH

Saving Money on Mobile Service

The data plans for mobile phones and other devices can be expensive. You can save money, however, by taking advantage of the options offered by different carriers. For instance, most carriers allow you to share a data plan among multiple devices—perhaps two family phones and a tablet or two sharing one data plan. In such a case, if one user needs a data allowance but doesn't use it much, the users of the devices share the monthly data allowance provided by the plan. At least one wireless carrier (AT&T)

offers a data "day pass"; it lets you use the Internet with your device periodically for a reasonable fee (much less than you would spend for a monthly data plan). Another way to save is to have a small data plan and connect through wireless networks whenever possible. Most smartphones can connect to a home or other wireless network and through these connections avoid using the data allowance.

also sign in to file and project sharing systems hosted by the employer. Telecommuting employees might also participate in online video calls or meetings using forms of digital communication that are personal, immediate, and interactive.

Of course, the same tools that enable telecommuting also facilitate collaboration among employees working at multiple sites. Employees can work online with team members, as well as outside vendors and contractors, in other cities and countries.

Entertainment and Social Connections

Internet users of all ages take advantage of computers for entertainment purposes. A computer with the right components and accessories can imitate almost any entertainment device. You can play games, listen to music, and even watch movies and TV programs on your computer. You can also message or chat with friends, participate in online social platforms and services (such as online dating sites), place carryout orders or make dinner reservations, and connect socially with others in just about any way imaginable.

Today's dedicated gaming consoles have internal hardware similar to a personal computer (PC) and attach to a TV for display. For gaming, most of these consoles connect to the Internet. Mobile phones, tablets, and other portable devices (such as the iPod Touch) can also be used for online gaming and other forms of entertainment. To play online, the user must have a cellular or wireless Internet connection for the device.

An enormous number of both paid and free games are available online, including traditional games such as backgammon, checkers, and bridge. Users must buy software to play some games—for example, EVE Online and World of Warcraft. But most (if not all) games can be purchased online and then downloaded or played online.

Playing games with other users online (sometimes called *social gaming*) is just one way to make social connections using the Internet. Options for social media and other online social activities are expanding at a fast pace. Consumers spend a lot of money on online gaming. According to one research firm, worldwide revenue from social media, including income from social gaming, is growing rapidly (see Figure 5.3).

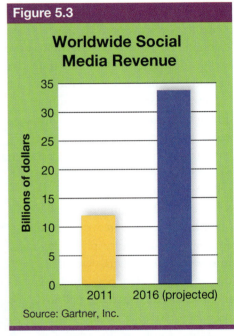

Figure 5.3

Worldwide Social Media Revenue

Source: Gartner, Inc.

Revenue from social media has grown rapidly worldwide—a trend that's expected to continue.

Electronic Commerce

Electronic commerce (e-commerce) involves exchanging business information, products, services, and payments online. E-commerce is commonly divided into two categories defined by the target audience: business to consumer (B2C) and business to business (B2B).

Online shopping makes up most of B2C e-commerce. The top retail category is clothing, followed by books, music, videos, auction items, toys, and computer hardware. Each year, retail e-commerce sales continue to grow. By the third quarter of 2015, sales had reached $87.55 billion, or 7.4 percent of all US commerce, according to estimates from the US Department of Commerce.

Many retailers post online catalogs that potential buyers can look through. The buyer can select items of interest and add them to a "shopping cart." This virtual shopping cart functions just like a real shopping cart, allowing the buyer to put items in the cart and remove them later, as desired. When the buyer finishes shopping, he or she proceeds through a virtual checkout. The buyer pays for the purchase by entering a credit card number or using another method of electronic payment. Within a few days, the purchased items arrive at the buyer's "ship to" address.

In addition to selling and advertising products and services to consumers, businesses are using the Internet for other purposes: to advertise products, buy goods from manufacturers and wholesalers, order raw materials, recruit employees, file government reports, and perform many other activities. These activities make up the B2B category of e-commerce. New ways for businesses to use the Internet are being discovered every day, and current uses are continually being improved to make them even more successful.

Consumers can purchase nearly any good or service online and have it shipped to a specific location, such as a home or business.

Research and Reference

The **World Wide Web (web)** is the part of the Internet that enables users to browse and search for information. Because of the web, thousands of opportunities have been created for people interested in research. Aided by the web's increasingly sophisticated search platforms, users can explore a wide range of topics, from anacondas to Zen Buddhism. Students, writers, historians, scientists, and other curious individuals rely on web-based resources to find and share facts and data as part of their pursuit for knowledge.

The numerous resources available on the web include materials from libraries and universities, government agencies, and databases around the world. Researchers can access online books, periodicals (magazines and journals), encyclopedias, photos, videos, and sound files from nearly any location. Users can also perform tasks such as verifying the spelling and use of a word in an online dictionary, answering a health question using medical and science sites, finding a mailing address using a people-search site, looking up property records on a government site, and getting directions to a location using a mapping site. In most cases, users can both read the information online and download it for later use.

Using a search engine within a web browser, the researcher has the tools needed to find practically anything on the web. Most college research projects today begin on the web, rather than in the library, using the student's favorite search engine. Searching for information on the Internet is discussed in section 5.6, "Searching for Information on the Internet," on page 209.

Tech Career Explorer

Checking Out TED

The mission of the nonprofit organization TED (Technology, Entertainment, and Design) is to spread inspired and innovative ideas worldwide. TED's primary means of spreading ideas is through recorded video talks by interesting and thought-provoking people. If you want to learn cutting-edge ideas about technology, personal and global challenges, and more, you can watch free TED Talks on those topics. Complete this exercise to explore a tech field that might interest you as a career.

Distance Learning

Many colleges and universities offer online courses and study programs in a form of education referred to as **distance learning**. Distance learning involves the electronic transfer of information, course materials, and testing materials between schools and students. A college or university typically delivers distance learning courses (also called *online courses*) to students using a type of online computing platform called a **learning management system (LMS)**.

Ready-made LMS platforms are available and provide a range of features. Typical features include pages that provide information about the course, communication tools such as online chat and email, online posting and grading of tests, and learning resources that support course content. The top two LMSs—WebCT and Blackboard— merged in 2006. The LMS has continued under the Blackboard name and includes the best of both original platforms. With Blackboard (see Figure 5.4), instructors can provide their own course content or use Blackboard-ready content developed by textbook publishers. Other LMSs are Moodle, Edmodo, and Desire2Learn.

Distance learning has become increasingly popular with students of all ages. It's especially popular with people whose interests aren't met by the course offerings of a standard or nearby college or university. Distance learning is also an attractive option

Figure 5.4

Blackboard provides numerous tools for online course delivery, including an activity stream feature and the ability to post content for both instructors and students.

Practical TECH

Free Online Learning Opportunities

You don't have to be working toward a degree to try online learning. Numerous online courseware sites have partnered with colleges, universities, and organizations such as museums to offer free online courses. One leading site, Coursera, offers more than 1,500 online courses from 100-plus partners. Another site, TED-Ed (**http://CUT6.emcp.net/TED-Ed**), offers more than 150,000 free online lessons. Some of these courses are based on

TED Talks, which are available at the TED website (**http://CUT6.emcp.net/TED**).

The number of free online courses continues to expand and includes offerings from Wikiversity, Udacity, and the OpenCourseWare Consortium, among others. See the section "Distance Learning Platforms" on page 226 to learn even more about these courses, including massive open online courses (MOOCs).

for students whose schedules or careers make it difficult to attend regular classes. Some business schools have distance learning programs and other options for individuals who want to earn a degree while working full time. For example, Duke University's Fuqua School of Business offers blended or hybrid courses in the master's in business administration (MBA) program. Blended or hybrid courses include both distance learning and onsite (at the school) study, providing students with the opportunity to earn a degree on a more flexible schedule while pursuing a career. The Duke MBA program provides online courses with weekend onsite study. Four-year colleges and universities, as well as many community colleges, offer distance learning courses as a low-cost, high-convenience way to get an education.

Recheck 5.1

Recheck your understanding of the concepts covered by this objective.

Precheck 5.2

Check your understanding of the concepts covered by this objective.

5.2 Connecting to the Internet

Billions of people throughout the world can connect to the Internet. Within each country, high-capacity networks operated by large telecommunications companies form the backbone of the Internet. Other organizations, including ISPs, purchase bandwidth from these high-capacity network providers, each of which is also known as a **network service provider (NSP)**. An **Internet service provider (ISP)** is an organization that provides user access to the Internet, usually charging a subscription fee. An ISP may share data with other ISPs and networks through **Internet exchange points (IXPs)**, as well as provide Internet connections to customers through a **point of presence (POP)**. High-volume, fiber-optic transmission lines form the Internet backbone and move data between the various connection points on what are known as *trunk lines*. In the United States, trunk lines are usually high-speed digital data transmission lines called *tier 1 (T1)* and *tier 3 (T3) lines*. A typical single T3 line to a location can operate from 28 to nearly 30 times faster than a single T1 line. The Internet backbone uses even faster fiber-optic transmission lines called *optical carrier (OC) lines*. The OC-768 lines in some sections transmit data at up to 40 gigabits per second. Carriers are continuing to update backbone networks to 100 gigabit speeds in the United States.

Businesses and organizations with high Internet bandwidth needs might pay the high cost of having a T1 or T3 connection. In some parts of the United States, high-speed fiber-optic connections are available for both commercial and residential users. However, most residential and small business users typically connect using some type of broadband connection, such as digital subscriber line (DSL), cable connection, or satellite Internet. Only a small number of users now connect via a traditional telephone landline.

Hands On

Setting Up a New Internet Connection in Your Operating System

No matter what type of broadband connection you have, once you have received the connecting hardware, called a *modem*, you will need to set up an Internet connection in your computer's operating system. If your ISP sends out an installation technician, he or she will usually set up the connection for you. This service is typical with satellite ISPs, for example. But if you purchase a modem independently or one is shipped from your ISP and you prefer not to use the installation software, you will need to set up the connection yourself. Follow the guidelines in this resource to connect a broadband modem directly to a Mac OS X or Windows operating system. (Setting up a wireless network and connecting the broadband modem to it is covered in Chapter 6.)

Figure 5.5

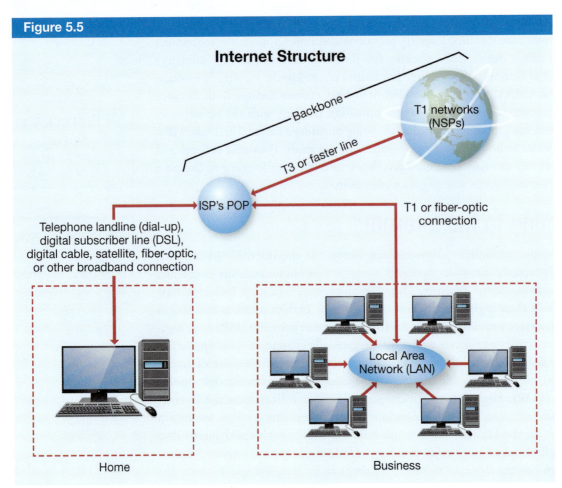

Internet Structure

Backbone

T3 or faster line

T1 networks (NSPs)

ISP's POP

Telephone landline (dial-up), digital subscriber line (DSL), digital cable, satellite, fiber-optic, or other broadband connection

T1 or fiber-optic connection

Local Area Network (LAN)

Home

Business

The structure of the Internet makes it possible for large volumes of data to be delivered to home and business users.

 **Activity 5.2.1**

Practice
The Structure of the Internet

Figure 5.5 illustrates the overall structure of the Internet, from the backbone to the connection provided to a user's home or business. Chapter 6 will provide more information about setting up a network.

Hardware and Software Requirements

The following equipment and software are required to connect to the Internet:

- A computer with an internal wireless or wired network adapter or wireless/ wired network card or USB adapter; a tablet device; or a smartphone
- A modem compatible with your connection type (DSL, cable, and so on)
- An account with an Internet service provider (ISP) or value-added network (VAN), including any locally installed equipment required, such as a cable connection or an Internet satellite dish
- Wireless and/or wired network equipment, if you want to share the Internet connection among multiple devices
- A web browser

As defined earlier, an ISP is a company that provides Internet access. Having access usually requires paying a fee but is sometimes free. (Firms that provide free access usually require subscribers to view advertisements when viewing web pages.) A **value-added network (VAN)** is a large ISP that provides specialized service or content, such as reports from the Reuters news service or access to a legal database. Nonetheless, all ISPs and online services can reach the same email users and websites.

The best-known ISPs offer service at a national level. But in the United States, some ISPs offer service only within a particular region based on the limits of the physical network. For example, a landline phone company might offer only dial-up or DSL Internet service in the states that it serves. Large ISPs provide local telephone numbers in several cities so that customers who travel outside their local areas can make dial-up connections without paying for long-distance calls. Today, most people access the Internet via wireless connections when traveling.

Types of Internet Connections

Users can get online using several types of Internet connections: dial-up, digital cable, DSL, wireless, fiber-optic, and satellite. All of these connection types except dial-up are considered broadband, or high-speed, connections. In 2015, about 67 percent of Americans over age 18 had DSL, digital cable, or satellite service, according to the Pew Research Center.

Table 5.1 compares the connection speeds used to **download** (receive) and **upload** (send) information. Internet transfer speeds are measured according to how many bits of data are transferred per second. Each **Kbps (kilobit per second)** represents 1,000 bits per second, and each **Mbps (megabit per second)** represents 1,000,000 bits per second. A **Gbps (gigabit per second)** is a billion bits per second.

Table 5.1 Comparison of Internet Connection Speeds

	Connection Hardware	Download Speed*	Upload Speed*
	Dial-up access with 56 Kbps modem	40–50 Kbps	28 Kbps
	Cable	Up to 105 Mbps	400–600 Kbps
	DSL	Up to 6 Mbps	Up to 768 Kbps
	Wireless and mobile	Varies widely	Varies widely
	Fiber-optic cable	Up to 1 Gbps	Up to 1 Gbps
	Satellite	Up to 15 Mbps	Up to 3 Mbps

* Download speed measures how quickly one computer can receive a file from another. In most cases, download speed is more important than upload speed. Upload speed measures how quickly a file can be sent from one computer to another.

Connection speeds vary depending on the type of plan purchased from the ISP; more expensive plans generally provide faster download speeds. Of course, having a fast download speed allows data to arrive and display more quickly on your computer and device. Having a fast download speed is also needed to perform activities such as viewing online videos and making calls over the Internet; both require high speeds to operate effectively.

Most of the connection types discussed in this section can be shared among several devices by connecting the modem to a local area network (LAN). For example, most users today share a connection at home by setting up a wireless LAN using a wireless router, which connects to a broadband modem, which then connects to the ISP service through a cable. Having a wireless setup makes it possible to connect computers and accessories (such as printers) to the network without wires. It also makes it possible for all of the connected computers and other devices (such as tablets and smartphones) to access the Internet connection. Figure 5.6 illustrates how a wireless Internet connection operates.

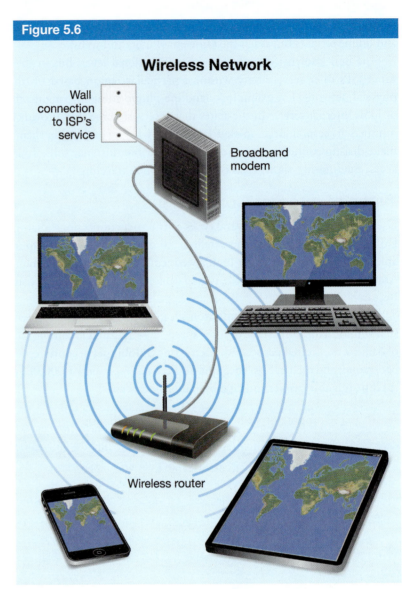

Figure 5.6

Wireless Network

Wall connection to ISP's service

Broadband modem

Wireless router

Having a wireless network enables numerous devices to access a single Internet connection.

Dial-up **Dial-up access** allows connecting to the Internet over a standard land-based telephone line by using a computer and a modem to dial into an ISP. Dial-up access is a feature typically included with the software provided by the ISP. After installing the software, the user can add a shortcut icon on his or her computer desktop; double-clicking on that icon will launch the connection.

Dial-up access is relatively inexpensive because of the slow connection speeds it provides, as noted earlier. To get faster connection speeds, the vast majority of US Internet users have upgraded to a **broadband connection**, or high-speed, Internet connection. Broadband connection speeds are better suited to online activities such as viewing videos. In some rural areas, power companies offer a form of Internet service called *broadband over powerline (BPL)*. BPL delivers Internet access over powerlines, similar to services that deliver access over phone lines.

Cable The same coaxial cable that provides cable TV service to a home or business can also provide Internet access. Cable TV companies such as Comcast and Time

Warner Cable provide a special modem and software for broadband. Having this type of connection allows simultaneous TV viewing and Internet usage. This service is available only in areas in which the provider has installed cable, however, which rules out many rural locations. In addition, with this type of service, the connection speed slows down as more subscribers sign up in a neighborhood or location. Comcast calls its service XFINITY Internet. Time Warner Cable offers several different Internet plans with names such as Ultimate and Extreme.

Digital Subscriber Line **Digital subscriber line (DSL) Internet service** is a form of broadband that's delivered over standard telephone lines. It's as fast as service using a cable modem and provides simultaneous web access and telephone use, but it has limited availability. DSL service is usually available only to users within three miles of the telephone carrier's digital subscriber line access multiplexer (DSLAM). A digital subscriber line is dedicated to one household and isn't shared with neighbors.

You can buy DSL service in a bundle with phone service from your phone company, or you can buy a naked DSL service, a connection without the accompanying phone service. Like dial-up, DSL has become less and less popular in the United States as consumers have shifted to faster broadband technologies.

Wireless One fast-growing segment of Internet service involves wireless broadband connections. Millions of wireless access points, or **Wi-Fi hotspots**, have sprung up worldwide, and the number is expected to continue to grow (see Figure 5.7). Using these hotspots, you can access the Internet in public places and even aboard airplanes using a computer (equipped with a wireless network card) or mobile device (such as a tablet or smartphone).

Just like you can create a wireless network at home, the owner of a coffee shop or other public location can create a Wi-Fi hotspot by sharing a broadband Internet connection through a wireless network. In some cases, the owner may protect the password for the wireless network so that only authorized customers can use it. In many other cases, though, using a Wi-Fi hotspot is free for customers and designated users. Some wireless service providers and private operators also charge a fee to provide access to their hotspots.

Wireless connections to the Internet can be slower than wired connections. Even so, they provide a great deal of flexibility and portability, because you aren't required to plug into a connection in a wall.

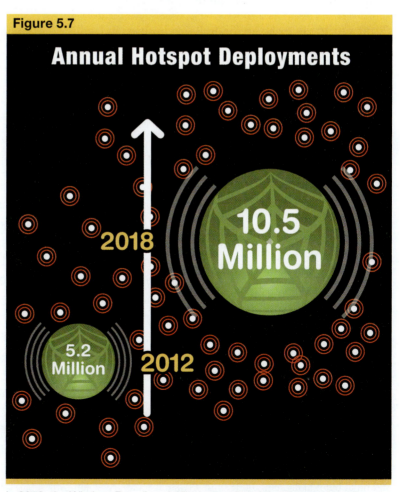

Figure 5.7

Annual Hotspot Deployments

2018 — 10.5 Million

2012 — 5.2 Million

In 2013, the Wireless Broadband Alliance predicted that the number of wireless hotspots worldwide would double within five years.

To guarantee that you will have access to hotspots while traveling, check the services offered by your mobile phone provider. Some providers offer access to a network of hotspots, either bundled as part of a plan or as an add-on service. Some providers also let you purchase short-term, prepaid access to enable your devices to connect to Wi-Fi hotspots. For example, AT&T offers prepaid DataConnect Pass plans in more than 100 countries, as well as global plans and both daily and weekly plans. AT&T also offers On the Spot one-time access, which lets you buy a session at one of its more than 30,000 hotspots for several dollars or less, depending on the location and session time. You can purchase this access even if you aren't an AT&T customer.

Wireless ISPs (also known as *Wi-Fi ISPs*) provide another form of wireless Internet access—one not many people know about. A Wi-Fi ISP uses directional antennas to direct wireless radio signals from one location to another within a particular area. Directing these signals creates a large hotspot, in effect, which provides continuous service within that area. Some cities have experimented with building this type of network to offer free wireless Internet access to the people that live and work in the area. Small wireless ISPs have also emerged in rural areas to offer a choice of services to customers who may not have access to other types of broadband. Service may be poor, however, in areas with lots of hills or trees.

Fiber Optic To make up for declining business in landline telephone service, large telecommunications providers in the United States and other countries are offering other services. Specifically, these telecom companies are delivering digital phone, TV, and Internet service to homes using fiber-optic cable. Verizon calls its service FiOS, and AT&T calls its service U-verse.

Hands On

Get Ready with Airplane Mode

To make sure you will be ready for your next trip, find airplane mode on your mobile device. Follow the steps presented in this resource.

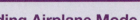 **Activity 5.2.2**

Video
Wireless Access Point

Hotspot

Understanding Airplane Mode

Making a call using a mobile phone during a commercial airline flight is prohibited by the Federal Aviation Association (FAA). However, the FAA does allow passengers to use some personal electronic devices (PEDs) during all phases of a flight, including takeoff and landing. Most major airlines offer Wi-Fi service, so now you can use your ebook reader or tablet throughout a flight. (Because of the sizes of notebook computers and certain devices, you must still stow them during takeoff and landing.) As of early 2014, additional rule changes with regard to the use of cell phones were also under consideration. Each carrier also may set its own specific policies for use of personal electronic devices, as well as setting fees (if any) for online wireless services.

There's one catch for using your device in flight—you must put it in airplane mode or otherwise disable cellular service in the device's settings. (Depending on the device and manufacturer, you may see another name for airplane mode, such as *flight mode*, *offline mode*, or *standalone mode*.) Using airplane mode prevents the device from sending and receiving calls, text messages, and other forms of data. Enabling airplane mode may also turn off additional signaling features that could interfere with the plane's avionics.

While in airplane mode, devices generally consume less power. This means that using airplane mode will help preserve battery life, which can be an advantage on a long flight.

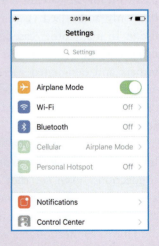

A fiber-optic cable bundles many strands of thin glass or plastic cable within an external sheath. In terms of service, fiber optics offers the advantages of freedom from electromagnetic interference and reduced signal loss; it also provides the greatest bandwidths over the longest distances. (Network bandwidth is discussed in more detail in Chapter 6.) A fiber-optic connection not only offers the speediest Internet downloads, but it can also carry digital TV and phone (voice) signals. This means that fiber optics allows the bundling of Internet, TV, and phone services. Some providers offer promotional discounts and free or discounted equipment to new bundle subscribers.

The biggest limitation of fiber optics is availability. Fiber-optic lines are expensive to install, so major providers have been slow to roll out this type of Internet service. The competition for providing fiber-optic cable is growing, however. Well-funded companies that haven't previously provided Internet or other content delivery services see the potential of fiber optics and are getting into the business. For example, Google Fiber has launched a digital Internet and TV service in several US cities, with more cities to follow. Google Fiber's unique hardware eliminates the need to have a separate modem and Wi-Fi router. Wireless network capability is built into Google's Network+ Box gigabit router. Google's TV Box can connect wirelessly to the signal from the Network Box and deliver HDTV.

Another great feature included with many fiber-optic TV bundles and some cable and satellite TV providers allows playing live TV or streaming other shows to a mobile device. After installing a free app on the device and entering the user name and password for the Internet account, you can watch content wherever a wireless connection is available.

Satellite Like having satellite TV, having a satellite Internet connection involves installing a dish at the service location. For a basic plan, the dish might be as small as a satellite TV dish, but for a plan with high download speeds, a somewhat larger dish will probably be required. Advances in the technology have reduced the sizes of satellite dishes over time, however.

Google Fiber uses a powerful Wi-Fi router to deliver crystal clear HDTV.

Installing a satellite Internet dish requires hiring a trained technician. The technician will know how to point the dish in the precise southern direction and angle

Practical TECH

Shopping for an ISP

When shopping for an ISP, consider more than just what type of connection is available in your area. With the exception of dial-up access, ISPs offer most types of connections through a variety of service plans based on download speeds, number of email addresses, and other features. Some plans even bundle services by combining cable TV or telephone with Internet for a single monthly fee.

You can find out what providers serve your area, what types of connections are available, and how much different plans cost by doing some research. Go to the library to use its Internet-connected computers or take your notebook or tablet to a place with free wireless service. To learn about service options, go to an ISP's website and look for a link or button for setting up a new service. You will likely have to enter your phone number or address to see whether service is provided in your area, as well as what plans and features the ISP offers and what they cost. If telephone or cable service is already available at your location, it's likely that your existing carrier offers Internet service too. If that's the case, then start with that ISP's website.

needed to communicate with the satellite carrying the service. The satellite ISP might lease space on the satellite or own the satellite outright. For example, leading satellite ISP HughesNet was purchased by EchoStar in late 2011, and in 2012, EchoStar launched its own EchoStar 17 satellite to provide more capacity to HughesNet. Exede (owned by ViaSat) is the other major satellite ISP offering services to residential and business customers in the United States.

A satellite dish must be installed where there's a clear line of sight to the satellite. At some locations, this requires installing the dish away from the building, whether a home or office, and mounting it on a metal pole. Coaxial cable runs from the dish to the building and connects to a satellite Internet modem. (The cable is buried if the dish is installed away from the building.) The modem is then connected to the wired or wireless network router to provide a broadband connection.

Downloading data can be quick via satellite, but uploading is slower. (This is also true for most other types of broadband connections.) Some satellite ISPs allow bundling of TV, Internet calling, and other services. The costs of satellite plans are also similar to those of other types of broadband services. Costs will vary depending not only on downloading speed but also on the amount of data downloaded. Because satellite capacity is limited, satellite ISPs charge users more for downloading large amounts of data (similar to the data plan for a mobile device). For example, a plan might limit you to downloading 15 gigabytes (GB) of data per month, which might not be enough if you stream a lot of video. Satellite ISPs usually offer ways to get around data limitations. For example, you might be able to purchase additional data allowances as needed or to download more data during low-traffic periods (such as 2 a.m. to 7 a.m.). Satellite Internet service has long been offered in rural areas with no other forms of broadband connection available, a great advantage.

Mobile Hotspots If you need to connect to the Internet frequently while on the go and don't want to constantly look for Wi-Fi hotspots, you can bring your own hotspot with you. Major carriers such as Verizon offer mobile hotspot devices. To use the device, you have to purchase a mobile data plan for it. You tell the device to connect with the mobile network, and once it's connected, it wirelessly shares the Internet connection. The number of users or devices that can connect at any time varies depending on the device and provider. (See the section "Using a Cell Phone as a Hotspot," in Chapter 6 on page 275, for instructions on setting up your phone as a hotspot.)

A hotspot device enables multiple devices and users to connect to the Internet wirelessly from any location. A mobile data plan is required and service is provided by the mobile network.

If you need only a single connection while on the go, you may be able to use your smartphone as a hotspot—a setup called **tethering**. Many models of smartphones are equipped to act as mobile modems. To use this function, you must pay for a monthly hotspot data plan. Once you have activated the proper plan, you can turn on the hotspot feature by changing a setting on your phone. The phone will display a request for a sign-in password to make the connection. The wireless networking hardware on your computer or tablet should discover the new wireless network (the phone hotspot). When it does, you will select that connection and enter the password to sign on. Your computer or tablet will then be connected to the Internet using your mobile phone provider's network. Any data that you download will be charged against your data plan.

Recheck 5.2

Recheck your understanding of the concepts covered by this objective.

5.3 Navigating the Internet

Once you have connected your computer or tablet to the Internet, you can start **surfing**, or navigating between pages and locations on the web using the browser. To navigate the web effectively, you should also know about Internet Protocol (IP) addresses and uniform resource locators (URLs) and how they are used to identify and locate resources on the Internet.

Web Browsers

A **web browser** or browser program displays web pages on the screen of a computer or mobile device. The Microsoft Windows operating system comes with the Microsoft Edge and/or Internet Explorer browser built in (see Figure 5.8). The Apple OS X and iOS operating systems come with the browser Safari built in. Google's Chrome browser works on Android and Chrome OS devices. Google also offers versions of Chrome that you can install and use instead of the default browsers on the Windows and OS X operating systems. A number of other browsers are also available for computers and other devices, such as Mozilla's popular Firefox browser and Opera Software's Opera browser.

As a feature of the Internet, website content must be built and accessed using consistent technology. Because of this, most browsers have similar features, including the following:

- The ability to interpret and display HTML code (the language of web pages).
- Support for compiled programming languages (such as Java) and scripting languages (such as Perl, PHP, and Ruby). The programs or scripts written in these languages extend the web browser's capabilities—for example, adding the ability to stream video. In some cases, an additional software component—either a plug-in or a runtime environment—must be installed within the browser to enable it to run the mini-programs or scripts.
- An easy-to-use interface that allows navigating backward and forward, tracking favorite websites, and more. You will learn more about these features later in the chapter.

Activity 5.3.1

Article
Browser Evolution

Figure 5.8

Use a browser such as Microsoft Edge to display a web page.

IP Addresses and URLs

Web browsers locate specific material on the Internet using an **Internet Protocol (IP) address**. An IP address works like an Internet phone number. Every device connected to the web can be located using its IP address.

Currently, the vast majority of IP addresses follow the **IPv4** format and use a four-group series of numbers separated by periods, such as 207.171.181.16. Using the IPv4 format, only 4.3 billion addresses can be created, and some of these addresses must be reserved for special purposes on the web. Because of the recent explosion in the number of devices connecting to the Internet, a new IP format has been developed, **IPv6**. An IPv6 address uses eight groups of four **hexadecimal digits** (that is, numbers with a base of 16), and the groups are separated by colons (:), as in 2001:0db8:85a3: 0000:0000:8a2e:0370:7334. (The IPv6 format can be abbreviated or stated in other ways. For example, you could remove the leading zeros within each group between colons, so that :0000: becomes just :0: or :0370: is just :370:.) Each IPv6 address is also called a **128-bit address**, which means it allows for 2^{128} addresses. That is:

340 undecillion, or
340,000,000,000,000,000,000,000,000,000,000,000,000, or
340 billion billion billion billion.

IPv6 is slowly replacing IPv4; the two protocols aren't compatible.

Because remembering IP addresses would be difficult, every website host has a corresponding web address called a **uniform resource locator (URL)**. URLs generally use descriptive names rather than numbers, so they are easier to remember. For example, to go to the home page of Amazon, you type the URL http://www.amazon.com, not the IP address. A system called **Domain Name Service** maps the URL to the host's underlying IP address.

The Path of a URL

A URL consists of an address that indicates where the information can be found on the Internet. It contains several parts that are separated by slashes (/), a colon (:), and dots (.). The first part of a URL identifies the communications protocol to be used. One protocol is Hypertext Transfer Protocol (HTTP); it's designated by *http://* (as in the Amazon URL mentioned previously). The other protocol is Hypertext Transfer Protocol Secure (HTTPS); it's designated by *https://* and indicates a secure connection.

Immediately after the protocol is the overall **domain name**, divided into various parts. First may come format information, such as *www* for World Wide Web pages. Following the format information is the **second-level domain**, which identifies the person, organization, server, or topic (such as Amazon) responsible for the web page. The **domain suffix,** or *top-level domain (TLD)*, comes next (*.com* in the Amazon example). After that, there may be additional folder path information (with folder names separated by slashes), as well as the name of a specific web page file or object. To go directly to a specific folder or file, you must type the full path and file name portions of the URL. Figure 5.9 illustrates the various parts of a URL.

Activity 5.3.2

Video
URL Structure

Figure 5.9			
Parts of a URL			
Protocol	**Domain name**	**Path**	**File name**
http://	www.nasa.gov/	audience/forstudents/	index.html

The domain suffix, or TLD, identifies the type of organization or the country of origin. In the Amazon example, the domain suffix *.com* stands for *commercial organization*. A web-based enterprise is often referred to as a **dot-com company**, because the company's domain name ends with *.com*. Table 5.2 lists other domain suffixes that are in common use.

In 1998, the US Department of Commerce created the Internet Corporation for Assigned Names and Numbers (ICANN) and assigned it the task of expanding the list of existing domain suffixes. In late 2000, ICANN completed this task and approved a number of new suffixes (see Table 5.3). These suffixes serve very specific purposes and may be reapproved for use on a limited basis. You may not see them used a lot for national organizations, but you may see local organizations using them.

Some URLs also include a two-letter country abbreviation. Table 5.4 lists the country abbreviations.

Table 5.2 Common Domain Suffixes Used in URLs

Domain Suffix	Type of Institution or Organization	Example
.com	commercial organization	Ford, Intel
.edu	educational institution	Harvard University, Washington University
.gov	government agency	NASA, IRS
.int	international treaty organization, Internet database	NATO
.mil	military agency	US Navy
.net	administrative site for the Internet or ISPs	EarthLink
.org	nonprofit or private organization or society	Red Cross

Table 5.3 New Domain Suffixes

Domain Suffix	Type of Institution or Organization
.aero	airline groups
.biz	business groups
.coop	business cooperatives
.info	general use
.museum	museums
.name	personal websites
.pro	professionals

Table 5.4 Country Abbreviations Used in URLs

af	Afghanistan	fr	France	nz	New Zealand	ch	Switzerland
au	Australia	de	Germany	no	Norway	tw	Taiwan
at	Austria	il	Israel	pl	Poland	uk	United Kingdom
be	Belgium	it	Italy	pt	Portugal	us	United States
br	Brazil	jp	Japan	ru	Russia	yu	Yugoslavia
ca	Canada	kr	Korea	za	South Africa	zw	Zimbabwe
dk	Denmark	mx	Mexico	es	Spain		
fi	Finland	nl	Netherlands	se	Sweden		

Typing a URL into a browser and pressing Enter or Return sends a request to the Internet (see Figure 5.10). Routers identify the request and forward it to the appropriate web server. The web server uses the URL to determine which page, file, or object is being requested. Upon finding the item, the server sends it back to the originating computer using the HTTP or HTTPS protocol, so the browser can display the delivered page on the screen of the computer.

Figure 5.10

Connecting to the Internet

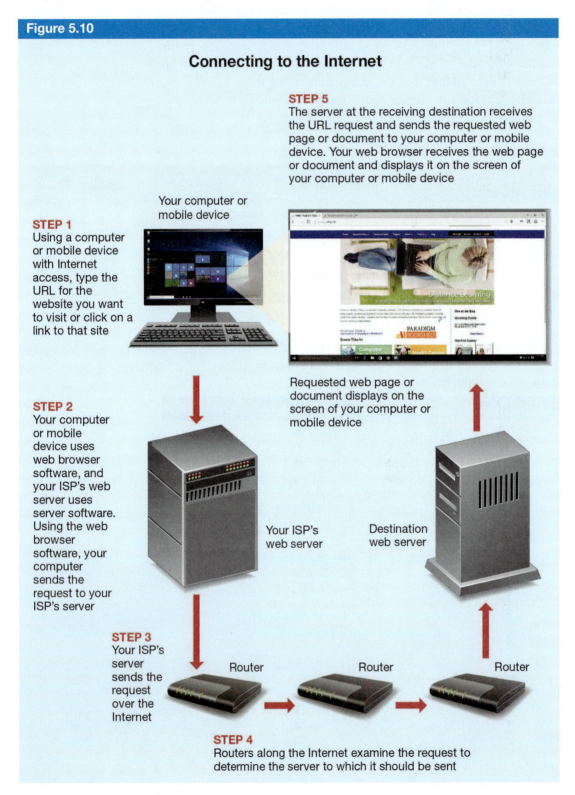

STEP 5
The server at the receiving destination receives the URL request and sends the requested web page or document to your computer or mobile device. Your web browser receives the web page or document and displays it on the screen of your computer or mobile device

Your computer or mobile device

STEP 1
Using a computer or mobile device with Internet access, type the URL for the website you want to visit or click on a link to that site

Requested web page or document displays on the screen of your computer or mobile device

STEP 2
Your computer or mobile device uses web browser software, and your ISP's web server uses server software. Using the web browser software, your computer sends the request to your ISP's server

Your ISP's web server

Destination web server

STEP 3
Your ISP's server sends the request over the Internet

Router   Router   Router

STEP 4
Routers along the Internet examine the request to determine the server to which it should be sent

Packets

A file isn't sent over the Internet as a single file. Instead, messaging software breaks the file into units called **packets** and then sends the packets over separate paths to a final Internet destination. The packets are reassembled when they reach that destination. What paths individual packets take depends on which routers are available. This process of breaking a message into packets, directing the packets over available routers to their final Internet destination, and then reassembling them is called **packet switching**.

Figure 5.11 shows the journey of an Internet message sent from a computer in Seattle and received on a computer in Miami. The message is broken into three packets, and each packet follows a different route to the final destination. If a packet arrives at a node (that is, a router or other communications switching equipment) that is not the final destination, the network passes it along to the next node. At the destination, the computer receives the packets and reassembles the file. If any packet is missing, the receiving computer requests that it be sent again. This re-requesting of information explains why web pages sometimes appear incomplete and some portions take longer than others to fully load.

The idea of dividing files into packets originated during the Cold War (1945–1991). During that era, the Internet was thought of as a system for maintaining communication among the military and other government agencies in the event of a

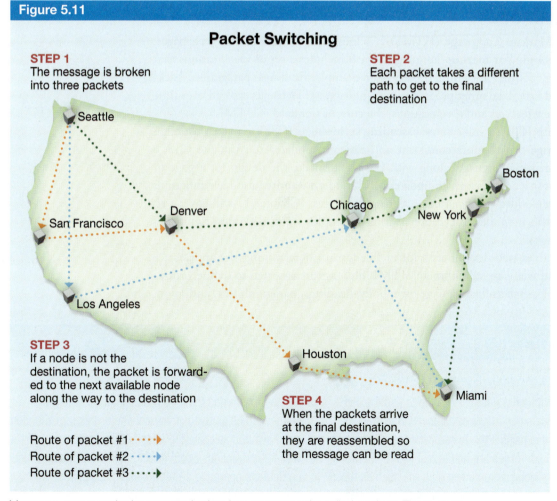

Figure 5.11

Packet Switching

STEP 1
The message is broken into three packets

STEP 2
Each packet takes a different path to get to the final destination

Seattle

Boston

Denver

Chicago

New York

San Francisco

Los Angeles

STEP 3
If a node is not the destination, the packet is forwarded to the next available node along the way to the destination

Houston

STEP 4
When the packets arrive at the final destination, they are reassembled so the message can be read

Miami

Route of packet #1 · · · · ▶
Route of packet #2 · · · · ▶
Route of packet #3 · · · · ▶

Messages sent over the Internet are broken into separate units called *packets*. The packets are directed by routers and reassembled when they arrive at the final destination.

nuclear war. To prevent breakdowns, the system was designed to keep working even if part of it was destroyed or not functioning. A packet sent from New York to Los Angeles, for example, might attempt to travel through Denver or Dallas. But if both of those systems are busy or unavailable, the packet could go up to Toronto and then on to Los Angeles. This design feature, called **dynamic routing**, is part of what makes the Internet work well even with a heavy load of traffic.

IPv6 enables routers to handle packets more efficiently than IPv4. Because of this and many other differences between the two protocols, the Internet will have to operate using the two protocols as side-by-side networks until IPv6 has been fully implemented. Special translation gateways and some other translation technologies enable limited traffic to flow between the IPv4 and IPv6 networks.

Recheck 5.3

Recheck your understanding of the concepts covered by this objective.

5.4 Understanding Web Page Markup Languages

Precheck 5.4

Check your understanding of the concepts covered by this objective.

Text files created with a word-processing program follow a particular file format that the program can display. Similarly, web page files follow a particular format that a web browser can display. Web page files are different, however, because special software isn't needed to create them. You can use practically any word-processing program that you want. However, to describe the content for a web page so that the browser can display it, you must use a specific language.

HTML and CSS

Hypertext Markup Language (HTML) has long been used to create web pages. HTML is a tagging or **markup language**, which includes a set of specifications that describe elements that appear on a page—for example, headings, paragraphs, backgrounds, and lists. Like other programming languages, HTML has evolved over time to include new features and specifications; the current standard is HTML5.

Along with HTML, you can use **cascading style sheets (CSS)** to make the design for a web page or site more consistent and easier to update. You can use CSS, a separate formatting language, along with HTML to make the design for a page or site more consistent and easier to update. Most modern websites also have functions that have been added using various scripting languages. (Chapter 11 will cover web development in more detail, because creating a complex website requires significant programming skills.)

HTML gives web developers a lot of freedom in determining the appearance and design of web pages. Within an HTML file, tags are inserted to define various page elements, such as the language type, body, headings, paragraph text, and so on.

Practical TECH

Is Your Computer System IPv6 Ready?

Most new computer systems are set up to use the IPv6 protocol, so users don't have to do anything to start browsing to sites using IPv6. To see what your computer's IPv4 and IPv6 addresses are and to test your computer's IPv6 readiness, you can run a test on a site such as **http://CUT6.emcp.net/test-ipv6**. For some older computers, it's possible to add the IPv6 protocol for the Internet connection being used. If you encounter this rare situation and have trouble browsing to specific websites, search the web for instructions about adding the IPv6 protocol to your computer's operating system. Making this change might solve the problem.

A **tag** is enclosed in angle brackets, and tags must be used in pairs: an opening tag and a closing tag. (The closing tag includes a forward slash.) As shown in Figure 5.12, the opening tag *<html>* should appear at the top of the document (below the *<!doctype>* tag). The closing tag *</html>* should appear at the bottom of the document to indicate that all of the text in the document is HTML code. The tag pair *<body>* and *</body>* define what should appear in the main browser window, *<title>* and *</title>* indicate the page title, and so on.

A web page also typically functions as a **hypertext document**, presenting information that's been enhanced with **hyperlinks** (also called *web links*) to other websites and pages. The user clicks a link to access additional information on another web page. Links most commonly appear as underlined text, but they can also take the forms of buttons, linked photos or drawings, navigation bars or menus, and so on.

Figure 5.12

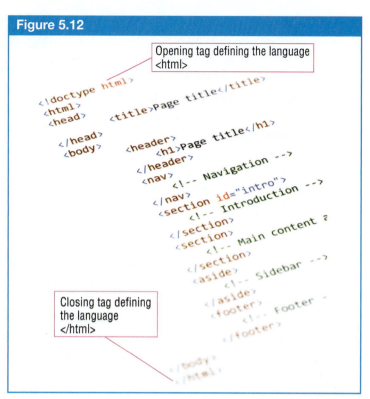

HTML tags are enclosed within angle brackets (< >) and used in pairs. An opening tag and closing tag define the text between them as a particular type of element for the web browser to display.

XML

Whereas HTML defines the format of a web page, **Extensible Markup Language (XML)** organizes and standardizes the structure of data so computers can communicate with each other directly. XML is more flexible than HTML, because it's really a **metalanguage**, a language for describing other languages. XML allows developers to design custom languages that work with limitless types of documents and file formats.

Web developers frequently use XML to manipulate and present information for large online databases. Many commonly used applications, such as Microsoft Excel and Access, can now import and export XML data. This compatibility makes XML the ideal tool for facilitating data sharing between the web and other platforms.

Activity 5.4.1

Article
Using XML to Share Information

Website Publishing Basics

You can create a simple website with just a little knowledge of HTML. (As noted earlier, Chapter 11 will provide more information about the scripting languages used for web programming.) Many ISPs include storage for a basic website and supply a predetermined URL based on the information in your account name. You can upload your web page to that location, often using a method called *File Transfer Protocol (FTP)*, and have your site ready to go. (You will learn more about FTP later in this chapter.) However, if you want to have your own domain name, the process requires a few more steps:

Activity 5.4.2

Video
Creating a Simple Web Page

1. **Obtain your domain name.** You can check to see if a particular domain name (for example, www.mydomainname.com) is available by using name registration services such as GoDaddy (at http://CUT6.emcp.net/GoDaddy) and Network Solutions (at http://CUT6.emcp.net/NetworkSolutions). If the name you want

is available, you can register it by paying a fee. Registration services also enable you to renew your domain name, and in some cases, they allow you to bid on names already owned by others.

2. **Obtain hosting.** The Internet hosting service operates the web servers that will store your website's content and deliver it to the web. The monthly or annual fee you pay will vary depending on the level of hosting services you need; you can usually get started for a low monthly cost. (Of course, a large organization might have its own servers to self-host the website.) GoDaddy and Network Solutions are among the many national hosting companies; you might also find local hosting companies that you can work with.

3. **Create your site content.** You can create your own HTML and other content from scratch, or you can use fee-based or free online tools such as Google Web Designer, Joomla, WordPress, and Drupal. (Keep in mind, however, that the features you build in may require a higher level of web hosting to support them.) If you include graphics files, use the file formats JPEG (Joint Photographic Experts Group), PNG (Portable Network Graphics), and GIF (Graphics Interchange Format). These files are smaller and preferred because they download more quickly. Similarly, for any video or audio you include, use an appropriately compressed file type, such as MP4 for video and MP3 for audio.

4. **Upload your content if needed.** Some hosting services include built-in tools for transferring files using FTP or another method. In other cases, you will need FTP software to complete the transfer.

Also keep in mind two more points. First, most hosting services require the home page for a website to have a specific file name (such as index.htm). Following this practice ensures that when a user navigates to your domain name (URL), the correct page will display. Second, some users take advantage of popular blogging websites (such as WordPress.com and Blogger) to get content creation tools and hosting services in one package. A URL may also be included in that package (although typically, the URL will include the name of the blogging website). WordPress.com will let you use your custom domain URL if you pay a small additional annual upgrade fee.

5.5 Viewing Web Pages

A **web page** is a single document that's viewable on the World Wide Web. A **website** consists of one or more web pages devoted to a particular topic, organization, person, or the like, and generally stored on a single domain. When you navigate to a website, the first page displayed is usually the site's home page. Like the table of contents in a book, the **home page** provides an overview of the information and features presented in the website.

This section covers some of the basic actions for using a web browser program to view, find, and mark online information. It also introduces the basic elements incorporated within today's multimedia sites.

Figure 5.13

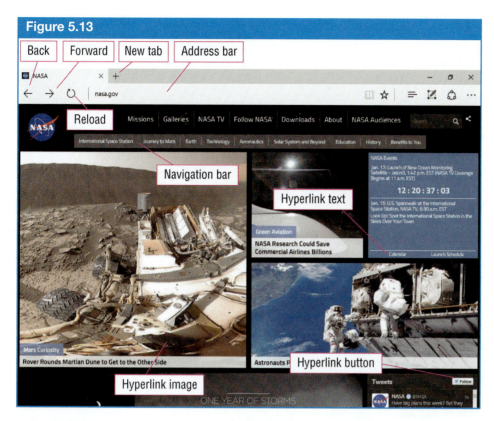

Back Forward New tab Address bar Reload Navigation bar Hyperlink text Green Aviation Hyperlink button Hyperlink image

 **Activity 5.5.1**

Practice
Web Browsing Features

Use these tools to browse the web.

Basic Browsing Actions

Various web browsers look a little different and offer some varying features. Even so, the basic browsing actions work the same no matter which browser you are using. Look at Figure 5.13 to see where to find the bars, buttons, and links used to perform these actions:

- **Go to a URL.** Select any address in the Address bar, type a new URL, and then press Enter or Return.
- **Go back, go forward, and reload.** Click the Back button to return to the previous page and click the Forward button to return to the previous page. Click the Reload button to reload a page that didn't display properly. While a page is reloading, the Reload button changes into the Stop button. Click this button to stop the reloading (which you may want to do if it's taking too long, for example).
- **Add a new page tab.** Click the New tab button, type the URL for the new web page, and then press Enter or Return.
- **Browse by following a hyperlink.** Click the hyperlinked text, image, or button in the body of the page, on the navigation bar, at a drop-down list, or elsewhere on the page.

Audio, Video, and Animation Elements

As the web grows more sophisticated, multimedia elements such as video and sound are being incorporated into web pages both to grasp viewers' attention and to expand the range of activities a web page can perform. Various applets and scripts make adding the elements possible, as do plug-ins such as Apple QuickTime, Adobe Acrobat Reader, Macromedia Shockwave, and Macromedia Flash Player.

 Activity 5.5.2

Article
Plug-ins, Applets, ActiveX Controls, and Scripting Languages

Java Applets and Scripts **Java** is a programming language that website designers frequently use to produce interactive web applications. It was created for use on the Internet and is similar to the C and C++ programming languages. Applets are small Java programs that web browsers run. (*Applet* is the term for a miniature program.) Like macros, Java applets provide the ability to program online games and highly interactive interfaces.

Other scripting languages, such as JavaScript and Ajax, enable web developers to add web page functions, such as user login tools, shopping carts, dynamically loading content (such as articles that update periodically), and more. (Numerous scripting languages are available, including Perl, PHP, and Ruby; they will be discussed again in Chapter 11.)

Cookies A **cookie** is a very small file that a website places on a user's hard drive when he or she visits the site. Often, these files are harmless and even helpful. For example, one type of cookie may be used to verify whether you are currently logged in to your subscription account on a site such as an online newspaper. Sometimes, however, websites use cookies to track the surfing habits of users without their knowledge. One website might place a file on your computer that indicates what sites you have visited and then allow related sites to read this information and track your actions. You can adjust the security settings on your browser to warn you when cookie files are being accessed or to prevent their operation altogether.

Plug-Ins Sometimes, a website will ask for approval to add a plug-in to your web browser. A **plug-in** is a mini-program that extends the capabilities of web browsers in a variety of ways, usually by improving graphic, sound, and video elements. A missing plug-in often causes viewing errors on a web page, such as a message that a video can't play because the appropriate plug-in hasn't been installed.

Most plug-ins don't carry hidden or destructive features that can cause problems. However, as a general rule, it's a good idea to perform a web search and verify that a plug-in is safe and legitimate before giving permission to load it onto your computer. If you think the website recommending the plug-in download is trustworthy, click the Refresh button on the browser. Doing so will reload the page and redisplay the prompt to install the plug-in. Follow the prompts to install the plug-in for your browser.

One widely known plug-in is Shockwave, by Macromedia. Sites that use Shockwave normally take longer to load but offer higher-resolution graphics, superior interaction, and streaming audio. Macromedia Flash Player and Apple QuickTime are two other popular plug-ins that let users experience animation, audio, and video.

Ads

Advertising on a company's or individual's website produces income. For some companies and individuals, this ad revenue supplements the primary revenue stream. For example, the giant online retailer Amazon not only promotes the products it sells, but also sells ad space to companies that want to feature their products or services on Amazon's prime web "real estate." For other companies and individuals, income from ads posted on their websites provides the majority of their revenue. A social media site such as Facebook, a news media site such as CNN.com,

Tech Career Explorer

IT for Space Travelers

NASA's research and exploration efforts require the skillsets of many people in addition to astronauts. If you are excited about being part of NASA's research and contributions to humankind but aren't sure how your skills and interests might fit in, complete this exercise to learn about job opportunities that involve an information technology (IT) role at NASA.

and an individual blogger's website may all rely heavily on ad-generated revenue.

Website advertisers typically pay for the advertising on a per-click basis, but other payment models are followed as well. A website may also present ads in many different formats, including ad banners and pop-up windows. Users should be aware that some less-than-legitimate content can masquerade as ads, including blind links and hijackers.

Banners A **banner ad** invites the viewer to click it to display a new page or site selling a product or service. Banners were originally rectangles that appeared across the tops and bottoms of web pages, but today, they can take any shape and appear in any location on a page. Many banners include bright colors, animation, and video to attract attention, as shown in Figure 5.14.

Banners can provide helpful information to people interested in the product being advertised. Also, banners often provide special pricing when the user clicks the banner to go to the linked product site.

Pop-Ups An online ad may also appear as a **pop-up ad**, as shown in Figure 5.15. Named for its tendency to appear unexpectedly in the middle or along the side of the screen, a pop-up ad (or *pop-up*) typically hides a main part of the web page. When the window pops up, that part of the page may also darken or flicker.

On most devices, you can click a Close (X) button in the pop-up to remove it from the screen. However, some pop-ups are extremely persistent—reappearing immediately after you close them or even lacking a Close button or any other means for shutting them. On a Windows computer, you might be able to close a pop-up window that doesn't have a Close button by pressing the keyboard shortcut Alt + F4. Most web browser software includes **pop-up blocker** features that you can activate to avoid this sort of nuisance. (Chapter 9 will explain more about web privacy and security, including pop-up blocking.)

Blind Links A link sometimes misrepresents its true destination, taking you to an unexpected page when you click on it. For example, a link such as <u>Next Page</u> might actually take you to an advertising web page. Called a **blind link**, this type of deceptive device appears only on websites that aren't trustworthy, such as some free-host sites. Free-host websites don't charge a fee for hosting web pages. However, they do require that the pages display banners and other forms of advertising chosen by the companies that host the pages.

Hijackers Web hijackers can disrupt your browsing experience and expose you to unwelcome ads. A **hijacker** is usually an extension or plug-in that's installed with your web browser. It functions by taking you to pages you didn't select—generally, pages filled with advertisements.

Figure 5.14

Websites sell advertising space in the form of banner ads. Many users prefer to avoid ad-heavy websites.

Figure 5.15

A pop-up ad covers part of the web page and prompts the user to buy a product or subscribe to information.

Hijackers typically install on your computer without your awareness and sometimes attempt to make you pay a fee to remove them. You can often get rid of hijackers by working with the security settings in your web browser and by deleting or uninstalling web browser extensions. In extreme cases, you may need to reinstall your computer's operating system.

A new form of hijacker replaces ads that the publisher sold with ads from the company that created the hijacker. Each time a user clicks one of these ads on the publisher's website, the hijacker company—not the publisher—receives revenue.

Web Page Traps Some websites can change your browser's settings permanently or attempt to prevent viewers from leaving by continually popping up more windows and disabling the Back button. To avoid this so-called **web page trap**, change your web browser's settings to increase the level of security. Having higher security settings may cause the browser to prompt you whenever it comes across suspicious behavior, as shown in Figure 5.16. Unfortunately, having higher security settings may cause the browser to prompt you constantly, even when you are visiting legitimate websites.

If you fall into one of these traps and are using Windows, press the key sequence Control + Alt + Delete to open the Task Manager. (Depending on your Windows version, you may have to press this sequence twice.) From the Task Manager, you can choose to reboot the computer or close the web browser.

Hotspot

Wireless, USA

The move to go wireless could spread nationwide. In early 2013, the Federal Communications Commission (FCC) proposed a plan to create a free wireless network covering all of the United States. The network would use some of the wireless spectrum currently used for TV broadcasting. Having such a network would make it possible for all types of devices to remain connected to the Internet at all times and at no cost to users—a reason that some companies support the proposal. Of course, companies that currently provide fee-based ISP services have expressed concerns about the proposal.

Figure 5.16

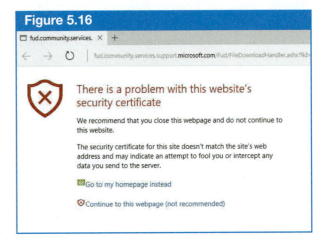

This warning indicates a problem with the site's online security certificate, which verifies the site's authenticity to users. The certificate might have expired, for example.

Cutting Edge

Introducing Web 3.0, the Semantic Web

The term *Web 2.0* was coined in 2004 by Tim O'Reilly at a conference sponsored by the company he founded, O'Reilly Media. At that time, interaction and collaboration were beginning to occur online, most notably through websites such as Facebook and Twitter. Now that Web 2.0 is part of the Internet's "present," experts are increasingly using the term *Web 3.0* (or sometimes *Semantic Web*) to describe the Internet's future. Possibilities for Web 3.0 developments may include machine-generated (rather than human-sourced) information, three-dimensional (3-D) simulations and expanded or enhanced reality (including

the widespread use of sensors), greatly expanded use of high-quality video by computers and other devices, and much more.

Figure 5.17

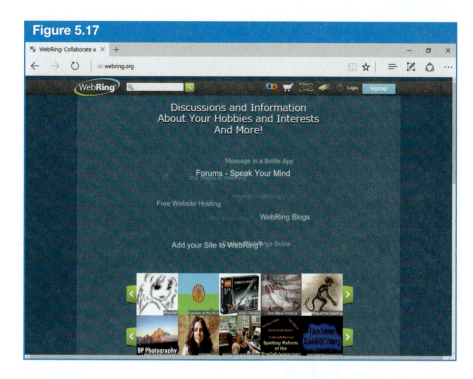

The WebRing home page has listings for hundreds of different WebRings organized around different topics.

WebRings

One relatively safe way to move from site to site on the Internet is by using a **WebRing** (see Figure 5.17). Each site on a WebRing maintains links to the next site and the previous site, forming a ring (hence, the name). WebRings link sites devoted to a similar theme or topic. Sites dedicated to hobbies or special interests typically include this navigation feature.

WebRings are usually moderated by people who want to help others find websites they would probably not find on their own. Taking advantage of WebRings is an excellent way for hobbyists to find like-minded individuals who share their passion for falconry, old cars, nineteenth-century tea sets, or hundreds of other hobbies. WebRing.org, shown in Figure 5.17, can help you find a WebRing in one of dozens of topic areas. You can search for a topic to find a list of matching WebRings. For example, if you search for waterfall, the matching rings include the Waterfalls WebRing, as well as rings on travel photography and more.

Recheck 5.5

Recheck your understanding of the concepts covered by this objective.

5.6 Searching for Information on the Internet

More than 90 percent of adult Internet users search the Internet to tap into the global library of limitless data that's available on practically any topic. Some experts now estimate that the World Wide Web holds more than 1 trillion pages of information. Finding any particular item among so much information requires the proper search tools and techniques.

Users can search for and retrieve information from web pages by using a search engine in a web browser. A **search engine** is essentially a website or service you use to locate information. You type search criteria or **keywords** in the site's search text box or in your browser's address or location bar. The leading search engines include Google, Yahoo!, and Bing.

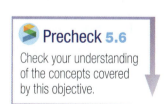

Precheck 5.6

Check your understanding of the concepts covered by this objective.

Suppose you want to find information about the Battle of Vicksburg for a history class report. You will begin by typing the search criteria—in this case, the words *Battle of Vicksburg*—in the search text box and then pressing Enter or clicking the Search button. Doing so will cause a list of hyperlinked articles to appear in the browser. Clicking on an article's title will make the article display and allow you to read it. Most search tools provide a basic search page that contains a search text box with a search command button beside or below it (see Figure 5.18).

Search Engine Choices

The search engine that was set up as the default when you installed your web browser may not be the one you prefer to use. However, every web browser program enables you to change the default search engine. In addition, most browsers enable you to add another search engine of your choice.

Not all search engines offer the same features, and some search engines perform certain types of searches better than others. Search results differ depending on the search algorithm (step-by-step search method) and software tools used to generate the results. Search results also may differ depending on the number of web pages an engine indexes (catalogs) and on the methods it makes available for refining a search. Also consider that some search engines accept fees for placing websites at the top of search results lists. This means that the first few websites in a results list are likely to have paid for that premier position and may not contain the information that's most relevant for you.

In addition to working with a single search engine, you can use a metasearch engine. A metasearch engine sends your search request to multiple search engines at once, and may also search other libraries and directories or paid-placement services. Metasearch engines include Search.com, Dogpile, and Excite.com.

Hands On

Adding a Search Engine to Your Browser

The process for adding a search engine to your browser depends on the browser. You can try methods like the ones described in this resource.

Figure 5.18

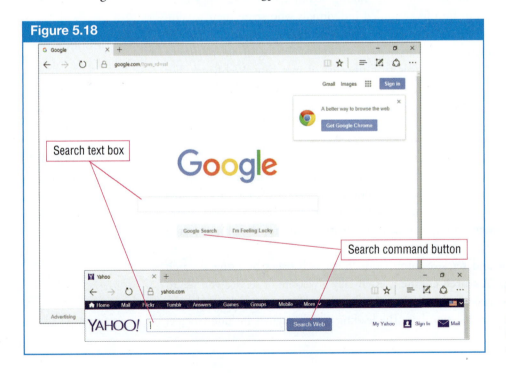

Google and Yahoo! are two frequently used search engines. Both provide a basic search page with a search text box and a search command button.

Default Search Engine

You can change the default search engine in your browser at any time. For example, you might prefer to use Google for most searches but switch to the Wikipedia Visual Search engine when you are looking for content with images for reference. Most browsers enable you to switch between search engines easily, but keep in mind that the new search engine you choose will remain the active or default engine until you choose another one.

Advanced Search Techniques

To get the most targeted results from any Internet search, you must enter the right keyword or keywords in the search engine's search text box. Using too many keywords will produce hundreds or even thousands of search results, which you will need to wade through to find what you are looking for. Using vague, obsolete, or incorrectly spelled terms will further reduce the chances of conducting a successful search. Think carefully about what combinations of words most likely appear in the material you need. Some search engines, such as Google, let you work with an advanced search page that prompts you to enter details about the information you want, as shown in Figure 5.19.

The first and often overlooked method for getting more accurate search results involves using quotation marks. If you enter the phrase *four score and seven years ago,* you will get different results than if you enclose the phrase in quotation marks, for example *"four score and seven years ago".* For a well-known phrase such as this, the results might be similar due to the advanced intelligence of the algorithms used by

Hands On

Choosing the Active or Default Search Engine in Your Browser

The method for changing the current search engine depends on your browser, but you can try techniques such as those described in this resource.

Figure 5.19

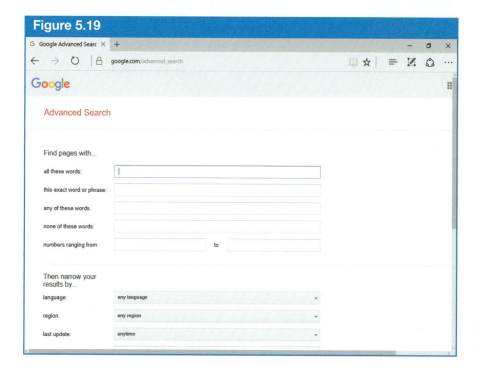

The Google Advanced Search page prompts users to provide details that will return more specific information.

today's search engines. However, for a less common phrase or a special item such as a name, enclosing the phrase or name in quotation marks will produce more targeted results.

Other advanced searching methods use a logic statement containing one or more **search operators** to refine searches. Three common search operators are AND, OR, and NOT:

- AND (or the plus sign, +) connects search terms and returns search results that contain references to all of the terms used. For example, asking the search engine to search for *dogs AND cats* (or *dogs + cats*) will return only sites containing references to both dogs and cats.
- OR returns results that contain references to any of the search terms. Asking the search engine to search for *dogs OR cats* will return sites that have references to either dogs or cats or both. OR is usually the default logic option on a search engine.
- NOT is used to exclude a keyword in a search. Searching for *dogs NOT cats* will produce only sites that refer to dogs but don't mention cats.

You can use search operators along with phrases contained in quotation marks to conduct even more detailed searches.

Bookmarking and Favorites

If you frequently use the web for research, you can mark and organize web pages to make it easier to find them again later. Some web browsers (such as Chrome and Firefox) call a marked page a **bookmark**, while others (such as Microsoft Edge and Safari) call it a *favorite*.

Once you have navigated to the page to mark, choose the button or command for marking favorites in your browser; this happens to be a star icon in the upper-right corner of both Chrome and Microsoft Edge. If needed, click the Add or Add to Favorites button, edit the name to use for the site,

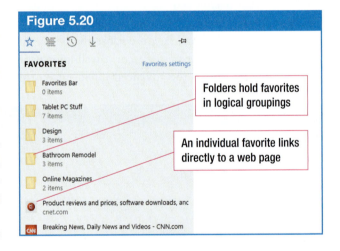

Figure 5.20

Folders hold favorites in logical groupings

An individual favorite links directly to a web page

choose or create the folder to store the bookmark in, and then click Save, Add, or Done. Using folders enables you to organize the sites you visit by subject matter or type, as shown in the folders listed in Figure 5.20. To use a bookmark or favorite, simply display the list or pane that holds them in your browser, expand a folder if needed, and click the bookmarked web location to visit.

Recheck 5.6

Recheck your understanding of the concepts covered by this objective.

5.7 Using Other Internet Resources and Services

The Internet originated as a platform for communication and information sharing. As its infrastructure and underlying programming technologies have evolved, the Internet has become a platform for many activities beyond communication and research. This section provides a detailed look at the broad variety of applications and activities that you can take advantage of when online.

Precheck 5.7

Check your understanding of the concepts covered by this objective.

Communicating with electronic devices might sound cold and impersonal, but in reality, the Internet continues to evolve as a primary channel for staying in touch with others. Less than a dozen years ago, you could use the Internet to communicate in only a handful of ways, but now, new digital platforms for connecting and sharing with others online emerge almost daily.

Electronic Mail

Electronic mail (email) remains one of the top activities performed on the Internet. In fact, nearly 90 percent of adults have sent or read email, and there were more than 4.4 billion active email accounts in 2015 (see Figure 5.21). You can use email to create, send, receive, save, and forward messages in electronic form. Email is a fast, convenient, and inexpensive way to communicate.

A typical Internet account includes at least one email address, and some ISPs allow you to create multiple email addresses per account. Other web-based email services (such as Gmail, Yahoo! Mail, and Outlook.com) allow you to set up an email address independent of a particular ISP. Gmail, Yahoo!, and Outlook.com accounts are free, but paying a small monthly fee will typically let you upgrade your account with features such as additional storage space.

You also can choose to work with and manage email in two different ways, depending on your ISP's capabilities and your own preferences. One way is to use an email application that's installed on your computer, such as Microsoft Outlook or Mozilla Thunderbird (a free alternative). Both Windows and Mac OS X include built-in applications for reading and sending email. After installing the software (if necessary), you set up your email account information so the software can connect with your ISP to send and receive messages. Email applications typically download all messages to your computer or device. However, you can choose to have messages stored online, as well, so that you can access them from other computers or devices.

The other way to work with and manage email is to use **webmail**. This method has become more common as users have increasingly wanted to access email via a smartphone or tablet in addition to a computer. With webmail, you use your web browser to navigate to your email account on your ISP's website. Depending on your service, you may have to navigate to a particular URL (such as *webmail.earthlink.net*) to access your ISP's sign-in page. After you sign in with your account information, you can send, receive, and

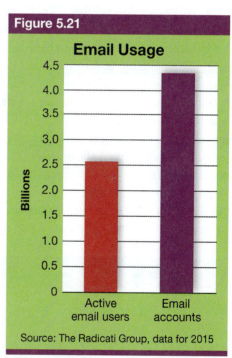

Figure 5.21

Email Usage

Source: The Radicati Group, data for 2015

Practical TECH

Mail on Mobile

If you use a tablet or smartphone for email, you can probably download an email app to make the process simpler than logging on through the device's web browser. For example, you can download apps for Gmail and Yahoo! Mail. To find apps specific to other email providers, search the app store for your device type.

For some other types of accounts, such as Outlook.com, you enter the email account information in the device's settings and use the device's mail app to work with your email. Windows Phone, iOS, and Android devices all have built-in mail apps.

view messages online. Some ISPs even offer a separate URL for signing in with a mobile device, such as *m.webmail.earthlink.net* (see Figure 5.22).

Even though Gmail, Outlook.com, and Yahoo! Mail are all webmail services, they also enable you to access your email for free through an email application such as Outlook. For Gmail and Yahoo!, the process for connecting to your email application typically means making sure that the POP email protocol is enabled in your online account settings and then setting up the account information in your email program. (Table 6.2 in Chapter 6 covers communications protocols such as POP.)

Figure 5.23 shows common features of both email applications and web-based email as they appear in Gmail. These features allow you to perform the following actions:

- Organize messages in folders.
- Assign priorities to the messages you create.
- Sort the messages in a folder.
- Change settings.
- Mark messages as "Read" or "Unread."
- Print messages and save attachments.

Whether you are using an email application or webmail, the process for sending an email message generally works the same. You click the command or button for composing a new message, provide the recipient's email address, type a subject in the *Subject* text box, type a message, and then click the Send button. In addition to sending messages that contain text, you can attach various types of files to email messages, including reports, spreadsheets, photos, and video files. Recipients can then open the attached files to view or save them.

In most email programs and webmail systems, you insert an attachment by clicking an Attach button (which often has a paper clip icon). Some email programs allow you to insert other types of information in a message as well. For example, if you click the

Figure 5.22

You can view webmail using your mobile device browser.

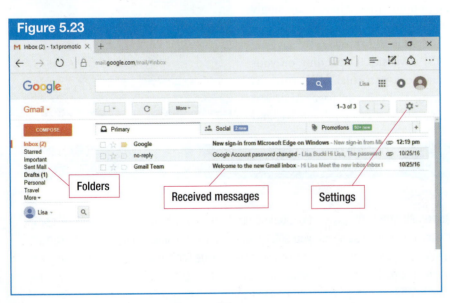

Figure 5.23

Google's Gmail is a free email service that includes many valuable features.

Figure 5.24

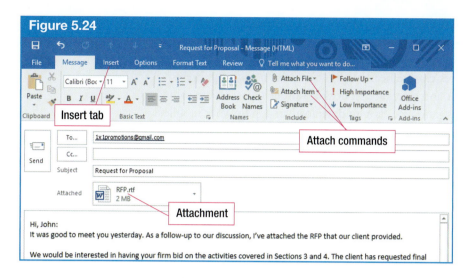

In the Outlook message window, click the Attach File button to select a file to send with a message or use the options available on the Insert tab to include other types of content.

Insert tab in an Outlook message window (see Figure 5.24), you will find options for inserting or attaching a calendar item, virtual business card, table, and more.

You may want to compress or "zip" large file attachments or multiple files. A **compressed file** or **zipped file** is smaller than the original file, which means it takes less time to send and download (copy from the host's computer to the recipient's computer). The recipient can then open or "unzip" the received file to view its contents.

Be aware that because malicious software can be hidden within certain types of files, some ISPs and IT departments block certain types of file attachments—including zipped files, image files, and executable files. It's a good idea to check with the recipient before sending a very large file or a file in a special format. If sending and receiving such files causes problems, you can use the FTP method (covered later in this chapter) to transfer the information.

Also be aware that most ISPs enable you have some control over spam, or unwanted junk emails. You can often change the overall level of spam filtering in your account settings or within your email program and block specific senders. You also can mark messages as spam, so that messages from that sender will automatically be directed to a Spam or Junk folder (also called the **spam trap**) in the future. The only drawback to this screening feature is that legitimate messages sometimes end up in the spam trap. Be sure to check this folder routinely for messages you might want.

Social Media, Sharing, and Networking

One new genre of web services enables people to create personal online spaces and interact socially. **Social networking services**—such as Facebook, Twitter, Pinterest, LinkedIn, and Reddit—have become popular, boasting hundreds of millions of users. These free sites give anyone the opportunity to open an account and share content.

For example, Facebook users can personalize their Timelines with profile information, photos, music and video, and status updates. Animal rescue groups use their Facebook pages to raise funds and place animals in adoptive homes.

Twitter operates differently, allowing people to share 140-character messages called *tweets* with anyone who cares to follow and read their messages. Celebrities and journalists use their Twitter accounts to connect with millions of fans and followers. Twitter recently purchased Vine (Vine.co, which is different from the Vine.com retail site), a mobile social video app for sharing six-second videos from a mobile device.

 **Activity 5.7.1**

Article
Internet Social Networks

Some sites bring together content from a variety of sources, either organizing it by tags or letting contributors rank or vote on its value. When tagging, the publisher or users apply a tag or keyword to identify a particular type of content.

New types of social media sites emerge nearly daily to address nearly any interest. Table 5.5 lists a variety of popular and emerging services of various types. To use some social media services, such as Instagram, you have to download an app for your mobile device. Other services simply work within your web browser.

Chat and Instant Messaging

Using **chat** and **instant messaging (IM)**, users can engage in real-time dialog, or live, instantaneous online conversations, with one or more participants. Chat and IM used to be thought of as two different services, with chats taking place in special online locations called *chat rooms* and IM usually taking place between two people in a back-and-forth dialog, like a typed phone conversation. Many users now call IM interactions *chats*; for example, some sales and help websites give you the option of initiating a chat (IM) session with a customer service representative.

ICQ ("I seek you") offers web-based chat room environments, where users can discuss a variety of topics, such as climate change and stocks. IM used to require having a specific application, such as Windows Messenger or AOL Instant Messenger. However, most IM services have been moved to a web-based platform or rolled into another service, such as Skype. Internet Relay Chat (IRC) is a form of instant messaging (even though it includes the word *chat* in its name) that requires specific software, such as mIRC (**http://CUT6.emcp.net/mIRC**). In addition, Google Hangouts incorporates text chat along with other messaging features for communicating with another user or a group.

Table 5.5 Popular Social Media Services Beyond Facebook and Twitter

Service	Description
Pinterest	Pinterest lets you pin or bookmark items from around the web on a virtual corkboard or scrapbook; you can also follow other users' boards.
Instagram	Instagram lets you capture photos from your mobile device, apply fun filters, and then share the photos at other social sites, such as Facebook, Twitter, and Tumblr.
tumblr. / reddit	Some social sites aggregate (or collect) a particular type of content and allow users to follow and interact. Tumblr aggregates more than 150 million blogs, and Reddit acts as a social news service.
Linked in	LinkedIn is a professional social network, on which users can create an online résumé, search for jobs, and share information about business topics.
DEVIANT ART / flickr	Some social sites let you share and distribute content you have created. Digital artists and others can share and sell their creations on DeviantArt. Using digital photocentric services such as Flickr, you can upload and share images, have printed items made, and distribute images for a fee or under Creative Commons licensing.
G+	Google+ falls somewhere between Facebook and LinkedIn in terms of the services it provides. Like Facebook, Google+ allow you to share information with circles of users, view other posts in an ongoing feed, and join special interest groups called *communities*. Like LinkedIn, Google+ tends to be professional in tone, and it lets users create and attend online events called *Hangouts*.

Most online and social services provide some form of chat or messaging. Gmail enables you to chat with your online contacts, and Facebook enables you to exchange **private messages (PMs)**, also sometimes called *direct messages (DMs)*, which are visible only to you and others invited to the conversation. With these types of social services, you can initiate a chat or message when you see one of your contacts or friends online. Type a comment and then press Enter or click Send to send it to the other person, who can respond to you in the same way. The messages remain visible in the message area as you continue the typed conversation, much like text messaging using a smartphone.

The corporate world is increasingly implementing forms of chat as a business communications tool. For instance, the team communication platform Slack lets users communicate by DMs or channels. Many shopping and customer service websites offer users the option of having an interactive conversation with a customer service representative via a chat or message window. Employees accustomed to instant messaging in their personal lives also find it convenient to communicate with coworkers and clients using this medium.

Message Boards

A **message board**—often called a *discussion forum* or simply a *forum*—presents an electronically stored list of messages that anyone with access to the board can read and respond to. Like a classroom or dormitory bulletin board, a message board allows users to post messages, read existing messages, and delete messages.

Similar to chat rooms, most message boards center on particular topics. Yahoo! Finance provides a message board for almost every stock so that investors can discuss a company's performance and stock price (see Figure 5.25). InvestorVillage is a stand-alone website that also offers a variety of boards about specific stocks and general investing topics. In the InvestorVillage message boards, you can read and respond to posts and typically assign ratings to comments by others. Because the messages remain in a message board (unless deleted by a moderator), you can typically search a board to find information posted by a particular user or information about a particular keyword. This searchability feature makes many message boards useful bodies of information that users can access for future reference or research.

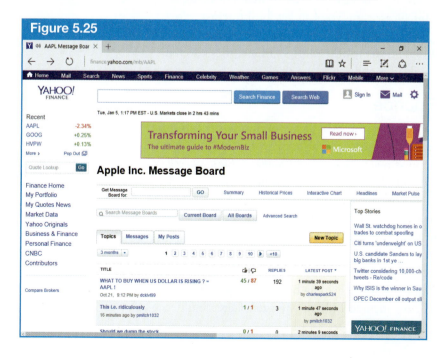

Figure 5.25

Users go to message boards, like this one from Yahoo! Finance, to read and post messages about topics of interest.

Blogs

A **blog** is a frequently updated journal or log that contains chronological entries of personal thoughts and web links posted on a web page. (It was originally called a *weblog*—a combination of the words *web* and *log*.) The content and style of blogs vary as widely as the people who maintain them (who are called *bloggers*). In general, though, blogs serve as personal diaries or guides to others with similar interests. Collectively, the world of blogs is known as the **blogosphere**. Users can start and publish blogs at websites such as Blogger and WordPress.com.

Many corporate websites now include one or more blogs to communicate with employees, customers, and partners. Bloggers add a personal, informal tone to company communications and provide information that's more timely and relevant than the content traditionally provided in a glossy marketing brochure.

Tech Ethics

Keeping Clean in Company Communications

Electronic communications in the workplace often involve legal privacy issues. Companies generally keep backups of communication in the event of a data loss, but some industries require that all forms of digital communication be archived for legal reasons. For example, the financial industry requires that all email and instant message content be kept for several years. Doing so is necessary to ensure it will be available as evidence in the event of an investigation by the Securities and Exchange Commission or another legal body.

Employees should keep the content of email and instant messages in the workplace professional and courteous, because their employers will have digital records of who said what and when.

News and Weather

Many users are turning away from print and TV sources of news and weather and relying instead on mobile and standard web versions of their favorite information sources. For example, CNN, ABC News, and other national networks offer free news online, 24/7. Some print-based publications, such as the newspapers owned by the Gannett company, attract readers by offering limited online articles to individuals who don't subscribe to the print edition and unlimited online articles to print subscribers. Other publications, such as the *New York Times* and the *Wall St. Journal*, offer digital (online-only) subscriptions.

Other more topical information sites are offshoots of popular subscription TV channels, such as ESPN and The Weather Channel. Some sites have more video content than other news sources and may offer localized content as well. For example, at many weather news sites, such as Intellicast.com, you can get local forecast information by entering your zip code. So you can read and access vital information while on the go, most news and weather sites (and many of the informational sites covered in the next section) enable you to download mobile apps.

Business, Career, and Finance

While plenty of entertainment can be found on the web, plenty of business resources are available as well. If you are looking for business news or strategy information, you can consult online editions of such popular magazines as *Fast Company*, *Businessweek*, *Entrepreneur*, and *Forbes*. You can also consult web-only business news sources, such as *Business Insider*. You will find content covering a variety of business segments and niches in specialty online publications such as *Wired*, and you will find informative publications and newsletters at the website of the trade or professional association for the industry you work in.

Most news and business sites offer a "Career" or "Job Postings" section, and some sites are dedicated to helping people find jobs (or to helping businesses that are hiring find employees). The top job search sites include Indeed, Monster, CareerBuilder,

GlassDoor, and Simplyhired. Some job search sites are specific to professions, such as Dice for IT professionals. Job-hunters of all types can also connect with target companies through LinkedIn. There are even sites to help people find freelance work, such as Elance and Guru.com. Most of these sites enable you to post your résumé, so it's available to all potential employers, and provide career statistics and help with career development.

If you are interested in news specific to the stock market, the Internet has what you need. Many major players—including Google, Yahoo!, Bloomberg, and Marketwatch—provide daily stock market and company news, along with stock quotes, charting, and more. Some sites also allow you to track a portfolio of stocks, and most provide information on topics such as personal finance and commodities.

Government and Portals

Any website with the domain .gov is a government website. Many .gov websites are operated by federal agencies. For example, you can go to the top of the US government by visiting WhiteHouse.gov. Other .gov websites are operated by governments at the state, county, and local or municipal levels. These sites not only offer information about government departments and services, but they also publish important announcements, including those required by public meeting laws.

A special type of website called a **portal** acts as a gateway for accessing a variety of information. A portal serves as a "launching pad" for users to navigate categorized web pages within the same website or across multiple websites. The US government's USA.gov website (**http://CUT6.emcp.net/USA.gov**) is an example of a portal (see Figure 5.26). The majority of the material on the USA.gov site is located on the USA.gov servers, but links also take users to individual federal, state, and local government agency websites. The home page for USA.gov provides an overview of the information contained within the site.

Figure 5.26

The official website of the US government, USA.gov, is a portal that offers access to information about all aspects of the federal government. The USA.gov home page provides links to information on millions of government web pages.

FTP and Online Collaboration

As mentioned earlier in the chapter, **File Transfer Protocol (FTP)** enables users to transfer files to and from remote computers. FTP was the original method used for transferring files on the Internet, and it remains an option for transmitting files that can't be emailed because of their large size or because they are blocked by the recipient's system.

Although most web browsers can be used to connect with an FTP server, heavy FTP users usually prefer to use some type of FTP client software, such as the free program FileZilla (shown in Figure 5.27). Most FTP servers are secure, so a user name and password are needed to sign on, but some site operators allow users to log on anonymously.

Typically, you can download files from the FTP site to your computer and upload files from your computer to the FTP site. FTP allows any kind of file to be transferred. For example, a student can download lecture outlines that an instructor has made available on a school's FTP site, or an engineer can download and view blueprints that an architect has placed on the firm's FTP site. And of course, telecommuting employees and contract workers can submit completed projects and documents via FTP and download resource documents.

While FTP used to be the main way to transfer documents for telecommuting and other forms of remote work, more modern online workspaces have evolved over the years. Online workspaces have developed both in conjunction with web-based email services and as standalone services implemented by corporations and other organizations. For example, when you have an Outlook.com account, you also have an online storage area known as your *OneDrive*. You can upload, download, and even share documents from your OneDrive with other users. Corporate-level collaborative platforms include SharePoint, which allows online file sharing and real-time file collaboration. (You will learn more about using online sharing and collaboration features in Chapter 7.)

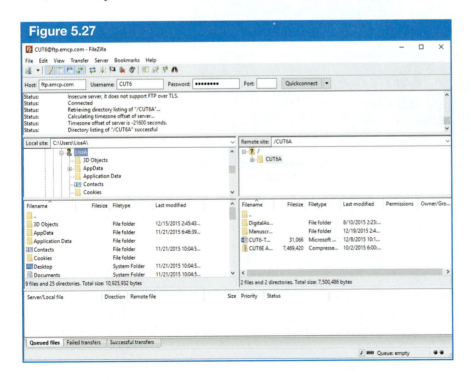

Figure 5.27

The authors of this textbook used FileZilla to upload all of the manuscript and image files to the publisher's FTP site.

Peer-to-Peer File Sharing

Peer-to-peer (P2P) file sharing has caused a lot of controversy on the Internet. P2P enables users to download material directly from other users' hard drives, rather than from files located on web servers. Napster, the famous pioneer of peer-to-peer file sharing, operated by maintaining a list of files made available for sharing by subscribers to the system. For example, someone would let Napster know that he had 50 music files on his hard disk that he would be willing to share. Other users could then use Napster to locate these files and request that they be sent to their computers. Newer P2P systems remove the central server entirely and allow user computers with the fastest connections to provide the search function and keep track of which computers have shared a file. P2P is a powerful idea that allows every computer to function as both a server and a client.

Napster was launched in 1999, and in less than a year, it had more than 20 million users. At its peak, Napster had more than 70 million users worldwide and was being used to download music files by almost 70 percent of US college students. Unfortunately, many of the files being shared in this way were copyrighted material. Napster was forced to shut down in 2001 after two court injunctions ordered it to stop doing business. After filing for bankruptcy and being acquired by Roxio, Inc., Napster was relaunched as a music download service in 2003 and eventually was incorporated into Rhapsody, one of many services chasing market leader iTunes.

Today's P2P technologies allow sharing any types of files, including games, movies, and software programs. Since Napster, the biggest file sharing technology has been BitTorrent. Industry research firms estimate that BitTorrent usage accounts for 35 percent of all Internet traffic. Although some individuals use BitTorrent to illegally find and download copyrighted files, others use the software to share their own files, which is legal. Also, software and media companies such as TimeWarner are interested in the distribution technology as another sales channel.

Using P2P technology to harness the individual contents of millions of computers around the world represents a vast opportunity for communications. However, with additional access come additional security risks.

Voice over Internet Protocol (VoIP)

Through an application of **Internet telephony** (digital communications using different IP standards) technology called **Voice over Internet Protocol (VoIP)**, two or more people with good-quality connections can use the Internet to make telephone-style audio and video calls around the world. The process digitizes the voices and videos, breaking them down into packets that can be transmitted anywhere, just like any other form of digital data.

VoIP can be used in three different ways: from device to device, via Internet-ready phones, and via an analog telephone adapter (ATA). Through popular device-to-device services, such as Skype, the user at each end of the connection downloads and installs software that uses the sound features in the computer, mobile device, or Skype-ready TV. Adding video requires having a webcam. The software enables the users to connect through a "call" over the Internet. Then, it translates the words spoken

Tech Career Explorer

Telecommuting Techs

Telecommuting has its own set of challenges, including being self-motivated, avoiding distractions, dealing with interruptions, and maintaining effective communication. If you like these kinds of challenges and you like IT, you might be interested in exploring how to combine the two. Complete this exercise for a brief introduction to various types of IT jobs and the skills and responsibilities involved in them.

into the microphone by the sender into sounds that are heard through speakers by the recipient, with video transmitting simultaneously.

Two-camera models of the iPhone, iPad, and iPod Touch, as well as some recent MacBook models, have the ability to make FaceTime audio and video calls over a Wi-Fi network. These devices all come loaded with the FaceTime software.

Having a Gmail account enables you to use a feature called *Google Voice* to call telephones of other Gmail account holders. These individuals can make free calls within the United States and Canada.

Although less common now than in the past, Internet-ready phones provide another option for users. This type of phone plugs directly into an Internet connection and performs the same translation without separate software. An ATA device takes the analog signal from a traditional phone and converts it into digital data that can be transmitted over the Internet.

You can make audio and video calls over the web using your computer or mobile device.

Using VoIP service eliminates the need to have long-distance telephone service, which sometimes involves paying extra charges. To take advantage of this savings, some users eliminate traditional telephone lines from their homes and make all calls using VoIP service along with a mobile phone. Vonage pioneered VoIP service, but many high-speed ISPs now offer VoIP calling plans, including TimeWarner Cable, SBC Communications, and HughesNet. Juniper Research has estimated that mobile VoIP usage would reach one billion users (or one in seven mobile subscribers) by 2017.

Audio, Video, and Podcasts

To watch a video or listen to a song stored on the Internet, users previously had to download the file to a computer and use a dedicated application to open it or download the file to a digital media player, such as an iPod.

Now, you can either download the file or stream it online.

Cutting Edge

Accelerating Innovation

The development of advanced, high-speed Internet applications and technologies is being facilitated by the Internet2 research platform. Internet2 is a consortium of more than 200 universities that are working in partnership with industry and government. It enables large US research universities to collaborate and share huge amounts of complex scientific information at amazing speeds. The goal is to someday transfer these capabilities to the broader Internet community.

Internet2 provides a testing ground for universities to work together and develop advanced Internet technologies, such as telemedicine, digital libraries, and virtual laboratories. An example of this collaboration is the Informedia Digital Video Library (IDVL) project. IDVL uses a combination of speech recognition, image understanding, and natural language processing technology to automatically transcribe, partition, and index video segments. Doing so enables intelligent searching and navigation, along with selective retrieval of information.

Internet2 has partnered with Level 3 Communications to launch the Internet2 Network backbone, which is capable of supporting speeds of more than 100 gigabits per second (Gbps). To learn more about Internet2, visit the Internet2 website at http://CUT6.emcp.net/Internet2.

Downloading The most popular music download service, Apple's iTunes, works with a variety of devices, including Windows-based computers. Most music download websites charge a per-track or per-album download fee. You "own" the music but can only sync or copy it to a limited number of devices.

For some time, the most widely used music file format for downloads was Moving Pictures Expert Group Layer III **(MP3 format)**. The MP3 compression format reduces the size of CD-quality sound files by a factor of 10 to 14. It reduces file sizes by removing recorded sounds that the human ear can't perceive. The MP3 format creates files that are much smaller and easier to download.

Compression and file size are an issue of some controversy for audio fanatics. iTunes files use the **Advanced Audio Coding (AAC) format**, which is thought to provide higher audio quality with comparable compression. Windows has another format: **Windows Media Audio (WMA) format**. Other enthusiasts prefer the **Free Lossless Audio Codec (FLAC) format**. This open source method provides efficient, **lossless compression**, which means none of the original sound information is eliminated.

iTunes and Windows Media Player, as well as other digital music management programs, enable you to **rip** (copy) songs from a CD and choose the file format and compression level you prefer. Once you have downloaded or ripped a music file to your computer's hard disk, you can transfer the song to a portable digital music player or smartphone for mobile playback.

You can view downloaded video files using an application such as Microsoft Windows Media Player. Many formats are used for digital movies, such as **MPEG (Moving Picture Experts Group) format** and the newer **MP4 format** and **WMV (Windows Media Video) format**. Because video files are very large, downloading movies or long clips takes a long time unless you have a high-speed Internet connection.

Some online audio and video files are called *podcasts*. In some ways, a **podcast** is like a typical downloadable audio or video file (or even a PDF or ebook file), but it's different in the sense that each download is often part of an ongoing series. Podcasts may be offered as daily or weekly episodes or as parts of a larger, comprehensive broadcast. Although most users typically listen to podcasts on portable devices, you can also play them back on a computer using applicable software for the podcast file format.

Streaming An alternative to downloading a song or video from the Internet is a technique called *streaming*. **Streaming** sends a continuous stream of data to the receiving computer's web browser, which plays the audio or video. Old data is erased as new data arrives, which means no complete copy of the material downloads. Streaming protects the owners of copyrighted materials to some degree, because it eliminates the possibility of copying and sharing.

The entertainment and rich media (streaming and interactive media) that are offered on the web have become increasingly full of features and easier to use. Sites such as YouTube and Pandora have become the Internet standard in video and music streaming.

YouTube enables people to upload, view, share, and comment about videos. The videos range from political commentaries to music videos to product reviews, plus some clips of random silliness. YouTube streams many videos at low resolutions to speed download and viewing time, but some are high-definition (HD) quality. YouTube is free to users, because the service is supported by advertising.

Pandora is a free, ad-supported online radio service that personalizes the songs it plays for listeners. It selects songs for you by analyzing what songs you have listened to previously. In 2013, Apple launched a similar service, iTunes Radio, offering more than 250 stations of music.

Using a portable music player is a convenient way to listen to songs downloaded from the Internet.

Other services offer fee-based video and music streaming or offer some free content along with the option to pay for additional content. For example, the Rhapsody music streaming service allows you to play music and share it on a limited number of devices or to stream it through an Internet-connected "smart" TV. Hulu offers some free online TV episodes and other content (such as documentaries), but it also lets you upgrade to Hulu Plus's more advanced content for a fee. And of course, the monthly subscription service Netflix enables you to stream TV and movie content to a variety of devices. Google Play also enables you to purchase movies and music.

It's also possible to view TV shows, music videos, movies, and other types of videos from a variety of websites. Many news networks and newspapers offer video on their websites. You can click on a story and then view a short video newscast that gives you all of the details.

Downloading versus Streaming   So which is better: downloading or streaming audio and video content? The answer depends on your preferences. If you like to control the cost on a case-by-case basis and "own" the content, then you should rip or download and purchase your media. But if you love to sample new music and movies, you will prefer the variety available through streaming subscription services.

Purchasing media allows you more control over access to the content. Every online service has usage agreements with particular artists and content providers. If any of those agreements changes, the service may have to remove certain songs and videos from its catalog. Should that happen, subscribers would no longer have access to that content.

Activity 5.7.2

Article
Streaming Media

Audio Books and Ebooks

Online books represent the latest "battleground" in terms of competition among digital entertainment services. Audible.com and other services provide downloadable audio books that users can play on digital music players. Amazon's Kindle reader spawned the first large group of **ebook** consumers. Amazon's Kindle eBooks store is the leading ebook retailer, holding a significant share of the market. Even if you don't have a Kindle, you can download a free Kindle app for another device and then purchase ebooks and read them using the app. You can also buy downloadable ebooks at Apple's online store, the Barnes & Noble NOOK Book Store, and the Google Play service, along with a other ebook stores and publishers.

While publishing hard copies of a book can be expensive, publishing a digital book is much less costly. With the right software and expertise, virtually anyone can publish an ebook. You can learn the ins and outs of the different file formats required by various ebook retailers, or you can produce and promote your ebook using a service such as BookBaby. These services produce and promote your ebook for a flat fee and, in some cases, a commission on royalties received from the digital retailer. Although ebooks

Hotspot

Replacing TV with Telephone?

InMobi (a mobile ad company) surveyed individuals about smartphone watching versus TV watching. According to the survey, the average person spends more minutes a day watching his or her smartphone than watching TV. At least 77 percent of users reported using their phones for online entertainment, including video and music.

Be aware that streaming media uses a lot of data. Know the data limit on your phone plan, and watch the amount of data you are using. You can reduce the amount of data you use through your phone service by connecting to a wireless network whenever possible.

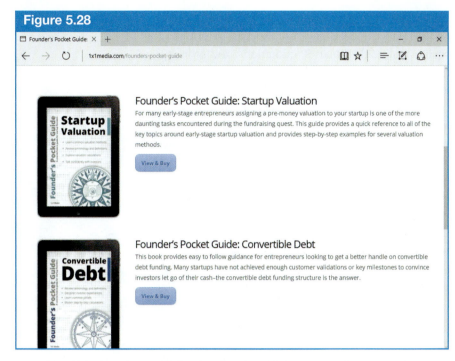

Figure 5.28

Ebooks are available for sale from digital booksellers and publishers, such as independent publisher 1x1 Media.

typically sell for less than print books, ebook publishing can offer a great money-making opportunity for individuals and independent publishers (see Figure 5.28).

iBooks Author from Apple enables creation of a new generation of ebooks. Using this free app, you can create interactive iBooks for iPad and Mac OS X. iBooks makes it possible to include not only videos but also galleries, interactive diagrams, 3-D objects, and more.

Health and Science

The web now also teems with medical information. Your personal medical providers and local medical facilities all likely have websites with basic information about location, hours, contact numbers, and service offerings. Some sites also offer health news and information that you might find useful, such as details about upcoming wellness programs. National health resources are also online, such as WebMD and MayoClinic.org. Sites such as these provide both current medical news and information about specific diseases and conditions, treatments, and medications.

If you are scientifically minded, you might enjoy exploring the range of resources available on the web. You can check out the online versions of popular publications, such as *Science* (Sciencemag.org), *Science Daily* (ScienceDaily.com), and *Popular Science* (Popsci.com). You can also check out the science offerings of media outlets such as Discovery Channel and National Geographic. At their websites, you can search to find serious scientific research and publications or fun science in the form of home science experiments.

Online Reference Tools

If you are a writer or researcher, you may feel overwhelmed by the huge number and variety of resources on the web. To make your search more efficient, use one of the reference tools available online, such as Refdesk.com. Refdesk.com, which calls itself the "Fact Checker for the Internet," serves as a dashboard to other core resources for researchers. It includes direct connections to all of the most popular search sites. In addition, it provides thought provokers such as "Fact of the Day," "Word of the Day," and "This Day in History"; links to news and weather sites; games and other diversions; translation tools; links to online encyclopedias and more specific information sources; and writer's resources, such as online dictionaries, quotations, and style and writing guides.

Other reference sites address specific subject matter or provide specific types of help. For example, About.com and HowStuffWorks offer instructions and information about a lot of tasks and topics. By searching, you can find sites offering useful information about everything from cleaning to legal advice. Of course, the websites of many schools and universities offer reference information about their programs. A search might turn up school-approved writing guidelines or research results of a study performed conducted by a particular department.

Wikipedia represents another valuable reference resource: a wiki. A **wiki** works like an online encyclopedia, but it allows anyone to contribute information. Users can post new articles about subjects, or they can edit or contribute to existing articles, add "Notes" or "See also" entries, or respond to questions or disputed information in an article. The idea behind a wiki is that having many users' contributions will improve the quality of the information in the article. Another popular wiki, wikiHow, is devoted to teaching users how to do anything. You also may see user-created "Help" and "How-to" wikis for open source software.

One potential drawback about using wikis applies to many online reference resources: Make sure the resource is credible and has a good reputation. In other words, know your sources.

Gaming and Gambling

Online gaming and gambling have grown into popular Internet pastimes for many people. Users can play by themselves or compete with other players, often in very real online worlds. For example, **virtual reality (VR)** involves a computer simulation of an imagined but convincing environment or set of surroundings. Games enhance the VR effect by enabling each player to select a virtual body, called an **avatar**, which serves as his or her point of view in the game world.

Millions of players pay monthly fees to play World of Warcraft, the most popular online game in the world. Many users also spend significant time gaming on mobile devices; in fact, apps for games are some of the most frequently downloaded mobile apps. Users also enjoy gaming through other platforms, such as Facebook.

Online casinos are a unique and controversial form of entertainment. Users can log on and gamble online in a virtual casino. Although online casinos are prohibited by law in many areas, they are difficult to police because they may be located in any part of the world. The experience may seem like playing a game, but any losses are real and will be billed to the user's credit card.

Distance Learning Platforms

As discussed earlier in this chapter, online or distance learning platforms serve the needs of degree-seeking and non-degree-seeking learners around the world. These platforms have developed in response to the rising costs of advanced education and the ongoing need for skills development and training. Some universities provide fee-based online learning services, such as online or hybrid (part online, part on campus) courses. MBA programs are offered online by a number of major business schools.

As noted earlier, you can also take advantage of free online courses from websites

Activity 5.7.3

Article
Earning a Degree Online

such as Coursera. A **massive open online course (MOOC)** provides free and open access and frequently offers the best content from top schools and partners. MOOCs typically include online video lectures with accompanying project assignments and tests. Some provide a completion certificate (either free or for a fee for some Coursera courses), which can be used as an employment credential. In addition to Coursera, other MOOC providers include Udacity and edX, whose partners include the Massachusetts Institute of Technology (MIT), Harvard University, and the University of California, Berkeley.

Some universities have adopted MOOCs to offer online degree programs. Using this successful technology has allowed schools to offer low-cost educational opportunities to a broader range of students than they can normally serve. While these programs aren't free, they are offered at a reduced cost. Students therefore have the chance to earn a college degree online for a reduced cost, compared with an on-campus degree. In 2013, the Georgia Institute of Technology (Georgia Tech) became the first top-ranked university to offer an online master's degree program. The cost of earning the degree online was less than one-fourth what it would cost students to earn the degree on campus. Twice as many students enrolled in the online program than in the standard program.

Research about the success of distance learning programs is ongoing. However, even the early data suggest that students stay more motivated when taking online courses than regular courses. Offerings for distance learning and online degree will most likely continue to expand in the next decade.

Web Demonstrations, Presentations, and Meetings

Not only educators are using the web as a platform for information delivery. In addition, businesses and organizations are using the web increasingly to share information and provide education. For example, many companies create media-rich and interactive product demos to show potential buyers product features and options.

Microsoft's PowerPoint presentation graphics program enables you to share a presentation online with users that you invite. A tool will prompt you to invite the users and then lead you through starting the online presentation. So, while you are holding a conference call, for example, your colleagues can view the presentation you have prepared as you walk them through it, slide by slide, over the phone.

Other online meeting services offer a more robust experience, including audio and video (of both participants and information), whiteboard-style brainstorming, and more. Team members around the country or the world can participate in live meetings via computer or mobile device. These services go beyond what can be done with PowerPoint and similar one-way presentation programs, because they allow all of the participants to interact with the online content. The leaders in these services include WebEx and GoToMeeting.

Sometimes, organizations use online meeting services to host a webinar, or web-based seminar. Conducting a webinar allows communicating directly with customers and others. A service such as AnyMeeting allows users to conduct online webinars and meetings with up to 200 participants. (Chapter 7 discusses other forms of online collaboration and teamwork.)

Recheck 5.7
Recheck your understanding of the concepts covered by this objective.

5.8 Respecting the Internet Community

Precheck 5.8
Check your understanding of the concepts covered by this objective.

Internet users around the world form a community, and like members of any community, they exhibit the entire range of behaviors possible—from considerate and creative to insulting and damaging. Unfortunately, the anonymous nature of Internet interaction tends to bring out the worst in some people. The fear of embarrassment or shame that sometimes governs behavior in face-to-face encounters fades away when people interact on the Internet. This means that some individuals act very differently than they would if they were in a public forum. These individuals ruin the Internet experience for others but experience few consequences themselves.

Guidelines for good net behavior have been developed to encourage people to be considerate and productive. Providing moderated environments is another way to manage inappropriate behavior. In addition, a number of technical and legal issues influence the direction and development of the Internet. Companies and individuals insist that standard protocols and increased transmission bandwidths be provided, consumers worry about the privacy and security of Internet communications and transactions, and copyright holders want stronger protection for their intellectual property.

Netiquette

Netiquette (*net* and *etiquette*) is a collection of guidelines that define good net behavior. Netiquette is based on the idea that people should treat others as they would like others to treat them.

Some points of netiquette address problem behaviors such as **flaming**, which is the Internet equivalent of insulting someone face to face. By taking advantage of the anonymity that's offered online, some people are as rude as possible, to the point that they drive others away. So-called flame wars are instances of flaming that are traded back and forth, often among multiple parties.

Other points of netiquette deal with Internet conventions that users should learn to avoid offending others unintentionally. For example, new email users commonly type messages in all capital letters without realizing that, by convention, using all caps is equivalent to shouting. Without meaning to, these email writers may make people

Practical TECH

The Internet Is Forever

The fact that Facebook and Twitter feeds seem to scroll off and SnapChat Snaps seem to disappear immediately may tempt you to act out or reveal too much information online. You should remember, though, that the servers hosting your data may archive it for a long time, and other users may capture and keep your material. For example, it's possible for a recipient to make a screenshot of a SnapChat Snap and post it on another service, such as Facebook or Twitter. In short, don't put anything online that you wouldn't want a future employer or anyone else to see. If you must post "selfies," avoid photos that show you nude, behaving badly, and so on.

uncomfortable or even angry. Knowing the common rules of netiquette listed in Figure 5.29 can help you avoid this and other unintentional offenses.

Having some specific suggestions for composing and sending email and other types of digital messages (including text messages and posts to social media) may help you better understand netiquette. Because composing and sending email is so quick and easy, you should be careful to avoid mistakes that you might regret later. Keep in mind these important points when writing and sending email messages and making posts:

- In most cases, an email message can't be retrieved after it's been sent.
- A permanent copy of any email message probably exists somewhere on the Internet.
- Others can easily forward or copy your email messages and posts.

For these reasons, it's a good idea to avoid sending or posting any message that you have written in anger or haste. Save the message and then look at it again later, after you have cooled down. If you still feel the message should be sent or posted, you will still have that option. However, in most cases, you will realize that you would have regretted sending or posting the original message.

Figure 5.29

Core Rules of Netiquette

Rule 1
Remember the human

Rule 2
Adhere to the same standards of behavior online that you follow in real life

Rule 3
Know where you are in cyberspace

Rule 4
Respect other people's time and bandwidth

Rule 5
Make yourself look good online

Rule 6
Share expert knowledge

Rule 7
Help keep flame wars under control

Rule 8
Respect other people's privacy

Rule 9
Don't abuse your power

Rule 10
Be forgiving of other people's mistakes

Source: Adapted from *Netiquette*, by Virginia Shea (Albion Books, 1994)

Moderated Environments

Many people who want to avoid the seedy side of the Internet interact with others in moderated environments. Many chat rooms, message boards, and mailing lists have a **moderator**, an individual with the power to filter messages and ban people who break the rules. Rule violations can range from making insults to not staying on topic. A moderator running a chat room on travel, for example, might warn or ban people for discussing their favorite movies at length. Usually, a moderator has complete power over the situation and can discipline people any way he or she sees fit. If a moderator is too harsh, however, people might switch to another group.

Net Neutrality

A common principle among networks is that of *network neutrality*, often shortened to **net neutrality**. Net neutrality is a doctrine or code of fairness that states that all Internet traffic will be treated with equal priority. In other words, one packet won't be favored or ignored over another, no matter who the sender or receiver might be.

Following this policy has several benefits. One key benefit is that the system's job of transmitting data is simplified. No data is more important than other data; it's all the same in value. This means that the system simply passes on whatever data it gets to the intended destination without judging the content. The policy of net neutrality also provides for greater innovation. When a new website is put up on the web, it's treated by the internal structure of the Internet with the same respect as the most popular site on the planet. By "leveling the playing field" in this way, the policy allows new sites to grow rapidly. In 2015, the FCC ruled in favor of net neutrality and issued new net neutrality rules.

Privacy Issues

Privacy is a major concern for many Internet users, particularly with email communications and e-commerce transactions. Most users know that email messages can be intercepted and read by others. In the workplace, employees' email messages may be read by their supervisors, and current law gives employers the right to do that. Monitoring employees' email is becoming more common as businesses discover that their workers are spending time surfing the web for personal reasons, instead of doing their work. (For more on employee monitoring, security, and similar privacy topics, see Chapter 9.)

Copyright Infringement

Many of the materials found on the web are copyrighted, and copying and using them without permission is illegal. Most websites include a copyright notice that states general guidelines for how the site's content may be used (see Figure 5.30 for an example). Nevertheless, users frequently ignore copyright laws, and some violators end up in court, such as those who used P2P services to obtain copyrighted music files.

Because most copyright laws were written with printed materials in mind, the US Congress passed a law in 1998 that addressed the major issues related to protecting digital content on the Internet (which can include text, videos, music, and many other file formats). The **Digital Millennium Copyright Act of 1998 (DMCA)** generally prohibits people from disabling software encryption programs and other safeguards that copyright holders have put in place to control access to their works. Entertainment companies have tried to protect their movies on DVDs by including security codes, but hackers have already developed programs capable of cracking them. A key provision of the Digital Millennium Copyright Act makes the use and distribution of security-cracking codes illegal, and the penalty involves civil damages ranging from $200 to $2,500. Repeat offenders face criminal penalties of up to $1 million in fines and 10 years in jail.

Figure 5.30

© 2016 The New York Times Company | Contact Us | Work With Us | Advertise | Your Ad Choices | Privacy | Terms of Service | Terms of Sale

The copyright notice on the *New York Times* home page reminds visitors that the content of the site is copyrighted.

Recheck 5.8

Recheck your understanding of the concepts covered by this objective.

Chapter Summary

➡️ *An interactive **Chapter Summary**, **Study Notes**, and a **Slide Presentation** with audio are available from the links menu on this page in your ebook.*

5.1 Exploring Our World's Network: The Internet

The Internet is used for communication, working remotely (**telecommuting**) and collaboration. Computers can be used for social connections and entertainment purposes, including playing games, listening to music, and viewing movies and videos. Electronic commerce (e-commerce) refers to the Internet exchange of business information, products, services, and payments. The Internet is a vast source of information to support both research and **distance learning**.

5.2 Connecting to the Internet

To connect to the Internet, the user must have an account with an **Internet service provider (ISP)**, which is a company that provides Internet access. The ISP will give the user a user name and password. Several types of Internet service are available. The older type of **dial-up access** is being replaced by **broadband connections**; they include cable, **digital subscriber line (DSL)**, wireless, satellite, and fiber-optic connections. Many users can share an Internet connection over a local area network (LAN), which is often wireless, or from a wireless **Wi-Fi hotspot**.

5.3 Navigating the Internet

Surfing the Internet means gaining access to and moving about the web using a browser. **Web browsers** locate material on the Internet using **Internet Protocol (IP) addresses**. Every IP also has a corresponding web address called a **uniform resource locator (URL)**, which is a path name that describes where the material can be found. The Internet breaks files into many pieces of data called **packets** and sends them out over separate routes in a process called **packet switching**.

5.4 Understanding Web Page Markup Languages

Web pages are usually created using **Hypertext Markup Language (HTML)**. **Extensible Markup Language (XML)** is a new and improved web language that allows computers to manage data more effectively. A **hyperlink** is any element on the screen that's coded to transport viewers to another page or site.

5.5 Viewing Web Pages

A **web page** is a single document that's viewable on the World Wide Web. A **website** is a collection of web pages about a particular topic. You use a web browser program to view and navigate between web pages and websites. The **home page** appears initially when you go to a website. You can enter the URL for a page in the browser Address bar and then press Enter to load the page. Website designers frequently program using **Java** and a variety of other scripting languages. A **plug-in** is a mini-program that extends the capabilities of web browsers in a variety of ways. Companies advertise on websites using **banner ads** and **pop-up ads**.

5.6 Searching for Information on the Internet

Search engines help you look for information using **keywords** (search terms). Advanced searching requires the use of logic statements known as **search operators**; using these operators will refine searches and improve results.

5.7 Using Other Internet Resources and Services

Most ISP accounts provide free email, but users also have the option of choosing a web-based service such as Gmail, Yahoo! Mail, or Outlook.com. Another option is to use **webmail**, rather than email software, to access email with a variety of devices, including mobile devices. Dozens of new **social networking services** enable users to connect and interact online for social and professional purposes. Users can also set up **blog**s to write articles about various topics and share them online. **Voice over Internet Protocol (VoIP)** technology provides free video and voice calling service over the Internet, rather than the telephone network. Tiny video cameras called *webcams* allow video to be included in the calls. Rather than download a piece of music or a video, users can access it using **streaming**. Streaming online entertainment to a variety of devices represents a fast-growing use of the Internet. Similarly, many users are purchasing and downloading **ebooks**, which can be read on computers, mobile devices, and even special readers such as Kindles. Users also enjoy a variety of gaming and gambling opportunities on the web. Students can take advantage of **massive open online courses (MOOCs)** to learn new skills or even get college degrees. Online presentation and meeting services improve businesses' productivity through webinars.

5.8 Respecting the Internet Community

Guidelines for good online behavior, called **netiquette**, have been developed to encourage people to interact politely and productively. **Flaming** is one of the most frequently encountered examples of rude Internet behavior. Providing a **moderator** is another way of managing inappropriate behavior. Other concerns for Internet use include net neutrality, privacy, and copyright infringement. **Net neutrality** is the policy that all Internet traffic will be treated with equal priority. Privacy is a concern particularly with email communications and e-commerce transactions. Copyright infringement occurs frequently on the Internet. The **Digital Millennium Copyright Act of 1998 (DMCA)** generally prohibits people from breaking software encryption and other safeguards.

Key Terms

Numbers indicate the pages where terms are first cited with their full definition in the chapter. An alphabetized list of key terms with definitions is included in the end-of-book glossary.

 *An interactive **Glossary** is available from the links menu on this page in your ebook.*

Chapter Exercises

Complete the following exercises to assess your understanding of the material covered in this chapter.

 *Interactive **Flash Cards** and an interactive **Game** are available from the links menu on this page in your ebook.*

Go to your SNAP Assignments page to complete the Terms Check, Knowledge Check, Key Principles, and Tech Illustrated exercises.

Terms Check: Matching

Match each term with its definition.

a.	packet	f.	e-commerce
b.	HTML	g.	browser
c.	netiquette	h.	banner
d.	spam	i.	zip file
e.	keyword	j.	dynamic routing

___ 1. A common type of compressed data file.

___ 2. A term used to find information using a search engine.

___ 3. Business conducted using the Internet.

___ 4. Unwanted messages sent in large numbers and often repeatedly over the Internet.

___ 5. A program that allows users to retrieve information on the World Wide Web.

___ 6. Small, rectangular advertisements used to promote products and services on web pages.

___ 7. The method used to send packets by a variety of different routes to their final destination.

___ 8. The code of guidelines for appropriate behavior for Internet users.

___ 9. The programming language long used to create web pages.

___ 10. A small amount of data sent across the Internet.

Knowledge Check: Multiple Choice

Choose the best answer for each question.

1. The first screen that's usually visible when entering a web site is called the
   a. webmaster.
   b. home page.
   c. banner.
   d. hyperlink.

2. Of the following types of Internet connections, which generally provides the slowest connection speed?
   a. dial-up
   b. DSL
   c. wireless
   d. All of these are about the same.

3. To transmit data over the Internet, messaging software breaks files into
   a. attachments.
   b. clip-ons.
   c. plug-ins.
   d. packets.

4. When you use your smartphone to connect to the Internet, you are using it as a(n)
   a. dial-up modem.
   b. roaming modem.
   c. cable modem.
   d. hotspot.

5. HTML stands for
   a. High-Tech Marketing Language.
   b. High-Tech Markup Language.
   c. Hypertext Markup Language.
   d. Hypertext Marketing Language.

6. Files added to email messages are known as
   a. attachments.
   b. clip-ons.
   c. plug-ins.
   d. packets.

7. ISP stands for
   a. international satellite phone.
   b. Internet satellite protocol.
   c. Internet service provider.
   d. international satellite provider.

8. How is chat or instant messaging different from email?
   a. You have to pay for IM service.
   b. With chat or IM, you type messages back and forth in real time and they stay onscreen.
   c. There is only one provider of IM services.
   d. None of these

9. A leading social media site for business users is
   a. LinkedIn.
   b. Facebook.
   c. Instagram.
   d. Pinterest

10. FTP enables you to
    a. organize emails in folders.
    b. chat on Facebook and save the conversation.
    c. send and receive files that can't be sent via email.
    d. program a website with styles.

Key Principles: Completion

Complete each statement with the appropriate word or phrase.

1. The graphic persona of a player in a virtual reality game is called a(n) _____.

2. A small file stored on a web surfer's hard drive that might be used to track his or her behavior is called a(n) _____.

3. The part of a URL that comes last and identifies the type of organization is called the _____.

4. Another way of accessing email via the web is _____.

5. A four-group series of numbers separated by periods represents a(n) _____.

6. An advertisement that appears within a rectangular portion of a web page is called a(n) _____.

7. Unwanted email messages that are transmitted over the Internet are called _____.

8. The design feature that describes how packets are moved around the Internet by the best available route is called _____.

9. The user's approval is often requested on a website before a _____ is downloaded and installed to provide additional functionality.

10. _____ sites, such as Facebook, enable you to interact with other users online.

Tech Illustrated: Figure Labeling

Fill in the blanks with the correct labels.

1. Packet switching

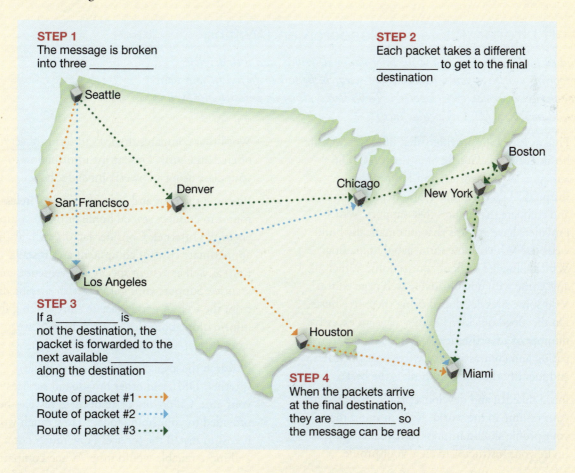

STEP 1
The message is broken into three _____

STEP 2
Each packet takes a different _____ to get to the final destination

STEP 3
If a _____ is not the destination, the packet is forwarded to the next available _____ along the destination

Route of packet #1 ····▶
Route of packet #2 ····▶
Route of packet #3 ····▶

STEP 4
When the packets arrive at the final destination, they are _____ so the message can be read

2. URL structure

a. _____   b. _____   c. _____   d. _____

http:// www.nasa.gov/ audience/forstudents/ index.html

Tech to Come: Brainstorming New Uses

In groups or individually, contemplate the following questions and develop as many answers as you can.

1. Smartphones, household appliances, vending machines, road systems, and buildings are just a few of the things that can be connected to the Internet for control and monitoring purposes. How will developing new uses for the Internet change its nature and how we think about it? What other new applications might be possible if roads can tell us how much traffic there is, if cars can tell how much fuel they have left, and if refrigerators can tell us there's no more juice?

2. Chat and instant messaging (IM) technology have grown from forms of social media to tools for business communication. Financial services and retail websites offer customers live "chat" with customer service representatives, and colleagues within organizations can chat to meet informally whenever the need arises. How will the use of chat and IM likely evolve as video messaging and calling become more popular? What additional benefits will this technology provide for businesses, both internally and externally?

Tech Literacy: Internet Research and Writing

Conduct Internet research to find the information described, and then develop appropriate written responses based on your research. Be sure to document your sources using the MLA format. (See Chapter 1, Tech Literacy: Internet Research and Writing, page 38, to review MLA style guidelines.)

1. Find at least four providers that offer free website hosting, such as Google Sites (**http://CUT6 .emcp.net/GoogleSites**) and Homestead (**http://CUT6.emcp.net/Homestead**). Identify and compare the features they support. Which providers have wizards that automatically build websites? Which allow form-based uploading? Which allow FTP client connections? Which, if any, come with downloadable web page editors? Visit some sites developed using these free hosts. Do they load quickly? Do they have an excessive number of advertisements? Write a report comparing and contrasting these free host providers, and identify the one you think is the best.

2. Join LinkedIn and develop a profile that presents your résumé to the world. Keep in mind that your profile should impress potential employers. Invite your instructor to view your profile.

3. Find out what ISPs are available in your area. Which one would best meet your needs? If you don't have access to a computer at home, assume that you are researching this information for your school. For each ISP, identify the services, speeds, and other account features it offers. Also find out information about the costs of the services. Then create a chart in Excel or

Word that compares the ISPs in terms of services offered and costs. Present the information to your class using a PowerPoint slide show.

4. Research the pros and cons of using a wireless router to connect several home or office computers to the Internet. Consider factors such as the approximate costs of equipment and installation, as well as system speeds, convenience, and security. Support your answers with specific data from the web. A good place to start looking for information about this equipment is Newegg .com (**http://CUT6.emcp.net/Newegg**).

5. Research the availability and cost of cable Internet, DSL, and other broadband services in your area. Could any or all of these services be provided to your home today? How much would it cost to install the service? How much faster and more reliable would it be? When comparing the costs, include the cost of a second phone line for a dial-up system; the faster systems have the advantage of not tying up the phone.

6. Find a web page that uses Flash animation. Game advertisements from companies such as Disney, Sony, and Microsoft tend to use Flash animation frequently. At the web page, were you asked you to download a plug-in? Are the

resulting graphics superior? How much longer does it take to load a page with Shockwave graphics compared with a page with simple HTML? (Be sure to mention the type of Internet connection you are using.)

Tech Issues: Team Problem-Solving

In groups, develop possible solutions to the issues presented.

1. Should federal and state governments invest heavily in providing high-speed Internet connections to schools and libraries? Why or why not? If the government pays for Internet service, should it have a say in how schools and libraries use the Internet? After the technology has been perfected, should high schools and colleges require students to use electronic versions of textbooks downloaded from the Internet? What would be the advantages and disadvantages of requiring this?

2. Many people use the web to operate their own businesses or to telecommute. If you were to consider working from home, what advantages and disadvantages would you consider? Would more risk be involved? More freedom? Less work or more work? What would be your greatest concern? Support your answers by conducting web research on this topic.

3. Experts claim that the "shelf life" of knowledge is only two to three years in many fields, including areas as diverse as medicine, technology, engineering, and history. How can distance learning and web-based tools help address this issue? Given this problem, should college diplomas be stamped with an "expiration date"? Why or why not?

Tech Timeline: Predicting Next Steps

Listed below is a timeline of some of the major events in the history of cybercrime. As you review the list, think of what major events might occur next, in terms of both hacker actions and the government's response. Use your predictions to complete the timeline through the year 2025.

1984 The press learns of several high-profile incidences of criminals breaking security systems and uses the term *hacker* to describe these criminals.

1986 The Electronic Communications Privacy Act and the Computer Fraud and Abuse Act both pass Congress.

1988 Robert Morris, a college student, releases a worm that brings much of the Internet to a halt.

1990 On January 15, AT&T's long-distance telephone switching system crashes, disrupting 70 million phone calls.

1990 In May, Operation Sundevil commences. Sundevil was the code name for the government's sweeping effort to crack down on cybercrime.

2000 In January hackers shut down Yahoo.com, Amazon.com, CNN.com, and eBay.com, among others, for one hour.

2000 In March, a 13-year-old hacker breaks into a government security system that tracks US Air Force planes worldwide, damaging a "secret" system.

2001 A cyberwar flares up between Chinese and American hackers after a US Navy plane collides with a Chinese fighter aircraft, killing the Chinese pilot. Each group of hackers attacks thousands of sites in the other nation.

2002 The Federal Bureau of Investigation (FBI) arrests three men who gained unauthorized access to credit reports and caused consumer losses of more than $2.7 million.

2003 The Department of Justice, FBI, and Federal Trade Commission conduct a major cybercrime sweep called *Operation E-Con* that results in 130 arrests and $17 million in property seizures related to Internet auction scams, bogus investments, credit card fraud, and identity theft.

2004 The fastest-growing Internet scam is now "phishing," in which criminals pretend to represent a legitimate web site or institution and request updates to individuals' financial records.

2005 Hackers favor the use of keystroke-logging technologies to steal sensitive information.

2005 Hackers crack Microsoft's antipiracy system within 24 hours after its launch.

2006 Jeanson James Ancheta pleads guilty to four felony charges for creating and selling so-called botnets: thousands of computers infected with malicious code and turned into zombie computers to commit crimes.

2009 An 18-year-old hacker going by the name GMZ cracks a Twitter staffer's password and gains access to high-profile celebrity Twitter accounts.

2010 The Stuxnet worm is deployed to disable equipment at Iran's nuclear facilities.

2013 In July, US Army soldier Chelsea Manning is convicted of violating the Espionage Act by releasing digital copies of classified documents to the public.

2013 In August, US National Security Agency contractor Edward Snowden flees the United States after copying and releasing classified documents and is granted asylum in Russia.

2015 Ross Ulbricht, creator and owner of Silk Road, an online black market for illegal goods, is sentenced to life in prison. He appeals the sentence. (Silk Road is part of the dark web, or areas on the Internet that require special software or authorizations to access.)

Ethical Dilemmas: Group Discussion and Debate

As a class or within an assigned group, discuss the following ethical dilemma.

The appeal of message boards is often the anonymity that the medium provides. In minutes, you can create a user name, log on to a board, and discuss the board topic with other a group of strangers—all without revealing your true identity. But what consequences would you face if the message board operator shared your account information with,

say, your family, employer, or law enforcement authorities? What prevents the board operator from doing this? Would you have any recourse against the operator? Does thinking about this dilemma change your view on what you would and would not say on a message board?

Chapter 6

Networking and Communicating with Computers and Other Devices

Chapter Goal

To understand how networking technology enables communication between computing devices

Learning Objectives

6.1 Explain the characteristics of data transmission.

6.2 Distinguish between wired and wireless communications media.

6.3 Differentiate among network types by architecture, coverage, and users.

6.4 Distinguish between network topologies.

6.5 Identify common types of networking hardware.

6.6 Describe the software that a network requires and the protocols used in network connections.

6.7 Explain how to set up and use wireless networks.

Green go-online icons indicate resources that are accessed from the links menu in your ebook.

SNAP icons indicate interactive resources that are available in SNAP. Go to your SNAP Assignments page to complete these quizzes, activities, and exercises.

functional limit of a dial-up modem). Nowadays, however, 256 Kbps is considered very slow, even though it's technically broadband; typical networking speeds start at around 10 Mbps and go upward from there.

Parallel and Serial Transmission

Data transmission can take place in either serial form or parallel form. Recall from Chapter 2 that a byte is eight bits. A **serial transmission** sends one bit at a time. As an analogy, think about a narrow path that only one person can walk on at a time. If eight people need to get to the end of the path, each person will have to walk through individually, one person after the other. At the destination, the party of eight will reassemble.

In contrast, a **parallel transmission** sends many related bits at a time. To use the same analogy, with a parallel transmission, there are eight separate paths, and each person takes a different path to the destination. Some people may arrive at the destination faster than others; if so, the early arrivers will wait until all eight people in the party have arrived before moving to the next step of their journey. Figure 6.2 compares the data movement through a serial cable versus a parallel one.

In the early days of computing, there was more data to be sent than there was available bandwidth to carry it. A serial pathway would be pushed to the limit with a backlog of data waiting to be sent and received. Parallel transmission was developed for devices that required higher bandwidth rates than the serial ports of the day could

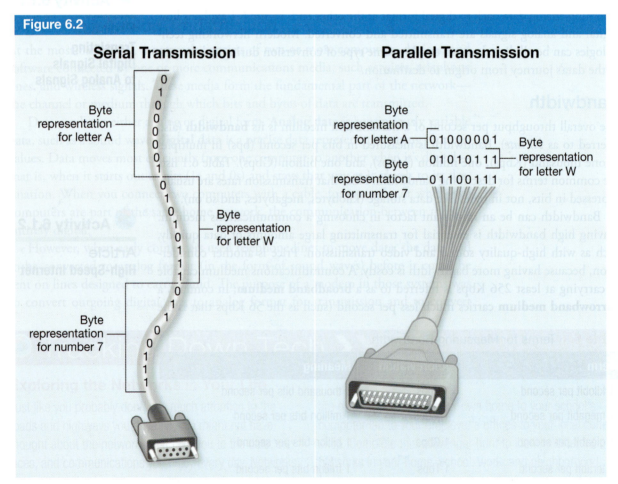

Figure 6.2

In serial transmission, all the data bits travel one at a time. In parallel transmission, a group of bits travel simultaneously over different paths.

handle. The most common parallel data pathways were from the motherboard to the hard disk drive (which was a parallel interface) and to the printer (also a parallel interface). Parallel transmission had its problems, though. The cable length was limited to about 6 feet, and the farther the data had to travel, the more latency (waiting) there was for the eight bits in a byte to catch up to one another.

Today's serial cables and ports can handle much higher bandwidth, so there's little reason to use parallel transmission anymore. The original uses for parallel transmission (hard drives and printers) now use serial transmission in most systems (serial ATA for hard drives and universal serial bus (USB) for printers).

Parallel transmission has never been very popular for networking. In the early days of computing, users sometimes connected two computers via their parallel ports (LPT ports) for a makeshift network for file sharing, but this setup was never optimal. Serial transmission has always been and continues to be the mainstay of network transmission.

Cutting Edge

Fiber-Optic Multiplexing

Multiplexing doesn't apply just to basic copper wires and TV systems; it can be implemented on fiber-optic cable too. Dense wave division multiplexing (DWDM) is a technology that uses different wavelengths of laser light to enable multiple data streams to be transmitted over a single optical fiber. The prohibitive cost of constructing new fiber-optic networks makes DWDM an attractive option for dealing with the increasing demand for high-speed Internet access.

Duplexing and Multiplexing

With **simplex transmission**, data is sent in only one direction. An example of a simplex transmission is an announcement made over a public address system in a school or sports arena. Communication can flow from the announcer's microphone to the crowd but not vice versa. A **half-duplex transmission** allows two-direction communication but not simultaneously. For example, a CB radio or walkie-talkie allows only one person to speak at a time on any particular channel. A **full-duplex transmission** occurs when two people talk on the telephone. In full-duplex transmission, both people are able to speak and hear at the same time. Duplexing is an issue mostly for analog data transmission; it isn't usually a factor with digital communication. Dial-up modems, which convert digital signals to analog, have a duplex setting for the analog data—half-duplex or full-duplex.

Multiplexing is a method by which multiple data streams (either analog or digital) are combined and carried on a single wire. For example, multiplexing enables several telephone calls to be carried over one wire or several TV channels to be carried over one coaxial cable.

 Recheck **6.1**
Recheck your understanding of the concepts covered by this objective.

Practical TECH

Evaluating Broadband Internet Services

When shopping for Internet connectivity from a cable or digital subscriber line (DSL) provider, you might have a choice of speeds. For example, a cable company might offer several different plans with speeds ranging from 3 Mbps to 100 Mbps, each at a different price. Not everyone needs the fastest Internet service available. People who stream music and movies online or play online games with complex graphics and fast action will benefit from the highest speeds, but people who use the Internet primarily for viewing web content and sending email won't be able to tell much difference between the speeds. When signing up for Internet service, consider starting with a lower-speed plan. If you are unhappy with that speed, you can upgrade to a faster-speed plan. Most providers will allow you to upgrade at any time, even if you have a service contract.

6.2 Distinguishing between Types of Communications Media

 Precheck 6.2

Check your understanding of the concepts covered by this objective.

Users must have access to communications media to transmit data or information between computing devices. A **communications medium** is a connection that enables computers in different locations to send data to one another. Communications between distant computers may take place through a combination of media, some of which the user may never see. Communications media are broadly classified as wired and wireless.

Wired Media

While many computers, devices, and networks now communicate using wireless technologies, many others continue to use lines and cables. In addition, most of the Internet is based on lines and cables (also called *wired media*). Wireless communication is used only at the end points—that is, the points at which individual computers connect to the network. Wired media include copper telephone lines, twisted-pair cables, coaxial cables, fiber-optic cables, and T lines. The medium chosen for a particular purpose depends mainly on user requirements related to availability, cost, speed, and other factors.

Copper Telephone Line The slowest and oldest method of remote computer communication is through a dial-up modem over ordinary copper telephone lines. As you learned in the section "Digital and Analog Transmission," on page 240, a modem is required at each end of the communications channel to translate the data between digital and analog formats. Dial-up networking has a maximum speed of about 56 Kbps, and you can't use your telephone line while the modem is using it.

Digital subscriber line (DSL) Internet service (which you learned about in Chapter 5) is technically not a separate transmission medium, because it uses the same existing copper phone lines that a home phone system does. DSL is able to carry data much faster than dial-up networking, because it uses optimized switched connections at the phone company's central office. (The term *central office* does not literally refer to an office, but instead refers to a switching station that manages the DSL hardware.) DSL breaks voice and data into separate channels and creates a digital loop between the user and the DSL hardware at the central office. As a side benefit of this split, users can make phone calls and use the Internet at the same time. The main drawback to DSL is that it's available only within about 3 miles of the central office. If your computer is farther away than that, performance will suffer badly. In fact, most phone companies won't provide DSL service outside a 3-mile radius.

Twisted-Pair Cable The copper phone cables discussed in the previous section are a type of cable known as *twisted pair*. Twisted-pair cable is one of the older types of communication media, but it's still widely in use.

A **twisted-pair cable** consists of pairs of copper wires, in which each wire is individually wrapped in plastic and all the wires are bound together by another plastic

 Activity 6.2.1

Video
DSL versus Cable

 Activity 6.2.2

Video
How Twisted-Pair Cable Carries Data

casing (see Figure 6.3). The pairs are twisted together to reduce the effects of **electromagnetic interference (EMI)**, which is the magnetic field generated when electricity passes through a wire. The pairs are often bundled in packs of hundreds or thousands, buried in underground electrical conduits (pipes), and run to various locations (such as buildings and rooms), where they can be connected to standard jacks. Twisted-pair cable is used in telephone systems and in most end points for networking. The cable used to connect an individual user's computer to a network is almost always a twisted-pair cable.

Twisted-pair cable comes in two varieties: **shielded twisted-pair (STP) cable** and **unshielded twisted-pair (UTP) cable**. STP cable is more expensive and is used in environments where EMI might be a problem, such as for a cable that passes over a fluorescent light fixture in a ceiling. UTP cable is by far the more common type.

UTP cable is available in different categories that are often referred to using the shortened term *Cat*—as in *Cat5*, meaning "category 5." The higher the category number, the faster the data transmission the cable can reliably support. The lower category numbers aren't used for modern networking. The only categories you will find in use today are the ones listed in Table 6.2. Notice that Cat5e and Cat6 cables have the same maximum speed. The difference is that Cat6 cables have a physical separator between the pairs, which helps cut down on EMI inside the cable. Cat6a, Cat7, and Cat7a all have the same speed.

The cables in Table 6.2 all use an RJ-45 connector on each end. An RJ-45 connector is like a telephone cable connector except slightly wider. If you look closely at the connector, you will see eight contacts; each represents one of the wires in the cable. A phone cord, in contrast, has two or four contacts. Figure 6.4 shows an RJ-45 connector.

Coaxial Cable **Coaxial cable** is commonly used for cable TV connections, in telephone networks, and in some computer networks. This type of cable consists of an insulated copper center wire grounded by a shield of braided wire (see Figure 6.5). Coaxial cable is more expensive than twisted-pair cable, but it's less susceptible to EMI and can carry much more data.

Broadband coaxial cable is the type most people are familiar with today; it has several channels, each of which can carry about 10 Mbps. Broadband is used for cable and satellite TV, as well as satellite Internet. Several other types of coaxial cable were previously used in types of networks that are now obsolete.

Figure 6.3

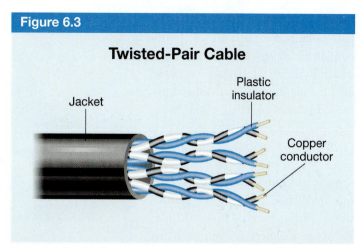

Twisted-Pair Cable

Jacket | Plastic insulator | Copper conductor

Twisted-pair cable is an inexpensive connector designed to reduce EMI.

Table 6.2 UTP Cable Categories Used in Modern Networks

Category	Maximum Speed
Cat5	100 Mbps
Cat5e	1,000 Mbps (1 Gbps)
Cat6	1,000 Mbps (1 Gbps)
Cat6a	10,000 Mbps (10 Gbps)
Cat7 and 7a	10,000 Mbps (10 Gbps)

Figure 6.4

RJ-45 Connector

A UTP cable has an RJ-45 connector on each end.

Figure 6.5

Coaxial Cable

Coaxial cable consists of a copper core surrounded by insulation and then shielded by braided wire.

Fiber-Optic Cable A twisted-pair cable and a coaxial cable both contain copper conductors and transmit electrical signals—streams of electrons. In contrast, a **fiber-optic cable** uses a string of glass to transmit photons—beams of light.

Figure 6.6 shows a simplified version of a fiber-optic cable. An actual fiber-optic cable can consist of hundreds of clear fiberglass or plastic fibers (threads), each approximately the same thickness as a human hair. Data is converted into beams of light by a laser device and transmitted as light pulses. Billions of bits can be transmitted per second. At the receiving end, optical detectors convert the transmitted light pulses into electrical pulses that computing devices can read. The advantages of using fiber-optic cables include faster transmission rates (up to 1 trillion bits per second), no EMI (because there's no electricity and therefore no magnetic field), better security (because criminals can't hack into a fiber-optic cable without destroying it), and a longer cable life.

Fiber-optic cable can transmit a large amount of data very quickly, so it's often used for a **network backbone** (the central pathway of a network). In the main data pathways that the Internet uses nationwide and worldwide, for example, many fiber-optic cables work together as a superhighway. Fiber-optic cable isn't typically employed at end-user sites, so most nonprofessional computer users will never work with it. The drawbacks of fiber-optic cable are that it's expensive and that it can be difficult to install because of the risk of breaking some of the glass fibers.

T Line The generic term **T line** refers to any of several types of digital high-speed, long-distance telephone lines that are capable of carrying multiple types of signals, including both voice and data. A T line is actually not a single line but a bundle of lines—for example, 24 lines are bundled for a T1 line. Because of this bundling, a T line allows a company to combine voice and data services in a single connection. A T line can be configured to dedicate a certain number of its internal lines to voice and

Figure 6.6

Fiber-Optic Cable

Protective jacket · Strengthening fibers · Plastic coating · Cladding · Glass or plastic core

Fiber-optic cable transmits beams of light through a glass or plastic core.

Activity 6.2.3

Article
Fiber-Optic Cable

This photo shows one type of connector on a fiber-optic cable. There are many types of fiber-optic cables, each using a different connector type.

Cutting Edge

Hollow-Core Fiber Optics

The current version of fiber-optic cable uses a glass core to transmit light waves, but a new version uses hollow-core optical fibers that guide light through hollow tubes filled with air. Doing so results in much lower light dispersion, allowing signals to travel two to five times farther than in conventional fibers. Increasing the distance the signal can travel reduces the overall cost of installing and operating a fiber-optic network because fewer cable segments are required, as well as fewer optical repeaters (devices that boost and rebroadcast the signal). For more information, check out the article at http://CUT6.emcp .net/FiberOpticTechnology.

a certain number to data, and as the company's needs change, its configuration of the T line can change.

A T line isn't a cable you buy in a store; rather, it's a connection you lease from a telephone company. One key advantage of a T line is that it's secure and dedicated. The bandwidth isn't shared, so other users' activities can't reduce the speed or reliability of your connection. A disadvantage of T lines is that they are very expensive compared with other types of Internet connections.

A **T1 line** carries data at 1.5 Mbps over its 24 internal lines, with each line running at 64 Kbps. When T1 lines were first developed, this was very fast. However, nowadays, cable and DSL speeds surpass this speed by multiples, so T1 Internet connectivity is no longer the high-speed solution it used to be.

A **T3 line** contains a larger bundle of individual lines: 672 of them. Working collectively, these lines can transfer data at up to 43 Mbps. One popular use for T3 lines has been to connect Internet service providers (ISPs) to an Internet backbone, but with the development of fiber-optic cable, T3 lines have become less popular for this purpose.

Wireless Media

Wireless media aren't really media in the same sense as cables; they can more accurately be called *wireless technologies*. Wireless technologies transmit information through the air in much the same way a battery-operated radio sends radio waves. Individual users, businesses, and organizations are rapidly embracing wireless technologies as workers become more mobile and wireless devices become more powerful. The most popular wireless transmission methods in networking today include Wi-Fi, WiMAX, Bluetooth, cellular, satellite, microwave, and infrared.

Activity 6.2.4

Video
Wireless Media

Wi-Fi Technology   The most commonly used wireless technology today is **Wi-Fi**, which is also called **IEEE 802.11**. *IEEE* stands for the Institute of Electrical and Electronics Engineers—the organization that maintains the standards for various types of computer and communication technologies. *802.11* is the number of the standard that governs Wi-Fi.

Several versions of standard 802.11 have been approved by the IEEE as Wi-Fi technology has evolved, each one with a different combination of speed, maximum distance, and frequency range—which is often referred to as a **band**. The version 802.11n was the most popular standard at the time this textbook was written. That standard is capable of carrying data at up to 300 Mbps over a range of up to 230 feet indoors and 840 feet outdoors. A new standard, 802.11ac, was approved in January 2014, and most new wireless networking devices now support it. The 802.11ac standard uses dual-band technology, so it supports simultaneous connections on both the 2.4 and 5 gigahertz (GHz) bands. It's backward compatible with standards 802.11b, 802.11g, and 802.11n. Table 6.3 summarizes the 802.11 Wi-Fi standards and their speeds and ranges.

Activity 6.2.5

Article
802.11 Wi-Fi Standards

Table 6.3 Wi-Fi Standards

Standard	Speed	Frequency Range (band)	Distance (indoors/outdoors in feet)
802.11a	54 Mbps	5 GHz	115/390
802.11b	11 Mbps	2.4 GHz	115/390
802.11g	54 Mbps	2.4 GHz	125/460
802.11n	Up to 300 Mbps	2.4 GHz or 5 GHz	230/860
802.11ac	Up to 1.3 Gbps	2.4 GHz or 5 GHz	230/860

Figure 6.7

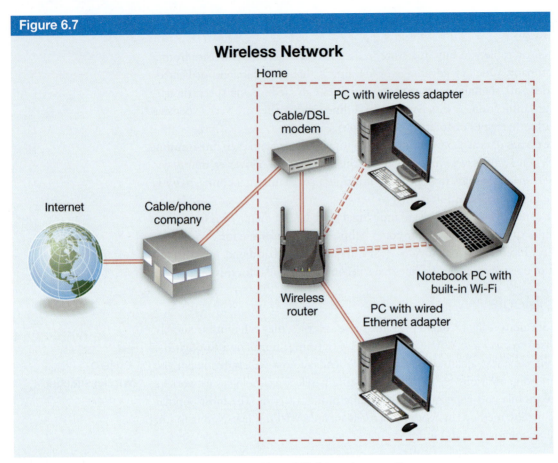

Wireless Network

A wireless access point can be used to share a cable or DSL Internet connection among multiple computers.

To use Wi-Fi, a device must be in close proximity (usually within 150 feet indoors or 300 feet outdoors) to a wireless access point. A **wireless access point** is a hardware device that communicates wirelessly with Wi-Fi capable devices. A Wi-Fi hotspot is a location that has one or more wireless access points. Many restaurants, hotels, school campuses, and airports provide Wi-Fi hotspots for a fee or at no charge. Home and small business networks can also take advantage of Wi-Fi by adding a wireless access point to a cable or DSL modem, as shown in Figure 6.7. For example, a hotel or coffee shop might share its Internet access with customers this way.

When a Wi-Fi device connects to a wireless access point, it's said to be operating in **infrastructure mode**. An alternative is to operate in **ad hoc mode**, which occurs when two computers connect to one another directly without an access point. To learn how to set up your own Wi-Fi network, see the section, "Setting Up a Wireless Home Network," on page 273.

WiMAX Technology WiMAX is a wireless technology with a larger usable range than Wi-Fi, with its own IEEE standard (IEEE 802.16). WiMAX is suitable for a metropolitan area network (MAN), in that it can provide network/Internet access to all locations in a large radius of a base station (up to 3000 square miles, although that's not common). An area can be covered by multiple WiMAX towers, somewhat like a cell phone network covers an area. Sometimes described as "Wi-Fi on steroids," WiMAX promises to give traditional Internet technologies some competition for consumer business, especially for customers who have difficulty getting cable or DSL service at their location. Its current data rates are around 30 to 40 Mbps, but a new standard approved in 2011 provides for more than 300 Mbps.

One benefit of WiMAX is that the signal is available anywhere within the service area, not just in one home or office. That means if you move several times a day between different buildings, such as between your home and your office in the same neighborhood, you don't have to change wireless networks. To use WiMAX, you need a WiMAX wireless network receiver in your computer that supports it. Some notebook computers come with WiMAX support built in, and others can add it in via a mini PCIe card or external USB device. The main drawback of WiMAX is its limited availability. To see if WiMAX is available in your area, go to **http://CUT6.emcp.net /WiMAXNetworks**.

Bluetooth Technology **Bluetooth** is a short-range wireless networking standard used to connect peripheral devices to computers, tablets, and smartphones. Bluetooth creates a point-to-point temporary network that can exchange both voice and data. Its range is limited to about 15 to 20 feet, so it's suitable only for helping local devices work together, not for connecting computing hardware devices that are physically separated. Common uses for Bluetooth include connecting a computer to a printer, a microphone headset to a smartphone, and a cordless mouse or keyboard to a tablet.

Bluetooth is the networking technology that allows devices to work together wirelessly.

Cellular Technology People can communicate wirelessly to and from nearly anywhere in the world using **cellular technology**. Cellular phones and devices work by maintaining contact with cellular antennae (which resemble metal telephone poles) positioned throughout a cellular calling area. Each area, called a **cell**, has its own antenna encompassing an area approximately 10 to 12 square miles in diameter. As a user moves from cell to cell, the closest antenna picks up the signal and relays it to the appropriate destination.

Cellular networks can carry both voice and data, and cell phones are fast becoming a popular alternative to using personal computers for accessing the Internet. A smartphone, as you learned in Chapter 1, is a cell phone that's equipped for other tasks besides making phone calls, such as running applications and accessing the Internet using a variety of applications. Cellular carriers offer high-speed data service via cell phones, with the level and speed of service depending on the cell that's being used.

Practical TECH

Bluetooth LE

Small portable devices that use Bluetooth to connect to other devices may have very limited power, and the Bluetooth networking consumes quite a bit of it. Bluetooth Low Energy (LE), also called *Bluetooth Smart*, is a new type of Bluetooth that reduces the power requirements. One popular use for Bluetooth LE is in wireless medical sensors used in physicians' offices, including thermometers, blood glucose meters, and blood pressure monitors that can send measurements wirelessly to the medical office's computer system for each patient, eliminating the possibility of data entry error. Most operating systems that support regular Bluetooth already include native support for Bluetooth LE.

Cellular service is classified as either 3G or 4G. The term **3G** stands for *3rd generation*; it's a class of mobile broadband service that provides about 3 Mbps throughput. **4G** stands for *4th generation*; this class is capable of around 9.5 Mbps throughput. When 3G or 4G service is used in a moving vehicle, the throughput rate drops considerably because of the need to change cells as the vehicle moves out of the range of each one.

Activity 6.2.6

Article
**3G and 4G
Cellular Service**

Satellite Systems A **communications satellite** is a solar-powered electronic device containing several small, specialized radios called *transponders*. A **transponder** receives signals from a transmission station on the ground called an **earth station**. Communications satellites are positioned thousands of miles above the Earth. A satellite receives transmitted signals, amplifies them, and then retransmits them to the appropriate locations on Earth (see Figure 6.8). Satellites orbit the Earth at the same

Figure 6.8

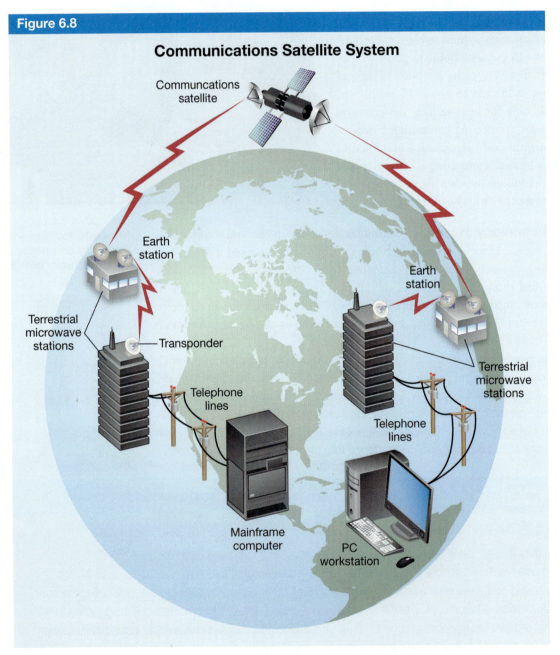

A communications satellite receives signals transmitted from Earth, amplifies them, and then retransmits them to the appropriate locations back on Earth.

speed that the planet rotates, making them appear stationary when viewed from the ground. This is called a **geosynchronous orbit**.

One benefit of satellite systems is the small number of satellites needed to transmit data over long distances. In fact, a small number of satellites properly positioned can receive and transmit information to any location on Earth.

Communications satellites are capable of transmitting billions of bits per second, making them ideal for transmitting very large amounts of data. Because of the time it takes to send and receive data across long distances, satellites are more appropriate for one-way communications, such as TV and radio transmission, than for interactive applications, such as video conferencing and Internet access. Satellite Internet access is available to individuals and businesses, but the **latency** (delay) involved in this communication medium limits the performance of this service to levels far below those of cable and DSL. The expense involved in building a satellite, sending it into orbit, and maintaining it is very high. Companies often share satellite technology, as individual companies are unable to bear the full cost of operating their own systems. Several satellites now in orbit handle domestic and international data, video, and voice communications for owners and subscribers. For instance, banks use satellites to transmit millions of customer transactions to other banks.

Activity 6.2.7

Video
Satellite Internet Service

Microwave Systems In general, a *microwave* is a high-frequency waveform. In the case of microwave transmission, it's a high-frequency radio signal used to carry data securely from one point to another. A **microwave system** enables a business to connect two locations wirelessly, for example (see Figure 6.9). Because the wave oscillates quickly, the communication speed is high.

Microwave transmission requires line-of-sight connections between the communication points, because the radio signals can't bend around objects; this means there can't be any visible obstructions between points. For this reason, microwave transmitters/receivers are often placed high up on buildings, towers, and mountains. The terrain and visibility determine the maximum distance between microwave units, but it's rarely more than 25 miles.

Microwave technology was developed in the 1930s. While newer technologies, such as fiber-optic cable and T lines, are more popular nowadays for connecting locations, microwave still has one important advantage: it can carry a secure, dedicated signal across very rough terrain, where there's no easy way to run cables. The

---

Figure 6.9

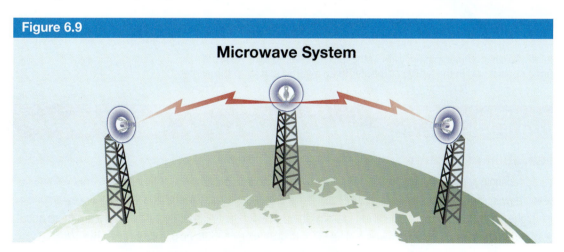

Microwave System

In a microwave system, data is sent as radio signals through the atmosphere from one microwave station to another. The stations must be positioned at relatively short line-of-sight intervals.

US military often uses microwave technology to create communications networks at remote locations with rugged terrain and little existing communications infrastructure. Satellite communication (described in the section "Satellite Systems," on page 250) can also connect remote locations wirelessly, but because satellite transmissions go through a shared satellite, they are less direct and less secure.

Microwave frequency ranges can be either licensed or unlicensed. If a company acquires a license from the Federal Communications Commission (FCC) for the use of a particular frequency range, that range is solely for that company's use. The US military owns certain frequency ranges, for example. There are also unlicensed frequency ranges that anyone may use, but they are shared by the people who have the equipment to use them and so may be more congested and offer slower data throughput.

Infrared Technology **Infrared technology** transmits data as light waves, instead of radio waves. One drawback to infrared technology is that objects placed between sending and receiving devices can interrupt transmissions, because the light waves must follow a line-of-sight path.

TV remote control units typically use infrared technology. Before Bluetooth was developed, many wireless computer peripherals used infrared to connect to the computer (see Figure 6.10). An infrared sensor in the computer (or attached to it via a port) would communicate with a wireless device, such as a keyboard, mouse, or

Figure 6.10

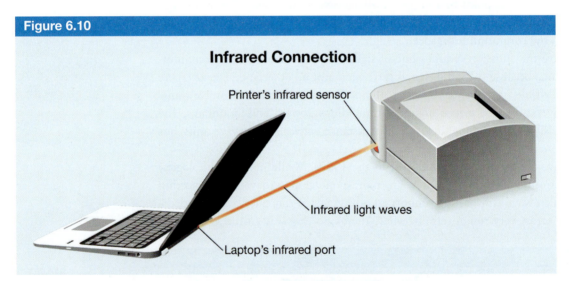

Infrared Connection

Printer's infrared sensor

Infrared light waves

Laptop's infrared port

In this example of wireless communication, data in the form of infrared light waves is transmitted from a special port in the laptop computer to an infrared sensor in the printer.

Cutting Edge

A New Generation of Infrared

Traditional infrared technology may be old and nearly obsolete. However, new infrared-based technologies on the horizon promise higher transmission rates than Wi-Fi, as well as greater security. An infrared signal requires a clear line of sight, but the hardware for it is very inexpensive. A system called *optical wireless* blankets an area with multiple infrared sensors, so that the signal bounces among them until it hits its target destination. To learn more about this technology and its possibilities, go to **http://CUT6 .emcp.net/OpticalWireless**.

printer. Notebook computers and hand-held devices commonly had infrared ports that would enable them to connect to other nearby infrared-capable devices to form temporary ad hoc networks. The standard for this type of infrared connection is called **IrDA**, which stands for *Infrared Data Association*—the organization that developed the standard.

Recheck 6.2

Recheck your understanding of the concepts covered by this objective.

6.3 Identifying Network Types

Networks vary enormously, from simple interoffice systems connecting a few personal computers and a printer to complex global systems connecting thousands of computers and computer devices. Networks can be classified by their architecture, by the relative distances they cover, and by the users they are designed to support.

Precheck 6.3

Check your understanding of the concepts covered by this objective.

Networks Classified by Architecture

The term **network architecture** refers to the way a network is designed and built, just as the general term *architecture* refers to the design and construction of a building. Client/server and peer-to-peer are the two major architectural designs for networks.

Client/Server Architecture In **client/server architecture**, a **client** (such as a networked personal computer, workstation, or terminal) can send requests to and receive services from another typically more powerful computer called a *server* (see Figure 6.11). The server can store programs, files, and data that are available to authorized users. The client PCs don't share the responsibility of keeping the network running, because the server takes care of that.

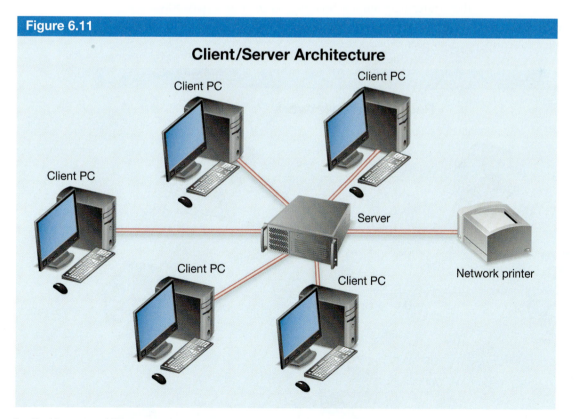

Figure 6.11

Client/Server Architecture

In client/server architecture, one or more servers is responsible for managing the network traffic and sharing network resources.

Client/server architecture is the predominant type used in all but the smallest networks (those with fewer than 10 to 12 computers). A client/server network can supply clients with stored data (from file servers), printing services (from print servers), Internet access (from Internet servers), and more, depending on what servers are used and how they are configured. For example, one of the servers could be set up with Microsoft SharePoint, enabling all the client PCs to participate in collaborative project management and data storage, or with Microsoft Exchange, providing email services to all the client PCs.

The major advantage of client/server architecture is that the network runs smoothly and efficiently, with little processing burden on the client PCs. A disadvantage is that it requires at least one computer to be dedicated to functioning as a server, and this computer requires a server operating system. Client/server is also overkill for very small networks (such as those in homes and small businesses that need to share just a few files and printers).

Peer-to-Peer Architecture **Peer-to-peer architecture** (sometimes called *P2P architecture*) is a network design in which there is no dedicated server. Another name for a peer-to-peer network is **workgroup**; this is the preferred name in Microsoft Windows. In a peer-to-peer network, each workstation shares in the network's administrative burden, and each workstation can communicate directly with all the other workstations, as shown in Figure 6.12.

Compared with client/server networks, peer-to-peer networks are usually simpler to install and maintain and are less expensive. However, they may not perform as well as client/server networks. The network traffic adds to each computer's burden, and the more computers there are, the greater that burden becomes. Peer-to-peer networks work best with fewer than 10 to 12 computers. Microsoft Windows contains the software needed to set up a peer-to-peer network.

 **Activity 6.3.1**

Video
**Peer-to-Peer
and Client/Server
Networks**

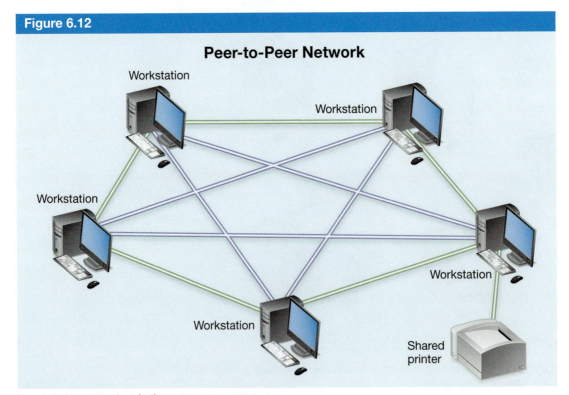

Figure 6.12

Peer-to-Peer Network

In a peer-to-peer network, there are no servers.

Networks Classified by Coverage

Another way to classify networks is according to the sizes of the geographical areas they cover. The smallest area networks may serve only single individuals, while the largest are used by major corporations, governments, and institutions.

Personal Area Network (PAN)   A **personal area network** (**PAN**) has a very small range and is used primarily by one person (see Figure 6.13). It's typically wireless, using either Bluetooth or IrDA technology. For example, when you have a wireless headset connected to your smartphone or a Bluetooth printer connected to your notebook PC, you have a PAN.

Figure 6.13

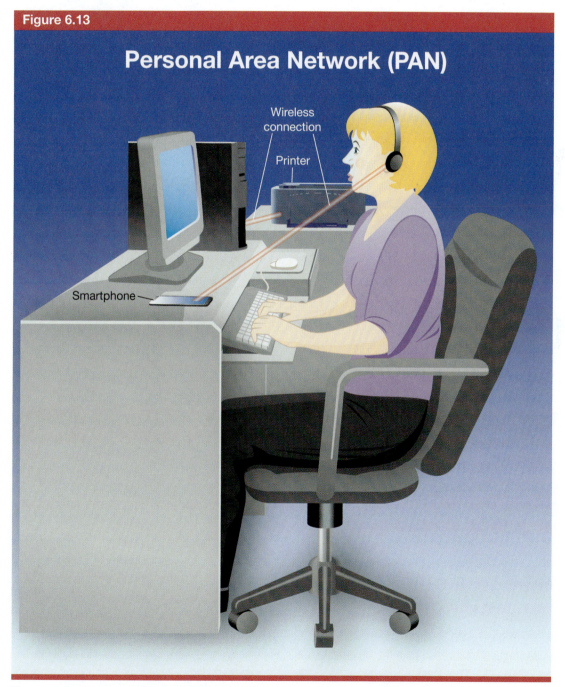

The network of devices within an individual's workspace is a PAN.

Local Area Network (LAN) A **local area network (LAN)** is a private network that serves the needs of a business, organization, school, or residence with computers located in a single building or group of nearby buildings, such as a college campus (see Figure 6.14). Working within a LAN makes it convenient for multiple users to share programs, data, hardware, software, and Internet access. A LAN may contain

Figure 6.14

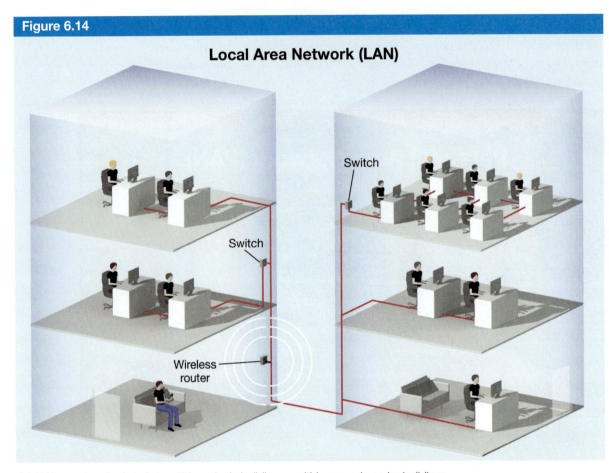

Local Area Network (LAN)

A LAN is a network of devices within a single building or within several nearby buildings.

Cutting Edge

Out There with the Outernet

The Outernet is a worldwide information service that addresses the fact that a large portion of the world's population still lacks access to information on the Internet, either due to lack of service availability or affordability, or due to censorship. The Outernet functions as an information broadcast service. Ground stations uplink selected content to miniature satellites called *CubeSats* that broadcast the information worldwide. The broadcast loops for better signal quality and updating. Users with mobile phones can request information from the Outernet, and other users will be able to use low-cost devices and receivers to access information. Portable ground-based receiver dishes also can be used to receive and store information for streaming to wireless devices for viewing via a web browser.

Outernet began by delivering news and information, educational material, emergency communications, and some applications and content, including all of Wikipedia. Over time, Outernet expects to build the library of available content according to a priority list based on user input. While Outernet provides only one-way broadcasts from outside the Internet, it enhances the potential ability to learn, be informed, and be entertained for billions more people around the world.

hundreds of computers and several servers; it isn't necessarily a small network. Its defining characteristic is that it's confined to a relatively small geographical region. This type of network typically has a wired backbone (fiber-optic or twisted-pair copper cable) plus some wireless access at the end points for individual users.

Metropolitan Area Network (MAN) One step up from a LAN in geographical range is a **metropolitan area network (MAN)**. As the name implies, a MAN is a network with the geographical range of a metropolitan area. Coverage may be provided by a combination of wired and wireless technologies. A MAN might be owned and operated by one company or organization, or it might be a cooperative venture among several organizations, including local government or public utility companies. A MAN is commonly

If the company you work for has a metropolitan area network (MAN) with wireless access, you might be able to work from a park near your office on a nice day.

implemented to provide Internet access, for example. With an Internet MAN, the range may vary from several blocks of buildings to an entire city and its suburbs.

Wide Area Network (WAN) A **wide area network (WAN)** spans a large geographical area, connecting two or more LANs. A business might use a WAN to communicate between a manufacturing facility in one state and its corporate headquarters in another. Governments, universities, and large corporations use WANs to share data among separate networks. WANs typically make use of high-speed leased telephone lines, wireless satellite connections, or both.

A special type of Internet-based WAN has become increasingly popular among large businesses that need a cost-effective way to expand their networking options. This specialized WAN is called a **virtual private network (VPN)**. Instead of leasing T lines to connect distant offices across the country, a company establishes a VPN by having each branch office set up a local Internet connection. Additional software and security procedures overlay these public Internet connections to create a secure, private network that allows offices to communicate as if they were within the same corporate network—even though they are actually using the Internet. Factors that make a VPN an attractive option are the cost savings, the reliability and wide availability, and the nearly unlimited bandwidth capacity of the Internet.

Networks Classified by Users

Networks can also be classified by the groups of users they are designed to accommodate. This classification includes intranets and extranets.

Intranet An **intranet** is a private network within an organization that uses the same basic protocols as the Internet but is restricted to only the staff of that company. Outside access to an intranet is typically prevented by a firewall, which consists of special

Tech Career Explorer

Network Administrator

A network administrator is an IT professional who manages the day-to-day operations of a network. A network administrator's duties might include setting up a LAN, configuring a server, and assigning user names and passwords. To get started as a network administrator, you should have at least an associate degree in computer technology or a related field plus CompTIA Network+ certification or some other equivalent networking certification. For more information, complete this exercise.

Figure 6.15

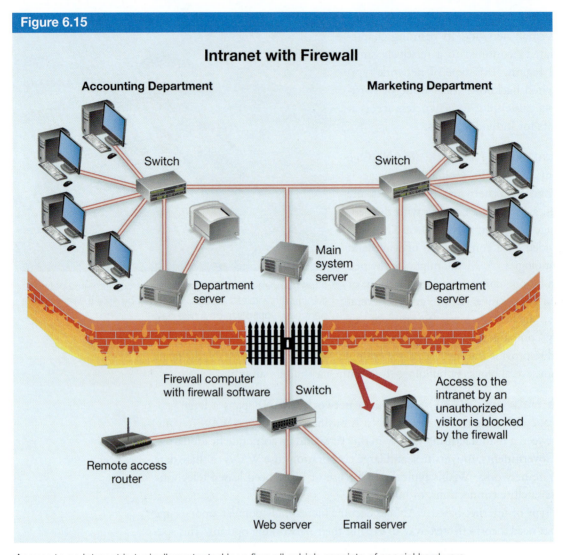

Access to an intranet is typically protected by a firewall, which consists of special hardware and/or software that limits usage to authorized users.

hardware and/or software that restricts access to and from a network. Figure 6.15 shows how a firewall protects an intranet. An intranet functions in the same way as a LAN that isn't connected to other networks outside the organization. Stored information is available only to authorized users, and certain kinds of information may be available only to specific persons, groups, or departments within the organization. For example, access to a company's new product designs may be restricted to employees in the research and design department who have special passwords.

Extranet An **extranet** is an extension of an intranet that allows specified external users (including employees, customers, and business partners) access to internal applications and data via the Internet. An extranet allows an external user with a valid user ID and password to pass through the firewall and access certain resources in the organization's network. Different user accounts may be assigned different usage permissions on the extranet. Workers may be allowed to send and receive email messages, for example, and an extranet may also allow fax transmission. A properly designed and implemented extranet can provide many useful services. Many companies use extranets to allow workers to access systems from remote locations. Mobile workers

Figure 6.16

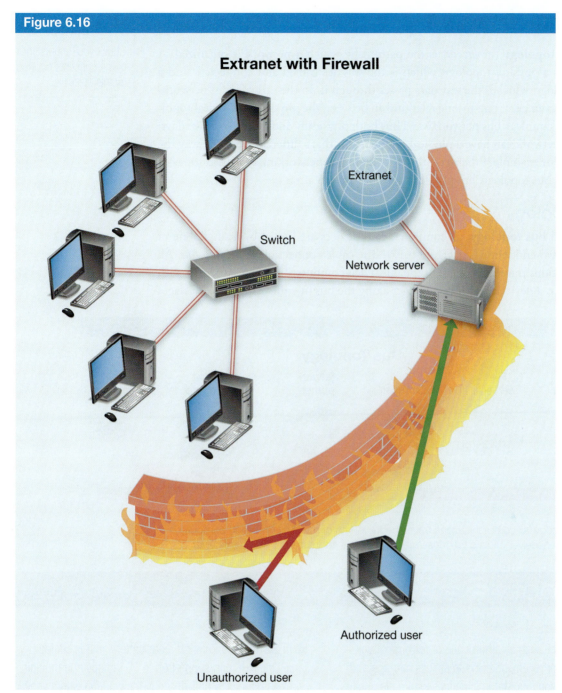

Extranet with Firewall

Extranet

Switch

Network server

Authorized user

Unauthorized user

An extranet allows authorized users to access a company's internal systems via the Internet but prevents unauthorized users from doing so.

can connect their notebooks or hand-held computers to a company extranet via a communications medium such as a telephone line. Figure 6.16 illustrates an extranet as well as the process by which an authorized user can access systems behind the organization's firewall.

Like an intranet, an extranet can be used for a variety of business activities. For example, an automobile manufacturer can post a request for bids for raw materials, such as engine parts, seat covers, and tires. Providing an electronic bid form with the request allows potential suppliers to submit their bids for supplying these materials.

Activity 6.3.2

Practice
An Extranet with Firewall

Recheck **6.3**
Recheck your understanding of the concepts covered by this objective.

6.4 Exploring Network Topologies

 Precheck 6.4

Check your understanding of the concepts covered by this objective.

A **network topology** (or *layout*) is the pattern by which a network is organized. A network has a physical topology, which is the way it's cabled and connected, and a logical topology, which is the way data passes through it. In the early days of networking, there was an exact one-to-one relationship between the physical and logical topologies—for example, a bus network was a bus both physically and logically. Nowadays, however, a network can have a physical arrangement that's different from the way the data flows. For example, Ethernet—the most common networking type used today—is logically a bus topology, but physically, it's most often a star.

Bus Topology

In a physical **bus topology**, all computers and devices are linked by a single line of cable with two endpoints (see Figure 6.17). The cable connection is called a *bus*. All communications travel the length of the bus. Each computer has a network card with a **transceiver**, a device that sends messages along the bus in either direction. Messages

Figure 6.17

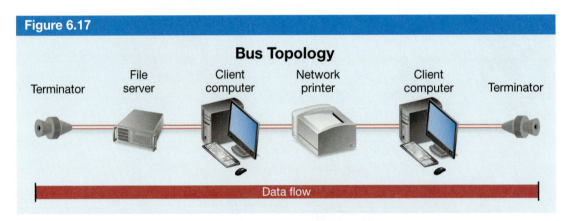

Bus Topology

Terminator   File server   Client computer   Network printer   Client computer   Terminator

Data flow

In a bus topology, all communications travel the full length of the bus, and each computer's networking transceiver checks the message to see if it is addressed to that transceiver.

Hotspot

Network-in-a-Box

After a disaster such as a hurricane or terrorist attack, the first task of relief workers is to assess damage and coordinate resources. But in situations where electricity has been cut off and phone lines are down, workers' ability to respond rapidly and effectively is severely hampered. NetHope is a consortium of 39 humanitarian organizations that focuses on exactly this issue: the need to deliver information and communication technology to relief workers. With the help of Cisco System engineers, NetHope has developed a network-in-a-box that can provide instant, durable communications in the most extreme conditions.

The box is called the *Network Relief Kit (NRK)*, and it consists of off-the-shelf components packed tightly into a small suitcase-size box with a handle. The NRK can be set up in 20 minutes, runs off a car battery, and is cooled by fans. One NRK can support up to 50 laptops and multiple wireless phones. A half-dozen NRKs working with a vehicle equipped with networking technology and a satellite broadband connection can cover 350 square miles.

When a tsunami hit Southeast Asia, thanks to the NRKs used in Indonesia and Thailand, relief workers who were hours or miles away from the central field office could focus immediately on food distribution, medical programs, psychological crisis intervention, and relocation without waiting for electricity and phone lines to be restored. NetHope has also focused on bringing reliable Internet access to relief workers in Dadaab, Kenya, the world's largest refugee camp, housing more than 320,000 people.

contain data, error-checking code, the address of the node sending the message, and the address of the node intended to receive the message. As the communication passes, each computer's network card checks to see if it's the assigned destination point. If the computer finds its address in the message, it then reads the data, checks for errors in the transmission, and sends to the sender of the data a message acknowledging that the data was received. If the computer's network card doesn't find its address, it ignores the message. The ends of the bus are terminated to prevent the signal from bouncing back.

Problems can occur if two or more computers send messages at the same time, which creates an interference pattern. When one of the computers detects this pattern, it jams the network, stopping all transmissions. A computer sending a message then waits and resends it—a process that's repeated until the message gets through without being blocked. Another problem with linear bus topology is that a broken connection along the bus can bring down the whole network. The official term for this error detection and correction process is **carrier sense multiple access with collision detection (CSMA/CD)**. CSMA/CD is used in all networks that use a logical bus, even if their physical topology is different.

Bus topologies commonly use coaxial or fiber-optic cable. Bus topologies are less expensive than some other network layouts but may also be less efficient.

Ethernet, which is the most widely used networking standard, originally was a bus topology both physically and logically. Today's Ethernet can function as a physical bus, star, or mesh, but it retains the basic data delivery and error correction of the original bus design, including using CSMA/CD for error correction.

Star Topology

In a physical **star topology**, multiple computers and peripheral devices are linked to a central gathering point—typically, a switch or a router (see the section "Routers," on page 266)—in a point-to-point configuration resembling a star (see Figure 6.18).

Figure 6.18

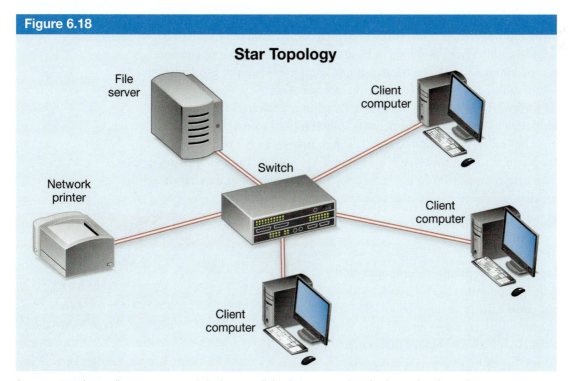

In a star topology, all computers and devices are linked to a central gathering point, through which all communications travel.

Figure 6.19

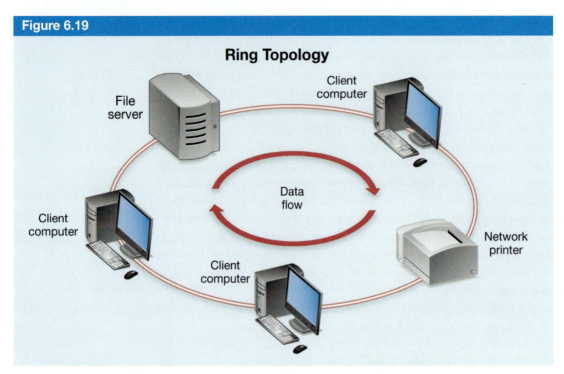

In a ring topology, each computer or device is connected to two or more other computers or devices in a circular path.

The switch or router acts as a switching station, reading the addresses of the messages sent by the nodes and routing the messages accordingly. Most small networks use a physical star topology, with each computer or device connecting to a switch or router through cables or wirelessly.

Ring Topology

In a physical **ring topology**, there is no central hub; each computer or device is part of a circle of computers and devices, as shown in Figure 6.19. This physical arrangement of computers is seldom used anymore, because if one computer or device is removed or one segment of cable has a break in it, the entire network fails.

The logical form of ring topology is called *token ring*. In the **token ring topology**, a computer is allowed to send data to the network only if it has a **token**, which is not a physical object but rather permission to speak. The computers in the network constantly pass the token among themselves; if a computer has nothing to send, it passes the token to the next computer in the circle. Because only the computer that has the token can put data on the network, data collisions aren't an issue in this topology.

Mesh Topology

Mesh topology connects multiple computers and devices to multiple computers and devices, so that many different paths exist from any one location to any other location. This topology ensures that the network won't fail to function if some of the computers or devices stop functioning. Mesh is the physical topology of the Internet. Hundreds of thousands of

Hands On

Using the TRACERT Command

You can use the TRACERT (Trace Route) command to see mesh topology in action. When you send a request for data to a website online, that request hops from router to router until it gets to its destination, and then the reply hops back from router to router. Follow the steps in this resource to trace a route in your local network.

Figure 6.20

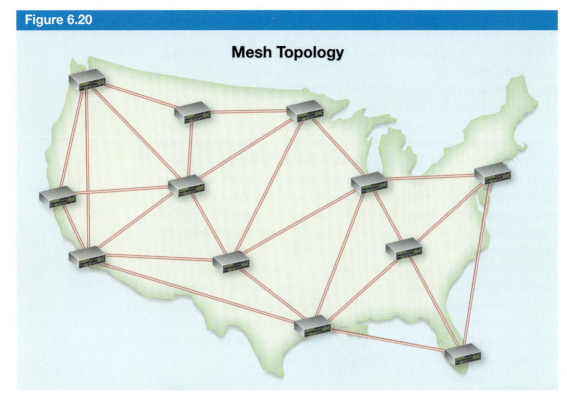

Mesh Topology

In a mesh topology, each computer or device is connected to multiple computers or devices, so network traffic can continue even if one or two pathways are blocked.

routers all over the world participate in the Internet, each one connected to several others. If any router fails, traffic is simply rerouted around the failure point. See Figure 6.20 for an illustration of the mesh topology.

Hybrid Topologies

Some businesses prefer using one kind of topology throughout the organization, while others prefer to use several different kinds. Indeed, the more common practice is for companies to combine network layout types to suit their particular situations. A system that mixes topologies in a network is called a **hybrid topology**. For example, each department may have a physical star topology for the computers in its area, and those stars may be joined using a backbone that's a physical bus topology.

6.5 Identifying Common Types of Network Hardware

Setting up a computer network generally requires special hardware to link all the computers and to facilitate communications. LANs and WANs may require different hardware devices. The most common network hardware devices include servers, switches, routers, repeaters, gateways, bridges, and network adapters.

Servers

A server is an essential part of a client/server network, which by definition must have one or more servers. Several types of server hardware are available to today's network administrator.

In a very small network, you might need only one server or possibly two. Such networks don't require a whole closetful of equipment—just an extra PC that can be

 Recheck 6.4

Recheck your understanding of the concepts covered by this objective.

 Precheck 6.5

Check your understanding of the concepts covered by this objective.

set up to run a server operating system. This type of server is called a **tower server**, which is a reference to the tower-style case common to most stand-alone servers. Each tower server requires its own complete workstation setup, including a monitor, mouse, keyboard, and network adapters.

The traditional type of server used in business is a **rack-mounted server**. Each rack-mounted server is more or less a fully functioning computer, although it lacks a keyboard, mouse, or monitor. It's typically mounted in a rack unit with other servers, which is how it gets its name. (It doesn't literally have to be in a rack; that's just the way multiserver systems are commonly set up to make the most of the available space.) A rack server isn't that different from a regular personal computer; it may have more RAM and a faster processor than is typical for a client PC, but it would be capable of running a client operating system if you chose to stop using it as a server. This type of server doesn't need a keyboard, mouse, or monitor, because a network administrator manages it remotely, using another computer as the terminal.

Rack servers (and their racks) are 19 inches wide and can vary in height. The height is measured in units (abbreviated U); 1U is 1.75 inches high (approximately the height of a pizza box). Large models can be 5U or even 8U in height. The larger the server, the greater the expansion possibilities—more expansion slots, more drive bays, and so on. Other components (such as backup batteries, network switches, and RAID units) are commonly stored on the rack with the server.

A rack-mounted server is typically mounted in a rack unit with other servers to make use of the space available.

A **blade-mounted server** isn't a full, stand-alone PC. It doesn't contain all the components of a computer, and to function, it must be mounted in a blade enclosure, which provides components such as the power supply, cooling fans, and networking components. Blade servers get their name from the fact that they are extremely thin—about three-fifths the height of a 1U rack-mounted server, or a little over 1 inch high. In networks that run multiple servers, companies can save money by installing multiple blade servers in a single blade enclosure. But because a blade enclosure has a single power supply and cooling system, it can be a point of failure. One hardware problem can take down an entire rack of servers, whereas a hardware problem with a rack-mounted server will take down only one server.

A blade-mounted server must be mounted in a blade enclosure, which provides components such as the power supply, cooling fans, and networking components.

Switches

A **switch** is a hardware device that physically connects computers within a LAN. When multiple computers connect to a switch via cables, a star topology is formed, as shown in Figure 6.18 on page 261. A switch is able to read the data in each incoming data packet, determine its destination, and then forward it to the correct computer. An earlier version of a switch, called a **hub**, did the same job physically but was unable to forward packets to specific ports. With a hub, every connected computer got a copy of every packet and had to determine whether it should be read or discarded. Hubs are now obsolete. A wireless switch is called a *wireless access point*.

A simple consumer-level switch may have four or five ports in which to connect cables. A business-class switch is a much larger box with dozens of ports; large organizations typically have multiple racks of switches with hundreds of cables running to and from them. These switches are usually stored out of the way in closets and other enclosures; a closet designed to store networking equipment (such as switches) is called a **wiring closet**.

This switch supports dozens of fiber-optic connections.

Routers

A **router** directs network traffic, like a switch does, but it's able to do so on a larger scale. Whereas a switch sends data to the correct device that's directly plugged into it, a router can send data to other networks, passing it off to other routers or switches outside the local network. A simple consumer-class router manages network traffic in a home or small business network and sends traffic to and from an Internet connection. It may be either wired or wireless; a wireless router typically allows wired connections too, providing several ports to which to connect cables. Some cable and DSL modems have both a wired and a wireless router built into the same unit.

A business-class router is able to route traffic to and from multiple networks, like a postal sorting facility. The Internet has hundreds of thousands of powerful routers, all working together to deliver messages and data from place to place.

A home router enables you to share Internet connectivity with all the computers in your home. This capability is sometimes built into a cable or DSL modem, eliminating the need for a separate router.

Repeaters

Information often travels a long distance, but the wires and cables used in that transmission may not be designed to carry messages the full distance. A **repeater** (also called an *amplifier*) is a specially designed electronic device that receives signals along a network, increases the strength of the signals, and then sends the amplified signals along the network's communications path (see Figure 6.21). Thus, a repeater helps solve the problem of information not being able to go the full distance of that path. It functions much like an amplifier in a home stereo system. A network spread over a wide distance may use several repeaters along the way.

Gateways and Bridges

A **gateway** is hardware and/or software that enables communication between dissimilar networks. For example, a gateway is needed to connect networks that use different

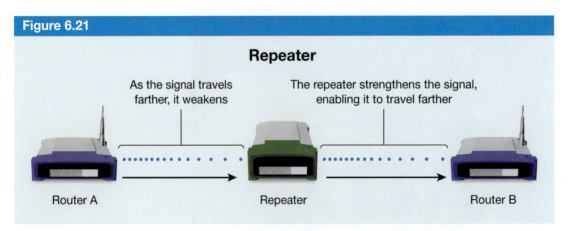

Figure 6.21

Repeater

As the signal travels farther, it weakens

The repeater strengthens the signal, enabling it to travel farther

Router A   Repeater   Router B

A repeater amplifies the data signal, allowing it to travel a longer distance than it could without help.

Figure 6.22

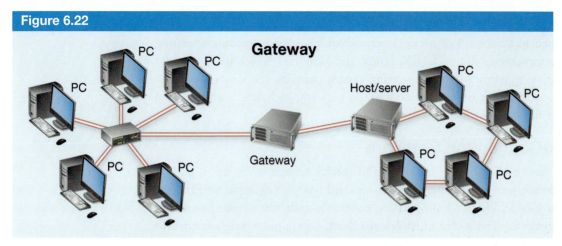

A gateway is a combination of hardware and software that allows dissimilar networks to communicate. This gateway is a server connecting a star network to a ring network.

topologies or different physical connection media. Figure 6.22 illustrates a gateway that joins a star topology network to one with a ring topology.

Whereas a gateway joins dissimilar networks, a **bridge** consists of hardware and/or software that allow communication between similar networks. For example, a bridge might be used to connect the networks in two different buildings or departments of a company, both of which are set up using the same topology.

Network Adapters

For a computer to communicate on a network, it must have a **network adapter**—that is, hardware that supports connecting to a network. The network adapter can be wired (with a jack for a cable) or wireless (with a Wi-Fi or Bluetooth transmitter/receiver), and it can be built into the computer's motherboard or added as an expansion device called a **network interface card (NIC)**. The term *NIC* is sometimes used generically to refer to any network adapter, although doing so isn't technically accurate.

Almost all portable devices (notebooks, tablets, smartphones, and so on) have Wi-Fi and Bluetooth capability built in, so installing a network adapter is an issue mainly for a desktop PC. A NIC for a desktop PC typically fits into one of the computer's PCI or PCIe slots. A NIC for a notebook PC may fit into a mini-PCIe slot or an ExpressCard slot, or it may connect to a USB port.

Each network adapter has a unique hardware identifier called a **media access control (MAC) address** (sometimes called a *physical address*). This address is unique in all the world to that particular network adapter. Part of the process of sending data on a network involves finding and specifying a device's MAC address to make sure the data is delivered to the right device. A MAC address is a 12-digit number consisting of six two-digit pairs, like this: 00-12-34-56-78-90.

A network interface card adds networking capability to a computer that doesn't already have it.

Recheck 6.5

Recheck your understanding of the concepts covered by this objective.

6.6 Understanding Network Software and Protocols

Network software has multiple components, and each operates at a different level of the process. Your operating system provides a whole suite of networking applications, drivers, and helper files—all of which work together to create and maintain your network connection.

Precheck 6.6

Check your understanding of the concepts covered by this objective.

Server Operating Systems

As you learned in Chapter 3, a network server requires a server-capable operating system to perform server duties. UNIX, Linux, and Windows Server are all popular server operating systems. A server operating system contains the drivers, utilities, services, and applications needed to administer a network, including authenticating users, sharing files, and managing network traffic.

Network Connection Software

Client PCs don't usually require installation of special network software to participate in a network, provided the network is a standard type (for example, an Ethernet network that uses TCP/IP). Most operating systems include the standard protocols and utilities needed to connect to a network as a client. Less popular types of networks may require installation of some client software.

The OSI Model and Network Protocols

Sending and receiving data on a network may seem simple and instantaneous, but it's actually quite a complex process involving several steps. To help make sense of all the steps in this process, engineers and educators have developed a seven-layer model to explain how different kinds networking software work together. This model, called the **Open Systems Interconnection (OSI) reference model**, applies no matter what networking technology, topology, or operating system is in use.

Figure 6.23 shows how the OSI reference model works. When a computer wants to send data to another computer on a network, it starts out at the top (Layer 7, the

Activity 6.6.1

Article
**Protocols
and Transmission
Standards**

Activity 6.6.2

Practice
**The OSI Reference
Model**

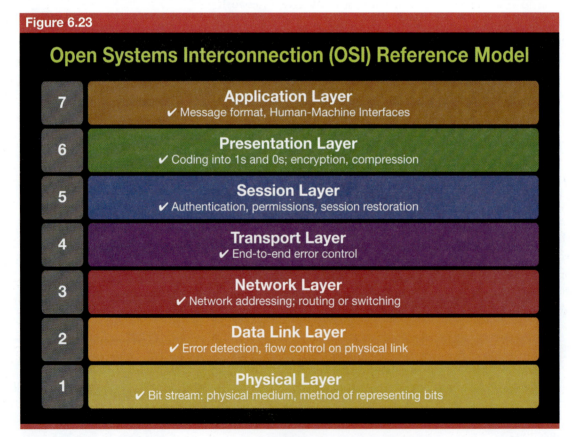

Figure 6.23

Open Systems Interconnection (OSI) Reference Model

7 **Application Layer**
✔ Message format, Human-Machine Interfaces

6 **Presentation Layer**
✔ Coding into 1s and 0s; encryption, compression

5 **Session Layer**
✔ Authentication, permissions, session restoration

4 **Transport Layer**
✔ End-to-end error control

3 **Network Layer**
✔ Network addressing; routing or switching

2 **Data Link Layer**
✔ Error detection, flow control on physical link

1 **Physical Layer**
✔ Bit stream: physical medium, method of representing bits

The OSI model provides a way of understanding the layers of software that network communication passes through.

Application layer) and works its way down to the bottom (Layer 1, the Physical layer), where the data is physically placed on the network via the network adapter. When the response comes back, it comes in at the Physical layer and proceeds up to the Application layer, where the application that originally requested the data can use and display it.

Here is a brief walkthrough of the steps involved in sending data:

7. **Application layer.** An end-user program at the Application layer (such as an email client or web browser) needs some data and requests it.

6. **Presentation layer.** The request is compressed, encrypted, and made into a common uniform format that the layers below can understand.

5. **Session layer.** A session is created between the two locations; they authenticate each other's identity and establish permission to send and receive. This layer starts and stops the session and maintains order.

4. **Transport layer.** A set of rules for transportation is agreed on, including a means of error control. The agreements cover topics such as what size of packets the data will be segmented into and how received packets will be acknowledged. This layer shields the upper layers from the networking process by making all the arrangements needed to transport the data.

3. **Network layer.** The data is placed into packets, which are parcels of data with network addressing attached to them. At this point, it's decided what physical path the data will take over the network, and the MAC address of the destination is determined. This layer routes the traffic to different networks based on the network address.

2. **Data link layer.** The packets are placed into frames containing the physical addresses of the locations. This is like placing letters into envelopes and writing the destination address on the outside of each one. This layer error checks and acknowledges the receipt of frames sent and received. It also makes sure the frames are reassembled in the correct order at the other end, if they arrive out of order.

1. **Physical layer.** The data is physically placed on the networking hardware and then sent out over the network.

At each of these levels, protocols are at work. A **protocol** is a set of rules for how things will happen. Communication can occur only if the communicating devices can agree on a common protocol at each level they interact. Networking can involve an alphabet soup of acronyms for various protocols, but if you keep in mind that each protocol operates at a certain level of the OSI model, the process may seem less complicated.

Application-Level Network Protocols The Application layer deals with individual applications that use the network, such as web browsers and email clients. Its protocols are high level, dealing with the data in human-readable form. A web browser uses primarily **Hypertext Transfer Protocol (HTTP)** to receive and display web pages. An email application may use some combination of **Post Office Protocol 3 (POP3)** to receive mail, **Simple Mail Transfer Protocol (SMTP)** to send mail, and **Internet Message Access Protocol (IMAP)** to manage a server-based email interface. Other application-specific protocols include File Transfer Protocol (FTP), which is used to transfer files quickly between FTP file servers, and **Telnet**, which provides a command-line interface for interacting with remote computers.

TCP/IP The protocols used at the Transport and Network layers can vary depending on the network type, but the most common protocols are **Transmission Control Protocol (TCP)** at the Transport layer and **Internet Protocol (IP)** at the Network layer. They are most often referred to together as **TCP/IP**. TCP/IP is a suite of inter-related protocols. It's the main protocol suite used today for Internet networking, as well as most business and home networks. TCP/IP is installed when you install your operating system; you don't need to do anything to enable it.

One of the key features of the IP portion of TCP/IP is IP addressing, which you learned about in Chapter 5. Each device on a network has a unique IP address—usually. A LAN may have its own IP addressing scheme, with privately assigned numbers. When its router is connected to the Internet, your ISP assigns an Internet-usable IP address to the router, and all the devices connected to the router use that same IP address through the router's **default gateway**. The default gateway is the port through which data leaves the router to go to another network. The devices share the same IP address in a process called **network address translation (NAT)**, which automatically changes the IP addresses on the data going in and out of the router as needed.

As you learned in Chapter 5, the Internet currently uses IPv4 addresses. IPv4 addresses consist of four numbers between 0 and 255 separated by periods (like this: 207.171.181.16), making up one 32-bit binary number when translated to binary. Only 4.3 billion such addresses are available, however, so as the Internet grows, these addresses have become in short supply. An organization called **Internet Assigned Numbers Authority (IANA)** is responsible for global coordination of the assignment of IP addresses. At some point, the Internet will change over to IPv6 addresses—128-bit numbers that the planet should never run out of.

Ethernet

At the Data Link layer, the protocols for the network type come into play. Among these protocols—which include Ethernet, token ring, and Fiber Distributed Data Interface (FDDI)—the main one to know about is **Ethernet**. Ethernet has become such a popular type of network that you can assume that any network is Ethernet unless otherwise specified. Officially, the term *Ethernet* covers both the wired and wireless forms, but in popular usage, the term has come to refer to the wired form, whereas *Wi-Fi* has come to refer to the wireless form.

Ethernet is logically a bus topology, using CSMA/CD to detect and correct collisions, as you learned in the section "Bus Topology," on page 260. An Ethernet network can physically be a mesh, star, bus, or hybrid topology, although star is the most common. It generally uses UTP cable (with a length limit of about 325 feet), but it can also use STP or fiber-optic cable. Very early forms of Ethernet used thick coaxial cable, but those forms are now long obsolete.

There have been different forms of Ethernet over the years. As hardware technology has continued to develop, Ethernet has used different cable types and carried data at different maximum speeds. Early Ethernet was referred to as *10Base2 (Thinnet)* or *10Base5 (Thicknet)*, for example. The most common form found on the market today is **10000BaseT**, also called *10 Gigabit Ethernet*. The number at the beginning of the name represents the maximum speed (such as 10 Mbps or 10,000 Mbps), and the number or letter following *Base* refers to the type of cable (*2* and *5* refer to two different thicknesses of coaxial cable, and *T* refers to twisted-pair cable).

Activity 6.6.3

Article
IP Addressing

Activity 6.6.4

Article
Ethernet

Recheck **6.6**

Recheck your understanding of the concepts covered by this objective.

6.7 Setting Up Your Own Networks

You don't have to be a networking professional to create simple networks. In the following sections, you'll learn some practical ways that you can use networking in your everyday life.

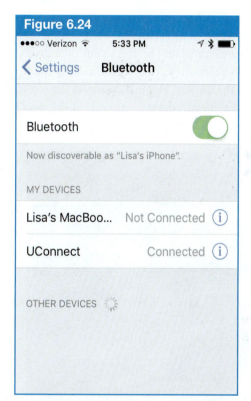

Precheck 6.7

Check your understanding of the concepts covered by this objective.

Connecting Bluetooth Devices

As you learned in the section "Bluetooth Technology," on page 249, Bluetooth is a short-range technology that creates personal area networks (PANs). To **pair** (connect) a Bluetooth-enabled peripheral device, such as a headset or printer, to a computer or smartphone, you follow this general process:

1. Make sure the devices are near each other—at least in the same room. Put the peripheral device in Discoverable mode. This enables the computer or smartphone to see the device and connect to it. Some devices are always discoverable when they are powered on; others require you to press a certain sequence of buttons or keys. Check the device's documentation for help in locating and adjusting these settings.

2. Use the Bluetooth software on the computer or smartphone to search for nearby Bluetooth-enabled devices. On a smartphone or tablet, the setting is probably located within the Settings app. In Windows, the Bluetooth settings are located in the Control Panel. Figure 6.24 shows a smartphone searching for Bluetooth devices.

3. Click the name of the device you wish to pair, click *Pair*, and then allow the operating system to complete the pairing process.

4. If you are pairing two computing devices, a passcode appears on the screen of each device. Verify that the passcodes are the same on both screens, and then click OK or Yes on each device.

Figure 6.24

A smartphone with Bluetooth enabled will search for nearby devices.

Note: The first time you use a certain device, the operating system may require you to install a driver for it. If you see a message requiring that installation, follow the prompts to download and install the driver.

5. If prompted to confirm on either device, follow the prompts to do so.

Not all Bluetooth devices can be paired with all other devices. In most cases, one of the devices must be some type of computer (a PC, laptop, tablet, or smartphone). For example, you would not be able to pair a mouse with a camera or a keyboard with a printer.

You may find that having Bluetooth enabled all the time drains the connected device's battery faster than normal. If battery life is an issue for you, you might want to go back into the device's Settings and turn off Bluetooth when the paired device isn't in use.

Connecting a Mobile Device to Wi-Fi

When a Wi-Fi connection is available, your device may pop up a message letting you know and inviting you to connect to it. If you don't see such a message automatically, you can manually search for nearby wireless networks.

Most devices have a Settings app that contains a *Network* or a *Wi-Fi* section. Use that section to make sure that Wi-Fi is turned on (that is, that the wireless network adapter is enabled). Look for the network you want to connect to, click it, and then click *Connect*. On a Windows PC, such as a laptop, you can click the Network icon in the notification area to view a list of available networks. Figure 6.25 shows the Network Settings pane in Windows 10.

Most wireless networks are set up with security, so that you must have a password to connect. The first time you connect to a secure network, you will be prompted for the password, or key. This password is associated with the wireless access point or router you are connecting to. If it's your own device, look for a label or sticker on the device that tells its default password code. If the device belongs to someone else, ask that person for the key. Figure 6.26 shows the screen of a Windows Phone prompting a user for the password for a network. A wireless network can also be set to Open status, which means it can be accessed without a password.

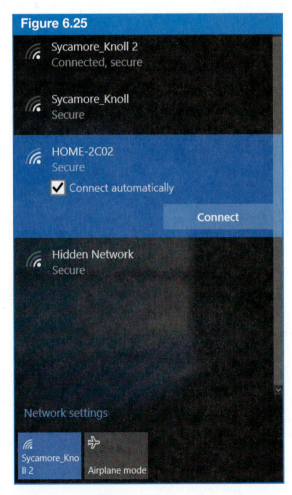

At the Network Settings pane in Windows 10, you can view a list of available networks, click a network to select it, and then click *Connect* to complete the connection.

The first time you connect a device to a secure network, you will see a prompt like this, asking you to enter the password.

Some newer routers and combination modem/routers have a Wireless Protected Access (WPS) button on them. If you press this button, the router becomes open briefly to connections from new devices. You can then click a prompt on the screen of the device you wish to connect to it to establish a connection without having to type the password.

Setting Up a Wireless Home Network

If you have cable or DSL service and your modem and router functions are combined into a single unit, a professional installer might have come to your home and set up your service for you. If that's the case, you already have a wireless network ready to go, and all you need to do is connect each wireless device to it, as described in the preceding section. If, however, you are starting from scratch, this section will provide a roadmap of how to proceed.

You will probably want to share your broadband Internet connection on the wireless network, so first make sure your Internet connection is working. To do so, connect an Ethernet cable from the modem to any computer, and check for Internet access. If you have access, the modem is working.

If the modem doesn't have a built-in router, you will need to purchase a wireless router. Look for one that's compatible with the 802.11n standard (or 802.11ac, if available). Power on the router. It should be ready to go right out of the box but with no security on it. That's good, at first, because you will want to make sure the wireless capability is working before you turn on the password. (Configuring network security is covered in the next section.) Try to connect to the router with one of your wireless devices. If it connects successfully, try to access the Internet. If it works, then you are ready to set up the security on the router. If not, check the router's documentation and online support for help.

Configuring Wireless Network Security

To change the security settings on a wireless network, you must connect to the router via its IP address using your web browser. Start by typing the router's IP address in the Address bar. (Check the documentation that came with your router to find out the IP

Activity 6.7.1

Article
**Setting Up
a Home Network**

Tech Ethics 🏛 🏛 🏛 🏛 🏛 🏛 🏛

Sharing Wireless Broadband

In urban areas, a router's Wi-Fi signal may extend far enough to reach several people's homes. Because of this, sometimes several neighbors go together on Internet service, with one neighbor paying for it and the others reimbursing him or her for part of the expense. On the surface, this might seem like a good idea, but it's problematic for several reasons.

First and most important, the terms of service of most broadband Internet service providers prohibit this type of sharing. The bottom line is that this kind of sharing amounts to stealing, because it deprives the ISP of revenue.

There are also potential complications that many people don't think of when they consider saving a few dollars a month. For example, what if you share with a neighbor who is a heavy Internet user (constantly streaming movies, for instance), so that your own Internet speed suffers? Or what if you share with a neighbor who gets involved in something illegal using an Internet connection that's set up in your name? There are service-related considerations too. For example, suppose the router is in your neighbor's home and he or she goes on vacation for a month. What if during that time, the router needs to be reset to troubleshoot a problem?

When you start adding up the negatives and risks, saving a little money each month might not seem like such a good deal.

address to use, or look it up online.) You may be prompted to enter a user name and password for the router. (Check the router's documentation for this information too, or look up the router's default user name and password online.) Turn on security and the authentication type, and specify a password to use.

Figure 6.27 shows an example setup screen. The setup screen for your router may look quite different, because the names of the sections and settings vary widely depending on the router's make and model. Check your router's documentation or online help as needed.

Different types of security are available on most wireless routers, including a security mode and an encryption method. Wi-Fi Protected Access II (WPA2) is the most commonly used security mode; when setting up your own network's security, it's a good choice. The encryption methods available depend on the security mode; for WPA2 on a small network, choose AES or TKIP. (It's not important to understand the details of these settings to set up your network.)

Figure 6.27

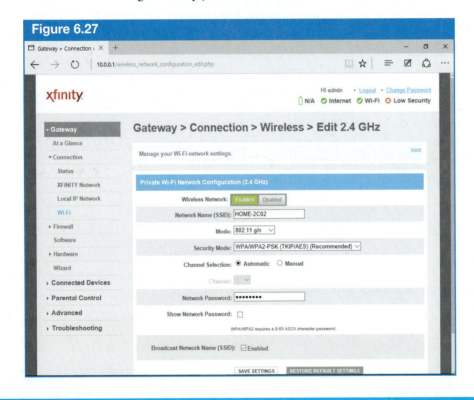

The setup screen for your router may look different than this one, depending on the make and model of your router. Follow the prompts on the screen, referring to the documentation and online help for your router as necessary.

Practical TECH

Near Field Communication

Near field communication (NFC) is a technology for establishing a temporary wireless connection between two devices by touching them together or bringing them in very close proximity to one another. Using NFC, cell phones can exchange contact information with one another, for example, and you can make a payment by waving an NFC-enabled credit card in front of an NFC sensor rather than swiping it through a card reader. Some payment systems, such as Apple Pay, enable consumers to store their credit card information on a cell phone and then pay for purchases without the card being present. NFC allows the phone and the credit card processing equipment to share the needed data. Like Bluetooth LE, NFC uses very little power.

Using a Cell Phone as a Hotspot

Many models of smartphones can be used as Wi-Fi hotspots, providing Internet connectivity for multiple Wi-Fi-enabled devices wherever you happen to be. The phone becomes a broadband modem, using its own Internet connection through the 3G or 4G network to supply Internet service to the devices.

The steps for enabling your phone's hotspot capabilities depend on the phone's operating system, but here are the general steps:

1. Open the Settings app on the phone. (It may be called something other than *Settings*, depending on the operating system.)

2. Select the Internet sharing feature, and turn it on. (The name of this feature also varies depending on the operating system; for example, it might be called *Internet Sharing*, *Personal Hotspot*, or *Tethering & portable hotspot for Android*.) Figure 6.28 shows the Internet sharing feature on a Windows phone.

3. Adjust any settings as needed.

4. On the computer that you want to use to connect to the Internet, detect new Internet connections available (as you learned to do in the section "Connecting a Mobile Device to Wi-Fi," on page 272), and then select and connect to your phone as if it's a wireless router or access point.

A possible downside to using your smartphone as a modem is that you will probably use more data. If you have an unlimited data plan, this won't be a problem. However, if your data plan is limited and you use more than it allows, you will likely be charged extra. Monitor your data usage very carefully if you are using your phone as a hotspot, to avoid extra charges, and turn off the Internet sharing feature on your phone when you are done using it.

Figure 6.28

Enable Internet sharing on your phone to make it operate as a hotspot.

 **Recheck 6.7**
Recheck your understanding of the concepts covered by this objective.

Chapter Summary

➡ *An interactive Chapter Summary, Study Notes, and a Slide Presentation with audio are available from the links menu on this page in your ebook.*

6.1 Understanding Data Transmission Basics

A **network** consists of two or more computers, devices, and software connected by one or more communications media, such as wires, telephone lines, and wireless signals.

Data moves most efficiently in **digital** form, but some communications media require data to be converted to **analog** form. The conversion between analog and digital is done using a modem. Data throughput per second is called **bandwidth**, and it's measured in bits per second. A **broadband medium** is one that carries data at least at 256 Kbps. A **narrowband medium** delivers data more slowly than that. Data can be transmitted via **serial transmission** (that is, one bit at a time) or via **parallel transmission** (many bits at a time). With some data transmission, data is sent in only one direction (**simplex transmission**). If data is sent in both directions but not simultaneously, it's **half-duplex transmission**. If it's sent in both directions simultaneously, it's **full duplex transmission**. **Multiplexing** is a method by which multiple data streams can be delivered on a single wire.

6.2 Distinguishing between Types of Communications Media

A **communications medium** is a connection by cable or by some wireless method. Most elements of a network are connected using cables; wireless connections are used only at the end points in most cases.

Copper telephone lines are one common type of cable used in communications. They are **twisted-pair cables**; the wires are twisted to reduce **electromagnetic interference (EMI)**. Twisted-pair cable can be either **shielded twisted-pair (STP) cable** or **unshielded twisted-pair (UTP) cable**. Shielding provides protection from EMI that originates from outside the cable. UTP is much more common. It's graded in categories, with Cat5e and Cat6 being suitable for modern home and business networking. A UTP cable has an RJ-45 connector at each

end, which looks like a wider version of a telephone connector.

Coaxial cable is commonly used for cable TV and in some computer networks. **Fiber-optic cable** uses glass threads to transmit beams of light in patterns that can be read as data. Fiber-optic cable is often used for the **network backbone** because of its speed and long maximum cable length.

A **T line** is a high-speed, long-distance telephone line leased from the phone company. It isn't actually a single line but rather a bundle of lines. A **T1 line** carries data over 24 internal lines at a combined rate of 1.5 Mbps. A **T3 line** carries data over 672 lines for a combined rate of up to 43 Mbps.

Wireless media transfer data through the air using either radio waves or light waves. **Wi-Fi** uses radio signals in the 2.4 GHz or 5 GHz band, according to the **IEEE 802.11** standard. There are several versions of Wi-Fi, including 802.11 a, b, g, n, and, most recently, ac. A Wi-Fi device connects to a **wireless access point** (in **infrastructure mode**) or directly to another Wi-Fi enabled device (**ad hoc mode**). **Bluetooth** is a short-range wireless networking standard for connecting devices to peripherals.

Cellular technology is the basis for the cell phone communication system. A geographical area of about 12 square miles, known as a **cell**, is covered by an antenna that communicates with any cell phones in its range. Cell phones that contain applications and Internet connectivity capabilities are called *smartphones*.

A **communications satellite** orbits the Earth. A **transponder** in the satellite receives signals from a transmission station on the ground called an **earth station**. Satellites orbit the Earth at the same speed as the Earth's rotation, so they seem stationary when viewed from the ground; this is called a **geosynchronous orbit**. Satellites are useful for some communications, but their inherent **latency** makes them inappropriate for Internet access.

A **microwave system** connects two locations point to point and requires a clear line of sight. It's sometimes used as a substitute for cables over very rugged terrain.

Infrared technology transmits data as light waves. **IrDA** is the standard for that type of transmission. TV remotes use infrared, and so did early mobile devices. Bluetooth has mostly replaced it, however, because infrared requires a clear line of sight and Bluetooth does not.

6.3 Identifying Network Types

Networks can be classified by their architecture, by the distances they cover, and by the users they are designed to support. The term **network architecture** refers to the way a network is designed and built. In **client/server architecture**, one or more servers manages the network. In **peer-to-peer architecture** (also called a **workgroup**), each computer shares the networking burden.

A **personal area network (PAN)** is a network that has a very small range and is used primarily by one person. A **local area network (LAN)** is a private network that serves an organization in the same building or a group of nearby buildings. A **metropolitan area network (MAN)** serves a metropolitan area, such as a city and its suburbs. A **wide area network (WAN)** spans a large geographical area. A **virtual private network (VPN)** uses the Internet instead of a leased line to create a virtual WAN.

A TCP/IP-based network that's housed within an organization to serve internal users is called an **intranet**. An **extranet** is an extension of an intranet that allows selected external users to have access.

6.4 Exploring Network Topologies

A **network topology** is the pattern by which a network is organized. A network has both a physical topology and a logical topology. For example, an Ethernet network is logically a bus topology but physically may be any of several topologies.

In a physical **bus topology**, the computers are linked with a single cable with two endpoints, called a *bus*. Data collisions are avoided using **carrier sense multiple access with collision detection (CSMA/CD)**. Bus topologies typically use coaxial or fiber-optic cable.

In a physical **star topology**, the devices are connected to a central gathering point, which can be a switch or a router. In a **ring topology**, there is no central hub; each computer is part of a circle of devices. The logical form of ring topology is called **token ring topology**. Permission to send data requires the device to have the **token**. In a **mesh topology**, multiple devices are connected to multiple others, creating a fault-tolerant web. A **hybrid topology** combines two or more physical topologies.

6.5 Identifying Common Types of Network Hardware

A server is an essential part of a client/server network. An organization with one or two servers may choose for each server to be a stand-alone unit, called a **tower server**. An organization with more servers may use **rack-mounted servers**, which can be stored compactly in a rack and don't need their own keyboards, mouses, or monitors. An organization that needs many servers may find **blade-mounted servers** most economical; multiple servers share a blade enclosure that has a single power supply and cooling fans, as well as some other shared components.

A **switch** physically connects computers within a LAN. It has ports for connecting cables from all the computers to be connected. A switch is able to route traffic between the connected devices; an earlier version called a **hub** didn't route traffic but served the same function physically. Racks of switches are sometimes stored compactly in a **wiring closet**. A **router** is like a switch except that it's able to direct traffic to other routers. A **repeater** strengthens and amplifies a network signal. A **gateway** joins dissimilar networks; a **bridge** joins similar networks. A **network adapter** is the network hardware inside an individual network device, such as a client PC or a printer. When the network adapter is an add-on board in a desktop PC, it's called a **network interface card (NIC)**. Each network adapter has a unique hardware identifier called a **media access control (MAC) address**.

6.6 Understanding Network Software and Protocols

Network software includes both server operating systems and the network connection software within client operating systems. **Protocols** work at various levels to transmit and receive data within the client and server operating systems. The **Open Systems Interconnection (OSI) reference model** provides one way of understanding the levels of communication.

At the application level, web browsers use **Hypertext Transfer Protocol (HTTP)** to send and receive data. Email programs may use some combination of **Post Office Protocol 3 (POP3)**, **Simple Mail Transfer Protocol (SMTP)**, and **Internet Message Access Protocol (IMAP)**. Other application-level protocols include File Transfer Protocol (FTP) and **Telnet.**

Transmission Control Protocol (TCP) and **Internet Protocol (IP)** form a suite of protocols **(TCP/IP)** on which the entire Internet is based, as well as most private networks today. It identifies computers using IP addressing. A router is assigned an IP address as a **default gateway**, which is the door into and out of the router to and from other networks. **Network address translation (NAT)** automatically changes the IP addresses going to and from another network (such as the Internet) that has different addressing requirements. IP addresses on the Internet are assigned by the **Internet Assigned Numbers Authority (IANA).**

Ethernet is the most popular networking standard in the world. Most networking hardware sold today is Ethernet. Wi-Fi is a form of wireless Ethernet. It islogically a bus topology but physically can be a star, mesh, or bus. There have been several versions, each with its own cable type and maximum speed. The current standard is **10000BaseT** also called *10 Gigabit Ethernet*, operating at 10,000 Mbps (1 Gbps) using twisted-pair cable.

6.7 Setting Up Your Own Networks

To connect Bluetooth devices, you pair them. Use the Settings or Control Panel on a PC or other computing device to make itself available to find Bluetooth devices, and then follow the prompts that appear to choose an available device and **pair** it with the computer.

To connect a mobile device to Wi-Fi, locate the setting on the device for enabling Wi-Fi. Available Wi-Fi networks should automatically appear on a list for selection; you choose the one you want. You may need to enter the network's password.

To set up a wireless home network, you will need network adapters for the devices and a router. Connect your Internet connection to the router and power it up. Look for the router in the available networks and connect to it on each device. To set up a router's wireless security, go into the router's settings using a web browser by specifying the router's IP address.

To use a cell phone as a hotspot, find the setting on the phone that turns on the Internet sharing or hotspot feature and enable it. Connect to it as you would any wireless router or access point with each device.

Key Terms

Numbers indicate the pages where terms are first cited with their full definition in the chapter. An alphabetized list of key terms with definitions is included in the end-of-book glossary.

 *An interactive **Glossary** is available from the links menu on this page in your ebook.*

Chapter Exercises

Complete the following exercises to assess your understanding of the material covered in this chapter.

Interactive **Flash Cards** and an interactive **Game** are available from the links menu on this page in your ebook.

Go to your SNAP Assignments page to complete the Terms Check, Knowledge Check, Key Principles, and Tech Illustrated exercises.

Terms Check: Matching

Match each term with its definition.

    a. serial transmission
    b. Bluetooth
    c. infrared technology
    d. network backbone
    e. Wi-Fi
    f. router
    g. switch
    h. broadband
    i. communications
    j. coaxial cable

__ 1. Describes a communications medium capable of carrying at least 256 Kbps.

__ 2. A hardware device that physically connects computers within a LAN.

__ 3. A form of data transmission that sends one bit at a time.

__ 4. A short-range wireless networking standard used to connect peripheral devices to computers, tablets, and smartphones.

__ 5. The most commonly used wireless technology today.

__ 6. Transmits data as light waves instead of radio waves.

__ 7. Directs network traffic across different network segments, such as between LANs.

__ 8. The central pathway of a network.

__ 9. Orbiting device containing several transponders.

__ 10. Commonly used for cable TV connections.

 ## Knowledge Check: Multiple Choice

Choose the best answer for each question.

1. The overall throughput per second of a transmission medium is its
   a. network architecture.
   b. bandwidth.
   c. broadband.
   d. topology.

2. Which type of data transmission allows two-directional communication but not simultaneously?
   a. simplex
   b. half-duplex
   c. full-duplex
   d. multiplexing

3. Which type of communications media uses a string of glass to transmit beams of light?
   a. copper telephone lines
   b. twisted-pair cable
   c. coaxial cable
   d. fiber-optic cable

4. Which type of network architecture has no dedicated servers?
   a. client/server
   b. client/client
   c. peer-to-peer
   d. peer-to-hub

5. Which network coverage classification describes a private network of computers located in the same building or group of nearby buildings?
   a. PAN
   b. LAN
   c. MAN
   d. WAN

6. Which network user classification restricts access to only the staff of a company?

a. intranet
b. Internet
c. extranet
d. innernet

7. Which physical network topology links multiple computers and peripheral devices to a central hub?
   a. bus
   b. star
   c. ring
   d. mesh

8. Network hardware that strengthens and amplifies a network signal is called a
   a. repeater.
   b. switch.

c. router.
d. hub.

9. Which application-level network protocol is used to send email?
   a. HTTP
   b. POP3
   c. IMAP
   d. SMTP

10. The most commonly used wireless technology today is
    a. cellular technology.
    b. communications satellites.
    c. microwave systems.
    d. Wi-Fi.

Key Principles: Completion

Complete each statement with the appropriate word or phrase.

1. _____ transmission sends and receives several related bits simultaneously.

2. A cell phone that can run applications and access the Internet is referred to as a(n) _____.

3. A network that spans a large geographical area, connecting two or more LANs, is called a(n) _____.

4. An extension of an intranet that allows users to access data via the Internet is called a(n) _____.

5. Hardware and/or software that enables communication between dissimilar networks is called a(n) _____.

6. To receive and display web pages, the protocol a web browser primarily uses is _____.

7. The most popular networking standard in the world is _____.

8. The way a network is designed and built is referred to as network _____.

9. The pattern by which a network is organized is referred to as network _____.

10. A set of rules for how things will happen is called a(n) _____.

Tech Illustrated: Figure Labeling

Fill in the blanks with the correct labels.

1. Wireless network

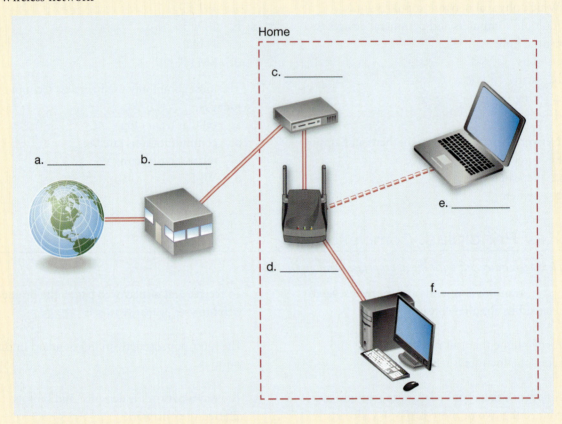

2. Star topology

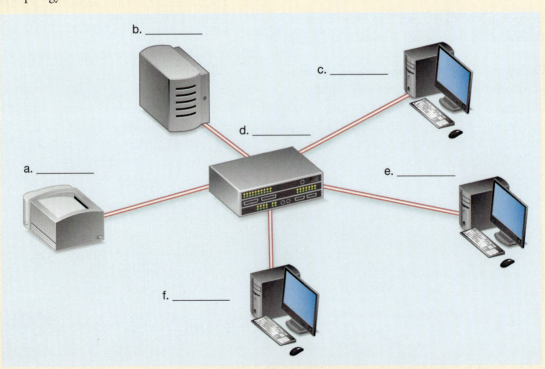

Tech to Come: Brainstorming New Uses

In groups or individually, contemplate the following questions and develop as many answers as you can.

1. New York City has found a use for its pay phone booths and kiosks, which are nowadays rarely used. It's turning them into Wi-Fi hotspots that provide free Internet access. Discuss how other cities could use or modify this idea to provide hotspot locations throughout the city.

2. Today, wireless technology is found in many homes. Wi-Fi is used to access the Internet, to send documents to the printer, and to connect to telephone service. What are some other wireless devices available for your home? Predict what devices will become wireless in the future. What issues could occur as the use of home wireless devices increases?

3. The availability of cloud storage and cloud-based apps has had positive impact on the way businesses operate and maintain their networks. From a network management point of view, what are some of the advantages of moving to cloud storage and cloud-based apps? As the use of cloud computing expands, what are some issues that could occur on networks?

Tech Literacy: Internet Research and Writing

Conduct Internet research to find the information described, and then develop appropriate written responses based on your research. Be sure to document your sources using the MLA format. (See Chapter 1, Tech Literacy: Internet Research and Writing, page 38, to review MLA style guidelines.)

1. Analyze the configuration of a local network. You could use your school network or the network of a local business or organization. Investigate the type of network, network topology, number of computers on the network, and communications media used, as well as whether the network is wired or wireless. Sketch and label the network configuration, and then describe the hardware and software used. Write a summary explaining why the organization or business established this particular setup. What were its primary needs, and how does the network meet those needs?

2. Intranets are found in most large corporations. Research a corporation (such as Coke or IBM) and describe the content accessible on its intranet. If possible, include a screen capture of the corporation's intranet home page. Next, research intranets in general and summarize considerations or tips that should be followed when launching an intranet.

3. What are the benefits to businesses of providing Wi-Fi access for customers in their establishments? Choose two or three businesses (near you, if possible) that provide Wi-Fi access to their customers. Possibilities include restaurants, cafes, and shopping malls. Determine whether customers need to provide personal information to use the Wi-Fi and whether limitations or costs are associated with using the Wi-Fi. Reflect on what benefits businesses can realize by providing this access to customers, and discuss issues businesses may have to deal with when they do provide Wi-Fi access.

4. Some cities, such as San Francisco, have explored digital inclusion strategies in an effort to provide free citywide wireless access and increased access to digital technology. Access to the Internet and digital technology has become increasingly important for employment and education, leaving residents who don't have access at a disadvantage. Research the digital inclusion strategy in San Francisco or a similar strategy in another city, summarize the progress of the initiative, and explain what obstacles or issues have occurred as a result of this type of initiative.

Tech Issues: Team Problem-Solving

In groups, develop possible solutions to the issues presented.

1. Some companies and individuals find it difficult to obtain high-speed Internet access or cell service because they are located in small or remote areas. What do you think can be done to help these businesses and individuals? Do you think people have a right to high-speed Internet access and cell service? Should the government play a role in solving this problem?

2. Most companies and organizations have network usage agreements that employees must sign before obtaining access to the network. Prepare a list of policies or conditions you feel should be included in a network usage agreement. Explain why you think these policies or conditions are necessary.

Tech Timeline: Predicting Next Steps

Look at the timeline below outlining major benchmarks in the development of the Internet. On the basis of your knowledge and any research you might conduct, think of three changes that may occur between now and 2025, and then add them to the timeline.

1958 Just after the Soviet Union's launch of *Sputnik I*, the United States forms the Advanced Research Projects Agency (ARPA).

1966 ARPA introduces its plan for a national network.

1973 The first international connections are made to the ARPANET.

1986 The National Science Foundation (NSF) creates NSFNET.

1990 The World Wide Web is invented.

1999 The first full-service, Internet-only bank is opened.

2000 The US Department of Justice, FBI, and National White Collar Crime Center launch the Internet Fraud and Complaint Center (IFCC).

2002 US online retail sales reach $45 billion.

2003 Nielsen NetRatings estimates there are 580 million Internet users worldwide.

2005 The number of worldwide Internet users tops 1 billion.

2009 63 percent of American adults have broadband Internet connections at home.

2012 Facebook reaches 1 billion monthly active users.

2013 51 percent of US adults bank online.

2014 Half of US adults age 55 and over own smartphones.

Ethical Dilemmas: Group Discussion and Debate

As a class or within an assigned group, discuss the following ethical dilemma.

As companies realize the consequences of security breaches in their computer systems, they are looking for experienced computer security specialists to help protect their systems from intrusions. Some companies hire former hackers (many of whom are convicted criminals), because they believe that these individuals' experience in finding security holes is extremely valuable. Other companies won't even consider hiring former hackers because of the security threats they pose to their employers.

Find an example of a hacker who got hired by a major company. Share your example with the group and then reflect on the following:

If you were responsible for the security of a large company's network and systems, would you hire a consultant who is an experienced hacker or a security consultant without a record of hacking?

How would you convince management that you made the right decision?

What safeguards would you put in place with the consultant to make sure that he or she would not use any sensitive information gained during the process of the analysis to compromise your company's security or privacy?

Chapter 7

Taking Advantage of the Cloud: Teamwork, Apps, and Storage

Chapter Goal

To learn how to make the most of the shift from device-based data storage and computing tasks to cloud-based data storage and computing tasks

Learning Objectives

7.1   Compare and contrast the cloud's offerings and infrastructure.

7.2   Explain how to use the cloud as an individual.

7.3   Describe how teams use cloud computing to collaborate.

7.4   Describe the various categories of cloud services.

Green go-online icons indicate resources that are accessed from the links menu in your ebook.

SNAP icons indicate interactive resources that are available in SNAP. Go to your SNAP Assignments page to complete these quizzes, activities, and exercises.

7.1 Understanding the Cloud

Precheck 7.1

Check your understanding of the concepts covered by this objective.

Chapter 6 explained the ins and outs of networks, and Chapter 5 explored the Internet, which is an online network of networks. This chapter brings together those concepts to cover **cloud computing**, the new way to think of how the Internet and other networks deliver content and services to computer users. For many of us, the Internet is the **cloud**. But depending on your viewpoint, the term *cloud computing* can have two meanings.

One meaning of *cloud computing* looks at things from the end user's standpoint. For an individual, working in the cloud means using a free or subscription service delivered over the Internet. For example, rather than installing a graphics program on your computer and using it to edit photos, you might use an online photo editor—such as Pixlr, FotoFlexer, or PicMonkey. Rather than making a backup of your files to an external hard disk or network storage, an online service uploads the backed-up data to the cloud for you. And of course, the social media and networking sites and webmail that you use "live" in the cloud. Smartphones, tablets, and other devices can also connect to the cloud to access content and services as needed. You can access applications and services in the cloud 24/7, and they update automatically, so you don't have to worry about downloading and installing updates. Figure 7.1 illustrates how quickly the scope of the cloud services market has grown.

The second meaning of *cloud computing* comes from the viewpoint of an information technology (IT) organization. In this case, *the cloud* refers to the infrastructure and software used to deliver services online. The cloud consists of many networked clusters of servers connected to the Internet. For example, large cloud providers (such as Amazon) operate data centers. A **data center** is a location housing a large computing operation with numerous networked servers. The provider sells the server space, computational power, and some software services to other companies and organizations. Data centers deliver information and

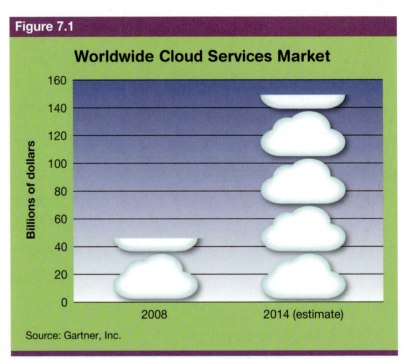

Figure 7.1

Worldwide Cloud Services Market

Billions of dollars

2008   2014 (estimate)

Source: Gartner, Inc.

Tracking Down Tech ≫≫≫≫≫

Trying Your Take on What Should Live in the Cloud

As you will learn in this chapter, *the cloud* refers to data storage and services that are available online. Using the cloud you can perform activities such as sharing a file with a group of users or using an online app from multiple devices. More and more organizations are moving large databases to the cloud, so that customers can retrieve information. Complete this scavenger hunt to discover content or services in your campus or local library that could be moved to the cloud.

Figure 7.2

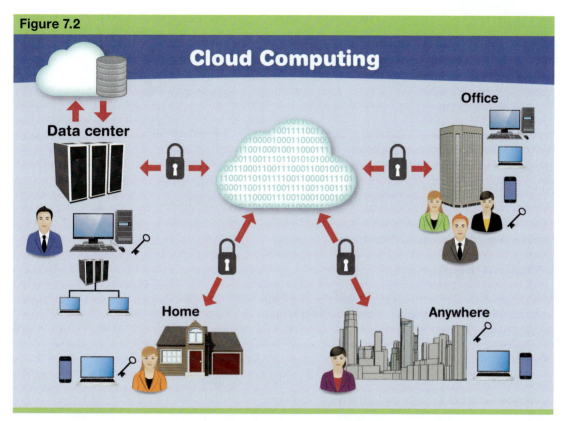

Data and services placed in the cloud by a data center can be accessed securely anywhere that the Internet is available.

services to the cloud. End users access the information or services, often via a secure Internet connection, from home, the office, or anywhere else. This second meaning of *cloud computing* emerged from a similar concept—**utility computing**—in which providers bundled and sold computing resources. Figure 7.2 illustrates this meaning of *cloud computing*. Most cloud providers use a variety of security techniques (indicated by the locks and keys in the figure) to ensure that data remains safe and private in the cloud.

Cloud computing enables companies and other organizations to provide online services with a smaller initial cost. This means they can roll out new services more quickly than would be possible if they had to build an internal server infrastructure from scratch. Suppose that a company wants to introduce a new consumer app. By operating in the cloud, the company can purchase space and basic software infrastructure from a cloud provider, rather than buy its own servers and IT services. (The company could also build its own cloud infrastructure, as discussed in the "Private" section on the next page.)

Virtualization and Scalability

In general terms, the cloud consists of high-power, large-capacity physical server computers located in data centers. More importantly, each physical server typically hosts multiple **virtual servers**—servers created by software rather than separate hardware. For example, a single physical server might be set up to operate five or six virtual servers.

A technology called **virtualization** makes this possible. Virtualization software (such as VMware) can create multiple distinct operating servers that run simultaneously on a single physical server machine, effectively turning that one server into two

Activity 7.1.1

Video
Virtualization

or more. Such a software-based server is a **scalable server**, which means it can be made larger or smaller or moved around easily. There's no need for physical hardware changes and no disruption to the app or service being delivered. In addition, these virtual servers typically operate in a self-service fashion, allowing IT staff to add and remove new cloud services at will, a configuration or setup process known as **provisioning**.

Consider a simple example. Suppose that a physical server is running two virtual servers. Virtual Server A uses 20 percent of the physical server's capacity, and Virtual Server B uses 30 percent; thus, 50 percent of the physical server's capacity remains available. If the organization that's purchasing capacity for Virtual Server A encounters more traffic or needs more storage for the content it delivers, it can scale up to using another 20 percent of the server's capacity on the fly (and pay for that additional capacity as required). Doing so will bring the organization's usage to 40 percent and reduce the server's remaining capacity to 20 percent.

Types of Cloud Computing

You will find numerous ways to deploy (that is, engineer or set up) a cloud infrastructure, such as a community cloud. Three types of cloud **deployment** models dominate: private, public, and hybrid.

Private A cloud setup created for and used by a single organization is called a **private cloud**. A private cloud can be hosted and managed internally at a company's own data center. Alternatively, it can be hosted internally but managed by a third party or hosted by a third party but managed by a company's IT staff. When a private cloud is hosted at a third-party data center, servers and software resources must be dedicated to the single organization.

Why might an organization choose a private cloud? It might want to create a specific operational or business environment, or it might want to be able to enforce specific security standards. In a private cloud, the resources may or may not be shared to the larger Internet cloud.

When an organization hosts its private cloud at its own data center (see Figure 7.3), it gives up some advantages, such as avoiding upfront hardware costs and physical setup of the servers. But it can also gain some advantages, such as the ability to operate the servers without virtualization (virtualization can slow down server performance somewhat). For this reason, some large providers of cloud services (such as Google and Facebook) manage their own private clouds.

Despite the drawbacks of private clouds, International Data Corporation (IDC) estimated the worldwide market for hosted private cloud, would reach $40.6 billion in 2019. IDC also estimated that spending on the cloud IT infrastructure would reach $53.1 billion by 2019.

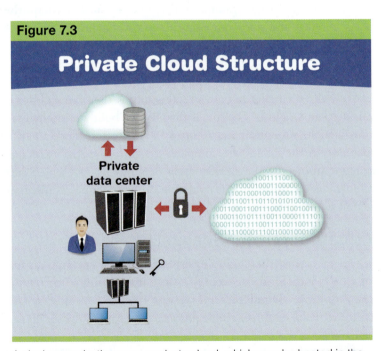

Figure 7.3

Private Cloud Structure

Private data center

A single organization uses a private cloud, which may be hosted in the organization's private data center or be a dedicated part of an external data center. The private cloud may or may not share its resources to the larger Internet cloud.

Public The resources for a **public cloud** exist for use by any organization (see Figure 7.4). A **cloud service provider (CSP)** operates one or more data centers, and organizations buy cloud capacity from a CSP as they need it. Doing so allows organizations to take advantage of the benefits of visualization and scalability.

Table 7.1 lists some of the many CSPs that sell public cloud capacity and services, along with websites where you can learn more about those CSPs. Each provider operates with a different **cloud management system**, or combination of software and other solutions used to run the provider's services. In addition to considering the

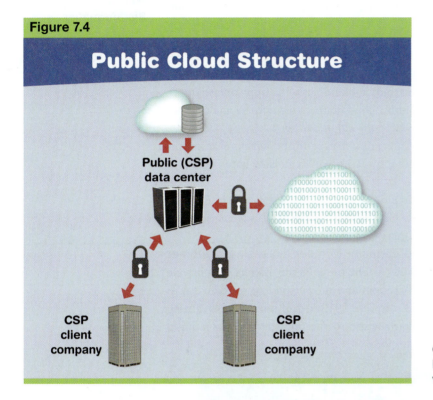

Figure 7.4

Public Cloud Structure

Public (CSP)
data center

CSP
client
company

CSP
client
company

Activity 7.1.2

Practice
**The Structure
of a Public Cloud**

Cloud service providers (CSPs) provide Internet-connected server space to a variety of clients and organizations.

Table 7.1 Cloud Service Providers (CSPs)

Provider Name	Website
Amazon Web Services	http://CUT6.emcp.net/AmazonWebServices
Bluelock	http://CUT6.emcp.net/BluelockCloud
CenturyLink	http://CUT6.emcp.net/CenturyLinkCloud
Dell	http://CUT6.emcp.net/DellCloud
Google Cloud Platform	http://CUT6.emcp.net/GoogleCloud
HP Cloud	http://CUT6.emcp.net/HPPublicCloud
IBM Cloud	http://CUT6.emcp.net/IBMCloud
Joyent	http://CUT6.emcp.net/JoyentCloud
Microsoft Cloud	http://CUT6.emcp.net/MicrosoftCloud
Oracle	http://CUT6.emcp.net/OracleCloud
Rackspace	http://CUT6.emcp.net/RackspaceCloud
Verizon	http://CUT6.emcp.net/VerizonCloud

capabilities of the cloud management system, an organization buying capacity from a CSP should consider whether the security and governance systems provide adequate protection.

The services and offerings of various CSPs vary widely. They may include different levels of consulting and private cloud hosting or assistance, as well as public cloud hosting. Some CSPs offer stronger scaling and traffic management packages, while others offer more features for heavy data processing. For example, Amazon offers Amazon Elastic MapReduce (Amazon EMR) for such powerful tasks as web indexing, data warehousing, machine learning, financial analysis, scientific simulation, and bioinformatics.

Activity 7.1.3

Article
Bioinformatics

Hybrid Some organizations choose to use both private and public cloud infrastructure—an arrangement that's called a **hybrid cloud**. An organization's hybrid cloud consists of its internal private cloud, plus public cloud capacity from one or more CSPs (see Figure 7.5). The private and public cloud connect securely to one another to exchange data, and they connect securely to the cloud overall.

Using a hybrid structure enables an organization to expand and tap cloud resources as needed. In fact, Gartner, Inc., predicts that by 2017, half of all large enterprises will use a hybrid cloud structure.

An organization might choose a hybrid cloud simply to avoid the costs of expanding its own private cloud for a particular new service. A company might also use a hybrid cloud structure for three other primary reasons:

- **To supplement its private cloud capacity to meet increasing customer demand, including demand spikes.** At one time, Netflix had its own private cloud data center for streaming TV shows and movies (video) on demand to customers, among other services. But by late 2012, it had moved its streaming service and much of its other infrastructure to the public cloud. Creating a

Figure 7.5

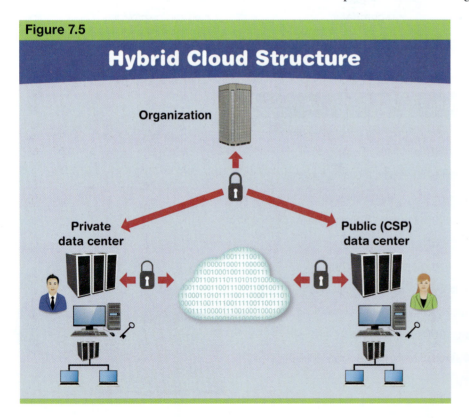

An organization can supplement its own cloud resources with a secure connection to cloud capacity from a CSP to create a hybrid cloud.

hybrid structure ensured that Netflix would be able to expand to meet increased customer demand on the fly. Some companies meet demand spikes using a technique called **cloud bursting**. In cloud bursting, the private cloud handles the average workloads or demands, and when demands ramp up to a specified threshold, public cloud resources come online automatically to handle the extra demand or activity. This method can be cost effective, as well, because the company pays for the cloud capacity only when it actually uses it.

- **To take advantage of a particular CSP's cloud management system and tools.** Small companies and startup businesses generally don't have the funds to build a sophisticated data center, including software and services such as powerful analytics (involving the use of computational power to find patterns in large volumes of data). For example, consider Etsy, an online market for vintage and handmade items. As Etsy grew, it opted to supplement its in-house capabilities with those of a public cloud provider because of the provider's analytics offerings. About 1 billion users view the Etsy website each month, so it needs substantial computing power to analyze the resulting view data and then make product recommendations.

- **To offer services via the public cloud while keeping some data more secure in the private cloud.** A variety of corporate, nonprofit, and governmental organizations that provide online apps and services want to allow public access to their services yet keep certain data private. For example, an online music streaming service might keep some of its customer data (such as user playlists) on its private cloud, where it can maintain the desired security practices. However, it might keep the digital music streaming software and content on a public cloud, where it can add more capacity as it posts new music releases.

Advantages and Disadvantages for Consumers

The cloud has enabled organizations of all types to create a new variety of online services and systems to serve customers. You will learn about some of the ways individuals and groups work with these offerings later in this chapter. As with any technology, the cloud provides many benefits but also some potential drawbacks. The following sections look at some of the factors that end users or consumers should consider.

Access to Data Across Platforms and Devices You can use any number of services to store your data in the cloud and then access it through a variety of operating systems and devices. For example, you can use the Microsoft Edge browser on your Windows computer at work to upload files to your own private storage area in Microsoft's OneDrive, and then use the Safari browser on your Mac computer at home to go to your OneDrive space and download a file. You can also access the files from your OneDrive files on a smartphone or tablet.

Similarly, many types of online services deliver a huge range of data that you can access from computers running Windows, Mac, and Linux operating systems or from any smartphone or tablet with the applicable cloud service app installed or using the device's browser. For example, if you subscribe to the Rhapsody streaming music service

Tech Career Explorer

Running the Cloud

Even experienced IT professionals have needed to upgrade their competencies to respond to the need for professionals who can set up and run cloud services. Complete this exercise to gain an understanding of the broad set of skills involved in supporting cloud computing.

and create playlists stored in Rhapsody's cloud, you can access your account and playlists via any computer's web browser and stream music stored in Rhapsody's cloud. (See the section "Streaming from the Cloud," on page 305, to learn more about this technology.) In addition, Rhapsody supports dozens of other devices. You can download a Rhapsody app for iPod Touch, iPhone, or iPad from the Apple App Store; download a Rhapsody Windows phone app; or download an app for Android phones and tablets from Google Play. Each of these apps enables you to log on to your Rhapsody account, and stream your selected music from the cloud.

Cloud-based services enable you to access content from a variety of platforms and devices. Rhapsody, shown here, streams data from an Internet-connected device to a car audio system using Bluetooth.

If you install the Rhapsody for Windows software for your computer, you can use it to transfer playlists and music via a USB connection to a music player that isn't cloud-connected, such as the Sansa Fuze+. Rhapsody also is compatible with the Xbox 360, and you can download a Rhapsody app to enable you to stream music from smart TVs made by LG, Panasonic, Samsung, Sharp, and Vizio, and even some Blu-ray disc players and home theater systems. Rhapsody works with the Sonos Wireless HiFi System, which delivers whole-house wireless music. And you can even stream Rhapsody music from your smartphone app to a Bluetooth-enabled compatible car audio system. Social media, webmail, online banking, and many other cloud services enable you to access your account and information from a variety of devices.

The ability to access cloud services via multiple devices offers advantages such as not having to copy data to every device you use, not having to create multiple accounts based on the device you are using, and in some cases, not having to synchronize information between devices. The main drawback is that occasional connection errors and service downtime might interrupt your ability to use the service.

Ability to Work from Anywhere You Can Connect When you can access files, business software, and services over the Internet, you can work anywhere that you can connect. Perhaps you like to take your laptop to a local coffee shop and soak up a different environment while you work. (You may have been doing this for years.) But what if you haven't copied a key document to your computer? With the cloud, you can access your files and work with them wherever you go—often, from a variety of devices.

For example, Apple offers mobile app versions of some of its productivity applications, including the Pages word-processing program. You can install the Pages app on your iPad, iPhone, or iPod Touch. Suppose you are in a cab on your way to a meeting, and you realize that you made a mistake in a document you just sent to a colleague. You don't have a wireless Internet connection in the cab, so you can't use your notebook to correct the document. However, you can use the Pages app on your iPhone to connect to the Internet via the cellular network, correct the document stored on your iCloud, and then share the corrected document with your colleague (This process may require upgrading to the latest operating system version and also upgrading to iCloud Drive.)

The ability to handle your business and personal tasks wherever and whenever needed trumps the drawbacks. In the Generations 2010 survey conducted by Pew Research for its Internet Project, 71 percent of respondents agreed that most people would do their work using online apps for computers and smartphones, rather than applications installed on a computer, just as in the previous example. On the downside, if you don't have the right app or connection available, you may not be able to do your work online in every instance. And if you are using cloud-based apps for your work, you may experience periodic connection difficulties or service downtimes.

Easier Collaboration Collaborative team platforms make it possible for users to meet in virtual spaces online and to share files and communicate from remote locations. For example, services like GoToMeeting and PeopleLink enable a user to schedule an online meeting and invite other participants. Once the meeting starts, participants join by calling in or using Voice over Internet Protocol (VoIP), and they can send video using a webcam. The meeting presenter can share his or her desktop to give an onscreen demonstration and even share keyboard control to allow participants to edit live documents on the screen.

Services like GoToMeeting and PeopleLink (shown here) allow real-time cloud collaboration for a team of users.

Cutting Edge

The Cloud's Bright Future

Experts predict that cloud technology will continue to gain momentum, both benefiting from and spurring new developments in hardware and software. For example, by 2020, low-cost hardware will drive even more powerful data centers. As chip companies continue to make lower power processors for better battery life in mobile devices, low power processors in computing equipment also will drive down the total cost of electricity used to operate large data centers.

Other changes will occur with regard to the types of cloud-connected devices and technologies available for end users. Some experts predict that eventually, all software will be delivered via the cloud, resulting in devices that have far more memory and far less storage. Some devices may feature push-button cloud backup and syncing built in. Because data on the cloud is subject to government subpoena and cybersnooping, other devices will enable individuals to turn their personal drives into a personal or private cloud, enabling secure sharing with specified friends and colleagues. From there, cloud access and integration will be added to many other appliances and equipment. For example, Delphi Automotive and Verizon have partnered on mobile hotspot technology for cars, meaning that passengers can connect to the cloud via in-car Wi-Fi. And expect to see many more cloud-connected wearable devices.

Other cloud collaboration platforms enable team members to store files and manage versions of them, even when operating from different states and countries. Online collaboration and file sharing allow teams to get results quickly and can eliminate costly travel.

Data Security and Privacy Concerns One potential drawback of cloud-based services (or even private network data that's accessible via the Internet) frequently grabs headlines: their vulnerability to hacking. Well-publicized examples include users' credit card and account information being stolen from the online databases of major retailers and financial organizations (such as Experian in 2015) and currency disappearing from major online exchanges (such as the bitcoin exchange Mt. Gox in 2014). These and similar cases demonstrate that information security remains a core concern for anyone placing personal data, content, and other property in the cloud.

Chapter 9 will go into more detail about privacy on the Internet, especially what you can do as a user to protect yourself. You probably know that you should use strong passwords and limit the type of information you share about yourself on social media sites, such as Facebook. The same guidelines apply when using services in the cloud—don't share anything that you want to keep private. Beyond that, the security of your personal information and data depends on the security measures and practices of the organization that's hosting it in the cloud.

Advantages and Disadvantages for Organizations

For an organization that provides services, moving those services to the cloud (particularly the public cloud) can bring a number of benefits. For example, without the cloud, a bank or financial services company can offer customers only limited interactions. After such an organization places its services in the cloud, however, it can increase

Tech Ethics

Content Controversies and the Cloud

In 2002, Google Books began a project to partner with various libraries to scan entire collections. This program, called the *Library Project*, was intended to create a searchable card catalog in the cloud. At first, Google Books scanned only works in the public domain—that is, works whose copyrights have expired or that were produced by organizations such as the US government (and therefore not copyrighted). But when Google Books made deals that involved scanning some works still under copyright, controversy erupted.

Copyright law has long protected published content in the United States. This body of law includes a fair-use policy that states how much of a work can be quoted in another document or in online search results. Google argued that it could scan books that are out of print but still under copyright (so-called *orphan books*) and then deliver only snippets of those books to users of its service—claiming that sharing these snippets might generate future

sales and thus benefit copyright owners. The opposition argued that Google Books was overstepping the fair-use policy, because it was scanning entire books even though it said it would show only limited numbers of pages in search results. The opposition also argued that Google Books was creating a monopoly in digital book content.

A settlement reached in 2008 actually increased the amount of each copyrighted work Google Books could show in search results. The settlement also required Google Books to pay $125 million for the copyrighted works it had already scanned and to pay royalties (percentages of earnings) to copyright holders on any fees collected for viewing digital books online.

What do you think of this settlement? In your opinion, who should receive more legal protection: the creator or copyright holder of a book or the company that digitizes the book and makes it available online? What is the reasoning behind your answer?

customer interactions (because customers no longer need to visit bricks-and-mortar locations). The organization can also offer new services that reduce its own costs, such as mobile depositing of checks. Other potential advantages include reduced expenses with pay-as-you-go services, easier deployment and agility, scalability, and enhanced reliability and security.

Reduced Expenses with Pay-as-You-Go Services When an organization moves to the public cloud, it can have few or no setup costs. The organization takes advantage of the services the CSP has already developed, rather than make its own up-front investment in costly equipment and software development. When the organization needs more capacity from the CSP, it simply accesses and pays for those services.

In this pay-as-you-go model, the organization doesn't have to wait years to see a return on the large investment that's needed to create a data center. This makes the services more cost effective and (potentially) profitable to provide right from the outset. In fact, many companies say that after moving to the cloud, they save money and can reduce their internal IT operations. Figure 7.6 shows the results of a survey by IT consulting firm NSK, Inc., regarding the number of companies reporting savings from moving to the cloud.

Easier Deployment and Agility Developing and rolling out a new online service can be a lengthy and costly endeavor that involves not only purchasing and setting up expensive server and communications hardware but also licensing and writing the software needed to deliver the cloud service. By using a CSP's existing cloud software and technology or by developing an internal platform to support additional cloud services, an organization can save a lot of money.

For example, the US government is thought to be one of the largest cloud users in the world, with up to half its services now in the cloud via "commercial cloud services, private clouds, shared clouds and using new policies, processes, and tools," and spending up to $2 billion annually according to NSK, Inc. The government spends a large portion of its budget supporting existing (legacy) systems, but by moving to the cloud and sharing common infrastructures, it can speed its service development and reduce costs. In fact, in a survey conducted by MeriTalk (a public–private partnership), federal IT executives reported that 77 percent of new software

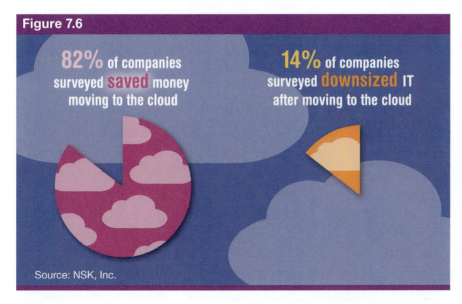

Figure 7.6

82% of companies surveyed **saved** money moving to the cloud

14% of companies surveyed **downsized** IT after moving to the cloud

Source: NSK, Inc.

Using a CSP's pay-as-you-go services can save a company money and enable it to reduce internal IT costs.

development was vital to their agencies' missions. Also, 71 percent reported that they were transitioning to cloud-based services to support faster application development. The potential annual savings is projected at $20.5 billion.

For nongovernment organizations, the cloud enables them to get new features to market more quickly. Social media companies, organizations known for their Internet portals (such as Yahoo!), and other organizations often take advantage of this flexibility. For example, when Facebook changed from having a user wall to having the new Timeline feature, it rolled out the service to users without having to rebuild its entire platform or replace other features. The new feature fit seamlessly into Facebook's existing platform. In this way, the cloud lowers the risk of introducing new services and reduces failures.

Scalability   As discussed earlier, the term *scalability* refers to the fact that virtualization enables an organization to increase capacity on demand, rather than have to build a physical server infrastructure. This factor gives public cloud providers an edge over a private cloud—in particular, because CSPs have the servers in place, with extra capacity ready to allocate to clients when they request it. For example, Google Cloud Platform promotes its scalability as a cost-effective substitute for building a private cloud infrastructure (see Figure 7.7). Even though a private cloud can take advantage of virtualization and scalability, the organization hosting the cloud has to pay upfront for the required hardware and other technology. According to Gartner, Inc., more than half of the server workload is virtualized, with the percentage of virtualization increasing rapidly.

Enhanced Reliability and Security   The cloud offers the benefits of reliable storage and enhanced security. Through virtualization and other tools, an organization can seamlessly back up data on its private cloud or take advantage of a CSP's data protection tools. **Small and midsize businesses (SMBs)**, in particular, can realize improved data security and more reliable system availability after moving to a CSP and accessing its services. (SMBs include small businesses with fewer than 100 employees and $50 million or less annual revenue, and midsize businesses with

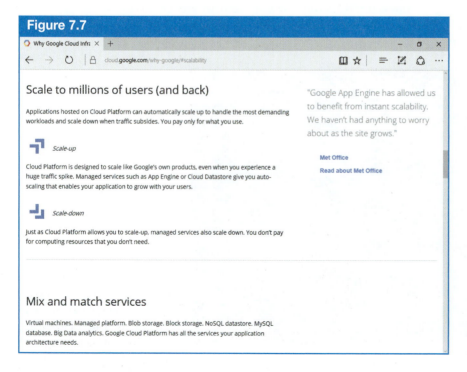

Figure 7.7

Why Google Cloud Infr × +

cloud.google.com/why-google/#scalability

Scale to millions of users (and back)

Applications hosted on Cloud Platform can automatically scale up to handle the most demanding workloads and scale down when traffic subsides. You pay only for what you use.

Scale-up

Cloud Platform is designed to scale like Google's own products, even when you experience a huge traffic spike. Managed services such as App Engine or Cloud Datastore give you auto-scaling that enables your application to grow with your users.

Scale-down

Just as Cloud Platform allows you to scale-up, managed services also scale down. You don't pay for computing resources that you don't need.

"Google App Engine has allowed us to benefit from instant scalability. We haven't had anything to worry about as the site grows."

Met Office
Read about Met Office

Mix and match services

Virtual machines. Managed platform. Blob storage. Block storage. NoSQL datastore. MySQL database. Big Data analytics. Google Cloud Platform has all the services your application architecture needs.

Google Cloud Platform touts its scalability for cloud applications and services.

Figure 7.8

Benefits Reported by SMBs Moving to the Cloud

94 percent increase in security technology, such as up-to-date systems and up-to-date antivirus and spam email management

62 percent increase in the level of privacy protection

75 percent improvement in service availability

Source: Microsoft, 2013

100 to 999 employees and up to $1 billion in revenue.) Figure 7.8 shows some of the benefits reported by SMBs that have moved to the cloud.

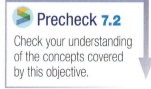

Recheck 7.1

Recheck your understanding of the concepts covered by this objective.

7.2 Working on the Cloud as an Individual User

While services such as online shopping have been available for a while, they have involved little in the way of your putting personal content online. Newer cloud services help you expand on the activities you already perform on your computer and other devices. When your email, documents, and apps reside in the cloud, you can access them from any device, not just your computer (see Figure 7.9). This section looks at

Precheck 7.2

Check your understanding of the concepts covered by this objective.

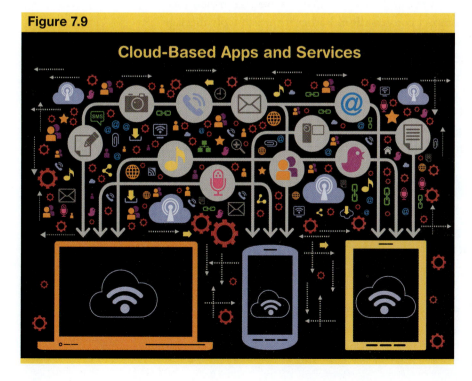

Figure 7.9

Cloud-Based Apps and Services

Cloud-based apps and services continue to expand rapidly.

how you can take advantage of the cloud for sending and retrieving email; storing, sharing, and backing up documents online; and working with apps to perform tasks.

Web-Based Email

Chapter 5 introduced the overall concept of email, or messages sent and received via the Internet. That discussion focused primarily on traditional email using email client software. Now, let's take a closer look at webmail, short for *web-based email*.

With a webmail service, you can do all the things you do from client software email, such as send and receive messages, create and save message drafts, organize messages into folders, and change settings to protect against spam. As with most Internet service providers (ISPs), there are limitations on how large any file attached to a message can be when you send it. Many free webmail services include news and weather information on the home pages of their websites.

Client email programs typically download messages from the email server—often because ISPs place space limits on accounts. Most webmail providers offer greater amounts of storage, even for free accounts. Having extra storage enables you to leave your messages in the cloud so you can view your email using multiple devices. For example, you can send an email to a friend from your home computer before going out to run errands. When you stop to grab lunch, you can check your email from your smartphone and respond to your friend's reply. Later, when you sign back on to your webmail from your computer, you will still be able to read the reply message from your friend, as well as check for other messages.

You can find many free cloud-based webmail services, and the most popular ones provide more than just email. For example, both Yahoo! Mail and Gmail enable you to chat or message others and include a calendar for organizing your schedule. Gmail and Outlook.com integrate with cloud storage. Some free services, such as Yahoo! Mail, are supported by advertising (see Figure 7.10). In some cases, you can hide the ads by changing a preference or installing a plug-in. In other cases, the only way to remove the ads is to upgrade to a paid account.

Some webmail providers, such as Yahoo! Mail and Gmail, enable you to view each message and its responses as a compact **conversation**. Rather than each reply message appearing as a separate item in the message list, all the messages appear grouped together in the message, with unread messages within the conversation appearing in bold, like other unread messages. This conversation feature makes it easier for you to follow a discussion and helps you avoid missing important messages in your Inbox folder.

When choosing a webmail provider, be sure to check the amount of free cloud storage provided for your messages (and other data, if applicable). Although most providers offer the option of upgrading to a paid account with more storage, upgrade

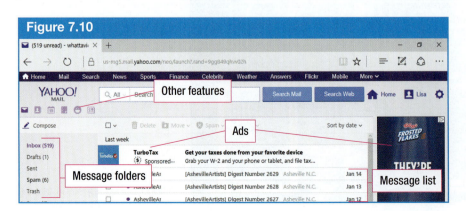

Figure 7.10

Activity 7.2.1

Practice
Webmail Features

Yahoo! Mail and other providers offer a number of features in addition to free webmail.

Table 7.2 Free Webmail Providers

Provider Name	Website	Free Message Storage Space
AOL Mail	http://CUT6.emcp.net/AOLMail	Roughly 5,000 messages, or up to 2 gigabytes (GB)
Gmail	http://CUT6.emcp.net/Gmail	15 GB, shared among Gmail, Google Drive, and Google Photos
GMX Mail	http://CUT6.emcp.net/GMXMail	Unlimited
iCloud Mail	http://CUT6.emcp.net/iCloudMail	5 GB, shared among iCloud backup, app data, stored documents, and iCloud Mail
Inbox.com	http://CUT6.emcp.net/Inbox.com	5 GB
Mail.com	http://CUT6.emcp.net/Mail.com	Unlimited
Outlook.com	http://CUT6.emcp.net/Outlook.com	Unlimited, although a fast increase in inbox size may prevent you from sending and receiving more messages
Yahoo! Mail	http://CUT6.emcp.net/YahooMail	1 terabyte

fees can add up quickly, especially if you need and use multiple webmail providers—perhaps one for your personal email and another for your professional email. Table 7.2 reviews some popular free webmail providers.

Getting an account from a webmail provider usually takes only a few minutes. Generally, you sign up for the account at the provider's website by providing some basic information about yourself. You provide your desired username, which will become your email address on the service, including @ and the service domain. Your account name and email address might be YourName123@gmail.com, for example. You also specify a password, which you can use to sign in to your email account from any device.

With some services, including Gmail and Outlook, you can read your email via an email client app. For example, you can turn on POP email (refer to Chapter 6 to see what the POP protocol is) in Gmail and then set up a program such as Outlook to download the mail to your desktop computer. (You would need to configure Outlook

Practical TECH ⚙⚙⚙⚙⚙⚙⚙⚙

How to Access Webmail

If you don't have your own Internet service and can get online only by using your smartphone and the cellular network or by taking your portable device to a location with free wireless, then you need a free webmail account to start communicating. Social networking services (such as Facebook and LinkedIn) include some email capability, but you typically need a separate email address to set up an account with any of them. You will get more features with a webmail service, such as Yahoo! Mail or Gmail.

If, on the other hand, you already have Internet service from an ISP (such as Earthlink or HughesNet), you likely don't need to set up a new email address. Accounts with ISPs such as these typically include five to 10 free email

addresses, which can be set up for members of a household or small business. You might have to access webmail through a variation of the ISP's main web address—for example, webmail.earthlink.net for Earthlink. Note that when an ISP doesn't have a dedicated mobile app for email, yet another variation of the URL may be provided for mobile—for example, m.webmail.earthlink.net.

If you are operating your own website, you may have to purchase email services for your domain separately. For instance, GoDaddy.com will host email for your website's domain for an annual fee, and you can sign on to your email account at GoDaddy's login.secureserver.net page.

to leave messages on the mail server to ensure that your Gmail messages remain available on other devices.) As another example, you can set up the Mail app in Windows to read your Outlook.com email.

With many webmail services, you can download a free app for your tablet or smartphone to make reading email easier (see Chapter 5). The Mac OS X and iOS systems automatically send iCloud Mail to the Mail app after you set up your iCloud services.

Using Cloud Storage

Just as organizations can move their data and services to a server hosted by a CSP in the cloud, you can use a cloud storage service to store your documents, digital photos, and other files in a secure online location. **Cloud storage** is simply a service that provides users with a set amount of file storage space in the cloud.

Using a cloud storage service offers these benefits:

- You can access your files using various devices and operating systems at any time from any location with an Internet connection. You can also make sure that files are updated on all devices (a process called *syncing*).
- You can share your files to other users, such as photos that you have stored online with a family member.
- Your data will be safer, because it will be in a secure location and will not be on a device that you could lose, such as a USB flash drive. In addition, the upload process copies files instead of moving them, so you can use cloud storage to create backups of important files.

You can take advantage of a number of free options for online cloud storage. As with webmail plans, in most cases, online file storage providers enable you to buy more space when needed for an additional fee. Table 7.3 lists leading free online storage providers. As the table shows, some cloud storage services combine webmail and cloud storage, while others offer only cloud storage.

Table 7.3 Free Cloud Storage Providers

Provider Name	Website	Amount of Free Storage and Additional Features
4shared	http://CUT6.emcp.net/4shared	15 gigabytes (GB), but files can be shared only with other registered 4shared users
Box	http://CUT6.emcp.net/Box.com	10 GB, but upgradeable for a fee to add more users and storage
Dropbox	http://CUT6.emcp.net/Dropbox	2 GB
Google Drive	http://CUT6.emcp.net/GoogleDrive	15 GB, shared among Gmail, Google Drive, and Google Photos; requires installing Drive apps; can also install Drive for file syncing
Hightail	http://CUT6.emcp.net/Hightail	Unlimited, 5 spaces
iCloud	http://CUT6.emcp.net /iCloudStorage	5 GB, shared among iCloud backup, app data, stored documents, and iCloud Mail; requires setup on all devices, including downloading iCloud for Windows
OneDrive	http://CUT6.emcp.net/OneDrive	15 GB; Start screen app built into Windows 10, 8.1; desktop app also built into Windows 10, 8.1; desktop app available for Windows Vista, 7, or 8 and Mac OS X, as well as apps for tablet and phone

Storing Your Files Generally, placing a file in cloud storage involves uploading the file, or transferring a copy of the file from your computer or device over the Internet to your online storage account. The method you use will vary depending on the service you are using, the operating system on your computer, and the device you are working on. In most cases, one of these three methods will work:

- **Use the upload feature of the cloud storage service.** If you are using a service via your browser only (such as 4shared or Dropbox), navigate to the service website in your web browser and then sign in to your account. Create folders, if needed, to organize your files, and then select the folder to which you want to upload one or more files. Click the button or choose the command for uploading, select the file(s) to upload in the dialog box that appears, and click Open (or the command for sending). You can use this method for the other services, too, when you don't want to use specific software. Figure 7.11 illustrates uploading a file to a Google Drive account.

- **Use an app in your operating system.** You can use an app in the operating system on your device or a software tool to upload the file. For example, in Windows 10, you can use the OneDrive app on the Start menu to connect with your OneDrive and upload a file to a folder. If you use the OneDrive features built into Windows, all you need to do is copy or move the file (up to 2 GB in size) into a folder within the OneDrive folder in File Explorer. From there, the file will upload automatically to the corresponding OneDrive folder in the cloud. Google Drive has a similar app. The link for downloading it appears below the folder list at the left in Figure 7.11.

  In Mac OS X, only certain applications—such as the latest versions of the iWork applications (Keynote, Pages, or Numbers), TextEdit, and Preview—work directly with iCloud. Once you have set up iCloud on your Mac, when you open an application such as TextEdit, it may prompt you to add files to

Figure 7.11

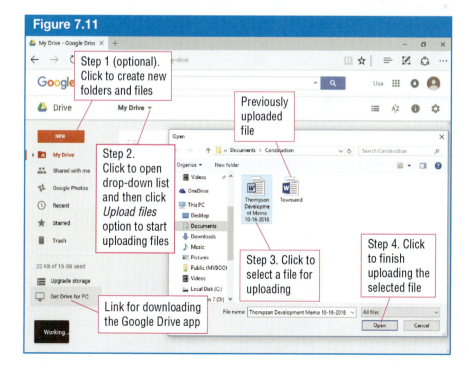

You can upload files to a cloud storage account such as Google Drive, shown here.

Figure 7.12

An iCloud-enabled application such as TextEdit may prompt you to move your files to the cloud after you enable iCloud.

your iCloud storage by dragging files from the Finder or other apps, as shown in Figure 7.12. The latest version of Mac OS X enables you to open your iCloud Drive folders in Finder.

- **Save or move the file directly from another application.** Another way to upload a file to your cloud storage is to save or move a file directly from an application. For example, in Windows applications such as Word 2016, when you choose the *Save* or *Save As* command on the File tab, you can choose your OneDrive from the list of places to which you can save, and then either click one of the Recent Folders or click the Browse button to select a OneDrive folder in which to save the file. In recent Windows versions, there's also a global setting for making your OneDrive the default save location.

  Similarly, in Mac OS X, you can create a file in an iCloud-capable application, use the *Save* command on the File menu, select *iCloud* from the *Where* drop-down list, and then select a folder if needed before finishing the save. (Some applications require upgrading to iCloud Drive for all Mac OS X file storage and editing operations.)

Sharing Your Files **Sharing** a file means making it available from your cloud storage for viewing, editing, and downloading by other designated users. As for uploading, the sharing process and capabilities vary by cloud service. Some services only allow

Tech Ethics 🏛 🏛 🏛 🏛 🏛 🏛 🏛

Working Outside the Company Cloud

Many companies ask employees to follow security and compliance policies for transferring, storing, and sharing files electronically. Some companies even go so far as to forbid employees to store company files on outside cloud storage services such as DropBox for security reasons. This can create difficulty when a company has a "bring your own device" policy. In such cases, an employee whose device is not compatible with company systems may feel compelled to use online file storage and services to work effectively. In fact, a survey by one enterprise storage company found that as many as 20 percent of employees may store and share company work files via online services, despite policies against that practice. Do you think employees who violate company policies and store files online are doing the wrong thing? What solutions might a company offer to reduce this issue?

users to download files you posted. The service generates a link to the file, and you copy and paste that link in an email message to the users who you want to access the file. For OneDrive and Google Drive, you click a button to share the file, enter the user's name or email address, and then specify whether the recipient can view, edit, or comment on the file (see Figure 7.13). Both OneDrive and Google Drive enable you to notify the invitees directly from the sharing box via email. Or, you can create, copy, and paste a link to share to your own email message or share the link via social media. For iCloud, you have to open the document to share in Pages, Numbers, or Keynote for iCloud. You can then use the Share button, add a password if needed, and email or copy the link to the file. Recipients don't need an iCloud account to edit the file, and all collaborators can see each other's edits in real time. For all three services, the link enables recipients to use a web browser to open and work with the file, assuming it was created in an online app or the user has the software needed to edit the file. Otherwise, recipients may be prompted to download the file.

By default, OneDrive has three folders: Documents, Music, and Pictures. All three folders are private folders by default. You have to share a link to a folder to grant other users access to it, and change the permissions to allow editing of specific files as needed.

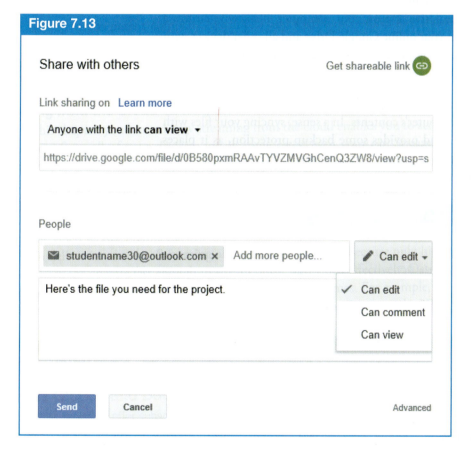

Figure 7.13

When sharing a file from Google Drive (and some other cloud services), you can specify what activities collaborators can perform with the file.

GO service that enables HBO subscribers to stream to mobile devices was so overwhelmed by demand to stream the show that the site crashed.

Despite the occasional glitches and crashes, streaming audio and video can be a good alternative for finding entertainment on demand, from a variety of locations. You could spend your morning commuter train ride watching streamed video clips from your favorite local or national news outlets to be up to date on current events by the time you hit the office. How you view various types of streamed content depends on the device you're using and the service. For example, you can view YouTube videos in your computer web browser, or via an app on your smartphone, tablet, or Smart TV. Similarly, you can join the growing number of people who listen to streaming music services such as Pandora and Rhapsody either through a web browser or a mobile app (see Figure 7.15).

Cloud storage locations hold the massive amount of entertainment content that you can stream to your PC, tablet, smartphone, or smart TV.

Broadly speaking, the content you can stream from the cloud falls into three categories:

- **Free.** Free streaming content can be delivered via the cloud from a variety of sources. For example, the Public Broadcasting Service (PBS) offers videos for craft projects for parents and kids. The Smithsonian Institution also offers free content, as do other educational and governmental websites. Vevo focuses on free music videos.

- **Ad supported.** On the video side, YouTube, Vimeo, and OVGuide have free ad-supported streaming videos. Many YouTube videos include embedded advertising, and YouTube also carries popular free content from Vevo. Vimeo enables you to rent streaming content for a fee, much like Netflix. Both YouTube and Vimeo organize some content in channels that you can subscribe to for repeat visits. Hulu also offers TV episodes and movies with embedded ads. On the audio side, there are numerous free streaming services. Some—like Pandora,

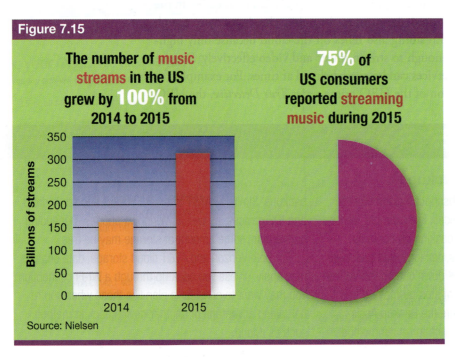

Figure 7.15

The number of **music** streams in the US grew by **100%** from 2014 to 2015

75% of US consumers reported **streaming** music during 2015

Billions of streams

Source: Nielsen

Shoutcast, iHeartRadio, and Beats 1 Radio—work much like radio stations. You sign on to your account and choose the station you want to listen to. Others, such as Spotify, enable you to choose music on demand, sometimes in addition to selecting broadcasts or stations. (Some of these free services do have some limits on the amount of content you can listen to for free.) And of course, the websites for most local and national TV and radio stations stream their own content, supported by the overall advertising revenues of the site and station.

- **Subscription or purchase.** Some sites require you to have a membership or purchase content for viewing. For example, Hulu Plus, Netflix, and Sony Video Unlimited require a monthly subscription to stream movies and TV shows. Rhapsody, Apple Music, and Sony Music Unlimited all offer subscription

Stream music on the go with an ad-supported service such as Beats 1 Radio.

streaming of on-demand music. With Rhapsody, you can create your own **playlist**—saved list of songs that you can select and replay at a later time.

Cloud Apps

As noted earlier in the chapter, many companies provide services in the cloud, including apps that you can use to perform various tasks. Many of the apps discussed here duplicate the familiar word-processing, spreadsheet, and presentation application software that you can install on your PCs and some mobile devices.

While the cloud or web versions of apps may not have all the features found in the installed versions, they offer a few advantages. First, as expected, you can access them

Practical TECH

Your Free (or Nearly Free) Cloud Library

Some organizations have made efforts to bring free and low-cost ebook content available to users of the cloud. Project Gutenberg offers more than 40,000 ebooks that are free because their copyrights having expired. Owners of Kindle eBook readers can take advantage of the Kindle

Owners' Lending Library to borrow more than 500,000 books. Some public libraries enable residents to check out ebooks and audiobooks as the ability to access streaming content grows. You could read quality books on your devices for years with little or no expense.

from any computer and many devices simply by signing in to the same account associated with one of the major end user cloud storage providers you've already learned about. Second, these web apps can save directly to the associated cloud storage, so once you have shared files, other users can easily view and edit them using the same web apps. Finally, you don't have to download and install any software updates; all the app updates occur in the cloud and appear seamlessly in your account.

Now take a look at the three major cloud apps services—Microsoft Office Online, Google Docs, and iWork for iCloud—as well as other web-based apps that perform specialized functions.

Activity 7.2.2

Article
**Cloud
Operating Systems**

Office Online One of the best-known suites of apps in the cloud is Office Online; it provides cloud versions of Word, Excel, PowerPoint, and OneNote (the Office program for organizing notes, images, hyperlinks, and more by project or topic). If you sign in to your account at OneDrive.com, you can access the Office Online apps by clicking the button with the boxes on it on the bar at the top, or by clicking New and then clicking one of the choices for creating a particular type of file. The Office Online apps have a ribbon interface just like the installed desktop applications. As you create your file, the app saves it to OneDrive automatically. You also can download a copy of a file or open it in the desktop application (assuming you have it installed) directly from the Online app. This compatibility between the Online app and the desktop application expands your options for working where and when you want.

Hands On 👆👆👆👆👆👆

Creating and Sharing a File from OneDrive

Follow steps like the ones in this resource to practice creating a document in the Word Online app and sharing it with your instructor.

Google Docs Once you're signed in to Google Drive, you can click the New button to use its Docs, Sheets, Slides, Forms, Drawings, and My Maps apps to create various types of files (see Figure 7.16). You also can install a Google Drive app on your Android or iOS device to be able to use the file creation apps on the go. As with the Office Online apps, each Google Docs app saves your work as you go along—in this case, to your Google Drive storage. The tools in these apps resemble those found in many desktop-based apps, such as tools for drawing shapes and lines in the Drawing app.

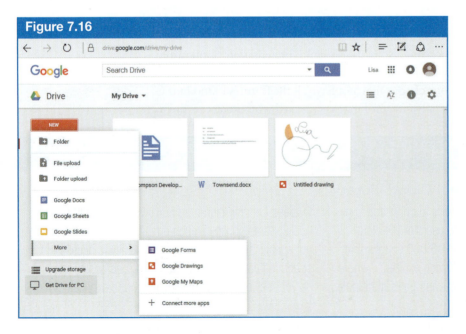

Figure 7.16

Google Docs includes six basic apps, and you can connect even more.

The File menu in the Google Docs apps provides options for emailing a file to collaborators or downloading it (converting it) to other formats, such as PDF. Even better, the Docs apps are compatible with other common file types. So, for example, if you have uploaded a Microsoft Word file to Google Drive, you can open the file in the Google Docs app and edit it there.

Google Docs also enables you to connect to a Template Gallery filled with file templates contributed by other users. If you click New in Google Drive and point to More, you can then click the *Connect more apps* command at the bottom of the menu that appears, you can set up additional web apps from third parties to work directly with Google Drive. This content and app ecosystem may make Google Docs a good choice when you and your collaborators need to perform a wide variety of different activities with cloud-based apps.

iWork for iCloud Apple's iCloud offers a set of three online apps based on its iWork desktop suite: Pages for iCloud, Numbers for iCloud, and Keynote for iCloud. As the names suggest, these are word-processing, spreadsheet, and presentation apps, respectively. All three are compatible with the corresponding apps for Mac OS X and iOS.

After you go to iCloud.com from your Windows or Mac OS X computer or mobile device and sign in, you can click the Pages, Numbers, or Keynote icon to get started creating a file. After responding to an introductory screen or two, you can select a template for a blank document, or choose from a collection of other templates to get started (see Figure 7.17). As with the other suites of web apps, the iWork online apps save your work automatically, and when you later close the editing window and review your documents, you can rename files as needed. You also can use the Tools menu while editing to download or email a copy of the file.

Special-Purpose Cloud and Mobile Apps In addition to the cloud-based apps associated with the major cloud storage services, you can access a wide selection of standalone cloud apps for a variety of purposes. Let's touch on just a few:

- **Prezi.** The wildly popular cloud-based presentation graphics app Prezi boasts 60 million users. You can use Prezi from your web browser, desktop, iPad, or iPhone. It syncs presentations automatically across all your devices. Prezi offers professionally designed templates, and you can look at popular "prezis" created and shared

Figure 7.17

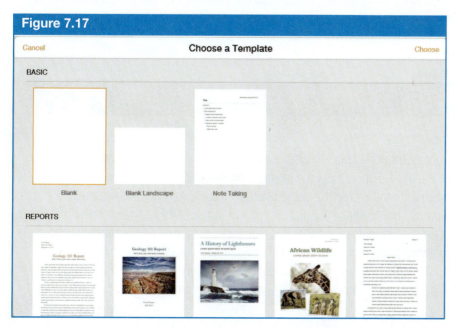

Many web apps, such as Pages for iCloud (shown here), enable you to take advantage of templates, just like applications installed on the desktop.

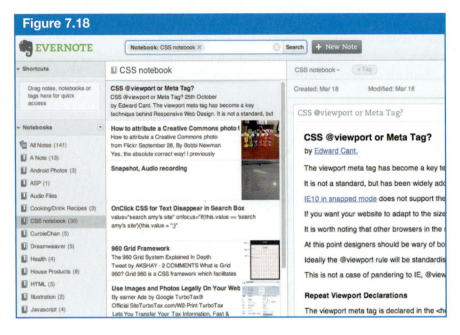

Figure 7.18

Organize notes, web page snips, and more by topic in Evernote to streamline your note taking.

by other users from around the world for further inspiration. You can get a public Prezi account (where all your presentations can be viewed publicly) with 100 MB of storage for free. Free prezis carry the Prezi logo. To use your own branding (logo) and have private prezis and 500 MB or 2 GB of storage, you can upgrade to another account level for a reasonable monthly or annual fee.

- **Evernote.** With an Evernote account and app, you can save notes and more to the cloud (see Figure 7.18). You can take notes, snip parts of web pages, and upload recorded audio and images. You also can upload documents you might need while on the move, such as reservation confirmations and maps. Evernote works great for collaborating on projects as well, because you can share notes with colleagues and classmates. Evernote even offers add-on apps, such as Skitch for annotating photos to point out important parts.

Tech Career Explorer

Tech in K–12 Education

While many consider IT a specific, dedicated career field, in truth, tech skills increasingly need to be in the toolkit for professionals in a number of fields, including teaching. The ConnectED Initiative, a national public-private effort to equip educators to bring students into the digital age, has set specific goals for bringing the best learning technology to students and teachers. Complete this exercise to consider the technical resources needed to meet this initiative's goals.

Hotspot

Find My iPhone

While not strictly a wireless service because it works over the cellular network, Find My iPhone is a handy feature for your wireless devices from Apple. When you enable iCloud on your iPhone, iPad, or MacBook, you can also enable Find My iPhone. If you lose your iPhone or other device, you can sign in to your iCloud account from another computer or device, and then click *Find iPhone*. After repeating the sign-in, this app displays a map that shows the locations of your various devices. You can select the lost device from the *All Devices* list that appears at the top, and in the box that appears, you can choose from among several options. For instance, if you think you have misplaced the device in your own house, you can have the phone play an alert sound. But if you believe the device is truly lost or has been stolen, you can lock it down by selecting *Lost Mode* or even erase its contents.

- **TurboTax Online.** Many cloud services such as Intuit's TurboTax Online enable you to accomplish tasks online that you tackle only periodically. You can use TurboTax Online with a desktop computer and your web browser. Alternatively, you can use the TurboTax SnapTax app to file from your iPhone or Android phone, or the TurboTax iPad app to file from an iPad. These solutions all work for uncomplicated tax returns.
- **Mobile banking.** Many banks offer online access to basic services, such as checking account balances, transferring funds between accounts, and even making deposits. Although you may have security concerns about doing your banking online, your banking information is already in the cloud in most instances, whether you like it or not.

 Recheck 7.2
Recheck your understanding of the concepts covered by this objective.

7.3 Working on the Cloud as a Team

In addition to single-user and small-group cloud services, more robust team collaboration platforms and services have emerged to take advantage of the cloud. Some can work in the private cloud, while others already exist for use in the public cloud. Many of these services require a large work group to be cost effective, but some are available for modest subscription fees. This section highlights the features available in some of these services, as well as the services themselves.

 Precheck 7.3
Check your understanding of the concepts covered by this objective.

File Storage and Sharing

Some of the services listed in Table 7.3 (on page 300) are free for basic end user plans, but can be upgraded for a monthly or annual fee. For example, you might be able to bump up to a plan designed for independent (self-employed) professionals, a plan for a small team or business, a plan for a larger business, or an enterprise-wide plan covering multiple separate operational areas of a single large company. Box, Dropbox, and Hightail all enable you to upgrade to plans offering expanded storage and other capabilities.

Plans and pricing vary widely by service. For example, Dropbox for Business offers unlimited space and versioning, as well as tools that enable company admins to restrict file access and track sharing, but charges a monthly fee per user. Box and Hightail also charge a monthly fee per user, with different plans and storage levels. Many of these plans allow access via mobile devices, and include administrative and file collaboration features. Some integrate with email services or clients and with the Microsoft Office desktop applications, in addition to having their own cloud-based apps.

Storing potentially sensitive files in the public cloud on services like these can be a controversial topic among IT professionals. Cloud-based services can experience data breaches, in which client and private corporate data could be stolen or exposed. Also, in industries that have to comply with federal and state laws about data practices (such as finance and banking), using a public cloud storage service can cause compliance difficulties. Because of these security concerns, some employers forbid the use of cloud storage services for internal company business.

File Versioning

One useful feature that comes with some team- and business-level public cloud storage is **file versioning**. In file versioning, the file system saves multiple previous versions of a file, creating a **version history** of what the document contained after each team member's edits. Depending on the service, you may be able to access 25, 50, or more previous versions of a file. Generally, you can view an older version of a file and, if

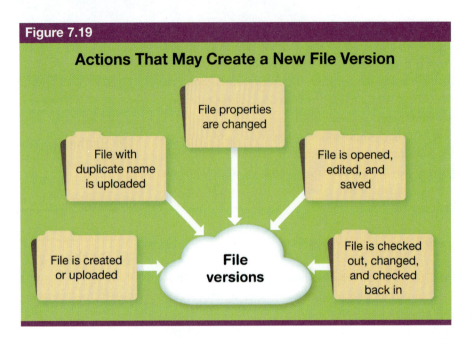

Figure 7.19

Actions That May Create a New File Version

File properties are changed

File with duplicate name is uploaded

File is opened, edited, and saved

File is created or uploaded

File versions

File is checked out, changed, and checked back in

On some business-level cloud storage and collaboration services, different actions such as these can create a new version of a file in the file library or version history.

needed, even restore an older version of the file if the most recent version has errors or other problems. For example, Google Drive enables you to view and manage file revisions or versions.

In some instances, such as the Microsoft SharePoint collaboration (groupware) platform, a user can check out a document for editing and check it back in afterward. **Check out** shows other users the name of the person currently editing the shared document. **Check in** shows other users that the shared document is now available for them to check out and edit.

Depending on the system being used, any of several methods might create a new file version tracked by the cloud storage system. Figure 7.19 illustrates some of the actions that may create a new file version in the version history.

Communicating

Some team- and business-level cloud collaboration tools can in part replace business travel and face-to-face meetings. These tools offer online meetings that include voice or VoIP calling and shared video. The basic account level generally includes the ability to share your desktop, a whiteboard, or applications with other meeting attendees. From there, the different plan levels allow more users and include more storage and features, such as high-definition (HD) video, phone call-in, and desktop remote control.

Practical TECH ⚙⚙⚙⚙⚙⚙⚙⚙⚙

Going Basic with Conferencing

For solo practitioners or businesses for which full-blown conferencing services are too expensive (beyond free trials or basic plans) or more than what's needed, other free voice and video services can work just fine for remote meetings. Both Skype (available as a free Windows download) and FaceTime (included with Mac OS X and iOS) enable video calling. Google Voice allows for audio-only calling, while Google Hangouts works for groups and can include videos, photos, and locations in the conversation. Microsoft offers Skype for Business voice and video messaging as a standalone service for a low monthly fee. A service called *join.me* offers free desktop sharing and VoIP for basic accounts, and you can add more features such as audio and recording by upgrading to a Pro or Enterprise account for a monthly fee per user.

Generally speaking, on each of these services, you can schedule a meeting and invite attendees. When the meeting time comes, you as the administrator or moderator (also sometimes called the *meeting organizer*) set up your audio and join the meeting. Invitees also must set up audio (and in some cases, video) and join the meeting. You decide what to share with the others in the meeting, such as your desktop, a whiteboard, or a file. You also might have the ability to record the meeting for later distribution. When the meeting concludes, everyone signs off.

The leading online meeting services are as follows:

- **WebEx.** The WebEx service from Cisco (see Figure 7.20) offers a free plan for small teams, and other packages for meetings with up to 100 attendees. The meeting organizer can record the meeting. Meetings can be conducted or viewed via a variety of mobile platforms, including iPhone, iPad, Android, and Blackberry. WebEx also enables users to schedule a meeting from within Outlook (the desktop version).

- **GoToMeeting.** The GoToMeeting service from Citrix offers a free trial. Its two plans allow up to 25 or 100 attendees per meeting for a set monthly or annual fee. Whether you're using this service on the desktop or a mobile device, you have to download the GoToMeeting software. In addition to features already described for WebEx, GoToMeeting allows cooperative onscreen editing and the ability to quickly change presenters. It also offers a centralized administration feature so usage can be monitored across an organization.

- **MY Web Conferences.** The newer MY Web Conferences service from MYTrueCloud offers features similar to those of WebEx and GoToMeeting. You can check out the free trial and then pay a monthly subscription thereafter. One feature that differentiates My Web Conferences is its optional proprietary two-factor authentication platform. This brings more security, because meeting attendees must verify identity twice. The company also offers products for specific industries, such as healthcare and pharmaceutical companies.

All of these providers offer services for a large online meeting, often called a **webinar**. While no hard and fast number defines the size of a webinar, for most of these providers, a webinar includes 100 to 1,000 attendees.

Figure 7.20

Users can sketch on a shared whiteboard with online meeting software, such as WebEx.

Collaborating

Other collaboration platforms combine file storage and versioning with features like shared communications. In contrast to the cloud meeting platforms just described, which work well for hosting occasional meetings, collaboration platforms often work best to serve a functional work team over the duration of a project. Examples of collaboration platforms include the following:

Activity 7.3.1

Video
Team Collaboration Platforms

- **SharePoint.** The **Microsoft SharePoint** collaboration platform is popular in the corporate world. While SharePoint technically is software deployed on server-level equipment, you'll often hear users refer to "a SharePoint." That's because SharePoint is typically used by large organizations to set up web- (cloud-) based team collaboration spaces. Organizations often use SharePoint to create multiple team project sites in their private cloud. Each team can manage its files on the SharePoint, as well as post messages for the team, "like" and "tag" information, add notes, upload and edit shared files, and more. Only team members added by the administrator can sign on to the team's site. The SharePoint also typically includes a public website so the team can share information with outside stakeholders. When the team completes the project or venture, that individual SharePoint site can be shut down while team project sites remain active within the organization.

- **Office 365.** Based on SharePoint, **Microsoft Office 365** gives even smaller businesses the opportunity to combine the Microsoft Office suite applications or web apps with a SharePoint-based space in Microsoft's public cloud (see Figure 7.21). Microsoft offers various Office 365 plan levels, for a monthly subscription per user. Office 365 Small Business plans require the user to have the Office desktop software, if desired. Higher-level plans include software downloads for users, such as Skype for Business (and sometimes InfoPath), which integrates Microsoft's voice, video, and chat messaging services. All plans provide integrated email and calendars, online conferencing, messaging and calling, a public website, SharePoint-based file sharing on a team site, simplified file sharing

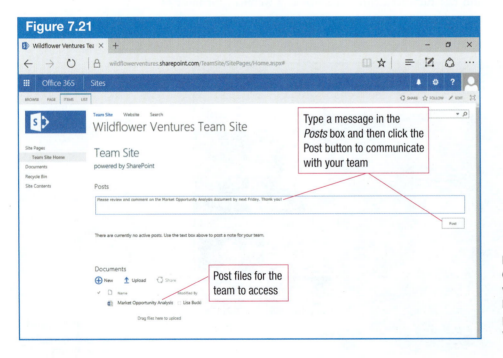

Figure 7.21

Microsoft Office 365 integrates Office suite applications or web apps with a SharePoint-based team workspace in the public cloud, accessible via a web browser.

with 1 TB of OneDrive for Business space, and mobile apps. Microsoft uses Microsoft Exchange Online (the hosted email service based on the **Microsoft Exchange** business email software and services) to manage email for Office 365. You can easily administer your site without IT experience, and the service is backed by Microsoft's security and support.

- **Zoho.** Zoho provides free apps and collaboration to as many as 10 million users. It divides it's apps into a variety of categories, such as Business Process and Sales & Marketing. The finance apps tackle such operations-oriented tasks as invoicing and managing finances. The collaboration apps include chat and social features, as well as project tracking and email. Other apps cover the standard word-processing, spreadsheet, presentation, calendar, and note-taking activities. Zoho apps can be integrated with Google apps for expanded collaboration possibilities.

Special Cloud Tools

Beyond file storage and sharing, file versioning, communicating, and collaborating, cloud-based tools for business tend to be far more specialized, and may even include dedicated hardware devices. For example, Dell Wyse Cloud Connect plugs into the high-definition multimedia interface (HDMI) or mobile high-definition link (MHL) port on a TV or monitor and turns it into a cloud-connected device that can connect to an available wireless network. Because each device can be administered via the Wyse Cloud Client Manager, it can be configured for one user and provide access to predefined apps and services in the cloud.

Other specialized cloud-based services are purely software oriented. Beanstalk provides private code hosting for software development teams, and GitHub provides a platform for software-building collaboration. Salesforce provides cloud-based customer relationship management (CRM) services to help salespeople track customer leads and close deals. LiquidPlanner is an online site for collaboratively managing all types of projects.

No matter what your team or business wants to accomplish, chances are you can find a cloud-based service to help you manage activities and reach your goals.

Recheck 7.3

Recheck your understanding of the concepts covered by this objective.

7.4 Examining the Various Cloud Services Categories

Now that you have had a chance to review some actual cloud services in action, it's time to look at some overall classifications for cloud services. While various experts may have identified a dozen or so of these categories, the three key ones you should know about are Software as a Service (SaaS), Platform as a Service (PaaS), and Infrastructure as a Service (IaaS). Other familiar cloud services include Email as a Service (EaaS), Database as a Service (DaaS), Security as a Service, Testing as a Service, and Storage as a Service.

Precheck 7.4

Check your understanding of the concepts covered by this objective.

Activity 7.4.1

Article
Cloud Services Categories

Software as a Service (SaaS)

Software as a Service (SaaS) means software delivered on demand from the cloud (Internet), usually via a web browser. Many of the web apps discussed so far—including the Microsoft Office Online, Google Docs, iWork for iCloud, and Zoho apps—function as SaaS. This is one of the fastest-growing areas of end-user cloud services, given the appeal of being able to create and edit documents across platforms.

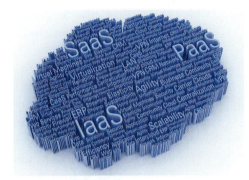

Some companies, such as Adobe, are in the process of migrating away from traditional downloaded (or installed from optical media) programs to hybrids that include installed software sold as a subscription and integrated with other cloud-based features.

In some cases, these subscription models have met with resistance because they prove far more expensive for the user over time. Even so, the trend toward selling subscriptions and moving software to the cloud seems intact.

Platform as a Service (PaaS)

Platform as a Service (PaaS) refers to the collection of services typically provided by CSPs and some other industry-specific providers. With PaaS, the CSP or other provider offers a choice of tools (security, application design and testing, and so on) and services (database integration, web service integration, and more), along with the physical infrastructure (network, servers, and storage) for a client to build cloud infrastructure.

As mentioned earlier in this chapter, the US government has been reorganizing its IT offerings using a PaaS model. Rather than have each federal agency build its new web-based services for the public from scratch, the government is developing a suite of cloud tools that individual agencies can implement as needed. MeriTalk estimates $20.5 billion in software development costs could be saved annually through this initiative.

Salesforce provides a unique hybrid of SaaS and PaaS. It offers services through its predefined suites, such as Sales Cloud, Service Cloud, and Marketing Cloud. Salesforce customers do not have to deploy any infrastructure, as all of the company's services are delivered over the web.

Infrastructure as a Service (IaaS)

Infrastructure as a Service (IaaS) provides the lowest level of service compared with SaaS (the highest) and PaaS. With IaaS, the CSP or other entity provides the physical hardware, the virtualization resources, and some other basic level of technology to cloud clients.

VMware, mentioned earlier, is a commonly used virtualization tool. Some IaaS offerings use Apache CloudStack open source software. CloudStack enables an organization to set up and manage large networks of virtual machines. CloudStack provides high scalability and is in use in private, public, and hybrid clouds.

Recheck 7.4

Recheck your understanding of the concepts covered by this objective.

Cutting Edge

Opening Up the Cloud

A much larger project aims to enable organizations to create cost-effective cloud computing services. The OpenStack project, founded by Rackspace Hosting and NASA, offers the OpenStack software code for free under the Apache 2.0 license. (The Apache Software Foundation manages and licenses various software projects and raises funds to support its projects.) Its community of more than 16,000 developers and other experts operate in more than 130 countries. OpenStack provides the benefit of running on more standard hardware rather than requiring any customizations. Its standardization can make it easier for one administrator to manage more cloud servers, another way to reduce costs. Expect OpenStack skills to increase in demand in the IT hiring community.

Chapter Summary

*An interactive **Chapter Summary**, **Study Notes**, and a **Slide Presentation** with audio are available from the links menu on this page in your ebook.*

7.1 Understanding the Cloud

Cloud computing enables organizations to offer services that exist in the Internet, rather than as software installed on an end user's computer. **Clouds** often run on **virtual servers**—servers created by software so each physical server can host multiple virtual servers—making them **scalable servers** and speeding **deployment**. A **private cloud** exists within an organization's own **data center**, while a **public cloud** exists for use by any organization and runs in the data center of a **cloud service provider (CSP)**. A **hybrid cloud** combines both public and private cloud services.

7.2 Working on the Cloud as an Individual User

Individuals can take advantage of a variety of services and functionality delivered in the cloud. In addition to using webmail for communications, people can use a **cloud storage** service for storing files online. After **uploading** a file, a user can **share** it with other users. Some cloud storage services, such as OneDrive and Google Drive, enable **syncing** data and files between devices. Other services include backing up your files, streaming music and movies, using online presentation and note-taking tools, and more.

7.3 Working on the Cloud as a Team

The cloud provides numerous opportunities to improve collaboration for far-flung teams. Team sharing platforms such as **Microsoft SharePoint** and **Microsoft Office 365** enable users to communicate and to access files stored in the cloud's team site. A user can **check out** a file to edit it, and **check in** a file when finished editing. Actions such as these may be part of a process of **file versioning**, in which the online platform keeps a **version history** for a file, so team members can review when changes occurred or even go back to an earlier version of a file. Other team tools make it possible to conduct online meetings and **webinars** using various services.

7.4 Examining the Various Cloud Services Categories

Because the cloud provides nearly endless capabilities, many different categories of cloud-based services now exist. These include **Software as a Service (SaaS)**, which is software delivered on demand from the cloud; **Platform as a Service (PaaS)**, which is the collection of tools, services, and infrastructure typically provided by CSPs and some other industry-specific providers; and **Infrastructure as a Service (IaaS)**, which is the lowest level of service and in which the CSP or other entity provides the physical hardware, virtualization resources, and some other basic level of technology.

Key Terms

Numbers indicate the pages where terms are first cited with their full definition in the chapter.
An alphabetized list of key terms with definitions is included in the end-of-book glossary.

*An interactive **Glossary** is available from the links menu on this page in your ebook.*

Chapter Exercises

Complete the following exercises to assess your understanding of the material covered in this chapter.

 *Interactive **Flash Cards** and an interactive **Game** are available from the links menu on this page in your ebook.*

Go to your SNAP Assignments page to complete the Terms Check, Knowledge Check, Key Principles, and Tech Illustrated exercises.

Terms Check: Matching

Match each term with its definition.

a.	cloud computing	f.	public cloud
b.	file versioning	g.	hybrid cloud
c.	virtualization	h.	conversation
d.	data center	i.	syncing
e.	private cloud	j.	cloud storage

___ 1. Can be hosted and managed internally at a company's own data center.

___ 2. An arrangement in which an organization chooses to use both private and public cloud infrastructure.

___ 3. A process that updates files on all the user's devices.

___ 4. A tracking system in which the file system saves multiple previous versions of a file; it captures what the document contained after each team member's edits, so older changes can be reviewed and reinstated if needed.

___ 5. In webmail, a feature in which all the message replies appear grouped together with the original message, rather than being listed as separate messages.

___ 6. A service that provides users with a set amount of online file storage space.

___ 7. The infrastructure and software used to deliver services online; also, a user accessing a free or subscription service over the Internet.

___ 8. Cloud resources that exist for use by any organization; an organization may buy cloud capacity on an as-needed basis to take advantage of the benefits of visualization and scalability.

___ 9. A location that houses large computing operations with numerous networked servers.

___ 10. A technology in which software can create multiple distinct operating servers on a single physical server.

Knowledge Check: Multiple Choice

Choose the best answer for each question.

1. A single physical server might actually be set up to operate five or six
   a. optical servers.
   b. peripheral servers.
   c. data centers.
   d. virtual servers.

2. One of the largest providers of public cloud services is
   a. Google Books.
   b. Microsoft Office 365.
   c. Amazon Web Services.
   d. GoToMeeting.

3. When private cloud resources come online automatically to handle a surge in demand or activity, it's called
   a. cloud bursting.
   b. cloud management system.
   c. data mining.
   d. expansion storage.

4. The Microsoft service that enables you to upload files and then access them using nearly any device that can connect to the web is called
   a. Office Cloud.
   b. Windows Live.
   c. Office 365.
   d. OneDrive.

5. The ability of an organization to increase cloud capacity on demand, rather than have to build its own physical server infrastructure, is called
   a. digital data.
   b. scalability.
   c. cloud management system.
   d. private cloud.

6. The Microsoft service that provides webmail is called
   a. OneDrive.
   b. Office 365.
   c. Office Online.
   d. Outlook.com.

7. The process of making sure that the files you have in all storage locations and devices are the same is called
   a. downloading.
   b. sharing.
   c. syncing.
   d. uploading.

8. Which is a popular cloud-based presentation app?
   a. Evernote.
   b. iVisual
   c. Prezi
   d. TurboGraphics

9. Which cloud collaboration tool is designed to replace business travel and face-to-face meetings?
   a. Find My iPhone
   b. iConversation
   c. TurboTax
   d. WebEx

10. Which cloud services category refers to software delivered on demand from the cloud, usually via a web browser?
    a. Database as a Service (DaaS)
    b. Infrastructure as a Service (IaaS)
    c. Platform as a Service (PaaS)
    d. Software as a Service (SaaS)

 ## Key Principles: Completion

Complete each statement with the appropriate word or phrase.

1. A cloud setup created for and used by a single organization is called a(n) _____.

2. When an organization uses both private and public cloud infrastructures, the arrangement is referred to as a(n) _____.

3. Google _____ offers 15 GB of online storage space, some of which is shared with Gmail.

4. Transferring a copy of a file from your computer or device over the Internet to your online storage account is called _____.

5. _____ a file means making it available from your cloud storage for viewing, editing, and downloading by other designated users.

6. Apple's _____ online storage syncs documents between devices, but it also syncs other information, such as your Contacts and Calendar.

7. _____ audio and video can be a good alternative for finding entertainment on demand from a variety of locations.

8. Many streaming music services enable you to create your own _____, which is a saved list of songs that you can select and replay at a later time.

9. _____ provides cloud versions of Word, Excel, PowerPoint, and OneNote.

10. Large online meetings are often called _____.

 Tech Illustrated: Figure Labeling

Fill in the blanks with the correct labels.

1. Cloud computing

2. Hybrid cloud structure

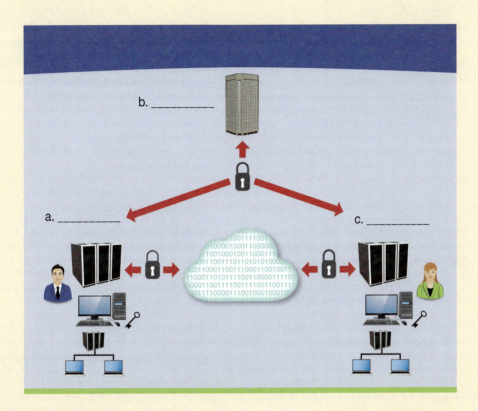

Tech to Come: Brainstorming New Uses

In groups or individually, contemplate the following questions and develop as many answers as you can.

1. Cloud services already facilitate device convergence and substituting new types of devices for a computer. For example, because you can leave your data in the cloud, you can use either your computer or a smartphone app to edit it. What other types of devices do you see converging or substituting for one another over time?

2. Many businesspeople already collaborate using virtual meeting tools. What dilemmas do you see arising from this? What new technologies might evolve in this space?

Tech Literacy: Internet Research and Writing

Conduct Internet research to find the information described, and then develop appropriate written responses based on your research. Be sure to document your sources using the MLA format. (See Chapter 1, Tech Literacy: Internet Research and Writing, page 38, to review MLA style guidelines.)

1. Imagine you are starting a new business and want to choose the free online webmail, cloud storage, and app suite that will best suit your needs. Go online to research the various choices, including the offerings from Microsoft, Google, and Apple mentioned earlier in the chapter, as well as any others you prefer. Choose the online services that will best meet your needs, and write a paragraph explaining why you selected this particular set of cloud-based tools.

2. The cloud enables you to take advantage of a huge variety of services while at home, at work or school, or on the go. Prepare a written report explaining what cloud-based services you currently use (navigation, gaming, and so on) and how they affect your life. Then research three additional cloud-based tools you might want to try and explain why.

3. Go online and search for a free, prerecorded webinar on a topic of your choice. (You can find an archive of webinars about Microsoft Office programs at **http://CUT6.emcp.net /MSOfficeBlogs**). Or, if you have time, find and participate in a live webinar. Write a brief report about the pros and cons of learning via webinar.

Tech Issues: Team Problem-Solving

In groups, develop possible solutions to the issues presented.

1. Today's classrooms in most US cities and towns have Internet connectivity, and in many cases, wireless connectivity. Brainstorm ways in which cloud services might replace current interactions among students, teachers, and parents, and describe each example in a group report.

2. Chapter 5 touched on some pros and cons for telecommuting, rather than working daily in an office. Based on what you know now about cloud services and tools, are concerns about telecommuting warranted? How do team leaders

and team members benefit from cloud-based tools? Write a brief group report addressing your conclusions about these issues.

3. Take a brief survey of your group members to identify the cloud-based services each person uses (such as webmail and free online file storage), and record the results in a table. If you discover that some students use few cloud-based services, expand the report to identify the barriers to usage and propose possible solutions.

Tech Timeline: Predicting Next Steps

Look at the timeline below, which outlines some of the major events in the history of the Internet and the cloud. As you review the list, think of what major events might occur next. Use your predictions to complete the timeline through the year 2030.

1993 World Wide Web technology and programming is officially proclaimed to be in the public domain and available to all.

1997 The number of web and Internet connected users surpasses 50 million.

1999 Salesforce.com becomes one of the first companies to deliver applications via a simple website.

2002 Amazon Web Services launches.

2003 Apple Computer establishes itself as an online music business with its iPod MP3 player (first introduced in 2001) and iTunes Music Store (launched in 2003).

2004 Wireless computer devices—including keyboards, mice, and wireless home networks—become widely accepted among users. More than 69 million US homes use broadband connections.

2005 Smartphones become the most widely used mobile device.

2007 Dropbox is founded by two students at the Massachusetts Institute of Technology (MIT).

2008 Microsoft introduces SkyDrive, which allows users to upload, share, access, and sync files through cloud storage, and provides access to Office Web Apps, which are limited, online versions of Word, Excel, PowerPoint, and OneNote.

2009 Browser-based applications such as Google apps emerge.

2010 The first iPad is released by Apple.

2011 Smartphones outsell personal computers, marking a milestone in how users access information over the Internet.

2013 Adobe's Creative Cloud software is subscribed to by over 1 million people.

2013 Microsoft releases Microsoft Office 2013 with integrated support for SkyDrive and subscription purchases available through Microsoft Office 365.

2014 Microsoft changes the name of SkyDrive to OneDrive due to a legal dispute and increases cloud storage to 1 TB for Office 365 subscribers.

2015 Microsoft moves further toward online software delivery, with the release of Windows 10 and Office 365 subscriptions.

Ethical Dilemmas: Group Discussion and Debate

As a class or within an assigned group, discuss the following ethical dilemma.

Because of breaches such as hacked consumer credit card information, many users have concerns about dealing with companies that store data in the public cloud.

In your group, discuss the issue of protection for consumers' data. Should US companies be required to improve their security practices now—for instance, by using a more secure form of credit card, as is already done in Europe? If so, should consumers or the companies have to pay for the improvements? Should companies pay automatic legal penalties for data breaches, or should consumers have to file lawsuits to recover damages?

Chapter 8

Maintaining and Managing Your Devices

Chapter Goal

To understand how to purchase, use, maintain, and troubleshoot computers of various types

Learning Objectives

8.1 Identify best practices for purchasing and setting up computing devices.

8.2 Explain how to clean, back up, secure, and configure computing devices.

8.3 Describe how to troubleshoot problems with computing devices.

8.4 Discuss how to avoid potential health problems caused by using computers.

Green go-online icons indicate resources that are accessed from the links menu in your ebook.

SNAP icons indicate inter-active resources that are available in SNAP. Go to your SNAP Assignments page to complete these quizzes, activities, and exercises.

8.1 Evaluating and Purchasing Computers and Mobile Devices

 Precheck 8.1
Check your understanding of the concepts covered by this objective.

When buying computers and other computer-related electronics for yourself, your family, or your business, there's more to think about than just the brand and model you want. For example, where will you buy your new device, and how will you make sure you get a good deal? Will you buy any extras for it? How will you get it set up?

Deciding Where to Buy

Many options are available for buying most brands and models of computers. Figure 8.1 shows some of them.

You can buy direct from the manufacturer—for example, buying an iPad from the Apple Online Store or an Apple retail store at a mall. When you buy from the manufacturer, you typically pay full retail price. However, it's easy to return or exchange the device, and you can choose from among the widest selection of devices and accessories, not just one or two models. Salespeople are available who are well educated in the products and who can help you make good buying decisions.

Third-party bricks-and-mortar stores, such as Best Buy and Walmart, may also have the device you are seeking. These retailers may offer discounts and limited-time sales, and be just as easy with returns and exchanges. However, you might not be able to find

Figure 8.1

Ways to Buy Computing Devices

Feature	Manufacturer's local store	Manufacturer's website	Local retail store	Third-party website	Online auction
Price	High ☹	High ☹	Varies 😐	Low 😊	Low 😊
Customer service	Good 😊	Good 😊	Good 😊	Varies 😐	Varies 😐
Immediate availability of product	Yes 😊	No ☹	Yes 😊	No ☹	No ☹
Exchanges and returns	Easy 😊	Easy but not immediate 😊	Varies 😐	Varies 😐	Usually not allowed ☹
Availability of knowledgeable consultants	Yes 😊	Yes 😊	Varies 😐	Not usually ☹	No ☹

Choose where to buy your computing devices based on the right balance of price and customer service for your needs.

🌀 Tracking Down Tech ››››››

Observing How People Use and Maintain Their Devices

It's easy to find good—and bad—examples of computer management and ergonomics all around you. Think about how people use devices at home, in coffee shops, and at a mall, for example. Complete this scavenger hunt to find instances of people interacting with and maintaining computers on campus and beyond.

all the models and options available at these stores. Salespeople are available but may not be knowledgeable about the products. These stores may also have websites from which you can order models that might be back ordered at your local outlet.

For the best discount, consider a third-party online store. You can find the lowest price for an item on a price comparison site and the order via the lowest-priced company's website. However, it's uncommon for a knowledgeable salesperson to be available to speak with; most phone representatives are simply order takers. If you need to return or exchange the item, or if it's defective, you must mail it back, and you might have to wait weeks to get a replacement or refund. Online auction sites such as eBay may also be good sources of bargains, although reliability and customer service depend on the seller you choose.

When you shop at a retail store, knowledgeable salespeople may be available to answer your questions.

Practical TECH

Comparison Shopping Online

Shopping for the best price online for a particular brand and model is easy, due to the many price comparison websites available. For example, PriceGrabber.com enables you to search dozens of online stores, and sorts the results by lowest price including shipping. Try it out now: go to a manufacturer's website for a computer you would like, and get its model number. Once you have the model number, go to PriceGrabber.com (http://CUT6.emcp.net/PriceGrabber) and search for that number to find out how much you could save by buying online. Some websites won't be included in the search results, such as sites that don't show the price of an item until it's added to the shopping cart. Therefore, an even better deal may be available than the ones you see listed. However, PriceGrabber.com will give you a baseline for comparison.

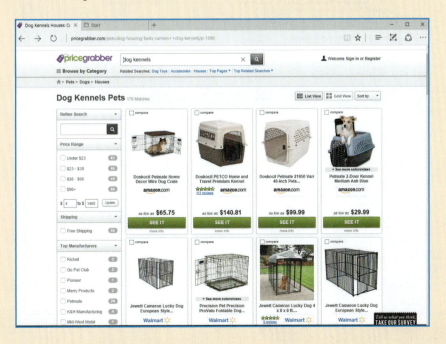

Choosing Accessories

Here are some accessories you might consider when purchasing a computing device.

Alternative Input Devices If you don't like the input devices that come with your computer, in most cases, you can buy others to replace them. For example, on a desktop PC, the model you choose might come with a very basic wired keyboard and mouse, but you may prefer something with more features, such as wireless connectivity or a built-in wrist rest. You can simply swap out the old for the new, because a desktop PC's input components connect with standard USB connectors. You can also use alternative types of input devices, such as swapping out your mouse for a trackball or adding a joystick or steering wheel for playing games. You can also add input devices to a notebook PC via the USB ports; the old versions are built in, but you can ignore them and use your add-on devices instead.

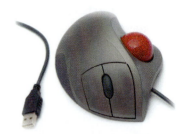

You might choose to add other types of input devices to your computer system, like this trackball.

Practical TECH

Using an External Monitor with a Notebook PC

If you connect an external monitor, keyboard, and mouse to a notebook computer, you have effectively created the equivalent of a desktop computer. You can keep the notebook computer folded up, and it will function the same as a desktop's system unit.

You may run into a problem, though, when you close the lid on the notebook PC. Most notebooks are set to automatically shut down or put themselves in Sleep mode when you close the lid. To get around this in Windows, right-click the Start button on the Taskbar and then click *Power Options*. In the Navigation pane at the left, click *Choose what closing the lid does*. Set the *When I close the lid* settings to *Do nothing* for both *On battery* and *Plugged in*. Click the Save changes button to apply your changes.

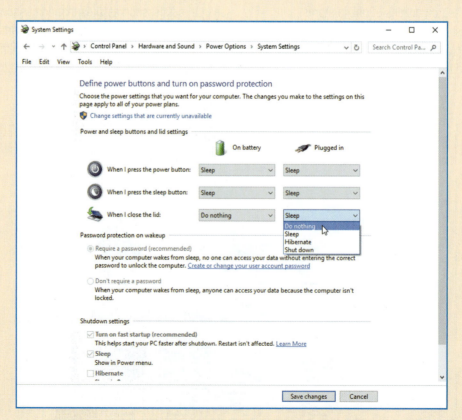

Alternative Monitors You can also choose a different monitor for a desktop PC. In fact, many desktop PCs don't come with a monitor at all, enabling you to purchase one separately or use one you already have. Most monitors use the same connectors—DVI, VGA, or HDMI—so it's a simple swap. If your notebook PC has the right port, you can also connect an external monitor.

Multimedia Add-Ons Desktop computers may come with a set of inexpensive stereo speakers; notebooks and tablets may come only with small built-in speakers. If you use your computer to play music or movies frequently or to play games that include sound, you might want to add a better speaker set, such as a Dolby Surround 7.1 system.

By connecting an external keyboard, mouse, and monitor to a notebook PC, you can create a complete desktop workstation.

You can also get wireless speakers that connect to the computer via Bluetooth.

You might also want a microphone (or a better microphone than the one that came with your computer) if you plan on recording your voice or using your computer for video chatting. Most notebooks have a built-in microphone; most desktop PCs do not. A headset with a combination of headphones and a microphone works well if you are going to be having long voice conversations through your computer's interface. For example, you might play an online game in which you voice chat with other people while playing as a group. If you don't need the headset, you might prefer a desktop microphone with a stand. Figure 8.2 shows both types. The headset shown in the figure is a Bluetooth model, so it can connect to the computer wirelessly.

Spare Power Cords and Batteries For a notebook or tablet computer, a reliable source of power is essential. When the computer is plugged into a wall outlet, it charges its battery. Depending on the device and what you are doing with it, a battery's charge

---

Figure 8.2

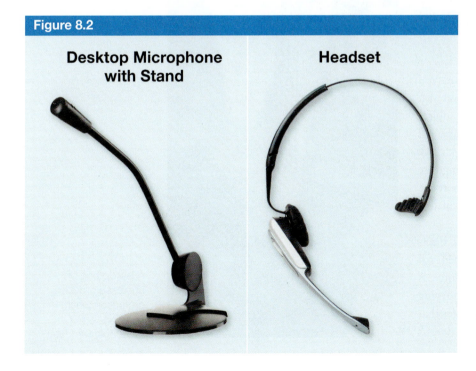

Desktop Microphone with Stand

Headset

You can add an external microphone to your computer.

can run the computer anywhere from 2 to 10 hours. When the charge runs out, you are done until you can plug back into an AC wall outlet. Some notebook computers have removable batteries, allowing you to carry a fully charged spare battery with you at all times so you won't run out of power at a critical moment. You can buy a spare battery when you buy the computer direct from the manufacturer, or you can buy a spare battery later from a discount battery supplier online.

A computer relies on its power cord to charge the battery. If something happens to the power cord (such as a dog chewing it up or someone dropping it in water), you won't be able to charge the battery or use the computer on AC power. Because the power cord is such an essential component, you might want a spare one of these too. Desktop computers use a standard, generic power cord that you can buy anywhere, so you might not need to keep a spare on hand for these. Tablet computers typically use a standard USB or similar interface to charge, so having a spare power cord for a tablet isn't important either. However, notebooks use a variety of power cord types and wattages, and you probably won't be able to walk into just any store and replace a notebook power cord. Therefore, if it's critical that you have access to your computer at all times, it makes sense for you to buy and carry a backup power cord.

Mobile Accessories Accessories for tablets and cell phones can extend the capabilities of those devices in some innovative ways. For example, the Square credit card processing system adds a credit card reader to an iPad or to some mobile phone models, so you can accept credit cards for your small business from anywhere you are. Many accessories target specialty niches, such as fitness monitors that enable you to monitor your heart rate on your phone as you exercise and mounting devices that allow you to attach your phone or tablet to a vehicle to serve as a GPS.

Protecting Your Investment

A computer represents a substantial investment of money. Besides accessories that enhance your user experience, you might also want accessories that protect your computer from damage and theft.

Cases and Protectors Because you are taking them with you wherever you go, portable computers may be subject to some harsh treatment. They may get accidentally dropped, bumped, kicked, or jostled along the way. A carrying case can be a smart purchase for a portable device, to minimize the impact of any rough treatment it may receive.

For a notebook computer, a briefcase, bag, or backpack designed for carrying a computer is a good choice. A model designed specifically for carrying a computer may have extra features that a normal backpack or satchel doesn't

A laptop bag or briefcase provides protection when traveling with a notebook computer.

have, such as extra padding in the compartment where the computer fits, pockets for small accessories, Velcro straps to hold cords, and a compartment sized to snugly fit a particular size of notebook.

To protect their tablet computers, many people use a padded cloth sleeve like the one shown in the bottom left photo, rather than a heavier (and bulkier) bag. The sleeve offers protection against scratches but doesn't add much to the bulk or weight of the tablet.

For some tablets, such as iPads, you can also buy a foldable protective **smart cover** that has some special features. The cover attaches with magnets to the side of the tablet, so it can be easily removed and replaced. When the cover is closed over the screen, the tablet puts itself to sleep automatically; then when you fold the cover open, the tablet wakes up again When the cover is open, it can be bent back to create a stand for the tablet. You can also purchase protective cases for smartphones, and you can purchase and install clear film screen protectors that prevent a touchscreen from becoming scratched with use.

A padded cloth sleeve provides protection for a tablet computer without adding much to its weight or bulk.

This magnetic smart cover can fold up into a stand and also wakes the tablet and puts it to sleep.

Practical TECH

Laptop Bags and Airport Security

If you travel through a security checkpoint at an airport, you will likely be asked to remove your laptop computer from its carrying case when it goes through the X-ray machine. Some models of bags, however, are considered *checkpoint friendly* by the Transportation Safety Administration (TSA). If you use a checkpoint-friendly laptop bag, you don't have to remove the computer. This can save a lot of effort if you travel a lot.

For a bag to be considered checkpoint friendly, it must have these features:

- The bag must have a designated laptop-only section.
- The laptop-only section must completely unfold to lay flat on the X-ray belt.
- There can be no metal snaps, zippers, or buckles inside, underneath, or on top of the laptop-only section.
- No pockets are allowed on the inside or outside of the laptop-only section.
- Nothing can be packed in the laptop-only section other than the computer.

Surge Suppression Electrical devices rely on the power coming from the wall outlet to maintain a certain well-defined voltage range (around 110 to 120 volts). However, the actual range may be different because of problems with the local electricity provider, wiring in the home or office, or environmental conditions. Sometimes there are outages, power surges or spikes, and sags, all of which can inflict damage to a computer.

A **surge** and a **spike** are basically the same thing: too much voltage. The term *spike* is used to describe a more dramatic surge. Power surges and spikes should be avoided because they can damage hardware. Computer components are designed to operate at precise, low voltages, and they are easily damaged by voltages that are too high. Modems that connect to phone lines are especially vulnerable to power spike damage. A lightning strike at or near your home can send a spike of high-voltage electricity not only in through your AC power outlets, but also through your land-based phone line, to which a dial-up or DSL modem is directly connected. Power spikes can also damage other circuit boards in the computer, including the motherboard.

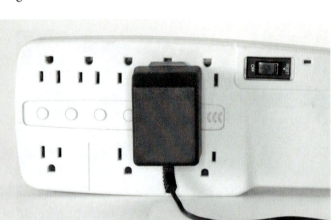

Activity 8.1.1

Video
**How Surge
Suppression Works**

External devices can help compensate for the various failings of household and office electricity. A **surge suppressor** is basically an extension cord with multiple plugs on it, but inside it is a metal oxide variable resistor (varistor)—sometimes abbreviated *MOV*—that can absorb any excess power during a surge or spike, preventing it from reaching the plugged-in devices. Some surge suppressors also include a pass-through for a telephone line, adding surge protection to it as well. Surge suppression capability is measured in joules. A **joule** is the energy required to sustain one watt for one second. The higher the joule rating, the greater the protection provided by the surge suppressor.

A surge suppressor provides protection against power spikes and surges.

Power Conditioning and Power Backup A **power sag** is insufficient voltage. Power sags don't usually damage hardware, but they can cause it to temporarily malfunction, resulting in memory storage errors that can cause the operating system (OS) to unexpectedly freeze up or restart. When that happens, you may lose the unsaved data in any applications you are working with.

A **power conditioner** includes the features of a surge suppressor, but also contains a feature that bolsters the voltage to the devices when the voltage coming from the AC outlet sags. It does this by storing extra voltage in a capacitor, and then discharging that extra voltage onto the power line when it detects a low-voltage condition.

An **uninterruptible power supply (UPS)** is a combination surge suppressor, power conditioner, and battery backup. It handles power surges in the same way that a surge suppressor does, but it has the added bonus of being able to power devices for a few minutes when a complete power outage occurs. This feature is very useful because it helps avoid problems that occur when a computer is shut down incorrectly, such as storage errors. A UPS connects to the PC (usually via a USB cable) to allow the operating system to interact with the UPS. When the OS receives information from the UPS that the AC power is off and the battery has begun providing power, the OS

Activity 8.1.2

Video
Two Types of UPSs

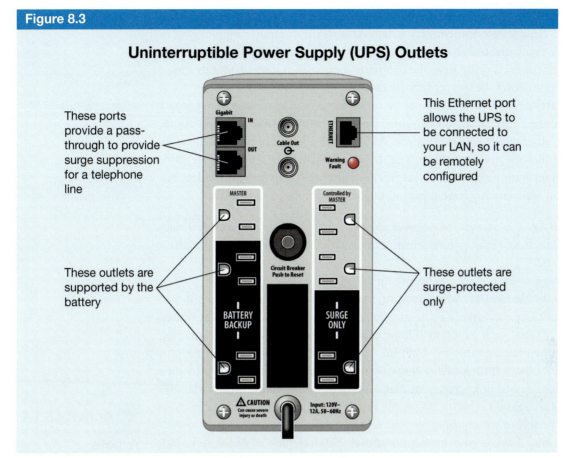

Figure 8.3

Uninterruptible Power Supply (UPS) Outlets

These ports provide a pass-through to provide surge suppression for a telephone line

This Ethernet port allows the UPS to be connected to your LAN, so it can be remotely configured

These outlets are supported by the battery

These outlets are surge-protected only

A UPS provides outlets that include a battery backup, so devices remain powered in the event of a power outage.

Activity 8.1.3

Practice
**Understanding
UPS Outlets**

can shut itself down automatically. Figure 8.3 shows a standby UPS suitable for home or small-office use; much larger models are available for servers.

Antitheft Tools Unfortunately, computers are popular targets for thieves because they are expensive and easy to resell. In addition, many people aren't as vigilant as they should be about keeping their computers safe and accounted for.

In an office environment, a desktop computer may be secured to a specific desk with a steel cable that passes through the computer's case, wraps around the desk (if the desk is built-in) or through a wall-mounted ring, and is secured with a lock. Only someone with a key to the lock can remove the computer from the office.

On some notebook PCs, there is a slot or hole in the side of the computer for connecting a special type of lock that connects to a steel cable. This is called a *Kensington security slot* (**K-slot**), named after the company that created and sells the lock. The lock may be a combination lock or key-opened lock, depending on the model. If the computer doesn't have a K-slot, you might use a lock that attaches to the notebook's monitor port as an alternative, or use a lock that's glued onto the cover of your notebook.

Some notebooks include a K-slot for connecting a Kensington lock like this one.

More high-tech security measures are also available. For example, you can attach a USB-based cable alarm. You connect a steel cable to the computer by plugging in a USB device that's attached to one end of the cable and setting a security code. The USB device disconnects easily from the computer, but when it does, it sounds a loud alarm if you don't enter the correct security code.

When traveling with your computer or smartphone, you may want to employ a **separation alarm**. This consists of two small devices; you attach one to the computer and hold the other somewhere close to you. As long as the two devices are within close range of one another, nothing will happen. However, if they get separated, an alarm will sound. A separation alarm can be helpful not only when your laptop is stolen, but also when you inadvertently leave it behind as you move from place to place.

Data Security The data stored on your computer may be even more critical than the hardware itself, and may include sensitive information that you don't want to share with onlookers.

To protect your data, there are three main action plans:

- **Authenticate the user who's logging in.** In addition to using a password, you might choose a biometric authentication method, such as a fingerprint reader. Some devices, such as recent iPhone models, even have fingerprint scanning and authentication capability built in.
- **Prevent others from looking at the screen.** You can install a screen filter on a monitor or notebook screen that makes the screen unreadable except when it's viewed straight on. This means people sitting beside you or standing above you won't be able to see anything on your screen.
- **Track and disable your stolen computer.** Services such as Absolute LoJack enable you to track the location of your stolen computer and lock it up so it can't be used. Some services can even wipe out the data on the hard drive.

Activity 8.1.4

Article
Tracking Stolen Computers

Evaluating Service Plans and Warranties

Most computers come with a basic one-year **warranty** against manufacturing defects for no additional charge. With some devices, you can choose to purchase an extended protection plan from the retail store where you bought the device. Read the terms and conditions carefully for this type of plan, and weigh its costs against its benefits.

Service and support plans commonly offer three main types of extended coverage:

- **Extension of original warranty.** This type of plan extends the duration of the original warranty for several years. For example, you might choose to extend the warranty on your desktop PC from one year to three years. The coverage itself doesn't change, only the duration. A warranty typically covers only defects in workmanship or reliability but not damage resulting from accidents. For example, if you drop your iPad into the bathtub, the warranty won't cover it.
- **Preferred or premium support.** You may choose to purchase a support plan that guarantees you shorter wait times when you call the manufacturer to troubleshoot problems. This support may also include access to professionals who can answer your questions about how to use the device, not just fix problems with it.
- **Accidental damage and breakage insurance.** You may be able to buy insurance coverage from the manufacturer, so that if something happens to your device, it will be fixed or replaced, regardless of what happened or who was at fault.

Setting Up a New Device

When you get a new device, you will probably be excited and in a hurry to start using it. If you hurry too much, though, you may miss some important steps in the setup process.

Unpacking Your New Device When unpacking your new device, be careful not to damage or discard any of the packing materials until you are sure the device is working properly. You may still want to save them for at least 30 days, in case the device malfunctions. If the device goes bad within 30 days and you still have all the packing materials, you may be able to return it to the store where you bought it for a refund, rather than have to go through the device manufacturer's warranty claim process. Also be careful when unpacking the device that you don't overlook and discard any small pieces or accessories that might be in the packing materials.

Connecting the Cables Follow the instructions that came with the device to connect its cables (if it has any). The connections may be obvious to you if you're familiar with the various ports on the device (covered in Chapter 2).

For a desktop PC, the connections are fairly standard between models:

- Connect the computer's power cord to the computer (on the back) and to the AC wall outlet or to a surge suppressor or UPS.
- Connect the monitor's power cord to a wall outlet, and connect the monitor's data cable to the VGA or DVI port on the computer.
- Connect the keyboard and mouse to the computer via USB ports. If the input device is wired, it will have a cable with a USB connector on one end. If it is wireless, it will come with a USB transmitter.
- If you are using a wired Ethernet connection, connect an Ethernet cable from the router or cable modem to the RJ-45 port on the computer.

When you unpack a new computer device, be careful not to discard any of the pieces—including accessories, warranty information, and instructions.

Figure 8.4 shows the basic connections for a desktop PC. The connections for other devices will vary.

A notebook computer is ready to go right out of the box. All you have to do is connect the power cord to the notebook and to the wall outlet. Any add-on devices can be installed later, after you get the basic system up and running.

Some tablets and smartphones do not have a power cord per se. Instead they have a data port, such as a USB port, and a USB cable that can optionally plug into an AC adapter, like the one in Figure 8.5. The device charges when the cable is plugged into an AC wall outlet; that same cable serves as a data connection when it's plugged into another device, such as a computer.

Figure 8.4

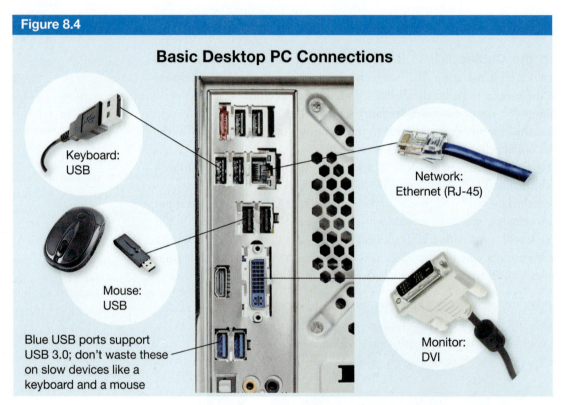

Basic Desktop PC Connections

Keyboard: USB

Network: Ethernet (RJ-45)

Mouse: USB

Blue USB ports support USB 3.0; don't waste these on slow devices like a keyboard and a mouse

Monitor: DVI

For a desktop PC, the monitor, keyboard, and mouse all connect to the system unit. The monitor connects via VGA or DVI, and the keyboard and mouse connect via USB. In this case, the keyboard uses a wired connection (a cable) and the mouse uses a wireless connection (a transmitter).

Figure 8.5

A USB Cable and AC Adapter with USB Port

Instead of having a power cord, some small devices connect to a USB cable that plugs into an AC adapter.

Tech Career Explorer

Computer Installer

If you love setting up computers, you might enjoy a job that consists mainly of new installations, either in residential or business settings. A computer installer's duties include unpacking and checking new hardware, making all the connections, and performing basic startup tasks, such as creating user accounts, connecting to the Internet, installing operating system updates, and installing any new software the customer may have requested. To find out more about this job, complete this exercise.

Charging the Battery If the device has a battery, you may need to plug it into an AC outlet and wait for the device to charge before you use it for the first time. For example, you should wait until a smartphone is charged before going through its Setup process to ensure that the power doesn't run out at a critical point in the process. Most devices charge faster if they remain powered off while charging.

Configuring the System The first time you turn on the device, you may be prompted to work through a Setup utility. This utility may walk you through setting up Internet connectivity, user accounts, and appearance preferences. It may also offer to import settings from another device.

Setting Up Wireless Connectivity For a mobile device, establishing wireless connections may be part of the initial configuration or may be accomplished separately. You may need to go into the device's Settings or Properties screen to find the networking configuration settings. A device may be able to find available networks and connect to them automatically, or it may need your help. The steps are different for each device, so you will need to check the device documentation. See "Setting Up a Wireless Home Network" in Chapter 6 to learn more about wireless connectivity.

Recheck 8.1

Recheck your understanding of the concepts covered by this objective.

8.2 Performing Basic System Care and Maintenance

Precheck 8.2

Check your understanding of the concepts covered by this objective.

By performing some simple preventive maintenance activities, you can give your computer a longer life and make it more pleasant to use, as well as protect your data.

Protecting the Computer from Damage

Computers today are surprisingly impact resistant, and can usually withstand some rough handling and minor accidents, such as dropping a tablet onto a carpeted floor or kicking over a system unit that sits on the floor as you walk past it. Monitors and screens are somewhat more fragile, and can crack or stop working if dropped on a hard surface.

A computer has two vulnerable areas, though: electricity and water. As you learned in the sections "Surge Suppression" and "Power Conditioning and Power Backup" on page 332, surge suppression and power conditioning are important ways of protecting your computer from power surges and sags.

Static electricity—also known as **electrostatic discharge (ESD)**—is also harmful to computer components. ESD is a risk mostly when working inside a computer, directly touching the circuit boards, so it's not an issue for most casual computer users. To avoid ESD damage, ground yourself by touching the computer's metal frame before you touch any internal components, and handle circuit boards only by the edges (if you must handle them at all).

Water is dangerous to a computer because water conducts electricity very well, and if there is water on a circuit board, the electricity will prefer to travel through the water rather than over the path through the circuits that it's supposed to take. When this happens, a **short circuit** occurs, which can not only cause the component to malfunction temporarily, but can sometimes cause permanent damage. Here are some tips for keeping your computer and its components dry:

- Don't use your computer when you are in or near water, such as in a bathtub.
- Don't use your computer outside when it's raining or snowing.
- When a computer has been in a cold environment and you bring it into a warm environment, give it time to warm up before turning it on. That way, if there's any frost or condensation on the components, it will have time to evaporate.

Cleaning a Computer

Computers can survive without cleaning, but they are much more pleasant to use when the surfaces you see and touch are clean. In some cases, a computer will even perform better after cleaning, such as removing any blockage from a fan vent. In the following sections, you will learn how to clean each part of a computer.

Cleaning the System Unit Desktop computers can get very dirty over time, accumulating large clumps of dust, hair, and other debris from the environment inside the case. This happens because of the nature of the case design. A typical desktop computer has multiple fans that draw in air to help keep the internal components cooler. Along with that air comes whatever is nearby, including animal hair and dander and dust. A small amount of debris inside the case won't cause a problem, but large clumps can contribute to overheating because they block the flow of air to the hot components that need the airflow to cool down. At a minimum, clean inside a desktop PC once a year.

To clean the inside of a desktop PC, turn the computer off and unplug it. Open up the case and manually remove any visible clumps of debris. Blow out the inside of the case with **compressed air** (sold in aerosol cans at most computer stores). Each aerosol can comes with a detachable thin plastic tube that you can use to direct the airflow precisely. You may want to take the case outdoors when using compressed air on it, to avoid blowing dust all over your work area.

Do not use any cleaning products, either aerosol or liquid, inside the computer. For cleaning anything that involves circuit boards, you must stay away from liquids, especially water. If some kind of moisture is absolutely necessary, use rubbing alcohol on a cotton swab. Brush off the circuit boards with a small soft paintbrush (like the kind used by an artist or the kind used to apply cosmetics). The circuit boards don't need to be sparkling clean; they just need to have the major clumps of dust removed. A handheld vacuum designed for electronics can come in handy, if available. Avoid touching the circuit boards with your fingers or loosening the cable connectors.

A can of compressed air typically comes with a tube you can attach to the nozzle to direct the airflow precisely.

Other parts of the computer that tend to accumulate dust include the fan on the power supply, the fan on the CPU, and the air vents in the case. Wipe off the air vents with a damp paper towel. For the power supply, point the compressed air nozzle at an angle to the fan opening, rather than blowing straight down into it. Doing so avoids driving the dirt even deeper into the power supply box instead of blowing it out.

Notebook and tablet PCs aren't designed to be disassembled for cleaning; they shouldn't need it anyway. Use compressed air to blow any dust or debris from visible areas of a notebook or tablet. For example, if USB and Ethernet ports aren't used, dust can accumulate inside them and should be blown out.

The outside plastic or metal casing of a computer can be cleaned anytime it's dirty. Use a soft cloth and a cleaning product designed for computers, or use a mild soap and water. Be careful not to get liquid in any of the openings.

Cleaning the Screen Always turn a monitor off before cleaning it. If any liquid gets inside, it can air dry without worries of short circuiting. It's also much easier to see spots on the monitor screen when the screen is dark.

To clean a computer screen (desktop, notebook, tablet, or smartphone), use a cleaning product designed specifically for computer screens. If you are using liquid from a spray bottle, don't spray it directly on the screen; spray a soft cloth, and then wipe the screen with the cloth. Don't use ordinary glass cleaner, because it may contain ammonia or other chemicals that can damage a monitor screen.

Cleaning the Keyboard Since it's always at the forefront of activity, the keyboard can get very dirty. Users may type with unwashed hands or eat, drink, smoke, and play with their pets while they use the computer. All of this activity leaves dirt, oil, and other residue on the keyboard.

To clean a keyboard, make sure the computer is off. Turn the keyboard upside down and gently shake it over a trash can to get rid of any loose debris. Spray a soft cloth with a liquid cleaning product designed for computers, and wipe each key individually. Use a folded cloth to reach between the keys. Avoid letting the liquid drip between the keys; if some liquid does drip, wait 24 hours before using the keyboard to ensure the liquid has dried (to avoid short circuiting). The reason for using a cleaning product designed for computers is that it may have antistatic properties (that is, properties that help cut down on static electricity, which is also harmful to computers), whereas ordinary household cleaning products do not.

One way to clean between the keys of a keyboard is with a folded cloth.

Removing the keys to clean under and between them isn't a good idea, because it can be difficult to get them back on again, especially the spacebar, which may have a spring behind it. If you have access to one, a small, handheld vacuum designed for working with electronics can be useful in sucking the debris out from under the keys.

If liquid is spilled on a keyboard, unplug it immediately from the PC and try shaking it upside down to release all of the excess liquid; then let it dry. If the liquid was plain water, the keyboard will probably be fine after it dries; just clean the outside as well as possible. But if the liquid contained sugar, the keyboard may never be completely clean again. Some people have successfully cleaned sticky keyboards in a dishwasher. To try this (there is little to lose with a keyboard that's otherwise on its way to the trash can), place the keyboard on the upper rack, wash without using the heat-dry feature, remove it after the wash, rinse it, and set it in a dish drainer for several days to dry out.

Cleaning the Mouse or Trackball A mouse or trackball, like a keyboard, gets very dirty because it's constantly being handled. When a mouse or trackball is so dirty that the sensors or rollers are blocked from sending reliable data to the computer, the on-screen pointer may jump or stutter, or moving the mouse in one direction (vertical or horizontal) may result in no action at all.

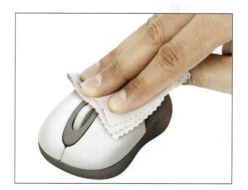

Clean the outside of a mouse with mild soapy water or a special cleaning product.

To clean the outside of a mouse, wipe it down with a soft cloth dampened with mild soapy water or a cleaning product designed for computers, just as with any other external PC component. If you have an older ball-style mouse, or a trackball, you can also remove the ball from its chamber and clean the rollers inside it with a cotton swab dipped in alcohol.

Backing Up Data

Because storage media such as hard drives can fail, it's important to make regular backups of your important data files, including business and personal documents and photos, financial records, and email and contacts. You may also want to make backups of the favorites you have saved in your web browser.

If the computer is at your workplace, a business **backup system** may be in place that automatically backs up your data files for you. Check with your supervisor to find out. If there is such a system, you don't have to back up your individual PC or its data.

Personal Backups If you need to manage your own personal backups, there are several ways to keep your data files backed up:

- Store your files in the cloud instead of on your local hard drive. That way, the files are available whenever and wherever you have Internet access. However, you won't be able to access them if you're not online.
- Use a cloud storage service that automatically mirrors files between the cloud and your local storage. For example, Microsoft's OneDrive service has an optional Windows application that keeps copies synced between your computer's local OneDrive folder and the copies on the cloud.
- Subscribe to an **online backup service**. The primary copies of your files remain on your local computer, but backup copies are made to the online server at intervals you specify. You may have to pay for this service.
- Use a backup utility to back up your files at specified intervals. This used to be the most popular method, but more convenient online methods have become feasible as the average user's Internet speed has increased in recent years.

Windows versions 7 and earlier came with a Backup utility that you could use to back up your files to the backup medium of your choice. Windows 10 doesn't have this application, however, so if you want a backup utility for a Windows 10 computer, you will need to buy a third-party product. Mac OS X comes with a backup application called *Time Machine*.

Whatever backup method you choose, make sure you select the files to be backed up wisely. Don't back up files that you can restore in other ways. For example, don't back up the Windows folder on your hard drive, because you can get those files back in the event of a complete system loss by reinstalling Windows. On the other hand, make sure you back up all the files you will need to put your system back in the event of a complete loss. Here are some suggestions for what files to back up for a Windows system:

- **The complete contents of your user account's folder from the Users folder**. This folder includes most of the files you will want to keep, including Internet Explorer and Microsoft Edge browser favorites and the contents of your Documents, Pictures, Videos, and Music folders.
- **Any data files from applications you use to store important data**. This might include data files for financial programs like Quicken and QuickBooks, and contact management and email data files for Outlook and other mail or personal information management applications.
- **Other data files that aren't stored in your user folders**. In addition to data files, this might include documents and photos.
- **Documents containing information you will need to restore any applications you might have to reinstall.** This might include product keys and registration numbers for any applications you have purchased online.

Business Backups Business data, such as customer and inventory records, can be much more valuable than the computers on which the data is stored. Can you imagine, for example, what would happen to Amazon. com if they lost their product database? Or if an airline lost the database of the scheduled flights and the reserved passengers? Because business data is so very valuable, companies make backup a priority.

Tech Career Explorer

Storage Backup Specialist

In large companies, planning and maintaining the backup systems is a full-time job. It's important that the backups be run on a regular schedule and that the backup media be maintained safely at off-site facilities. A storage backup specialist (or storage administrator) is the person responsible for the company's backup systems and disaster recovery plans. Complete this exercise to learn more about this career.

Data backups for business focus on these areas:

- **How efficiently can we back up our data, both in terms of cost and time spent?** Many large companies don't rely on ordinary servers for backups; they have advanced backup appliances that back up data from the network at a very high transfer rate. The latest backup technologies and systems cost more initially, but they can pay for themselves in reduced labor costs (fewer employee hours spent monitoring the backup processes) and reduced hardware costs when fewer drives are needed to store backup files.
- **How reliable are those backups, should we ever need to use them?** Are there any scenarios in which our backups might fail or be inadequate? How much reliability risk are we willing to take to keep costs down? Many companies store their backup files off-site, either by backing up through a network to another building or by having IT employees hand-deliver backup media to a remote location every day.
- **How quickly can the data be restored?** Every hour that a business is not conducting business because of a computer problem is money wasted. In the event of a major data loss, how long will it take for IT professionals to get new hardware and software up and running and restore the backups? A good backup system is not only quick to back up, but also quick to restore.

Most businesses have not only everyday routines for backups, but also a disaster recovery plan. This plan outlines all the possible scenarios for loss of computer capability and data, and provides step-by-step instructions as to how to proceed to get the company's computer systems back up and running as quickly as possible. For example, what happens if the building where all the IT data is kept burns down? What happens if there is a flood? a hurricane? a terrorist attack? A disaster recovery plan might authorize IT specialists to purchase all-new computer hardware and start recovering the data from backups right away, for example, rather than waiting on an insurance settlement. It might instruct them whether or not to retain components that are damaged by water, smoke, or radiation, and where to store those components for later forensic use.

Changing System Settings

Most operating systems allow users to change a multitude of system settings—from the current time zone to the color of the desktop background. In Windows 10, you

Cutting Edge

Deduplication in Business Backup

One problem with backing up business servers is that there's a huge amount of redundancy. Suppose you have 20 servers, and each one runs the same server operating system. Each day, you back up the files that have changed, and each week, you do a full backup of each server. Over 50 percent of the files on each server are the same, and only about 15 percent of the content of any particular server changes from week to week, on average. That's a lot of duplication, and duplication drives up the cost of the backup system exponentially because of the huge amount of data that must be moved from the original location to the backup every single week.

To streamline the backup process both in terms of the time it takes and the hardware it requires, many companies are moving toward deduplication systems. A *deduplication system* reads each chunk of data to be backed up, and if there's already an identical copy on the backup device, it inserts a pointer to that existing copy rather than recopying the original. A *deduplication backup appliance* consists of a combined deduplication hardware and software package from a specific vendor. Many companies find that using a deduplication backup appliance cuts down on their data backup costs so dramatically that it pays for itself in a very short time.

access most system settings via the **Control Panel**, shown in Figure 8.6. To access the Control Panel in Windows 10, right-click the Start button on the Taskbar and then click *Control Panel*.

Windows 10 also offers an alternative way of accessing certain system settings via an app style of interface. To access the Settings app, click the Start button and then click *Settings*. Figure 8.7 shows that interface. The Control Panel and the Settings app overlap in the settings they control, but some settings are available in only one place or the other.

Hands On

Adjusting Mouse Settings

One of the many ways you can change how your computer's operating system works is to adjust the mouse settings. Follow the steps in this resource to explore your mouse's settings in Windows.

Figure 8.6

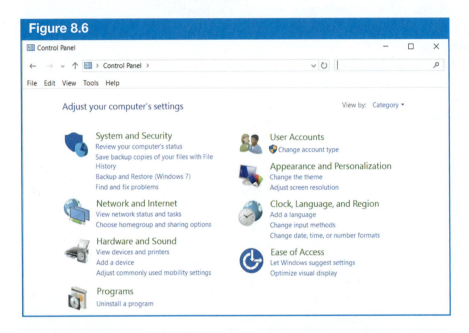

Use the Control Panel in Windows 10 to control many system settings.

Figure 8.7

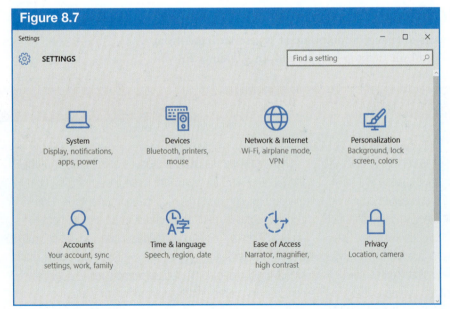

Windows 10 offers a Settings app as an alternative to the Control Panel.

Figure 8.8

In Mac OS X, you can control how the operating system works via System Preferences.

In Mac OS X, you access most settings through **System Preferences**, shown in Figure 8.8. To access System Preferences, click *System Preferences* on the Dock, or navigate to the System Preferences folder inside the Applications folder.

Performing Software Updates

The companies that develop operating system and applications frequently release updates for them. These updates may add features, fix bugs, enhance the performance of certain hardware, patch security holes, and provide updated data for utilities such as virus and spyware checkers. In the following sections, we'll look at some of the updates available.

Operating System Updates Most operating systems' default settings specify that updates will be automatically downloaded and installed without any user intervention. This is true for both Windows and Mac OS X. As long as you are connected to the Internet, your computer will automatically update itself.

In some cases, however, you might not want this to occur. For example, in a business that uses some proprietary software, installing certain updates might prevent the software from working properly. The system administrator may decide not to allow employees to download updates individually in such cases. Instead, the system administrator may test each update as it becomes available on a single computer and then roll out an update via the company's network containing only the updates that have been determined not to cause problems.

On a Windows 10 computer, to adjust the **Windows Update** settings, open the Settings app, click the *Update & Security* icon, and then click *Advanced Options*.

Figure 8.9

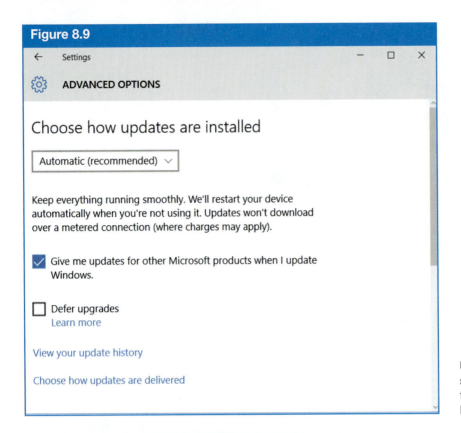

Use the Change settings screen to choose how updates to Windows will be downloaded and installed.

Figure 8.10

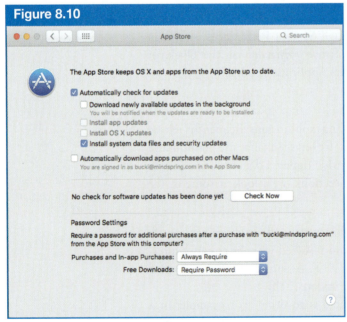

Use App Store to choose how updates to Mac OS X will be downloaded and installed.

Change the *Choose how updates are installed* setting from the drop-down list (see Figure 8.9).

In Mac OS X, you can access a similar dialog box by opening System Preferences and choosing *App Store*. As shown in Figure 8.10, in App Store, you can control whether updates will be automatically found, downloaded, and/or installed.

Application Updates In Windows 10, Microsoft desktop applications such as Microsoft Office can be updated automatically along with Windows. To activate this feature, mark the *Give me updates for other Microsoft products when I update Windows* check box, shown in Figure 8.9.

For Mac OS X applications, the same settings that control the operating system updates also control the updates for apps, as you saw in Figure 8.10. Mark or clear the *Install app updates* check box to choose whether to receive application updates.

Other applications may let you know individually when an update is available. Some applications keep a monitoring program running in the background at all times so that you will be notified immediately of updates; other applications check the product website when you open the application. If you see a message that a new version is available, you can follow the prompts to install it.

Mobile Device OS Updates On a tablet or smartphone, you might have to open the Store app to get updates for your installed applications. When you do so, the Store app will let you know what updates are available and allow you to choose which ones to install. Figure 8.11 shows a Windows Phone with available updates to be installed, for example.

When a major update is available, such as a new version of the operating system, the update might not be installed automatically. For example, Figure 8.12 shows an iPad with an iOS update ready

On a Windows Phone, open the Store app to see and install updates.

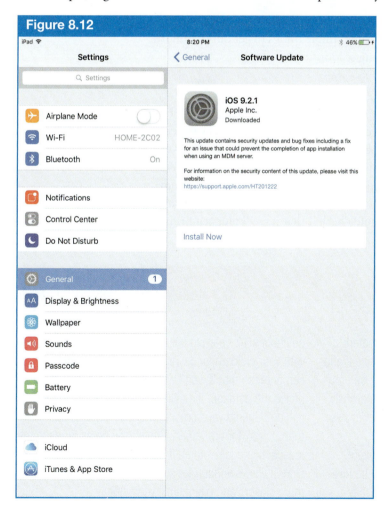

An iOS update is ready to be installed on this iPad.

Figure 8.13

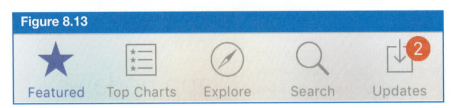

The Apple Store app shows available updates via a number on the Updates icon at the bottom of the screen.

to be installed from the Settings app. To complete this update, you would click the app and then click *Install Now*.

Application updates are retrieved through the Apple Store app on iOS. For example, Figure 8.13 shows the bar along the bottom of the Apple Store app screen, where it indicates that four updates are available. You would click the Updates icon to see a list of updates and choose which ones to install.

Recheck 8.2

Recheck your understanding of the concepts covered by this objective.

8.3 Diagnosing and Dealing with Issues

Precheck 8.3

Check your understanding of the concepts covered by this objective.

Even though today's computers are fairly reliable, problems do still sometimes occur. Determining the exact cause of a problem can be difficult in many cases because multiple problems have similar symptoms. For example, if your monitor doesn't show any image, it could be a problem with the monitor itself or its connection to the computer, or it could be that the monitor and its connection are working just fine but the computer isn't sending the monitor anything to display. It also could be that the display adapter is faulty.

As a nonprofessional computer user, you will likely run into problems that you can't solve on your own. However, you can do some simple things to get out of minor jams, and those fixes are covered in the following sections.

Checking Connections

When a computer has worked fine and suddenly starts having a problem, it may be because a connector has come loose. When you jostle a desktop computer's system unit or one of its attached components, the cables can sometimes become loose, so that the connectors aren't snug anymore. This can cause intermittent or complete failures of data moving from one place to another, such as data moving to or from a disk drive or a printer. Similarly, when an external monitor, mouse, or keyboard suddenly stops working, the first thing you should check is that it's still plugged firmly into its port.

Tech Ethics

Who Is Responsible for Computer Damage?

Children today are often more adept at using computers than adults, but that also means they're more confident and will experiment with computers and sometimes cause problems. It's important to monitor their computer use carefully, not only to protect the children from adult content, but also to protect the computers from the children.

When a child causes damage to a computer system that's expensive to fix, or causes important data to be lost, who is responsible? Consider this scenario. Suppose a neighbor's 12-year-old child is visiting your house playing with your children, and while he's there, he damages your computer so that it won't work anymore. By the time you notice the damage, the child has gone home. What should you do? Should you contact the child's parents and ask them to pay for the repair? Should you go as far as to take legal action against them if they refuse? Or should you consider it your own fault for not having supervised the children more closely, and pay the bill yourself?

Troubleshooting Dead Computer Issues

If the computer appears completely dead, it's probably not getting any electricity. Check to make sure there's an uninterrupted connection from the computer to a working power outlet or surge suppressor. Keep in mind that some surge suppressors have on/off switches.

Another possibility is that the PC may have been placed into a low-power Sleep mode and can't wake up for some reason. To check for that, press and hold down the PC's power button for 10 seconds and then release it. Doing so will terminate any low-power modes and shut off the computer completely. Press the Power button again to try to start the computer from scratch.

If you have installed new hardware and your computer is suddenly dead afterward, it's probably the new hardware's fault. Uninstall it and try again. If your computer is still dead, look at the device manufacturer's website for information about what might be happening.

If a mobile device such as a tablet or phone is dead, read the manual or look online to find the procedure for resetting the device. It probably involves holding down multiple buttons on the device at the same time or pressing a sequence of keys in a certain order. There may be separate instructions for a hard reset and a soft reset. A **hard reset** wipes out everything, returning the system to the exact state it was in when you first got the device. A **soft reset** corrects some types of errors but leaves your data and settings intact.

Responding to System Error Messages

If you see an error message as the computer is starting up, you have some information to work with in troubleshooting. Look up the error message online. Some error messages have obvious meanings, like *Keyboard stuck;* others may have a variety of causes.

If your device is running Windows and you see an error message on a bright-blue screen, Windows has encountered a serious error and has shut itself down. The error is usually hardware related and can occur when memory or some other piece of hardware is failing or incompatible with the rest of the computer. This screen is sometimes jokingly referred to as the **Blue Screen of Death (BSOD)**. The messages on BSODs were usually very technical and cryptic in earlier versions of Windows, but in Window 8.1 and later, the messages are much more friendly and less detailed, as shown in Figure 8.14.

Figure 8.14

:(

Your PC ran into a problem and needs to restart. We're just collecting some error info, and then we'll restart for you. (0% complete)

If you'd like to know more, you can search online later for this error: HAL INITIALIZATION FAILED

A Windows blue-screen error message indicates a serious problem that requires you to restart.

Addressing Disk Errors

Disk errors occur when the file system on your hard drives malfunctions. It can be a hardware error, such as a flaw in the disk surface that makes whatever is stored there unable to be read. It can also be a software error, such as the disk's file allocation table (that is, its table of contents) having incorrect information about what's stored in a particular spot. Disk errors occur almost exclusively on mechanical disk drives, such as hard disk drives, and not on solid-state drives. The main symptom of a disk error is an error message in the operating system telling you that it can't read or write to the disk.

When you see such an error in Windows, run the **Disk Check** utility to find and fix any problems. To access this utility, open File Explorer, click *This PC*, right-click the icon for the disk drive, and then click *Properties*. On the Tools tab of the disk's Properties box, click the Check button and then follow the prompts.

On a Mac, you can check a disk by running **Disk Utility**, which is in the Applications/Utilities folder. Choose the Mac hard drive from the Navigation pane on the left, and then click the First Aid tab. Click *Verify disk*, and wait for the utility to check the disk.

Deciding When You Need Professional Help

As a nonprofessional computer user, you may not be able to fix every problem on your own. You may need to ask a tech-savvy friend for help or use a repair service. There are many tutorial videos online that can walk you through the process of doing major repairs yourself, but these videos aren't authoritative, and may give bad advice that can cause you to damage your computer. Consult a professional in any of these situations:

- A hardware component is malfunctioning.
- The OS won't start and you have tried everything suggested in this chapter.
- You think your computer is infected with a virus, and your antivirus program can't remove it.
- The computer is overheating.
- Your computer is making multiple beeping sounds when you turn it on, and nothing appears onscreen.

Don't be shy about consulting a professional any time you run into a problem that you can't solve on your own. It's better to pay someone to fix the problem the right way than to experiment with various fixes that might make it worse.

 Recheck 8.3

Recheck your understanding of the concepts covered by this objective.

8.4 Avoiding Potential Health Problems

Computers can be a great benefit to people, but there are also some health and wellness issues associated with computer use. In the following sections, you'll learn how to make your computing experience as healthy as possible.

 Precheck 8.4

Check your understanding of the concepts covered by this objective.

Ergonomics

As you learned in Chapter 2, *ergonomics* is the study of the interaction between humans and the equipment they use. Research has shown that it's possible to reduce strain on the human body by designing hardware that makes it easy for the body to move in more natural ways, and by positioning hardware and humans correctly in relation to one another. Ergonomic input devices are available that are designed with human comfort in mind, such as keyboards that have a split design and a wrist rest. Ergonomic devices can help users avoid painful **repetitive stress injuries**, such as tendonitis and carpal tunnel syndrome in the hands and forearms.

Body positioning is also an important part of ergonomics. Look at Figure 2.17 in Chapter 2 on page 82 to review the correct angles at which a human body should interact with a computer at a desk to avoid body strain.

Eyestrain

Computer vision syndrome is the name given by the medical community to the array of symptoms that people experience from overusing their eyes at a computer. Symptoms can include headaches, loss of focus, burning or tired eyes, blurred or double vision, and neck and shoulder strain. Fortunately, there are some things you can do to minimize the ill effects of computer usage on your eyes.

- **Eye breaks**. As you work, take frequent "eye breaks" in which you stare off at something distant for 20 seconds every 20 minutes. You should also take longer breaks; rest your eyes for 15 minutes every two hours.
- **Lighting**. Light shining directly on a monitor can reflect back, creating glare that makes it harder to see the onscreen image. Use indirect lighting when possible, and avoid using your computer in direct sunlight or in front of a sunny window where the sun shines directly on the monitor. If glare is unavoidable, consider getting an **antiglare filter** for your monitor, to reduce reflection from your screen.
- **Positioning**. Position your monitor so that when you are sitting upright in front of the computer, the monitor is just slightly below eye level. Doing so keeps your head and eyes pointing straight forward (not tilted down or up). If you are using a notebook computer, this may not be possible; if you experience neck or eye problems, consider attaching an external monitor.
- **Refresh rate**. CRT monitors (the old, boxy types of monitors) can be run at different refresh rates. You can control that setting in the monitor's Properties in the operating system. The higher the refresh rate you use, the less flicker you will get from the screen, the more stable the image will appear, and the less eyestrain you will likely experience when looking at the monitor for long stretches at a time. Adjust the refresh rate for a CRT to at least 100 Hz if possible.
- **Resolution**. As you learned in Chapter 2, you can change the screen resolution in your operating system so that everything appears larger on your monitor (at a lower resolution). Review the section "Display Performance and Quality Factors" on page 71 for more information about changing the resolution of the display.

Activity 8.4.1

Article
Computer Vision Syndrome

Hotspot

Ergonomics for Mobile Phones

Mobile phones may be popular, but using one is not particularly good for your body. Looking at a tiny screen for long stretches can cause eyestrain, and hunching over the phone to type long text messages can place strain on your shoulders, back, and neck. The best way to avoid ergonomic problems is an obvious one: simply use the phone less. Rely instead on desktop and notebook computers to do the majority of your communicating. But if the phone is your only option, there are some things you can do to minimize the impact on your body:

- For voice calls, use hands-free headsets, rather than holding the phone up to your head or, worse yet, wedging it between your ear and your hunched-up shoulder.
- When texting, take advantage of the phone's voice recognition program, and dictate most text messages.
- When texting, don't hold the phone in your lap so that you have to bend your neck far forward to see the screen. Hold it close to your chest, so you bend less.

For more information about mobile phone ergonomics, check out http://CUT6.emcp.net/PhysioAdvisor.

Chapter 9

Understanding Your Role as a Digital Citizen: Security, Privacy, and Ethics

Chapter Goal

To understand the security, privacy, and ethical issues involved in modern computing

Learning Objectives

9.1 Assess the risks involved in using computers and networks.

9.2 Explain the threats posed by computer viruses.

9.3 Describe strategies for protecting computer systems and data.

9.4 Explain the role of ethics in computing.

9.5 Describe privacy protection issues in computing.

9.6 Discuss property protection issues in computing.

9.7 Discuss personal and social issues related to computer and Internet use.

 Green go-online icons indicate resources that are accessed from the links menu in your ebook.

 SNAP icons indicate inter-active resources that are available in SNAP. Go to your SNAP Assignments page to complete these quizzes, activities, and exercises.

9.1 Assessing the Risks of Computing

 Precheck **9.1**

Check your understanding of the concepts covered by this objective.

As we become increasingly dependent on computer systems to facilitate our jobs, our personal lives, and the infrastructures of our communities and country, the proper operation of computers becomes more important. With the explosive growth of the Internet and networks in general, an enormous body of computers and data is now accessible by members of the general public—not all of whom are trustworthy. **Cybercrime**—crime committed using a computer—has reached epic proportions. Cybercrime can include stealing corporate and personal data, using the Internet to carry out crimes such as embezzlement and fraud, and creating viruses that disrupt business operations and destroy data, hardware, and software.

To protect their systems adequately, organizations need to assess the level of security risk that they face. Two factors help determine the level of risk for an organization: threat and vulnerability. **Threat** refers to the severity of a security breach—in other words, how bad the consequences would be if the security breach occurred. Would the breach just create a minor annoyance, or would it bring the whole company to

Cybercrime—crime committed using a computer—is growing worldwide. You can make your computers and data less vulnerable to attack by implementing basic security practices, which you will learn about in this chapter.

🌀 Tracking Down Tech ⟩⟩⟩⟩⟩

Protecting Yourself against Computer and Privacy Threats

Computer security and privacy threats are all around us every day. To become more aware of these risks, you need only take a quick look at the computer devices and systems you encounter on a regular basis. Complete this scavenger hunt to discover ways that people's security and privacy are being safeguarded on computers—well, poorly, or not at all—on campus and beyond.

a halt? **Vulnerability** refers to the likelihood of a security breach of systems or data. Some types of security breaches are extremely unlikely, whereas others have a realistic chance of happening. Both factors can be plotted along a spectrum of low to high (see Figure 9.1). Plotting levels of threat and vulnerability can help an organization set its priorities for addressing security concerns.

The Internet has been likened to the physical world of the last millennium, before it was explored on a large scale. Both represent vast new territories to investigate, with great opportunities for development that can benefit people as individuals and as nations. The physical world offered explorers large expanses of land, rich with natural resources. The Internet offers an ever-expanding body of information and the ability to communicate instantly 24 hours a day.

Like the uncharted wilderness, the Internet lacks borders, and it is this inherent openness that makes it so valuable and so vulnerable at the same time. Over its short life, the Internet has grown so quickly that the legal system hasn't been able to keep pace. Legal systems aren't designed to adjust for rapid technological changes, and often, a new technology has become commonplace when laws and enforcement agencies are finally in place to govern its use.

Security is a major concern, especially in electronic commerce transactions. Businesses selling products and services over the Internet have discovered that many potential customers are reluctant to use credit cards for payment. Stories abound about hackers penetrating computer systems and using stolen credit card numbers. To ease these fears, major retail companies have instituted sophisticated encryption systems that protect customers' financial information.

Activity 9.1.1

Practice
Using a Risk Assessment Matrix

Figure 9.1

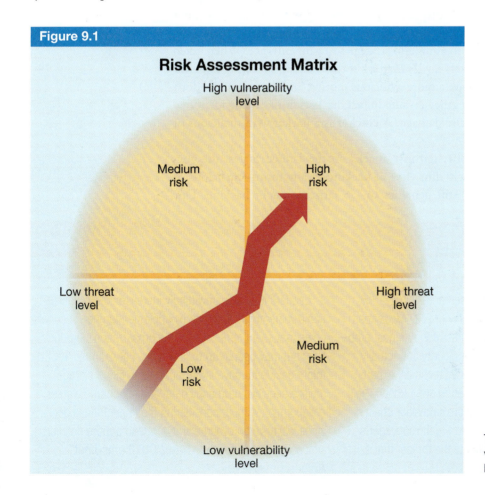

The higher the level of vulnerability and threat, the higher the level of risk.

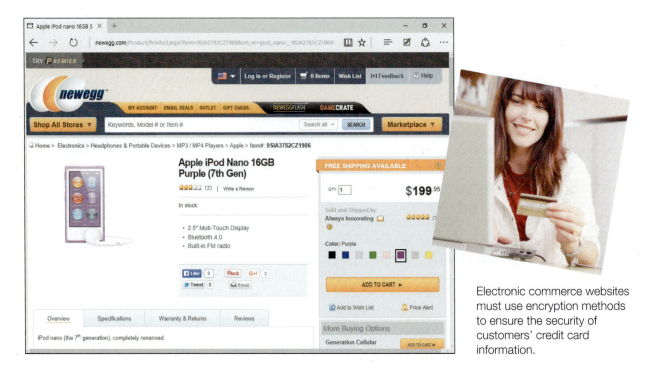

Electronic commerce websites must use encryption methods to ensure the security of customers' credit card information.

User Authentication and Unauthorized Access

Unauthorized access to a system is the most common security risk. Hackers carry out most cases of unauthorized access to computers and networks. A **hacker** is a computer expert that seeks programming, security, and system challenges. Some hackers exploit websites and programs with poor security measures in place. For more challenging sites, hackers use sophisticated programs and strategies to gain entrance. When asked why they like to hack, most hackers say it's merely for the challenge of trying to defeat security measures. They rarely have a more malicious motive, and they generally don't aim to destroy or damage the sites they invade. In fact, hackers dislike being identified with individuals who seek to cause damage. A **cracker** is a hacker with malicious or criminal intent.

Since the September 11, 2001, terrorist attacks on the United States, the government has taken an increasingly dim view of hacking in any form—malicious or not. Law enforcement imposes stiff penalties to US citizens caught hacking. Due

Tech Ethics

Uninformed Management = Vulnerable Organization

According to the 2013 State of Cybercrime Survey (co-sponsored by the US Secret Service, *CSO Magazine*, and Carnegie Mellon University), some of the biggest problems an organization faces in cybersecurity are actually problems with its management, not its technical experts. The top leaders of an organization often don't know who's responsible for cybersecurity, so there's no clear chain of accountability. Because leaders aren't technical experts themselves, they may underestimate the threats that exist, as well as their consequences.

Leaders may also unwittingly increase their organization's vulnerability to attack by implementing new technologies that seem beneficial for the organization's productivity but may open it up to new risks. For example, a CEO might decide to move important data to cloud storage, digitize sensitive hard copy data, and encourage worker collaboration without considering the impact those decisions will have on cybersecurity. To read a more detailed synopsis of the data, go to **http://CUT6.emcp.net /CybercrimeSurvey**.

A hacker is someone who gains unauthorized access to data, but he or she may not do anything malicious with it. A cracker is a hacker with malicious or criminal intent.

Learning a person's user ID and password is the most common way that hackers gain fraudulent access to a victim's data.

to the proliferation of the Internet, however, many hackers live in foreign nations and are therefore difficult to catch. Groups of international hackers sometimes also become involved in **cyberwar**: attacking sites in countries where the rival hackers live. Cyberwar has yet to prove serious, but this may change as we come to depend increasingly on the Internet.

User IDs and Passwords Most hackers focus on gaining entry over the Internet to a secure computer system by finding a working user ID and password combination. User IDs are easy to come by and are generally not secure information. Sending an email, for example, displays the sender's user ID in the return address, making it very public. The only missing element then is the password. Hackers know from experience what kinds of passwords are common, and they have programs that generate thousands of likely passwords and try them automatically over a period of hours or days. In the section "Authentication" on page 382, you will learn how to create a strong (difficult to guess) password.

System Backdoors Programmers sometimes provide another unintentional entrance to a network or information system. A **system backdoor** is a test user ID and password that provides the highest level of authorization. The "backdoor" often is created innocently in the early days of system development to allow programmers and other team members access for fixing problems. Through either negligence or design, the user ID and password are sometimes left behind in the final version of the system. Perhaps years later, when the backdoor has been forgotten, people who know about it can then enter the system, bypassing the security.

Spoofing A sophisticated way to break into a network via the Internet involves spoofing. **Spoofing** is fooling another computer by pretending to send packets from a legitimate source. It works by altering

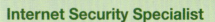

Tech Career Explorer

Internet Security Specialist

For every "black hat" villain who writes and distributes malware or hacks into a system, there is a "white hat" hero who saves the day, detecting the intrusion and creating a patch that fixes the vulnerability. If you're interested in being that hero, consider a career in network and Internet security. Many colleges and universities offer a specialty in computer security, and in such a program, you will learn the techniques that hackers, crackers, and all kinds of cybercriminals use to do their dirty work. You will also learn how you can harden your network security to keep most of them out. To learn more about this career, complete this exercise.

the address that the system automatically puts on every message sent. The address is changed to one that the receiving computer is programmed to accept as a trusted source of information.

This type of attack was very successful in the earlier days of the Internet, but now defensive systems exist to guard against spoofing. Software worms, described in the section "Avoiding Computer Viruses," on page 372, often use spoofing as a technique. The first known worm on the Internet, which was created by Robert Morris Jr. in November 1988, used spoofing to infect more than 6,000 core servers and effectively halted the Internet.

Information Theft

Information can be a company's most valuable possession. Think of a sales database, for example, listing all of a company's clients, with contact information and sales history. This database represents years of work and expensive research. A competitor who gains access to this information will have a huge advantage. He will know exactly how much to bid to gain a sale, which clients to call, and what products they like to buy.

Stealing corporate information—a crime included in the category of **industrial espionage**—is easy to do and difficult to detect. This is due in part to the invisible nature of both software and data. If someone steals a jetliner, it's easy to see that the plane isn't in the hangar. But with software, if a cracker breaks into a company network and manages to download the company database from the network onto a disk, nothing seems wrong. The original database is still in place, working the same way it did before. Even the disk containing the stolen information looks the same as it did when it was blank.

Data theft can be difficult to detect, because the data is still there after the theft has occurred. Employees and others can steal data by copying it to an optical disc or a USB drive.

For safety's sake, organizations regularly make many copies of their databases. Unfortunately, having multiple copies creates an additional security risk, because it's difficult to track the copies. If an extra backup is made one day and then simply vanishes, the crime might go undetected.

Unauthorized Data Browsing Unauthorized data browsing is a crime that involves an invasion of privacy. Workers in many organizations have access to networked databases that contain private information about people. Examples include a college admissions staffer who has access to students' transcripts and an IRS employee who has access to citizens' tax returns. Out of curiosity, or occasionally malice, these employees may "browse" through the private documents of famous individuals and personal acquaintances. Accessing this information may provide details for good lunchroom gossip, but doing so without an official reason is against the law, even if the person doing the browsing does not use that information for financial gain.

The IRS had a particularly large problem with data browsing in the late 1990s, when the activity became so common and involved so many employees that it turned into a scandal. Some employees were fired, and the rest were given specialized training in appropriate conduct.

Unauthorized Use of Wireless Networks The growing number of wireless devices has created a new opening for data theft. Wireless devices—including security cameras, smartphones, notebook computers, and input and output peripherals—are inherently less secure than wired devices. Home users, in particular, tend not to bother turning on security controls on their wireless routers, such as requiring a password to surf the web. A wired connection, such as a cable between a keyboard and a computer, can't be as easily intercepted as a wireless radio transmission. To intercept company emails on a wireless LAN, all a competitor needs to do is park a computer-laden van outside the building and listen. This is far easier than splicing into a network that's connected by wires.

Wireless devices bring with them more security risks, because they don't need to be physically connected to a network to access it. Home users, as well as business users, can help protect their data from theft by enabling security controls on their wireless routers.

In theory, a domestic Wi-Fi network comes armed with a high degree of security. The wireless router that's central to a domestic Wi-Fi network has several built-in protection features. Firewall software intercepts hackers' attempts, and encryption devices scramble data inside the network so that it isn't readable without an encryption key. Wireless networks also usually employ some type of password-based security to prevent unauthorized use. See the section "Configuring Wireless Network Security" in Chapter 6 to learn how to set up wireless security on your home Wi-Fi router.

Such features only work, however, if users activate them. The process of setting up a home wireless system can be overwhelming. By the time users get to the complicated steps involved in securing the system—changing the default password, installing the security software, turning on the encryption device—many give up or do it wrong, leaving their networks wide open.

Danger also lurks in **rogue hotspots**. A laptop user may be sitting in a trusted wireless coffee shop, unaware that the latte drinker at the next table has equipment in her backpack that's jamming the legitimate base station and sending a stronger signal with a look-alike login. When the victim logs onto the rogue hotspot, his data is ripe for the taking.

Using a motorized vehicle and a laptop, some hackers cruise the city streets in search of vulnerable networks. Using a GPS, antenna, and software readily available on the Internet, hackers can collect information on wireless access points or break into networks. This is known as **war driving**.

Consumers and business users can protect their data by taking the time to figure out how to implement the safety features of their computers, software, and networks. Industry analysts recommend making protection features more user friendly or building them into the wireless products, so it's not left to end users to "put on the armor."

Practical TECH

Ad Hoc Networks and Rogue Hotspots

Sometimes in public venues, an individual user will set up an open wireless network. When you view the list of available networks in such a venue, you might see a tempting-looking network, like the "Free Wi-Fi" one shown here.

Notice, however, the different icon for the connection. This icon indicates that the connection is an ad hoc network: one that's between computers directly and not going through an access point. This type of network is likely to be a trap designed to steal information from your computer. Don't connect to an ad-hoc network in a public venue; it won't provide Internet access, and you may put your computer at risk.

Not all rogue hotspots can be detected by looking at their icons; some may appear to be legitimate access points. When you are using the free wireless access at a public place, ask someone who works there for the name of the network, and don't connect to any network that doesn't match that name.

Denial of Service Attacks

One type of computer crime generally attributed to organized hackers is known as **denial of service (DoS) attack**. In a DoS attack, one or more hackers participate, each running multiple copies of a program that simply asks for the same information from a website over and over again—not just a few times but thousands of times a second. Soon, the system is flooded and essentially shut down (see Figure 9.2).

To understand how a DoS attack operates, think of what has to happen when you click a link on a web page or select a favorite website to visit. Your computer sends a

Activity 9.1.2

Practice
**Denial
of Service
Attack**

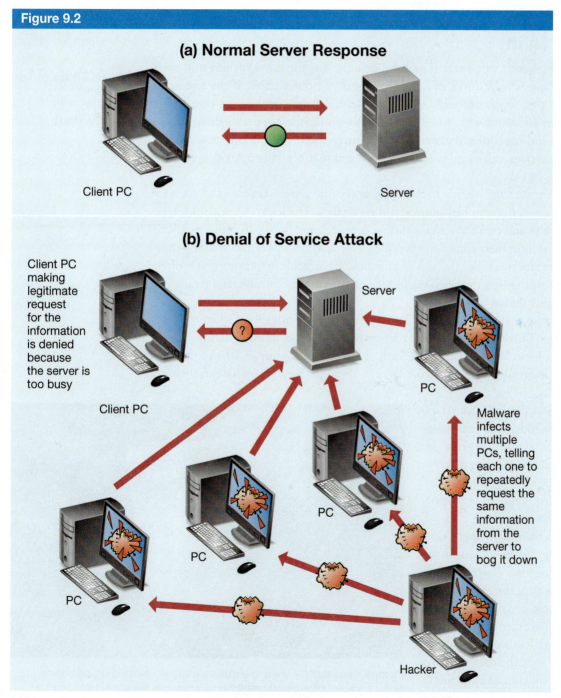

Figure 9.2

(a) Normal Server Response

Client PC   Server

(b) Denial of Service Attack

Client PC making legitimate request for the information is denied because the server is too busy

Client PC

Server

PC

Malware infects multiple PCs, telling each one to repeatedly request the same information from the server to bog it down

PC

PC

PC

Hacker

(a) Normally, when a computer makes a request of a server, the server is able to respond.
(b) In a DoS attack, multiple requests are made simultaneously, thus overwhelming the server and leaving it unable to respond.

message to the host computer, generally asking for the information stored on the home page. To respond to your request, the host computer sends the information across the Internet, and your computer then displays it on the screen. This process works fine if a reasonable number of people ask for the information simultaneously, but if thousands of requests are received, even by the fastest computers, things slow down.

Have you ever gone to a website and had to wait a very long time for the page to load, even though it usually works quickly, and the other sites you have been surfing have popped right up? This delay usually occurs because many people are requesting the same information that you are. Imagine the system overload if thousands of requests are arriving each second.

Identity Theft

Hackers and crackers who break into websites and cause them to slow down or even shut down have several direct effects on personal computer users. If the site is an e-commerce site, legitimate users will be prevented from ordering products. The greater danger associated with hacking into websites is the theft of personal credit card information and other private data. Called **identity theft**, this hacking crime is the one that the average citizen probably fears most and that prevents many people from buying goods online.

Identity theft occurs when a hacker gains entry into a web database and copies a person's social security number, address, and credit data. The hacker then assumes the person's identity and uses the stolen personal data to apply for credit cards, a driver's license, and so on. Then comes the spending spree, which leaves the victim with a long list of unexpected bills. This sort of crime can be difficult to unravel, and it often leaves the victim with a damaged credit rating and years of bureaucratic wrangling with credit institutions.

Another way that individuals can lose control of their private information is by giving it away. **Phishing** is an activity that involves attempts to fraudulently acquire another person's sensitive information, such as a credit card number. The term refers to the use of increasingly sophisticated lures to "fish" for users' financial information and passwords.

In a typical phishing situation, the criminal sends an official-looking email or instant message in which she masquerades as a trustworthy person or business. The message often appears legitimate and may even include a copy of a legitimate company's logo. The unsuspecting victim is asked to click on a link that directs him to another web page, on which he is asked to enter a password, credit card number, or other personal data. Once the data has been submitted, the criminal uses the data to make credit card purchases, transfer funds from the victim's bank account, or engage in other illegal activities.

Activity 9.1.3

Article
Identity Theft

By stealing a person's online credentials, a cybercriminal can gain access to all the personal information and financial resources those credentials unlock. Once the thief has a social security number and other personal information, she usually wracks up huge debts in the victim's name.

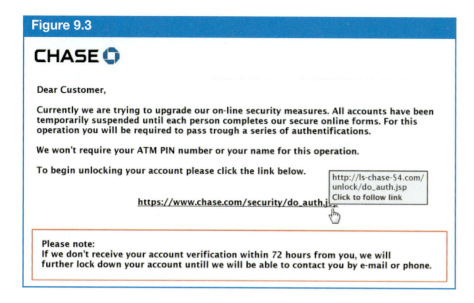

Figure 9.3

This phishing email is attempting to get the recipient to disclose private information in an online form. Although the logo looks almost exactly like the logo of a well-known bank, several clues in the email suggest that the message didn't come from the bank.

Figure 9.3 shows a phishing email that looks like it's from a reputable bank, but several clues indicate that it's not. For example, the email contains several typographical errors and awkwardly worded sentences. The entire email is also in bold type, which isn't customary in professional communications. Even though the URL listed in the email appears to be from the bank's own website, hovering the mouse pointer over the URL shows a ScreenTip that indicates that the hyperlink's actual address is a completely different site. The email threatens to "lock down" the account—something a bank would never do if you didn't comply with an email. It's also unlikely a bank would use the words *lock down* to describe this action. Finally, it's generally not customary for a bank to require customers to complete any types of online forms, so any email you receive asking to update your account information is likely fraudulent.

Consumers can decrease the chance of having their credit card information stolen by dealing only with web merchants who encrypt credit card numbers and other private data. Recall that a secure site is indicated by an *s* following *http* in the URL. It's important for users to protect themselves from phishing attempts by critically reading any request before responding with private information. Users should never provide sensitive, private information without confirming the legitimacy of the request.

Employee Theft

Although accurate estimates are difficult to pinpoint, businesses certainly lose millions of dollars a year in stolen computer hardware and software. In large organizations, such theft often goes unnoticed or unreported. Someone takes a computer or a scanner home for legitimate use, and then leaves the job sometime later but keeps the device. Sometimes, employees take components to add to their home PC systems. And occasionally, thieves break into businesses and haul computers away. Such thefts cost far more than the price of the stolen hardware. They also involve the cost of replacing the lost data (if, indeed, the data is replaceable), the cost of the time lost while the machines are gone, and the cost of installing new machines and training people to use them.

Mobile computing has created new opportunities for computer theft, as the devices are smaller and more easily taken. In response to this threat, employers are stepping up efforts to monitor employees, using security systems of the types outlined in the following section on security strategies.

Recheck 9.1

Recheck your understanding of the concepts covered by this objective.

9.2 Avoiding Computer Viruses

One familiar form of risk to computer security is the computer virus. Recall from earlier chapters that a computer **virus** is a program written by a hacker or cracker that's designed to perform some kind of trick on an unsuspecting victim. In some cases, the trick is mild, such as drawing an offensive image on the screen or changing all the characters in a document to another language. Sometimes, the trick is much more severe, such as reformatting the hard drive and erasing all data or damaging the motherboard so it can't operate properly.

Worms are often confused with viruses, but they operate in quite a different fashion. Rather than add itself to another program and wait for a user to execute an attachment or open a file with a macro, a **worm** (also called a *software worm*) actively attempts to move and copy itself. Operating in most cases on the Internet, a worm uses spoofing techniques to fool computers into accepting and executing copies. The worm then transmits itself to other machines and performs its prime function, whatever that may be. Today, worms are commonly used as hacking devices. They seek computer systems to break into and leave a route for later entry by a hacker or cracker.

Who Creates Viruses and Worms?

Together, viruses and worms are a form of computer vandalism. They are destructive and attack victims randomly, often causing millions of dollars in damage. Viruses have effects that range from annoying to catastrophic. Nuisance viruses, espionage viruses, and data-destructive viruses are the common types of viruses that may be encountered.

An interesting note is that computers running Microsoft Windows are more prone to viruses than those running the Mac OS. This vulnerability may be because Windows is more popular and therefore targeted as a platform on which a virus can spread more easily, or it may be because of anti-Microsoft sentiment among some radical programmers who believe that all software should be free.

According to FBI profiling, the typical virus or worm creator in the past was a young, male computer science major working on a graduate degree. In some circles, creating and releasing a virus, like hacking, is a "rite of passage." Some virus creators are trying to express their creativity, and others are responding to increased antivirus capabilities by finding new methods to inflict damage.

More and more often, however, viruses are written for the purposes of selling products that are basically without value. Today, viruses and worms are constantly being created and defeated. The Internet has accelerated the rate of virus creation and distribution, but at the same time helped speed up the distribution of defenses against them.

Viruses and the Law

When someone steals or damages another person's physical property, it's a prosecutable offense. But what about cybercrimes, such as intrusion or theft involving data or communications lines? This is an area in which the legislative bodies of governments struggle to keep up with the times.

In the United States, the Electronic Communications Privacy Act of 1986 makes it illegal to intercept and make public any private communications over computer networks and telephone lines. In addition, the Computer Fraud and Abuse Act of 1986 provides stiff penalties for breaking into a computer system or intercepting an electronic transmission to copy, alter, or destroy data. Most cybercrimes involving hacking and data leaks are covered by one of these federal acts.

 Precheck 9.2

Check your understanding of the concepts covered by this objective.

 Activity 9.2.1

Video
Software Worms

Legal sanctions against individuals who create and spread viruses have taken awhile to develop, however. Federal legislation has dealt mainly with offenses against government-owned computers and networks. Therefore, almost every state has adopted its own legislation to punish individuals who spread viruses. Virus creators can also be punished under statutes aimed at property damage, rather than computer viruses.

How Viruses Infect Systems

A virus can't enter a computer uninvited. It must enter disguised in another file (usually an email attachment or a download from a website). A virus typically hides in the binary code of an executable file, and its instructions are executed when the program runs. Viruses may also reside on storage media and even on legitimate copies of software direct from manufacturers.

Many viruses today are transmitted as attachments to email messages sent over the Internet. When a user opens an attachment infected with a virus, the virus is installed on the computer and unleashed to do its damage. New viruses appear every day, because they are easy to create and can spread across the globe in a few days through the use of flash drives, email, and network or Internet contamination (see Figure 9.4).

A virus hides in the executable code for a program file and executes when the program runs.

 **Activity 9.2.2**

Video
Email Viruses

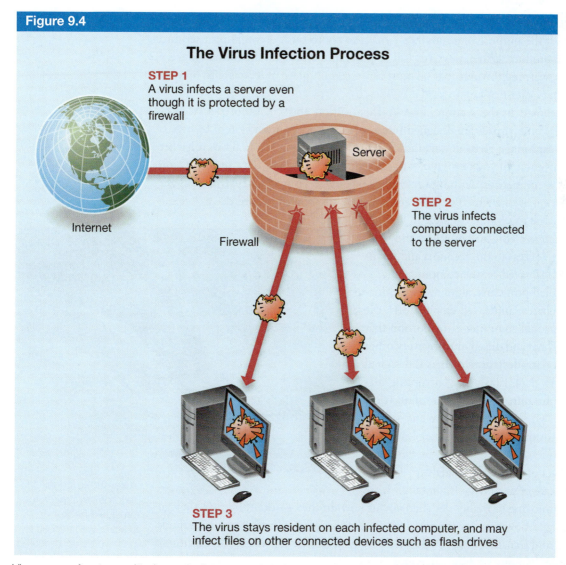

Figure 9.4

The Virus Infection Process

STEP 1
A virus infects a server even though it is protected by a firewall

Server

Internet

Firewall

STEP 2
The virus infects computers connected to the server

STEP 3
The virus stays resident on each infected computer, and may infect files on other connected devices such as flash drives

Viruses are often transmitted over the Internet and through shared devices such as flash drives.

Some of the signs of a virus infection are as follows:

- When booting your computer, an error message is displayed requiring a reboot or not allowing you to boot up at all.
- Some of your files become corrupted and suddenly don't work properly.
- A specific program (such as Microsoft Word or Excel) doesn't operate properly.
- Programs or files have suddenly vanished.
- Unknown programs or other files appear on your hard drive.
- Strange messages or images display on your monitor.
- Your system has less available memory or disk space than it should.
- A disk or volume name has been changed.
- Unexpected sounds or music are played at random times.
- You receive the same email message repeatedly from the same people.

You can protect your computer from viruses in several ways. One way is to use antivirus software on a regular basis. In addition, users can avoid viruses in email by simply not reading spam and by never clicking a link or downloading an attachment from an unknown source.

Types of Viruses

A **nuisance virus** usually does no real damage but rather is just an inconvenience. In most cases, the purpose of a nuisance virus is to try to bully a computer user into purchasing a product. Often, the virus will be programmed to pop up a window every few minutes, warning the user that he must buy a certain piece of software to prevent some imaginary catastrophe.

As you learned in the section "User Authentication and Unauthorized Access," on page 364, some viruses are designed to create a backdoor into a system to bypass security. An **espionage virus** doesn't inflict immediate damage, but it allows a hacker or cracker to enter the system later for the purpose of stealing data or spying on the work of a competitor. A common type of espionage virus is a **keystroke logger** (also called a *keylogger*), which stores every typed keystroke on the hard drive. Later, a hacker can access this file and analyze it, looking for things such as credit card numbers and passwords to allow access to the accounts and financial information saved on the computer.

The installed programs, along with the documents, databases, and saved emails, form the heart of a personal computer—the portion that makes it personal and different from every other computer. A **data-destructive virus** is designed to destroy this data. Erasing or corrupting files so that they are unreadable is a common trick. Some viruses go for the easy route and simply attempt to format the entire drive, leaving it blank. Data-destructive viruses can eliminate computer data or make it unreadable.

A keystroke logger records keystrokes to provide a hacker or cracker with access to passwords and secured information at a later time.

Viruses can create effects that range from minor and annoying to highly destructive, but how do they work? Where do they go on the disk, and how are they launched by another program? The following methods of operating and transmission provide another way of classifying viruses. Some viruses fall into more than one of these categories.

Tech Ethics

Ransomware

Ransomware is the term coined for malicious code that tries to extort cash from victims. In ransomware, a program will seize control of a computer until the user agrees to the attacker's demands. The extortion usually calls for the victim to transfer funds via e-gold or another money transfer service. Some famous examples include the following:

- The Kovter Lock Screen program scares a victim by pretending to be a federal agency that has shut down his or her computer because it may have been used to download and distribute illegal content. The program tries to extort money from the victim to resolve the case without prosecution.

- The Archiveus program holds a user's data for ransom, telling victims that they must purchase a certain amount of pharmaceutical drugs from a Russian online drug store in order to get their files back. Archiveus sneaks into a computer's My Documents folder, where it scrambles all the files and deletes the originals. An attached ransom text file lets victims know that they can obtain a password to unscramble their files by purchasing from one of three overseas pharmacies.

- In a similar vein, Ransom.A attacks a computer and then threatens to destroy one file every minute until victims wire $10.99 via Western Union to a specified account.

- DigiKeyGen finds its victims by appealing to people's baser instincts. This program pops up as an advertisement promising access to a free pornographic website. Once downloaded, it covertly installs software that generates nonstop hard core ads. Then it offers to sell victims an antispyware program for $49.99 to clean up the mess.

Security software experts say that much of ransomware is "more bark than bite." The key to unlocking files is usually somewhere in the ransomware file itself. In the case of Archiveus, an antivirus company cracked the code within weeks and put the solution online.

Even if the threat or demand is a bluff, there's always a first wave of victims who fall prey to ransomware. Antispyware experts emphasize the importance of creating backups for systems and files—and to always be suspicious of something for nothing.

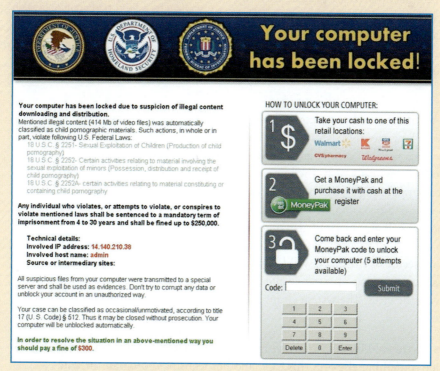

A type of ransomware called the *Kovter Lock Screen program* uses official language and logos to imitate a federal agency, trying to scare victims into paying bogus fines for downloading and distributing suspicious content with their computers.

Polymorphic Viruses Some viruses, in order to counter detection and prevention methods, are programmed to change themselves and their behaviors to fool the programs meant to stop them. This type of virus is called a **polymorphic virus** (or *variant virus*).

Stealth Viruses A **stealth virus** tries to hide from the software designed to find and destroy it. A stealth virus masks the size of the file it's hiding in by copying itself out of the file to another location on the victim's hard drive. Some varieties of stealth viruses avoid detection by disabling the antivirus software on the computer, either completely or partly.

Macro Viruses A macro is a small program that allows users to customize and automate certain functions in an application. Microsoft Word, Access, and Excel allow users to create macros, for example.

A **macro virus** is written specifically for one program, such as Microsoft Word. The program becomes infected when it opens a file with the virus stored in its macros. The applications will sometimes give a warning, asking if the macros should be activated. If the user clicks *Yes* and activates the macros in the infected document, the macros will then infect the application, which means every file created or edited using that application on that computer will also be infected. Reinstalling the application will remove the virus, but the program will become infected again the moment it opens an old file containing the virus. A macro virus usually does little harm, but it can be difficult to remove.

Macro viruses were a serious threat at one time, but Microsoft now takes steps to protect users by employing macro security within each application. Microsoft has also made the default file format for each application a type that doesn't allow viruses, making the virus-capable file format available as an alternative.

Hands On

Exploring Macro Security Settings in Word

In Microsoft Word 2016, you can choose whether macros can or can't run in documents. You can also distinguish between digitally signed macros (which are verified by a third-party authentication service to be harm free) and nonsigned macros. Follow the steps in this resource to see how Word 2016 protects against macro viruses.

Boot Sector Viruses The **boot sector** of a hard disk contains a variety of information, including how the disk is organized and whether it's capable of loading an operating system. When a disk is left in a drive and the computer reboots, the operating system automatically reads the boot sector to learn about that disk and to attempt to start any operating system on that disk. A **boot sector virus** is designed to alter the boot sector of a disk, so that whenever the operating system reads the boot sector, the computer will automatically become infected.

Fortunately, most boot sector viruses can be easily detected, since the size and nature of the boot sector of a disk are well known and normally don't change much. Antivirus software can identify any strange alteration, warn the user, and provide the option of removing the virus. The system cleans the disk by simply rewriting a normal boot sector onto it.

Trojan Horse Viruses Like its namesake from a Greek legend, a **Trojan horse virus** hides inside something else—in this case, another legitimate program or data file. This type of virus is quite common with downloaded games and other types of shareware files, such as screen savers. Sometimes, even downloaded movie clips and audio files can be infected. The downloaded file may install and run without a problem, but unknown to the victim, a virus is included in the software, installing itself with the other files. The virus may cause damage immediately, or it may delay acting for a time.

To prevent infecting your computer with a Trojan horse virus, it's a good idea to download shareware programs from the original creator's website or a site the creator recommends. Other sites, such as fan sites, may be less monitored. The bottom line? Make sure you trust the website from which you are downloading software.

Multipartite Viruses A **multipartite virus** is named for its ability to attack a computer in several different ways. The virus may first infect the boot sector and then move on to become a Trojan horse type by infecting a disk file. Multipartite viruses are more sophisticated and therefore more difficult to guard against than other types of viruses. They are also more rarely encountered.

Logic Bomb Viruses A successful computer virus, like a successful biological virus, must spread before it can kill the host. If a biological virus killed its first victim more or less instantly, it wouldn't have a chance to infect more people. The same is true of a **logic bomb virus** (also called a *time bomb virus*), which typically doesn't act immediately but rather sits quietly dormant, waiting for a specific event or set of conditions to occur.

A famous logic bomb virus was the widely publicized Michelangelo virus, which infected personal computers and caused them to display a message on the artist's birthday. A destructive type of logic bomb virus that occasionally has been built into systems involves placing a virus within a company's employee database. The virus is tied to a specific employee and programmed to "explode" when the employee is terminated, thus destroying the database.

Named after the Trojan horse from a Greek legend, a Trojan horse virus hides within a legitimate program or data file but contains instructions that perform harmful actions.

A logic bomb virus works like a time bomb, waiting to explode at a specific time.

 Recheck 9.2
Recheck your understanding of the concepts covered by this objective.

9.3 Protecting Computer Systems and Data

Our increasing reliance on computer-based systems means a corresponding rise in threats to computer security. If online banking and shopping are the norm, for example, it only makes sense that bank robbers and shoplifters will be online. The increasing complexity of the Internet and the constantly changing technologies also leave new gaps for cyber rogues to slip through.

As the Internet has evolved and computer technology has become more sophisticated, IT managers, computer experts, and security specialists have developed security strategies to prevent damage and losses. These strategies are covered in the following sections.

 Precheck 9.3
Check your understanding of the concepts covered by this objective.

 Activity 9.3.1

Article
Protecting the Internet from Terrorists

Locking cables can secure mobile computing devices to fixed objects to deter theft.

Physical Security

One important way to mitigate the risk of security breaches is to physically protect computing devices. Physical security has two major components: the locations of devices and the use of locking equipment. Expensive or mission-critical equipment should be located in a controlled-access building or room. Biometric or security card access can be used to control who is authorized to enter a computing area. For notebook and laptop computers, a locking cable should be used when the device will be unattended. The cable, which connects to the computer, should be secured to a fixed point, such as a heavy desk or shelf.

Firewalls

Developed originally to prevent security breaches such as spoofing and hacking, firewalls run on computers that are attached directly to the Internet, as was explained in Chapters 3 and 6. A firewall will generally allow normal web browser operations but will prevent many other types of communication. It works similarly to a security guard at a private club who checks membership cards before allowing people in.

A firewall checks incoming data against a list of known, trusted sources. If a packet doesn't fit the profile of anything on the list, then it's rejected. If there's a special need for an additional piece of software that uses an unconventional route to transmit data into the system, the firewall's "trusted" list can be altered to allow it to accept the incoming data. Most employers have firewalls for their networks, which is why computer games and certain other consumer-type programs may not operate properly in the workplace.

Activity 9.3.2

Video
Firewalls

Network Sniffers

A **network sniffer** is a software package that displays network traffic data. It can be used to spy and monitor, or to prevent unauthorized activity. In the workplace, for example, it shows which resources employees are using and the websites they are visiting. Network sniffers can also be used to troubleshoot network connections and improve system performance.

Most network administrators run a network sniffer all the time, so while you are on a network, keep in mind that somewhere, someone likely has the power to look over your shoulder. Although abuses of older technology (such as telephones and written mail) are forbidden by strict laws, online privacy rights are still emerging.

Browser Security Settings

Most web browsers have security settings designed to minimize the risk that websites with malicious code will infect or harm the user's computer. Most of these settings are enabled by default, but you can adjust them.

Figure 9.5 shows Internet Explorer's Internet Options dialog box, in which you can set security settings on the Security tab. Each icon at the top of the Security tab represents a security zone. A zone represents a certain level of trust in the site. You can specify which zone a certain site belongs to. If a site isn't assigned to a zone, it falls under the Internet zone. After selecting a zone, you can drag the *Security level for this zone* slider up or down to change the settings for that zone. Other browsers offer equivalent security features to those in Internet Explorer, but not all browsers enable you to configure different settings for multiple zones.

When you adjust the security level for a site, you change the settings for various types of active content on web pages, such as Java, Flash, and **ActiveX** controls. Each of these is a type of program that runs on a web page. Each is useful but can potentially open up the computer to security threats of varying levels. In the security settings

Figure 9.5

Internet Explorer offers security presets for different levels of trust assigned to sites.

for a level, a content type is set to *Enable*, *Disable*, or *Prompt*. The *Prompt* setting causes IE to display a dialog box when that content type tries to run, asking you what to do each time.

ActiveX controls are perhaps the most risky of these types, because they copy files to your hard disk that persist after the browser is closed. Because of this risk, a security system called *signing* certifies an ActiveX control to be harm free. IE's security settings permit more liberal security to signed ActiveX controls than unsigned ones. For a full picture of the security settings and how they change with a particular level choice, click the Custom Level button in the Internet Options dialog box.

To make users less vulnerable to phishing scams, a browser may include antiphishing tools. In IE, this tool is the SmartScreen Filter. It is a **phishing filter** that works by comparing a site's URL to a list of known phishing sites and alerting the user if there's a match. This tool also scans the pages you visit for suspicious signs that the site might not be legitimate. This feature is enabled by default in IE.

Antivirus Software

Because viruses often corrupt or erase data and open up systems to unauthorized access, every computer system should have antivirus software, such as that provided in Symantec Endpoint Protection. This software is quite successful in detecting and removing known viruses.

The trouble with any antivirus software is that it can detect only viruses with known signatures. A **virus signature** is a telltale string of characters that can be used to identify a particular virus. There are 10 to 20 new viruses reported daily, and your virus program must be updated with the latest signatures to protect against them. Most antivirus software updates itself online automatically. Antivirus software was covered in more detail in Chapter 3.

Data Backups

One crucial element of any prevention scheme is to be prepared for the worst. What if a fire burns up your company's offices and computers? Will all employees have recent backups on hand to replace their critical files? Backing up data and placing the backup in a safe spot are necessary chores, because if antivirus software misses a bug or if a disaster occurs, you don't want to be left with nothing.

 **Activity 9.3.3**

Article
Virus Detection and Prevention

Practical TECH ⚙️✳️⚙️✳️⚙️✳️⚙️

National Cyber Security Alliance

There are lots of little things you can do to your computer that will add up to having a much safer computing environment, such as boosting your browser security settings, making sure your firewall is active, and being cautious when opening email with suspicious attachments. One great resource for learning more about personal computer security is the Stay Safe Online website (**http://CUT6 .emcp.net/StaySafeOnline**), sponsored by the National Cyber Security Alliance. There you will find articles about many types of threats, tip sheets and white papers, and the latest information about new ways that criminals are finding to break through people's computing defenses.

Organizations can choose from many backup methods. Beyond the obvious move of having a complete copy of programs and data in a safe place, companies tend to take additional measures, particularly concerning the primary database. If something goes wrong with the backup, a company may find itself out of business quickly. Organizations normally keep more than one backup of important databases and update the backups on a daily or weekly basis.

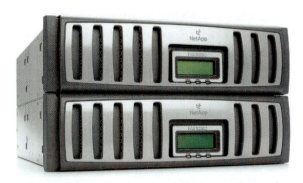

An external backup appliance helps protect system data.

To create a more reliable backup, some companies employ a **rotating backup** scheme. For example, a company might have seven copies of data, one for each day of the week. On the eighth day—for example, on Monday morning—the administrator takes the previous Monday's backup and overwrites it, saving the new backup on an old tape and erasing the oldest copy. This scheme has several advantages. It saves time, as only one backup needs to be made per day. Also, if the database is lost or corrupted, many copies exist, some of which may predate the beginning of the problem. For example, if a virus infects a database on Thursday and isn't detected until the following Monday, it will be possible to reload Wednesday's version and go back to a safe, clean copy with no virus in it.

One major issue with backing up is redundancy. If you back up the same 10,000 files each day, perhaps only 100 of those files will change on any given day. That means you are backing up 9,900 files that haven't changed—files that are already included in the previous day's backup set. To alleviate this problem, many companies use differential or incremental backups.

An **incremental backup** includes only the files that have changed since the last backup of any kind. For example, you might do a full backup on Monday, and then an incremental backup on each subsequent day. Each file has an *Archive* attribute that can be set on or off. When a file changes, the operating system flips on the *Archive* attribute automatically. When a backup program performs a full backup, it flips off the *Archive* attribute for every file. Then, during an incremental backup, it backs up only the files for which the *Archive* attribute is on, and it turns off the *Archive* attribute for the files it backs up. With an incremental backup, you save the maximum amount of time and media, because no files are backed up except those that aren't included in another backup set. However, if disaster strikes and you have to restore files, you may have to restore them from several backup sets. For example, if the system crashes on Thursday, you will first restore Monday's backup set, then Tuesday's set, and then Wednesday's set.

A **differential backup** offers a compromise between efficiency and convenience. It backs up only the files that have changed since the last *full* backup. When it backs them up, it doesn't turn off the *Archive* flag, so each file remains marked to be backed up until the next full backup is performed. So, for example, you might do a full backup on Monday, and then a differential backup on each subsequent day of the week. If the system crashes on Thursday, you will first restore Monday's backup set and then Wednesday's backup, and you will have an up-to-date copy again.

A company may employ a special computer system called a **backup appliance** that's designed specifically for performing and storing backups. Such an appliance may be configured to perform **deduplication** operations, which reduce the amount of redundancy in a backup set by not backing up identical copies of certain folders and files multiple times. Unlike a simple incremental or differential backup, which simply looks at each file's *Archive* attribute to determine whether to back it up, deduplication software examines each file to be backed up, and if an identical copy of it is already backed up, the software uses a pointer to refer to the existing copy, rather than re-copy it to the backup set. In a large organization, a deduplication-capable backup appliance can save a great deal of time and money.

A Disaster Recovery Plan

A **disaster recovery plan** is a safety system that allows a company to restore its systems after a complete loss of data. A companywide disaster recovery plan details how the company will respond to various disasters, including how it will recover lost data.

A disaster recovery plan typically answers these questions:

- What data backup procedures will the company follow on a daily and weekly basis to ensure that data is consistently backed up? You learned about some of the options for backup plans in the previous section.
- Where will data backups be stored to ensure they will be safe if the building is destroyed? A company may have a procedure in place in which an employee manually carries backed-up data media to another location, or the data may be backed up via a network or Internet connection to a remote location.
- What storage-level appliances or drives will be used to make sure data lost due to a failure of the storage medium can be recovered? The most common storage-level protection used is redundant array of inexpensive disks (RAID), covered in Chapter 3.
- When a disaster occurs, what procedure will be followed for getting the most critical data and computer systems back up as quickly as possible?

A disaster recovery plan should include a clear chain of accountability, as well as a detailed procedure for each type and scope of disaster.

Authentication

Authentication is the process of proving that a user is who he says he is, and confirming that he is authorized to access an account. The stronger the authentication mechanism, the more secure the system. Common forms of authentication include personal identification numbers (PINs), user IDs and passwords, smart cards, and biometrics.

Personal Identification Numbers A personal identification number (PIN) is a number that is used in place of a password for authentication before completing certain transactions. For example, an automated teller machine (ATM) card is issued with a PIN that the customer types into a numeric keypad. The card itself has an account number printed on it, and a magnetic strip with that same number encoded on it. Because only the owner of the card should know the PIN, access to the account is granted when the correct PIN is entered for the card that was inserted.

An ATM requires a digitally encoded card combined with a PIN for access to an account.

User IDs and Passwords A major player in nearly every computer security system is the combination of a user ID and password. The user ID is the known portion of the combination: the identification of the user relative to which account the user is seeking access. The password is the core security element that's used as authentication. The user ID is generally publicly known. The password is secret—the part that a hacker or other type of criminal seeks.

Since a password is a critical element of any security system, it's important to create one that isn't easily guessed. A good password has two somewhat contradictory characteristics: It must be easy to remember and hard to guess. A password that's hard to guess is known as a **strong password**. It is simple to think of a long, random string of letters and numbers that no one would ever guess, but while this password is definitely strong, it is not a good password unless you can remember it. A password is of little use to a user who forgets it. A complicated password tends to leave the user no option but to write it down, which is a major breach of security.

It's just as easy to come up with a password that's of no value because it's so obvious. This type of password errs on the side of being memorable, but again provides little security because anyone can come up with it by guessing. For this reason, a password that's identical to the user ID, the name of the user, or some other familiar thing in the user's life is a weak choice. Other types of ineffective, generic passwords are words such as *password* and *qwerty* (made by typing an obvious sequence of letters on the keyboard).

To create a secure, memorable password, use one or two common or familiar words connected with a number or other symbol, or substitute numbers or symbols for one or two letters in a familiar word, mixing up uppercase and lowercase letters. Examples include the following:

light3n1ng
dog+wingS
justice&acquittal
5COW&duck5

Smart Cards Authentication to computer systems can also be provided by the technology in smart cards. A **smart card** is a plastic card, similar to a credit card, that contains stored information in a computer chip inside it. This information can be used to authenticate a user on a computer system, to allow access to a building or secured area, to provide information about the holder of the card, and so on. Some smart cards are swiped in card readers, whereas others with radio frequency identification (RFID) enabled chips just need to be in proximity to the computer to authenticate the user and provide access to the system. Smart cards provide quicker access to systems than typing in a user ID and password, but there are security drawbacks, since there is no proof that the person with the smart card is the owner of it.

Biometrics Many companies now use biometric authentication systems to make sure that only authorized employees are allowed to enter secure areas, such as research buildings. A **biometric identifier** is a physical attribute that's unique to an individual and can be used to authenticate identity. Through a biometric authentication system, a computer can effectively measure a biometric identifier such as a voice, a fingerprint, hand geometry, facial geometry, a retinal pattern, an iris pattern, or a handwritten signature. Biometric devices automatically recognize human beings in a variety of ways. Essentially, each device focuses on one characteristic or body part and uses a computer to compare known patterns against a measurement taken by the device.

A **fingerprint scanner** makes a digital image of a person's fingerprint, like a scanner or copier makes an image of a page. A computer then compares the image against a known set of fingerprint images stored in a database. If the image matches up, the system knows who is requesting access and will act appropriately. A fingerprint scanner

Activity 9.3.4

Video
Biometric Identification

Encryption Methods Many different encryption methods may be used for coding and decoding data, and an encryption key may use more than one method. Table 9.1 illustrates four ways data can be encrypted.

The two basic types of encryption methods are secret key (also called *private key*) and public key encryption. With **secret key encryption**, both the customer and the business use the same encryption key to encrypt and decrypt the data. **Public key encryption** uses two encryption keys: a public encryption key, which all authorized users know, and a secret encryption key, which only the sender and the receiver know. For example, a public key might be used to encrypt customer data being transmitted, and upon receipt of the data, a secret key might be used to decrypt it. A popular public encryption technology used to transmit data over the Internet is **RSA**, named for its developers, Rivest, Shamir, and Adleman.

Encryption Protocols Several security and encryption technologies have been developed to ensure the protection and confidentiality of personal data and messages being transmitted over the Internet.

Secure Sockets Layer (SSL) and **Transport Layer Security (TLS)** are cryptographic protocols that provide secure communications on the Internet for transmitting data such as that used in credit card activities, emails, faxes, and banking transactions. The two protocols are very similar; TLS is SSL's successor, and was originally released as an upgrade to SSL. Each uses two keys to encrypt data: a public key known to everyone and a private or secret key known only to the recipient of the message. URLs that use the SSL or TLS protocol start with *https* instead of *http* (see Figure 9.7). **Hypertext Transfer Protocol Secure (HTTPS)** is a secure form of Hypertext Transfer Protocol (HTTP) that provides encryption for data sent through a web-based connection.

Table 9.1 Ways Data Can Be Encrypted

Encryption Method	Word in Plaintext (English Format)	Word in Ciphertext (Coded Format)	Explanation
Replaces characters with different characters.	COMPUTER	XMRCEYLZ	Each character is replaced with a different character.
Inserts an extra character after each character.	JOHN	JBOBHBNB	The letter *B* is inserted after each character.
Removes and stores characters.	INFORMATION	INFRMAION	Every fourth letter (*O, T*) is removed and stored.
Switches characters.	PAYMENT	APMYNET	Beginning at the left, pairs of letters are reversed.

Figure 9.7

Sites that use SSL or TLS have URLs that begin with *https* instead of *http*.

Another protocol for transmitting data securely over the World Wide Web is **Secure HTTP (S-HTTP)**. Whereas SSL and TLS create a secure connection between a client and a server, over which any amount of data can be sent securely, S-HTTP is designed to transmit individual messages securely.

These technologies can be seen as complementary rather than competing. All three have been approved by the Internet Engineering Task Force (IETF) as standards.

Monitoring and Auditing

Companies realize that unauthorized access to systems and information may come from inside the organization. Many companies have implemented monitoring of employees' online and offline activities while at work. Software packages used for monitoring include keystroke loggers (discussed in the section "Avoiding Computer Viruses," on page 372) and Internet traffic trackers, which record the web sites that employees visit for later auditing. Some employers also use video surveillance through webcams or closed circuit cameras to observe activities that occur around critical systems or data storage areas.

In the United States, privacy laws are quite lax in the area of preventing video surveillance. In many states, there are essentially no laws preventing someone from videotaping even a person's most private moments without his knowledge. Court battles are underway and new laws are being written, but the process is slow and action is unlikely until there is a high-publicity case. In the meantime, employers are videotaping their employees and store owners are carefully watching customers. In

 **Activity 9.3.5**

Article
Surveillance Technologies

Practical TECH

Heartbleed

SSL and TLS are fairly secure, but they aren't immune to attack. This was proven in 2014, when the Heartbleed security bug was discovered to have made vulnerable up to half a million secure servers that relied on OpenSSL, a widely used version of TLS. This vulnerability left 17 percent of the Internet's secure web servers open to the theft of private information, including user passwords. (Not every vulnerable computer was actually attacked.)

In a nutshell, here's how Heartbleed did its dirty work. TLS links computers by having one computer send a "heartbeat request" message, usually a text string, along with the string's length. For example, it might send the text string "dog" and the string length "3." The receiving computer then sends back the same thing, and that's how the computers know they are in sync. The Heartbleed exploit sends a malformed heartbeat request that contains a small string and a misreported long length. For example, it might send the text string "dog" and the string length "497." The receiving server returns the short string as it was sent, but then also returns 497 letters of extra information that it happens to have in its active memory—which might be anything. It might

be sensitive information, like a credit card number or a user name and password, or it might be junk. But if the attacker is patient and repeats the process thousands of times, information might be acquired that can be used for financial gain or privacy invasion.

Forbes columnist Joseph Steinberg wrote, "Some might argue that [Heartbleed] is the worst vulnerability found (at least in terms of its potential impact) since commercial traffic began to flow on the Internet." Server administrators worked quickly to apply patches and warn users, but the entire web industry was shaken to its core by the broad scope of the servers affected, the huge potential for security and privacy damages, and most of all, that nobody saw it coming. Heartbleed serves as a reminder not to rely too much on computer security keeping your data 100 percent safe.

many states, it isn't illegal for employers to monitor the activity of their employees in many different ways. If there are restrictions, companies can easily get around them by having employees sign a waiver as a condition of employment, allowing the monitoring without consent. Many people don't realize what they are signing when they take that new job.

Auditing involves a review of monitoring data and system logins to look for unauthorized access and suspicious behavior. A security or audit officer typically reviews reports created by keystroke loggers, Internet traffic analyzers, and usage of systems. The officer is looking for abnormal patterns of behavior or login failures that suggest inappropriate access to data. The gathered data can provide evidence in prosecuting an attacker, and may also indicate areas of system vulnerability that need to be reviewed and improved.

9.4 Understanding the Role of Ethics

Ethics are the principles we use to determine the right and wrong things to do in our lives. Most ethical beliefs are learned during childhood and are derived from family, society, and religious tradition. For example, many people in our society hold to the belief that telling a lie, stealing, driving under the influence of alcohol, and exhibiting racist behavior are ethically wrong behaviors. If we have internalized a code of ethical principles, we grow up instinctively knowing the right thing to do without consciously reflecting on the ethical basis for our decisions.

 Recheck 9.3

Recheck your understanding of the concepts covered by this objective.

 Precheck 9.4

Check your understanding of the concepts covered by this objective.

Activity 9.4.1

Article
Ethics in Society

Ethics are the principles we use to determine what's right and wrong and to help guide our choices and actions, in both our personal lives and our business lives.

Occasionally, however, situations arise that force us to consciously recall our ethical principles in order to choose the right thing to do. This often occurs when we are faced with a novel or unfamiliar situation. If examining our own ethical guidelines fails to assist us in new situations, we may have to adopt other ethical guidelines or modify our own guidelines to arrive at a correct decision.

Ethics aren't the same as laws or regulations. Ethics are internalized principles that influence the decisions we make. A law is an external rule that if violated is punishable by society. Laws usually stem from ethical principles, but because people differ in what they consider to be ethical behavior, some individual or group will always find some laws unethical. For example, in the world of computer use, not everyone agrees that it should be illegal to share copyrighted digital music clips. Similarly, not everyone agrees that the government or another controlling body should prohibit viewing and distributing pornography on the web.

Ethics are not the same as laws, but ethics do inform the shaping of the laws. Laws are external rules that if violated are punishable by society.

For many people, violating their ethical principles is worse than violating the law. Such people believe their first duty is to follow their conscience if there is a conflict between the two. Life would be easier for many of us if there were only one clear-cut ethical standard, and if right and wrong were always easy to distinguish. In reality, however, there is not always consensus on what constitutes ethical behavior. Even if consensus is reached, disagreements often arise in determining how ethical beliefs should be applied to real-life situations.

Ethics and Technology

Computer technology is constantly evolving and presenting novel or unfamiliar situations requiring us to make ethical decisions. New technologies often create ethical dilemmas because they allow humans to act in new and unforeseen ways. The typical initial response to dealing with ethical issues raised by new technologies is to attempt to fit them into traditional ethical and moral frameworks. But the difficulty often lies in determining how to categorize the new issues in order to know which ethical rules or principles to apply.

Email is a good example of this problem. If email is regarded as similar to its nonelectronic counterpart, paper mail, then the ethical rules concerning privacy (which are already well established for letters) will apply to email. However, because email technology easily allows the forwarding of messages to thousands of people at the touch of a button, perhaps it should be considered more like sending a postcard— an act that has significantly lower expectations of privacy. As a third alternative, we might decide that email doesn't fall into either of these traditional categories, thus necessitating that new ethical concepts be created and applied.

Each new generation of computers permits us to do things that we could only imagine a few years ago. As a result, computer technology continually poses numerous ethical dilemmas. Adapting traditional ethical thought and behavior to these issues has resulted in new interpretations of the old rules, and these new interpretations have, in turn, led to the formation of a branch of applied ethics called **computer ethics**. As with all ethical issues, whether computer ethics offers a unique set of ethical behaviors or merely new interpretations of traditional ethical categories is still under debate. However, classifying the important ethical issues raised by computer technology under the title *computer ethics* provides us with a convenient way to discuss and analyze ethical dilemmas unique to computer technology.

Electronic computers have been around since 1941. Early computers were large mainframe devices maintained by a team of engineers and programmers. Ethical decision making involving computers and their capabilities was limited to the relatively small group of people involved in the design and use of these large mainframes. Beginning in the early 1980s, however, personal computers became widely available. Technology has advanced so rapidly that the capabilities of personal computers and newer computing devices far exceed those of early mainframes. The development of the Internet has also vastly increased the technical capabilities of the average computer user.

The widespread availability of personal computers, devices, and the Internet means that a large group of people now face the ethical responsibilities inherent in controlling a powerful technology. Computers impact almost every facet of our lives. Anyone using a computer faces a variety of ethical challenges.

Hotspot

Wired to Cheat

With Tour de France bicyclists using performance-enhancing drugs and home run slammers taking steroids, it should come as no surprise that intellectual games are also being sullied by cheats. The only difference is that electronically transmitted data, not chemicals, provides the edge.

Chess is a game played under a code of honor, but that hasn't stopped some players in the past from sneaking peeks at chess books and consulting with friends during bathroom breaks at tournaments. As computer technology has become smaller and more connected, some players have found ways to cheat digitally as well.

In 2006, for example, during the World Open Chess Championship, two players were suspected of receiving unauthorized help via computer technology. The first player raised eyebrows when as a low-ranking player he beat three high-ranked masters and had an error-free game against a grand master. Such marked improvement in an adult player is extremely rare. Officials ran his game against the grand master with commercial chess-playing software and noted that 25 of the player's moves were identical with those made by the software. Feeling the heat, the player disappeared into the restroom. Nothing was found in the stall, but his advantage was apparently flushed away, because he quickly lost the next three games.

A second player was expelled because the "hearing aid" he was wearing turned out to be a wireless receiver, which he used to communicate secretly with another person. It is speculated that the other person was reproducing the game's moves on a portable computer and feeding suggestions to the player. The player, clad in a bulky sweater a little too warm for July, refused to be searched and was expelled.

Since then, there have been numerous confirmed cases of chess cheating in national and international competitions using portable devices such as smartphones to get software help or communicate with someone who has access to software help during breaks. In one case in Australia, a 14-year-old boy was caught consulting the Chessmaster software on his PlayStation Portable device in a restroom, for example. This has led to many organizations banning the possession of cell phones by contestants during tournaments.

Personal Ethical Guidelines for Using Technology

Computers and the Internet are very powerful tools. With a few taps on a keyboard, users have the ability to do much good or to create great damage. A doctor can use the Internet to diagnose a patient many miles away. Companies can use the Internet to sell products and services around the world. Every day, users benefit by being able to use email to contact friends and relatives and to conduct business. On the other hand, computer technology can be used to spread damaging viruses, break into computer networks to steal or damage material, use copyrighted material unlawfully, spread hatred and promote violence, and create numerous other problems for society.

What can be done to prevent unethical behavior on computers and the Internet? Certainly, laws can be passed to punish the most egregious violations. But legislation is never the only, or even an adequate, answer to an ethical dilemma. Rather, the application of sound ethical principles must begin with the individual.

For starters, all computer users should be aware of the power of a computer. They should understand its capacity for good or harm, and they should realize the societal and personal consequences of perpetrating illegal or harmful behaviors with a computer. Moreover, users should read, think about, and consider adapting for their own use a **computer code of ethics**. Researchers C. Dianne Martin and David H. Martin compared four such codes of ethics adopted by major organizations and determined that the codes included 10 common themes (see Figure 9.8).

Figure 9.8

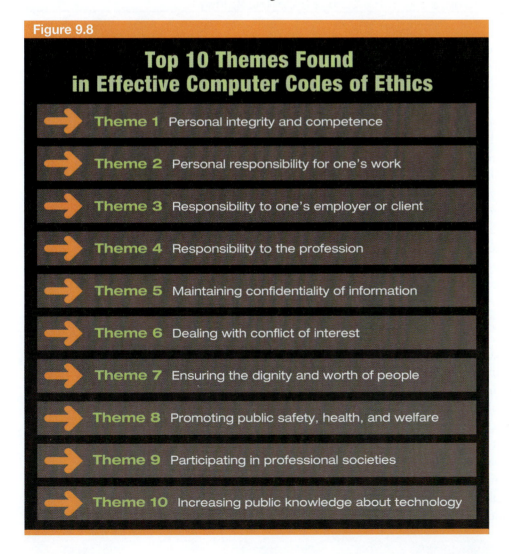

Top 10 Themes Found in Effective Computer Codes of Ethics

→ **Theme 1** Personal integrity and competence

→ **Theme 2** Personal responsibility for one's work

→ **Theme 3** Responsibility to one's employer or client

→ **Theme 4** Responsibility to the profession

→ **Theme 5** Maintaining confidentiality of information

→ **Theme 6** Dealing with conflict of interest

→ **Theme 7** Ensuring the dignity and worth of people

→ **Theme 8** Promoting public safety, health, and welfare

→ **Theme 9** Participating in professional societies

→ **Theme 10** Increasing public knowledge about technology

Table 9.2 Software Engineering Code of Ethics and Professional Practice

Relationship	Obligations
Public	Software engineers shall act consistently with the public interest.
Client and Employer	Software engineers shall act in a manner that is in the best interests of their client and employer consistent with the public interest.
Product	Software engineers shall ensure that their products and related modifications meet the highest professional standards possible.
Judgment	Software engineers shall maintain integrity and independence in their professional judgment.
Management	Software engineering managers and leaders shall subscribe to and promote an ethical approach to the management of software development and maintenance.
Profession	Software engineers shall advance the integrity and reputation of the profession consistent with the public interest.
Colleagues	Software engineers shall be fair to and supportive of their colleagues.
Self	Software engineers shall participate in lifelong learning regarding the practice of their profession and shall promote an ethical approach to the practice of the profession.

Source: IIEE Computer Society, version 5.1, excerpted from "Short Version" (http://CUT6.emcp.net/CodeOfEthics). Copyright 1999 by the Institute for Electrical and Electronics Engineers, Inc. and the Association for Computing Machinery, Inc.

Table 9.2 is an example of a code of ethics for software engineering developed jointly by the Institute of Electrical and Electronics Engineers and the Association for Computing Machinery.

In fact, Martin and Martin noted in their review that computer codes of ethics were remarkably similar to those created for noncomputer professionals. This isn't surprising, since such codes fall into the category of normative ethics: a set of prescriptions for what behaviors should be adopted or actions performed. A code of ethics for computer use is thus helpful in terms of providing general guidelines for behavior. However, users need to bear in mind that they will still have to make hard decisions when applying such principles to real-life situations.

Because of the number and complexity of issues involved in the rapidly evolving world of computer technology, it's unlikely that a consensus will ever be reached on a single ethical code for the computer industry. Still, all users should consider it a point of personal integrity to use computers and the Internet ethically at all times.

> **Recheck 9.4**
>
> Recheck your understanding of the concepts covered by this objective.

9.5 Exploring Privacy Protection Issues

> **Precheck 9.5**
>
> Check your understanding of the concepts covered by this objective.

Most people have information about their personal lives that they wish to keep private. These confidential matters may be as simple as birth dates, telephone numbers, and email addresses, or they may involve information about indiscretions, opinions, and preferences that could embarrass an individual or even harm him or others if revealed to the public.

Even in a society that values the right to privacy, we realize that this right is not absolute. We need to reveal personal information at certain times, such as when we apply for a job, a loan, and a credit card and when we visit a doctor. Most people are generally willing to reveal personal information if it's absolutely necessary, but they expect that this information will be closely guarded.

Any communication over the Internet makes us increasingly vulnerable to monitoring and data-gathering activities that can compromise our privacy. While most of this activity doesn't have a malicious intent, the cumulative effect of many different methods of gathering, processing, and sharing personal information can be disastrous. For example, today many medical records (for instance, test results and prescription information) are stored on networked databases

In a society where more and more personal information is available online, many people are stepping back and looking for ways to create privacy barriers between their personal and business lives and the world at large.

that can be shared among professionals such as doctors, lab technicians, and pharmacists. If this information falls into the wrong hands, it might be used in unauthorized and unforeseen ways—perhaps for marketing purposes, for denying insurance coverage or employment, or even for stealing a person's identity. In the following sections, we will examine threats to privacy from the public availability of information, and from commercial, government, and workplace sectors.

 **Activity 9.5.1**

Video
Personal Privacy

Public Information Availability

A controversial privacy issue concerns the use of publicly available data. A wide range of personal information has always been available through public records such as birth records, marriage licenses, divorce records, drivers' licenses, and bankruptcy records. Even though in the past this information was available to the public, it was scattered across a wide range of jurisdictions and often stored in dusty record books. Access was difficult for all except knowledgeable researchers. Now, all this has changed. Database companies have combed these records and created electronic databases that can provide this information to anyone with a credit card and access to the web.

Many people are justifiably worried about their personal information being misused. A case in Washington State illustrates how such abuse may occur. An anonymous website appeared that contained the names and salary details of police officers in many western Washington communities. So far, the site hasn't listed addresses or phone numbers, although ominously, empty columns are already in place for this data. Police officers and their families are concerned, of course, but they have few options for responding. The information on the site was obtained from public records, and no malicious threats were made against the police officers. However, if the site begins to list the addresses of the officers, it has the potential to expose them to harm.

Another controversial type of public information available on the Internet is the listing of criminal records. Several states have posted websites identifying prison inmates and their criminal histories. Privacy advocates worry that

The federal Health Information Portability and Accountability Act (HIPAA) helps protect individuals' health information from inappropriate access and use.

Figure 9.9

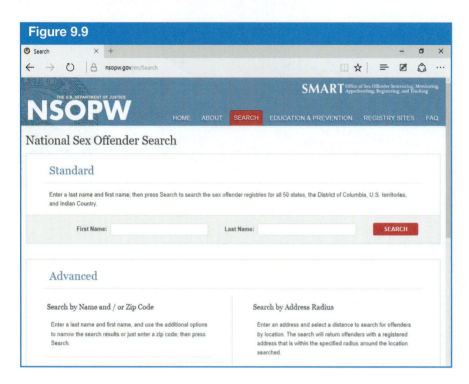

The US Department of Justice maintains the National Sex Offender Public Website, which provides the names, addresses, photographs, and conviction information of sex offenders. Information is searchable by name, county, city, or zip code.

this information will be used against criminals who have served their time and are trying to re-enter society. Easy access to information on their criminal backgrounds may compromise their ability to find jobs and housing. However, many people have supported the online availability of sex offender information as a protection for their families.

The National Sex Offender Public Website is an online database provided by the US Department of Justice that can be searched to identify sex offenders living in a community (see Figure 9.9). Photographs, addresses, and criminal conviction information are available through this resource. Additional organizations have provided the capability for people to receive email alerts when a sex offender moves into their zip code.

One area in which US law has been proactive in protecting citizens' information is healthcare. When computers began to become the standard for medical record keeping, many consumers were concerned that their healthcare records could fall into the wrong hands, and be used against them. For example, a potential employer might access the medical records of a job applicant to make sure she's in good health, to avoid hiring someone likely to make costly medical insurance claims on the company's policy. To prevent such misuses of health information, Congress passed HIPAA in 1996, which puts in place a number of regulations that govern how healthcare providers must collect, store, and safeguard medical information.

Interception of Wireless Communications

Limiting access to wireless networks isn't just a security issue (as discussed in the section "Unauthorized Use of Wireless Networks," on page 367), but also a privacy issue. Wireless communications devices such as smartphones and tablets are extremely vulnerable to interception by others, partly because they transmit data into the air, where anyone can intercept it. Wireless security is thus an important issue, and is becoming more so as the use of wireless devices increases. For example, many medical personnel carry tablets that store sensitive patient medical information. Creating better security for wireless communications devices is a major challenge currently facing the computer industry.

Commercial Privacy Issues

One key threat to privacy comes from e-commerce activities. Since the earliest days of e-commerce, users have expressed serious concerns about the potential abuse of personal data they enter on the Internet. Whenever purchases are made over the Internet, buyers must provide certain information to pay for the goods or services. At a minimum, completing a financial transaction online involves revealing names, mailing addresses, and credit card numbers. Many commercial sites also seek information about consumer preferences and buying habits, although providing this type of information is usually optional.

Once entered on the Internet, personal information can be used to create a consumer profile. A **consumer profile** contains information about an individual's lifestyle and buying habits that marketers can use to more effectively target and sell their goods.

Cookies To some extent people can control the amount of information they voluntarily disclose when making purchases on the Internet. However, online tracking technologies allow websites to gather personal data without consumers' permission or even their knowledge.

One of the most controversial of these technologies is the cookie. Recall from Chapter 5 that a *cookie* is a small data file created and placed on a computer's hard drive by a certain website. The original purpose of cookies was for the convenience of Internet users. Some cookies can remember passwords and user IDs, avoiding the necessity of having to enter such data each time the user visits the site that placed the cookie. Cookies can also contain details about user preferences, automatically customizing a site to those preferences during repeat visits. In addition, cookies record information about the user's IP address, browser, computer operating systems, and URLs visited. Microsoft Windows 10 stores cookies for the active user in a folder called *INetCache* (see Figure 9.10).

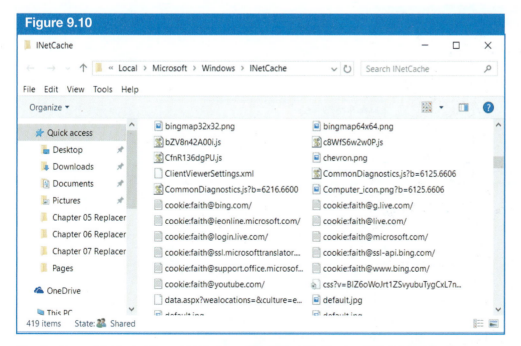

Figure 9.10

The Cookies subfolder in Microsoft Windows 10 is called *INetCache*. With Internet Explorer, you can manage how cookies are stored in this subfolder.

Although cookies have the potential for data-gathering abuse, when used as intended, they aren't a threat to privacy, because the information they contain is only readable by the cookie's originator. But to circumvent this restraint, some companies have created coded cookies used by websites that join their networks. Such companies then gather customer information from these networked websites to compile detailed marketing profiles, usually used to effectively target web advertising banners to appropriate consumers. The gathered cookies can reveal very specific details about user interests and preferences, because they track a trail of websites visited, including the length of time a consumer spent at each site.

Because of the potential misuse of third-party information, browsers have different settings for first-party and third-party cookies (see Figure 9.11). A **first-party cookie** is created by the actual site you are visiting. A **third-party cookie** is created by an ad on a site, where the ad is owned and managed by a different company.

Global Universal Identification Another tracking technology with the potential for misuse is **global universal identification (GUID)**, which is a globally unique identification number that can be coded into both hardware and software. It is also called *globally unique identifier*. The general idea of GUID is that each person has a single, permanent identification number that is used across all communication media. The widespread use of GUIDs could eliminate the relative anonymity that Internet users now enjoy.

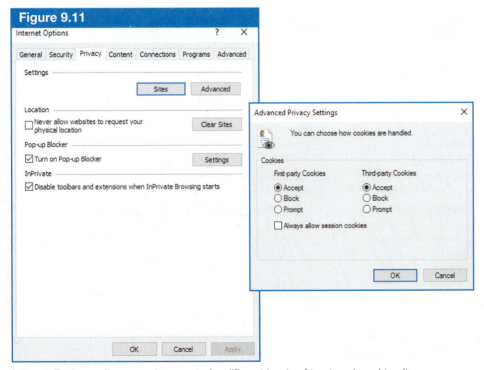

Figure 9.11

Internet Explorer offers security presets for different levels of trust assigned to sites.

Several companies have been forced to withdraw GUID features from their products when it became known that they were in place, including Intel, Microsoft, and RealNetworks. If the use of GUIDs becomes widespread, it will be possible to track down the originators of almost all unpopular or controversial messages or ideas that are communicated over the Internet—a severe blow to Internet privacy.

Location Tracking Most cell phones are equipped with a global positioning system (GPS) chip that can pinpoint the location of the phone within a few dozen feet. This feature was originally included in cell phones for 911 emergency service dispatching, but other uses have been developed to take advantage of these features. The uLocate service, for example, allows online tracking of a cell phone after uLocate software has been loaded on it. Many smartphone applications can also use the location data to show local weather and business information.

Although locating technologies might be useful to find lost children, monitor the locations of teenagers, and dispatch emergency services, there is a potential for abuse as well. Suppose, for example, that as a condition of receiving a company car or an employer-provided cell phone, an employee agrees to allow its location to be monitored 24/7. The employer could use the data gathered to find out personal information about the employee's habits, such as what clubs he attends, what stores he shops at, and how late he stays out at night. If the employee is suspected of committing a crime, law enforcement could potentially subpoena that information and use it to prosecute the case.

Industry Self-Regulation Seeking to allay consumer privacy concerns, many commercial websites adopt a privacy policy. A **privacy policy** (or *compact privacy policy*) is a statement promising that a site will protect the confidentiality of any information a customer reveals. Some browsers, such as Internet Explorer, treat sites with a compact privacy policy more liberally than sites without one when it comes to accepting cookies.

To lend greater credibility to its privacy policy, a company can use one of a number of third-party organizations formed to foster industry self-regulation, including BBBOnLine, TRUSTe, and WebTrust. These organizations offer seals for display by websites that meet their privacy guidelines. (In the case of TRUSTe, the seal indicates that the company has gone through a certification process and adheres to the agency's program requirements.) E-commerce industry representatives believe such policies show that the industry can police itself in the matter of consumer privacy.

The Online Privacy Alliance (OPA), an industry coalition of more than 80 computer companies, was formed to promote online privacy. OPA members believe that a combination of regulatory and self-regulatory measures can protect users against online invasions of privacy. Members also believe that because of OPA's approach, no new legislation is needed in the area of computer privacy. Some of OPA's high-profile members include Microsoft, Apple, Compaq, Dell, IBM, Sun Microsystems, Yahoo, and Xerox. Among other measures, OPA advises websites to adopt privacy policy statements that address such important matters as disclosure of information and data security. OPA also recommends that websites use independent monitoring organizations, such as BBBOnLine and TRUSTe, to ensure that their stated policies are carried out properly.

In 2013, the Federal Trade Commission voted unanimously to endorse a self-regulatory plan submitted by the Network Advertising Initiative (NAI), a consortium of major Internet advertising companies. These companies include many of

Activity 9.5.2

Article
P3P

Websites may display the TRUSTe or WebTrust seal if they meet that agency's privacy guidelines.

the largest advertising firms online, including 24/7 Media, AdForce, AdKnowledge, Double-click, MatchLogic, Engage Technologies, NetGravity, and Real Media. These companies have agreed to allow consumers to do the following:

- Opt out of the collection of anonymous data on the Internet for the purpose of profiling
- Determine whether they want to allow previously collected anonymous data to be merged with personally identifying information
- Give or deny permission for the collection of personally identifying information at the time and place it is gathered on the Internet

Yet despite the best efforts of OPA, NAI, and other organizations, high-profile breaches in data privacy have led some to believe that government regulation provides a more satisfactory solution.

Government Regulation A number of bills to protect online consumer privacy have been proposed at local, state, and federal levels, but only one major piece of federal legislation has been passed. The **Children's Online Privacy Protection Act (COPPA) of 1998** is aimed at protecting children under the age of 13 from privacy violations. It prohibits the gathering and sharing of personal data without the permission of a child's parents or legal guardians. COPPA applies to any website directed at children or any operation that believes it may be dealing with children.

Privacy advocates are pushing for similar legislative protection for adults. Much of the debate over privacy legislation concerns whether consumers should have the right to choose to opt in and receive cookies or to opt out and not receive cookies. Industry advocates prefer the opt-out feature, while privacy advocates worry that many consumers will be unaware of the need to opt out or won't have the computer skills to select that option.

If self-regulation by the Internet commerce industry fails to satisfy consumers and government watchdogs, answers to privacy issues will inevitably be provided by creating new laws. However, some experts believe that existing legislation is sufficient

COPPA protects children by prohibiting the gathering and sharing of personal information about them without permission of the their parents or guardians.

to handle most if not all problems. As you can see from Table 9.3, no major privacy protection laws have been enacted in the United States since 2003.

Table 9.3 Major US Privacy Protection Laws

Act Title	Year	Description
Do Not Call Implementation Act	2003	Established the FCC's National Do Not Call Registry to facilitate compliance with the Telephone Consumer Protection Act of 1991. This registry is intended to give US consumers an opportunity to limit the telemarketing calls they receive.
Controlling the Assault of Non-Solicited Pornography and Marketing (CAN-SPAM) Act	2003	Attempts to control the distribution of spam messages, particularly unwanted pornographic text and images, by imposing penalties on distributors.
Uniting and Strengthening America by Providing Appropriate Tools Required to Intercept and Obstruct Terrorism Act (USA PATRIOT Act)	2001 (renewed 2006 and 2011)	Enacted in response to the 9/11 terrorist attacks against the United States, and dramatically expanded the authority of US law enforcement agencies for the stated purpose of fighting terrorist acts in the nation and abroad. Has also been used to detect and prosecute other alleged potential crimes, such as providing false information on terrorism.
Children's Internet Protection Act	2000	Requires public schools and libraries to filter Internet materials to prevent children from being exposed to undesirable information, such as pornography. Libraries that refuse may be denied the use of federal E-rate funds, available from the government for the purchase of computer technologies.
Financial Services Modernization Act	1999	Contains privacy provisions to require financial institutions to notify consumers of their policies for sharing information with affiliates and third parties. Also allows consumers to opt out of information sharing with nonaffiliated third parties.
Children's Online Privacy Protection Act (COPPA)	1998	Applies to the online collection of personal information by persons or entities from children under 13 years of age. Details what a website operator must include in a privacy policy, when and how to seek verifiable consent from a parent or guardian, and what responsibilities an operator has to protect children's privacy and safety online, including restrictions on marketing to children under age 13.
No Electronic Theft (NET) Act	1997	Extends copyright protection to include materials sent over the Internet, even if no money (payment) is involved. Includes downloading and accessing MP3 files, even if they are available on the Internet for free.
Health Insurance Portability and Accountability Act (HIPAA)	1996	Sections protect the receipt of health insurance coverage for workers and their families when they change or lose their jobs and address the security and privacy of health data. A main purpose is to improve the efficiency and effectiveness of the nation's healthcare system by encouraging the widespread use of electronic data interchange in the US healthcare system.
Computer Fraud and Abuse Act (CFAA)	1986	Makes it illegal to knowingly use a computer without authorization to obtain personal financial information, to use a computer to defraud, and to knowingly transmit a computer virus that causes damage to other computers.
Electronic Communications Privacy Act (ECPA)	1986	Extends government restrictions on wiretaps from telephone calls to include transmissions of electronic data by computer. Prevents unauthorized government access to private electronic communications, and protects individuals' communications against government surveillance conducted without a court order from third parties with no legitimate access to the messages.

Consumer Self-Protection In the absence of effective industry self-regulation or government regulation, computer users can take a number of steps to reduce the likelihood of their personal privacy being violated. First, make sure you conduct e-commerce transactions only on sites protected by encryption programs, such as SSL and TLS, as described in the section "Encryption Protocols" on page 386.

Second, look for sites with privacy statements, and read each statement carefully to see what protection the site offers. Sites that pledge compliance to third-party privacy programs offer an even higher level of security against potential abuse.

Third, to avoid Internet profiling and the possible abuse of data gathered from cookies, set your browser either to warn you when cookies are going to be placed on the hard drive or to reject them altogether. (You may find, however, that constant notifications of cookies is annoying, and that failing to accept cookies limits the functionality of your favorite websites.) You can also find software programs that deal with cookies, providing you with the option of accepting or rejecting them as you see fit. If a cookie is from a site you trust, you may wish to accept it because of the customization functions it can provide.

Fourth, never volunteer more information than is absolutely necessary to complete an e-commerce transaction. Providing details about your lifestyle, habits, interests, and shopping preferences only increases the chance that this information will be passed on to third parties for marketing purposes.

Finally, take advantage of any special privacy protection modes that your browser offers when visiting a site that you don't want to track you. For example, Internet Explorer and Microsoft Edge will run in a protected mode called **InPrivate Browsing**, so that cookies, spyware, and downloaded applications will be isolated from the main operating system. To start a new InPrivate session in Internet Explorer, click the Tools button, click *Safety*, and click *InPrivate Browsing*. To start a new InPrivate session in Microsoft Edge, click the More button and then click *New InPrivate window*. A new window opens in InPrivate mode (see Figure 9.12). In Internet Explorer, you will see an InPrivate indicator in the address bar. InPrivate mode persists until you close the browser window.

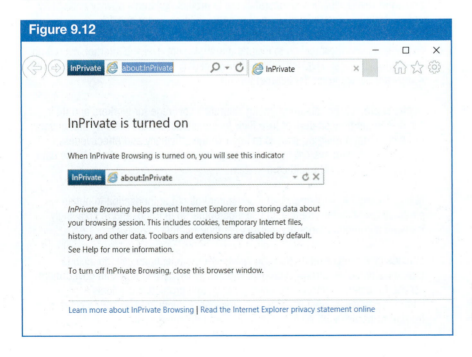

Figure 9.12

Use InPrivate mode in Internet Explorer to browse without leaving any trace of your session behind.

Government Issues

According to the FBI, organized crime groups and other criminal associations routinely use the Internet to conduct their activities. The FBI believes that the ability to intercept these transmissions to discover evidence of criminal wrongdoing is essential. In fact, FBI statistics show that electronic surveillance has enabled tens of thousands of felony convictions.

The FBI and other law enforcement agencies contend that if they aren't allowed to monitor crime organizations under certain circumstances, society as a whole will suffer. They also worry that today's increasingly sophisticated encryption technology will provide criminals with powerful tools that law enforcement won't be able to counter. While many people understand the FBI's concerns, some critics believe government agencies themselves need careful policing to ensure that they do not step over the line and invade the privacy of innocent citizens.

Eavesdropping To develop its capability to monitor email messages, the FBI devised a series of Internet wiretap programs in the late 1990s. These programs—named Omnivore, Carnivore, and DCS1000—could intercept communications while ignoring messages they weren't authorized to intercept. During a criminal investigation, the FBI would install the software at the office of the suspect's Internet service provider (ISP). In 2005, the FBI dropped its homegrown programs in favor of commercially available surveillance software.

The Uniting and Strengthening America by Providing Appropriate Tools Required to Intercept and Obstruct Terrorism Act—commonly known as the *USA PATRIOT Act*—was enacted by Congress in 2001 and renewed in 2006 and 2011. The act's intended purpose of fighting terrorism allows law enforcement agencies, including the FBI, to eavesdrop on private telephone messages and to intercept and read email messages sent by individuals and groups. Many individuals and groups consider this legislation to be a controversial violation of their right to privacy guaranteed by the US Constitution. Some fear their innocent messages may be misinterpreted, resulting in their being charged with criminal action or intent. There have been several legal challenges to this legislation, but none has been successful.

Encryption Restrictions One difficulty faced by the FBI and other law enforcement officials in monitoring email transmissions is the widespread availability of sophisticated encryption programs. Many of the programs using public key encryption are virtually unbreakable. As you will recall from the section "Data Encryption," on page 385, public key encryption uses both a public and a private key for encrypting and decrypting messages. The public key is open to anyone, and can be used for encoding messages. The private key is held only by one person, who can use it to decode messages created using the public key. The FBI has warned that its role in protecting the nation from criminal activities will be negatively affected by the uncontrolled availability of encryption programs.

Protection from Government Threats to Privacy Most citizens recognize that at times, it's necessary to allow the government to intercept and read messages. With court permission, government law enforcement agencies can intercept personal communications under certain circumstances if they can demonstrate that evidence of criminal activity is strongly suspected. The conditions for such interception are rigorous. The intercept must be for the purpose of gathering hard evidence of law breaking, not merely for intelligence gathering.

However, there is always the real danger that interception privileges will be abused and violate the rights of ordinary citizens to communicate freely using the Internet. Most of the objections to wiretapping and eavesdropping programs have centered on the initial lack of information about the programs' designs and protection features. To answer these objections, the FBI set up an independent review committee to examine its programs. While not everyone agreed with the findings, the committee supported the FBI by stating that the programs worked as claimed, intercepting targeted messages while ignoring those that weren't targeted.

Another issue that continues to cause widespread concern is the federal government's tapping of individuals' telephone conversations and email messages as part of the war against terrorism. Although everyone agrees that terrorism is a major security concern, many individuals and groups contend that these government actions violate their right to privacy. The main worry is that innocent messages by individuals may be misinterpreted resulting in senders and recipients facing criminal charges. As a result of court challenges and congressional hearings, Congress adjusted the federal wiretapping statutes in 2008, but the issue remains contentious, and the laws may be changed further.

An equally controversial issue is that of encryption. The top-secret NSA restricted the use of encryption programs for many years. Eventually, NSA control over these programs was loosened as commercial interests needed them to protect data sent over computer networks and the Internet. One of the results of this move was the development of the SSL protocol used today to protect the transmission of credit card data over the web. ATMs also use sophisticated encryption programs to protect their data.

Even after loosening controls, however, the government maintained tight restrictions over the export of encryption programs.

The NSA and the administration continue to grapple with the challenge of gathering information about potential terrorist threats through electronic surveillance while maintaining an individual's right to privacy.

Tech Ethics

Edward Snowden: Traitor or Hero?

In 2013, a computer professional named Edward Snowden came to international attention when he leaked roughly 1.7 million security-classified US government documents, which he acquired when working as an NSA contractor. Thousands of these documents were subsequently published on several websites, and the US government suffered serious security and privacy violations, as well as international embarrassment, as many of the leaked documents implicated the government in illegal surveillance activities, including the mass gathering of cell phone records from private citizens who weren't suspected of any crimes.

Snowden fled the United States before he could be prosecuted, and took refuge in Russia. Some people consider Snowden to be a hero of people's information rights who leaked this information not for personal gain but as a whistleblower against the illegal actions of the government, in the interest of the public knowledge. Others see Snowden as an unpatriotic cybercriminal who has cost his country billions of dollars and untold embarrassment, as well as putting intelligence workers at risk.

Is Snowden a traitor or a hero? Should patriotism involve loyalty to one's government institutions or to one's fellow citizens, if a choice has to be made between the two? Read more about Snowden (at http://CUT6.emcp.net/EdwardSnowden) and decide for yourself.

The government's fear was that other countries would employ these programs to protect their spying and surveillance activities against the United States. The fact that many foreign countries didn't enforce such restrictions placed the American software industry at a disadvantage by not allowing it to offer state-of-the-art encryption. But recently, restrictions on foreign distribution of encryption software have been considerably relaxed, although certain restrictions remain in place. These restrictions don't pertain to the sophistication of the programming, but instead apply to the destination of the product.

Given the rapid advances in technology, government control of encryption technology will no doubt fail to be effective. Encryption programs can now be transmitted electronically at the press of a button, and once released, they can't be recalled. Moreover, the latest encryption programs claim to be unbreakable.

Workplace Issues

Many employees now have Internet access at their workplaces and can send and receive email messages using the Internet or company intranet. However, companies want to ensure that their employees are concentrating on their jobs and not sending personal emails and browsing the web. Therefore, some employers have chosen to use special software programs that monitor workers' behavior. These programs track the numbers and types of keystrokes employees enter on their keyboards, read the messages employees send and receive, and even capture what's on employees' computer screens at any given time.

Employers today can know exactly what their employees are doing from the time they enter the workplace to the time they leave. Even if a worker erases material, she has no guarantee of privacy, because a stored copy of the erased material is likely to exist somewhere in the company's archives. Many employees find this kind of monitoring of their work demeaning, and they question the employer's right to do it.

Protection from Workplace Threats to Privacy What privacy rights do workers have when on the job? The answer may surprise you: almost none. There are no laws preventing electronic surveillance of employees in the workplace. In the eyes

According to the law, an employer has the right to monitor employee activity in the workplace.

Table 9.4 A Fair Electronic Monitoring Policy for Employers
(American Civil Liberties Union)

In order to prevent abuses, employers can and should adopt a policy that includes the following features:
• Notice to employees of the company's electronic monitoring practices
• Use of a signal to let an employee know he or she is being monitored
• Employee access to all personal electronic data collected through monitoring
• No monitoring of areas designed for the health or comfort of employees
• The right to dispute and delete inaccurate data
• A ban on the collection of data unrelated to work performance
• Restrictions on the disclosure of personal data to others without the employee's consent
Source: American Civil Liberties Union (http://CUT6.emcp.net/ElectronicMonitoringPolicy).

of the law, employees who are on the job are using company property, and the company has the right to monitor the use of that property. Many businesses believe they have a right to ensure that employees are doing their jobs, instead of wasting time on personal activities. Furthermore, businesses insist such snooping is justified to prevent employees from engaging in activities that might result in liability for the company.

Companies have a legal obligation to adhere to their own official policies on employee privacy. If the company has pledged to respect any aspect of employee privacy, it must keep that pledge. For example, if a business states that it won't monitor employee email or phone calls, by law it must follow this stated policy. However, a company is not legally required to notify its employees if and when monitoring takes place. Therefore, it's wise for employees to assume they always are being monitored and act accordingly.

Privacy advocates are calling for this situation to be changed. They acknowledge that employers have the right to ensure that their employees are doing their jobs, but they question the need to monitor employees without warning and without limits. The American Civil Liberties Union has, in fact, proposed a Fair Electronic Monitoring Policy to prevent abuses of employee privacy (see Table 9.4).

Protection of Anonymity

With all the layers of tracking and monitoring on the Internet, anonymity might seem like an impossible dream to those who desire it. It seems like everyone is continually watching everyone else, whether it's to make sure they aren't committing crimes or to monitor their shopping habits to predict what they might buy next. However, thanks to programmers who believe that Internet anonymity should be possible, several tools and services are available that can make your Internet experience untraceable.

For example, the Invisible Internet Project (I2P) is software that creates a "network within a network," somewhat like a VPN does when it creates a secure tunnel on the Internet. I2P allows applications to exchange files, send email, web surf, chat, and post blog entries in privacy. It can also be used to host anonymous websites.

Tor (which stands for The Onion Router) is software that conceals its users' identities and locations by separating identification and routing. Tor protects against a form of Internet surveillance known as *traffic analysis*, which logs information about the end points of a communication and its duration. Tor encrypts a communication

Activity 9.5.3

Article
I2P and Tor

and then bounces it through a network of relays run by volunteers all over the world to ensure privacy.

For more basic anonymity, you don't need any special software. You can use the InPrivate Browsing function of Microsoft Edge or Internet Explorer, described in the section "Consumer Self-Protection," on page 400, to browse websites without leaving any traces of the communication on your own PC and without the websites you are visiting harvesting any information from the transactions. Other browsers may also offer special privacy modes; check the documentation for your favorite browser to find out.

Recheck 9.5

Recheck your understanding of the concepts covered by this objective.

9.6 Examining Property Protection Issues

Precheck 9.6

Check your understanding of the concepts covered by this objective.

The ability to link computers through the Internet offers many advantages. With linked computers, we can quickly and easily communicate with other users around the world, sharing files and other data with a few simple keystrokes. A report written in New York can be attached to an email and arrive on someone's desk in London within minutes. Digital images can be placed on web pages for downloading and viewing by users around the world.

However, the convenience provided by linking computers through the Internet also can lead to unauthorized sharing of copyrighted text, photos, music, videos, and computer programs, infringing on the rights of the original owners to control and profit from their distribution. There is already a solid legal framework ensuring the protection of personal property, but computers have created many new issues that challenge conventional interpretations of these laws.

Plagiarism

Plagiarism is using others' words and ideas without attributing the original creator(s) as the source. Examples include copying from an encyclopedia or book for an academic paper without citation, reusing text found on the Internet in a political speech, and failing to give credit in a research report to the authors of previous studies on which the new research is based.

Plagiarism is a major problem in high schools and universities. Students mistakenly think it's OK to copy and paste data from the Internet into a research paper without attributing the sources, and to cobble together an entire paper by pulling data from multiple sources. Or worse yet, students know it's wrong but do it anyway, thinking they won't get caught. Many professors aren't vigilant about checking papers for plagiarized content, and don't educate students about proper citation use.

Fortunately, the same technology that allows plagiarism to happen so easily—the Internet—also provides antiplagiarism tools that instructors can use. See the Cutting Edge feature "To Catch a Plagiarist" in Chapter 4 on page 157 to learn how using antiplagiarism software helps instructors detect plagiarism in students' academic papers.

To avoid plagiarism in your work, make sure you provide appropriate citations when quoting the work of others. Microsoft Word includes a citation management feature that automatically formats citations correctly for a particular citation standard (such as APA or MLA).

Intellectual Property

Intellectual property includes just about anything that can be created by the human mind. To encourage innovation and improvement and thus benefit society as a whole, the US legal system grants patents to individuals who invent new and better ways of doing things. A **patent** awards ownership of an idea or invention to its creator for a fixed number of years. Doing so allows the inventor the right to charge others for use of the invention. If a person invented a new type of electric motor and received a patent, for instance, any other person wishing to make use of the invention would have to gain permission from the inventor before proceeding.

To encourage and protect artistic and literary endeavors, an author or an artist is awarded **copyright** to created material. Copyright provides the right to control use of the work and charge others for its use. A **trademark** establishes ownership of a certain identifying symbol or logo.

The **World Intellectual Property Organization (WIPO)** is a specialized agency of the United Nations dealing with intellectual property rights (see Figure 9.13). WIPO administers international treaties addressing various aspects of intellectual property, and 183 nations belong to the organization. WIPO divides intellectual property into two categories: industrial property (which includes invention patents, trademarks, and industrial designs) and copyright (which includes books, films, music, and art).

Patent and copyright violations are punishable by law, and prosecutions and convictions are frequent. The legal framework protecting intellectual property has come under constant challenge as technology has moved forward.

One of the most common copyright violations online is the illegal distribution of copyrighted music and video files. Most movie and music sharing sites that offer free downloads operate illegally and cannot withstand legal prosecution, but they persist for a while through legal loopholes and delays in arrests. They also sometimes persist because they are hosted in countries that either do not have strong laws against sharing copyrighted content or lack the law enforcement resources to quickly and aggressively pursue copyright violators. Peer-to-peer file sharing systems such as BitTorrent make it more difficult for authorities to identify the person or company violating the copyright because individuals who have no role in the original copying of the material may be participating in its distribution.

Figure 9.13

The World Intellectual Property Organization (WIPO) "is dedicated to developing a balanced and accessible international intellectual property (IP) system, which rewards creativity, stimulates innovation and contributes to economic development while safeguarding the public interest."

Peer-to-peer file sharing copyrighted material online may seem like an easy way to get movies and music. However, it is illegal, and those who are caught can face large fines and even jail time.

Because of the legal system's limitations in stopping illegal file sharing, content owners such as movie studios and record labels have stepped up to work with ISPs. A movie studio or record label might monitor the IP addresses of computers that illegally distribute their content, and then notify that user's ISP, asking the ISP to make the illegal distribution stop.

The Internet also makes it very easy to access and copy written works that may be protected. Today, authors are increasingly dismayed to find copies of their works appearing on the Internet without their permission. An author may indeed have given permission to a website to print her work, but once a single website has posted it, anyone can copy it for his own use. The same problem, of course, occurs with graphic and artistic images on the Internet, such as photographs and artwork. Once placed on the web, they can be copied and reused numerous times. In fact, unauthorized copying of items appearing on websites is difficult and sometimes even technically impossible to prevent.

Software is also subject to copyright laws. Unauthorized software copying and distributing is a multibillion-dollar problem for the software industry.

Fair Use

In some situations, it's perfectly legal to use other people's written work. It's always been permissible to use another person's material without permission as long as the use is acknowledged, is for a noncommercial purpose, and involves only the use of a limited amount of protected material (such as no more than 300 words of prose and one line of poetry). Such use is called **fair use** and is outlined by the US Copyright Act, Section 107. Here is what Section 107 states:

> [T]he fair use of a copyrighted work, including such use by reproduction in copies or phonorecords or by any other means specified by [other sections of the law], for purposes such as criticism, comment, news reporting, teaching

(including multiple copies for classroom use), scholarship, or research, is not an infringement of copyright. In determining whether the use made of a work in any particular case is a fair use, the factors to be considered shall include—

1. the purpose and character of the use, including whether such use is of a commercial nature or is for nonprofit educational purposes;
2. the nature of the copyrighted work;
3. the amount and substantiality of the portion used in relation to the copyrighted work as a whole; and
4. the effect of the use upon the potential market for or value of the copyrighted work.

The fact that a work is unpublished shall not itself bar a finding of fair use if such finding is made upon consideration of all the above factors.

Even under the fair use provision, it's important to acknowledge the source of the material. Plagiarism may be punished by law, and in many educational institutions, it can result in suspension or even expulsion.

Intellectual Property Protection

Intellectual property owners face two basic problems in the digital age. First, new technology has presented new difficulties in interpreting previous understandings of the protection of intellectual property—for instance, in applying the fair use provision to Internet material. Second, the new technical capabilities brought about by digital technologies have greatly increased the ease with which intellectual property can be appropriated and used without authorization, making policing and protecting intellectual property very difficult. Dealing with these problems has involved making changes to existing copyright legislation. Moreover, intellectual property owners have formed new organizations to ensure the protection of their property.

Fair Use and the Digital Millennium Copyright Act   The difficulty in determining what constitutes fair use has increased with the proliferation of computers and the Internet. Digital technology allows (even requires) using material in ways that were never envisioned before, and applying fair use guidelines isn't always easy.

To deal with these issues, the Digital Millennium Copyright Act of 1998 (DMCA) was enacted. The DMCA updated copyright laws to reflect new digital age realities. In addition, this law brought US copyright laws in line with WIPO treaties, to which the United States is a signatory. In 2001, the European Union passed similar legislation called the *European Union Copyright Directive (EUCD)*.

Among DMCA's key provisions are thwarting efforts to get around copyright protection systems, clarifying the concept of fair use as it applies to digital works, and dealing with the issue of an ISP's liability for hosting copyrighted materials. DMCA also makes a number of exceptions for digital fair use. For example, libraries are exempted from certain copyright provisions to allow them to carry out their research and information-sharing functions. Another exception was granted to repair shops, which are allowed to make copies of programs involving maintenance or repair of products. In addition, DMCA states that ISPs won't be held liable for copyright violations that occur solely as a result of their hosting function.

Industry Efforts to Enforce Copyright Protection Because of the difficulty and expense of going after violators of music, video, and software copyrights, many distributors have focused on developing and implementing copy protection technologies, called **digital rights management (DRM)**. For example, most movie DVDs have a 40-bit encryption called the *content scramble system (CSS)*. It's an algorithm that commercial DVD players have the code to decrypt. This encryption can't be copied to writeable DVDs, so encrypted home copies can't be made. However, this code was cracked within three years of its introduction, and software was developed that could strip the encryption from a movie and then copy to a DVD. The movie industry can't change the code without rendering all old DVD players obsolete, so they are stuck. However, a new, harder-to-break code was developed for Blu-ray discs and players. Called the *advanced access content system*, it uses several hundred different keys, each of which can be revoked should it be cracked (so that future disc releases can't use it).

Some software has copy protection built into it to prevent users from easily making copies of discs. A common protection scheme for software is to require that the installation CD be present in the drive whenever the program runs. Making copies of the CD with a burner, however, easily fools this protection scheme. It can also be fooled with a workaround that involves copying extra files from the CD to the hard drive and redirecting the software to check the hard disk for these files instead of the CD. Some game companies are taking the extra step of making duplication difficult by scrambling some of the data on their original CDs, which CD burners will automatically correct when copying. When the copied and corrected CD is used, the software will check for the scrambled track information. If the error isn't there, the software won't run. A common goal of hackers and crackers is to crack software protection schemes. **Cracking** is a method of circumventing a security scheme that prevents a user from copying a program or installing it on multiple computers.

Most people agree that copyright protection serves an important function in a free market economy. However, some detractors argue that strict enforcement of copyright protection is counterproductive and may cost software manufacturers more money in consumer ill will than they would lose from illegal copying. For example, in 2005, Sony BMG added software on CDs—unbeknownst to buyers— that when inserted in a computer would install a hidden, difficult-to-remove utility on the computer and would then interfere with CD copying. In terms of public relations, this software was a disaster for Sony. It reported back to Sony on the user's private listening habits, contained code from other software it was legally entitled to use, and hid itself from the operating system. Worst of all, third-party developers quickly released malware that exploited the software. Public outcry was intense, and led to a boycott of all Sony music CDs. In 2006, Sony BMG recalled some of the affected CDs and made consumer settlements, and in 2007, the company suspended all its CD copy protection efforts.

There are trade organizations that help copyright owners enforce their rights. For software, two key organizations are the Software & Information Industry Association (SIIA) and The Software Alliance (also known as *BSA*, because it was formerly the Business Software Alliance). Both organizations actively pursue the use of illegal software. The violators they catch face stiff fines and even jail sentences. Similar organizations exist for music and videos.

Recheck 9.6
Recheck your understanding of the concepts covered by this objective.

9.7 Thinking about Personal and Social Issues

Precheck 9.7

Check your understanding of the concepts covered by this objective.

In addition to raising privacy and property concerns, computers have had an unanticipated impact on numerous personal and social issues. The solutions to these issues are often complicated because of a lack of consensus on what, if anything, should be done to deal with them.

Online Gambling

Most gambling occurs at casinos, but the availability of **online gambling** is attracting a growing number of gamblers, including both adults and teenagers. (Teens are prohibited by law from visiting bricks-and-mortar casinos.) Online gambling has become a $12 billion industry. Until recently, it has been based almost entirely outside the United States, although about half its customers live in the United States.

Online gambling is a growing personal and social problem. Because individuals often bet with credit cards, they often don't realize how quickly they are losing money.

Tech Ethics

Gambling Addiction

Gambling can be as addictive as alcohol or drugs. Not everyone who participates will become addicted, but a sizable minority will, and the life effects can be devastating. According to Jeffrey Deverensky, a leading authority on youth gambling addiction, "Online and mobile gambling is going to be a big thing, and those ages 18 to 25 have the highest prevalence of gambling-related problems among adults." He estimates that between 5 and 8 percent of university students are at-risk gamblers, and an additional 2 to 4 percent suffer from a serious gambling addiction.

Deverensky says that one hard part of dealing with this issue is "getting parents and teachers to realize the dangers of gambling are often no less severe and sometimes much greater than drinking, reckless driving, drugs, and unprotected sex." He explains that many addicts are addicted to high-risk behavior in general, and will substitute one high risk behavior for another. The fifth edition of the American Psychiatric Association's *Diagnostic and Statistical Manual of Mental Disorders (DSM5)* notes that when "individuals are engrossed in Internet games, certain pathways to their brains are triggered in the same direct and intense way that a drug addict's brain is affected by a particular substance."

All forms of Internet gambling were illegal in the United States since well before the Internet was even invented. The Wire Act of 1961, which outlawed using interstate or international communications methods such as phone lines to transmit gambling wagers on sporting events, was interpreted by the courts to include all forms of gambling. The Unlawful Internet Gambling Enforcement Act (UIGEA) of 2006 strengthened that connection by preventing gamblers from using credit cards to bet online and allowing authorities to work with ISPs to block access to gambling websites.

However, in 2011, the US Attorney General's office issued a legal opinion that reinterpreted the Federal Wire Act of 1961 as applying only to sporting events or contests. This ruling lifted the long-time federal ban on nonsport betting on the Internet, such as poker and slots. As a result, companies in several states, including Nevada, Delaware, and New Jersey, have recently rolled out real-money gambling websites and smartphone apps.

Critics of online gambling cite concerns about gambling addictions, fraudulent gambling sites, and the inability to identify underage players. They feel that widespread gambling is not good for individuals or for society in general, and oppose efforts to make gambling more convenient and accessible. In 2014, the attorneys general of 16 states wrote to Congress, asking it to restore the previous interpretation of the Wire Act and go back to a federal prohibition on online gaming.

Protection of Freedom of Speech

The Internet as we know it actually began as a research project of the US Department of Defense. It was purposely designed without any controlling authority. To protect the system in the event of a natural disaster, military attack, or widespread loss of connectivity, developers created it so data could travel along any of several different paths before being reassembled at the receiving end.

Activity 9.7.1

Video
Freedom of Speech

This decentralized, and now internationalized, network makes it difficult for any government to control content. As a result, the Internet contains materials that wouldn't be allowed in many jurisdictions if it were received by more traditional means, such as paper mail and TV. Examples of these types of materials are hate speech, cyberbullying, and pornography.

Hate Speech The freedom of speech guaranteed by the US Constitution allows great latitude in what people can say. Consequently, a great number of websites contain written materials that many individuals find offensive. This includes materials inciting hatred against people of certain races, religions, and beliefs. Some hate speech sites use foul and inappropriate language, and some even post dangerous information, such as how to make illegal drugs and explosives.

Cyberbullying **Cyberbullying**, which includes texting and sending harassing email messages, along with posting embarrassing photos, is a problem that affects not only students but also people in the workplace. In work situations, the practice is usually called *cyberstalking*. In either case, the purpose is to harm another person's reputation or self-image.

According to the National Crime Prevention Council, about half of all high school students have reported being victims of cyberbullying. The council's research also suggests that this destructive online behavior is increasing. Some states have passed laws against digital harassment, and proposals to criminalize cyberbullying have been introduced in Congress. On the consumer front, prominent social networking sites, such as Facebook and MySpace, are working with corporations and legal groups

Figure 9.14

Facebook's Help page provides links to a form users can use to report abuses of its terms of use, such as cyberbullying and hate speech.

to educate and protect the online community from this malicious form of digital conduct. Facebook and other such sites also provide tools to help users recognize and report cyberbullying and other abuses (see Figure 9.14).

Pornography *Pornography* is material containing sexually explicit images or text that's deemed unacceptable or harmful by society. The borderless nature of the Internet and the technical ease with which pornography can be distributed make it available to anyone with an Internet connection.

Pornographic websites were among the first sites to spring up on the Internet, and they pioneered many of the features e-commerce sites now use. Despite their contributions to e-commerce, their content is unwelcome in many homes, especially where children or certain vulnerable adults might view it.

Protection against Unwanted Material

Little can be done to prevent people from using the Internet to present or distribute offensive or pornographic materials. The freedom of speech guaranteed by the US Constitution has been interpreted as protecting both acceptable or well-received expressions and unacceptable or unpopular expressions. Unless a website contains materials that overtly and directly threaten the livelihood or well-being of an individual, a group, or the government, it enjoys protection as free speech.

For computer users, the best protection against offensive or unwanted material on the Internet is just to avoid it. If you happen to stumble across materials that are pornographic or disturbing in any way, merely click the Back button on your browser (see Figure 9.15) and leave the offensive site. Many children and vulnerable adults, however, are less able to exercise judgment in what constitutes undesirable or harmful materials. Parents and guardians are therefore advised to take measures to protect these users from viewing such materials.

Measures might include installing filtering programs similar to the programs used in schools. With filtering software, parents and guardians have a powerful tool to aid them in making sure children and vulnerable adults don't view or read inappropriate or unapproved materials on the web. Similar to antivirus software, filtering software must be constantly updated to keep track of any new sites containing unwanted material.

Figure 9.15

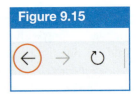

One effective way to avoid exposure to unwanted Internet content is to hit the Back button if you accidentally land on an inappropriate site.

Legislation against Internet Pornography Although few real restrictions have been put in place on adult pornography on the Internet, strict legislation does forbid the use of children in pornography on the Internet. A series of federal laws, including the Child Pornography Prevention Act of 1996, enact harsh penalties for people distributing or possessing child pornography. According to the Executive Office for US Attorneys (EOUSA), 1,732 cases of child pornography, coercion, or enticement were referred to US Attorneys' offices in 2006.

Almost all pornographic websites carry disclaimers requiring people entering the sites to declare that they are over 18 years of age and are aware that they are logging on to a site containing pornographic materials. In fact, some sites subscribe to services that verify the ages of potential users.

Internet Filters After much debate, Congress passed a law in 2000 that was designed to protect schoolchildren and library patrons from being exposed to pornographic sites and other types of restricted materials. Called the **Children's Internet Protection Act (CIPA)**, the law requires public schools and libraries to install Internet filtering software on their computers. The American Library Association challenged the law on the grounds that Internet filters could prevent access to materials protected by the First Amendment. The case was heard in March 2003 by the Supreme Court, which ruled that the law was constitutional.

A **filtering program** can prevent access to sites, keep track of sites visited, limit connection time, record keystrokes, prevent downloading, and allow users to view only those sites that have been accessed. One popular filtering program, Net Nanny (shown in Figure 9.16), contains features that protect against pornography, online predators, age-inappropriate content, and cyberbullying.

Organizations such as the Consortium for School Networking (CoSN), a nonprofit association, provide schools with guidelines for evaluating Internet filtering programs. These guidelines, along with information about educators' responsibilities, can be found at the CoSN website.

Figure 9.16

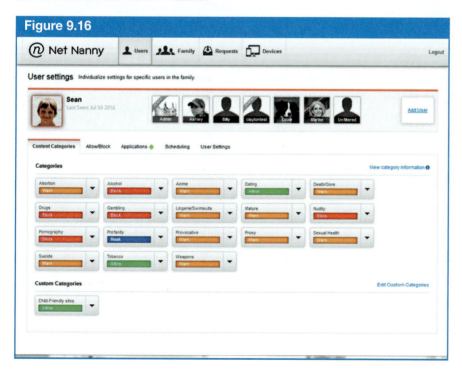

Filtering programs can help protect children from inappropriate websites.

Acceptable Use Policies Although CoSN doesn't necessarily endorse the CIPA, the group strongly recommends that every school district adopt an **acceptable use policy (AUP)** to guide users and administrators about Internet use. According to the National Education Association, an effective AUP contains six elements:

- a preamble that explains the goals and rationale
- a definition section that identifies key terms
- a policy statement that describes the computer services covered by the AUP
- an "Acceptable Uses" section that clearly defines appropriate use
- an "Unacceptable Uses" section that provides examples of inappropriate use
- a "Violations and Sanctions" section that tells users how to report violations and where to direct their questions

Typically, students and parents sign the AUP document to acknowledge that they are aware of Internet use restrictions and that the district isn't responsible for students who decide to violate the restrictions.

Protection of Children from Online Predators

Another worry for many people is protecting children from websites and chat rooms with harmful or inappropriate materials. A problem that law enforcement agencies have become increasingly aware of is the presence of online predators. An **online predator** is an individual (often a child molester) who uses the Internet to talk young people into meeting, exchanging photos, and so forth.

In general, children shouldn't have private, unmonitored access to the Internet. Organizations managing child access to the Internet often use a proxy system that's set up to make a URL check and disallow packets that transfer to and from websites that are off limits. This is how Internet connections at elementary schools protect children from accessing adult sites. A number of commercial software packages incorporate this feature for home use. Some also allow tracking of Internet use so that parents can monitor which websites their children have visited.

Bridging the Digital Divide

Today, many people in industrialized nations take for granted the availability of modern digital technologies. But of course, not everyone in the world enjoys such privileges. Even within developed nations, access to digital technology isn't evenly distributed. The gap between those who have access to computers and the Internet and those who do not has been called the **digital divide**.

In the United States, the availability of computers and high-speed Internet access varies depending on several demographic factors. Table 9.5 presents the demographic findings of the 2013 Pew Research Center Internet Project survey.

Pew Research also found that 15 percent of US adults don't use the Internet at all. The largest groups that don't use the Internet are senior citizens, adults with less than a high school education, and adults living in households earning less than $30,000 a year. Among nonusers, almost half stated that the main reason they don't go online is that they don't think the Internet is relevant to them.

Table 9.5 Demographics of Broadband Internet Users (percentage of all US adults who use high-speed Internet at home)

Demographic	Broadband Internet Users
All adults	70%
a. Men	71
b. Women	69
a. White, Non-Hispanic	74
b. Black, Non-Hispanic	64
c. Hispanic	53
a. 18–29	80
b. 30–49	78
c. 50–64	69
d. 65+	43
a. No high school diploma	37
b. High school grad	57
c. Some college	78
d. College+	89
a. Less than $30,000/yr	54
b. $30,000–$49,999	70
c. $50,000–$74,999	84
d. $75,000+	88
a. Urban	70
b. Suburban	73
c. Rural	62

Source: Pew Research Internet Project, Home Broadband 2013 (http://CUT6.emcp.net /BroadbandUseDemographics).

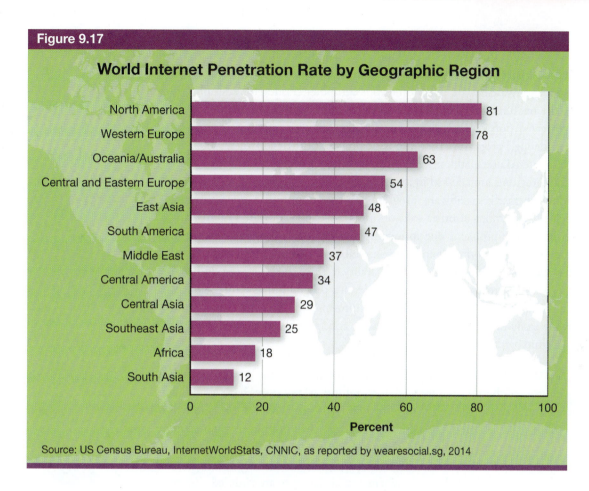

Figure 9.17

World Internet Penetration Rate by Geographic Region

Source: US Census Bureau, InternetWorldStats, CNNIC, as reported by wearesocial.sg, 2014

Globally, there's even more of a digital divide. Figure 9.17 shows the percentages of Internet penetration (that is, locations where the Internet is available) by continent as of January 2014.

Many charitable organizations have programs aimed at narrowing the digital divide. For example, a nonprofit group called One Laptop per Child has produced a $100 laptop that can be used in underdeveloped nations to help bridge the global digital divide.

The World Bank and other international bodies have created initiatives to overcome the digital divide around the world, but accomplishing this goal remains a daunting task in many impoverished parts of the world. Many underdeveloped nations must meet people's basic needs (such as providing reliable sources of water, medicine, and electricity) before even considering access to digital technology. Education and literacy rates are also low in many areas of the world, so many people wouldn't be able to use computer technology effectively even if they had it. While some progress has been made, the digital divide may widen worldwide in the coming years as computers become increasingly important to the economy and educational systems of industrialized nations, creating a striking gap between the prosperity of some of the world's nations and the poverty of others.

Software Quality and Accessibility Issues

When most people think about software and rights, they think about the rights of software companies that are protected by copyright legislation. But what assurances do software makers owe to the people who use their programs?

Bad software costs US businesses an estimated $100 billion a year in lost productivity. Poorly designed software has even been implicated in accidents that have resulted in deaths and injuries. Every day, computer users around the world experience problems attributed to poor software design. Every time your computer crashes, for example (see Figure 9.18), the malfunction stems from a software problem that the manufacturer should have corrected. Software companies continually work to improve their products and correct, or "debug," programs. They also issue updates of their software, which are usually free to registered users. Still, many consumers wonder why software errors aren't corrected before programs are released in the first place.

In defending themselves, software programmers point out that their software must interact with a number of other software programs and hardware systems, any one of which may cause problems due to incompatibility. While programmers try to ensure that their programs work well and are compatible with connecting software and hardware, they can't guarantee 100 percent reliability. Critics, however, respond that many companies simply refuse to do enough to reduce programming errors. Paul A. Strassmann, a consultant who worked as corporate information officer for Xerox, once stated, "Software easily rates among the most poorly constructed, unreliable, and least maintainable technological artifacts invented by man."

Software Quality If software doesn't perform according to the manufacturer's promise, the consumer's best option is to ask for a refund. Many stores have generous refund policies, and a consumer's right to return goods is protected by the Uniform Commercial Code (UCC). The UCC contains language covering buyers' rights and allowing buyers to reject any product, "if the goods or the tender of delivery fail in any respect to conform to the contract." But this protection covers only the right to return the product for a refund. In cases where actual damages are suffered due to the software, victims must pursue redress through the legal system by filing a lawsuit. Multimillion-dollar lawsuits have been filed over claims that defective software caused financial damage or other hardship.

Legal measures address only the unfortunate results of poor software design. In reality, the best protection against software problems is for software manufacturers and designers to produce better software programs in the first place. As a consumer, you can't control software quality directly, but you can choose which software to buy. If you are choosing an application that will hold and manipulate important data, you should gather as much information as you can about the application's quality and reliability before purchasing it. Read consumer reviews online to find out what problems other customers have had.

Figure 9.18

Mail quit unexpectedly.

Click Reopen to open the application again. Click Report to see more detailed information and send a report to Apple.

Ignore   Report...   Reopen

When an application crashes, the user can lose data, as well as lose valuable time restarting the application and in some cases the operating system.

Software Accessibility An estimated 30 million Americans have some sort of disability, and as the US population ages, this number will certainly increase. In fact, some individuals with disabilities refer to able-bodied people as *TABs*, or temporarily able bodied, since most people will experience some form of disability at some point in their lives. People with certain disabilities may be unable to use computers and the Internet.

In the early days of the Internet, it seemed a blessing for many persons with disabilities. Those with impaired vision could read email and web pages using text-to-screen readers, thus opening up a new window to the world. However, the development of graphical user interface (GUI) browsers and other web page enhancements (such as frames) has closed this window for many people with visual impairments. If web page designers don't provide alternative text attributes for images, their text-reading software is rendered speechless. One disabled activist has lamented that the new graphical browsers force people who are visually impaired to crawl the web, rather than surf it.

Other accessibility problems faced by segments of the disabled population involve the use of computer hardware. Individuals with motor impairments and missing limbs, for example, can't use a mouse and may also be unable to use a conventional keyboard. Individuals with visual impairments may experience difficulty viewing a monitor unless the screen is capable of providing an enlarged display.

Americans with disabilities have been active in asserting their right to improved accessibility to computer technology. In 1999, the National Federation of the Blind (NFB) filed suit against giant ISP America Online (AOL), because AOL software was incompatible with the screen access software used by people who are blind or visually impaired. AOL eventually reached an agreement with the NFB to remedy the problem.

In a decision with even wider implications, the US government issued new rules in late 2000 ordering almost all government websites to be fully web accessible to people with disabilities within six months. The only exceptions allowed are sites dealing with

Developing hardware that's accessible to individuals with physical impairments is important. This specially designed keyboard is one example of such technology.

national security. This decision was based on an interpretation of the Americans with Disabilities Act (ADA) of 1990, which protects people with disabilities against discrimination. ADA states that no individual shall be discriminated against on the basis of disability in the full and equal enjoyment of the goods, services, facilities, privileges, advantages, or accommodations of any place of public accommodation by any person who owns, leases (or leases to), or operates a place of public accommodation.

The decision by the US government to ensure accessibility also affects any sites receiving money from the government. Sites that fail to comply with the ruling face being denied public funds. Some legal observers predict that it won't be long before commercial enterprises are required to make their sites fully accessible as well.

To help website owners comply with these guidelines, and to make the web more accessible in general, the World Wide Web Consortium (W3C) has developed the Web Accessibility Initiative (WAI) with the mission "to lead the Web to its full potential to be accessible, enabling people with disabilities to participate equally on the Web." The WAI article "Introduction to Web Accessibility" (**http://CUT6.emcp.net /ProvidingWebAccessibility**) provides guidelines on making a website more accessible. A second article, "Web Accessibility Evaluation Tools: Overview" (**http://CUT6 .emcp.net/EvaluatingWebAccessibility**), provides guidelines for evaluating the accessibility of an existing website. The results of analyzing a website with one of these evaluation tools is shown in Figure 9.19.

People with disabilities, along with their supporters, point out that incorporating features making computers and web pages accessible to them isn't just a good idea from a legal point of view, but also makes sense financially. Improving access to computers and the Internet will increase the number of potential customers for these goods and services. In addition, if these features are incorporated in software and hardware during the design phase, the cost will be much less than if they must later be retrofitted into existing products.

Figure 9.19

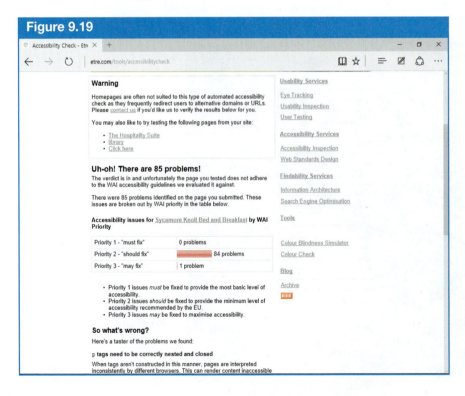

Etre is one of many websites that analyze a site for accessibility issues and provide a detailed report on what to do to fix any problems that it finds.

Both Microsoft Windows and Mac OS X include accessibility options designed to help users with special needs navigate the user interface more easily. In Windows 10, the accessibility features can be enabled using the Control Panel's *Ease of Access* section, and include the following:

- **Narrator.** Reads aloud the text from dialog boxes and windows
- **High-contrast themes.** Applies easy-to-see colors and effects to the display
- **Magnifier.** Magnifies one section of the screen
- **On-screen keyboard.** Allows the user to type by clicking onscreen buttons representing keys
- **Speech recognition.** Allows the user to input commands and data by speaking into a microphone
- **Mouse keys.** Allows using the numeric keypad to move the mouse pointer
- **Sticky keys.** Allows pressing key combinations (such as Ctrl+Enter) one at a time
- **Toggle keys.** Plays a tone when the Caps Lock, Num Lock, or Scroll Lock key is pressed
- **Filter keys.** Ignores or slows down brief or repeated keystrokes
- **Sound sentry.** Uses visual notifications for sounds

If you aren't sure which features to enable for your particular situation, the Ease of Access Center can provide recommendations based on your answers to a questionnaire, as shown in Figure 9.20.

Recheck 9.7
Recheck your understanding of the concepts covered by this objective.

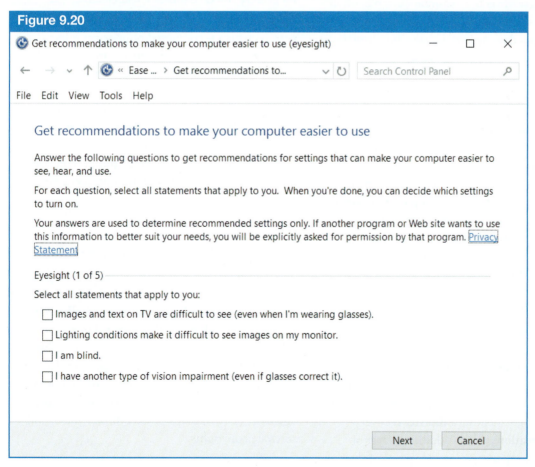

Figure 9.20

Windows 10 will suggest accessibility options appropriate to your situation.

Chapter Summary

*An interactive **Chapter Summary**, **Study Notes**, and a **Slide Presentation** with audio are available from the links menu on this page in your ebook.*

9.1 Assessing the Risks of Computing

A **threat** refers to the severity of a security breach of systems or data. **Hackers** gain access to a network by entering a **system backdoor** or by **spoofing**, which is fooling another computer by pretending to send packets from a legitimate source. Unauthorized data browsing is a crime that involves an invasion of privacy. Other more serious crimes include **identity theft** and **phishing**, which attempts to fraudulently acquire another person's sensitive information, such as a credit card number.

9.2 Avoiding Computer Viruses

Viruses and **worms** are used to infect computers. The **Trojan horse virus** is a common example, often downloaded with games and other shareware files. A **nuisance virus** does no real damage, but creates an inconvenience. An **espionage virus** allows a hacker to enter the system to steal data or spy. One common type of espionage virus is a **keystroke logger**. A **polymorphic virus** changes itself to avoid detection. A **stealth virus** tries to hide from anti-virus software. A **macro virus** is written in a macro that runs as part of a data file. A **boot sector virus** infects the **boot sector** of a disk so that the virus loads into memory at startup. A **Trojan horse virus** masquerades as a useful program but is actually malware. A **multipartite virus** infects a computer in multiple ways. A **logic bomb virus** sits dormant until a specific set of conditions exists.

9.3 Protecting Computer Systems and Data

Strategies for protecting computers include employing a **network sniffer** to display network traffic data, adjusting browser security settings, and downloading antivirus software. Companies can recover from total loss of data by implementing a **disaster recovery plan**. **Authentication** adds an additional layer of security by requiring users to provide proof of their identity such as a **strong password**, **smart card**, or **biometric identifier**. **Encryption** further protects against data compromise by scrambling information so the data becomes unreadable to spies.

9.4 Understanding the Role of Ethics

Ethics are the principles we use to determine what is right and wrong. Technology creates unfamiliar environments, requiring people to make ethical decisions based on new situations. A **computer code of ethics** is a statement of principles of ethical behavior when using computers.

9.5 Exploring Privacy Protection Issues

A commercial threat to privacy is a **consumer profile**, which is composed of personal information on the Internet that marketers use to target and sell their goods. A **cookie** is one form of Internet technology that compiles Internet user information, tracking websites visited along with time spent at each site. **Global universal identification (GUID)** also has the potential for misuse, eliminating anonymity on the Internet. **Privacy policies** on commercial websites are one way to protect confidential customer information.

9.6 Examining Property Protection Issues

The convenience of the Internet makes it easy to use words and ideas without giving credit to the original owners, known as **plagiarism**. Since **intellectual property** can include anything created by the human mind, a person needs a **patent** to claim ownership of the created material and hold the **copyright**. **Fair use** means that a work can be used for a noncommercial purpose as long as credit is given. **Digital rights management (DRM)** helps protect music, video, and software copyrights.

9.7 Thinking about Personal and Social Issues

Some Internet-related social issues include **online gambling** and **cyberbullying**, which includes texting and sending harassing email messages or posting embarrassing photos. Laws can protect users from these online activities, such as the **Children's Internet Protection Act (CIPA)**, which requires public schools and libraries to install Internet filtering software on their computers. A **filtering program** can prevent access to inappropriate sites in accordance with the **acceptable use policy (AUP)** established by the user or administrator.

Key Terms

Numbers indicate the pages where terms are first cited with their full definition in the chapter. An alphabetized list of key terms with definitions is included in the end-of-book glossary.

An interactive **Glossary** is available from the links menu on this page in your ebook.

9.1 Assessing the Risks of Computing

cybercrime, 362
threat, 362
vulnerability, 363
hacker, 364
cracker, 364
cyberwar, 365
system backdoor, 365
spoofing, 365
industrial espionage, 366
rogue hotspot, 368
war driving, 368
denial of service (DoS) attack, 369
identity theft, 370
phishing, 370

9.2 Avoiding Computer Viruses

virus, 372
worm, 372
nuisance virus, 374
espionage virus, 374
keystroke logger, 374
data-destructive virus, 374
polymorphic virus, 376
stealth virus, 376
macro virus, 376
boot sector, 376
boot sector virus, 376

Trojan horse virus, 376
multipartite virus, 377
logic bomb virus, 377

9.3 Protecting Computer Systems and Data

network sniffer, 378
ActiveX, 379
phishing filter, 380
virus signature, 380
rotating backup, 381
incremental backup, 381
differential backup, 381
backup appliance, 381
deduplication, 381
disaster recovery plan, 382
authentication, 382
strong password, 383
smart card, 383
biometric identifier, 383
fingerprint scanner, 383
hand geometry system, 384
computerized facial recognition (CFR), 384
iris recognition system, 384
retinal recognition system, 384
voice verification system, 385
signature verification system, 385
encryption, 385
ciphertext, 385

encryption key, 385
secret key encryption, 386
public key encryption, 386
RSA, 386
Secure Sockets Layer (SSL), 386
Transport Layer Security (TLS), 386
Hypertext Transfer Protocol Secure (HTTPS), 386
Secure HTTP (S-HTTP), 387
auditing, 388

9.4 Understanding the Role of Ethics

ethics, 388
computer ethics, 389
computer code of ethics, 391

9.5 Exploring Privacy Protection Issues

consumer profile, 395
first-party cookie, 396
third-party cookie, 396
global universal identification (GUID), 396
privacy policy, 397
Children's Online Privacy Protection Act (COPPA) of 1998, 398
InPrivate Browsing, 400

Chapter Exercises

Complete the following exercises to assess your understanding of the material covered in this chapter.

*Interactive **Flash Cards** and an interactive **Game** are available from the links menu on this page in your ebook.*

Go to your SNAP Assignments page to complete the Terms Check, Knowledge Check, Key Principles, and Tech Illustrated exercises.

Terms Check: Matching

Match each term with its definition. For interactive Flash Cards of key terms and their definitions, go to **http://CUT6.emcp.net/FlashCards**.

a. audit
b. macro virus
c. patent
d. system backdoor
e. polymorphic virus

f. network sniffer
g. consumer profile
h. spoofing
i. worm
j. fingerprint scanner

___ 1. A software package that monitors network traffic.

___ 2. An all-access user ID and password left behind by its original programmer.

___ 3. An executable virus stored within a Word data file.

___ 4. The process of fooling another computer into granting access by changing the address on packets so that they seem to come from a legitimate source.

___ 5. Malware that moves between networked computers rather than between specific files.

___ 6. A biometric security device.

___ 7. A type of virus that changes its behavior to avoid detection.

___ 8. Information about the lifestyle and buying habits of an individual.

___ 9. A review of monitoring data and system logins to look for unauthorized access and suspicious behavior.

___ 10. Ownership of an idea or invention.

Knowledge Check: Multiple Choice

Choose the best answer for each question.

1. Which term refers to a computer security weakness that could possibly be exploited if it were known?
   a. cybercrime
   b. spoofing
   c. threat
   d. vulnerability

2. Which is a type of computer crime where one or more hackers shuts down a system by flooding it with information requests?
   a. denial of service (DoS) attack
   b. industrial espionage
   c. phishing
   d. spoofing

3. Which is an attempt to acquire another person's sensitive information, such as a credit card number, by simulating a trusted website?
   a. spamming
   b. Denial of Service attack
   c. phishing
   d. spoofing

4. Which online security risk tricks the user to connect to a look-alike public wireless network, making his data vulnerable?
   a. cyberwar
   b. data browsing
   c. denial of service (DoS) attack
   d. rogue hotspot

5. Which type of virus allows a hacker to enter a system for the purpose of later stealing data or spying on the work of a competitor?
   a. data-destructive virus
   b. espionage virus
   c. nuisance virus
   d. polymorphic virus

6. Which biometric system uses the unique pattern of blood vessels on the back of the eyeball to identify an individual?
   a. computerized facial recognition
   b. iris recognition system
   c. retinal recognition system
   d. signature verification system

7. Which type of data backup only backs up files that have changed since the last backup?
   a. differential backup
   b. incremental backup
   c. rotating backup
   d. sequence backup

8. Which law was designed to protect school-children and library patrons from being exposed to pornographic sites and other types of restricted materials?
   a. Children's Internet Protection Act (CIPA)
   b. Children's Online Privacy Protection Act COPPA)
   c. Digital Millennium Copyright Act (DMCA)
   d. Family Educational Rights and Privacy Act (FERPA)

9. Which term refers to a set of principles that govern the responsible and competent use of computers?
   a. disaster recovery plan
   b. consumer profile
   c. computer code of ethics
   d. acceptable use policy

10. Which type of virus hides inside a seemingly useful program?
    a. boot sector virus
    b. logic bomb virus
    c. stealth virus
    d. Trojan horse virus

 Key Principles: Completion

Complete each statement with the appropriate word or phrase.

1. _____ refers to using a computer to commit a crime.

2. A _____ virus tries to hide from the software that's been designed to find and destroy it.

3. Active content on web pages may take the form of Java, Flash, or _____ controls.

4. Personal identification numbers (PINs), user IDs and passwords, and biometrics are common forms of _____.

5. A _____ determines a person's identity by measuring the dimensions of her hand.

6. Unreadable, encrypted text is called _____.

7. The successor to the encryption protocol Secure Sockets Layer (SSL) is _____.

8. A cookie created by the website the user is visiting is called a _____.

9. _____ is using others' words and ideas without attributing the original creator(s) as the source.

10. Texting or sending harassing email messages and posting embarrassing photos is called _____.

Tech Illustrated: Figure Labeling

Fill in the blanks with the correct labels.

1. The virus infection process

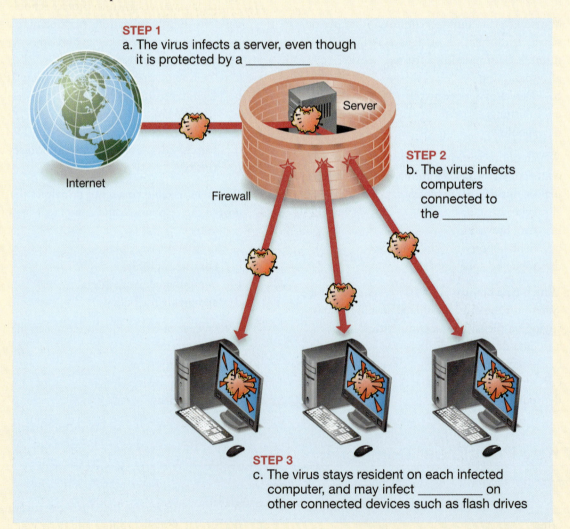

STEP 1
a. The virus infects a server, even though it is protected by a _____

Server

STEP 2
b. The virus infects computers connected to the _____

Internet

Firewall

STEP 3
c. The virus stays resident on each infected computer, and may infect _____ on other connected devices such as flash drives

2. Using an encryption key

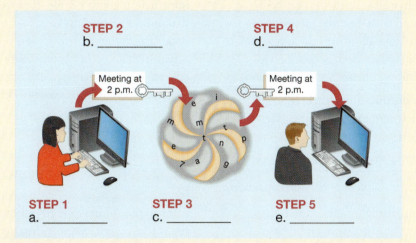

Tech to Come: Brainstorming New Uses

In groups or individually, contemplate the following questions and develop as many answers as you can.

1. In 2014, Apple was awarded a patent for an Automatic Avatar Creation technology that will allow devices to create a three-dimensional avatar that closely resembles the user captured in a photo or video. Research this patent, and then reflect on the potential of this technology. What do you think Apple will use the technology for? What other uses for the technology are related to online security and privacy issues?

2. Biometric authentication is used to identify individuals in a fast and reliable way through the use of unique biological characteristics. For example, fingerprint scanners are now widely used to log in to notebook computers. What other devices are currently making use of biometric technology? What devices do you predict with have this technology in the near future? Where else might this technology be used?

Tech Literacy: Internet Research and Writing

Conduct Internet research to find the information described, and then develop appropriate written responses based on your research. Be sure to document your sources using the MLA format. (See Chapter 1, Tech Literacy: Internet Research and Writing, page 38, to review MLA style guidelines.)

1. Research an actual data security breach, and summarize what happened. Include answers to these questions: How did the hackers or crackers gain access to the system? Was the company negligent in its security practices? Has the company changed its practices as a result of the breach? Were consumers or clients compensated? Were the hackers or crackers caught and charged with a criminal offense? How did the company handle the public relations aftermath?

2. Industrial espionage is often the basis for the plot in a movie, but it also occurs in real life. Research three high-profile industrial espionage cases, and summarize what happened in each. Also reflect on what the company could have done to prevent these incidents.

3. It's hard to avoid getting spam, or junk email. Sort through your email to find examples of potential identity theft, phishing, and viruses. Describe or copy each email, and then explain how it tries to trick the recipient. Research what you can do to protect yourself from these types of emails. How do you think your email address became a target?

4. As discussed in this chapter, companies are concerned with the physical security of their computers. Research and then describe precautions that companies can take to protect the physical security of their computers and electronic devices. Add visuals to enhance your description.

5. Workers in many organizations (such as hospitals and law enforcement agencies) have access to networked databases that contain private information about people. Research and describe data-browsing lawsuits that have occurred because individuals' privacy has been compromised. Reflect on how commonly data browsing occurs. What precautions can organizations put in place to avoid having unauthorized personnel engage in data browsing?

Tech Issues: Team Problem-Solving

In groups, develop possible solutions to the issues presented.

1. Review the section "Bridging the Digital Divide," and reflect on the demographic statistics within your small group. What could be done in your local area to reduce the digital divide? Brainstorm solutions, and then narrow your focus to one possible solution. Present your idea to the whole group.

2. Do you know how to determine whether the website you are visiting is secure? Many users don't realize that browsers display a variety of icons in the Address bar to indicate whether a site is secure. For example, Internet Explorer displays the lock icon to indicate a secure site, and it also uses different colors to indicate whether websites' certificates are valid. Research the security indicators used by three web browsers, and create a visual reference that summarizes the meanings of these indicators. Your visual might take the form of a handout, web page, or slide presentation.

Tech Timeline: Predicting Next Steps

Since the days of early civilization, people have found it necessary to send secret communications that require keys of some kind to decode them. Data encryption has become particularly important with the evolution of the Internet, since companies and individuals routinely store, post, and send private and secure information. Look at the timeline below, outlining the major steps in the history of encryption techniques. Then research the subject and add at least two more steps to the timeline.

5th century BC Greeks use numbers to represent letters in sending secret messages.

AD 16th–18th centuries Ruling monarchs use substitution cipher techniques (letters that represent other alphabet letters).

1942 During World War II, the US Marine Corps use Navajo code talkers, who use their native language to transmit secure communications.

1960 The first user authentication system (user ID and password) is introduced by MIT's CTSS (Compatible Time-Sharing System) as a way to limit scarce computing time.

1970s The data encryption standard (DES) algorithm is introduced.

1991 Pretty Good Privacy (PGP) is released as freeware and becomes a worldwide standard in data encryption software.

1994 Netscape releases Secure Sockets Layer (SSL) technology.

1997 The Advanced Encryption Standard (AES) is released by the National Institute of Standards and Technology (NIST) as a replacement standard to DES.

1999 Wired Equivalent Privacy (WEP) is ratified as a part of the Institute of Electrical and Electronics (IEEE) Engineers) 802.11 standard.

1999 The Transport Layer Security (TLS) 1.0 protocol is released.

2002 Advanced Encryption Standard (AES) becomes a standard for the US government.

2004 The 802.11i extension to the Wi-Fi standard is ratified as an improvement over the WEP standard.

2007 94 million credit cards are exposed when hackers take advantage of a weak encryption system at TJX, which owns Marshalls and TJ Maxx.

2013 According to reports by the New York Times and other major news media outlets, the US National Security Agency (NSA) has secretly succeeded in breaking much of the encryption used to keep personal data safe online.

2013 Google provides a free encryption service for all data stored in Google Cloud Storage. This action is designed to reassure consumers concerned over government surveillance of private online data.

2014 Microsoft activates Transport Layer Security (TLS) encryption for its webmail services Outlook.com, Hotmail.com, Live.com, and MSN.com.

Ethical Dilemmas: Group Discussion and Debate

As a class or within an assigned group, discuss the following ethical dilemma.

Employers have the legal right to track what their employees do online during work hours. Although many employers feel that such monitoring is necessary to keep workers focused and productive, many employees feel that monitoring is an invasion of their privacy.

Research the technology used to monitor employees and then discuss these questions:

- Should employees be warned they are being monitored?

- Can using web filters to block certain categories of websites (such as online shopping sites) be used as an alternative to monitoring employees?
- If employees use employer-provided laptops and cell phones after work hours or during work breaks, should companies monitor this use as well?
- Should an employee be fired for a first-time violation?

Chapter 10

Leveraging Technology in Business

Chapter Goal

To understand how information technology plays an expanding role in business operations, decision making, and commerce

Learning Objectives

10.1 Explain and give examples of information systems.

10.2 Discuss the considerations for planning and analyzing information systems.

10.3 Outline the process for designing and developing a new information system.

10.4 Describe the steps for implementing an information system.

10.5 Explain how to support and maintain an information system.

10.6 Describe e-commerce and online shopping, including venues, sites, apps, and examples.

10.7 List and give details about various e-commerce payment methods and explain how to use mobile devices for transactions.

10.8 Distinguish between consumer e-commerce and business-to-business (B2B) e-commerce, and describe major B2B technologies.

Green go-online icons indicate resources that are accessed from the links menu in your ebook.

SNAP icons indicate interactive resources that are available in SNAP. Go to your SNAP Assignments page to complete these quizzes, activities, and exercises.

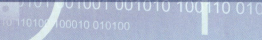

10.1 Understanding Information Systems and Their Functions

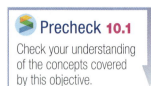

Precheck 10.1

Check your understanding of the concepts covered by this objective.

An information system is much more than computers or software. An **information system (IS)** combines hardware, software, networks, and other components to collect, store, and process data that people in organizations use to manage daily and long-term operations and create and sell various types of products. For example, an organization might use computerized information processing for taking orders, tracking inventory, and other transactions. Organizations also use ISs for organization-wide, long-term operations, including gathering and organizing the information necessary to make decisions about future growth and other strategic changes (see Figure 10.1).

Figure 10.1

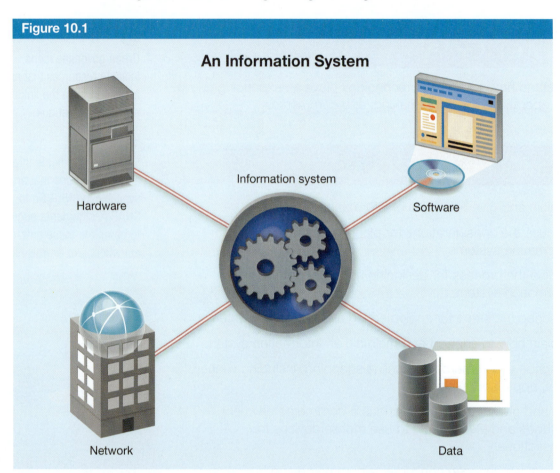

An information system combines hardware, software, networks, and other components to collect, store, and process data that people in organizations use to manage daily and long-term operations and create and sell various types of products.

Tracking Down Tech ❯❯❯❯❯

Finding Sales and Informational QR Codes

Thanks to technology, businesses of all types have more ways than ever to sell products to consumers. Start observing how common one digital sales method has become, by completing this scavenger hunt to find sales and informational quick response (QR) codes on campus and beyond.

A fast-food purchase transaction serves as an excellent example of how information systems function. A customer service associate takes an order, enters it into a customized cash register, and performs a cash or credit transaction, issuing a receipt. The "cash register" works as a sophisticated networked computer. It transmits the food order to the prep area or kitchen, where overhead terminals display multiple orders in sequence so that the food-prep workers know what food to prepare in what order. The information system database automatically removes the food ingredients from inventory as the associates prepare and conclude each order. In this type of system, the term **point of sale (POS)** or **electronic point of sale (EPOS)** commonly refers to the cash register system and supporting IS software and systems.

The restaurant manager and owner can use the information that the database in the POS system gathers and processes to create reports covering a variety of topics. Such a system makes it easy to review the day's financial transactions and totals, identify which items need to be reordered, and zero in on best-selling products. Members of the marketing team in the franchise or parent company headquarters can use the gathered information to improve the restaurant's financial results by deciding which products should be discontinued, promoted, or possibly sold at a reduced price.

Why do companies and governments use information systems? Simply put, computerized information management increases productivity and efficiency, making companies more competitive and service providers more efficient. Computer-based information systems offer four key advantages over traditional (precomputer) information systems:

- **Improved speed.** Companies perform daily operations more quickly, reducing production times and increasing employee productivity.
- **Improved efficiency.** Well-designed information systems result in more efficient production processes, saving time and money. Figure 10.2 shows how implementing an automated system can improve speed and efficiency even in a fast-moving service, such as toll collection.

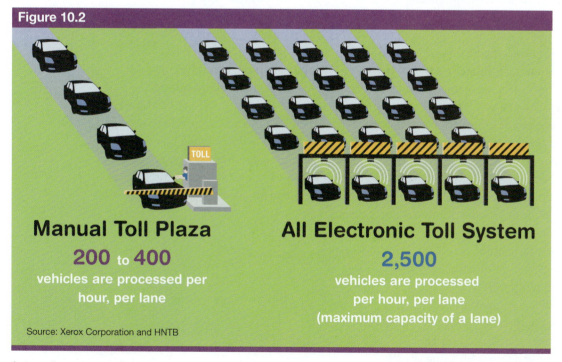

Figure 10.2

Manual Toll Plaza
200 to **400**
vehicles are processed per hour, per lane

All Electronic Toll System
2,500
vehicles are processed per hour, per lane
(maximum capacity of a lane)

Source: Xerox Corporation and HNTB

Automating a transaction system such as toll collection can improve speed and efficiency.

- **Improved quality.** Because computer-based information systems handle tasks previously handled by humans under traditional systems, they tend to reduce human error, enhancing product quality.
- **Improved measurability.** Computers can track most production factors, making it easier to organize recent data to find trends and abnormalities. Team members can then apply the resulting information to improve products and streamline the production process.

The first computerized information systems appeared in the 1950s. They were designed to handle tedious tasks such as sorting mail, printing checks, creating phone bills, and storing demographic data for the US Census Bureau. Now we accept various types of information systems as part of daily life. Bank ATMs and pay-at-the-pump stations allow us to make self-service transactions. Online shopping enables us to shop from the comfort of our home or dorm, or we can use a mobile app to buy products and make payments. Retailers use bar code readers to scan items and launch a series of actions: recording the price, deducting the item from inventory, and ordering a

Retailers use information systems that track pricing and inventory, as well as using scanning for faster checkout transactions.

replacement. New digital payment methods make it easier for small retailers to accept credit cards. Comparing the speed of these electronic operations with the time they once took to perform manually shows why computerized information systems are so valuable.

Computerized information systems continue to transform business and governmental activities that humans previously handled, both consolidating and expanding operations. Older systems compartmentalized information and maintained separate databases for various functions such as payroll, billing, sales, and work orders. Newer systems integrate such formerly separate databases, making data more accessible and increasing the variety of methods that users can employ to evaluate the resulting information.

Different types of information systems can be classified by function. Depending on need and size, an organization may implement a more limited or more broad type of system. For example, a small manufacturer might only need to employ a system to automate distribution, while a Fortune 500 company might put an organization-wide enterprise resource planning system into operation. In the following sections, you will learn more about these types of information systems:

- Distribution management
- Office information
- Management information
- Decision support
- Executive information
- Factory automation and plant operations
- Customer relationship management (CRM)
- Enterprise resource planning (ERP)

A distribution management system enables a company to manage product warehouse and delivery systems more effectively, especially for large-scale operations.

Distribution Management Systems

An information system designed to get products to customers more effectively can have a huge impact on business operations. A **distribution management system** enables a company to deliver products quicker, cheaper, and with fewer errors. A distribution management system includes an underlying database, but the structure also includes elements that may seem unrelated, such as the duties and schedules of forklift operators and truck drivers. Large retailers such as Amazon and Walmart rely on automated distribution and inventory management tools to increase efficiency in areas such as delivery time and product inventory levels.

Implementing a distribution management system typically enables a company to reduce inventory overhead—a major business advantage. Traditionally, distribution management systems involved making or ordering large quantities of finished goods in advance, manually tracking warehouse inventory (that is, counting products by hand and recording the count on paper) and deliveries, and then manufacturing or reordering large quantities based on estimates to restock the warehouse.

Now, distribution management systems form a critical part of supply chain management (SCM), which includes expertise in transporting and storing goods and materials from origin through manufacture to consumption. Experts in **distribution logistics**, who focus on delivering products and materials, use various distribution management systems to track orders, shipping, billing, and more. Many companies today also incorporate **telematics** systems that combine GPS, wireless communications features, and other technologies to plan more efficient shipping routes and monitor shipment locations.

In complicated businesses with large warehouses and diverse products arriving and shipping out, a sophisticated distribution management system can optimize the areas

Tech Career Explorer

Career Logistics

While many warehouse and distribution careers may seem low tech, logistics careers often demand complex problem-solving, analytical, and technical skills. In fact, the material handling industry trade group MHI has estimated that 1.4 million new logistics workers (270,000 per year) will be needed by 2018, with a median salary of $80,000. Look into logistics careers by completing this exercise.

Figure 10.3

Areas That a Distribution Management System Can Optimize

Warehouse layout and efficiency

Inventory slotting by demand or size

Compliance with regulations

Labor usage and costs

Shipping from vendors, and to and from customers

Shipped? YES!

Vendor and customer ordering and communications

listed in Figure 10.3. For example, modern warehouse systems use **radio frequency identification (RFID)** to enhance inventory tracking and placement (called *slotting*). In this technology, tags or labels include an integrated circuit and are able to receive and transmit a radio frequency signal.

Office Information Systems

An **office information system (OIS)** automates office work. This type of system collects, stores, and transmits data in a shared environment. An OIS typically provides standard operating procedures, connectivity, and electronic data processing.

Hotspot

Tagging Inventory

As you just learned, RFID tags work wirelessly. A company can attach RFID tags to palettes or boxes of products, or even individual items. Each RFID tag usually has a unique serial number (some are user programmable) that can be used to track the tagged inventory item. So, for example, when the tagged item is placed in a particular warehouse slot location, the warehouse employee can assign the appropriate tag number to the appropriate location slot in the inventory-tracking database. Depending on the specific type of tag and overall system in use, the tag may be tracked automatically, or the employee may need to use a handheld reader device to scan the tag when the inventory item is moved to a new location. Some tags use the Bluetooth wireless frequencies, while others use the 802.11 wireless network standard. RFID chips can be used for other types of tracking, as well. For example, pet identification microchips use RFID technology.

Standard Operating Procedures A **standard operating procedure (SOP)** includes a set of instructions describing how to perform a task. Workers follow the logical steps in SOPs to process information correctly. SOPs cover both manual and computerized processes, including data entry, report generation, and paperwork flow. In a college setting, there are typically SOPs for activities such as admitting students, entering them into the information system, processing scholarships, disbursing financial aid, and processing transcripts.

Connectivity **Connectivity** refers to the ability to link with other programs and devices. Connectivity enables office workers to move information faster and more accurately from one part of the information system to the next—without documents being lost or forgotten along the way. Connectivity is enhanced by computer networks that facilitate faxes, email, and other forms of electronic document transmission.

Electronic Data Processing **Electronic data processing (EDP)** is the use of computers to process data automatically. This function can take a variety of forms, from triggering electronic payroll deposits by using a payroll-processing system to creating new documents. Transactional processing is used for most situations involving standardized data entry, such as ordering systems in fast-food restaurants. Businesses handling large amounts of data input often use batch processing. For example, the banking industry uses batch processing to process the millions of checks and cash card transactions that need to be cleared every day. Batch processing is usually more efficient than updating the entire database every time a change is made.

Management Information Systems

With the exception of very small companies, nearly every business uses some form of a **management information system (MIS)**. As the name suggests, the purpose of an MIS is to provide information that assists in the management of business operations. Management information systems typically integrate information from different company departments or functions into one database. This combining characteristic is what enables the comprehensive reporting capabilities of an MIS. An MIS usually provides support to management in the form of regular reports, on either a periodic or an on-demand basis. Quarterly earnings, monthly cash flow, and other types of reports provide important information that helps managers improve productivity and profitability. Management information systems also can identify problem activity, such as an unusually high number of production errors or customer returns.

Decision Support Systems

A **decision support system (DSS)** helps managers make informed business judgments. An organization generally custom builds a DSS for each business case or problem to solve. A user can create a simple DSS using a spreadsheet program, while more sophisticated examples include artificial intelligence technology. A DSS might exist independently of an OIS or MIS, but it may use the same software and database information.

Decision support systems do more than track input data and print summary reports covering what happened during the previous month. A DSS includes a user interface as well as a database. In addition, a DSS uses a model, or data modeling, to analyze the data. **Data modeling** builds in decision factors and criteria to simulate a real-world situation. With data modeling systems, users can input numeric data into "what if?"

scenarios to predict outcomes, or make choices to arrive at data that meets goals or objectives. For example, company leaders can use data modeling to help them decide whether to open a new branch office or to determine loan payments at different rates of interest. The ability to visualize alternative scenarios is a valuable decision-making aid.

Many websites build in DSS technology to help you find products, services, and programs based on criteria you specify. For example, you might want to use a comparison site such as MSN Autos to search for a new or used vehicle that has the features you select, as shown in Figure 10.4.

Spreadsheets Used to Create DSS Applications In many ways, the popularity of spreadsheets as simple decision support systems drove the PC revolution in the early 1980s. Experts considered spreadsheet programs as "killer applications" that spurred early PC sales into the millions. People used spreadsheet programs to "run the numbers"—business jargon for performing a DSS-type "what if?" analysis. Recent versions of Microsoft Excel include specific functions and tools you can use to analyze data or perform "what if?" comparisons. For example, Figure 10.5 shows how Excel's Goal Seek feature calculated the selling price needed to achieve a 45 percent target margin with a $1.99 cost of goods.

Expert Systems An **expert system** is a sophisticated DSS that attempts to model an expert's knowledge of a topic. An expert system contains a set of facts and rules—called a **knowledge base**—about a specific, complex application. The system leads the user through a series of focused questions and then makes recommendations based on the user's responses. Expert systems exist to aid doctors in diagnosing rare diseases, to help geologists find oil and mineral deposits, and to troubleshoot network connections. Expert systems qualify as decision support systems but also represent a

Figure 10.4

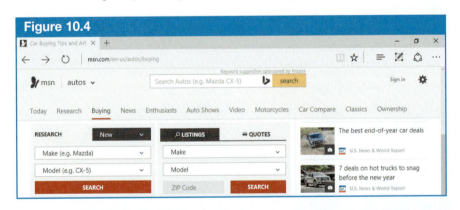

MSN Autos uses decision support system (DSS) technology to help users shop for cars.

Figure 10.5

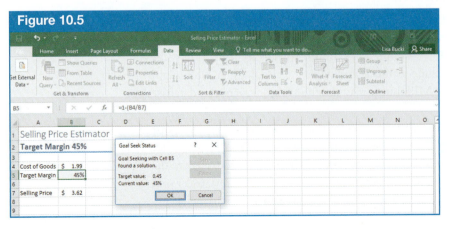

Microsoft Excel includes functions and tools you can use to support business decision making. In this example, the user enters the cost of goods in cell B4 as well as an example selling price greater than 0 in cell B7, and the desired target margin value for cell B5 in the Goal Seek feature. These values enable Goal Seek to calculate the selling price needed to achieve the target.

major component of the field of artificial intelligence. For more information about expert systems, see the section "Artificial Intelligence" in Chapter 13.

Online Analytical Processing Systems

An **online analytical processing (OLAP) system** defines and clarifies methods of handling "what if?" questions posed to large databases, as well as to massively distributed data systems such as the Internet. OLAP originated from a white paper commissioned by Arbor Software and written by Dr. E. F. Codd and others in 1993. A variety of OLAP software emerged from that point, as well as some software companies building OLAP capabilities into existing programs. The field

A doctor might use an expert system to help diagnose a rare disease.

continues to evolve, with a major focus on providing better ways to analyze the mass of data now pouring into databases, thus producing more useful results. (The section "Multidimensional Databases" in Chapter 12 explains more about using OLAP techniques to structure data.)

The information yielded through effective use of OLAP systems is called **business intelligence (BI)**. Some examples of business intelligence large corporations seek via OLAP systems include customer spending patterns and behavior, competitive positioning with other companies, and risk factors for credit or insurance purposes.

Executive Information Systems

An **executive information system (EIS)** functions as an upper-management tool. It's similar to a decision support system but is generally more intuitive and broader in focus. An EIS attempts to bring together information from an entire organization, rather than focus on any one department or group. It supports strategic decision making by facilitating the creation of high-level summary reports that executives can use to help make any number of important decisions. For example, an EIS can be used to evaluate accounting issues, such as cash flow, quarterly earnings, and dividends. In addition to knowing which burgers sell best, the CEO of a fast-food chain might want to know which locations are experiencing the best sales growth. This information can then be used to maximize profits by ensuring that new restaurants are opened only in the high-growth locations the EIS identifies.

Factory Automation and Plant Operations Systems

In addition to being used in offices, information systems are frequently found in factories. The types of systems used in factory automation include computer-aided manufacturing (CAM) and computer-integrated manufacturing (CIM). Statistical quality control (SQC) is another form of information system often used in plant operations.

Computer-Aided Manufacturing A **computer-aided manufacturing (CAM) system** involves the direct use of computerized systems to manufacture products. The use of robots in automobile manufacturing plants is a classic example of this technology. Another classic example is the use of common systems that monitor and report

Automobile manufacturing plants commonly use robots as part of computer-aided manufacturing (CAM) systems.

on assembly line progress. These CAM systems provide factory operators with information such as temperature readings, assembly line speeds, and quality test failure statistics. Any computerized system that directly aids in a manufacturing process is called a *CAM system*.

Computer-Integrated Manufacturing

A **computer-integrated manufacturing (CIM) system** offers much broader coverage than a CAM system. CIM systems focus not only on the factory floor but also on the company as a whole. A CIM system connects the factory floor to the executive offices, the accounting department, and the sales staff, making information available to anyone who might need it. As a much larger form of information system than a CAM, a CIM impacts everyone in a manufacturing company—from the president down to the mail clerk.

In an automotive company employing CIM, factory lines would use individual CAM systems to help operators monitor and control production. These CAM systems would be networked to a CIM that tracks production progress, errors, and goals, and this information would be automatically sent to headquarters for evaluation. Orders would also be sent from the management information system, telling the CAM lines what to produce and in what quantities.

Statistical Quality Control

A **statistical quality control (SQC) system** uses a combination of data tracking and data modeling to build a picture of how well a factory operates. An SQC tracks measurements of final product quality and compares them with the conditions present throughout the manufacturing process. For example, through the use of an SQC, a car manufacturer may discover that some supplied metal caused more defective parts than other supplied metal, or that one shift of workers generates better-quality products than another shift.

Customer Relationship Management (CRM) Systems

A **customer relationship management (CRM) system** gives a company a structured way to track interactions with current and potential customers. CRM systems start with tasks as simple as building a customer contact list, and from there build in features such as targeted marketing and promotions, mobile and social marketing, and customer service and support tracking.

Activity 10.1.1

Article
Customer Relationship Management

In terms of market share and sales revenue, the top CRM services include Salesforce Sales Cloud, SAP, Oracle Sales Cloud, and Microsoft Dynamics CRM (see Figure 10.6). The various services include a wide variety of pricing options and offerings, so an organization considering CRM options should consider the following factors:

- **Onsite versus cloud.** Some services, including Salesforce Sales Cloud and Oracle Sales Cloud, offer only web-based services, for which the charges can be hundreds per month per user. Other services, such as Microsoft Dynamics CRM, enable organizations to purchase and install the software onsite. Large organizations might save money in the long run with an installed application. Small businesses might consider Zoho CRM, which is free for up to three users.

Figure 10.6

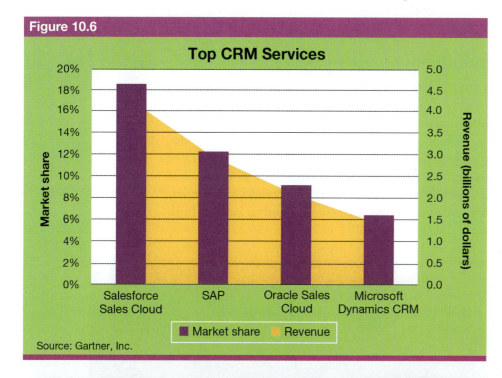

The top-four CRM services commanded more than 45 percent of that market and had more than $10 billion in sales in 2014.

Customer relationship management (CRM) systems give companies a platform for managing customer interactions. Some, including SugarCRM, integrate mobile apps.

- **Integration.** An organization may have other systems in place and need to integrate its CRM approach with existing data. For example, Oracle Sales Cloud integrates with other Oracle systems, and likewise, Microsoft Dynamics CRM integrates with Office 365. Insightly, a cloud-based solution, works well with Google apps, Gmail, Google Drive, and other services (such as Evernote). Nimble works well with social media offerings, and Zoho CRM integrates well with Intuit QuickBooks accounting software and more.

- **Mobile apps and customization.** Mobile capabilities and customization offerings vary widely among CRM providers. For example, Sage CRM enables clients to build custom modules they can use to manage events, tradeshows, projects, and more. SugarCRM and other services include well-integrated mobile apps for a variety of uses.

Enterprise Resource Planning (ERP) Systems

When a business or other organization grows large and complex, running all its diverse functional areas presents challenges. An enterprise needs to pull together information from many varied areas such as human resources, accounting, product planning and design, the manufacturing floor, the supply chain, and CRM and sales. An **enterprise resource planning (ERP) system** uses integrated applications or modules for the various business functions that work with the data in a centralized database. Depending on the system being used, there might be modules for planning, material purchasing, distribution, inventory management, accounting, business intelligence and reporting, and so on (see Figure 10.7).

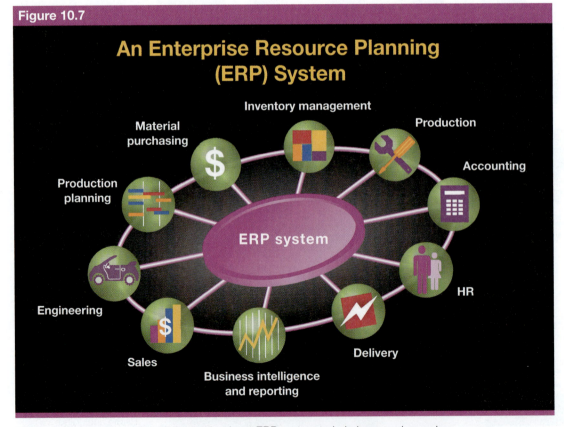

Figure 10.7

An Enterprise Resource Planning (ERP) System

Different functional modules work together in an ERP system to help large and complex organizations pull together information from varied areas.

IT professionals typically identify or classify ERP systems by industry or size. For example, a healthcare/medical organization typically uses a different type of ERP system than an aerospace or public sector (government) enterprise. Professionals in the ERP field also classify ERP solutions and their providers in tiers according to size:

- **Tier I, or large enterprise ERP systems.** Tier I providers serve the largest enterprises—usually companies with revenues exceeding $1 billion annually. Oracle, SAP, and Microsoft Dynamics ERP lead in this tier.
- **Tier II, or midmarket ERP systems.** Tier II providers sell to enterprises with $50 million to $1 billion in annual revenues. As expected, more providers compete in this tier, including abas-USA, Epicor, IFS, Infor Lawson, NetSuite, Plex Systems, QAD, and Sage.
- **Tier III, or small business ERP systems.** The Tier III market includes companies with $10 to $50 million in annual revenues and, generally, more simple business data needs. ERP providers such as Activant (part of Epicor), Consona, Aptean, Exact Globe, SYSPRO, and Visibility offer systems for this tier.

In some cases, enterprise customers may combine solutions from different vendors (when compatible) to customize an overall system. For example, IBM partners with Oracle to provide custom ERP solutions. Many ERP systems also include customizations such as language localization, cloud services, and mobile app integration. So, for example, an employee on a sales call could enter travel expenses from a mobile device to the ERP sales-tracking module.

 Recheck 10.1
Recheck your understanding of the concepts covered by this objective.

10.2 Planning and Analyzing Information Systems

 Precheck 10.2
Check your understanding of the concepts covered by this objective.

An organization might initiate the process of planning or updating an information system in response to a variety of factors. For instance, the company leadership may decide to "computerize" paper-based systems that worked well in the past but no longer keep up with today's marketplace demands. Or perhaps a company that uses systems and databases accessible only to a few people with specialized skills needs a new system to accommodate business expansion. For example, a small professional

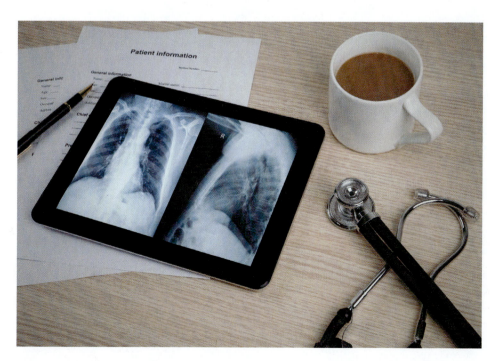

A well-designed information system can make resources and information more accessible. For example, a physician in an office can view a patient's X-rays added to the system by another physician treating the patient in the hospital.

office might join with several other offices to form a larger practice. Its billing and receiving information may be on one computer database, while its payroll and inventory systems may still reside on paper forms. The larger practice could utilize a new information system to integrate all the functions and records of its member offices, allowing access to the practice's data from any networked device.

System Development Life Cycle

The comprehensive process for building an information system is called the **system development life cycle (SDLC)**, a series of steps culminating in a completed information system (see Figure 10.8). Creating and executing a development plan includes several stages, some of which have already been set in motion as part of the decision to proceed with the project. The process includes planning, design, implementation, and support—always returning to the planning stage, to continue through the cycle again. The planning stage includes preparing a needs analysis, conducting a feasibility

Activity 10.2.1

Practice
**The System
Development Life Cycle**

Figure 10.8

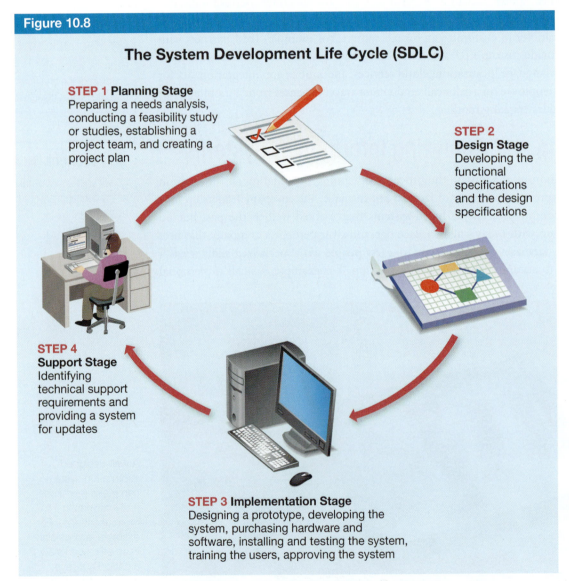

The System Development Life Cycle (SDLC)

STEP 1 Planning Stage
Preparing a needs analysis, conducting a feasibility study or studies, establishing a project team, and creating a project plan

**STEP 2
Design Stage**
Developing the functional specifications and the design specifications

**STEP 4
Support Stage**
Identifying technical support requirements and providing a system for updates

STEP 3 Implementation Stage
Designing a prototype, developing the system, purchasing hardware and software, installing and testing the system, training the users, approving the system

The development of an information system follows an ongoing system development life cycle (SDLC), which includes planning, design, implementation, and support.

study or studies, establishing a project team, and creating a project plan. In the design stage, the team develops the functional specifications and the design specifications. The implementation stage consists of designing a prototype, developing the system, purchasing hardware and software, installing and testing the system, training the users, and approving the system. The support stage incorporates identifying technical support requirements and providing a system for updates.

System Planning and Analysis

To understand how the information system development process works, imagine a scenario involving an automobile manufacturing company named Big Engines, Inc. Big Engines' management decides the company's old system operates poorly and sees an opportunity to improve current operations. After recognizing the need for a new system, management can contact either the company's own internal development team (if one exists) or an outside vendor.

Suppose Big Engines wants to upgrade its existing CIM. A **feasibility study** is conducted to investigate how large the project might be and how much it might cost. A large automobile company like Big Engines typically employs its own internal development team. However, the internal team may recommend hiring a systems vendor or integrator if the project is beyond the team's capabilities or if the team is too busy handling existing problems.

If management decides to hire a systems vendor or integrator, a **request for proposal (RFP)** is sent to one or more possible suppliers. The systems vendors or integrators send representatives to better determine system requirements before quoting a price. Big Engines then reviews each proposal response to choose the vendor best meeting the project requirements and desired pricing and schedule.

An RFP response typically requests a **project plan**, which includes an estimate of how long the project will take to complete, an outline of the steps involved, and a list of deliverables. A **deliverable** is a document, service, hardware, or software that must be finished and delivered by a certain time and date to keep the project on schedule. Big Engines' project team sketches out overall plan requirements before releasing the RFP. The vendor responses supply recommended details, including the cost and benefits of the project, references from client for whom similar work was completed, and résumés for the consultants who will work on the project. Most vendor agreements tie payments to the successful completion of project deliverables.

Project planning normally involves a large number of meetings. Systems analysts must meet regularly with potential system users and management personnel to learn precise needs, wants, and processes. Interviews, employee questionnaires, and simple observation of daily practices all factor into this process. Various project management tools are available to help schedule each phase of the project and to determine the priority of each step.

Planning is the first step in the system development life cycle. This stage includes preparing a needs analysis, conducting a feasibility study, issuing requests for proposals, establishing a project team, and creating a project plan.

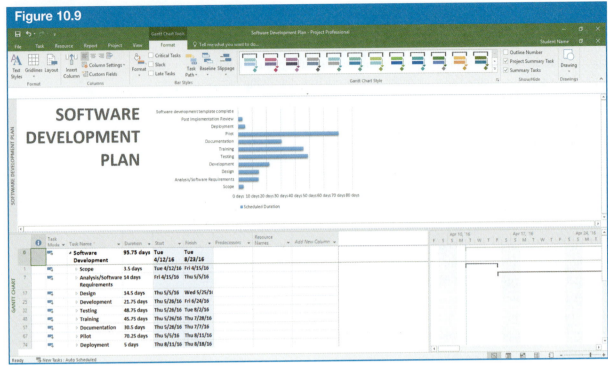

Figure 10.9

A Gantt chart helps to visually communicate the critical steps and schedule for a project. This example is based on a free Microsoft Project template developed by Microsoft.

The project manager probably uses specific planning tools to handle a large systems development project, such as a project management tool like Microsoft Project (Figure 10.9) or ProjectLibre (http://CUT6.emcp.com/ProjectLibre), both of which can create Gantt charts and other types of project timelines. A **Gantt chart**, named after Henry Gantt, uses bars to show the stages and tasks in a project and the order in which they must be completed. A Gantt chart graphically shows task beginning and end times to map out the schedule in detail. Other online project management systems work well too. Setting realistic time frames—one of the most difficult tasks in project management—contributes to the success of any project.

Creating a Project Team

Identifying and assembling a team of employees with the skills and expertise required to develop or implement a new information system comes early in any major system overhaul. A **business systems analyst** typically leads the early phases of systems development. Through interviews with management and users, the analyst defines the business problem and plans a solution. In response to the business systems analyst's recommendations, software engineers and programmers handle the design and implementation of the new system. The team may either base the new system on software from an outside provider or start from scratch.

Programmers specialize in writing the software code for new software, typically focusing on specific tasks. In contrast, software

The project team should ensure that any purchased information system includes adequate technical support, including on-site trouble-shooting and assistance as needed.

engineers create the higher-level software design, as well as focusing on the broader planning and implementation steps for the system. This set of activities overall comprises **software engineering** (sometimes also called **software development**). Larger-scale projects that also involve production and manufacturing systems may require input from a **systems engineer**: a technical expert who can help plan and develop the various parts of the information system that interact with other processes, such as an assembly line.

Any large software or system project requires creating a project team. That team usually includes a project manager, who acts as the team leader. Sometimes, the project manager also functions as a systems analyst, responsible for completing the systems analysis and making design recommendations. The rest of the project team includes software engineers, programmers, hardware techs, and in some cases, other internal experts who can provide feedback on how to address particular business functions. The software engineers and programmers deal with software issues, while the technicians handle hardware issues. (Note that different organizations may configure project teams differently, and often include external consultants and programmers, as well as company members, to ensure the team includes the proper skill sets.)

Evaluating the Impact of a New Information System

The decision makers in an organization should study the likely impact of a new information system in advance to determine the system's suitability. Replacing a traditional paper system or differing electronic solutions from various departments can result in a difficult adjustment process for some employees. Sometimes, a major information system upgrade—moving from using Excel spreadsheets to using an SAP ERP system, for example—makes almost as dramatic an impact as does the switch from a paper system to an electronic system.

While moving to a new information system results in both positive and negative effects, the negative effects typically work themselves out relatively quickly as users learn the system. As an infrastructure investment, a new information system may take time to provide a full return on the investment. The major effects of upgrading or switching to a computer-based information system include the following:

- **Expanded technical staff.** In the short term, new technology requires additional technical personnel, such as network technicians and programmers. The transition period can last a year or more for a large system project, and the company payroll will increase dramatically. In addition to paying existing staff to keep business rolling, the company must pay to retrain the current staff so they can operate the new system. Some organizations also train teams of "superusers" who can share their system knowledge with other employees.

- **Added equipment and upgrade costs.** The pricing for a new system should include the cost for upgrades. Many new systems require immediate hardware and software (such as operating system) upgrades, while for other systems, upgrades can take place over time. In some cases, the system may run on existing server hardware. In other instances, the team may decide to upgrade servers as well, to take advantage of the speed and performance boost provided by the latest server technology.

A new information system might trigger the need for hardware and software upgrades. The system development plan should include the necessary staffing and budget to handle equipment disposal and recycling.

- **Increased profit margins.** Any information system should pay off in the ability to do business faster or to grow the business. This effect usually takes time to materialize. Even in the case where a new information system doesn't reduce a company's expenses, it typically enables the company to grow and expand its business.

- **Enhanced product or service quality.** After the complete implementation of an information system, improvements in product and service quality should follow. For example, a manufacturing company might see raw materials arrive more quickly and with fewer errors in the received shipments. These changes can lead to higher-quality products, which mean more satisfied customers and therefore increased sales—the ultimate goal of making any business change.

- **Streamlined staffing.** Adding or upgrading an information system could reduce the need for team members in some areas of an organization. For example, computerized billing, order taking, and credit approval processes might translate into reductions in the staff needed to handle those functions. Any savings from reduced staffing should help offset the cost of implementing the system.

- **Temporary disruption.** On the technical side, hardware and software systems take time to perfect, and errors will emerge while implementing these systems. On the human side, switching systems stresses employees at all levels, as people learn new methods for accomplishing their jobs.

Choosing a New Information System

The purchase of an information system is a major decision, particularly for a small organization. In the early planning stages, decision makers may have only limited knowledge to guide them. It isn't uncommon for nontechnical people to find themselves in charge of deciding which hardware and software combination to purchase for their organization—without having any idea of how to make that decision. Decision makers should consider the following factors when choosing an information systems package:

Activity 10.2.2

Article
Value-Added Resellers and Original Equipment Manufacturers

- Internal development versus outsourcing
- User interface design
- Niche information system
- Turnkey system
- System support

Internal Development versus Outsourcing Once the organization has decided to proceed with a new system, the next decision revolves around how to bring the system into service. Although many IS solutions are purchased from large providers, an organization typically needs information technology (IT) team members familiar with the software to implement and develop any needed customizations for it internally. Otherwise, the organization may need to bring in external resources to implement and develop the new system.

The decision between using internal versus external resources is heavily influenced by the organization's size. Larger organizations usually have in-house IT staffs devoted to developing and maintaining information systems. Smaller organizations usually can't afford to pay or hire employees to implement and develop information systems, so they end up purchasing standard software packages or subcontracting their information system development and support work. Often called **outsourcing**, this practice involves hiring a third party to handle the project—usually, a consultant or

Activity 10.2.3

Article
The Buy versus Build Decision

Some organizations outsource the development and maintenance of the information system to a systems integrator as a more cost-effective way to meet the organization's technology needs.

a systems integrator. A **systems integrator** is a company that specializes in installing and supporting information systems.

As a company grows and its needs become more complicated, hiring IT experts for systems maintenance and support may become a necessity. Hourly consulting rates typically exceed those of internal tech staff.

User Interface When comparing systems to purchase and implement, the organization will want to consider each system's user interface. The interface design should be user friendly and intuitive, making critical information readily apparent. Examining and comparing a number of different interfaces can prevent costly mistakes.

Niche Information System A **niche information system**, also called a **vertical market system**, exists to serve a specially focused set of customers. For example, a number of niche systems—including products such as Shop Boss Pro and AutoBiz—provide tools for running an auto repair shop. (Similar products help users run wheel and tire stores and auto body repair shops.) Such a system includes key forms and reports, such as those for customer contact information, repair orders (see the example

 **Activity 10.2.4**

Article
Horizontal versus Vertical Market Software

Practical TECH

Your Piece of the IS Interface

In some cases, an information system can address user interface and interaction issues for external customers, as well as employees and vendors or partners. Take mobile banking apps, for example. When you download and install a mobile banking app on your smartphone or tablet, the app must be easy to use and navigate on your device, as well as communicate seamlessly with the bank's internal account and transaction systems. Most large and regional banks offer mobile banking apps, as do some smaller local banks. A mobile app can save you tremendous time, enabling you to make transfers and online payments—and in some cases, limited check deposits—from wherever you are and for no additional fees, depending on your account type.

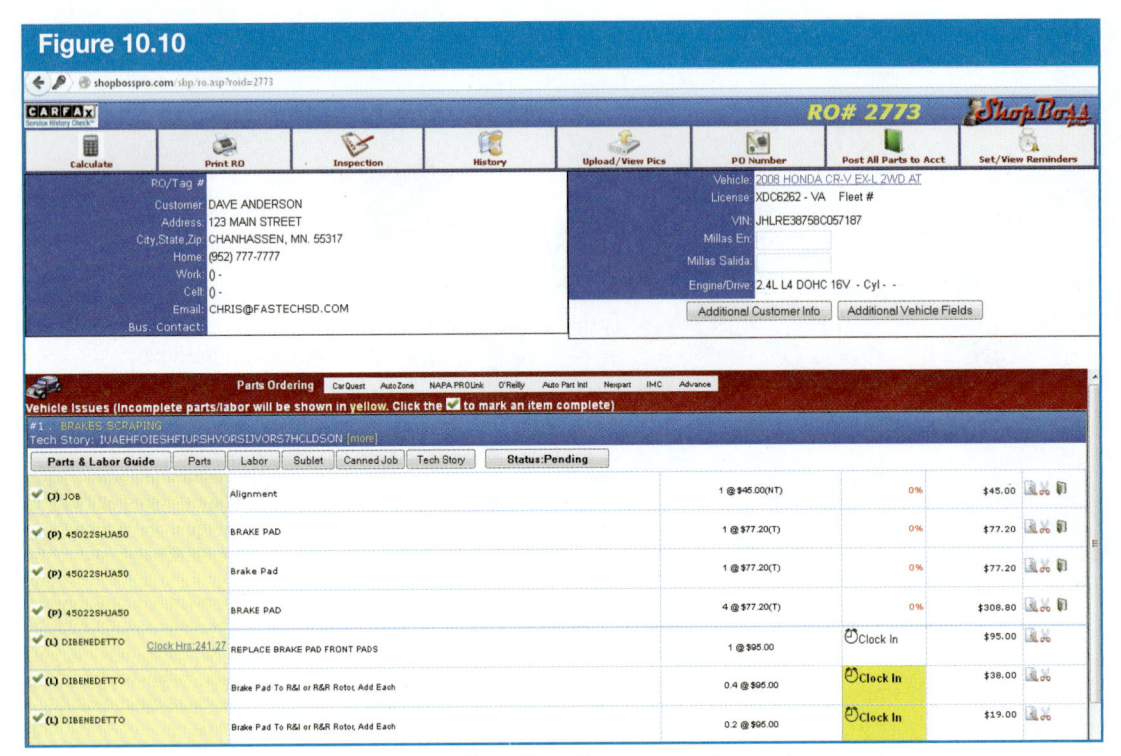

This screen showing a repair order from the Shop Boss Pro program for running an auto repair shop illustrates a typical niche information system designed for a specific business.

in Figure 10.10), work in progress, vehicle repair history, and so on. This type of information system typically serves an organization's needs well without requiring a lot of technical know-how or staff training.

Turnkey System   A **turnkey system** contains everything a business needs to get a new information system up and running. The name comes from the idea of simply being able to "turn the key," similarly to how you start a car by turning the key to start the engine. You shouldn't run into any complications or need any particular technical skills. Because turnkey systems feature heavy customization and may include support services to tailor them to an organization's exact needs, they can be quite expensive.

System Support and Maintenance   The organization must scrutinize the level of technical support included by the system provider, whatever the system under consideration. The client organization needs to know whether the system package price includes installation, staff training, and on-site service and repair. If it doesn't, the cost of these services needs to be investigated and factored into any calculation of the total cost for the system. All systems require technical support and maintenance, so the purchaser needs to clarify the included level of support—both on-site and phone support—before finalizing the system purchase.

For example, a company can easily customize an SAP system, such as by changing pricing information for specific customers over time. If a company doesn't have staff qualified to make SAP system changes and perform other maintenance, the company can purchase additional on-site and off-site expert consulting and support from SAP or an SAP partner company. Other information systems products—such as those geared for particular industries, like healthcare and shipbuilding—may be less customizable and may require working with the software vendor company or a partner company.

Article
Support Contracts

Recheck your understanding of the concepts covered by this objective.

10.3 Designing and Developing Information Systems

A project moves into the design stage once the project team has approved the plan, including the budget. The design process begins with writing functional and design specifications. In most cases, the project team creates the functional specification, describing what the system must be able to do. The company that wins the bid to do the project usually writes a second document, called the *design specification*. The project leaders must approve both documents before work can proceed.

The **functional specification**, usually written first, states exactly what the information system must accomplish. For example, one part of the functional specification may require that 20 computers be connected to a secure company database, with each workstation having access to particular cloud-based services. This document outlines only the functions the system will have to perform, not the kinds of computers and software needed to operate the system.

The **design specification** spells out how the goals laid out in the functional specification will be reached. It details hardware and software requirements necessary to execute the functions, including the operating system and platform, type of database to use, and user authorization and access.

Part of the design and development step requires the creation of a data dictionary listing all the information that must be handled (the data elements) and the types, names, and sizes these data elements require. For example, a manufacturer might want an inventory of all raw materials used in production. The company might also want records providing information for ordering new parts from suppliers. Most important will be sales orders and customer records.

Another significant part of any design specification is deciding whether to use packaged (off-the-shelf) software or custom software. A manufacturer might buy an off-the-shelf Oracle database and a CAM software package such as Wonderware, and then employ a large consulting firm, such as Deloitte or IBM, to use these products in the design and development of a custom information system. This software combination would be able to provide a good CIM system covering the entire operation.

10.4 Implementing Information Systems

The project can move into its next stage, implementation, once the development team and the systems vendor or integrator have developed the design specification and approved the plans. **Implementation** involves the actual work of putting the system together, including creating a prototype and completing the programming. In most cases, implementing the new system is the longest, most difficult step in the process.

Prototyping

Prototyping is the creation of a preliminary, not fully functional version of a program that demonstrates the user interface and functionality of the system. This process enables users to see what the final project will look like, often months before the project completion date. Users often generate many suggestions for changes after they review the

 Precheck 10.3

Check your understanding of the concepts covered by this objective.

 Activity 10.3.1

Video
Process Modeling: Entity Relationships

 Activity 10.3.2

Video
Process Modeling: Data Flow Diagrams

 Activity 10.3.3

Video
Process Modeling: Decision Trees

 Activity 10.3.4

Video
Process Modeling: Object Models

 Recheck 10.3

Recheck your understanding of the concepts covered by this objective.

 Precheck 10.4

Check your understanding of the concepts covered by this objective.

 Tech Career Explorer

Designing Your Own Systems Career

Controversy exists about whether the term *software engineer* or *software developer* should be used to describe particular technical jobs. A search for either job title on a major job search site, such as Indeed or Monster, typically returns good news: thousands of open positions with salaries from $50,000 to more than $130,000. To learn more about these challenging careers in designing software and systems, complete this exercise.

prototype. These suggestions will be easier to incorporate into the system if they are discovered at this early stage of the development life cycle.

Software Programming

The software programming occurs at the implementation stage, and the hardware team ensures that the new computer hardware works. The programming phase involves discovering problems and spending long hours to solve them, and it requires hard work on the part of the development team. The information system will normally use an existing software package, with customization required to make everything work as desired. For example, two different grocery chains might purchase the same information system package, but each chain will modify the software to ensure the system meets its needs. A company that can use niche package software tailored precisely to its industry can save considerable time and money.

Hardware and Software Purchasing

All the required hardware and software must be purchased and delivered before any system can be installed and considered up and running. In most cases, the software and service costs far outweigh the hardware costs, because the service requires many hours of highly skilled labor. Integrating all the system's computers and software and getting the entire system to work as planned involves significant expenditures of money and person-hours.

Installation and Testing

Beta testing begins once the computers and software are installed and operating. **Beta testing** is a period during which the system is rigorously tested for errors and failures in operation. The company continues to use any previously installed information systems during this time, with a duplicate of information from the old system copied to the new one for comparison purposes.

For example, a global manufacturing company would probably choose one of its many factories to test a new system. All the other factories would continue using the company's old system until the new one achieves performance goals. Once the new system has been approved, it would be installed in every plant—a process referred to as *rolling out the system*.

Purchasing and installing hardware for a new information system can be expensive, but software and service usually eat up by far the largest portion of the project budget.

User Training

User training normally takes place at the same time as beta testing. During this training, system users learn how to run the new software. This process can also result in the discovery of errors that were not detected during the design process. A number of things can go wrong with an information system, including lost records, network errors, system crashes, and the accidental display of confidential information (for example, employee salaries). All these things can require the development team to create an emergency patch, or correction, to the system. In the worst cases, errors may cause the team to go back to the planning stage to determine their origin.

Approval

Once an information system is installed and working, the committee or executive over-seeing the purchase of the system must inspect, test, and approve it. This is normally done after the system has proved itself during a successful beta testing period. Final approval is often tied to full payment being made to the suppliers. The approval period can be a stressful time for everyone involved if a system has problems.

Recheck 10.4

Recheck your under-standing of the concepts covered by this objective.

10.5 Supporting and Maintaining Information Systems

A system goes into the support stage after it has been accepted and approved. It's quite possible that undetected errors might still exist or that additional features may be requested. The IT staff performs different types of maintenance on the system, including the following:

Precheck 10.5

Check your understanding of the concepts covered by this objective.

- **Corrective maintenance** to identify and fix errors
- **Perfective maintenance** to enhance the software to meet new requirements
- **Adaptive maintenance** to address other environment changes, such as operating system upgrades
- **Preventive maintenance** to increase reliability and ease of maintenance

When maintenance needs exceed in-house capabilities, a **support contract** normally enables users to contact the system vendor or integrator for technical support and training, and sometimes for on-site troubleshooting. Even if the system was designed in-house, the responsible department often operates as an indepen-dent entity—sometimes even charging the department that acquired the system for maintenance expenses. The support stage continues until a new information system is proposed and developed, usually years later. At that point, the existing system is retired and no longer used.

The system development life cycle is referred to as a *cycle* because it operates in a circular fashion. Technology moves forward so fast that as soon as one cycle of devel-opment ends, a new development phase begins. If mistakes have been made, the team might have to "go back to the drawing board" and return to the planning stage. This can happen for many reasons, including changes in funding, development of new technology, errors in the original plan, and other unforeseen difficulties. In any case, the circular methodology helps foster continual refinements and improvements in the process, which in the end benefits all participants.

Recheck 10.5

Recheck your under-standing of the concepts covered by this objective.

Tech Ethics 🏛 🏛 🏛 🏛 🏛 🏛 🏛

Following the Code in Software Engineering

The Association for Computing Machinery, or ACM (which calls itself the world's largest educational and scientific computing society), and the IEEE Computer Society jointly developed and approved the Software Engineering Code of Ethics and Professional Practice (**http://CUT6.emcp .net/SECode**). The first rule of this code calls for acting in the best interest of the public, and the second rule calls for acting in the best interest of clients and employers. What might happen when those two standards come into conflict? What if you were a software engineer, and your employer asked you to create a system to do something illegal, such as alter mortgage application processing based on race or gender? What if you worked for a govern-ment agency and were asked to create a system that rigged a bidding process to favor large companies over small ones, no matter what the bid amount? How would you respond to such dilemmas?

10.6 Exploring Electronic Commerce and Online Shopping

Precheck 10.6
Check your understanding of the concepts covered by this objective.

Since the mid-1990s, computing technology has not only delivered great changes in how businesses operate internally, but it has also driven profound changes in the provider-consumer equation. Consumers increasingly use the Internet to purchase products and services and interact with retailers and service providers.

Electronic commerce (e-commerce) is the name for buying and selling products and services over the Internet. Through e-commerce tools such as shopping agents, live chat, and electronic payment systems, consumers can locate, evaluate, and purchase everything from cars to clothing to sporting goods to travel services to home improvement and grocery items online. Businesses can order supplies, schedule and track shipments, and communicate with customers within a few seconds. Increasingly, consumers make their online purchases using smartphones, tablets, and other mobile devices—a form of e-commerce called **mobile commerce (m-commerce)**. As illustrated in Figure 10.11, m-commerce purchases have grown rapidly in recent years.

If you follow print or online news sources about technology or business, you may have read the terms *business-to-business electronic commerce* and *business-to-consumer electronic commerce*. These terms identify two major categories of e-commerce. In **business-to-business (B2B) electronic commerce** (also called *e-business*), companies use the Internet to conduct a wide range of routine business activities with other companies, including ordering manufacturing parts and purchasing inventories from

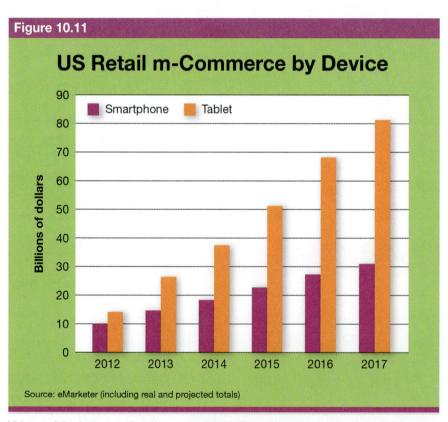

Figure 10.11

US Retail m-Commerce by Device

Source: eMarketer (including real and projected totals)

Using mobile devices makes it easy to place online orders almost any time, leading to significant growth in sales made via m-commerce.

wholesalers. In **business-to-consumer (B2C) electronic commerce**, companies use the Internet to sell products and services to consumers and to receive payments from them.

Simply put, B2C e-commerce is the marketing and selling of products and services to consumers over the web. A retail company that carries out electronic commerce is sometimes referred to as an **e-tailer**. Hundreds of well-known retailers—including Walmart, JCPenney, Best Buy, and Staples—now have websites where customers can purchase many of the same items stocked in the companies' retail store buildings. Additionally, many businesses, such as Amazon and Overstock (see Figure 10.12), sell their products and services exclusively over the web. A company that has no bricks-and-mortar presence is referred to as a **pure-play e-tailer**.

The retail stores and shops down the street or at the local mall where you buy goods and services have physical buildings, making them bricks-and-mortar retailers. A bricks-and-clicks retailer, in contrast, combines sales from bricks-and-mortar stores with sales from the Internet. Many bricks-and-clicks operations, including many home improvement and technology retailers, also enable customers to place orders online for in-store pickup.

Electronic commerce has experienced phenomenal growth since Tim Berners-Lee first introduced his concept for the World Wide Web in 1989. According to estimates from the US Department of Commerce, for the third quarter of 2015, e-commerce sales had reached $87.5 billion. That is a huge sum of money—but it was only 7.4 percent of all US commerce for the same time period. This shows that there is still a lot of room for e-commerce to grow.

Figure 10.12

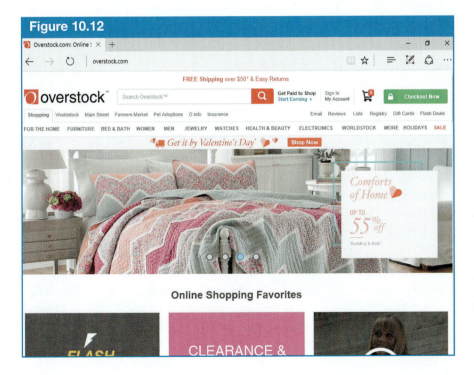

Overstock is an example of a pure-play e-tailer, because it markets and sells products only through the Internet. It offers merchandise in a number of categories.

Advantages of Online Shopping

Online shopping involves using a web-connected computer or mobile device to locate, examine, purchase, and pay for products. Although online shopping offers many advantages for both consumers and businesses, you should take care to be a savvy consumer, which includes understanding the online shopping process and knowing some guidelines for shopping online.

For the consumer, online shopping offers several distinct advantages over traditional shopping methods:

- Convenience
- Greater selection
- Easy comparison shopping
- Potential sales tax savings

Some US states do not require an online retailer to collect sales tax when the retailer has no physical location within the state; some states do. Other states, such as North Carolina, require taxpayers to estimate an amount of sales tax due for online sales even when retailers did not collect sales tax. The federal government has not passed any legislation regarding sales taxes for Internet sales, though proposals have been made to standardize sales tax collection practices.

Many bricks-and-clicks businesses encourage consumers to shop online because it saves employee time, thus reducing staff needs and costs for the company. For example, some major airlines offer special discounts to travelers who purchase their tickets online, and most are eliminating paper tickets altogether. In addition, with an airline ticket purchased online—called an **e-ticket**—a consumer can often check in

Cutting Edge

Home Trackers

Did you know the global positioning system (GPS) coordinates for the White House are 38.898648N latitude and 77.037692W longitude? Just as you can use GPS coordinates to pinpoint the exact location of the White House, the US government can use them to come within 40 feet of your front door!

The global positioning system consists of 24 satellites operated by the US government to provide users with positioning, navigation, and timing (PNT) data and services. Because taxpayers support these services, we as end users can use GPS receiver equipment to access the latest satellite data for free. Although critics complain that GPS makes it easier for the government to monitor citizens, tracking suspects via GPS without a warrant has been ruled unconstitutional. To learn the latest about planned upgrades to the current GPS, visit http://CUT6.emcp.net/GPS.

Companies also can take advantage of GPS data to improve operations, especially in the area of distribution logistics. Online retailers rely on package delivery services such as Federal Express (FedEx), the United Parcel Service (UPS), and the US Postal Service (USPS) to transport online purchases to customers. In late 2013, UPS launched its ORION software project, which uses historical GPS data about previous delivery routes and other telematics data to come up with more efficient routes.

ORION, which is short for On-Road Integrated Optimization and Navigation, not only helps make delivery times more predictable, but also yields substantial fuel savings. While ORION was tested between 2010 and 2012, UPS saved 3 million gallons of fuel. UPS estimates that once all its drivers are using ORION, it will save $50 million per year in fuel costs by taking just one mile a day off each of its drivers' routes.

for a flight and print a boarding pass online up to 24 hours prior to departure. See Figure 10.13.

Types of Online Retail Sites

Just as traditional shoppers can visit a variety of bricks-and-mortar retail outlets, Internet shoppers can visit several types of online shopping sites.

Online Stores An **online store** (also called an *online storefront* or **virtual store**) is a seller's website where customers can view and purchase products and services. The site groups the merchant's products and services in categories that link to lists of merchandise. The user points to or clicks a desired category to view pictures, descriptions, and prices of available products and services (see Figure 10.14).

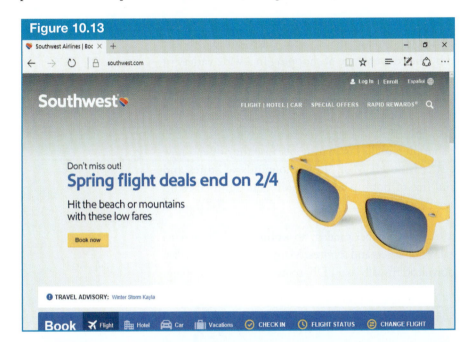

Figure 10.13

Most airlines, including Southwest Airlines, enable consumers to purchase e-tickets online. In fact, a recent trend among airlines is the elimination of traditional paper tickets.

Figure 10.14

Most online stores organize products in easy-to-navigate categories.

Online Superstores Like a bricks-and-mortar superstore, an **online superstore** offers an extensive array of products, from candy bars to clothing to tools to household appliances. Some well-known superstores—for example, Walmart and Target—also have online superstores. You can also find specialty online superstores that focus on particular types of products, such as Motorcycle-Superstore.com and ATGStores.com. ATGStores.com offers 3.5 million home improvement and décor products (see Figure 10.15). Similarly, Overstock.com specializes in deeply discounted surplus products from a variety of manufacturers. Huge selection and great pricing make online superstores especially popular with shoppers.

Shopping at an online superstore is generally the same as shopping at a single online store. However, you may find many more departments and categories of products. To help you find what you want, the home pages of most online superstores provide a search feature.

Online Shopping Malls When shopping malls were introduced in the 1950s, consumers were delighted by the convenience of shopping in a wide variety of stores physically connected under one roof. Similar in concept, an **online shopping mall** connects its stores via hyperlinks on the mall's home page. In fact, some businesses don't have individual online stores but instead offer their products and services only at an online shopping mall.

Many consumers find online shopping malls fascinating because they offer a new and exciting way to shop. One site, Mile Hi Mall, hosts thousands of stores and promises to be family friendly and free of pop-up ads. Fashionmall.com focuses on representing fashion and home retailers.

Online Catalogs Similar to a traditional paper catalog, an **online catalog** presents detailed information about a company's products and services. Many well-known retailers offer online catalogs that you can download (usually as a PDF) to use for offline shopping.

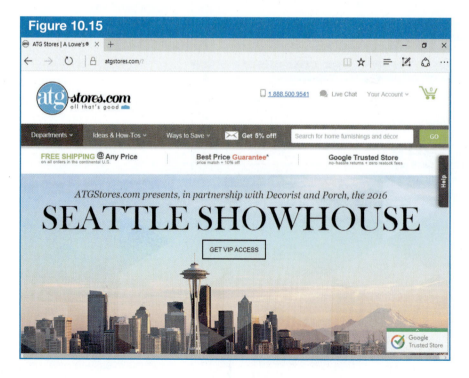

Figure 10.15

Online superstores like ATGStores.com may offer millions of products.

Customers can browse catalogs online and select items to purchase. In recent years, some online catalogs have become increasingly high-tech, and many now include multimedia enhancements, such as voice and video clips. Onlinecatalogs. com collects a variety of catalogs that you can browse and shop online.

Shopping Agents A **shopping agent** (also called a *comparison shopping website*) enables you to compare the prices that multiple online retailers charge for a particular product or type of product (see Figure 10.16). These sites use a variety of techniques to collect product information from various merchants. Some crawl (that is, continually search) the web for specific products and their prices. Others receive information directly from the merchant or manufacturer—sometimes in the form of a feed, where the product information follows a standardized format. Other sites even enable consumers to contribute data, such as particular prices.

A shopping agent site indexes products in its database, storing the price and the URL of the vendor's website. A shopper can search for a product to see the results from the shopping agent's database, saving time and money. Note, however, that shopping agent websites may be paid by the stores listed in a price comparison.

Examples of Online Services

Businesses continue to discover new ways to advertise and sell their services to consumers online. Consider Ticketmaster, where consumers can get information about entertainment in their area, find a date for an event through the company's dating service, book and print tickets, and make a restaurant reservation. At car-buying services such as CarsDirect, consumers can research hundreds of models, configure a car or truck with the options they select, and receive price lists. The service then works with a local dealer to deliver the car to the buyer.

That's not all. Many employers are now arranging to process and deliver workers' benefits online, savings millions of dollars in the costs of printing and distributing

Figure 10.16

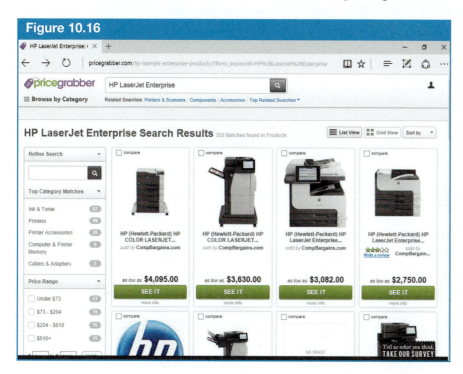

In this example, a search for *HP LaserJet Enterprise* using PriceGrabber yielded a variety of matches.

enrollment materials alone. Manufacturers such as Boeing and GE Aviation have also greatly reduced paper consumption and saved millions by issuing technical manuals, instructions, and parts lists online to their customers.

The following sections describe other examples of expanding and emerging online services. You can likely think of many more.

Online Streaming Services, Auctions, and More Websites offer a variety of online services or even work with other types of technology to deliver information via the Internet. While no list of services now available and emerging on the Internet can be exhaustive, consider these possibilities:

- **Online auctions.** Online auction services such as eBay enable you to purchase new, used, and vintage items either in a low-cost auction format or at seller-set prices.
- **Subscription software.** Some software publishers now deliver software via online delivery under a subscription plan. Microsoft Office 365, which you learned about in Chapter 7, works this way. So does the Adobe Creative Cloud suite of graphics programs. While a subscription model can be much more expensive for consumers, most of these plans include ongoing product updates, ensuring that the user gets the latest new features without having to pay a separate upgrade fee.
- **Media and music services.** The iTunes Store enables you to purchase songs and download them to a computer or other mobile device, listen to free podcasts, stream online radio music, and more. It requires special software that interacts directly with the web and your devices. The Hulu and Netflix websites enable you to subscribe to a service that streams movies and TV shows to your computer, mobile device, or PC. The DirecTV website acts as a supplement to DirectTV satellite TV service; you can order additional pay-per-view movies and events from the website to have them beamed to your connected TV.
- **Online support services.** Some sites offer expert advice and recommendations for a subscription or per-use fee. For example, subscribers to Angie's List get access to recommendations for local service providers, such as electricians and pet sitters. In other cases, you can purchase additional online support for software and hardware for a fee. Many real estate firms provide information on their websites about listings of properties for sale. While you generally can't purchase the property from a realtor's website, you can use the site to search for houses to see and a real estate agent to work with. And yes, you can even get a reading by a psychic via online chat, sometimes for a fee.
- **Online gaming.** While free online gaming can be fun, other popular games charge subscription fees. In still other cases, players must purchase virtual items, such as weapons and expansion features, to advance in a game.

Online Banking and Investing **Online banking** involves using a web-connected PC or mobile device to conduct routine banking transactions. As noted earlier, you can use your bank's online banking features to pay bills, transfer funds among accounts, purchase CDs (certificates of deposit), and perform other financial transactions over the web from the convenience of your home or office. Some services even enable you to send money directly to another user's checking account. Banks that offer online services generally provide their customers with instructions for conducting business online. Available online services vary among banks. Visit a particular bank's website to learn about the online banking services it offers to its customers.

 **Activity 10.6.1**

Video
Online Banking

Online banking activities continue to grow. According to Pew Research Center, as of late 2013, 51 percent of US adults banked online and as of late 2014, 57 percent used their mobile phones for banking. In addition to banking online with a traditional bank, such as Wells Fargo or Bank of America, consumers can choose an Internet-only bank, such as NetBank, Ally (Figure 10.17), or Discover Bank.

At some banking sites, customers can even apply for a loan online. In fact, some loan companies—for example, Quicken Loans and E-Loan—operate solely as online lenders. Another lender, Ditech, offers mortgages and home equity lines of credit only at its website.

Similarly, many investment and trading companies enable you to manage your accounts online via PC or mobile apps. For example, when you have your individual retirement account (IRA) with Fidelity, you can use the Fidelity website or one of the Fidelity mobile apps to access your account balances and stock (or other investment) positions, buy and sell stocks, and transfer funds between your account and a bank account. Other popular online investment companies include Charles Schwab, TD Ameritrade, and E*TRADE.

Figure 10.17

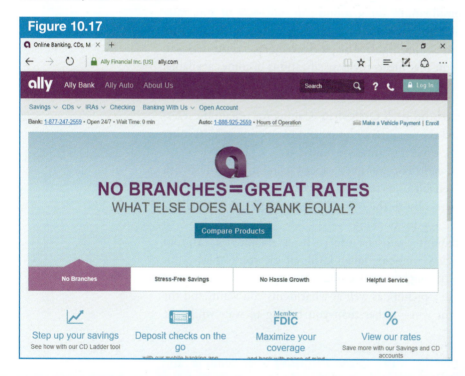

Online banking services such as Ally make it easy to perform transactions online or via a mobile device.

Practical TECH

Booking or Becoming a Vacation Spot

You can find great vacation rental deals on sites such as Airbnb, VRBO (Vacation Rentals by Owner), and HomeAway. On these sites, home and condo owners can list their property (or even rooms in their homes) for short-term rentals. Say you decide to go to your favorite music festival last minute, and you can't find a hotel room. You check Airbnb and find a condo you can rent two nights, splitting the space and cost with friends.

Not only are these services convenient for travelers, but they also enable homeowners to pick up cash when they'll be away for a while or have a second property. While you can also find rental deals on Craigslist, the specialized travel sites offer more details about property amenities and customer reviews and ratings. Airbnb also insures the homeowner again guest damages.

Online Travel and e-Ticketing Consumers are increasingly keen on getting the most value out of their travel budgets. With a huge increase in the number of travel-related venues online, consumers today have many options for comparison shopping. Some users surf the Internet to research destinations, transportation, and prices, and then they make their purchases off line at local travel agencies. But increasingly, consumers are both researching fares and flights and purchasing tickets online—a process called *e-ticketing*, as mentioned earlier.

Most attractive to many consumers today are online services that locate inexpensive airfares. For example, at Priceline.com, consumers specify the price they wish to pay for a particular flight, and the service searches to find that fare. Consumers can often find airfares well below the prices offered at traditional travel agencies. Expedia delivers price and schedule combinations for a round-trip, one-way or multiple-destination search, allowing users to sort options by airline, arrival and departure times, price, and even duration of the flight. And at Travelocity, consumers can request an email alert when a flight that meets their specifications becomes available. Most online travel services also provide regular email alerts about cheap travel deals.

Online Restaurant Reservations and Ordering Calling for restaurant reservations can mean working around the restaurant's hours and competing against other diners trying to call at the same time. Fortunately, online reservation services can help you get the reservation you want. For example, leader OpenTable partners with more than 32,000 restaurants to enable users to book reservations online for free. The restaurants (who want more diners) absorb the cost of the service. Many OpenTable users take advantage of its mobile app for booking.

Similarly, many major restaurant chains feature curbside pickup for carryout orders. Now, some chains, such as Carrabba's Italian Grill, enable you to place your curbside carryout orders online through their websites. You specify the restaurant location where you want to make a pickup, as well as what items you want, and the order will be hot and waiting for you—rather than you having to wait while the location prepares your order.

Peer Lending, Crowdsourcing, and Crowdfunding Peer lending and peer-to-peer lending services help individuals seek loans from and make loans to one another. Borrowers post information about their desired loans, including the amounts and purposes, and investors offer to loan money to the borrowers they select at specified interest rates. The peer lending site typically handles the monthly payment transactions, depositing each payment in the lender's account. The service Prosper leads the peer lending market.

Crowdsourcing and crowdfunding services depend on contributions from numerous users to create content, raise money, and so on. For

Practical TECH

Streaming Pizza Orders

Streaming video service Hulu includes an interactive advertising system. It even offers "in-stream purchase" ads. Partner Pizza Hut used this technology to enable viewers streaming to certain devices to place orders through ads in the streams. Consumers could enjoy the show—and pizza too!—with less interruption than having to call in a delivery order.

Practical TECH

What's Hot and What's Not

In addition to Angie's List, other social crowd opinion sites enable you to find great restaurants, hair professionals, and other businesses and services based on ratings posted by other consumers. For example, Yelp enables you to find popular local businesses and services in a number of cities in the United States and beyond. You can also consult the free Epinions website for consumer reviews of thousands of products.

Figure 10.18

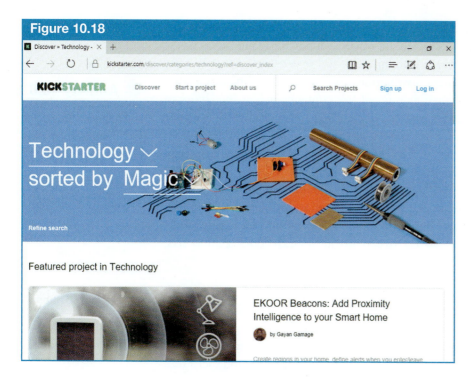

Crowdfunding sites such as Kickstarter enable crowd members to contribute financial support, typically in exchange for items related to the project.

example, CafePress enables users to design t-shirts, stickers, and other items and offer them for sale. Both Kickstarter (Figure 10.18) and Fundable help small ventures raise money for business projects and other small ventures. With these services, a band might seek funds for a new album project, offering final copies of the work, t-shirts, and other items in exchange for various levels of financial contributions. Start-up kinds of projects typically involve seeking contributions for the prototyping and initial production run, with contributors receiving one of the products from the first run. Other platforms, such as YouCaring.com, enable users to start campaigns to raise donations to help with causes such as assisting families with medical expenses or losses from home fires.

Digital Content Distribution Chapter 5 explained how the Rhapsody subscription music service enables you to stream music to a PC or a variety of other devices—even to a compatible car stereo system via a mobile phone and Bluetooth connection. Many other services deliver various types of media and information for a price, beyond streaming media and services such as iTunes, discussed previously. For example, photo-sharing sites, such as Flickr, enable users to share, license, and sell digital photos—sometimes for free or attribution only under Creative Commons licensing. (A Creative Commons license enables a work's creator to distribute it for free, subject to restrictions in the license—such as attributing the work to the original author or not using the work for commercial purposes.) Sites geared more toward professionals, such as iStock and Shutterstock, offer thousands of images that others can license to include in various publications.

Numerous sites—including the Kindle Store (Amazon), NookPress (Barnes & Noble), Google Play (Google), and iBooks (iTunes Store)—sell ebook downloads. Even if you don't have the right device for purchasing an ebook from a particular store, such as a Kindle for purchasing from Amazon, you can typically download an app that simulates the device's function and make your purchases from within the app. Other

 **Activity 10.6.2**

Video
Digital Media and Streaming Technology

 **Activity 10.6.3**

Article
Copyrights and Licensing for Digital Media

ebook stores offer PDF downloads, which are even more device independent. And of course, Amazon and the iTunes Store, among others, sell downloadable audio books that you can listen to while driving or working out.

Other examples of digital content distribution services include online newspapers and magazines. Many offer a limited amount of free content, such as the ability to view a certain number of articles per week. Beyond that, you need to sign up for an online subscription. The *New York Times* uses this model for its online edition, requiring a subscription if you want to view beyond a limited amount of free content. Similarly, many print newspapers include access to the online edition along with a subscription to the print edition. Still other types of publications, such as specialty newsletters and research reports, charge annual subscriptions or per-report fees. For example, many investing newsletters work by annual subscriptions. And many libraries are partnering with services like OverDrive to provide digital ebooks, audiobooks, and more for you to borrow and use.

Flash Sales, Deals, and Small Online Stores　Online retailing provides such flexibility for retailers that they can experiment with innovative methods such as flash sales. With a **flash sale**, the online retailer sells a small quantity or surplus of stock at a large discount for a limited period of time. Because the retailer promotes the flash sale using various low-cost methods—including email blasts, mobile alerts, and social sites such as Facebook—this type of sale offers a great, flexible way for retailers to clear out old inventory and maximize revenue.

Flash-type sales can work in a few different ways. For example, a regular online retailer might offer flash sales as part of its regular sales and marketing plans, to close out the stock on older items. Country Outfitter uses this approach, routinely featuring flash sales from the home page of its website (Figure 10.19).

Activity 10.6.4

Article
The Battle for Net Neutrality

Figure 10.19

Consumers can take advantage of deep discounts and online retailers can clear out old inventory via flash sales, like this one from the home page of Country Outfitter's website.

Other retailers rely on flash sales as the overall sales model, adopting more of a "daily deals" format. For example, Zulily calls its sales "events." Each event begins at 6 a.m. Pacific time and lasts 24 or 72 hours. Users who sign up for the free membership receive a daily email announcing new events. Rue La La and HauteLook follow a similar model, offering members-only sales on items from higher-end and luxury brands.

Other deal sites provide a way for small businesses to offer deals on their products and services to a wider audience. A merchant or service provider can arrange to offer a deal through Groupon. Users can sign up for a Groupon account by city (many deals are local). Groupon sends regular emails about current discount offers, called *Groupons*. Buyers can purchase a Groupon, print the Groupon certificate (or coupon), and then present the certificate to the small business to receive the discount. (Buyers can also use the Groupon mobile app to buy and redeem Groupons.) For example, you can easily find Groupons for discounted massages from local spas and meals at area restaurants. With a free membership, LivingSocial helps you find deals in select cities. Both Groupon and LivingSocial offer a wide variety of deals on anything from hotels to local tours and events.

One last type of store enables entrepreneurs and creators to get their products online without establishing a full-blown website. eBay enables small retailers and individuals to create their own eBay stores to sell new, used, and unique arts and crafts items. Shoppers can browse eBay Stores by searching on item categories or specific store names. Similarly, Etsy offers the ability to create small online stores. It focuses on artists, craftspeople, and designers in various fields, along with vintage items, and has 22.6 million active buyers, 1.5 million active sellers, and 36 million items listed.

The Online Shopping Process

Once a consumer finds an e-tailer's site that has items of interest, he or she should first take a few moments to evaluate the site carefully for quality, ease of use, and credibility. If the site passes the evaluation criteria, the consumer can then go ahead and check out the photographs, descriptions, and prices of the items.

When ready to make a purchase, the buyer should follow the directions given. At some sites, consumers make a selection by first clicking on the item; selecting settings such as size, quantity, and color, if applicable; and then clicking a button with a label such as "Buy" or "Add to Cart." This action electronically places the selected item in an online **shopping cart** (also called a *shopping basket*)—a virtual container for the items the consumer wishes to purchase. After the shopper has selected all the desired items, he or she can click a Shopping Cart button or link (Figure 10.20) to see a complete list of the items, along with each item's price and quantity and the total price, including any taxes and shipping costs.

To complete the checkout, the buyer enters a shipping address, selects a payment method, and enters information for the payment method (such as a credit card number and security code). After the buyer reviews the order information, a final screen appears confirming the order. Generally, the retailer also

Tech Career Explorer

SEO and E-Commerce

When consumers need to search for a new or specialty product to buy online, the order of the search results matters, because users most likely will check out the sites listed in the search results from the top of the list down. Search engine optimization (SEO) techniques help websites such as online retailers improve their rankings in search results. To learn more about careers in this emerging area, complete this exercise.

Activity 10.6.5

Article
How Shopping Cart Systems Work

Figure 10.20

Figure 10.21

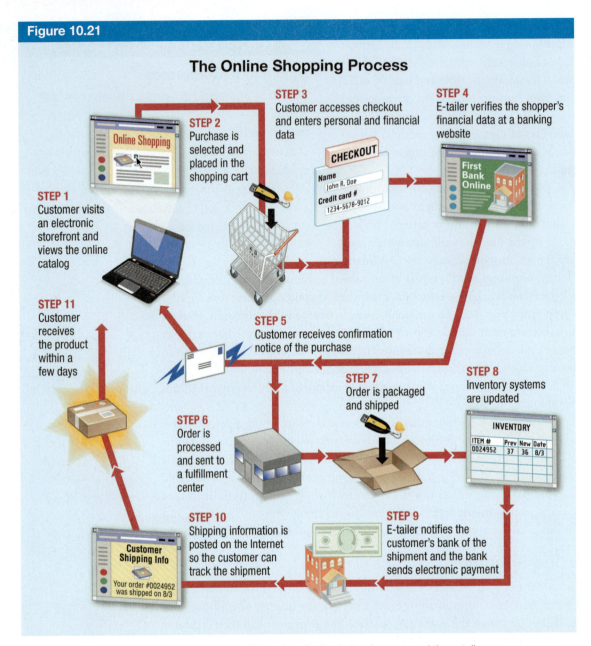

The Online Shopping Process

STEP 1
Customer visits an electronic storefront and views the online catalog

STEP 2
Purchase is selected and placed in the shopping cart

STEP 3
Customer accesses checkout and enters personal and financial data

STEP 4
E-tailer verifies the shopper's financial data at a banking website

STEP 5
Customer receives confirmation notice of the purchase

STEP 6
Order is processed and sent to a fulfillment center

STEP 7
Order is packaged and shipped

STEP 8
Inventory systems are updated

STEP 9
E-tailer notifies the customer's bank of the shipment and the bank sends electronic payment

STEP 10
Shipping information is posted on the Internet so the customer can track the shipment

STEP 11
Customer receives the product within a few days

The online shopping process includes a number of steps for both the shopper and the retailer.

follows up with an email message containing the order confirmation, as well as a later message containing the shipment notification and providing a shipment tracking link. The purchased items are then shipped to the address specified. Figure 10.21 illustrates the steps in the online shopping process.

Guidelines for Shopping Online

When consumers shop on the Internet, they need to be aware that online shopping differs from traditional shopping. In traditional shopping, consumers visit stores to find the items they want and may examine items carefully from all angles and ask questions of the sales clerks. However, when shopping online, consumers purchase items without being able to examine them fully.

Activity 10.6.6

Practice
The Online Shopping Process

Although online shopping is relatively safe, consumers need to take some precautions. The old adage "Better safe than sorry" is good advice when shopping from an e-tailer. Figure 10.22 offers a checklist of useful tips consumers should keep in mind to avoid trouble when shopping online. Consumers should keep security in mind as the number-one concern.

Figure 10.22

Tips for Shopping Online

 Tip 1
Buy only at secure sites. Secure sites use encryption to scramble credit card information so that no one except the site owner can read it. When you enter a secure site, a pop-up notice will appear in your browser, and then an icon of a closed lock will appear at the bottom of the browser.

 Tip 2
Read and understand the site return policy. For example, if you decide to return an item that isn't broken or damaged, some online retailers charge a restocking fee that could be up to 15 percent of the price of the object. In other cases, you might have to pay the shipping cost for returning the item.

 Tip 3
Find out the site's privacy policy before purchasing. Ask what information is gathered, how that information is used, and whether it will be shared.

 Tip 4
Answer only the required questions when filling out forms. Many sites put an asterisk next to each question that must be answered, and you should answer only the questions that have an asterisk to maintain as much privacy as possible.

 Tip 5
Never provide your social security number. There's no legitimate reason a site needs to know this.

 Tip 6
Look for sites that follow privacy rules such as those defined by TRUSTe. TRUSTe (http://CUT6.emcp.net/TRUSTe), a leader in online privacy, allows sites to post an online seal if they meet TRUSTe's comprehensive privacy certification requirements.

 Tip 7
Keep current on the latest Internet scams. The US Consumer Gateway (http://CUT6.emcp.net/USConsumerGateway) reports on Internet scams and tells consumers what actions the Federal Trade Commission (FTC) (http://CUT6.emcp.net/FTC) has taken against Internet scamsters. The Internet Fraud Watch, run by the National Consumers League (http://CUT6.emcp.net/NCL), is a great resource as well.

TRUSTe, a leader in online privacy, certifies websites that adhere to best practices for privacy in personal data collection and usage. Sites meeting its comprehensive privacy certification requirements can display the TRUSTe Certified Privacy Seal (see Figure 10.23). Shoppers also can click *Find Trusted Sites* on the organization's main website (http://CUT6.emcp.net/TRUSTe) to go to a page where they can search for an online retailer by name or URL to check its certification status.

Figure 10.23

To complete online transactions, consumers often must provide personal and financial data. The security on these transactions is therefore extremely important. Most surveys that ask shoppers to state their concerns about online shopping demonstrate that privacy issues—the security and confidentiality of personal and financial information—top the list. Because of these concerns, many companies now post privacy statements on their websites. In addition, the US government has enacted legislation to protect individuals against the theft, sale, or misuse of such information (see Table 10.1).

Although some websites still offer little or no transaction security, thousands of online stores and services now spend large amounts of money to ensure that consumers can enter personal data with confidence. Many such sites encrypt the personal and financial information the customers provide. As defined in Chapter 9, encryption is the process of converting readable information (called *plaintext*) into unreadable information (called *ciphertext*) to prevent unauthorized access and usage. Most encryption

Table 10.1 Milestones in Federal Privacy Legislation

Legislative Act	What the Act Does
Privacy Protection Act of 1980	Protects information stored in computerized databases and other documents
Electronic Communications Privacy Act of 1987	Makes it illegal for private citizens to intercept data communications without authorization
Computer Security Act of 1987	Requires the security of information pertaining to individuals
Consumer Internet Privacy Protection Act of 1997	Requires prior written individual consent before a computer service (such as an ISP) can disclose information about a subscriber.
Communications Privacy and Consumer Empowerment Act of 1997	Protects individual privacy in electronic (online) commerce transactions
Data Information Privacy Act of 1997	Restricts the use of personal data and regulates spamming
Children's Online Privacy Protection Act of 1998	Restricts the amount of personal Information gathered about children age 13 and younger and gives parents permission rights for controlling the information requested
Patriot Act of 2001	Expands the ability of the federal government to track Internet usage and emails

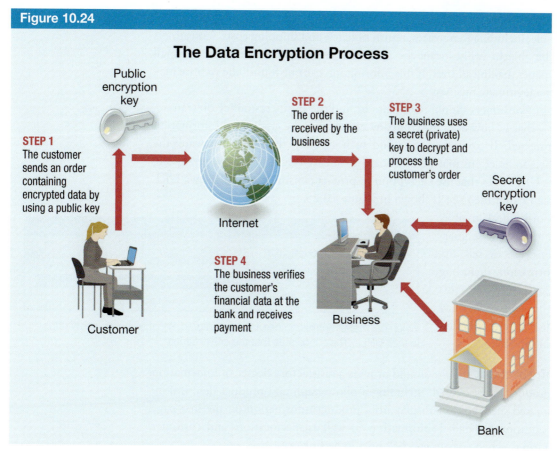

Figure 10.24

The Data Encryption Process

Public encryption key

STEP 1
The customer sends an order containing encrypted data by using a public key

Internet

STEP 2
The order is received by the business

STEP 3
The business uses a secret (private) key to decrypt and process the customer's order

Secret encryption key

STEP 4
The business verifies the customer's financial data at the bank and receives payment

Customer

Business

Bank

With data encryption, data is encoded when transmitted over the Internet and then decoded by the recipient.

systems work in the same way (see Figure 10.24). Here is a simple scenario of a typical online transaction:

- A customer visits a particular online shopping site and chooses items to purchase.
- After making her selections, the customer enters purchase, shipping, and payment information onto an online purchase form.
- As the customer enters this information, it is encrypted (encoded), making it almost impossible for anyone who might intercept the transmission to read it.
- When the order arrives at its destination, the information is decrypted (decoded), allowing the business to validate it and process the order.
- Following processing, the goods are shipped to the customer.

To ensure the security of online transactions by encrypting data, a business applies a formula that uses a code called an *encryption key*. The recipient of encrypted information (the business) uses an encryption key to decode the customer's information when it's received.

Evaluating Online Shopping Sites and Apps

What should consumers look for when visiting sites or selecting apps to use to shop online? (Some retailers offer specific apps you can use for shopping their websites.) Before making a purchase, a wise consumer will make certain that each online retailer website or shopping app provides the following information.

Selling and Security Terms   Consumers should find, read, and easily understand the terms of sale, including item prices, return policies, and shipping costs. Consumers should also be able to easily locate the customer service telephone number, email address, and paper mailing address. If this information can't be found, the website may not represent a legitimate business.

In addition, consumers should make sure to find the business's policy on transaction security—that is, how does the company ensure that the credit card information entered is protected? If consumers can't find such a policy, they should beware: the security of their transactions may be in jeopardy. An easy way to identify a secure site is to check its URL. Sites that use encryption to protect consumer data display a URL that includes an *s* after the *http*, as shown in Figure 10.25.

A final security check involves making sure the business guarantees it won't use or sell any personal information, including email addresses. Without this guarantee, the consumer may receive unsolicited telemarketing calls and email messages.

Figure 10.25

When payment information needs to be entered, most websites show *https* in their URLs. The *s* indicates that the site is secure.

Product Information   The site should provide a satisfactory degree of information about each product being offered, including a photograph and product description. Many highly rated sites typically display brief product information on the first page and provide additional, detailed information, as well as specifications and customer reviews and ratings, when consumers click on a hyperlink.

Keep in mind that retail mobile apps typically offer fewer functions than do retail websites. When an app might display limited product information, using the website instead can help ensure you make the best purchase decision—especially for complicated or expensive products.

Purchase Process   The directions for purchasing items at a site should be simple to follow. As noted previously, many sites offer a shopping cart format for selecting products and a summary page that tallies the items selected and their costs, the shipping charges for the order, and taxes. At any point in the purchase process, the consumer should have the chance to make a change to the order.

Hands On

Practicing Shopping on the Web

Follow the steps in this resource to browse an e-tailer's secure website and identify the security and privacy features.

Customer Service   An online shopping site should provide a high level of customer service, just as customers would expect from a high-quality bricks-and-mortar store. At many sites, users can provide feedback to the company about its website or about purchased products, get online help, and view useful product information, such as instructions for assembling a bicycle or setting up a new personal computer. Some sites provide links that identify a specific person or department to contact or a telephone number to dial.

More robust commerce websites include live sales chat support. In some instances, the shopper clicks a Chat or Live Help button or link to initiate the chat with a support representative. In other instances, the chat window opens automatically,

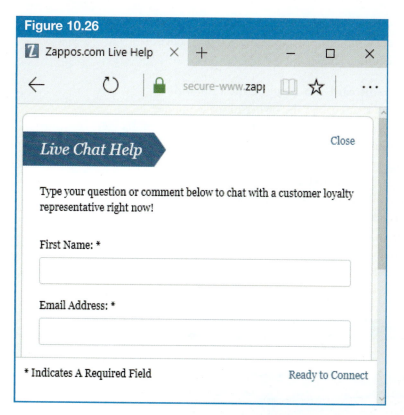

Figure 10.26

Many retailers enable you to use chat to ask questions about a product prior to buying it online.

prompting the shopper to speak with a customer service representative if needed, as shown in Figure 10.26.

10.7 Completing Electronic Commerce Transactions

Making online purchases requires having methods of online promotion and payment. Consumers can use a variety of technologies not only to find sales and deals but also to make online payments to e-tailers.

Transaction Payment Methods

When purchasing goods and services over the Internet, consumers must enter their credit card information to charge their accounts. However, the web offers new and improved payment technologies. Today's technology allows payments for goods and services purchased online to be made by a variety of methods, including electronic funds transfer, credit and debit accounts, smart cards, retailer branded credit cards and gift cards, and person-to-person payment systems.

Electronic Funds Transfer The term **electronic funds transfer (EFT)** refers to any transfer of money over the Internet. Actually, banks and other businesses were transferring money over the web long before this capability became available to the average user. Some recurring services enable you to set up automatic payments (or autopay), in which the monthly fee is deducted directly from your bank account via an EFT transaction. For example, you may set up your ISP or mobile phone account so the usage fee is deducted from your bank account on a monthly basis.

In other cases, the process works less directly, as with the PayPal online payment system. For example, if you prefer to use PayPal to pay for your online shopping transactions whenever possible, you can link PayPal to your bank account. Any payments

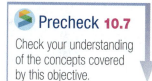

Recheck 10.6
Recheck your understanding of the concepts covered by this objective.

Precheck 10.7
Check your understanding of the concepts covered by this objective.

Activity 10.7.1

Article
E-commerce Business Models and Revenue Streams

you authorize will then be deducted from your account by the PayPal service. In this type of transaction, the PayPal service acts as a layer of security, because you don't have to provide your banking information to the online retailer.

Credit Cards and Debit Cards A **credit card** is a small plastic card with a magnetic strip containing owner information that enables the owner to make online and in-store purchases on credit. Using a major credit card—such as MasterCard, Visa, American Express, or Discover—a consumer can charge both traditional and online purchases to the credit account (Figure 10.27). A monthly billing statement lists all purchases made using the credit card, plus interest and other fees.

A **debit card** resembles a credit card and, like a credit card, is used as an alternative to cash when making purchases. Unlike a credit card, however, a debit card is linked to a checking or savings account. When a purchase is made with a debit card, the bank or credit union withdraws the funds directly from the linked account. Consumers also can buy prepaid debit cards and use them for making online payments. With one of these cards, you determine how much money to add to it, and you can refill it after

Figure 10.27

E-commerce sites require customers to submit payment information. Most users pay for online transactions with credit cards.

Practical TECH

Extra Credit Security

As a leader in online payments, PayPal protects users by shielding their credit account information. When you use PayPal to send money to an online retailer, a charity, a small business, or another user, the other party never sees your credit card or bank information. The Master-Card and Visa transaction systems (which handle both credit and debit card transactions) have added a similar feature. MasterPass (MasterCard) and V.me (Visa) enable you to check out in a more secure fashion at participating retailers. The bonus for all of these services is that you don't have to re-enter your credit card information for every transaction.

you have spent it down. With no associated bank account, prepaid debit cards eliminate security and overdraft concerns.

Smart Cards Major companies such as JPMorgan Chase, Target, and Neiman Marcus have experienced major data breaches by hackers, with thousands of reported security incidents involving hundreds of millions of customer records per year. Because of such incidents, the Visa and MasterCard payment networks in the United States have started shifting to new technology that replaces a credit card's magnetic stripe with a computer chip. This technology offers a greater level of security for in-store purchases. This form of card is sometimes called a *smart card*.

A smart card keeps personal and financial data on a small microprocessor embedded in the card. The user inserts the card into or waves it over a special electronic card reader that reads information on the card, and the transaction proceeds. Once your US credit cards have been upgraded to smart cards, you will still be able to use them to pay for online purchases of products and services, though the payment input method may change. Smart cards also work well for special applications, such as paying transportation fees, calling with specially equipped pay phones (more popular outside the United States), storing medical information for easy transmission to health care providers, and providing identification for security access to a building or office.

This PATH SmartLink Card allows a New York City subway rider to pay for admission to the subway. The rider waves the card past the sensor on the turnstile, and his or her account is debited.

Retailer Branded Credit Cards and Gift Cards Some e-tailers allow qualified customers to open store credit card accounts. In this arrangement, sometimes called a **credit account**, the online retailer charges purchases to the customer's account and the customer promises to pay for the purchases upon receipt of a monthly statement—just as for a regular credit card. Many online retailers now offer their own store branded cards. For example, Overstock.com enables customers to obtain an Overstock.com MasterCard, and Amazon offers the Amazon.com Rewards Visa Card.

PayPal's Bill Me Later service functions as a retail line of credit. When you qualify and add this feature to your PayPal account, you can use it to pay for purchases from online merchants that accept Bill Me Later. You will be billed for each purchase within a couple of weeks or so of the order shipping. Once you receive the statement, you can either pay the full amount immediately, or make smaller payments and pay interest on the balance.

Many online or bricks-and-clicks merchants offer gift cards that are good only for their stores. You might receive a gift card from a friend or relative, or order one as part of a cash-back arrangement on your credit card account. (Some companies also enable you to print a cash-back reward as an e-certificate, rather than have to send you a plastic gift card.) To use a gift card or e-certificate for an online purchase, you enter the card or certificate serial number for that payment method during the online checkout process.

Person-to-Person Payment Systems A **person-to-person payment system** enables consumers to transfer money (even a small amount known as a **micropayment**) to one another through a credit card or bank account. Popular uses for person-to-person payments include paying for online auction items and sending money to friends or family.

PayPal dominates in this area. To use its person-to-person payment system, the sender and receiver must each have an email account registered with the PayPal service. Each must also provide a bank account or credit card number from which money will be withdrawn or to which it will be deposited. Once the sender designates a recipient and pays the money, the recipient receives an email notification and the money is mailed by check, transferred to a bank account, or credited to a credit card account.

Similar systems enable users to make smaller-scale loans and donations. For example, YouCaring.com enables a person to start a campaign seeking donations in support of a cause. An individual can donate any amount of money, keeping his or her identity and the amount anonymous if desired. The campaign's creator can provide updates about the cause and how the donations will be used. Kiva brings together individual borrowers and lenders from around the world. Loans made and tracked via this service start at as little as $25.

Mobile Devices and Accessories Used for In-Person Commerce

The commerce landscape continues to change rapidly, with technology facilitating rapid changes in how consumers pay for goods and services, even when shopping in person in traditional bricks-and-mortar stores. Here's a look at just a few of the technologies gaining traction in digital commerce.

Digital Wallet (Mobile Payments) A **digital wallet** (such as Google Wallet) consists of an app—usually, a mobile app—that gathers all your credit card and loyalty payment information together. When you check out after making a mobile purchase, the wallet automatically transfers the appropriate payment information to the retailer. In stores, the methods for using digital wallets have been evolving. Some early systems called for providing your mobile phone number and a PIN. Other retailers may accept a more recent contactless payment system.

Cutting Edge

Cryptocurrency

Bitcoin originated in part as another person-to-person (P2P) payment method involving both the currency itself and an online payment system. Bitcoin is supposed to work as a consensus network supporting the encrypted currency (or cryptocurrency) through a public ledger called *block chain*, intended to provide the ability to track and verify every transaction for security purposes. This international Internet currency became popular quickly, initially driving up the value of each bitcoin. (Bitcoins and other cryptocurrencies are created in a controlled quantity via a process called *mining*.) However, several incidents marred the organization's reputation and decreased the value of bitcoins. As reported in the media, bitcoins have been used for illegal online transactions—most prominently, on the underground web's now defunct Silk Road site, where illegal goods and services such as weapons were brokered. Also, hackers inevitably attacked the bitcoin market, in one instance allegedly leading to the loss of millions of dollars worth of bitcoins from MtGox, one of the bitcoin exchanges. The exchange later filed for bankruptcy. Other cryptocurrencies exist and face the same challenges. For example, a hacker mined $620,000 worth of Dogecoin by infecting other users' storage devices with malware.

Figure 10.28

Digital wallet apps enable you to make in-person payments at some retailers.

Other systems enable you to touch or tap your phone on a compatible reader on the register to pay—a method called *tap and pay*. For example, the Android Pay app, shown in Figure 10.28, allows tap-and-pay transactions for more recent Android phones at retailers with compatible checkout terminals. In the Apple Pay system, you can use your iPhone 6 or later with near field communication (NFC) capabilities to make contactless payments on compatible terminals. You store credit card information for use with Apple Pay in the Passbook app.

Some digital wallets also enable you to store and carry additional types of information on your smartphone, such as event tickets that you have purchased. For example, Apple's Passbook app also can store movie, concert, and airline tickets, and loyalty cards and coupons. The Lemon Wallet app can hold your debit, credit, ID, insurance, and loyalty card information; it converts each to a barcode that the retailer can scan in the checkout line. Paypal has its own digital wallet app. Some bitcoin services and the Dogecoin cryptocurrency services offer a wallet app, as well.

QR Codes and App Coupons A **quick response (QR) code** provides a signal to a consumer that he or she can find out more about a product or service online.

Cutting Edge

A New Type of Swipe

Startup company Coin created a credit card-like device that includes a reprogrammable metal swipe strip. The Coin device can hold information for up to eight different credit cards or loyalty cards. You use a companion smartphone app and dongle (a security device that plugs into your smartphone and allows the app to run) to select which card becomes active in the device, reconfiguring the swipe strip for that particular card. (This process works via Bluetooth.) Then the merchant can swipe it through an existing credit card reader, just like current-generation swipe credit cards. For security, the Coin app monitors to make sure the card is in range. After the card has been out of range for a certain period of time, the app gives an alert. Shortly after that, the Coin will lock itself if still not reconnected to the phone, to prevent unauthorized usage.

When the consumer sees a QR code in a store or in a printed ad in a magazine or newspaper, he or she can scan the QR with a scanner smartphone app to jump right to information about the product or service in the phone's web browser. Some digital wallets also use QR codes for person-to-person money transfers. The user who wants to give the money displays a QR code in the wallet app, and the recipient scans the code with a smartphone to complete the transaction.

Similarly, many retailers now offer online apps that can send coupons and alerts about special sales deals to your smartphone. For example, the app for Earth Fare, a chain of natural foods supermarkets, shows deals for your local store and enables you to track your Tomato Bank loyalty points. And RetailMeNot offers a mobile app you can use to download coupons for thousands of products to your smartphone.

Hands On

Adding a QR Scanner to Your Mobile Device
Follow the steps in this resource to download and add a QR scanner to your smartphone.

Jump to product information by scanning a QR code with your smartphone.

Credit Card Reader Accessories Many small retailers now bypass using traditional POS cash registers altogether. They conduct sales transactions using an iPad, iPhone, or Android phone along with a reader accessory for swiping credit and debit cards. The company Square leads in this type of service. Retailers can use a credit card reader such as Square at their physical stores, and this type of system also works great for people who sell from a variety of locations, such as artists who travel to various art fairs.

iBeacon Apple created a technology called *iBeacon* that uses a Bluetooth low-energy signal to send smartphone alerts to shoppers within a store. The iBeacon works as sort of a mini hotspot. When a user with an iPhone and a compatible app nears the iBeacon location, the retailer's system automatically sends sale and deal alerts to the app in the iPhone. Macy's was the first retailer to implement a trial of iBeacon, beaming alerts to iPhones with the Shopkick app as the phones' owners entered the store. Qualcomm introduced a similar proximity system called *Gimbal beacons*.

 Recheck 10.7
Recheck your understanding of the concepts covered by this objective.

10.8 Understanding Business-to-Business Electronic Commerce

 Precheck 10.8
Check your understanding of the concepts covered by this objective.

Today, more and more businesses use Internet connectivity to enhance their operations. B2B electronic commerce is a segment of electronic commerce in which businesses or organizations use the Internet and e-commerce technologies to conduct a wide range of routine business activities with other companies. In a business-to-business e-commerce transaction, both the seller and the buyer are business organizations.

Virtually all business networks now connect to the Internet, enabling companies around the world to communicate easily with other businesses and individuals who are vital to their work processes. These vital contacts include suppliers, regulating agencies, shipping companies, customers, and a host of other companies, organizations, and clients that influence the day-to-day operations of the business. With B2B e-commerce, companies can order supplies, share information, coordinate operations, speed up product development, process financial transactions, improve customer response time, enhance collaboration between employees, and conduct numerous other business functions with significant savings in time and cost.

B2B electronic commerce transactions can also take place within a business. **Intrabusiness electronic commerce** involves the use of web-based technology that enables a company to handle transactions that occur within itself. For example, at a large corporation with offices throughout the world, technicians at various locations who are working on a product design can communicate ideas and share plans over the Internet.

You may be surprised to learn that today, most of the e-commerce that takes place on the Internet is B2B e-commerce. As more businesses integrate aspects of B2B e-commerce into their operations, the volume of business-to-business revenue rises—and this upward trend is expected to continue in the future. Those companies currently engaged in switching some or most of their operations to the Internet see the potential for future financial gains.

Beyond all their other functions, computer technology and the web have changed the way businesses and organizations process, transmit, and receive information. Computers enable people to obtain information that's more current, more accurate, and more comprehensive. From a business perspective, the Internet provides almost instant access to information about customers, suppliers, competitors, government agencies, and markets any place in the world

As covered in Chapter 5, in today's marketplace with its new work patterns, the web enables an increasingly mobile workforce to tap into company information from remote locations and to participate in meetings and conferences while at home or on the road. Sales representatives can use CRM tools to exchange information with customers and process orders faster using the web. The web enables organizations to work across nations and continents in ways never experienced before. Some analysts predict that this true revolution in business practices will continue to occur because of computer technology in information-driven areas of the economy, such as financial services, entertainment, healthcare, education, and government. Areas such as manufacturing and utilities have begun to respond more rapidly, as well.

The Internet changes the method for doing business, but not the reason. Ultimately, in a free market economy, a business survives only if it produces high-quality, in-demand products or services and keeps its costs low. But the power of the Internet to streamline the exchange of information will certainly be exploited more and more by companies that understand its extensive potential.

The Supply Chain: A B2B Model

Businesses today come in all shapes and sizes: from solo entrepreneurs to corporations with many thousands of employees and billions of dollars in annual sales. But whether large or small, all businesses depend on a host of outside vendors to help create, market, and distribute their products. This fundamental business characteristic is termed **interdependence**, and it means that a business's decisions and actions often depend on the decisions and actions of others. For example, a manufacturer's decision to increase its output may depend on whether its suppliers can deliver more materials and its shipping company can handle additional cargo.

A company's interdependence with others is best observed by considering the concept of the **supply chain** (also known as the *value chain*). The supply chain includes a series of activities a company performs to achieve its goals at various stages in the production process. Figure 10.29 illustrates the activities that might make up a supply chain; however, the structures of actual supply chains vary depending on the type of business and customer needs. Many of the activities, or "links," involve outside parties, such as parts manufacturers and trucking companies. The value added at each link in the chain contributes to the company's profit and enhances the product's value as well as the company's competitive position in the market. And for the supply chain to function most effectively, all parties involved need to be able to communicate quickly and to share information.

Table 10.2 lists the types of information that can be shared among employees, suppliers, and other business partners because of this type of model. Establishing, running, and refining a supply chain form an area of expertise called **supply chain management (SCM)**.

Activity 10.8.1

Video
The Supply Chain Model

Figure 10.29

A supply chain may include some or all of these activities.

Table 10.2 Types of Information Shared in the B2B Model

Category	Examples
Product	Product prices, specifications, and sales data
Customer	Sales forecasts and sales histories
Supplier	Product and parts availability, sales terms and conditions
Production	Production capacities and plans
Shipping	Carrier availability, schedules, and costs
Inventory	Inventory levels, capacities, and locations
Competitor	Competitor products and market shares
Sales and marketing	Collection of POS data and product promotions
Manufacturing	Manufacturing performance, product quality, delivery schedules, and customer satisfaction

Input and Output in a Supply Chain One way to think about supply chain activities is to classify each production stage as primarily input or output. Input is centered on **procurement**, which involves searching for, finding, and purchasing materials, supplies, products, and services at the best possible prices and ensuring they are delivered in a timely manner. In terms of output, businesses must often correlate the date and time of manufacture and delivery of a certain product to a customer's request—a process referred to as **just-in-time (JIT) manufacturing**. For example, a construction firm may contract with a steel manufacturer for a quantity of 20-foot steel beams to be delivered on a specified date, at which time the beams are to be installed in a new building. If the steel manufacturer fails to deliver on the specified date, construction delays result, and the project's price tag increases.

E-commerce makes it possible to streamline the operation of the supply chain to meet a company's input and output needs. Using the Internet, a firm can electronically link to suppliers, manufacturers, warehouses, distributors, shipping companies, business partners, and customers in one virtual operation. Suppliers can anticipate a company's needs simply by monitoring its inventory online and shipping supplies just in time.

Many contemporary software vendors offer supply chain management solutions to help companies automate their production processes. These vendors include IBM, Ariba (an SAP subsidiary), JDA, Oracle, and SAP. The nonprofit Supply Chain Council offers frameworks and methods companies can use to improve supply chain performance. For instance, the council's Supply Chain Operations Reference (SCOR) model can be used for diagnosing supply chain issues.

Internet Structures That Facilitate B2B Supply Chains A business or organization can use the Internet in several ways to communicate and exchange information with other companies and/or its supply chain partners, including websites, intranets, extranets, and virtual private networks (VPNs). The type of structure a particular firm chooses depends on its needs.

Activity 10.8.2

Article
B2B Exchanges

Creating a company website establishes Internet visibility to other businesses and vendors. A properly developed site can enable the company to conduct business-to-business activities with its suppliers, banks, and other organizations with which it operates. In addition, business-to-business sites often include links to other companies and to documents or forms that enable vendors to bid on supplying the company with products and services. The site should also be structured to provide customers with information about the business and its products. Links can take customers to catalogs, lists of products with prices, order forms, and shipment placement and tracking.

Thousands of businesses have installed intranets that provide for the efficient transfer and retrieval of information by authorized employees within the organization. An intranet makes it possible for a business to lower its costs by enabling users to access important information, such as manufacturing schedules and inventory lists, quickly and efficiently.

An extranet, on the other hand, makes it possible for people inside and outside the business to communicate and to access stored information that can aid them in their activities and relationship with the business. For example, a supplier of materials to a manufacturing company can use the company's extranet to access and fill purchase orders for the manufacturer, and a customer can use it to check on the status of an order.

A virtual private network (VPN) can help eliminate the problem of unauthorized persons intercepting and misusing transmitted data. A VPN uses encryption and other security technologies to ensure that only authorized users can access the network and that the data can't be intercepted. Suppose a company wishes to provide mobile or remote workers with secure access to company data stored in standard files, such as text-based documents, and in company databases. With secure access, off-site workers typically access the data through their normal Internet connections, but the VPN protects the communication.

One of the security technologies that a VPN uses to safeguard data is tunneling. **Tunneling** enables one network to send its data via another network's connections. It works by adding a network protocol within the encrypted packets carried by the second network. For example, Microsoft's Point-to-Point Tunneling Protocol (PPTP) technology enables a business or organization to use the Internet to transmit encrypted data across a VPN by embedding its own network protocol within the TCP/IP packets carried by the Internet. A computer or router at the receiving end decrypts incoming data.

Major B2B Technologies

Software manufacturers have produced a host of programs that are used in B2B e-commerce operations. Some are designed specifically for manufacturing, while others are designed for other types of businesses, such as service organizations, financial institutions, and transportation companies. Major types of B2B software include the following:

- electronic data interchange (EDI)
- payment and transaction systems
- security technologies

Electronic Data Interchange   Many businesses use **electronic data interchange (EDI)** to exchange specially formatted business documents, such as purchase orders, invoices, credit application and approval forms, and shipping notices. EDI automates repetitive business transactions—those that occur again and again in the course of a normal work cycle.

To exchange information through EDI, the recipient needs an EDI translator to convert proprietary data from the sender into a standard format that the receiver can read. Using a translator also provides data security by rendering the data unreadable if an unauthorized party intercepts it.

Using EDI offers some distinct advantages over performing the same transactions using paper mail:

- Lower transaction costs
- Faster transmission of forms and documents
- Less paper flow
- Reduced data entry errors at the receiving end
- More reliability in sending and receiving documents

Some companies even have developed EDI applications to the extent that orders from customers are automatically created, processed, and shipped without human intervention. For example, a retailer's EDI system may be designed to notify a supplier automatically when the inventory level decreases to a certain level. Upon notification, the supplier processes the order and sends the product to the company to replenish the

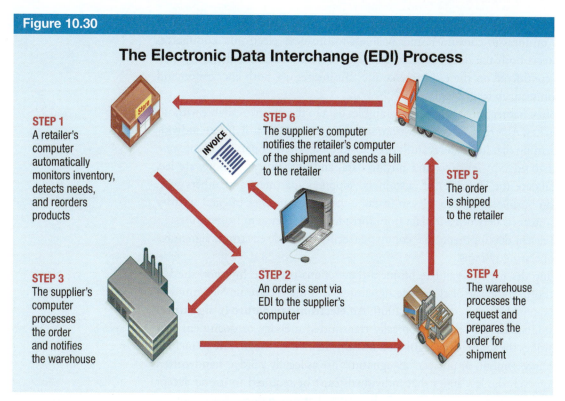

Figure 10.30

The Electronic Data Interchange (EDI) Process

STEP 1
A retailer's computer automatically monitors inventory, detects needs, and reorders products

STEP 6
The supplier's computer notifies the retailer's computer of the shipment and sends a bill to the retailer

STEP 5
The order is shipped to the retailer

STEP 3
The supplier's computer processes the order and notifies the warehouse

STEP 2
An order is sent via EDI to the supplier's computer

STEP 4
The warehouse processes the request and prepares the order for shipment

Electronic data interchange (EDI) can be used to streamline inventory ordering.

inventory. Figure 10.30 illustrates one example of how EDI could streamline inventory ordering.

Payment and Transaction Systems The payments required for exchanging products and services over the Internet may be delivered using financial electronic data interchange and automated clearinghouse transfers.

Numerous businesses use a form of EDI technology called **financial electronic data interchange (FEDI)** to transmit payments electronically. FEDI technology provides for the electronic transmission of payments and associated remittance information among a payer, a payee, and their respective banks. Using this technology lets businesses replace the labor-intensive activities of producing, mailing, and collecting checks. FEDI also eliminates delays inherent in processing checks through the banking system.

Many types of businesses now take advantage of FEDI technology. For example, AT&T offers FEDI as one billing and payment method for business customers. Healthcare providers—such as hospitals, doctors' offices, and ambulance services—use FEDI technology to bill private insurance companies and government agencies (such as Medicare) for patient services. In turn, some insurance companies and government agencies use FEDI technologies to remit payments for patient services.

An **automated clearinghouse (ACH)** is another type of automated banking network for transferring funds electronically from one account to another account. Some large banks have established their own private clearinghouses, while other smaller banks have joined together to form clearinghouses that serve member banks. ACH technology can process high-volume transactions, such as direct deposit payroll and vendor payments. The US Federal Reserve System operates one of the largest ACH networks in the nation.

Security Technologies Security concerns receive much attention by everyone involved in business-to-consumer and business-to-business electronic commerce. Security protects both the data stored in an e-commerce system and the individual transactions conducted on the e-commerce site. Businesses use both encryption and authentication security technologies.

Recall from Chapter 9 that *encryption* scrambles data so that it isn't readable without an encryption key. Also recall that *authentication* is the process of identifying an individual and confirming that he or she is authorized to access a system. Encryption software enables firms to encrypt sensitive and private data, and authentication software lets companies validate the identities of customers, suppliers, partners, and others with whom they do business. A company can install a firewall as another integral security measure to protect its network and data from intruders and its system from viruses.

The most recent developments in e-commerce security include electronic signatures and trusted operating systems.

Recognizing the need to validate business transactions over the Internet, the US Congress authorized the use of electronic signatures with the Electronic Signatures in Global and National Commerce Act in 2000. An **electronic signature (e-signature)** is a digital code attached to an electronically transmitted message or document that uniquely identifies the sender. The legislation broadly defined an e-signature to include "electronic sound, symbol, or process." E-signatures are as legally valid as handwritten signatures; however, the law states that individuals can't be required to use or accept e-signatures if they choose not to. The law also states that e-signatures don't apply to wills, divorce papers, and court orders.

Electronic signatures are especially important for e-commerce and are a key component of most authentication schemes. To be effective, e-signatures must be unforgeable (that is, unable to be faked in any way). Several encryption systems exist to guarantee a high level of security for digital signatures.

Any person can create and send an electronic signature using a desktop application such as Adobe Acrobat Pro (see Figure 10.31). Because the legal definition of e-signature is so broad, some businesses add an additional level of security by employing a digital signing service. This type of service issues digital IDs that allow organizations to verify identities and ensure valid signatures. In other instances, such as with the popular DocuSign service, you can upload a document that needs to be signed and identify who needs to sign it by email address. The service then emails each signer a link he or she can use to view and sign the document, which remains securely stored online.

Figure 10.31

SUBMITTED BY:

According to federal law, an e-signature—like this one created in Adobe Acrobat Pro—is just as valid as a physical signature on a piece of paper.

Taking a step beyond installing a firewall, a business that demands strong security for online transactions can use a **trusted operating system (TOS)** on its web server. Originally developed to ensure the security of military and government data, TOSs have evolved for business use. A TOS operates as a security-hardened version of a standard operating system. It isolates OS functions into separate compartments and restricts the ability of unauthorized users to access key areas of the OS. Many commercial operating systems allow for a single administrator account with complete access to the entire system. By contrast, a TOS isolates all of the OS services users need to access into individual compartments, each with distinct administrative accounts. An example of a TOS product is PitBull by General Dynamics C4 Systems.

Recheck 10.8

Recheck your understanding of the concepts covered by this objective.

Chapter Summary

➡ *An interactive **Chapter Summary**, **Study Notes**, and a **Slide Presentation** with audio are available from the links menu on this page in your ebook.*

10.1 Understanding Information Systems and Their Functions

An **information system (IS)** combines hardware, software, networks, and other components to collect, store, and process data that people in organizations use to manage daily and long-term operations and to create and sell various types of products. Computerized information management increases productivity and efficiency, making companies more competitive. Computer-based information systems offer four key improvements over traditional (precomputer) information systems in the areas of speed, efficiency, quality, and measurability.

Common functional classifications of information systems include **distribution management systems**, **office information systems (OIS)**, **management information systems (MIS)**, **decision support systems (DSS)**, **executive information systems (EIS)**, factory automation systems, **customer relationship management (CRM) systems**, and **enterprise resource planning (ERP) systems**. Within these categories are a number of types of information systems. For instance, **electronic data processing (EDP)** is a system within OIS, and **online analytical processing (OLAP)** is a system within DSS. Two systems are used in factory automation: the **computer-aided manufacturing (CAM) system** and the **computer-integrated manufacturing (CIM) system**. A **statistical quality control (SQC)** system is another form of IS often used in plant operations.

10.2 Planning and Analyzing Information Systems

The comprehensive process of building an IS is called the **system development life cycle (SDLC)**. Creating and executing a development plan involves four main stages: planning, design, implementation, and support. A **feasibility study** is conducted to investigate the difficulty and cost of developing or implementing a new system. If management decides to hire an outside systems vendor or **systems integrator**, a **request for proposal (RFP)** will be sent to one or more possible suppliers. An RFP response usually requests a **project plan**, which includes an estimate of how long the project will take to complete, an outline of the steps involved, and a list of **deliverables**. Developing or implementing a new IS involves identifying and assembling a team of employees with the necessary skills and expertise, including software engineers, programmers, and hardware techs. Sometimes, the project manager also functions as a **business systems analyst**, who is responsible for completing the systems analysis and making design recommendations.

The decision makers in an organization should study the likely impact of a new IS to determine its suitability. Upgrading or switching to a computer-based IS can be difficult for some staff, and it may take time for the new IS to provide a full return on investment. The major effects of upgrading or switching to a computer-based information system include expanded technical staff, added upgrade costs, increased profit margins, enhanced product or service quality, streamlined staffing, and temporary disruptions.

Once the organization has decided to proceed with a new system, the next decision is how to bring the system into service. At this stage, decision makers should choose an information systems package based on these factors: the use of internal versus external resources (**outsourcing**), user interface design, **niche information systems**, **turnkey systems**, and system support.

10.3 Designing and Developing Information Systems

A project moves into the design stage once the project team has approved the plan, including the budget. The design process begins with writing functional and design specifications. In most cases, the project team creates a **functional specification**, which describes what the system must be able to do. The **design specification** outlines the hardware and software necessary to execute the functions. Project leaders must approve both documents before work can proceed. Another significant part of any design specification is deciding whether to use packaged (off-the-shelf) software or custom software.

10.4 Implementing Information Systems

Once the development team and systems vendor or integrator have developed the specifications and approved the plans, the project moves into the next phase—**implementation**—which is usually the longest, most difficult phase. Implementation involves the actual work of putting the system together, including creating a prototype and completing the programming. A prototype is a miniprogram that demonstrates the user interface and functionality of the system. The **beta testing** period begins once the computers and software have been installed and are operating; during this period, the system is rigorously tested to ensure that it functions as designed.

User training normally takes place at the same time as beta testing; system users learn how to run the new software. This process can result in the discovery of errors, such as lost records, network errors, system crashes, and the accidental display of confidential information. Any of these problems can result in calling on the development team to create an emergency patch, or correction, to the system.

After the IS has been developed, the committee or executive overseeing its purchase must inspect, test, and approve it. This can be a stressful time for everyone involved if a system has ongoing problems.

10.5 Supporting and Maintaining Information Systems

After the IS has been accepted and approved, the project goes into the support stage. Users might still be dealing with errors in the system, or additional features may be requested. The support staff might conduct **corrective maintenance**, **perfective maintenance**, **adaptive maintenance**, or **preventive maintenance**. Having a **support contract** usually allows users to contact the system vendor or integrator for technical support, training, and troubleshooting. The support stage continues until a new IS is proposed and developed.

The system development life cycle operates in a circular fashion: as soon as one phase ends, a new one begins. If mistakes have been made, the team might have to return to the planning stage. Following this cycle helps ensure that continual adjustments and improvements are made, which ultimately benefits all participants.

10.6 Exploring Electronic Commerce and Online Shopping

Electronic commerce, or **e-commerce**, is the buying and selling of products and services over the Internet. There are two categories of e-commerce. In **business-to-consumer (B2C) electronic commerce**, companies use the Internet to sell products and services to consumers and to receive payments from them. In **business-to-business (B2B) electronic commerce**, companies use the Internet to conduct a wide range of routine business activities with other companies—for instance, ordering manufacturing parts and purchasing inventories from wholesalers.

A retail company that carries out electronic commerce is sometimes referred to as an **e-tailer**. A company that sells its products and services exclusively over the web is referred to as a **pure-play e-tailer**. **Online shopping** involves using a web-connected computer or mobile device to locate, examine, purchase, and pay for products. Online shopping offers several distinct advantages over traditional shopping, including convenience, greater selection, more product information, and easy comparison shopping.

Online shoppers can visit a number of online shopping venues. An **online store** (or **virtual store**) is a seller's website where customers can view, purchase, and pay for products and services. An **online superstore** offers an extensive variety of products at bargain prices. An **online shopping mall** connects stores via hyperlinks on its home page. An **online catalog** presents detailed information about a company's products and services. A **shopping agent** continually searches the web for specific products at the lowest possible priced.

Businesses continue to discover new ways to advertise and sell services to consumers online, including services that provide media and music, auctions, gaming, restaurant reservations and ordering, and borrowing and lending money. Two of the most popular online services today are **online banking** and travel services. Some of these services are free, but most require the user to purchase a subscription.

At most online shopping sites, the buyer electronically places selected items in a virtual **shopping cart**. To purchase the items, the buyer reviews a summary of the items and their costs, the total cost, and taxes, shipping, and other charges. To check out, the buyer enters a shipping address, selects a payment method, and enters information related to it. Many shopping sites use encryption to protect the personal and financial information consumers provide in online transactions. Encryption is the process of converting readable information (plaintext) into unreadable information (ciphertext) to prevent unauthorized access and usage. In evaluating online shopping sites, buyers should look for features such as clearly stated selling and security terms, a satisfactory amount of product information, a simple purchase process, and excellent customer service.

10.7 Completing Electronic Commerce Transactions

Today's technology allows consumers to make payments for goods and services purchased online using a variety of methods: **electronic funds transfer (EFT)**, **credit cards** and **debit cards**, smart cards, **credit accounts**, **person-to-person payment systems**, virtual currencies, and **digital wallets**. Consumers can also be alerted to products, coupons, and sales in a variety of ways. A **quick response (QR) code** provides a signal to the consumer that he or she can find out more about a product or service online. Similarly, many retailers offer online apps that send coupons and alerts about special sales deals to the consumer's smartphone.

To complete sales transactions, many small retailers bypass using traditional cash registers. They use an iPad, iPhone, or Android phone along with a reader accessory to swipe credit and debit cards.

10.8 Understanding Business-to-Business Electronic Commerce

Business-to-business (B2B) electronic commerce (or e-business) is a segment of e-commerce in which businesses and organizations use the Internet and e-commerce technologies to conduct a wide range of routine business activities with other companies. In a B2B electronic commerce transaction, both the seller and buyer are business organizations. B2B electronic commerce transactions can also take place within a business. **Intrabusiness electronic commerce** involves using web-based technology to handle these kinds of transactions.

All businesses depend on outside vendors to help create, market, and distribute their products—a fundamental business characteristic termed **interdependence**. A company's interdependence on others is best observed by considering the concept of a **supply chain**. A supply chain includes the series of activities a company performs to achieve its goals at various stages in the production process; in other words, it's the linked process by which a product moves from production to market. Supply chain activities can be classified as input or output. Input activities involve **procurement**: searching for, finding, and purchasing materials, supplies, products, and services at the best possible prices and ensuring that they are delivered in a timely manner. Output activities involve correlating the date and time of manufacture and delivery of a certain product to a customer's request; this process is referred to as **just-in-time (JIT)** manufacturing.

A business or organization can use the Internet in several ways to communicate and exchange information with other companies and organizations and/or its supply chain partners, including websites, **intranets**, **extranets**, and virtual private networks (VPNs). The type of structure a particular business or organization chooses depends on its needs.

Software manufacturers have produced a variety of programs that are now being used in B2B **e-commerce** operations. Some are designed specifically for manufacturing, whereas others are designed for service organizations, financial institutions, transportation companies, and other types of businesses. Major types of B2B software include **electronic data interchange (EDI)** and payment and transaction systems such as **financial electronic data interchange (FEDI)** and an **automated clearinghouse (ACH)**. The most recent developments in e-commerce security include **electronic signatures** (e-signatures) and **trusted operating systems (TOSs)**.

Key Terms

Numbers indicate the pages where terms are first cited with their full definition in the chapter.
An alphabetized list of key terms with definitions is included in the end-of-book glossary.

➡ *An interactive **Glossary** is available from the links menu on this page in your ebook.*

Chapter Exercises

Complete the following exercises to assess your understanding of the material covered in this chapter.

Interactive **Flash Cards** and an interactive **Game** are available from the links menu on this page in your ebook.

 Go to your SNAP Assignments page to complete the Terms Check, Knowledge Check, Key Principles, and Tech Illustrated exercises.

Terms Check: Matching

Match each term with its definition.

a.	digital wallet	f.	Gantt chart
b.	beta testing	g.	data modeling
c.	outsourcing	h.	person-to-person payment system
d.	tunneling	i.	QR code
e.	feasibility study	j.	e-commerce

___ 1. The buying and selling of products and services electronically over the Internet.

___ 2. A system that uses "what if?" scenarios to predict future outcomes.

___ 3. A visual that uses bars to show the stages and tasks in a project.

___ 4. A symbol a consumer can scan with a smartphone app to jump right to information about the product or service in the phone's web browser.

___ 5. A security technology used by a virtual private network to safeguard data.

___ 6. An app that gathers all your credit card and loyalty payment information.

___ 7. Enables consumers to transfer money to one another through a credit card or bank account.

___ 8. The rigorous testing of a system for errors and failures in operation.

___ 9. Conducted to investigate how large a project might be and how much it might cost.

___ 10. The process of hiring a third party to handle a project.

Knowledge Check: Multiple Choice

Choose the best answer for each question.

1. Which system is designed to help companies deliver products more quickly, more cheaply, and with fewer errors?
   a. decision support system
   b. distribution management system
   c. office information system
   d. standard operating system

2. Which system defines and clarifies methods of handling "what if?" questions posed to large databases?
   a. executive information (EIS) system
   b. expert system
   c. online analytical processing (OLAP) system
   d. electronic data processing (EDP) system

3. Which system involves the direct use of computerized systems to manufacture products?
   a. computer-aided manufacturing (CAM) system
   b. statistical quality control (SQC) system
   c. customer relationship management (CRM) system
   d. enterprise resource planning (ERP) system

4. Which system uses a combination of data tracking and data modeling to build a picture of how well a factory operates?
   a. computer-aided manufacturing (CAM) system
   b. computer-integrated manufacturing (CIM) system
   c. customer relationship management (CRM) system
   d. statistical quality control (SQC) system

5. In a project team, which individual typically leads the early phases of systems development?
   a. business systems analyst
   b. programmer
   c. software engineer
   d. systems engineer

6. Which of the following states exactly what an information system must accomplish but not how it will be accomplished?
   a. data model
   b. design specification
   c. functional specification
   d. prototype

7. Which form of commerce is used by consumers to make online purchases using a mobile device, such as a smartphone?
   a. bricks-and-mortar commerce
   b. business-to-business (B2B) electronic commerce
   c. mobile commerce
   d. smart commerce

8. Which of the following enables you to quickly compare the prices that multiple online retailers charge for a particular product?
   a. online catalog
   b. online shopping mall
   c. online superstore
   d. shopping agent

9. Which of the following legislative acts restricts the use of personal data and regulates spamming?
   a. Privacy Protection Act of 1980
   b. Electronic Communications Privacy Act of 1987
   c. Communications Privacy and Consumer Empowerment Act of 1997
   d. Data Privacy Act of 1997

10. Which of the following is a general term that refers to any transfer of money over the Internet?
    a. electronic funds transfer
    b. e-ticketing
    c. intrabusiness electronic commerce
    d. supply chain

Key Principles: Completion

Complete each statement with the appropriate word or phrase.

1. A system that combines GPS, wireless communications features, and other technologies to plan more efficient shipping routes and monitor shipment locations is called a(n) _____ system.

2. A set of instructions describing how to perform a task is referred to as a(n) _____.

3. _____ refers to the ability to link with other programs and devices.

4. The comprehensive process for building an information system is called the _____.

5. A system created to serve a specially focused set of customers is called a(n) _____.

6. A preliminary, not fully functional version of a program that demonstrates the user interface and functionality of the system is referred to as a(n) _____.

7. A system that contains everything a business needs to get a new information system up and running is called a(n) _____.

8. Businesses such as Amazon that sell their products and services exclusively over the web are referred to as _____.

9. When an online retailer sells a small quantity or surplus stock at a large discount for a limited period of time, it's called a(n) _____.

10. _____ is an Apple technology that uses a Bluetooth low-energy signal to send smartphone alerts to shoppers within a store

Tech Illustrated: Figure Labeling

Fill in the blanks with the correct labels.

1. An information system

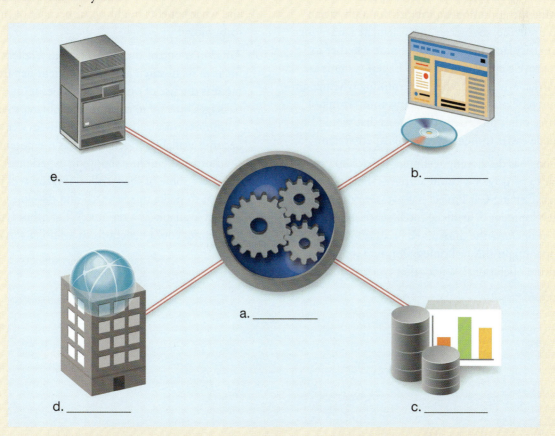

e. _____

b. _____

a. _____

d. _____

c. _____

2. The electronic data interchange (EDI) process

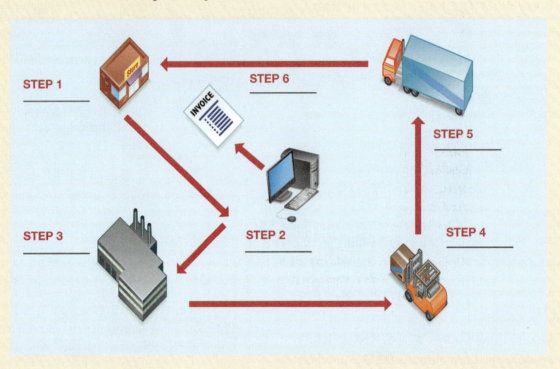

Tech to Come: Brainstorming New Uses

In groups or individually, contemplate the following questions and develop as many answers as you can.

1. Expert systems have been developed to determine the appropriate antibiotic for a physician to prescribe, to forecast the avalanche hazard for a particular area, and to determine whether to approve a credit application. Expert systems are particularly useful when determining whether an outcome may be costly or dangerous. Think of three other processes or decisions that would be made easier through the use of expert systems.

2. Google is developing technology that allows a car to be driven without a driver. The Google Self-Driving Car Project has overseen the development of artificial intelligence software that operates the unmanned or autonomous car. How might this technology impact Google's future operations? What other types of business could benefit from this technology? What issues and what benefits might occur because of this technology?

3. Amazon is one of the largest online retailers. A focus of its research and development department is the use of unmanned drones to fly packages directly to consumers' doorsteps within 30 minutes of placing orders. If this service does become available, it definitely has the potential to improve the online shopping experience. What are some of the hurdles Amazon will have to clear to make this research and development project available as a service? What other types of companies could benefit from a similar service?

Tech Literacy: Internet Research and Writing

Conduct Internet research to find the information described, and then develop appropriate written responses based on your research. Be sure to document your sources using the MLA format. (See Chapter 1, Tech Literacy: Internet Research and Writing, page 38, to review MLA style guidelines.)

1. Research a retailer that has bricks-and-mortar stores and offers online shopping. How much of its revenue is generated from online shopping? Analyze how online shopping has impacted the retailer's store operations. What types of payment methods does the retailer accept? Read its website privacy policy. How is your personal information protected if you make a purchase on the retailer's site?

2. Research one of the large automakers, such as Ford, to see how it uses robots to assemble and test its vehicles. Describe how the company's computer-aided manufacturing system works. How has this technology impacted jobs and the skills employees must have to work in this field?

3. Shipping, logistics, and courier companies have complex distribution management systems. Research UPS, FedEx, or a similar company and describe how its distribution management system works. Include statistics in your report.

4. Locate and read the Electronic Signatures in Global and National Commerce Act of 2000. Explain why Congress defined electronic signatures broadly to include "electronic sound, symbol, or process." Describe how to create an electronic signature and the decisions that must be made during the process. Are there limitations to when or where you can use an e-signature? How has the use of e-signatures affected the way certain professions (such as accountants and lawyers) do business? What risks are associated with e-signatures?

5. How many information systems are tracking your actions right now? Research the different kinds of records stored on government and corporate information systems. What might the IRS, police, and government officials know about you from records in their information systems? What rights do you have to access this data?

Tech Issues: Team Problem-Solving

In groups, develop possible solutions to the issues presented.

1. Imagine that you are opening a small restaurant. What functions will your information system have to perform for the restaurant to run efficiently? How can you use the IS to expand your business capabilities and increase sales?

2. e-Commerce has opened the door to a global marketplace for many companies. However, moving from a local to an international marketplace can be challenging. Brainstorm some of the issues companies face in moving to a global marketplace. How might some of these challenges be overcome?

3. You have been given the task of preparing an RFP to send out to vendors for the development of a new information system for a construction company. To select the best vendor for the job, you will need to gather information about how various vendors will complete the project. What questions should you ask in the RFP to gather information about each vendor's project plan and deliverables, including time and cost? What other factors do you need to consider before selecting the right vendor for the job?

Tech Timeline: Predicting Next Steps

Look at the timeline below summarizing major milestones in the development of electronic commerce. Based on your knowledge and research, predict at least three important milestones that could occur through the year 2030.

1995   Auctionweb.com, the origin of eBay is launched.

1998   E-commerce becomes a major economic player.

1999   Shawn Fanning founds Napster, a music file sharing program, during his freshman year at Northeastern University.

2000   Annual e-commerce sales exceed $200 billion.

2001   Napster is found guilty of allowing the illegal copying of copyrighted music. Warner Music, BMG Entertainment, EMI Group, and RealNetworks form a partnership called *MusicNet*, which licenses its MP3 technology and its partners' record titles for downloading.

2002   Online auctions become tremendously popular, with sales topping $13 billion.

2003   The IRS offers free electronic filing (e-filing) for federal tax returns.

2005   Fifty million US adults bank online.

2009   US retail e-commerce sales top $31.7 billion in the first quarter alone.

2011   eBay generates $11 billion in revenue.

2012   Amazon sales are over $61 billion.

2013   Online comparison shopping sites attract 72 million monthly visitors.

2014   Home furnishings retailer Williams-Sonoma reported that its e-commerce sales make up more than 50 percent of its revenues.

Ethical Dilemmas: Group Discussion and Debate

As a class or within an assigned group, discuss the following ethical dilemma.

A *cookie* is a file that a web server transmits to a user's browser so that the server can track the user's activity on a specific website, including which ads a user sees and how often a user visits the site. Many businesses favor the use of cookies, while many consumers are opposed. Businesses claim that cookies are harmless and that they enable companies to better serve customers by directing ads, sales information, and new product introductions to specific demographic groups. Conversely, some individuals and consumer groups argue that the use of cookies is an invasion of privacy and that cookies may result in security problems, especially if collected information is shared with other companies, organizations, and individuals.

What is your position on this issue?

Do certain situations justify using cookies to collect user information? Why or why not?

What are a business's ethical obligations, if any, concerning this matter?

What operating system features are available to block cookies?

Chapter 11

Using Programming Concepts and Languages

Chapter Goal

To understand how programmers use programming languages and development tools to create and modify software

Learning Objectives

11.1 List the steps in the software development life cycle.

11.2 Define the basic concepts of computer programming.

11.3 Describe the techniques and tools used in programming.

11.4 Identify several programming languages, and list their strengths and weaknesses.

11.5 Explain the programming tools available for web applications and content.

Green go-online icons indicate resources that are accessed from the links menu in your ebook.

SNAP icons indicate inter-active resources that are available in SNAP. Go to your SNAP Assignments page to complete these quizzes, activities, and exercises.

11.1 Describing the Software Development Life Cycle

Precheck 11.1

Check your understanding of the concepts covered by this objective.

Software development life cycle (SDLC) is the term used to describe the phases involved in the process of creating, testing, and releasing a new software product. This cycle is similar to the process used in developing an information system, except that in the SDLC, the cycle focuses on the creation and release of a software program, not the development of a customized information system. The SDLC is repeated every time a new version of a program is needed.

As shown in Figure 11.1, the software development life cycle includes these phases:
- Proposal and planning
- Design
- Implementation
- Testing
- Public release

Proposal and Planning

In the proposal and planning phase of a new software product, software developers describe the proposed software program and what it's supposed to accomplish. In the case of existing software, the proposal and planning stage can be used to describe new features and improvements. Older software programs are often revised to take advantage of new hardware and software developments and to add new functions and features.

Activity 11.1.1

Practice
The Software Development Life Cycle

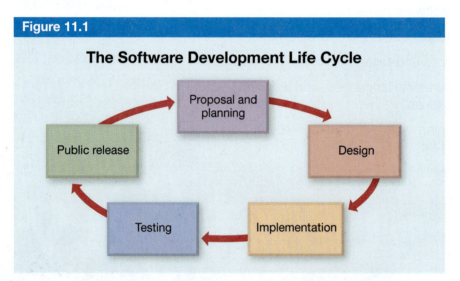

Figure 11.1

The Software Development Life Cycle

The software development life cycle involves proposing and planning, designing, implementing, testing, and releasing software.

⟩ Tracking Down Tech ⟩⟩⟩⟩⟩⟩

Choosing a Programming Language to Learn

Many technology experts recommend that everyone who plans to attend college (or is already in college) should take at least one semester of a programming language, because it teaches one how to think in a structured, orderly way. But how would you get started learning a language, and which language should you learn? Complete this scavenger hunt to find classes offered in your area, as well as advice on which language will be most valuable to potential employers.

Design

Developers are ready to begin the design process once the decision has been made to create or upgrade a software program. This step produces **specifications** documenting the details of the software to be written by programmers. Developers use the problem-solving steps described in the section "Problem-Solving Steps," on page 499, to determine appropriate specifications.

Implementation

The implementation phase of the software development life cycle is usually the most difficult. Development teams often spend late nights and weekends writing code and making it work. Large programming projects are much like engineering projects. They are too big for a single individual to complete, so they require a programming team. For example, a professionally released, mass-market software program may be the result of the combined efforts of five programmers, or of more than 500. Each programmer in a programming team is responsible for a small portion of the final program, and the team leader must carefully coordinate the efforts of team members to ensure that the program works as intended. Software engineers typically coordinate programming projects while working with programming teams.

If the planning and design efforts have been successful, this phase should go well, but unanticipated problems inevitably crop up and have to be solved. The end result of the implementation phase is the production of a prototype called an **alpha product**, which the development team uses for testing purposes. The alpha product can be revised to incorporate any improvements team members suggest.

Testing

A quality assurance (QA) team usually develops a **testing harness**, which is a scripted set of tests that a program must pass before being considered ready for public release. These tests might cover events such as very large input loads, maximum numbers of users, running on several different supported platforms, and simulated power outages.

Once alpha testing has finished, a **beta version** of the software program is created for testing outside the development group, often by a select group of knowledgeable consumers. Any suggestions they make can be used to improve the product before it's released to the general public.

Once the beta version has been finalized, the user manual is written or updated. At this point, the software developer sends the master CDs or DVDs to duplicators for mass production (called *release to manufacturing*, or *RTM*). Some software is released digitally online for distribution, so it does not require disc creation.

Tech Career Explorer

Software Developer

Software developers do much more than just programming. They are entrepreneurs or visionaries with ideas for new and innovative software. They manage and participate in the entire life cycle of the software, from concept to release. They determine whether the market needs and wants the proposed product, figure out how to create it, and assemble the team of programmers and other professionals. Complete this exercise to learn more about software development work.

Activity 11.1.2

Video
Beta Testing

After a software program has been carefully tested, the master is released for duplication if it will be distributed on disc.

Public Release

When the product is deemed ready for widespread use, it's declared "gold" and released to the public. A **gold release** is also referred to as a *generally available release* of the software.

At this point, the software development life cycle goes back to the beginning phase, as software developers think of new ways to improve the product. The cycle continues until a new version (revision) of the original product is ready for release.

Software usually has major releases and minor revisions, which are typically represented by different version numbers. For example, Adobe Acrobat Reader 11.0.08 was a newer minor revision of Acrobat Reader XI (11).

11.2 Understanding Programming Terms and Concepts

To understand how programmers create and modify software, you need to be familiar with some basic terms and concepts. A *program* is a set of instructions telling a computer how to perform various tasks, and programming is the act of creating these instructions. Programmers use a **programming language** to create a program. Programs are also referred to as *source code*. **Coding** is the term programmers use to refer to the act of writing source code. Programmers write code using various programming languages, standard building blocks, and specific problem-solving techniques—all discussed in the following sections.

Language Characteristics and Classifications

Programming languages contain smaller vocabularies than human (natural) languages and are much less complex. A typical programming language may contain 100 to 200 elements (words and symbols), whereas a human language (such as English) contains around 10,000 elements. The **syntax**, or structure, of a programming language also tends to be less complex than that of a human language. A programming language is therefore not as difficult to learn as a foreign language, such as French or German.

The process of writing a program is similar to the process of writing a term paper. The writer of a term paper chooses a topic and then thinks about how the topic can be

Recheck 11.1
Recheck your understanding of the concepts covered by this objective.

Precheck 11.2
Check your understanding of the concepts covered by this objective.

Activity 11.2.1

Article
Logic Tables and Control Structures

Cutting Edge

The Russians Are Coming

Many US software companies outsource much of their computer programming to businesses in other countries that can provide qualified programmers for lower per-hour rates. More and more countries—including Vietnam, Botswana, and Argentina—are competing for a piece of the American "pie," with India currently claiming the biggest slice.

But the new face at the table competing for programming work from the United States is not a third world country—it's Russia. Russian programming expertise lies in high-end, complex programming. The country has a highly educated workforce, with more than 50 percent of its students majoring in science, math, or computer science. UNESCO ranks Russia third in the world in terms of scientists and engineers per capita. Russia's homegrown IT sector, which receives strong government support, boasts almost 300 software companies.

Russia's relative proximity to the United States gives the Russians a slight edge over Indian and Southeast Asian programmers, as the end of the Russian programmer's workday overlaps the beginning of the workday on the US East Coast. Russian programmers command more money than their third world counterparts but still only one-fifth of US pay rates.

organized in a logical fashion to ensure that the paper will convey her intent. During the writing process, the term paper goes through several drafts, which are corrected and updated until the final version is ready. Programming follows the same steps, but uses a programming language and computers instead of a human language and word-processing software.

Programming is difficult mental work, not unlike the effort involved in writing a report for a college course. Programming actually requires more effort than writing a report, however, because a program must accomplish all of its goals with zero or little tolerance for error. A professor may gloss over a few minor punctuation mistakes and still give a paper an A, but a program with a single **syntax error** (a mistake in the way programming elements are written) won't work at all, and will therefore be worthless. This is the equivalent of a term paper being considered unreadable because of a single misplaced comma.

High-Level versus Low-Level Languages Computer languages can be classified as low level and high level. A *low-level language* is close in form to the thought processes computers use. Also called *machine language* or *machine code*, this type of programming language is a binary language consisting of 1s and 0s. On the other hand, a *high-level language* is relatively similar to natural languages, such as English, making this type of computer language easier to use than machine code.

Although high-level languages are easier to learn and use, low-level languages run faster and take up less disk space. This means that software companies can save time and money by using high-level languages to develop software programs. However, the programs will take up more space and run more slowly than programs developed using low-level languages.

Programming Language Generations A computer **programming language generation** is a type or group of programming languages that were developed at the same time, in a particular chronological order. The language of the most recent generation builds on the languages in the preceding generation. There are five generations of computer programming languages, as outlined in Figure 11.2. A computer language is

Activity 11.2.2

Article
Linear Programming and Simplex Method

Activity 11.2.3

Practice
Generations of Programming Languages

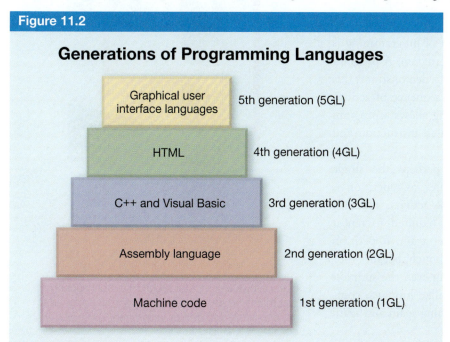

Figure 11.2

Generations of Programming Languages

Graphical user interface languages — 5th generation (5GL)

HTML — 4th generation (4GL)

C++ and Visual Basic — 3rd generation (3GL)

Assembly language — 2nd generation (2GL)

Machine code — 1st generation (1GL)

Each generation of programs builds on the contributions of the group of languages that preceded it.

sometimes described as belonging to a generation of languages. For example, a programmer might describe HTML as a popular fourth-generation language (4GL) used to design web pages.

The Basic Building Blocks of Programming

All computer programs contain four main programming elements, which work together as discrete units or in combined form. Together, these programming elements allow computers to process data and turn it into information for various uses. The four main programming elements are as follows:

- Variables
- Executable statements
- Looping
- Decision statements

Variables A **variable** is a data value stored in computer memory. A variable can be anything a programmer wants to keep and work with—a name, a number, or even a status indicator, such as yes/no. For example, a program for adding two numbers and producing a sum will have variables for the first and second numbers, plus a variable for the sum of those numbers. Variables normally have data types, similar to the possible data-type fields used in a database.

Executable Statements Statements are used to manipulate variables and to perform actions, such as sending output to a screen or printer. Some statements read input from the mouse and keyboard and store that data for later use as a variable. When run by a program, an **executable statement** performs an action and then proceeds to the next statement in the sequence.

Looping An essential element of programming is the ability to repeat parts of a program. A program for controlling a stoplight clearly demonstrates this capacity, as it repeats the same sequence of actions and decisions endlessly. **Looping** allows a program to return to a previously executed instruction and repeat it (see Figure 11.3).

The power of looping is perhaps the single greatest capacity of the computer, as repetition is the dullest part of any mental activity. Humans naturally become bored when required to repeat a series of actions over and over again. Repetition isn't a problem for computers, though, because they never get bored with performing even the simplest and most repetitive chores. Unlike humans, computers excel at doing the same thing again and again very quickly.

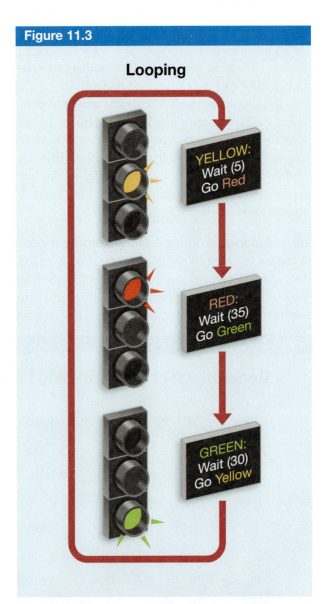

Figure 11.3

Looping

Looping allows a computer program to continuously repeat the same steps, such as a program designed to direct a traffic light to display yellow, red, and green lights at consistent intervals.

Decision Statements A program that simply follows a linear sequence of actions without variation is of limited use. However, if a program contains a **decision statement**—a point where different actions may be performed depending on specific conditions—then it will be more useful.

For example, the stoplight program shown in Figure 11.3 will be more helpful to pedestrians if the pattern can be interrupted when someone wants to cross the street. As illustrated in Figure 11.4, the program can be designed so that a crosswalk button controls the stoplight behavior using an **if-then statement**. This statement allows the program to perform differently depending on whether the button has been pressed. As this example shows, computers make decisions by comparing values in variables and then performing different sequences of actions depending on the outcomes.

Figure 11.4

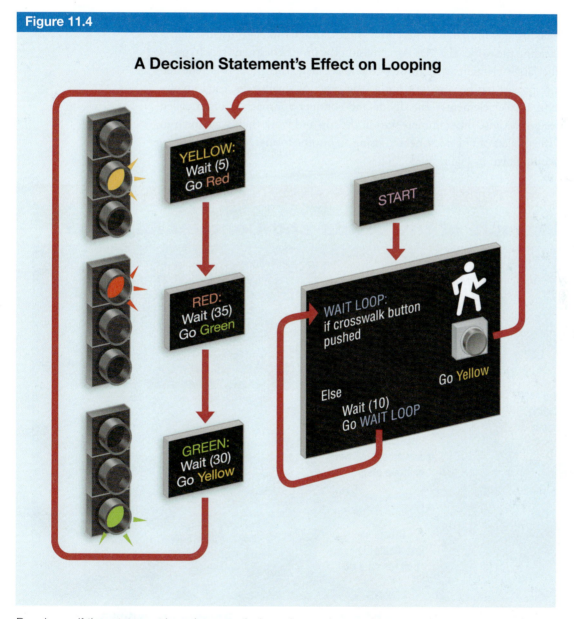

A Decision Statement's Effect on Looping

By using an if-then statement based on a particular action, such as pushing a crosswalk button, a program can interrupt a looping pattern. Decision statements make a program more useful—in this case, often allowing pedestrians to shorten the time they will wait to cross the street.

The Divide-and-Conquer Approach to Problem-Solving

Programming is a problem-solving process. For programmers, this means that technical knowledge alone isn't enough. To be truly successful, programmers must be creative analytical thinkers. In many cases, the technical details of a project are too complex for managers to deal with, so employers prize programmers with excellent problem-solving capabilities. Problem solving is as much an art as a science, but there are techniques for solving problems using logical processes, including the divide-and-conquer approach.

One technique for solving problems when developing software is to break down the large problem into several small problems. This technique is based on the idea that every program is like a giant puzzle. In the **divide-and-conquer approach**, programmers tackle one small piece of the puzzle at a time. They work on each piece until they solve it, and then they move on to the next one.

Before breaking down a large project into pieces, programmers must develop a strategy for tackling the work. The idea is to envision the project in its entirety in order to identify the larger elements that must be handled first. This process is repeated until the entire project has been reduced to a long series of small steps, each involving smaller and smaller elements. The divide-and-conquer approach is often called **top-down design**, because programmers start at the top and work their way down to the bottom. The process can be documented using an outline format, or in a hierarchy chart like the one shown in Figure 11.5.

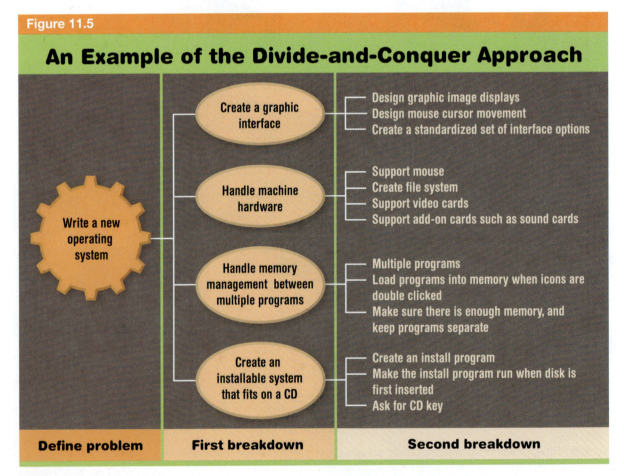

Figure 11.5

An Example of the Divide-and-Conquer Approach

Write a new operating system

Create a graphic interface
- Design graphic image displays
- Design mouse cursor movement
- Create a standardized set of interface options

Handle machine hardware
- Support mouse
- Create file system
- Support video cards
- Support add-on cards such as sound cards

Handle memory management between multiple programs
- Multiple programs
- Load programs into memory when icons are double clicked
- Make sure there is enough memory, and keep programs separate

Create an installable system that fits on a CD
- Create an install program
- Make the install program run when disk is first inserted
- Ask for CD key

Define problem   **First breakdown**   **Second breakdown**

The divide-and-conquer approach helps programmers break a large project into manageable parts. The breakdown process continues until there are no more steps to break out.

Problem-Solving Steps

Few jobs are more complex than computer programming. Because of the difficulty, programmers need to be the type of workers referred to as *self-starters*. They have to be prepared to take on programming projects with only vague goals and guidelines, and produce a working piece of software. To accomplish their tasks, programmers follow a standard set of problem-solving steps:

1. Identify the problem.

2. Analyze the problem.

3. Brainstorm solutions and choose the best one.

4. Write the algorithm.

5. Prototype the solution.

6. Implement and test the solution.

Identify the Problem Organizations that contract programmers' services aren't always sure of what they want. Sometimes they can describe their needs, but not in a way that will help programmers know where to begin. Programmers may hear statements such as "Our billing system is too slow—fix it" and "We would like to network all of our company offices."

Programmers must first hammer out the definition of the problem before they can begin to solve it. Programmers start every project like interrogators, beginning with a thorough set of questions covering every aspect that isn't clear. If programmers begin a project without correctly identifying the problem(s) that must be solved, they will very likely come up with the wrong solutions. This means they will end up losing valuable time, and quite possibly their jobs.

In the case of a slow billing system, programmers might start off with questions isolating the cause of the slowdown: Is the network running slowly? Are the computers old and out of date? Is there faulty hardware somewhere? A simple fix, such as new network equipment or a new printer, will often solve problems and avoid the need for expensive programming.

Before beginning work, a programmer must be able to communicate with the company's business leaders to understand the scope and needs of the project.

Analyze the Problem   After the problem has been identified, the next step involves analyzing it. At first glance, this may seem identical to the first step (identify the problem), but it's actually more complex. Analyzing the problem can involve learning new skills and concepts. For example, if a problem has been identified that requires installation of a network connecting 100 computers, the programmer must understand how networks function, what kind of software and hardware are needed, and how it all works. If the solution to an identified problem requires writing a program in Visual Basic, then part of understanding the problem includes understanding Visual Basic.

At this point, it's probably clear that the term *programmer* only partly covers what a computer specialist does. How broad a programmer's job becomes is partly related to the size of the organization that he works for. In some jobs, hundreds or even thousands of computer people work on a project, and in such cases, a given programmer's job is very focused. It's more common, however, to have a single programmer or a small group of programmers working on a given project. This arrangement widens the list of responsibilities for the individual.

Brainstorm Solutions and Choose the Best One   Once a problem has been identified, analyzed, and understood, programmers are ready to develop a set of solutions. Novice programmers sometimes ignore this critical phase. It may seem that the easiest approach would be to choose the first solution that comes to mind, but unfortunately, doing so often leads to less than optimal outcomes. The best strategy is to create a list of all possible solutions, evaluate them, and then choose the best one before proceeding.

By brainstorming, programmers can identify all possible solutions first and then evaluate them to determine the best solution.

Write the Algorithm The next step involves clearly defining the solution. If it's determined that new software is needed to solve the problem, part of this step may include deciding which language to use in creating the program. To assist in defining the solution, a program is first written out as an algorithm before being written in a programming language. An **algorithm** is a complete list of steps for solving a problem.

Algorithms usually are written in **pseudocode**, which is a very high-level language that computers can't read. Pseudocode is a useful tool for organizing the way a programmer thinks about a solution. The algorithm is later translated into a program the computer can interpret. Figure 11.6 shows an example of a pseudocode algorithm for changing a lightbulb.

Hands On

Writing Pseudocode

Follow the instructions in this resource to see how well you can describe a simple process in pseudocode.

Figure 11.6

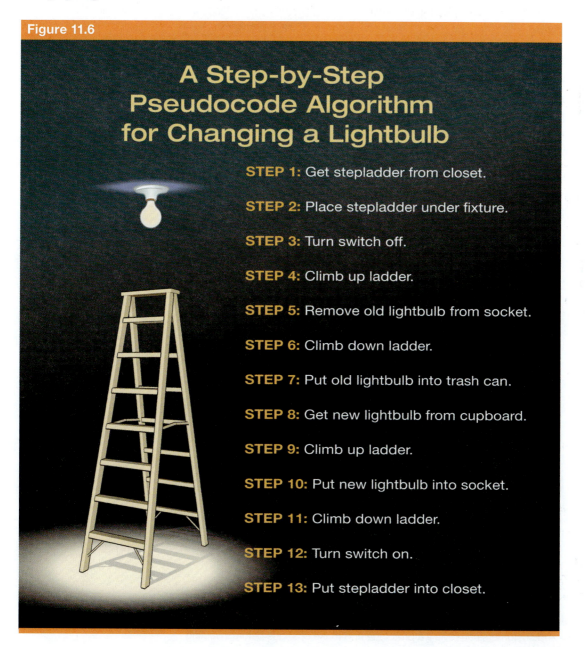

A Step-by-Step Pseudocode Algorithm for Changing a Lightbulb

STEP 1: Get stepladder from closet.

STEP 2: Place stepladder under fixture.

STEP 3: Turn switch off.

STEP 4: Climb up ladder.

STEP 5: Remove old lightbulb from socket.

STEP 6: Climb down ladder.

STEP 7: Put old lightbulb into trash can.

STEP 8: Get new lightbulb from cupboard.

STEP 9: Climb up ladder.

STEP 10: Put new lightbulb into socket.

STEP 11: Climb down ladder.

STEP 12: Turn switch on.

STEP 13: Put stepladder into closet.

Prototype the Solution For a large project—especially one that isn't a modification of an existing project—the next step is to prototype the solution. **Prototyping** means creating a small, semifunctional version of the solution to see if and how it works.

In a website example, a programmer might first illustrate or develop just the visual aspects of the main web pages. Then the customer requesting the website can review these pages. Doing this provides the customer with something tangible to look at before deciding on the final design. It's much easier for the programmer to make changes at this point rather than later, when the complex programming logic has already been coded. Building a prototype for customer review is a much less expensive way to assess a solution than completing the entire project for review.

Hands On

Prototyping a User Input Screen
Follow the instructions in this resource to try your hand at designing a data entry screen for a new application that will collect anonymous feedback about a product.

Implement and Test the Solution After a successful prototype has been created, the next step is to fully solve the problem. This is when the program is actually coded. Implementation is usually the most difficult and complex step in programming, especially if the problem is relatively new and unknown. Testing the solution frequently, as each step of the algorithm is translated into a program, helps ensure fast and accurate development.

Programmers and customers can review a prototype and make changes before investing more time in the development of software.

During the implementation phase, programmers sometimes learn that the planned solution simply isn't working. This means that an error was made earlier in the problem-solving process and that it's time to return to the beginning and complete the steps again. It may be that another solution must be chosen from the original list of solutions. Documentation, such as a user's manual, is often written at this stage of the project.

Recheck 11.2

Recheck your understanding of the concepts covered by this objective.

11.3 Applying Programming Techniques and Tools

Software developers have a variety of tools and techniques at their disposal to make their jobs easier. Over the years, programmers have developed some effective approaches to structuring programs that have become industry-wide best practices. Rather than reinvent the wheel with each project, today's programmers can use time-tested techniques for application development.

Precheck 11.3

Check your understanding of the concepts covered by this objective.

Development Techniques

As the programming industry has matured—with millions of programmers writing trillions of lines of code—some best practices have emerged. By following these practices, modern programmers can avoid making some of the mistakes their predecessors made. The following sections review a few of the important programming techniques that professional programmers use.

Structured Programming Programming was a new science in the early days of computing, and people wrote programs without applying rules to their development practices. Programmers were charting unknown territory, with no maps to guide them, so they tended to write whatever code they thought would work.

Structured programming forced order onto this chaos, and presented guidelines for an organized, logical approach to programming that focuses on thinking at a higher level. Rather than simply executing lines one after another and writing code line by line, the programmer thinks in terms of structured groups of instructions. For example, if a program is designed to print out a bitmap image on the screen (such as a photo of a person's face on a web page), the programmer builds a **routine** (sometimes called a *function*), which is a section of the program specifically created to handle such images. The code for that routine is then broken down into steps, which in the case of a bitmap will be to draw first one line of the grid, then the next line of the grid, and so on. This process of creating groups of instructions as independent elements is the essence of structured programming.

Modules One result of applying the divide-and-conquer approach to programming is the creation of **modular code**. Programmers work to create code modules that handle the separate components of a program. Like a single brick in a building, each module is a solid portion of a larger structure. Using this modular approach serves the purpose of making the code reusable, and also helps in tracking down the sources of errors. When something goes wrong, programmers can usually assume that it isn't the fault of the modular code, because that code typically has been tested and proved in use.

Programs are described in terms of their **modularity**, which is a measurement of how well the source code is divided into individual modules. The higher the modularity of a program, the more reliable the program.

Using modular code also saves time, because programmers don't have to "reinvent the wheel" every time they write a new program. An example of this efficiency is a code module that reads data from a mouse and interprets user input by analyzing the

Interpreting mouse movement as input is an example of modular code. Once mouse movement has been programmed, other programmers can reuse the code for that movement.

mouse's movements across the mouse pad. Once this module has been finalized, it can be used as a component of any program requiring mouse input.

A very simple type of modular code is a *macro* that's programmed into a spreadsheet or a document. A macro is a recording of steps to perform a repetitive activity. Although programming skills aren't required to create macros, macros are stored as a form of source code.

Object-Oriented Programming

Object-oriented programming (OOP) forces exacting rules on programmers. OOP is essentially an extension of the modularity concept, but it goes further by defining each module—called an **object**—with definite rules for interfacing and a protected set of variables.

For example, if a program object is built to handle the time of day, it might hold data such as the seconds, minutes, and hours. It might also have an *a.m./p.m.* flag, and the functions that control the setting of the time won't allow illegal values. Thus, if someone tries to set the clock using an hour value of 27, the program won't allow it.

Protected variables are one of the key advancements in programming, as they allow a programmer to prevent data from being altered during program execution. A programmer working with a team sets up rules for the legal use of an object's data, thereby reducing the chances for error when someone unfamiliar with the code tries to use it. This technology is a great help in team development projects, because programmers can use the objects without needing to learn how they work. Simply understanding an object's interface enables programmers to use it.

Rapid Application Development

Programmers began to experiment with **rapid application development (RAD)** techniques in the 1990s. Since labor costs constitute the major expense in software development, the primary focus of RAD was designing methods to reduce these costs by decreasing the time it takes to develop a project. Changes in the traditional approach to program development included eliminating labor-intensive written phases of the design stage by moving to early prototyping and by using higher-level languages. Visual Basic, Delphi, and other high-level languages with good interface capabilities are often used to aid in RAD.

Activity 11.3.1

Article
Object-Oriented Programming

🄂 Hands On 👆👆👆👆👆

Creating Macros

Microsoft Office applications enable the user to create macros to automate frequently performed tasks. To cut down on macro virus infection, the default file format in each application doesn't support macros; for example, Word's .docx and Excel's .xlsx formats aren't macro capable. However, you can use macro-enabled file formats instead when you want to save a document or template that includes macros; macro-enabled formats end in *m* rather than *x*, as in .docm and .xlsm. Follow the steps in this resource to create a macro that applies a certain type of formatting to cells in a new Excel workbook.

Programmers using RAD follow these guidelines:

1. Use visual development (4GL) tools whenever possible.
2. Rapidly prototype new projects to reduce redesign time.
3. Approach coding with these priorities:
   - Use existing code first.
   - Buy someone else's existing code second.
   - Write new code last.

Another focus of RAD is to allow nonprogrammers to perform simple programming tasks, so they do not have to rely on professional programmers for small projects. Managers, chemists, and various types of engineers often need to use computers in specialized ways that require some programming, but do not require a full application to be developed. Using RAD techniques reduces the level of programming knowledge and skill needed.

Agile Development Programming has traditionally been primarily a solitary activity. When large teams of programmers work together on major software products, each programmer is assigned a fixed, well-defined segment of the program to work on, and then set to work on that segment, alone, sometimes for weeks at a time with minimal feedback. Some new development methods, however, have been changing this paradigm.

For example, **Agile software development** radically redefines the accepted methods of software development by focusing on the following values, which were published in the Agile Manifesto:

- **Individuals and interactions over processes and tools.** Self-organization and motivation are important.
- **Working software over comprehensive documentation.** It is more important to show clients working software than it is to show them documents of how the software will work.

Cutting Edge

Sharing Code through Krugle

Working with open source software means sharing code—in other words, using software that others have already created to develop new and improved software. While this sharing may seem like a nice idea, most programmers actually prefer to write their own code from scratch. Finding the relevant bits of code they need is just too hard.

One company, Krugle, is dedicated to solving this problem. It started out by designing a search engine named *Krugle* to make it easier for programmers to find and share code. Krugle's creators hoped that by building an orderly, accessible library of freely available code, they could help programmers increase their work efficiency.

Krugle stands out from other source-code search engines in several ways. It lets programmers search by programming language, as well as annotate code and documentation, create bookmarks, and save search results in a tabbed workspace.

Now this company has taken its desire to help programmers one step further by releasing Krugle Enterprise. Krugle Enterprise is a system that helps software development companies keep their own comprehensive, searchable libraries of all the source code they use or have used. This appliance, which continues to grow and develop, has helped programmers become more efficient, thus saving companies time and money. Its success is also proving that when open source is combined with the right tools, it's more than just a nice idea. It can be a profitable one too.

You can explore the Krugle open source archives at **http://CUT6.emcp.net/KrugleOpenSource**. You can learn more about the company at **http://CUT6.emcp.net/Krugle**.

- **Customer collaboration over contract negotiation.** Customers cannot fully express their requirements upfront, so it's important to keep the customer involved throughout the development.
- **Responding to change over following a plan.** Being able to make quick adjustments to the product as well as to development processes is important.

Agile is not a brand-new concept; its predecessors include Scrum, Crystal Clear, and Extreme Programming. After the Agile Manifesto was published in 2001, these predecessors and others were collectively referred to as *Agile*.

Agile development breaks the big picture into small units called *iterations* that can be accomplished within a few weeks, and then assigns a cross-functional team to the iteration that handles the complete cycle for that unit: planning, requirements analysis, design, coding, unit testing, and acceptance testing. Each iteration results in a demonstrable result, which is then reviewed by stakeholders. Agile development includes daily status meetings in which team members report their previous progress and their plans for the coming day.

Agile development allows the software to develop organically as teams discover new ways of doing things. Not all software development projects are suited for this method. Agile methods work best with smaller projects, and with more experienced developers who don't mind if the requirements change frequently.

Development Tools

Programmers have a variety of tools at their disposal to make their jobs easier. For example, at some point, every program must be translated from its original source code into machine code so it can be executed. Tools such as compilers, interpreters, and debuggers are used to handle this translation task and fix any errors that may result. Some of these tools are freeware, while others cost thousands of dollars. Their capabilities also vary greatly.

Tech Ethics

Keeping Source Code Secret

Is it a crime to make a personal copy of the source code for a program that belongs to your employer, even if you don't do anything with the copied code? The answer to that question was crucial for Sergey Aleynikov. Aleynikov worked for Goldman Sachs from 2007 to 2009. When he left to go work for a competitor, he took some of Goldman Sachs' source code with him without permission. Goldman Sachs involved the FBI, claiming that someone who understood this source code could use it to build a program that would manipulate markets in unfair ways. Aleynikov did not give the code to his new employer, or use it to commit any market manipulation. Nevertheless, in 2010, a jury convicted him of two counts of theft of trade secrets and transportation of stolen property. He was sentenced to 97 months in prison.

In March 2011, Aleynikov appealed the conviction, and in February 2012, the US Court of Appeals for the Second Circuit ordered his conviction reversed and a judgment of acquittal entered, on the grounds that no crime had been committed. The court determined that the source code was not a stolen good as defined in current laws, and was not related to or included in a product produced for or placed in interstate or foreign commerce. Aleynikov spent 11 months in prison, got divorced, and depleted all his savings fighting the charges. Later in 2012, the State of New York tried charging him again, but he was acquitted on the grounds that the original arrest by the FBI was illegal and therefore most of the evidence collected by the FBI was inadmissible.

If someone were to do the same thing Aleynikov did today, however, it would be illegal. In December 2012, Congress passed an act declaring that unauthorized appropriation of source code would be a crime going forward, in the Theft of Trade Secrets Clarification Act of 2012.

When deciding which tools to use, a company or individual should consider a tool's cost and user-friendliness, as well as the performance of programs produced using the tool. Another important factor is whether the user is already familiar with the tool. Any training required must be included when calculating the tool's total cost. A sound purchasing decision can be made once all these factors have been considered.

Compilers and Interpreters Almost every computer language comes equipped with a *compiler*: a program that translates programming language source code into machine code, the language used by computer chips. A compiler reads an entire program prior to execution, and then displays a list of program errors that may be present. A compiler can only translate one language, and is specific to that language. A variety of compilers are available for most languages, each offering its own special features.

An *interpreter* differs from a compiler in that it translates instructions one by one as the source code is being executed, rather than all at once after reading through the entire program. Since an interpreter acts on just one line of instruction at a time, it identifies errors as they are encountered, including the line containing the error.

Practical TECH

What to Do with Scripting Error Messages

When a scripting error appears as you are running a program or viewing a web page, what should you do? Well, to start with, you can click the button to close the dialog box that reports the error. There may be a *Debug* option in the dialog box (for example, for some web scripts), but that's not for you; it's for the programmer who wrote the program. You may be asked whether you want to continue running scripts on this page. If you click *Yes*, other scripts on the page will attempt to execute; if you click *No*, they won't.

You can't fix the program, but you may be able to change the conditions that are making the error appear. For example, if the error is being generated by an application or the operating system, try restarting your computer. If the error is being generated by a script on a web page, try closing and reopening your browser and then renavigating to the page you were on. If that doesn't work, try a different web browser; some errors are caused by using a browser that doesn't support the script or application.

Another possible fix is to empty the browser's cache of temporary files. In Internet Explorer, you can clear temp files by clicking the Tools icon (looks like a gear), clicking *Internet options* in the drop-down menu, and then clicking the Delete button at the Internet Options dialog box. Make sure the *Temporary Internet files and website files* check box is marked at the Delete Browsing History dialog box, and then click Delete.

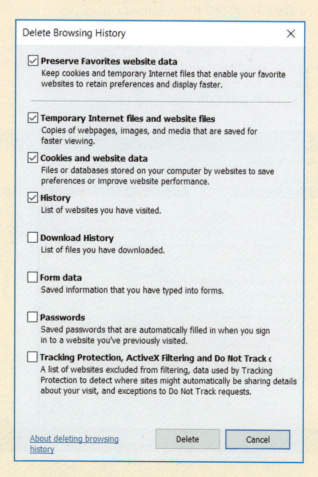

Compilers and interpreters have different strengths and weaknesses. Compiled programs tend to run much faster in their final form, and they use much less memory than interpreted programs. Compilers also offer software manufacturers the advantage of releasing only the unreadable machine code version of a product, while keeping the source code secret. This makes compilers popular with manufacturers of software distributed for retail sale.

However, interpreted programs are easier to develop and test. Since no separate compilation step is performed, programmers can click a button and execute the new program at any time. This ease of execution and testing speeds up development, saving programming fees. Another positive feature is that an interpreted language can be distributed without a binary file. This feature is popular with programmers, who can write special programs for the Internet that are many times smaller than comparable machine code files. The smaller size means these programs can be transmitted faster across the Internet. On the downside, interpreted programs run slower due to the time required to interpret lines one at a time.

Debuggers A **bug** is a computer error. The term was originally coined by Grace Hopper, the inventor of COBOL. When a moth crawled into a computer's circuitry and caused it to malfunction, she called the error (quite literally) a *bug*.

A **debugger** is a software tool that helps programmers find errors quickly. Debuggers also allow programmers to closely examine what's happening when a program runs. In most cases, debuggers are integral components of compilers and interpreters, just as spelling checkers are typically integrated with word processors.

Software Development Kit A software development kit (SDK) is a package of applications that work together to help you develop software in a particular programming language or set of languages. For example, Microsoft Visual Studio includes a development environment with a code editor, a compiler, and a debugger that can be used with several Microsoft-created programming languages, including Visual Basic and Active Server Pages (ASP) (see Figure 11.7).

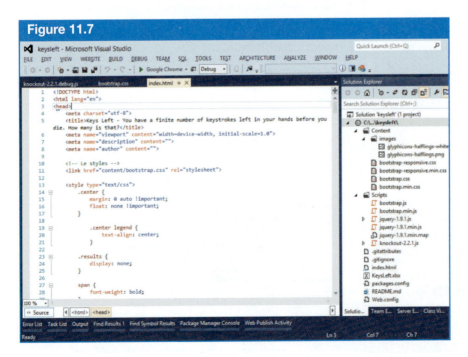

Figure 11.7

Microsoft Visual Studio is a software development kit for professional programmers.

Documentation Tools

Proper documentation is a key element of software development. **Documentation** consists of written notes that explain how a program works. Several tools exist to help with the creation of documentation, including flowcharts, CASE tools, and comments.

Flowcharts A **flowchart** provides a visual diagram of an algorithm. Instead of using pseudocode, a programmer can draw a flowchart showing the logic of a program with symbols that represent operations (see Figure 11.8).

Today's professional programmers rarely use flowcharts, as most software programs are too complex to be represented graphically in every detail. However, beginning programmers still use flowcharts to help visualize their algorithms and understand their programs before they attempt to write code. Figure 11.9 displays an example of a flowchart using standard flowchart symbols.

Activity 11.3.2

Article
Working with Pseudocode and Flowchart Documents

Figure 11.8

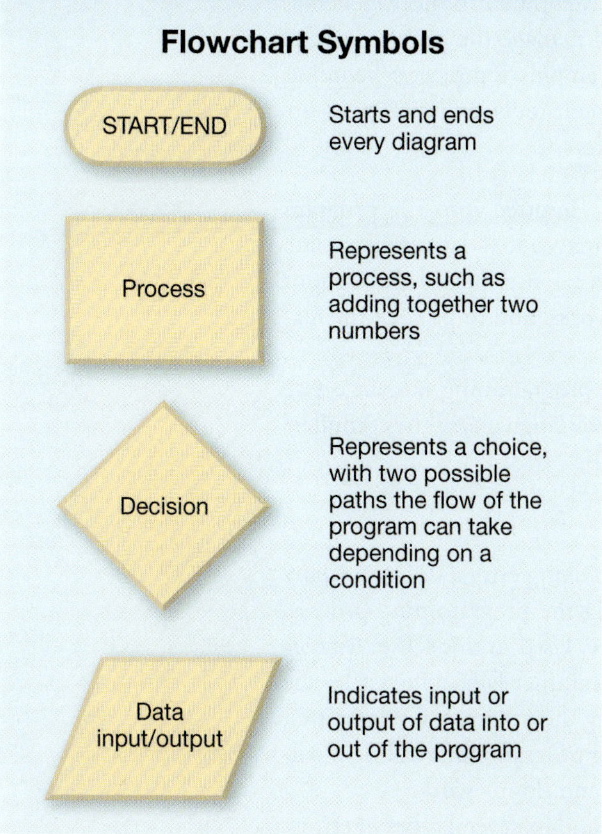

Flowchart Symbols

START/END — Starts and ends every diagram

Process — Represents a process, such as adding together two numbers

Decision — Represents a choice, with two possible paths the flow of the program can take depending on a condition

Data input/output — Indicates input or output of data into or out of the program

These symbols are used in flowcharts to represent operations.

Figure 11.9

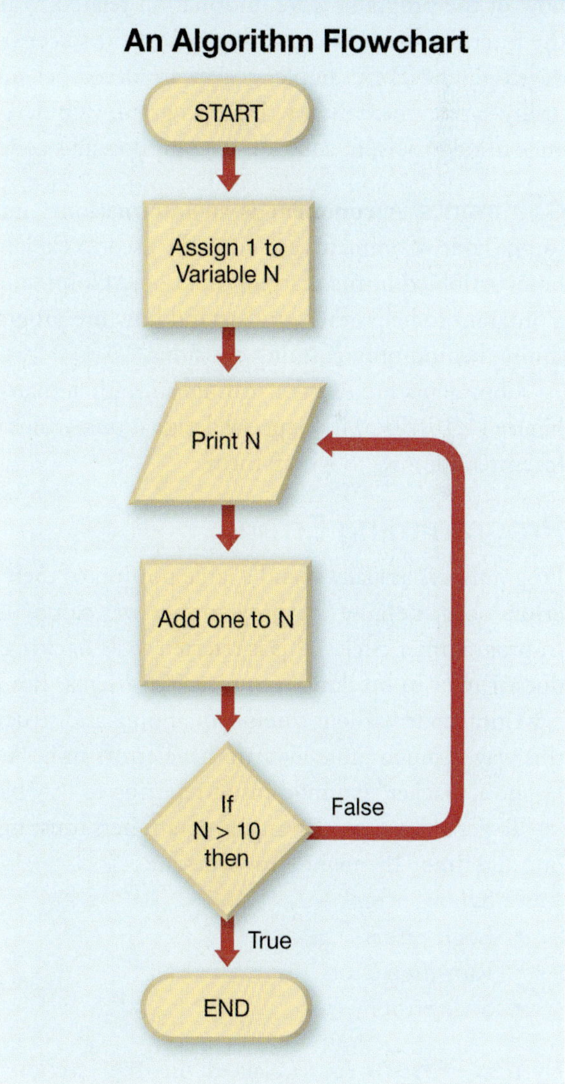

An Algorithm Flowchart

START
↓
Assign 1 to Variable N
↓
Print N
↓
Add one to N
↓
If N > 10 then — False →
↓ True
END

Creating a flowchart helps programmers visualize the steps in a software program.

🖑 Hands On 🖑🖑🖑🖑

Drawing a Flowchart

A flowchart can be created to describe a decision-making process. Follow the instructions in this resource to try drawing a flowchart similar to the one in Figure 11.9.

Figure 11.10

A C++ Source Code Fragment Containing Comments

```
int x;      // creates an integer variable called x
x = 12;     // sets the value of the variable x to 12
cout        << x << endl; // prints the value of x and goes
                         // to the next line
```

Comments are inserted into source code to help other programmers understand how a program works. A set of forward slashes (//) indicates the start of a comment, and a hard return indicates the end of the comment.

CASE Tools Teams that develop software don't do so with a pencil and paper, of course, or even simple applications like Notepad and Word. Instead they use suites of powerful applications that are specifically designed to help with project management, programming, user testing, and so on. These tools are collectively known as **computer-aided software engineering (CASE) tools**. CASE tools can diagram the flow of the program, store information related to the development project, generate the interface (such as the dialog boxes and screens), and manage the progress of the development. For example, a software developer might employ a project scheduling utility, a documentation writing program, web development tools, and quality assurance testing tools, in addition to compilers and code editors.

Comments A **comment** is an informational message inserted into the program source code. Comments are normally used to explain source code to later readers, like notes scribbled in the margins of a book. Comments can be interspersed throughout a program to help others understand how the program works, and to provide the reasoning behind programming decisions.

Comments are written in English, rather than in a programming language (see Figure 11.10). They have special designations, which vary by language, so the compiler/interpreter knows to ignore them.

Programming Errors

Programmers actually spend a large portion of their time fixing errors, or bugs. Many errors occur because the programmer was sloppy during the programming process. In programmer circles, this is referred to as **hacking code**. Used in this sense, *hacking* doesn't refer to breaking into security systems. If a programmer is hacking code, she is writing code without carefully planning and structuring the program. Code written this way is much more likely to have errors in it. Among programmers, calling a colleague a "hacker" is a mild insult referring to lazy habits and sloppy work.

To get a program working, programmers must isolate and fix several types of errors, one at a time. The main error types are

- Syntax errors
- Logic errors
- Run-time errors
- Style errors

Syntax Errors As explained in the section "Language Characteristics and Classifications," on page 494, syntax errors, like grammar errors, are usually due to typing mistakes and misunderstanding of the rules of a language. Computer languages are very structured and require programmers to use them flawlessly to create working programs. To use an analogy, if a program were created to read a paragraph in a newspaper, it might require that all sentences in that paragraph start with a capital letter and end with a period so it can recognize them. Any deviation from these requirements would prevent the computer from recognizing a string of words as a sentence, causing it to reject the newspaper and demand that the error be fixed.

Logic Errors A **logic error** occurs when a program's syntax is correct, but the program instructs the computer to perform an action incorrectly. For example, if a program is meant to add a column of numbers and instead multiplies them because of an incorrect instruction, this will be considered a logic error. The program might run, but it won't do what the programmer intended it to do. This type of error is very common and is the most difficult type of error professional programmers deal with because the error is not immediately obvious from a visual scan of the code.

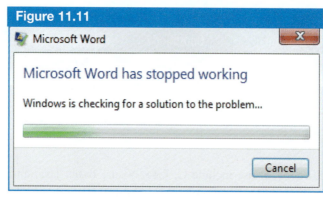

Figure 11.11

A crash bug, a type of run-time error, is one of the most dreaded programming errors, because it causes the program to stop running.

Run-Time Errors A **run-time error** refers to a mistake that occurs when an application is running. A **crash bug** is one of the most dreaded types of run-time errors, because it causes a program to stop running, or crash. If a program crashes, it's useless, so programmers usually attempt to solve this kind of bug first. Figure 11.11 shows a run-time error that has caused the program to crash.

Another common cause of run-time errors is an **infinite loop**, which is a programming mistake that causes a program to perform the same set of instructions over and over again, without any way of stopping. An infinite loop causes the computer to lock up or freeze—a state in which it no longer responds to input from the mouse or keyboard.

Style Errors A **style error** in programming code is similar to bad grammar in a term paper. A term paper with bad grammar may still be readable, but the grammar will detract from the reader's enjoyment (and most likely, the student's grade). In the same way, a program with style errors may still run, but programmers may be unhappy with the way it was written because the errors make the code bulkier, slower to execute, or more difficult to edit.

One style error programmers commonly make is writing dead code. **Dead code** is code that's "commented out," which means that it's marked with comments to notify the compiler to skip and ignore it. The presence of dead code makes it hard to read source code, because dead code appears to be part of the program but actually has no effect on how it runs.

Recheck 11.3

Recheck your understanding of the concepts covered by this objective.

11.4 Evaluating Programming Languages

The first programming language was machine code, since it's the language that computers use for their internal operations. Programming in machine code is difficult, because this code consists entirely of binary numbers. Assembly language was invented to make programming easier by attaching symbols and words to represent the different combinations of binary digits in machine code. Since the first assembly code was written, hundreds of high-level programming languages have been created, but today, only a few are used extensively for professional work. Popular programming language

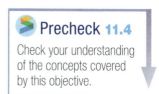

Precheck 11.4

Check your understanding of the concepts covered by this objective.

Table 11.1 Commonly Used Programming Languages

Language	Compiled?	Interpreted?	Object Oriented?
C	Yes	No	No
C++	Yes	No	Yes
Java	Yes	Yes	Yes
Visual Basic	No	Yes	No

currently in use include C, C++, Visual Basic, Java, and scripting languages (such as the many variants of HTML). Table 11.1 compares four common programming languages.

Machine Code

As previously defined, *machine code* is the computer programming language that computers actually read and interpret. The code is written using a series of binary strings. A *binary string* is a meaningful sequence of binary digits—1s and 0s. Computers can read and act on this code, because they "think" using the binary system. Programmers rarely write programs using machine code, because it's difficult for anyone to memorize the long binary strings that comprise this language.

Assembly Language

Assembly language is easier to use than machine language, but still not far removed from it. Assembly language uses symbols and words to represent the elements of machine code, making it possible for programmers to memorize them. Computers can't read assembly language, so it must be converted to machine code by an assembler before it can be used. Instructions written in assembly language are read into a program called an *assembler* (which is like a compiler), which translates the instructions into machine language.

Compared with programs created in other programming languages, assembly language programs run faster and use less memory. The chief drawback is that they are difficult to write because of the extreme level of detail required for every operation, and because of this development times are longer. Assembly languages are used wherever speed and memory are at a premium, and maximum possible efficiency is desired. Embedded computers—such as cell phones, calculators, and other electronic devices—are often programmed using assembly language.

Legacy Programming Languages

Many of the programming languages students learned 20 to 30 years ago are seldom used in new programming projects. However, programmers still need to know them in order to maintain large existing systems that were developed using them, such as those in government agencies like the IRS.

COBOL COBOL, which is an acronym for *COmmon Business-Oriented Language*, is used chiefly for business applications by large institutions and companies. As mentioned in the section "Debuggers," on page 508, it was developed Grace Hopper in 1959.

Although the use of COBOL is rapidly diminishing, many schools still require students to study it. Originally designed to be an English-like language for handling database processing, it has changed little since its creation. It's slow and cumbersome, but it has a large body of existing code and many programmers are familiar with it.

RPG **RPG**, an acronym for *Report Program Generator*, is commonly used in business environments, particularly in programs for IBM's AS/400. It's slow and inefficient, but simplifies the coding of database applications; it also has the advantage of being familiar to many programmers. Many midrange and mainframe computers rely heavily on RPG.

FORTRAN **FORTRAN** stands for *FORmula TRANslator* and for many years was the language of choice for math, science, and engineering projects. Created in 1954 by IBM and released commercially in 1957, FORTRAN dominated scientific and engineering programming for decades. FORTRAN is still in use today in factories and laboratories, although it isn't as common as COBOL.

BASIC Beginner's All-purpose Symbolic Instruction Code, or **BASIC**, is a high-level language that's friendlier and more natural than COBOL and FORTRAN. Originally designed at Dartmouth College as a teaching tool in the 1960s, BASIC is still used professionally in an updated form (Visual Basic).

BASIC is an interpreted language, which means it runs slowly. This drawback is somewhat compensated for by the fact that development in BASIC tends to go more quickly for the programmer. The original BASIC supports only command-line interfaces, rather than graphic point-and-click technology. A comparison of the BASIC sample code with C++ code (see Figures 11.12 and 11.13) shows why BASIC is considered easier to understand.

Visual Basic

Visual Basic (VB), developed by Microsoft and released in 1991, is currently the professional's language of choice for developing software prototypes, and for developing custom interfaces for Windows platforms. Programs written in VB aren't generally

Activity 11.4.1

Video
Visual Programming

Figure 11.12

An Example of BASIC Source Code

```
10   Rem This code sample prints out 1 through 10 on the screen.
20   For Count = 1 to 10
30   Print Count
40   Next Count
50   End
```

This sequence of BASIC code will print the numbers 1 through 10.

Figure 11.13

An Example of C++ Source Code

```
#include <iostream.h>
void
main()
{
        int count; // Create a variable called "count"
        for (count = 1; count <= 10; count++)   // Loop 10 times
                count << count << endl;         // Print 10 values
}
```

This sequence of C++ source code will print the numbers 1 through 10.

mass marketed. They are quick and easy to develop, but run slowly and are demanding of resources such as RAM and disk space. Visual Basic supports graphic interfaces, unlike the original BASIC of the 1960s. Because of this feature, VB is easier to use than languages such as C and C++.

C and Its Variants

C was developed in the early 1970s by Dennis Ritchie and Ken Thompson at Bell Labs for the early UNIX operating system. The language was named *C* because it built on an earlier language called *Basic Combined Programming Language* (*BCPL*), or *B*. C is a compromise between high-level and low-level languages, containing components of both BASIC and assembly language, but it's still considered a high-level language. C programs aren't as easy to read as BASIC programs, but they run considerably faster and use less space. C isn't quite as fast as assembly code when executing, but it's much faster than BASIC.

C++ (pronounced "see plus plus") is an adaptation of C. More specifically, it's a superset of C, and any C program should run without problems as a C++ program. This means that a compiler that compiles and understands a program written in C++ will also understand a program written in C. C++ is the same as C, but with added features such as object-oriented programming. Most professional software sold today is written in some form of C or C++. Figure 11.13 on the previous page shows a section of C++ source code that prints out the numbers 1 through 10.

C# (pronounced "see sharp") is a modern object-oriented language derived from C++ and Java. It combines the productivity of the simplistic Visual Basic with the power of the C++ language. C# programming allows the use of features in the Microsoft .NET Framework, C, and Microsoft's Component Object Model (COM).

Objective-C is a variant of the C programming language that Apple uses to create the OS X and iOS operating systems. It adds an object-oriented messaging component to the basic C feature set.

Swift is a new Apple-developed language that may soon replace Objective-C as the preferred programming language for developing the iOS and OS X operating systems as well as applications that run on those platforms. It is backward-compatible with Objective-C code, but it isn't based on the C programming language, so programmers are more free to implement more modern coding techniques.

Java

Sun Microsystems's *Java* programming language has become widely used on the Internet for specialized web page applications. Composed of small applications (each called an **applet**) that can run on all types of computer operating systems, Java was created to facilitate communication on the Internet among the wide variety of user platforms.

Central to the software is the **Java virtual machine (JVM)**, which converts general Java instructions into commands that a device or computer can understand. A JVM is currently built into most web browsers. It works with the operating system on embedded chip devices, such as smart cards and web-enabled cellular phones, or it may be integrated directly into them.

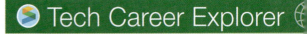

Tech Career Explorer

Java versus JavaScript

Java and JavaScript are two different languages. Java is a compiled language, whereas JavaScript is interpreted. Also, Java applications can run as stand-alone programs, whereas JavaScript runs only within a web page. However, the two languages use many of the same commands and structures, so if you learn one, you are more than halfway toward learning the other. This similarity makes Java and JavaScript attractive to study when preparing for a career in computer programming—not only because they are very popular languages, but also because you will acquire two different language skills without having to learn two completely different systems. Complete this exercise to learn more about what Java and JavaScript have in common.

> **Figure 11.14**
>
> ### An Example of JavaScript
>
> ```
> <head>
> <script type="text/javascript">
>
> <!--Comment: This JavaScript Code will cause three buttons to appear
> that can change the background color when clicked.-->
>
> <!--Begin
> function newcolor(aColor)
> {
> document.bgColor=aColor;
> }
> End-->
> </script>
>
> </head>
>
> <body>
>
> <div id="choices">
> <form>
>  <input type="button" value="Red" onclick="newcolor('red');">
>  <input type="button" value="White" onclick="newcolor('white');">
>  <input type="button" value="Blue" onclick="newcolor('blue');">
> </form>
> </div>
>
> </body>
> ```

Java is very similar to C++, but is designed to run either as an interpreted script transmitted over the Internet or as a compiled (machine code) executable program. This flexibility and its **cross-platform compatibility** to run on nearly any operating system have made Java very popular with programmers around the world.

This sequence of JavaScript code directs a browser to display buttons that users can click to change the background color within the web browser window.

Scripting Languages

A **scripting language** is an interpreted language that's relatively easy to learn and use. A scripting language is a **nonprocedural language**, meaning that it explains what the computer should do in English-like terms, but not precisely how the computer should do it.

Web pages are usually built with scripting languages, such as Hypertext Markup Language (HTML) and JavaScript. Advanced wizards and editors in programs using scripting languages allow people to build web pages without knowing the underlying HTML code. Users of these systems may not even realize they are programming. A variety of improved web page capabilities are provided by newer versions of HTML, including DHTML, XHTML, XML, and WML.

Other popular scripting languages used in building web pages are **Perl** (Practical extraction and report language), **VBScript** (loosely based on Visual Basic), and **JavaScript** (similar to Java, developed by Sun Microsystems). See Figure 11.14 for a sample of JavaScript. JavaScript can run as an interpreted script over the Internet or as a compiled executable program.

Recheck 11.4

Recheck your understanding of the concepts covered by this objective.

11.5 Developing for the Web and Mobile Environments

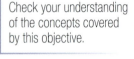

Precheck 11.5

Check your understanding of the concepts covered by this objective.

Programmers who write programs designed to be run on websites use a special set of tools. The main tool of a web developer is Hypertext Markup Language (HTML), which you learned about in Chapter 5. Most commercial websites, however, contain much more complex code than can be written with HTML alone. For example, a website may have drop-down menus that appear when you point at certain buttons, pictures that change every few seconds, applications that run on the page (such as a mortgage calculator, chat window, or game), and search tools that retrieve results from databases. Similarly, programmers who develop for mobile devices, such as smartphones, have their own special tools and challenges. In this section, you will learn about some of the programming tools used in these specialized environments.

HTML and Its Variants

HTML is an interpreted language used to create web pages. It's called a *markup language*, because it marks up plain text by adding bracketed tags that specify how the text should be laid out and formatted—for example, *<p>* to indicate a body paragraph and *<H1>* to indicate a first-level heading. Figure 11.15 shows an example of a simple HTML web page.

HTML generates static pages. A page loads in the web browser, and then nothing else happens until you click a link to display a different web page. To extend HTML's capabilities to allow for interactive content, such as menus that open and close when you point at certain buttons, Dynamic HTML is used. **Dynamic HTML (DHTML)** isn't a separate language, but rather a collection of technologies that work together to make websites more interactive. For example, on a web page that implements DHTML, you might be able to point at a button to see a fly-out menu. A DHTML page typically uses several programming languages to accomplish its effects, including standard HTML, cascading style sheets (CSS), and a scripting language such as JavaScript.

Cascading style sheets (CSS) is a markup language closely related to HTML; it's used for defining the formatting of a web page. CSS can be placed in an HTML document as an internal style sheet, or it can be placed in a separate file and referenced as an external style sheet by multiple pages.

Extensible Markup Language (XML) is similar to HTML, except it's completely programmer definable. Rather than sticking with prescribed tags, the programmer

Activity 11.5.1

Video
How HTML, CSS, and JavaScript Work Together

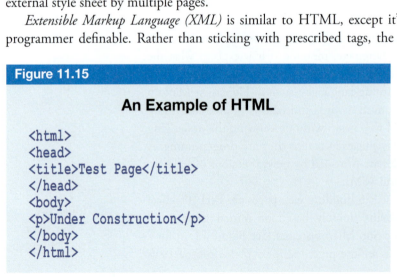

Figure 11.15

An Example of HTML

```
<html>
<head>
<title>Test Page</title>
</head>
<body>
<p>Under Construction</p>
</body>
</html>
```

This sequence of HTML code displays a web page with the message "Under Construction."

can create his own tags and codes. To take advantage of this extensibility, the entire HTML 4 language was re-created in XML, resulting in **Extensible HTML (XHTML)**. It was thought that web programmers would be able to use XHTML to extend HTML in whatever ways were needed to create more dynamic programming on web pages. Unfortunately, XTHML never really caught on.

What did catch on, however, was a new version of HTML called **HTML5.** It's officially still in beta testing, but many web designers have already begun using it, and the latest versions of all major browsers support it.

```
<html>
  <head>
    <title>My Homepage</title>
  </head>
  <body bgcolor=white>

    <table border="0" cellpadding="10">
      <tr>
        <td>
          <img src="images/logo.png">
        </td>
        <td>
          <h1>Hello</h1>
        </td>
```

HTML is the basis of almost all web-based content, so it's a very useful development tool for anyone to learn.

HTML5 has several benefits. One is that it uses semantic tags. A **semantic tag** is a tag whose name reflects its usage. For example, a *<nav>* tag indicates a navigation bar. Another benefit is that HTML5 contains many new tags for dynamic support, such as a *<details>* tag that shows a pop-up with more information when you point at the element on the web page, and a *<canvas>* tag to create a drawing space on a web page. HTML5 also simplifies the process of adding audio and video clips to pages with new *<audio>* and *<video>* tags.

Scripting Languages for Web Pages

Once a web page has loaded onto a user's screen, HTML is done with its part of the job. The page just sits there until another page loads. If the designer wants the page to do something active—such as display a menu when the user rolls the mouse pointer over a button—then some additional programming is required.

The most common way to add this programming is to use a scripting language, such as JavaScript. The developer pastes the code for the additional functionality into the HTML file, so when the HTML file loads, the script also loads and can be executed when it's triggered to do so (for example, by a button on the page). Although JavaScript is the most common scripting language used for web pages, some web pages use VBScript, JScript, Perl, or Rexx instead. (As noted in previous section, when this is done in conjunction with HTML and CSS, it's known as *Dynamic HTML*.)

Server-Side Programming

Because HTML is an interpreted language that executes on the fly when a web page loads, it has certain limitations. For example, it's not very good for querying an online database and reporting the results back, because each time an HTML page loads, it's essentially a stateless process—that is, each page is a blank slate that doesn't remember anything that happened on a previous page. Developers can get around this partially with cookies, but to execute complex activities on a website, some of the programming needs to be stored on the server. This is called *server-side programming*.

Hands On

Creating a Web Page in Notepad

HTML is very simple to learn compared to other languages, and it doesn't require any special development tools. You can create a complete web page using nothing but Notepad, the text editor that comes with Windows. Follow the steps in this resource to see how it works.

Several different programming languages can be used for creating server-side programs. **Server-side include (SSI)** is a simple interpreted scripting language that's used for very simple operations on the server, such as loading the same navigation bar or boilerplate text on every page. Not all web servers support SSI, however.

Sites like Google News and Amazon start with a simple HTML and CSS frame, and then draw data from a server to fill in the placeholders with the latest news and the latest products for sale. Languages such as **JavaServer Pages (JSP)**, **Active Server Pages (ASP)**, and **PHP (PHP: Hypertext Preprocessor)** are used to write the code on the server that tells it what to do. The data itself is usually stored in a database format, such as Structured Query Language (SQL).

Website Development Tools

It's technically possible to generate an entire website by writing plain text code in a simple text editor like Notepad, but it's tedious to do so. Most web developers use web creation software to accelerate the process of creating a site.

Web creation software can function as both a text editor and a what-you-see-is-what-you-get (WYSIWYG) preview application. That way, when a developer makes changes to the HTML code, the changes are visible immediately in the preview. Web creation software can also simplify formatting and layout by allowing the developer to apply formatting attributes with a point-and-click toolbar and by using preset templates to simplify page layout.

Web creation software can either be offline based or online based. An offline application, such as Adobe's **Dreamweaver** or Microsoft's **Expression Web**, is installed on a local PC—the same as any other software. The developer creates the site offline, and then uploads it to a server when the site is ready for use. WordPress.org provides a free application called *WordPress* that falls into this category as well. (Don't confuse WordPress.org with WordPress.com, where blogs are hosted.) Figure 11.16 shows a

Activity 11.5.2

Article
Using Office Applications to Create HTML Files

Figure 11.16

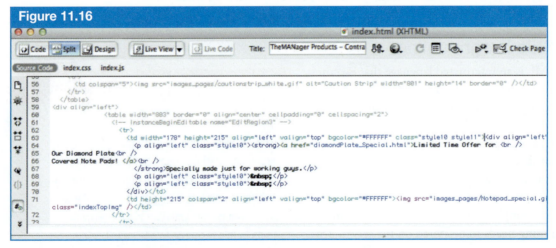

Dreamweaver was used to create this code for the website shown in Figure 11.17.

section of source code in Dreamweaver, and Figure 11.17 shows the portion of the web page that displays from that code.

Dreamweaver is an example of an application that generates standards-compliant code. The websites created with this software can be loaded onto any web server. Some online development tools, however, require certain software to be available on the server on which the site is hosted. For example, **Joomla** is an easy-to-use tool that many people find quicker and easier to use than traditional tools (see Figure 11.18). However, a Joomla-based site can be created and managed only on a server that supports it. Joomla is not a web development application per se, but rather a content management platform. You choose a design and upload your content, and Joomla puts the two together to display a website. An alternative to Joomla is **Drupal**, an open source content management platform.

Figure 11.17

The code created in Dreamweaver as shown in Figure 11.16 looks like this when displayed online.

Figure 11.18

The Joomla control panel allows users to manage the content for a website.

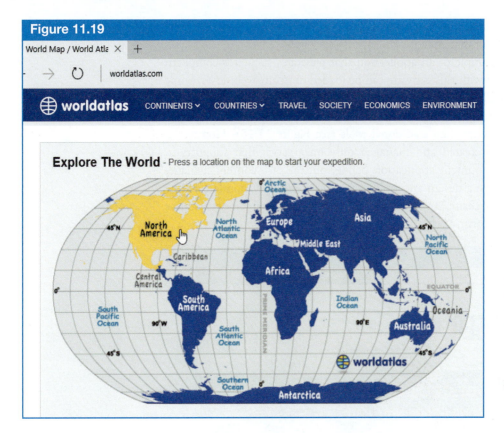

Figure 11.19

Each area of this world map has a separate hyperlink that takes visitors to a location-specific web page. When you point to one of these hyperlinks, the area turns yellow—as illustrated by North America.

Web Graphic Design and Interactivity Tools

Most of the static graphics on web pages are either photos or illustrations, much like the ones you learned about in Chapter 4. Photos typically are JPEG and PNG formats; both formats are compact and load quickly. Graphics that change every few seconds are usually GIF graphics, because GIF supports simple animation effects. A GIF graphic can hold several different images in the same file and then cycle between them when displayed on a web page.

In addition to ordinary graphics, web pages also can have graphics designed especially for online use. These graphics may have special properties, such as **hotspots**—that is, different hyperlinks assigned to different spots on the graphic. For example, a graphic showing a map of the world might have a different hyperlink assigned to each continent, as shown in Figure 11.19. Web graphics may also be animated in more sophisticated ways than simple GIF images can be.

Adobe leads the industry in tools for web-based graphic design. The most common applications used for web graphics are all Adobe products:

- Adobe Illustrator for creating 2-D and 3-D line drawings
- Adobe Fireworks for creating web graphics (discontinued in 2013 but still supported)
- Adobe **Flash** for creating animations, games, and interactive modules for websites

Web Page Development for the Mobile Platform

When designing web content, developers can no longer assume that users will display it on a traditional computer screen. More and more, users are accessing web content via smartphones and other small-screen devices, such as mini-tablets.

Developers designing for mobile devices have these considerations to think about:

- **Screen size.** Rather than specifying a certain width for a web page, developers create a fluid CSS-based layout so the page can adapt its content as the browser window size changes.
- **Touchscreens.** When designing the buttons to click on a page, developers must be aware that small-screen users won't be able to control the "click area" as precisely as mouse users can. Buttons to press or click should be fairly large.
- **Image optimization.** A small screen can show an image at a very low resolution without losing any image quality. Using low-resolution images helps keep the overall bandwidth usage down, which users on limited data plans will appreciate. Developers can query the browser for screen height and width and have several sizes of each graphic available to be delivered appropriately.

App Development for Mobile Devices

There is a huge market today for apps for mobile devices. A quick look at the Apple Store on your iPhone or the equivalent store on your Android or Windows Phone device will show you that thousands of apps are available for just about all purposes. Where do all these apps come from? Some of them come from well-established software companies, but many of them come from independent software developers.

For iOS applications, developers typically use Objective-C as a programming language; as you learned in the section "C and Its Variants," on page 514, Objective-C is the preferred programming language for developing Apple applications. Apple iOS apps can be developed only using the Mac platform, with the iOS software development kit (SDK). The development tool used most frequently is Xcode (shown in Figure 11.20). Both the iOS SDK and Xcode are available for free from Apple. Xcode, provides a graphic environment in which developers can create storyboards for an app.

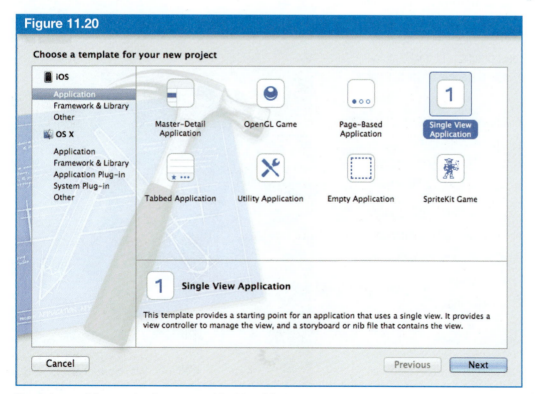

Figure 11.20

Xcode is a mobile app development tool for Mac OS X.

Android apps are written in Java, and the layouts are created in XML. Because Android was developed by Google, Google is the main player in creating and promoting Android development tools. Eclipse and Android Studio are two of the tools they provide for free. Android apps can be developed using Windows, Mac, and Linux operating systems.

Mobile developers can also use special development tools. For example, Adobe PhoneGap creates an app that runs on several different mobile device platforms. The user interface (UI) portion of the application is created using HTML, CSS, and Javascript, and then PhoneGap bundles those files into platform-specific packages for the various phone operating system, including iOS, Android, Windows Phone 7, Windows Phone 8, BlackBerry, and WebOS. Another example of a cross-platform tool is Appcelerator Titanium, which allows a developer to create a single UI, write the app's basic code in JavaScript, and then reuse as much of the code as possible in versions for different mobile platforms.

Tech Career Explorer

Write Your Own Apps

Developing video games and productivity apps requires teams of dozens or even hundreds of programmers. In comparison, writing a smartphone app is not that difficult. Individual hobbyists and students produce thousands of apps each year, and some of their results even hit the big time and are sold in the Apple Store, Google Play Store, and other app stores. Complete this exercise to see what's involved in creating an iPhone app.

Recheck 11.5

Recheck your understanding of the concepts covered by this objective.

Hotspot

Mobile Web Authoring

When accessing web pages on a small screen, such as on a smartphone or mini tablet, users have different priorities than when using a full-size computer. To address these differing priorities, the World Wide Web Consortium (W3C) has published some best practices for making a page small-screen friendly. Here are some of the highlights:

- Keep URLs short.
- Provide only minimal navigation at the top of the page.
- Do not use image maps.
- Do not use pop-ups.
- Use a consistent theme across pages.
- Do not create periodically auto-refreshing pages.
- Keep externally linked resources to a minimum.
- Limit the content to what the user has requested.
- Limit scrolling to one direction.
- Do not use graphics for spacing.
- Do not use frames.
- Do not use tables.
- Test pages on actual devices as well as emulators. Visit http://CUT6.emcp.net/MobileWebAuthoring for more details.

Chapter Summary

*An interactive **Chapter Summary**, **Study Notes**, and a **Slide Presentation** with audio are available from the links menu on this page in your ebook.*

11.1 Describing the Software Development Life Cycle

The **software development life cycle** involves planning, designing, implementing, testing, and releasing application software. During the design process, **specifications** document the details of the software to be written by programmers. A prototype called an **alpha product** is produced, which the development team uses for testing purposes. Once testing has been finished, a **beta version** of the software program is created, to be tested by a select group of knowledgeable customers until it is deemed ready for widespread use, referred to as a **gold release**.

11.2 Understanding Programming Terms and Concepts

Programmers use a **programming language** to create a program. They must be careful to avoid a single **syntax error**, which is a mistake in the way programming elements are written, or the program will be worthless. Basic building blocks of programming include **variables, executable statements, looping,** and **decision statements**. If a problem arises, programmers may use an **algorithm**, or complete list of steps for solving a problem. They can also create a **prototype** of the solution to see if and how it works.

11.3 Applying Programming Techniques and Tools

Software developers have a variety of tools and techniques at their disposal, such as **structured programming** or **modular code**, which handles the separate components of a program. A **debugger** is a software tool that helps programmers find errors quickly. Other tools include **documentation** explaining how a program works and **flowcharts**. Despite all the tools available, programmers can make programming errors. One of the most dreaded types of **run-time errors** is a **crash bug**, which causes a program to stop running.

11.4 Evaluating Programming Languages

Assembly language was invented to make programming easier by attaching symbols and words to represent the numbers in machine code. Some of the most popular programming languages currently in use include **Visual Basic (VB), C, C++, Java virtual machine (JVM)**, and scripting languages. A **scripting language** is a **nonprocedural language**, meaning that it explains what the computer should do in English-like terms, but not precisely how the computer should do it. Web pages are usually built with scripting languages, such as HTML and **JavaScript**.

11.5 Developing for the Web and Mobile Environments

Programmers use a special set of tools to write programs designed to be run on websites. **Dynamic HTML (DHTML)** is a tool that makes websites more interactive. Another tool is **HTML5**, which has the benefit of adding **semantic tags** whose names reflect their uses. Web creation software can either be offline based or online based. **Dreamweaver** and **Expression Web** are examples of offline applications. Some online development tools include **Joomla** and **Drupal**, an open source content management platform.

Key Terms

Numbers indicate the pages where terms are first cited with their full definition in the chapter. An alphabetized list of key terms with definitions is included in the end-of-book glossary.

 *An interactive **Glossary** is available from the links menu on this page in your ebook.*

11.1 Describing the Software Development Life Cycle

software development life cycle (SDLC), 492
specifications, 493
alpha product, 493
testing harness, 493
beta version, 493
gold release, 494

11.2 Understanding Programming Terms and Concepts

programming language, 494
coding, 494
syntax, 494
syntax error, 495
programming language generation, 495
variable, 496
executable statement, 496
looping, 496
decision statement, 497
if-then statement, 497
divide-and-conquer approach, 498
top-down design, 498
algorithm, 501
pseudocode, 501
prototyping, 502

11.3 Applying Programming Techniques and Tools

structured programming, 503
routine, 503
modular code, 503

modularity, 503
object-oriented programming (OOP), 504
object, 504
rapid application development (RAD), 504
Agile software development, 505
bug, 508
debugger, 508
documentation, 509
flowchart, 509
computer-aided software engineering (CASE) tools, 510
comment, 510
hacking code, 510
logic error, 511
run-time error, 511
crash bug, 511
infinite loop, 511
style error, 511
dead code, 511

11.4 Evaluating Programming Languages

assembly language, 512
COBOL, 512
RPG, 513
FORTRAN, 513
BASIC, 513
Visual Basic (VB), 513
C, 514
C++, 514
C#, 514

Objective-C, 514
Swift, 514
applet, 514
Java virtual machine (JVM), 514
cross-platform compatibility, 515
scripting language, 515
nonprocedural language, 515
Perl, 515
VBScript, 515
JavaScript, 515

11.5 Developing for the Web and Mobile Environments

Dynamic HTML (DHTML), 516
Extensible HTML (XHTML), 517
HTML5, 517
semantic tag, 517
server-side include (SSI), 518
JavaServer Pages (JSP), 518
Active Server Pages (ASP), 518
PHP (PHP: Hypertext Preprocessor), 518
Dreamweaver, 518
Expression Web, 518
Joomla, 519
Drupal, 519
hotspot, 520
Flash, 520

Chapter Exercises

Complete the following exercises to assess your understanding of the material covered in this chapter.

➡ *Interactive* **Flash Cards** *and an interactive* **Game** *are available from the links menu on this page in your ebook.*

Go to your SNAP Assignments page to complete the Terms Check, Knowledge Check, Key Principles, and Tech Illustrated exercises.

Terms Check: Matching

Match each term with its definition.

a. pseudocode
b. comment
c. cross-platform compatibility
d. Dreamweaver
e. Visual Basic

f. beta version
g. CASE tools
h. assembly language
i. gold release
j. debugger

___ 1. Software that helps design new software.

___ 2. An informational message inserted into the program source code.

___ 3. A tool that helps identify and correct problems in software code.

___ 4. A programming language that is similar to machine language but uses text-based commands.

___ 5. A step-by-step description of how a program should operate, using ordinary language (not a specific programming language).

___ 6. A software program that's ready for testing outside the development group.

___ 7. A Microsoft-developed programming language used for developing custom interfaces for Windows platforms.

___ 8. An application used for creating web pages.

___ 9. A software program that's ready for public release.

___ 10. Refers to the capability of a program to run on more than one operating system.

Knowledge Check: Multiple Choice

Choose the best answer for each question.

1. Which phase in the software development life cycle produces specifications documenting the details of the software to be written by programmers?
   a. design
   b. implementation
   c. proposal and planning
   d. testing

2. Which classification of computer languages is relatively similar to natural languages, such as English?

   a. low-level language
   b. high-level language
   c. machine code
   d. syntax

3. Which would be classified as a third-generation programming language (3GL)?
   a. assembly language
   b. HTML
   c. graphical user interface languages
   d. Visual Basic

4. When a program is run, which programming element performs an action (such as sending output to a printer) and then proceeds to the next statement in the sequence?
   a. decision statement
   b. executable statement
   c. loop
   d. variable

5. Which programming element allows a program to return to a previously executed instruction and repeat it?
   a. decision statement
   b. executable statement
   c. loop
   d. variable

6. Which type of programming statement allows a program to perform differently depending on whether a condition has been met?
   a. comment
   b. executable statement
   c. if-then statement
   d. loop

7. Which software tool helps programmers find errors quickly?
   a. compiler
   b. debugger
   c. flowchart
   d. interpreter

8. Which is the preferred programming language for developing Apple applications?
   a. HTML
   b. Java
   c. JavaScript
   d. Objective-C

9. The following sequence of code is written in which language?

```
<body>

<div id="choices">
<form>
    <input type="button" value="Red"
    onclick="newcolor('red');">
    <input type="button" value="White"
    onclick="newcolor('white');">
    <input type="button" value="Blue"
    onclick="newcolor('blue');">
</form>
</div>

</body>
```

   a. C++
   b. HTML
   c. JavaScript
   d. Visual Basic

10. Which type of error occurs when a program's syntax is correct, but the program instructs the computer to perform an action incorrectly?
   a. infinite loop
   b. logic error
   c. run-time error
   d. style error

Key Principles: Completion

Complete each statement with the appropriate word or phrase.

1. Phases in the software development life cycle include proposal and planning, design, implementation, testing, and _____.

2. When developing software, the result of the implementation phase is the production of a prototype called a(n) _____.

3. A program that has not yet been compiled is also referred to as _____ code.

4. A coding error, which is usually caused by a typing mistake or a misunderstanding of the rules of a language, is referred to as a _____ error.

5. A small, semifunctional version of a large project that is created to see how the solution works is called a _____.

6. _____ is a term that was originally coined by Grace Hopper and refers to a computer error.

7. In Microsoft Office, you can automate a frequently performed task by recording a _____.

8. A program that translates programming language source code into machine code and then reads an entire program prior to execution is called a _____.

9. If programmers develop software by tackling one small piece of the puzzle at a time, they are taking a _____ approach.

10. A _____ provides a visual diagram of an algorithm and is sometimes used instead of pseudocode.

Tech Illustrated: Figure Labeling

Fill in the blanks with the correct labels.

1. Flowchart symbols

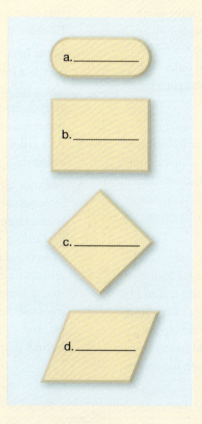

a. _____

b. _____

c. _____

d. _____

2. Characteristics of common programming languages

Language	Compiled	Interpreted	Object-Oriented
C	Yes	No	No
C++	a. _____	d. _____	g. _____
Java	b. _____	e. _____	h. _____
Visual Basic	c. _____	f. _____	i. _____

Tech to Come: Brainstorming New Uses

In groups or individually, contemplate the following questions and develop as many answers as you can.

1. Home automation devices are available that allow you to control your lights, entertainment devices, home security system, and heating even when you are away from home. How do you see this technology evolving in the future?

2. Even when modular code is used, programming is still very much a manual, time-consuming task. How might this change in the future?

Tech Literacy: Internet Research and Writing

Conduct Internet research to find the information described, and then develop appropriate written responses based on your research. Be sure to document your sources using the MLA format. (See Chapter 1, Tech Literacy: Internet Research and Writing, page 38, to review MLA style guidelines.)

1. Have you ever thought of a career as a programmer? Investigate the educational requirements certifications needed for this career, as well as the current job market and earning potential. Summarize your research and then reflect on whether this could be a viable career path for you.

2. Pick one of the languages discussed in this chapter, and research its current use in industry. Where is it being used? What are some examples of real-life applications that have been written in this language? Will this language continue to be used in the long term, or will it be eventually phased out?

3. Did you know that you can create an app and then submit it to Apple or Google for review and testing? If your app is successful, it could be sold in Apple's App Store or Google's Play Store. Research the idea of being an app developer, and document the steps you would have to go through to create and submit an app for review.

Include highlights of an individual or individuals that were successful in selling an app to Apple or Google.

4. What happens when software is released with a bug or a logic error? Research real-life disasters that have occurred because of software errors. In each case, describe what caused the problem, when it occurred, and what the outcome was. Also reflect on how the problem could have been avoided.

5. Software already controls many objects and tasks in our daily lives. Airplane autopilot software is an example of an intelligent program that performs a task normally associated with human expertise. How much of the time is a typical airliner under the control of a computer rather than a human? Do all major airliners use autopilot software? Can autopilot software land, take off, and fly a plane without any direction from human pilots?

Tech Issues: Team Problem-Solving

In groups, develop possible solutions to the issues presented, using the six problem-solving steps outlined in this chapter. Number the steps 1 through 6, and write a description of your efforts at each step.

Individual Issues

1. Starting a car.

2. Making a sandwich.

3. Deciding what to do for entertainment tonight.

4. Installing a wireless router.

Global Issues

1. Stopping an asteroid from colliding with the earth.

2. Providing fast Internet connections and making them accessible to everyone in the world.

Tech Timeline: Predicting Next Steps

Computer language development has seen much progress during the course of its history. Recent trends appear to lead toward "super-languages" that combine features of low-level and high-level languages, and operate as either compiled or interpreted languages. Look at the timeline below, and predict developments in programming languages to the year 2030.

1946 Coding of the world's first computer (ENIAC) is performed in machine code only.

1959–1961 COBOL, a high-level compiled language, is developed by a team led by Grace Hopper.

1965 BASIC, a high-level interpreted language, is released to the public.

1968–1973 C, a compiled language that's lower level and more machine-like than most previous languages, is developed.

1980 Object-oriented programming languages are developed, raising the level of modularity and making the programs more abstract (higher level).

1995 Java is released as a slightly higher-level version of C that runs in an interpreted fashion on the Internet.

1998 Microsoft releases Visual J++ as a competitor to the industry-leading Java from Sun Microsystems.

1998 The XML Working Group officially releases the first version of the XML special-purpose markup language (XML 1.0).

2000 Microsoft releases C# as part of the Visual Studio development toolkit.

2001 The Eclipse Project begins.

2002 Microsoft releases VB.NET, Visual C#, and ASP.NET for web development under the .NET framework.

2006 XML 1.0 Fourth Edition and XML 1.1 Second Edition are released.

2008 The first draft of HTML5 is released.

2011 Java 7 is released.

2014 Apple releases a new programming language called *Swift* for creating iOS and Mac OS X apps.

Ethical Dilemmas: Group Discussion and Debate

As a class or within an assigned group, discuss the following ethical dilemma.

As technology evolves and we rely more and more on software to function in our daily lives, ethical dilemmas emerge for programmers. With software running people's refrigerators, thermostats, alarm systems, and even their cars, a bug can have serious consequences. Reflect on programmers' responsibilities in situations like these, and then discuss the following:

- Does a programmer have any recourse if an employer is rushing a project and the rush may result in a flawed software release?

- If software malfunctions, such as in an alarm system, who is responsible?
- Should a programmer adhere to the exact letter of law when programming devices that will operate in the public realm, such as driverless cars? Should there be any exceptions? If so, what?
- How strict should testing standards be to deliver accurate code if it's going to be used for a critical use, such as the operation of traffic lights?

Chapter 12

Changing Everything with Big Data

Chapter Goal

To learn core database concepts such as database elements, types, models, and administration requirements, as well as understand new database technologies and techniques

Learning Objectives

12.1 Explain how databases work and identify their basic structural elements.

12.2 Describe the elements of a database management system (DBMS) and their functions.

12.3 Identify various database classifications by data model and function.

12.4 Explain how databases are designed.

12.5 Differentiate among methods of data processing.

12.6 Describe the areas of responsibility for a database administrator.

12.7 List procedures and examples for new techniques such as data mining and visualization.

Green go-online icons indicate resources that are accessed from the links menu in your ebook.

SNAP icons indicate interactive resources that are available in SNAP. Go to your SNAP Assignments page to complete these quizzes, activities, and exercises.

12.1 Understanding Database Basics

 Precheck **12.1**

Check your understanding of the concepts covered by this objective.

As you learned in Chapter 4, a **database** is a collection of data organized in one or more data tables stored on a computer. The database management system software used to manage the database enables the user to organize and store information in a structure enabling easy data search and retrieval. Businesses, government departments and agencies, private organizations, and academic institutions all use databases, and these applications represent the dominant use of computing power in the business world today. Without databases, the Internal Revenue Service couldn't collect income taxes, the American Red Cross couldn't allocate funds, and US colleges couldn't operate efficiently. Schools use databases to store and handle grades, class schedules, tuition payments, library fines, and other records relevant to education. Colleges typically use enrollment trend reports to plan for new courses and to branch out into new academic areas. In these cases, they might use not only their own database information, but also reports from national college associations and the federal government.

Databases are used for more than routine operations. Executives commonly consult company databases to produce information for use in decision making. When a company considers opening a new branch office, upper-level managers and other strategic planners can carefully examine databases describing the purchasing habits of local consumers to choose the best location. The US Bureau of Labor Statistics maintains a database about consumer pricing, employment, pay rates, spending, and productivity to help measure the country's economic health. And of course, companies maintain databases full of product information, making it possible for consumers

Information stored in a database can be retrieved in a variety of useful formats, such as graphs, charts, tables, and maps.

⬡ Tracking Down Tech ❯❯❯❯❯

Data in the Media

We humans track all sorts of statistics, from our weight and blood pressure measured at our annual medical visits to how many minutes we work out each week. On a larger scale, newspaper, radio, and TV media all relay historical statistics and data that when compared with current events, give more context to the day's events. Complete this scavenger hunt to find examples of database data being used in various media.

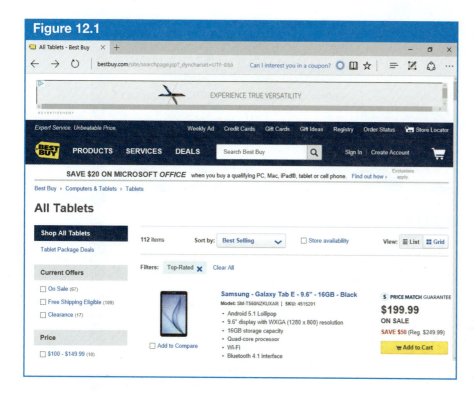

Figure 12.1

E-commerce sites use databases to record prices, sales, and other information about their products. This page from Best Buy's online site shows the results of a search for top-rated tablets.

to search online for products to purchase (see Figure 12.1). In addition, the company can monitor products' sales performance and reorder or put items on clearance to eliminate remaining inventory, adjust pricing, and so on. Larger databases might hold necessary customer information. For example, AT&T and Verizon keep call records in large databases for customer billing purposes, and financial organizations keep certain transaction and communications records in databases to comply with regulatory requirements. Even computerized club membership lists and customer lists for candy and cookie sales serve as basic databases.

Comparing Data versus Information

Data and information are key concepts in understanding the importance of computerized databases. Recall from Chapter 1 that data consists of raw, unorganized (unprocessed) content in the form of words, numbers, sounds, and images. Data processed and organized along with other useful data on the same topic becomes information.

The ability to associate or organize stored data in a variety of meaningful ways represents the power of database software. For example, an insurance company might store zip code information in its database, but a zip code alone can't identify a customer. However, when you provide other data—such as a name, an address, or a phone number—along with the zip code, this set of organized data becomes information that can be used to locate and identify a customer.

Note that the web and the cloud contain large quantities of unstructured data. The final section of this chapter will cover newer methods for dealing with unstructured data, such as analytics—but first, let's focus on traditional databases and file processing.

Reviewing Historical Database Forms

Primitive data storage systems existed long before computers came into being. Important records such as birth certificates, medical histories, income tax files, payroll records, and car license data were stored on paper forms before the first database

Figure 12.2

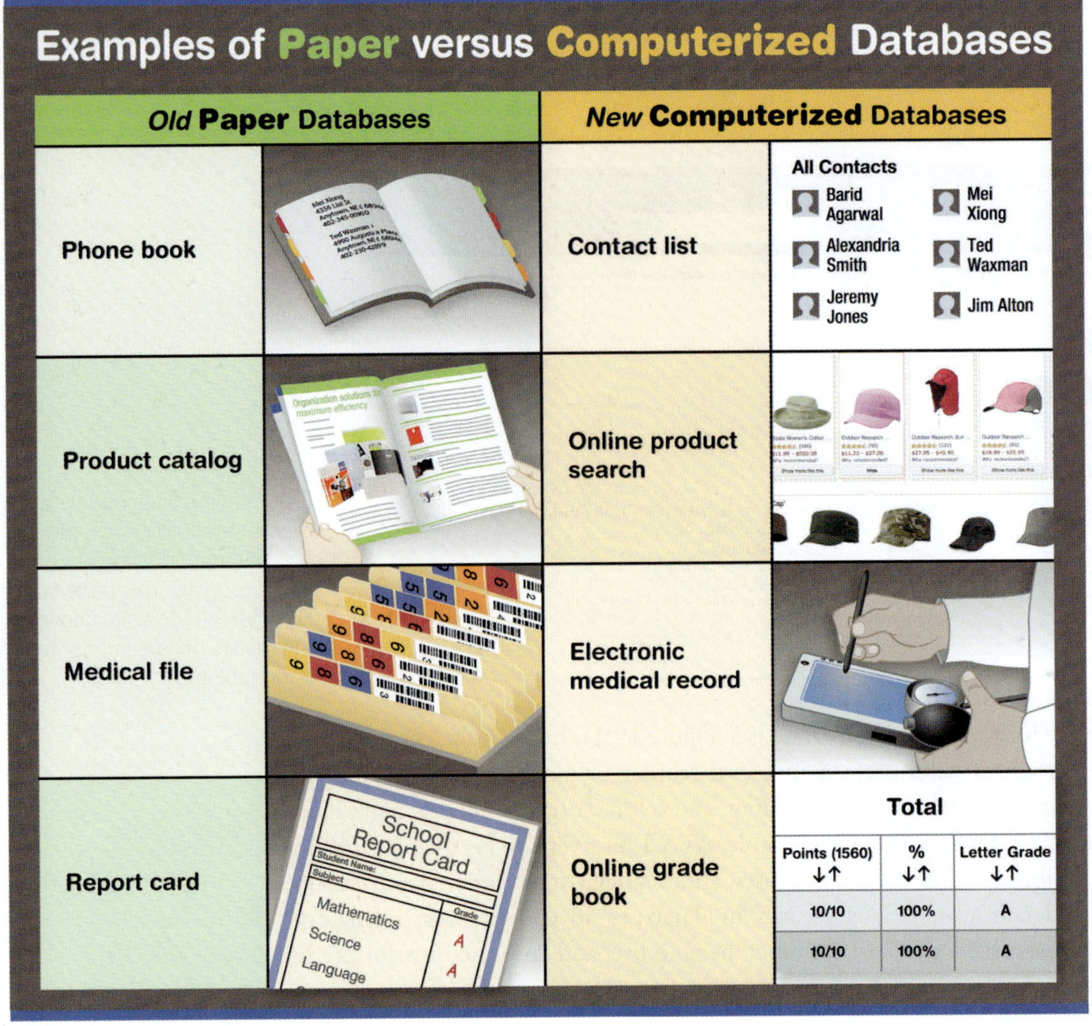

Examples of Paper versus Computerized Databases

Old **Paper** Databases		*New* **Computerized** Databases	
Phone book		Contact list	**All Contacts** Barid Agarwal · Mei Xiong Alexandria Smith · Ted Waxman Jeremy Jones · Jim Alton
Product catalog		Online product search	
Medical file		Electronic medical record	
Report card	School Report Card	Online grade book	

For the Online grade book:

	Total		
	Points (1560) ↓↑	% ↓↑	Letter Grade ↓↑
	10/10	100%	A
	10/10	100%	A

software was developed in the 1950s and 1960s. These printed documents were usually collected and organized in filing cabinets. Locating information and structuring it for various purposes was possible, assuming good filing habits helped maintain consistent organization. However, document retrieval often involved sifting through stacks of paper, identifying the desired data, and then writing or typing selected items on more paper so people could analyze the information. For example, if a health department wanted to determine if a flu outbreak had resulted in a significant increase in deaths within a certain age group, workers had to read mounds of death records and manually note the causes of death and the ages of the victims. Today, the same task could be executed in minutes or seconds using a computerized database.

Computerized databases have become so useful in all areas of personal and public life that paper-based storage systems are used less and less (see Figure 12.2). Even small, independent medical offices, small retail shops, and other types of small businesses have been rapidly moving to electronic systems. Likewise, many of us now use smaller digital database tools to manage our own personal information.

 **Activity 12.1.1**

Article

The National Electronic Disease Surveillance System (NEDSS)

Maintaining Accurate Data

Databases serve as records of events or situations, and therefore require prompt and frequent updates to maintain the data's accuracy. For example, suppose an insurance

Figure 12.3

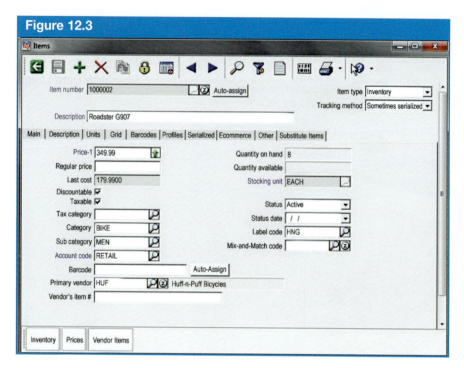

Accurate inventory data and sales data facilitate product and purchasing decisions in a retail business. Point of sale (POS) solutions like NCR Counterpoint integrate retail sales, inventory management (shown here), and more for retailers.

company maintains a database containing names, addresses, birth dates, and policy information. Several different departments in the company can access the database. The underwriting department sends out information whenever policy benefits change. The marketing department sends mailings to people who may be interested in new benefits. The accounting department uses the database to mail billing notices. Company managers regularly generate reports, or information combined from linked data tables, to forecast new directions for the firm. If a policyholder moves to a new address, buys a new vehicle, or experiences some other type of change, the database must be updated to reflect the change. Otherwise, the information the company uses will be incorrect, potentially resulting in an avalanche of problems throughout the departments, such as mailing a bill or policy update to the wrong address.

Paper forms stored in files served as a primitive type of database before records were computerized.

Data quality is particularly important when, as often happens, summarized information is used for decision making. In retail sales, the computer checkout system might automatically deduct items sold from the inventory in the database. Periodically, store personnel might perform a physical inventory, and compare those results with the information in the database. Even small retail companies need accurate inventory data. Sales information tracked in the database enables owners or managers to decide what products need to be ordered. Discrepancies between the database inventory counts and physical inventory counts might help identify problems with theft or excessive damage loss. Sales data from the database provides a constantly updated snapshot of revenue, as shown in Figure 12.3.

Identifying Levels of Data within a Database

The ability to organize and reorganize data for different purposes is provided by two database characteristics: their vast storage potential and the way they organize data. A traditional database organizes data in a hierarchical fashion, containing information about entities in the form of fields, records, and tables. (Some large-scale database

Activity 12.1.2

Video
Database Structure

Figure 12.4

Traditional Database Hierarchy

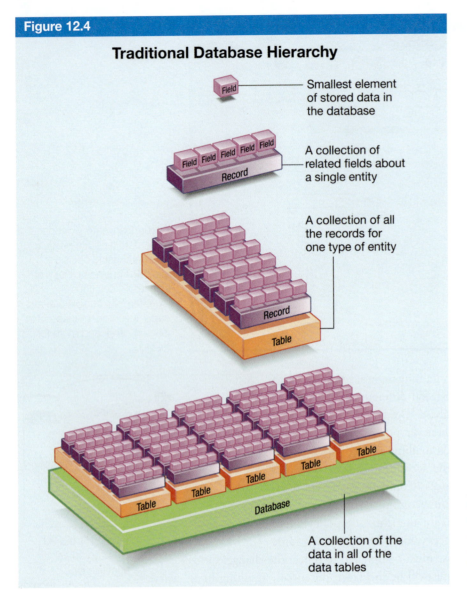

Field — Smallest element of stored data in the database

Record — A collection of related fields about a single entity

A collection of all the records for one type of entity

Record

Table

Database — A collection of the data in all of the data tables

A traditional database, shown here, organizes data in a hierarchy. A record collects multiple fields about an entity, and a table or data file holds individual records. The database collects the data tables or files.

systems may group tables in multiple data files and have the ability to use data from external files.) Figure 12.4 illustrates this hierarchy.

Entities An **entity** is anything you want to keep a record of in a database. It might be something that exists physically, such as a person or product that you want to track information about. Or it may be conceptual, such as a sales transaction that describes products removed from inventory and the amount of money received for those products. Other examples of conceptual entities include student grades, traffic violations, and mobile phone call records. Databases organize and store information about different entities using fields, records, and tables or files.

Fields The smallest element of stored data in a database is a field. A **field** is a single value, such as a name, an address, or a dollar amount. A field may have multiple properties, with these three being the most essential:

- **Data type.** The **data type** specifies the type of information the field will hold. Data types include, for example, numeric, alphanumeric (numbers and letters), and date.

- **Field name.** A **field name** is a unique name assigned to the field by the person developing the database.
- **Field size.** The size of a field is described as the number of characters that can be entered in it. For example, say a database contains a field with a size of 20 characters. If the user types an entry longer than 20 characters into the field, the database will automatically truncate the extra characters to fit the entry into the field.
- **Other.** Other field properties might include displaying a field with particular formatting, or specifying a list of entries that the user can make in the field.

Each field holds the data described by its field name. The most common data types are numeric and alphanumeric. **Numeric data,** or *integer data*, consists only of numbers. **Alphanumeric data,** or *text data*, consists of letters, numbers, and sometimes special characters. Other data types exist, such as logical yes/no fields, time and date fields, and long text or memo fields, which allow unlimited character input. The more unusual data types include pictures, movies, and sound. Table 12.1 describes various field data types.

Records A collection of related fields describing a single entity (person, place, thing, or event) is called a **record**. If a record holds a mailing address, it likely includes fields named *FirstName*, *LastName*, *Address1*, *Address2*, *City*, *State*, and *ZIPCode*.

Table 12.1 Common Field Data Types

Data Type	Description of Data
Attachment	Enables an external file such as a Word document or PDF file to be attached to the database entry or record
Calculated	Automatically performs a calculation using data from one or more other fields, such as multiplying an item's price times the tax rate to find a tax amount
Currency	Allows only dollar amounts, such as a bank account balance
Date/Time	Allows only valid dates/times, such as 11/12/18
Hyperlink	Enables a record to include a link you can click to display a web address or start a message to an email address
Logical or Boolean	Yes/No states (TRUE/FALSE behind the scenes), such as whether or not the person listed in the record is "married" or "retired"
Long Text or Memo (or Long)	Holds lengthy text information, notes, or history
Numeric or Integer (or Number)	Holds numbers such as a count of inventoried products
Object or OLE Object	Allows embedded nontextual information, such as pictures
Sequence or AutoNumber	Automatically increases the value of an integer whenever the user adds a new database entry or record; generally used to make a primary key that automatically assigns a unique new number to each new entry or record (row)
Text or Alphanumeric, also called *Short Text*	Holds textual information such as a person's name, with numbers also allowed, as in a street address

Tables or Files A **data table** (or in some systems a data file) is a collection of records of the same type. Some database programs, such as Microsoft Access, organize each set of records as a table within the main database file (see Figure 12.5), while other database systems store each collection of related records in a separate data file or might hold tables in multiple data files.

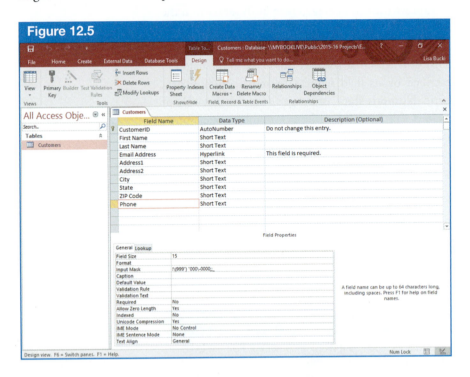

Figure 12.5

Database design includes deciding what fields to include in a table. In Microsoft Access, you set up table fields in table Design view, shown here.

Cutting Edge

Medical Records Go HITECH

Imagine you have just moved to a new city, and you need to see a doctor. What if your new doctor could access all of your medical records instantly just by clicking a mouse or tapping a screen? That's exactly what the government thinks doctors should be able to do, and why it's helping to fund the creation of a massive new networked database—one that will contain the electronic health records (EHRs) of every American.

On February 17, 2009, President Obama signed into law the Health Information Technology for Economic and Clinical Health (HITECH) Act, which provides federal stimulus money to healthcare providers who adopt a certified electronic system for keeping and exchanging patient medical records, and carries penalties or disincentives for those who don't do so. To receive funding, the provider must choose a system that is interoperable, meaning the records can be viewed and shared by other providers, among other criteria.

The pace for creating this network of electronic health record databases to modernize the medical system continues to exceed the government's interim goals. As of late 2014, the US Department of Health and Human Services HealthIT.gov division reported that more than 80 percent of office-based physicians and more than 90 percent of hospitals had implemented eligible systems, with many of them receiving incentive payments to do so.

Of course, physicians and other medical personnel needed to invest the time to learn the new systems. Some physicians have also turned to medical scribes (transcribers) to handle entering notes and recording details about patient interactions. The scribe (or remote scribe service) prepares the finished record, and the physician reviews and approves the record for entry into the system. The government believes that in the end, the system will save money, boost the economy, and most importantly, help Americans live healthier lives.

When designing and building a database, the designer must decide what records need to be tracked, which fields will be in those records, and which data type and size each field will use. Each record in the table or file appears on a single row and follows the same record layout. For example, if a company's database has a table called *Customers*, every record in the table will have *CustomerID*, *FirstName*, *LastName*, and similar fields for each customer listed. All the records will use the same set of fields. The list of all the records of the same type forms the data table or file. From this point on, the text uses the term *table* to refer to either a data table or a data file.

Examining Databases and Information Systems

Networked databases enable businesses to save time and money by coordinating their operations. If each department in a business kept its own customer records, there would be duplicate entries, wasting time and causing confusion. If the different departments share a single networked database, information has to be entered only once, and it can then be accessed freely by anyone needing it.

Many large-scale databases serve as information systems, which you learned about in Chapter 10. Information systems meet the information needs of a company, such as tracking income and expenditures, recording transactions, sharing resources, and planning for growth. A variety of information systems have evolved as software capabilities and market needs have changed over the years. This chapter reviews some information systems as they relate to databases.

Management Information Systems A management information system (MIS) database tracks and controls business operations through transactions entered in the database. A **transaction** is a business activity central to the nature of an enterprise. Examples include a product being sold, an airline flight being booked, or a college course grade being recorded. A database stores the information that serves as the core of any MIS system.

An MIS for an airline runs the flight departures and arrivals display, and thus needs to handle flight numbers, gate numbers, and expected departure and arrival times. Every ticketing agent's computer communicates with the MIS. When a flight departs, another MIS run by the Federal Aviation Administration (FAA) uses radar systems to track the flight's progress toward its destination.

Office Information Systems Today, an **electronic office**, or an office that implements an office information system (OIS) to automate office work, is the norm rather than the exception. Most organizations of all sizes use a computerized OIS to manage a variety of tasks. For example, a shipping company OIS database may hold records for every customer, so that the sales department can generate a report

An airline's MIS contains information about passengers, luggage, seat assignments, and flight arrival/departure times.

to identify key clients. When a client calls in, the customer service representative (CSR) can look the caller up in the database and immediately direct the call to the right sales representative. CSRscan also quickly access the orders database and check the status of any client order.

Decision Support Systems Rather than simply track the day-to-day operations of a business, a decision support system (DSS) is designed to help leaders make decisions about operations. A DSS might include a predictive model of the business that enables managers to work with "what if?" scenarios. For example, when a business considers expanding or releasing a new product, a DSS can help determine if the change will likely succeed or fail. The DSS database can provide information on past performance, which the business decision makers can use to judge the cost of the expansion and any changes to revenue that might result.

Factory Automation Systems Computer-aided manufacturing (CAM) and computer-integrated manufacturing (CIM) information systems support factory

CIM and CAM systems that automate manufacturing track detailed data about work in progress, inventory, and more.

Hotspot

The "World Cup of Selfies"

The 2014 FIFA World Cup Brazil soccer tournament played out at multiple new stadiums, each of which held tens of thousands of excited fans. Numerous technology companies—including HP, iBwave, and Lemcon Americals—provided various expertise and technologies to deploy the stadium wireless networks, which needed to handle traffic from thousands of users at any given time during each of the 64 matches. Fans could use the official FIFA app to access databases of players and league information, as well as accessing other information wirelessly and posting to social media. According to *RCR Wireless News*, the National Union of Fixed and Mobile Telecom Companies of Brazil (SindiTelebrasil) said that "more than 4.5 million phone calls were made and 4.5 million photos were sent, and that a total of 26.7 terrabytes [sic] of data were transmitted." The record amounts of data transmitted resulted in many in the media and beyond nicknaming the event the "The World Cup of Selfies."

automation. Generally, the term *CAM* refers to a system that runs an assembly line directly, controlling the manufacturing process from the shop-floor level of conveyor belts and robots. CAM systems form a portion of a complete CIM system. The term *CIM* refers to a higher-level concept, indicating a system that controls a manufacturing process from beginning to end. The database at the core of these systems stores information about factory operations, such as counters that automatically add all the items manufactured to inventory.

Recheck 12.1
Recheck your understanding of the concepts covered by this objective.

12.2 Looking at Database Management System Software

Precheck 12.2
Check your understanding of the concepts covered by this objective.

Database management system (DBMS) software (discussed in Chapter 4) enables a user to create and manage a computerized database. A DBMS also allows a user to create reports from stored data. IBM's DB2, Oracle Database (and other database products) from Oracle Corporation, SAP, and Microsoft's SQL Server dominate the enterprise DBMS market, and the open source (freeware) MySQL is also gaining in market share. In the small business and individual user markets, Microsoft Access enjoys wide use on Windows systems, while FileMaker (a product of an Apple subsidiary) runs on OS X systems and boasts millions of users. Other free and low-cost alternatives include Apache's Cassandra, often used in cloud applications.

In addition to maintaining the overall structure of the data, a DBMS handles many other functions. Database keys, query tools, security elements, metadata, and backup and recovery utilities all allow users to organize database data into useful information.

Database Keys

A **key** is an attribute that can be used to identify a set of information and therefore provide a means to search or sort a database. The database designer designates fields within a database as keys, setting the most important field in a table as the primary key. The **primary key** must contain only unique entries, such as unique ID numbers, so it can be used to locate records quickly. A *FirstName* field makes a poor key, because many people have the same first name. In a state government database that tracks traffic and parking violations, the car license *PlateNumber* field could be used as a primary key, because no two cars registered in the same state can have the same license plate number. Common primary keys include fields with unique entries, such as bank account, credit card, social security, reservation confirmation, and work order numbers. Primary keys can be large numbers, but they can also include letters, like many drivers' license numbers.

In some cases, a DBMS can give you help with creating a primary key. For example, when you create a new table in Microsoft Access and add a field using the AutoNumber data type (which forces a unique numeric entry for each record), saving the table will make Access prompt you to set up the primary key. If you click Yes, Access will automatically mark the AutoNumber field as the primary key. Otherwise, you can use the

Practical TECH

Databasing for Free

Apache's open source (free) OpenOffice suite also includes the Base database application. When you choose OpenOffice, you get not only this free, full-featured database, but other tools including word-processing, spreadsheet, and presentation capabilities. OpenOffice comes in versions for Windows, OS X, and Linux, making it a good choice when you need to work on multiple platforms. Even better, data from Base can easily be connected with or imported into many other DBMS systems. Go to http://CUT6.emcp.net/OpenOffice to learn more about Base and to download OpenOffice.

Figure 12.6

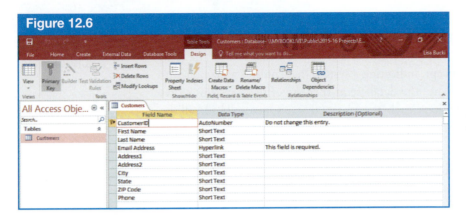

In Microsoft Access, use the Primary Key button to designate the table field that will function as the primary key. To activate the feature, display the table in Design view, click the field name, and then click the Primary Key button in the Tools group on the Table Tools Design tab.

Primary Key button in table Design view, shown in Figure 12.6, to set the selected field as the primary key.

It's possible to search or sort a database without using the primary key, but it might be more difficult, as other fields may not contain unique entries and therefore may return a confusing array of results. For example, let's say an online retailer's database uses the *OrderID* field as the primary key. After placing an order, the customer receives a confirmation email that includes the specific *OrderID* for his order. If the customer then calls the company to inquire about a shipping or billing error, the CSR will likely ask for the *OrderID*. As the unique primary key entry, that data enables the CSR to locate the order record quickly. If the CSR asked for a last name, she would have to sort through all the customer's order records, and perhaps even the records of another person with the same last name. Doing this would waste time, as a large database could contain thousands of duplicate last names. Managing the enormous amounts of information in a database would be nearly impossible without primary keys.

Users may need to browse records to find the desired information when a table lacks a primary key. **Data browsing** involves moving through a database file, examining each record, and looking for information. This strategy also works when a multifield search or a search on a secondary key returns many results that must be sifted through. Hunting through the best results returned by a search engine is a form of data browsing.

Query Tools

Database data resides in stored data tables or files until the system needs to perform **file processing** (that is, retrieve and perform some type of operation) on the data. At that point, the software copies the data into RAM. Database management systems include **query tools** that help users select matching information from within a larger set of data. A **query** enables users to specify criteria designed to retrieve needed information. For example, you could create a query in a grades database with the criterion of listing all students in the top 10 percent of academic achievement—the dean's list for that semester. You could then create and print a report based on the query results. Generally, you create a query, and then run it to display the results, or list of records that match the query criteria.

A query language, such as the popular **Structured Query Language (SQL,** pronounced "sequel")**,** enables users to request information from a database. SQL is simple when compared with a programming language, but it's also structured, meaning that it isn't as free form as some natural programming languages that mimic human speech. Widely supported, SQL works with most databases in use today. For this reason, users can employ SQL to bridge communications gaps between different database systems

Activity 12.2.1

Article
Open Source SQL Tools

or between database systems running on different operating systems.

The basic query command that SQL commands is the **SELECT command**, which asks a database to return records that match specified criteria. The command uses the keywords *SELECT [fields] FROM [table]* and specifies the table and fields from which the information is to be selected (see Figure 12.7).

Other database software uses a method called *Query by Example (QBE)* for creating queries. In **Query by Example (QBE)**, the user builds the query by selecting one or more tables to query, adding the fields to display in the results in a query grid, and then entering the entry to match or other criteria in applicable fields. Access uses this method for queries. The query grid serves as a visual means of guiding the user in creating the query.

You can set up one query to return data from more than one table (record source) through a process called **joining**, which matches data from fields in the specified data tables. The most common type of join matches the primary key field in one table with the field holding the same type of data in another table. As shown in Figure 12.8, for example, if student names (personal records) and grades were entered in separate data tables, the *StudentID* primary key in the personal records table could

Figure 12.7

▧ GPA

```
SELECT Student.StuID, Student.FName, Student.GPA, Student.Enrolled
FROM Student
WHERE (((Student.GPA)>3.49) AND ((Student.Enrolled)=Yes));
```

This SQL view of a query in Microsoft Access returns the top students in a table, with "top" defined as students who have a grade point average (GPA) above 3.49. Note that the syntax of the SQL statements allows for slight variations.

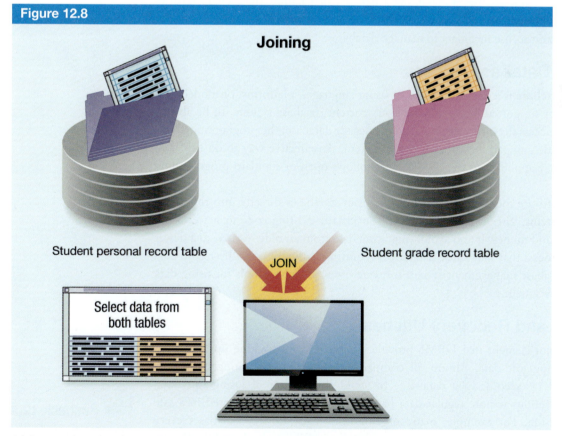

Figure 12.8

Joining

Student personal record table

Student grade record table

JOIN

Select data from both tables

Joining matches data from fields in specified data tables. Both the student personal records and student grade records files would have a common *StudentID* AutoNumber field, allowing the information from both tables to be returned in a single query.

be joined to a corresponding *StudentID* field in the grades table to find the grades by student in the query results. In some cases, Access creates joins automatically during the query design process. In other cases, the user must create the join manually. Unlike relationships, which are covered on page 546, a join exists only within the query that contains it.

Security Measures

A DBMS also includes **security measures** to protect and safeguard data. Payroll, accounts receivable, and email storage systems all contain sensitive information that must be protected against theft, alteration, and deletion. Competitors, hackers, crackers, and disgruntled employees can do a great deal of harm if they are allowed access to critical company databases.

Maintaining data security is a critical issue for database administrators. Security methods include restricting access by requiring user identification and passwords. Usually, only users with high levels of access can change the data in a database, and only those with the highest level of access can change the format of the data.

Metadata and the Data Dictionary

Metadata—or in this case, information about the elements in a database—describes the structure, specifications, and purpose of each element. The **data dictionary** (also called a *metadata repository*) collects the body of metadata for the entire database. For a field called *FNAME*, metadata might describe it as being a text field with a maximum length of 20 characters used for holding a person's first name. These characteristics might not be immediately obvious from the field name *FNAME*. Designers, users, and administrators use metadata to manage databases.

Legacy Database Access

A **legacy database** is a database that runs using languages, platforms, or models that are no longer supported by an organization's current database system. To be able to continue to access the information stored in a legacy database, the programming code must be made compatible with the newer system. An effective way to do this is to migrate legacy applications to a DBMS that follows open or standard programming interfaces.

Some software tools read the data from legacy databases directly into the newer database systems. This avoids the need to convert the existing code to newer code, saving time and money. It also avoids migrating data from an older format to a newer format, a process that may cause data errors requiring manual, record-by-record correction. Database management system software often integrates tools for using data from a legacy system.

Backup and Recovery Utilities

Another major element that DBMS provide is a method for backing up, repairing, and recovering lost data. Almost all companies keep sales, marketing, customer, payroll, and tax records in a database. To avoid the disaster of losing this data, most organizations require regular data backups, with the backups stored in a safe remote location. For example, many organizations back up key databases every 24 hours, during nonpeak usage time frames. It's also possible to back up DBMS data to a cloud service. In a **recovery**, or restoration of data, the database administrator uses the most recent backup, which typically contains the most recent and accurate data.

Recheck 12.2
Recheck your understanding of the concepts covered by this objective.

12.3 Exploring Types of Databases

Exploring Types of Databases

Databases are often categorized by the way they organize data (data models), or by their function (storing information for ongoing processes versus storing information for historical purposes).

Databases Classified by Data Model

A **data model** defines the structure of information to be contained in a database, how the database will use the information, and how the different items in the database relate to each other. The data model identifies the logical organization of the database contents.

The data model also defines how complex the operations performed on the data can be. Advanced data models tend to be more reliable and consistent, allowing for greater connectivity with outside systems. They also tend to be easier to work with and less expensive to develop and maintain. Common data models include flat file, relational, object-oriented, multimedia, multidimensional, XML, web, and hybrids.

Flat File Databases A traditional data file storage system that contains only one data table or file is known as a **flat file database**. Early desktop database programs—such as the databases in Microsoft Works and Apple Works—used the flat file model, keeping a single list of data in each database file. Another early database program, dBase, pioneered the .dbf file format. Some database programs can still output and open .dbf files, and Microsoft Excel also retains the capability to open lists of data in the .dbf file format. Simple and easy to use, flat file systems may be slower to respond to queries and other actions than relational databases, because each record must contain all the required fields and searches run sequentially, record by record.

Today, flat file databases exist, but often in the format of specialized freeware, shareware, or low-cost applications for very specific purposes. For example, such programs enable you to catalog your recipes, book collection, or movie collection. The

Hands On

Using Excel Online as a Flat File Database

While both the online and desktop versions of Excel function primarily as spreadsheet programs, you can use them to perform basic database-like functions, such as sorting (placing the records in a new order according to the entries in one field) and filtering (showing only records that match specified criteria, much like a query). For these functions to work, the data must be arranged properly as a list or table on a worksheet. Each field of data should appear in a column, and each row should hold a single record. If included, field names should appear in the top row of the list or table. Follow the steps in this resource to create a list of data in Excel Online and perform a basic sort and filter.

home inventory software shown in Figure 12.9 enables you to keep a list of your home possessions for insurance and other purposes. As shown in this example, some of these programs offer basic searching (find), sorting, and filtering capabilities. (Filtering displays a set of records matching criteria you specify.) This home inventory program also includes the ability to generate charts and reports about the data in the current file's list of items.

Flat files can be useful for organizing information, but relational database systems offer faster, more comprehensive reporting capabilities better suited for business applications.

Relational Databases Most modern databases use a **relational database** model, in which fields with similar data can be connected between data tables or files in the database, making it possible to retrieve data from the related tables. In a relational database, the data table (consisting of rows and columns) may be called a *relation*, each record is called a **tuple**, and a field is called an **attribute**. Many of the element definitions are the same as with a traditional flat file system. The primary difference concerns the organization of the tuples and fields or attributes, and any relationships between fields in different tables.

Compared with flat file models, relational database models offer the key advantage of being able to share, extract, and combine information from multiple tables fairly easily. For example, in a flat file system, an entity's address might be stored in several individual database files. If the entity's address information ever changes, its address records will have to be updated in each separate database file. If any record is overlooked, that particular file will contain outdated information, meaning that any output using that record will be inaccurate. In a relational database, rather than

Activity 12.3.1

Article
Relational Database Design

Activity 12.3.2

Video
Relational Database

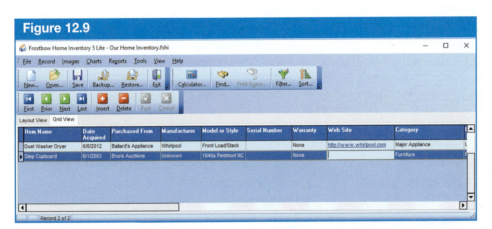

Figure 12.9

In a flat file database system, each file holds a single list of records. Some may offer basic search (find), sort, and filtering capabilities.

Hands On

Understanding and Creating a Delimited Text File

It's possible that the data you need to work with exists in a legacy database or other type of format that your current database system can't use. In many cases, you can work around that by exporting the file from the old software as a delimited text (TXT) file or comma-separated values (CSV) file, and then importing the resulting file into your current database. In a delimited file like this, each record appears on a single row, and a delimiter character separates the field entries. Not surprisingly, a comma-separated values file uses the comma character as the delimiter. A delimited text file might use a comma, a tab, a semicolon, or another character as the delimiter between the fields. Usually, the first row in the file contains the field names, but that isn't essential. In this resource, you find steps to create a comma-delimited text file in the Windows Notepad app.

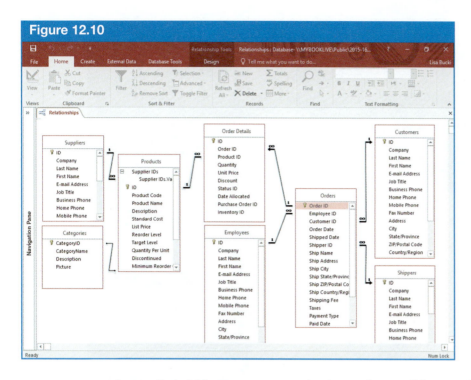

Figure 12.10

Microsoft Access shows the relationships between tables in a database. Attributes such as the customer's ID number, customer's street address, and customer's phone number are stored in the Customers table, and the customer number will also be found in the Orders table when a purchase has been made.

repeating an attribute called *Address* in many records, the attribute will be stored in only one data table, and related to multiple other tables as needed (see Figure 12.10). Thus, in a relational database, updating the attributes for one or more tuples in a single table will ensure that any query or report pulling data from the table displays the most current information.

Object-Oriented Databases An **object-oriented database** stores data in the form of objects (units of object-oriented programming logic). Each object contains both the data related to the object (such as the fields of a record) and the actions the user might want to perform on that object. A record object created for a payroll department might contain the salary of an individual, along with the calculations required to withhold taxes and calculate the final pay amount. Object-oriented databases allow for faster development and access times, speeding up database functions and making developing this type of database easier.

Multimedia Databases As computer storage and processing speeds continue to increase, so do the number of multimedia databases. In addition to the text and numbers a typical database model handles, a **multimedia database** allows the storage of pictures, movies, sounds, and hyperlinked fields. A multimedia employee database file, for example, could include snapshots of employees, along with recordings of their voices.

Multidimensional Databases In Chapter 10, you learned how online analytical processing (OLAP) systems help organize massive amounts of data in a database. An **OLAP Cube** structures data in multiple dimensions. (Even though it's called a *cube*, an OLAP structure may organize data in more than three dimensions.) A **multidimensional database**, therefore, uses a cube structure to organize data, and is typically optimized for OLAP applications. The basic cube structure typically includes dimensions for measures (measure attribute) such as sales quantity by product along one dimension, time (time attribute) along another, and scenarios or locations (feature attribute) such as regions along another. The ability to organize large sets of data makes

Figure 12.11

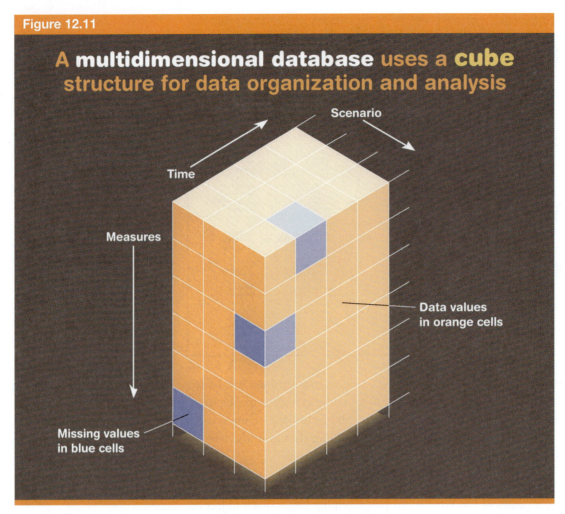

A **multidimensional database** uses a **cube** structure for data organization and analysis

Scenario

Time

Measures

Data values in orange cells

Missing values in blue cells

a multidimensional database the right choice for a large data warehouse operation, such as the data for a large online retailer. Figure 12.11 shows a generic, basic cube structure for a multidimensional database. Note that the cube structure may vary from this typical example—including dimensions for different attributes and more dimensions.

In contrast to a multidimensional database, a relational database contains data tables with only two dimensions: the record row dimension and the field column dimension. However, a multidimensional database might include data from an existing relational database, because a multidimensional database can integrate data from a variety of sources.

Generally speaking, a multidimensional database offers two advantages. First, it allows greater flexibility in the types of questions and queries the database can handle. Second, its organization allows for faster processing and results.

XML Databases As Chapter 5 touched on, XML (eXtensible Markup Language) is a metalanguage, a type of computer language used to describe other languages. XML has been combined with HTML to produce the next generation of HTML, known as XHTML (eXtensible HyperText Markup Language). The increasing number of XML documents and documents using XML-compliant languages such as XHTML has led to efforts to create and perfect XML databases.

In an **XML database**, the fundamental database structure consists of XML documents and elements, whereas in a traditional relational database, data is stored in tables organized in rows and columns. Using XML as a database structure means that

 **Activity 12.3.3**

Practice
Multidimensional Database Cube

XML documents can be stored in their entirety, instead of being broken down and stored in the different rows and columns of a relational database. XML documents can then be retrieved in their original format instead of being re-created from stored data. XML databases may be used in content management systems (CMSs), such as the system a news organization uses to process, organize, publish, and store articles. Forms of XML databases are also used in the engineering, banking, advertising, and aerospace fields, among others.

While XML databases work with XML documents as a whole, relational databases perform better for storing numbers and text; thus XML databases will likely complement rather than replace relational databases in the years to come.

Web Databases Organizations use a **web database** to hold information that will be accessed via a specific web page opened in a web browser. The web database may function on the organization's local network or via the web. For example, the local county government might make property records such as deeds accessible online via a searchable database. Online airline and hotel reservation sites use web databases to hold availability and pricing information. As might be expected, online shopping sites also use a web database to deliver product and pricing information in response to what the customer searches for or clicks on the site. Social media sites also rely on web databases to store user posts, photos, videos, and so on. And many mobile apps draw on data from web databases.

The actual database employed to deliver the data to the web page may vary. Many sites use an XML database to store the data accessed by the front end web page. Other database tools and types already discussed also can be used to create and serve as web database infrastructure. For example, Access offers a Custom web app template choice. After you select that template and specify a web-based SharePoint or Office 365 location to publish the database to, you can add a blank table to hold new data or create a table from existing data from Access, Excel, SQL Server, and other sources. Saving the app publishes the web database to the location specified earlier, making it available for sharing.

Hybrid Databases A database may use different models together to allow more effective data handling. This type of database is called a **hybrid database**. A combination of relational and object-oriented database models is a popular form of hybrid database, and as just noted, a multidimensional database might draw its data from the tables in a relational database. Relational databases can handle only simple mathematical calculations, such as addition and subtraction, so users may have to use separate applications and custom-programmed solutions to perform complex calculations.

Practical TECH

Taking Your Database to the Web

Database development sounds really complex, but as with other technologies, you can find some beginner-friendly and lower-cost tools for nontechnical people. For example, Zoho, a suite of free and low-cost tools, includes Zoho Creator. You can use it to create your own web databases (which it calls database apps) using a drag-and-drop builder. You can start using Zoho Creator for free and upgrade from there as your needs require. For more information, see http://CUT6.emcp.net/ZohoCreator. A similar tool called *knack* enables you to define a database, build an interface, and then share the data. After a 14-day free trial, knack charges a monthly fee that varies based on the plan you pick. Check this one out at http://CUT6.emcp.net/knack.

A database used for passport renewal might combine alphanumeric citizen data with a passport photo image in a hybrid database.

Combining relational and object-oriented data models allows for more sophisticated analysis within the framework of the relational database. The advent of the web and the increasing availability of multimedia files have also driven the popularity of this type of hybrid.

Databases Classified by Function

The two major functional classifications of databases are operational databases and data warehouses. Operational databases work as continually updating systems. For example, a supermarket may use an operational database that receives an update every time a shopper purchases an item. In contrast, a data warehouse system contains data that's periodically extracted and analyzed by a company's staff for use in making strategic decisions. A data warehouse typically doesn't receive modified or updated information on a continuous basis.

It's possible for a database system to perform more than one function at the same time. Also, these classifications don't pertain to specific data models. Operational databases, for example, might use flat file or relational structures. The list of database types continues to evolve, and new classes may emerge in the future.

Operational Databases An **operational database** works by offering a snapshot of a fluid situation. This type of system usually tracks a changing operation or situation, such as the inventory of a store. Examples of operational databases include inventory-tracking systems used by retail stores. An example is a store that offers products in stock and on the shelves for customers to purchase. As a checkout associate scans the bar codes on the items a customer has selected for purchase, the transactions automatically update a database that tracks the amount and location of each item in the store. When the stock of diapers or lawn chairs runs low, the database automatically orders more.

E-commerce websites typically rely on operational databases. These sites enable the user to place items in a virtual shopping cart and then enter credit card and shipping information, as discussed in Chapter 10. An order database tracks this data, including later shipping and payment information.

Depending on the amount of traffic they receive, website databases may be distributed databases. A **distributed database** spreads its data across multiple networked computers, with each computer storing a portion of the data. This type of database can hold more information than any one computer can contain, and allows for cheap and easy expansion, as in public cloud computing. Distributed databases offer advantages in cost, expandability, and storage capability. A major disadvantage is that they may not operate as quickly as a database stored on a single server or mainframe.

Data Warehouses A **data warehouse** stores data gathered from one or more databases. Unlike an operational database, a data warehouse doesn't change or delete the information it stores on an ongoing basis. In contrast, a data warehouse receives only periodic updates, or may rely on data from other sources for updated information. As the name implies, a data warehouse functions as a vast storage place for holding information that can later be used in a variety of ways.

Law enforcement records are one example of information that's stored using a data warehouse (see Figure 12.12), with vast collections of photographs and arrest records

The operational database at a grocery store is updated each time an item is scanned or entered at a checkout station.

Activity 12.3.4

Article
Data Warehousing and Data Mining

Figure 12.12

Data warehouses store large amounts of data for various purposes, such as online selling and mapping—in this case, mapping crime reports.

on file for reference or for statistical use. Companies also maintain data warehouses to test new ideas against past results, to provide CSRs with customer information, or create web-based sales tools to make product suggestions to customers. Many of the largest company databases contain information dating back to the 1950s. Companies are increasingly experimenting with these databases, using data-mining techniques (such as those described on page 564) to sift through information and identify previously unnoticed trends.

Recheck 12.3

Recheck your understanding of the concepts covered by this objective.

12.4   Planning and Designing Database Systems

Planning and designing a database system requires a combination of knowledge, skills, and creativity. This job is usually handled by a **database analyst**, sometimes called a *database designer*. A database analyst may also be responsible for administering the database after it's built. Like a structural engineer who designs buildings and draws blueprints, a database analyst uses experience to identify the project's needs and then design a structure or system to fulfill them.

Precheck 12.4

Check your understanding of the concepts covered by this objective.

The Database Management Approach

The development and maintenance of database structures and applications employs a methodology called the **database management approach** (sometimes shortened to the *database approach*). Using the software tools of a database management system (DBMS), a database analyst or database designer follows three broad steps in the planning process:

1. **Create an organizational structure for the data.** A designer focuses first on creating an abstract structure that imitates a real-life situation, drawing on an analysis of the information needs and the purpose(s) of the database. The analyst makes decisions about the kinds of records needed, the types of fields needed in each record, and how fields should be grouped to form records and tables. Choosing the data type and formatting for each field is another basic decision. With the field-record-table structure established, the analyst can decide how the database will accept data.

Activity 12.4.1

Video
Database Design

2. **Design an interface that makes the database user friendly.** Users don't need to understand the internal structure of a database. Their most important consideration is being able to easily enter data and request information. A **front-end interface**, or collection of modules or data entry forms, makes this possible. The interface elements interact with the DBMS—the software features or separate functionality that manipulates and manages the database. The front-end interface should also prevent users from entering erroneous data into the database. For example, it could incorporate techniques such as presenting a drop-down list of allowable entries for a field, and preventing entry of

A well-designed database interface helps users enter data easily with minimal errors, and also displays requested information in useful and logical formats.

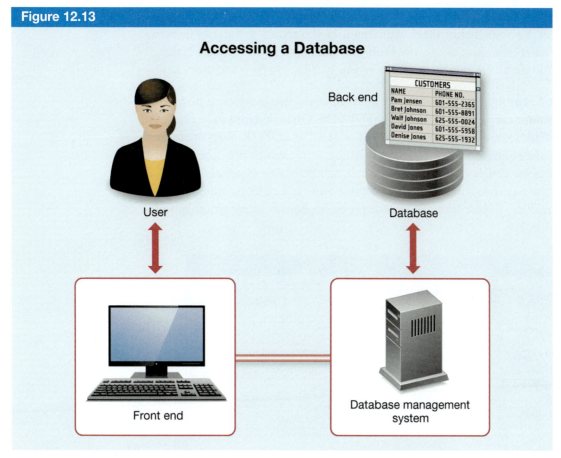

Figure 12.13

Accessing a Database

Back end

CUSTOMERS	
NAME	PHONE NO.
Pam Jensen	601-555-2365
Bret Johnson	601-555-8891
Walt Johnson	625-555-0024
David Jones	601-555-5958
Denise Jones	625-555-1932

User

Database

Front end

Database management system

The user requests and enters data through the front-end interface features. The database management system manages the retrieval and update functions of the database.

a record missing a vital piece of information, such as a zip code. Figure 12.13 shows the relationship of the DBMS, the front-end interface, and the database.

3. **Set up reporting capabilities to allow for inquiry and response.** Because inquiry and response functions represent the main tools for analyzing database information, they receive significant attention from the designer. A DBMS typically includes reporting features, and the designer chooses how and where in the system to make query and reporting features available.

Database Objects: Tools in the DBMS

A **database object** is an element within many types of databases, such as a form, a report, or a data filter. Database designers use database objects to build the system interface and the reporting features.

Forms A **form** is a screen or dialog box that allows the user to enter data into the database. The form includes a collection of fields, enabling the user to enter needed data in a way that many people consider easier and more friendly than working with tables. Even better, a form may include fields from multiple tables, streamlining the data entry process. The database designer can build in features to enable a form to detect and prevent erroneous or incomplete data input. The user also can search through data, move to other records, and make changes using a form. Many jobs involve working with forms in a database, such as airline ticketing and hotel front-desk work.

A well-designed form provides questions or prompts. The designer may include default entries for some fields; these will remain in the record if the user doesn't input alternate entries. Buttons on the form may prompt the user to take action, such as the Submit Claim button shown in Figure 12.14.

Reports A **report** presents output from a data table or query in a format designed to make the information easy to read (see Figure 12.15). Often designed to be printed out for later review, reports also can be emailed or saved as PDFs. Reports often use grouping to place similar data together and sorting to present data in the desired order. The database designer also might add totals, subtotals, averages, and other calculations to the report to summarize the data and make it a more meaningful tool for decision making. Report examples include monthly phone bills, report cards, and grade transcripts.

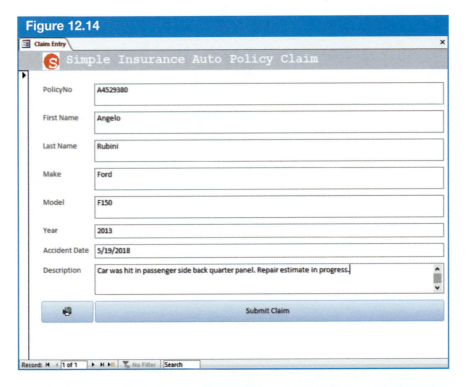

Figure 12.14

This form prompts the user to input data into an Access database.

Figure 12.15

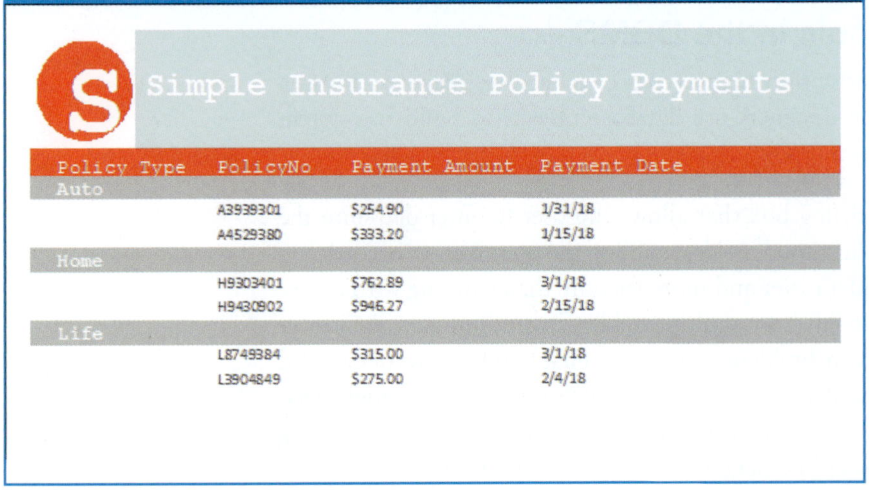

A report presents output from a database using an attractive, easy-to-read layout. Most databases can generate reports by request or automatically. This example report from Access groups insurance records by policy type.

A report can be generated by request or automatically. For example, a consumer credit report isn't issued regularly, but only at the request of a lending firm or the consumer. On the other hand, a lender automatically generates monthly billing statements for consumers—a type of automated report.

Data Filters and Queries Many databases enable the user to apply filtering criteria, called a **data filter**, which displays only a subset of the data. For example, if a user wishes to view only accounts receivable overdue by 90 days, applying a filter looking for dates greater than or equal to 90 days ago to the *DueDate* field in the Accounts Receivable data table will display that matching data.

Search engines on the web work much like data-filtering systems. Each search engine maintains a massive database of web pages, and the contents of each page are indexed for searching. If a user searches for "cat and dog," for example, a search engine will bring back pages containing both the words "cat" and "dog." The report generated—in this instance a web page displaying a list of matches—is transmitted to the user, with the matching pages highlighted as hyperlinks.

In general, more specific data filters yield more limited and focused results, increasing the likelihood of finding the desired content. Database designers can help end users by including a good, effective data filter as part of the user interface. Earlier in the chapter, you learned about query tools. Many database systems, such as Access, store queries as separate database objects.

Macros Chapter 4 introduced the concept of macros—a saved set of instructions in a program that you can execute by giving a single command. A database typically has a number of macros associated with other objects and events. For example, a macro attached to a Print button in a report would print the report when the user clicks the button. Another macro might be assigned to run automatically when a user opens the database or a specific form. Another macro might run when the user clicks a particular field on the form or tries to leave the field after making the wrong type of entry. Many database systems store each macro as a separate object.

 Recheck 12.4
Recheck your understanding of the concepts covered by this objective.

12.5 Using Databases

After the database designer creates and tests the database, users can begin to enter and work with data. The term **data processing** refers to the activities performed with a database, including various types of interactions and events. Database users perform data-processing activities as part of their job.

 Precheck 12.5
Check your understanding of the concepts covered by this objective.

Data Processing

The processing of database interactions can be set up using batch or transaction processing, or a combination of both methods.

Batch Processing With **batch processing**, data processing occurs at a scheduled time, or at a critical point in a process. Batch processing saves redundant effort by updating data all at once, rather than continuously. For example, a company may only process its payroll in a single batch after receiving weekly total work hours for its hourly workers. A massive database may take anywhere from several minutes to several hours to run a large process. In some instances, batch processing aids in workflow, enabling users to schedule certain tasks to occur automatically during off hours. However, batch processing can introduce some lag into a system. For example, if a

An air traffic control system is an example of a real-time system. Data must be kept accurate and current, requiring an update as soon as a change occurs.

brokerage receives new shares of stock into clients' accounts due to a stock split, clients who log on to their online accounts might not see the new shares until the brokerage's batch process updates that account information.

Transactional Processing **Transactional processing** occurs when the database updates immediately for each input. Smaller databases and databases that require all information to be absolutely current operate on a transactional basis. For example, a **real-time system**—such as a factory automation system or an air traffic control system—can't afford to wait until midnight to update. A system like this that performs critical functions requires data with second-by-second accuracy. In transactional processing, records of an *event*—such as the purchase of an item, the construction of an automobile part, or the departure of a flight—are processed in the database one at a time as they occur.

E-commerce transactions use **online transactional processing (OLTP)**. E-commerce websites require fast, always-on processing. OLTP systems offer the benefit of being in business 24 hours a day, because customers expect rapid order processing.

Mixed Forms of Processing Some systems mix transactional and batch-processing techniques. For example, in situations involving online orders, a transactional process may be used to handle credit card verifications, while batch processing may be used to handle pick-and-pack orders, requesting that items be taken from inventory and prepared for shipping to customers.

Managing and Updating Databases

Most people use databases as tools in performing their jobs but aren't involved in database design and management. An end user called a **data entry operator** types and changes database data as needed, ensuring that the contents of the database remain as up to date as possible. Without current, accurate data, the database can't deliver good information for use in business decision making and other activities. A database must be updated for every bill payment, address change, or order placed. Many professionals work with databases regularly as part of their job, including accountants, executives, and salespeople.

Database users perform a number of actions on databases on a daily basis. They add, modify, delete, and sort records, among other activities.

Adding Records Entering a new record adds a new record row to a specific data table. For example, when a student completes a course, an administrator adds a grade record to that student's transcript, listing the course taken, the date of completion, and the final grade received.

Modifying Records If a correction is needed to any existing entry, the record in question can be displayed and the change made in the applicable fields, such as changing a B letter grade to an A. Address information (such as street, city, state, and zip code) also requires frequent updates in many databases.

A student's grades are entered into and stored in a database. The individual grades are used to create a report, or transcript.

Deleting Records Deleting a record removes its field contents from the database. For example, when a retailer discontinues a product, it removes that product from its database system, because it no longer needs to track information about it.

Sorting Records As noted earlier, sorting involves arranging records in a particular order, such as alphabetically or numerically. For example, think about a cell phone bill for a family of four where each person has a phone. The mobile provider's database tracks calls, talk minutes, data minutes, and text messaging for each of the four phone numbers. The detailed bill that lists all the calls has had two sorts applied: calls have been sorted by phone number, and then all the calls for each phone have been sorted by date and time (from least recent to most recent). Sorting data in a database (based on the ordering of a key field) enables you to learn more about the data, such as which phone number on the bill had the most calls.

Most database systems sort records automatically on the basis of the primary key field. For example, many colleges use students social security numbers as primary keys, as they are unique and don't require students to learn new numbers. However, sorting records by primary key isn't helpful if the primary key for a student is unknown, and most people using the college's database will not know a particular student's social security number. If a professor wished to change a grade for a student, but didn't know that student's social security number, it could take a long search to find that one record. In that case, the database could be sorted by student name, and the results searched to isolate the correct student.

 Recheck 12.5

Recheck your understanding of the concepts covered by this objective.

12.6 Describing the Areas of Database Administration

Many factors affect database performance, and thus the quality of the information generated. Database designers must consider each factor, and then ensure that corrections for possible problems are built into the system. Once problems occur, it's the job of the database administrator to solve them.

Database administration—that is, operating and maintaining the database system—remains an important IT function, because databases typically form the core of a company's information systems. A **database administrator (DBA)** handles the day-to-day operations of the database. DBA tasks typically include installing and configuring the database, upgrading the database software as needed, ensuring

 Precheck 12.6

Check your understanding of the concepts covered by this objective.

 Activity 12.6.1

Article
Database Administration

that the database provides rapid response times to users, integrating security strategies so only authorized users can access the database, and completing backups of the data on a regular basis (see Figure 12.16).

Database administration combines application development, technical support, and technical training. DBAs maintain databases for existing applications and fix databases when things go wrong. Because DBAs must be intimately familiar with the structure of the database and application, they may also be responsible for teaching users how to operate the system. Larger systems require a team, or perhaps even an entire database and a department of people dedicated to the task.

A DBA performs varied duties, including editing and updating databases. Changes in organizational policy often result in changes to the company database. For example, if the billing information sent to customers needs to include new information, such as a change in credit terms, the administrator needs to edit and test the appropriate report.

Database administrators play a critical role in the success of any organization, because preventing computer **downtime**, or time in which the system is unavailable, falls on their list of responsibilities. Consider an airline reservation system. If it stops

Tech Career Explorer

Database Administrator

Given the ongoing transition from paper records to databases, the demand for skilled DBAs continues to increase. According to the US Bureau of Labor Statistics, employment in this field may grow by as much as 15 percent between 2012 and 2022. If you like working with data, and you like creating orderly, logical rules and seeing them implemented, you might enjoy database administration as a career. Many DBA certifications also can enhance your career prospects as a DBA, such as the Microsoft Certified Database Administrator (MCDBA). Numerous certifications exist for specific database systems such as Oracle. Learn more about this job by completing this exercise.

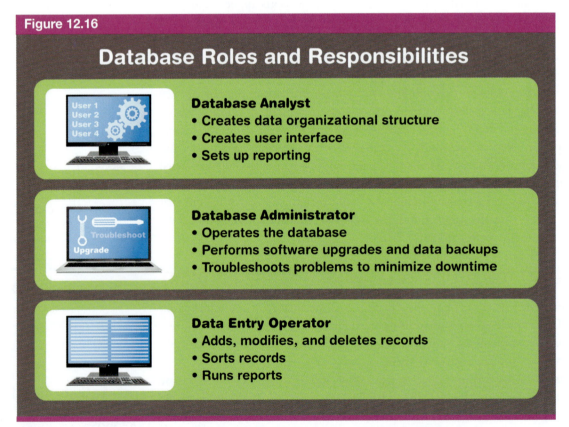

Figure 12.16

Database Roles and Responsibilities

Database Analyst
- Creates data organizational structure
- Creates user interface
- Sets up reporting

Database Administrator
- Operates the database
- Performs software upgrades and data backups
- Troubleshoots problems to minimize downtime

Data Entry Operator
- Adds, modifies, and deletes records
- Sorts records
- Runs reports

Database administrators are responsible for keeping databases up and running to support a company's operations.

running for a period, the airline can't sell tickets or perform any other reservation functions. Customers dislike waiting or being told "The computer system is down." That phrase usually means that a DBA is working feverishly to solve a problem.

Additional factors that database administrators must be aware of include the corruption and loss of data; backup and recovery operations; database response times; record locking; and data integrity, contamination, and validation.

Data Loss and Corruption

Data loss and data corruption are the most serious failures that can occur in a DBMS. Data loss occurs when previously input data can no longer be retrieved, perhaps due to an unintended delete action performed by a database user. **Data corruption** occurs when data is unreadable, incomplete, or damaged. Some database systems include tools for safeguarding and repairing data. For instance, Microsoft Access provides the Compact & Repair Database feature, shown in Figure 12.17. Data backup strategies, discussed next, provide a method for recovering lost or corrupted data.

Backup and Recovery Operations

Every database administrator should develop a **backup and recovery plan** for the DBMS. Data loss can result from a power interruption or equipment failure, and having a recent data backup available enables the administrator to recover the data.

Previously, tape systems were used as the backup storage medium, because tapes were a cheap mass storage medium that could be placed in an offsite safe for protection. While some organizations still use tape systems for backups, disk and flash storage systems now deliver improved backup speed and performance. Newer forms of enterprise data backup software and services enable large-scale backing up over a network, including consolidating backed-up data from multiple locations. Organizations can also use cloud backup systems, including public and hybrid cloud locations, for data backups.

Figure 12.17

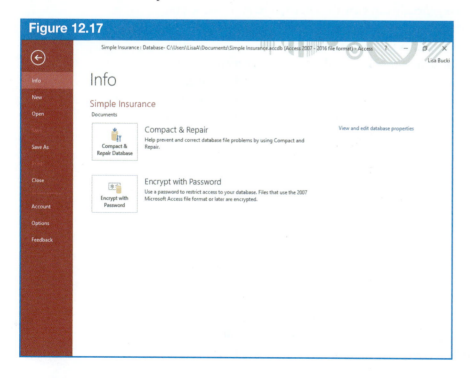

Microsoft Access includes a Compact & Repair feature to help prevent and correct data problems in a database file.

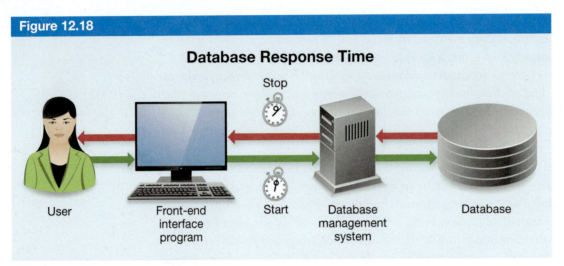

Database response time is the lag time between a user issuing a command and the database system taking action.

Database Response Time

The length of time a database operation takes depends largely on the server's processing and disk speed. The lag time between a user issuing a command and the database system taking action is called the **database response time**. Network conditions may also affect response time if someone is using a remote access method to perform database operations. A distributed database may magnify response time delays, as several servers may have to perform various parts of the entire operation. Figure 12.18 illustrates the lag that's often experienced in a distributed database.

Record Locking

Large database systems typically have many users working with records at any one time. Although two or more users generally can view the same record at the same time without issues, simultaneous attempts to update the same record can cause a problem. **Record locking** occurs when multiple users attempt to edit an existing record, automatically preventing changes from being written to the database, as a safety precaution. The database management system only allows one user at a time to edit or delete a record. While the DBMS processes changes to a record, it locks the record against other changes, displaying an error message for any other user attempting to open and change the locked record.

Data Integrity

The term **data integrity** (sometimes called *data quality*) describes the accuracy of the information provided to database users. A system with high data integrity provides more value to users than a system containing a large percentage of errors. For example, a sales database with high data integrity will produce mailing lists with few incorrect addresses, increasing the percentage of sales material that reaches intended targets and ultimately increasing sales.

   Redundancy, or the duplication of one or more fields of data in multiple tables, is an enemy of data integrity. Having the same field in multiple places creates opportunities for error. For example, an address stored in multiple data tables will need to be changed in all tables. If the address is changed in only one table, it will be accurate in that table but not the others.

Redundancy errors are difficult to weed out, and database administrators spend a good deal of time using up-front checks and data design strategies to locate them. Structuring a database by creating a separate table for each type of data helps normalize it. **Normalization** is the process of structuring a database to avoid redundancy (duplication of entries) and undesirable dependencies (relationships between entries). This makes the database more compact and responsive. Database developers use specific rules (referred to as *normal forms*) to ensure that a database is normalized. The first normal form (1NF) states that there can be only one value per field per record. For example, if a customer has two telephone numbers, you can't put them both in a single *Phone* field for that individual. You must create two different fields: *Phone1*, and *Phone2*.

▶ **Activity 12.6.2**

Article
**Database
Normalization
Basics**

Data Contamination

Once in the system, an error can cause a ripple effect known as **data contamination**. Data contamination involves the spread of incorrect information and can have serious consequences. For instance, in credit reporting, if a company database erroneously shows that a customer has defaulted on a credit purchase, that error will eventually be reported to a credit agency. The customer may then receive a poor credit rating, and the company may be liable for any damages resulting from its mistake. Data validation, described next, helps prevent data contamination.

Data Validation

Among database administrators, the concept of data validation is summed up by the phrase "garbage in, garbage out" (GIGO). As explained in Chapter 1, GIGO means that bad input will result in bad output. That's why administrators use data validation methods to prevent bad data (garbage) from entering a system.

Data validation techniques ensure that users enter correct and complete data into the system. Because errors are far more difficult to detect and remove once they are in the system, preventing errors from being entered in the first place works better to ensure that a database remains error free. Anyone who has ever tried to rectify a billing error will appreciate the difficulties involved in straightening out erroneous information.

Designers and administrators can use a variety of techniques to prevent false data from entering a system. Data validation checks are methods of restricting table and form input so that false data can't be easily entered into the system. Validation methods include checks for referential integrity, range, alphanumeric, consistency, and completeness.

Referential Integrity **Referential integrity** involves making sure that the records entered into tables remain consistent with the relationships between the tables. For example, if you deleted the accounting department record in one table, then all the employee records that listed a key to the accounting department would have an invalid reference to a record that no longer exists. To make sure this doesn't happen, a referential integrity confirms that when you delete a record, other records aren't depending on it for parts of their data to be valid. To continue with our example, to delete the accounting department record without creating an error, you would have to first delete all the employees or change their *Department* field entries to different departments before the database would allow the deletion of the accounting record. Generally, the database designer specifies what, if any, type of referential integrity check to use when creating the relationships.

Range Checks A **range check** is a simple error-checking system usually performed on numeric data entries. For example, to reduce errors in birth date entries, a range check could be created specifying that no birth date prior to 1890 be accepted, since it's unlikely that anyone born before that date is still alive.

Alphanumeric Checks When entering a value for a field, only certain kinds of characters may be allowed. An **alphanumeric check** allows only letters of the alphabet and digits to be entered. This check will prevent users from entering incorrect characters, such as a dollar sign ($) in a customer home address field and text in a date/time field; see the error message in Figure 12.19, for example. Some DBMSs also enable the database designer to set up a check based on specific formatting for the field, such as a particular date format applied to a field with the date/time data type.

Consistency Checks A **consistency check** is made against previously entered data that has already been validated. For example, a validation system will indicate an error if a user attempts to enter a phone number or social security number that doesn't match previously validated information for the item. Microsoft Access includes a Table Analyzer Wizard to help find and remove duplicated and mistyped information. The wizard also enables you to create a Delete query, to help find and remove unneeded data.

Completeness Checks A **completeness check** ensures that every required field in a record contains an entry. Given the natural human tendency to tire of entering data, users often try to skip fields during input. To prevent missing data in important fields, the database designer can mark a field as "required," so that when a user tries to save the record without an entry in that field, a warning like the one in Figure 12.20 appears. Having an empty field, for example, a credit card number without the expiration date—can prevent other steps, such as processing the order with the incomplete credit card information.

Figure 12.19

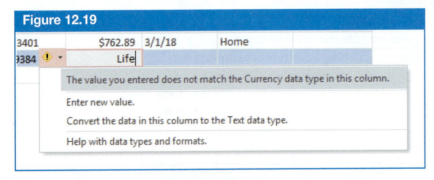

Data validation requires complete and accurate input. This Microsoft Access error displays if the user tries to enter a text value in a currency field.

Figure 12.20

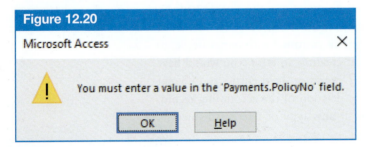

The user might see this kind of warning after failing to enter data in a required field.

Recheck 12.6

Recheck your understanding of the concepts covered by this objective.

12.7 Finding Meaning in Big Data

Precheck 12.7

Check your understanding of the concepts covered by this objective.

With the rise of the Internet and the cloud—as well as the new services that run on them, such as e-commerce and social media—the amount of data created and stored by human beings continues to explode (as shown in Figure 12.21). The term *big data* refers not just to the sheer amount of data being produced on a daily basis today. In addition, the term **big data** represents an emerging branch of information technology dealing with transforming large amounts of unstructured data into useful information using new methods. *Big data* also might refer to any sort of large and complex or unstructured data set.

What does *unstructured data* mean? Simply stated, any type of data that doesn't lend itself to being organized into records, tables, or cubes. For example, millions of users post on Facebook, tweet on Twitter, and upload on YouTube every day. The sorts of data involved in these actions don't lend themselves to storage and analysis in a traditional database system. Other sets of data are so vast and complicated that traditional systems lack the tools for extracting meaningful information from them. Examples of this type of data include the wealth of weather information gathered moment by moment around the world, the increasing amount of health information

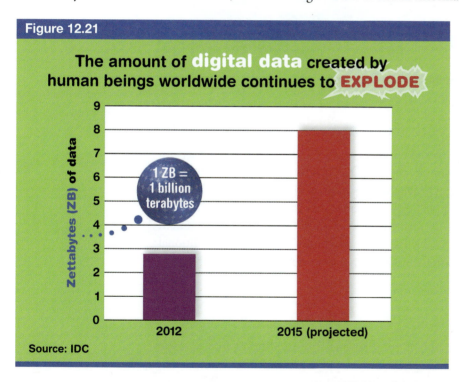

Figure 12.21

The amount of **digital data** created by human beings worldwide continues to **EXPLODE**

Zettabytes (ZB) of data

1 ZB = 1 billion terabytes

2012   2015 (projected)

Source: IDC

Tech Ethics 🏛 🏛 🏛 🏛 🏛 🏛 🏛

What about Data Privacy?

Data mining can reveal a lot about a person. For example, drugstore data about a person's purchases over time might give indications of whether he or she has particular ailments. Many organizations that gather data about customers and users by law have a privacy policy and must issue a written copy of that policy periodically. Banks and credit card companies routinely include privacy policy information with statements. Most medical providers also must now implement and follow a privacy policy.

How concerned are you about data privacy? Should you be more concerned? Why or why not?

Figure 12.22

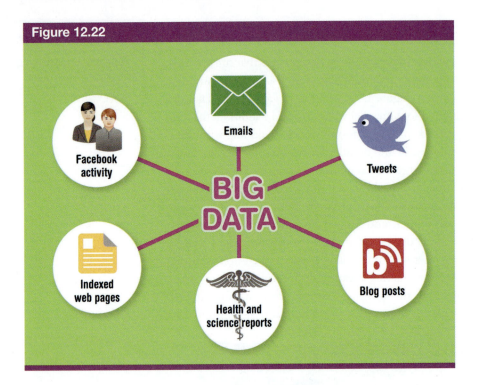

stored digitally, and even the number of web pages indexed by various search engines. Figure 12.22 illustrates some of these types of data.

Methods for Dealing with Big Data

Emerging new databases provide methods to start looking at dynamic ways to store and evaluate large sets of data. For example, the NoSQL open source standard, adopted in database products such as MongoDB, enables documents to be arranged without the use of organizational schemas, or via flexible schemas that can be changed as needed. These databases can store items by identifying key values (metadata), as document stores, or even as graph databases. Beyond those additional models, three additional emerging methods help organizations evaluate large collections of data:

- Data mining
- Analytics
- Data visualization

Data Mining **Data mining** involves using advanced computing to find patterns and relationships in large sets of data in order to apply an organizing structure and extract information. For example, a large retailer might process millions of POS transactions per day involving tens of thousands of different products. Data mining would help the retailer uncover hidden sales trends. A large health organization could use data mining to find emerging patterns of adverse drug reactions and then take action to protect people. Or data mining could uncover how certain weather readings evolve second by second over the course of a powerful storm.

The data-mining process involves using multiple disciplines—such as advanced statistics, artificial intelligence, and artificial neural networks (pattern recognition models that learn through training)—to summarize and extract the relevant data into a useful set of information. The process also typically involves a number of stages, from preparing the data to building and validating the model that will be used to examine the data.

Analytics Analytics takes the data-mining outcome further. In addition to discovering meaningful patterns in data, **analytics** includes communicating insights about data, as well as using data to make more informed business decisions in pursuit of improved business performance. Analytics often includes charts and other visual representations of the data. The business intelligence yielded by analytics helps companies target actions more effectively. For example, a company can analyze a set of customers based on past purchasing behavior, and extend special coupons and offers only to those customers most likely to act on them. Analytics requires serious computational power. For that reason, a big data analytics project or service might distribute the data across multiple computers that can perform computations in parallel (at the same time). A popular open source framework called *Hadoop* provides this capability, resulting in its growing use.

Web analytics services analyze and report on the behavior of visitors to a website. For example, Google Analytics (Figure 12.23) tracks how visitors to a particular website behave, so the website's operator can identify key audiences by a variety of metrics, including affinity categories (groups of people who share common hobbies, likes, and preferences), demographics, and location, as well as whether visitors viewed the site via a desktop system or a mobile device. Having these details can help the operator identify key audiences and evaluate what website changes will have a real impact.

In its Top 10 Technology Predictions for 2014, ICD predicted that big data analytics services spending would exceed $4.5 billion in 2014. Not only are organizations spending heavily on their own analytics projects, but they are also purchasing analytics capabilities. For example, a company might expand its data-processing capabilities via **Hardware as a Service (HaaS)**, essentially paying for hardware on an ongoing basis (like a subscription), rather than purchasing it outright. Or rather than build in-house analytics expertise, a company might use a **Big data as a Service (BdaaS)** provider, buying analysis tools and information from an outside company such as SnapLogic.

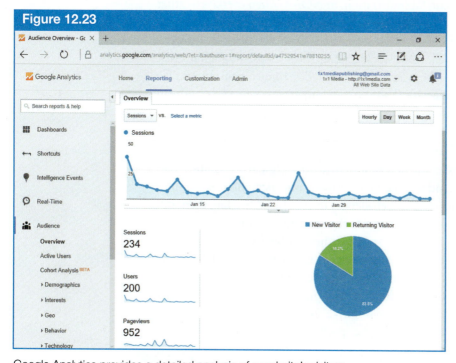

Figure 12.23

Google Analytics provides a detailed analysis of a website's visitors.

Figure 12.24

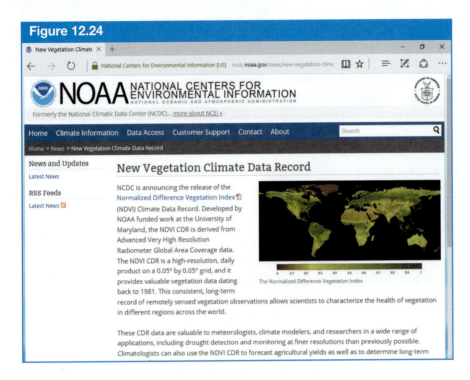

Visualization helps communicate complex data sets, revealing patterns, clusters, and extremes graphically.

Data Visualization Any method of presenting numeric data visually to help make the data more understandable represents the process of **data visualization**. For example, the charts and infographics included throughout this book serve as basic visualizations of the data they illustrate. Big-data analysts often prefer to use visualization to present data, because the visualization can reveal patterns and transitions that may be hard to pick up when reviewing numeric data alone.

For example, the National Centers for Environmental Information (part of the National Oceanic and Atmospheric Administration, or NOAA) often overlays weather and Earth surface data on maps (Figure 12.24), so viewers can review a visual representation of how the collected data evolved over time. Data visualization provides value in many other fields, as well, from stock trading "heat maps" to graphics that map hot topics and trends in social media. As with analytics, some organizations take advantage of **Visualization as a Service (VaaS)** to tap into experts who can transform the organization's data into stunning visuals.

More Big-Data Examples

In addition to helping businesses operate more efficiently, big data, analytics, and data visualization offer the potential to enhance human understanding of complex problems, potentially identifying risks and challenges to come, and heading them off. See big data, analytics, and data visualization in action in ways like this:

- Weather information organizations, such as the National Centers for Environmental Information, can take advantage of the data collected by many sources—for instance, ground-based weather sensors and highly accurate weather satellites—to make weather predictions for increasingly smaller micro areas. Better weather data can improve storm warnings and safety, as well as help farmers better prepare for the specific weather conditions in their immediate areas.

Figure 12.25

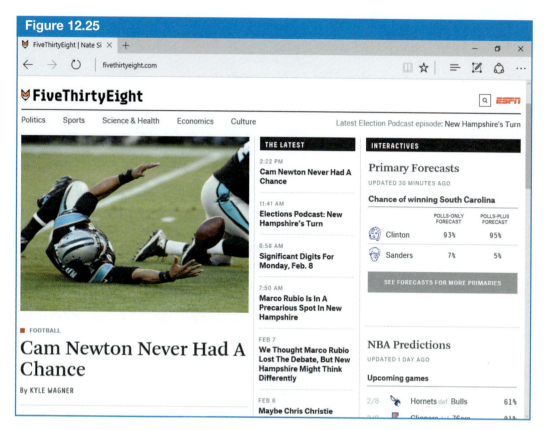

The website FiveThirtyEight, which was founded by Nate Silver, offers interesting news and data analysis on such diverse topics as politics, sports, science and health, economics, and culture.

- Geographic information systems (GISs) can store, analyze, and visualize geographic data for city and county government decision making and planning, such as emergency and disaster planning. Private entities also can take advantage of GIS data, sometimes called *spatial analytics*. The Open Geospatial Consortium (OGC) is an industry-based, international consortium focused on developing publicly available GIS interface standards to help make data and information services available for all types of applications. The ArcGIS desktop software by Esri even comes in a low-cost licensed version that home users can use to develop GIS skills or use them for volunteer projects.

- Political statistics expert Nate Silver gained notice for creating highly accurate models for predicting election outcomes, often presented in compelling graphical formats. Silver and his colleagues continue to present interesting and useful news and data analysis at the website he founded, FiveThirtyEight (see Figure 12.25).

- According to Gartner, Inc., "By 2017, 40 percent of utilities with smart metering solutions will use cloud-based big data analytics to address asset-, commodity-, customer- or revenue-related needs." Advanced metering will help utilities better manage the flow of electricity based on real-time data from the grid, balancing loads as needed and leading to more effective services. Customers will be able to use web interfaces to monitor their meter usage data and adjust their behaviors.

Recheck **12.7**
Recheck your understanding of the concepts covered by this objective.

Chapter Summary

➡️ *An interactive **Chapter Summary**, **Study Notes**, and a **Slide Presentation** with audio are available from the links menu on this page in your ebook.*

12.1 Understanding Database Basics

A **database** is a computerized system for storing information in an organized manner so that it can be searched for and retrieved when needed. Data associated with other useful data becomes information. Databases organize data in a hierarchical fashion, storing information about **entities** in the form of **fields**, **records**, and **data tables** or data files. The most common database application is an information system, which is a system of computer hardware, software, and operating procedures.

12.2 Looking at Database Management System Software

Database management system (DBMS) software controls databases. **Keys** are attributes that can be used to identify a set of information, and the designer designates the most important field in a record as the **primary key**. **Data browsing** is the process of moving through a database file, examining each record and looking for information. A **query** enables the user to specify criteria designed to retrieve matching information. **Structured Query Language (SQL)** is the most popular database query language. A DBMS also provides **security measures** to protect and safeguard data. **Metadata** is information about data, and a **data dictionary** holds the body of metadata for a database. Backup and **recovery** utilities provide methods for backing up and restoring lost data.

12.3 Exploring Types of Databases

Databases are often categorized by the way they organize data (**data models**), or by their function (**operational databases** and **data warehouses**). Common data models include **flat file databases**, **relational databases**, **object-oriented databases**, **multimedia databases**, **multidimensional databases**, and **hybrid databases**.

12.4 Planning and Designing Database Systems

The job of planning and designing a database system is usually performed by a **database analyst**. The development and maintenance of database structures and applications uses a methodology called the **database management approach**. A database designer uses **database objects** to build the **front-end interface** program and the reporting features. A **form** window enables the user to enter data into the database. A **report** presents a formatted body of output from a database. You can limit the records displayed in a table using filtering criteria called **data filters**, so that only the subset of matching data appears.

12.5 Using Databases

The activities performed with a database are referred to as **data processing**. With **batch processing**, data processing occurs at a scheduled time, or when a critical point has been reached. **Transactional processing** happens as the user makes changes to the database, and tends to be done with smaller databases or with operational databases that require all information to be current. **Online transactional processing (OLTP)** is used at e-commerce websites requiring fast, always-on processing.

12.6 Describing the Areas of Database Administration

A **database administrator (DBA)** maintains and updates the DBMS software. The DBA also develops and maintains the **backup and recovery plan** to recover data in the event of data loss or **data corruption**. Organizations may store backups on a variety of media, including tape, disk, flash, and cloud. The lag time between a user issuing a command and the database system taking action is called the **database response time**. **Record locking** is an automatic protection process that occurs when multiple users attempt to edit an existing record. **Data validation** is the process of making certain that the data entered into the system is both correct and complete. Validation ensures **data integrity** (or data quality) and protects against **redundancy**. The process of structuring a database so it avoids redundancy and dependency is called **normalization.** Other validation techniques check **referential integrity**, **range**, **alphanumeric**, **consistency**, and **completeness**.

12.7 Finding Meaning in Big Data

The term **big data** refers to working with large and complex data sets to uncover existing patterns, as well as the datasets themselves. **Analytics** applies additional statistical and other techniques to data to reveal predictive patterns for business decision making. Analysts often present analytics outcomes in graphic forms. **Data visualization** methods include ways of presenting data visually to make it more understandable. All three of these techniques now can be used by various public and private organizations to improve understanding and decision making.

Key Terms

Numbers indicate the pages where terms are first cited with their full definition in the chapter. An alphabetized list of key terms with definitions is included in the end-of-book glossary.

*An interactive **Glossary** is available from the links menu on this page in your ebook.*

Chapter Exercises

Complete the following exercises to assess your understanding of the material covered in this chapter.

 *Interactive **Flash Cards** and an interactive **Game** are available from the links menu on this page in your ebook.*

Go to your SNAP Assignments page to complete the Terms Check, Knowledge Check, Key Principles, and Tech Illustrated exercises.

Terms Check: Matching

Match each term with its definition.

a.	report	f.	flat file database
b.	data warehouse	g.	data corruption
c.	field	h.	form
d.	recovery	i.	metadata
e.	relational database	j.	query

___ 1. Describes the structure, specifications, and purpose of each element in a database.

___ 2. Takes place when the database administrator uses the most recent backup to restore data.

___ 3. The type of database in which fields with similar data can be connected between data tables in the database.

___ 4. A traditional data file storage system that contains only one data table or file.

___ 5. Presents output from a data table or query.

___ 6. A screen or dialog box used to enter data in a database.

___ 7. A single value, such as a name.

___ 8. Occurs when data is unreadable, incomplete, or damaged.

___ 9. Stores data gathered from one or more databases.

___ 10. Used to display a list of records that match specified criteria.

Knowledge Check: Multiple Choice

Choose the best answer for each question.

1. In a database, which field would be the best choice for the primary key?
   a. first name
   b. last name
   c. age
   d. social security number

2. Which data type is used to embed nontextual information, such as pictures?
   a. hyperlink
   b. object
   c. memo
   d. sequence

3. Which type of database runs using languages, platforms, or models that are no longer supported by an organization's current database system?
   a. flat file database
   b. legacy database
   c. object-oriented database
   d. multimedia database

4. In a relational database model, a *field* is called a(n)
   a. attribute.
   b. entity.
   c. object.
   d. tuple.

5. Which of the following is database management system software?
   a. Microsoft Access
   b. Microsoft DBMS
   c. Microsoft Word
   d. XML database

6. Which type of processing updates the database immediately after a transaction occurs?
   a. batch processing
   b. data filtering
   c. hybrid processing
   d. transactional processing

7. Which term describes the accuracy of the information provided to database users?
   a. data contamination
   b. data integrity
   c. data redundancy
   d. database normalization

8. Which term describes the ripple effect that can occur as a result of an error in a database?
   a. data contamination
   b. data integrity
   c. data redundancy
   d. data validation

9. Which type of check ensures that every required field in a record contains an entry?
   a. alphanumeric check
   b. consistency check
   c. completeness check
   d. range check

10. Which of the following involves using advanced computing to find patterns and relationships in large sets of data to apply an organizing structure and extract information?
    a. data browsing
    b. data mining
    c. data structuring
    d. data visualization

 Key Principles: Completion

Complete each statement with the appropriate word or phrase.

1. The most common data types are numeric and _____.

2. When data processing occurs at a scheduled time, the type of processing is called _____.

3. A popular query language is _____.

4. The body of metadata for the entire database is collected by the _____.

5. A database that uses different models together to handle data is called a _____.

6. A retail store's inventory-tracking system is typically classified as a(n) _____.

7. To display only a list of customers with last names that start with the letter *B*, you should apply a _____.

8. A _____ is a business activity that is central to the nature of an enterprise, such as a product being sold or an airline flight being booked.

9. The individual that handles the day-to-day operations of a database is called the _____.

10. _____ represents an emerging branch of information technology that deals with transforming large amounts of unstructured data into useful information using new methods.

Tech Illustrated: Figure Labeling

Fill in the blanks with the correct labels.

1. Data table design

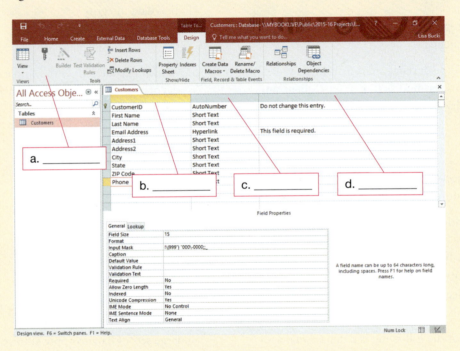

2. Accessing a database

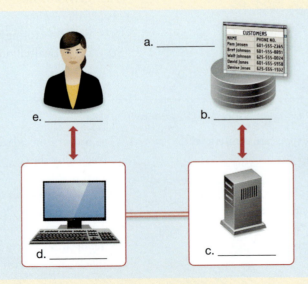

Tech to Come: Brainstorming New Uses

In groups or individually, contemplate the following questions and develop as many answers as you can.

1. An optical eye reader can identify your retina signature. Using this technology will allow an individual to glance at the reader and generate a positive identification. How might this technology affect the way databases operate? What type or types of databases could benefit from this technology?

2. Database performance is measured by the ability to read and write data from persistent storage.

Historically, persistent storage has been in the form of magnetic spinning disks. Solid state disk (SSD) technology allows for an increase in database performance. Research this technology. How widely is it used? Why should companies upgrade to this technology? Is there anything that would stop them from upgrading to this technology?

Tech Literacy: Internet Research and Writing

Conduct Internet research to find the information described, and then develop appropriate written responses based on your research. Be sure to document your sources using the MLA format. (See Chapter 1, Tech Literacy: Internet Research and Writing, page 38, to review MLA style guidelines.)

1. NoSQL databases have become an alternative to SQL databases. Explain the differences between an SQL and a NoSQL database. What are the benefits of using a NoSQL database?

2. Databases are used to track data about crimes, including DNA evidence. Conduct research on databases used by law enforcement agencies at the state and national levels to track crime data. Use actual case examples to explain how these databases help law enforcement officials to solves crimes and share information.

3. A lot of personal information is stored in online databases, which means privacy and security breaches are issues of concern. Is your personal data safe when you make an online purchase? Describe a recent security breach that happened to a major retailer or company. Who

is responsible when a security breach happens? What can you do to protect your personal data?

4. Major vendors in the database retail market include Oracle, MySQL, and Microsoft SQL server. Research these three vendors or other vendors in this market, and compare database features between products. Include a cost comparison and statistics on usage in the industry.

5. The widespread use of databases has created a demand for professional database administrators, designers, and developers. Research the database career path. What education is required? What technology and application knowledge are companies looking for? What type of salary is available? Analyze whether you think this is a good career path.

Tech Issues: Team Problem-Solving

In groups, develop possible solutions to the issues presented.

1. You have been hired to design a relational database for a new restaurant. What fields, records, and data files/tables will make up your database? Sketch the relationships you will create between the tables. What data validation techniques will you use to ensure the data is complete and correct?

2. Because so much valuable and important information is stored in databases, having a backup and recovery plan is critical. If you owned a business, how would you back up your database? How often would the database need to be backed up? If you needed to recover data, how would the recovery process work?

Tech Timeline: Predicting Next Steps

Look at the timeline below outlining the history of credit cards. Research this topic and try to predict the next logical steps by completing the timeline through 2030.

1914 Western Union gives out metal cards providing credit privileges to preferred customers. These cards come to be known as "metal money."

1924 General Petroleum Corporation issues the first "metal money" for gasoline purchases.

1938 AT&T introduces the "Bell System Credit Card." Airlines and railroads soon reveal their own similar cards.

1959 Many banks offer the option of revolving credit, allowing people to make monthly payments on balances owed, rather than having to pay them at one time.

1966 Fourteen US banks form Interlink (later known as *Visa Card*), a new association with the ability to exchange information on credit card transactions.

2000 Smart cards grow dramatically in Europe and Asia, becoming the dominant form of electronic payment.

2001 Disposable credit cards, good for one use only, become popular for online consumer purchases.

2003 Orbiscom introduces ControlPay technology, which allows the primary credit card accountholder to control spending limits and locations for various family members.

2004 PayPal reaches 50 million account holders worldwide for its online payment service.

2008 The average US household carries about $8,700 in credit card debt.

2012 56 percent of Americans are concerned about someone obtaining and using their credit or debit card information.

2013 278 million Visa cards are issued in the United States.

2015 Despite an October 1 deadline, the majority of cardholders had not received new, more secure chip-enabled credit cards and the majority of merchants did not have the required chip card terminals.

Ethical Dilemmas: Group Discussion and Debate

As a class or within an assigned group, discuss the following ethical dilemma.

Websites often collect and store data about users who have visited or purchased items from them. Sometimes, data collection is accomplished by placing "cookies" on the hard drive of a user's computer, which are read the next time the user navigates to that site. Other times, a website requires a user to register and provide personal information to access "premium" features on the site. Many users offer this information without thinking about the privacy implications of sharing their personal data. Because of consumer privacy concerns, websites typically post privacy policies that outline how they are storing visitors' personal information, what they do with it, and whether they share it with other parties.

Read the privacy policies on three sites that you visit frequently.

Do you feel differently about visiting this site or providing personal information to it after reading the privacy policy? Why or why not?

Research what actions you can take if a company violates its own privacy policy.

Glimpsing the Future of Computing

Chapter Goal

To learn about emerging technologies that are likely to impact the future of computing

Learning Objectives

13.1 Explain and give examples of how technology incorporated into traditional equipment and electronics improves performance and functionality.

13.2 Discuss the possible applications for 3-D printing and displays.

13.3 Explain what role special project labs play in pushing the technology envelope.

13.4 Describe the field of artificial intelligence and list some of its practical applications.

13.5 Distinguish between new and emerging computing methods such as quantum computing and older computing architectures.

Green go-online icons indicate resources that are accessed from the links menu in your ebook.

SNAP icons indicate interactive resources that are available in SNAP. Go to your SNAP Assignments page to complete these quizzes, activities, and exercises.

13.1 Making Old Tech New

Precheck 13.1
Check your understanding of the concepts covered by this objective.

The term *convergence* carries many meanings. In the worlds of business and technology, **convergence** occurs when differing technologies and industries merge to form a newer, better product or process. For example, Chapter 1 looked at a number of different consumer products that now include embedded computing technology, allowing consumers to control the products wirelessly via smartphone, among other activities. While adding computing and communications technology to small devices brings about significant changes for individual users, this section examines a few examples of how adding computing technology to larger-scale systems can bring benefits to all stakeholders—operators, individual users, and society at large.

The Smart Grid and Smart Power Meters

The electric power grid and home and business power management in the United States have until recent years lagged behind in integrating any form of computing or communications technology. This lag resulted in part from the daunting scale of modernizing power delivery and management infrastructure.

The power grid consists of wires, substations, transformers, switches, and many other types of equipment. As illustrated in Figure 13.1, the first part of the

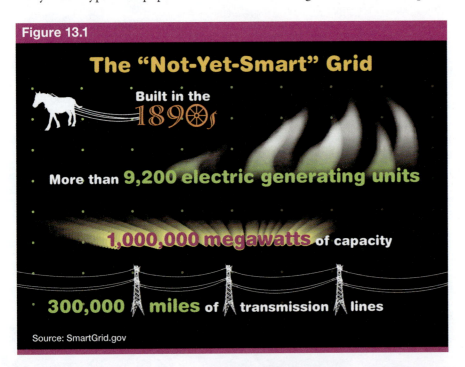

Figure 13.1

The "Not-Yet-Smart" Grid

Built in the 1890s

More than **9,200 electric generating units**

1,000,000 megawatts of capacity

300,000 miles of transmission lines

Source: SmartGrid.gov

Tracking Down Tech ❯❯❯❯❯

Back to the Future

Storytellers often predict events and developments that later become realities. For example, French science fiction writer Jules Verne predicted the development of the electric submarine, radio and TV newscasts, and video conferencing, among other technologies. To take your own look at how science fiction might predict real-world technologies like those that continue to emerge today, complete this movie scavenger hunt to find fictional technologies that may or may not have become real.

existing grid was built in the nineteenth century. As it grew and scattered local grids became tied together to form a national grid in the twentieth century, the size of the grid became a roadblock to modernization. The many millions of residential and business customers tied to the grid posed an additional challenge.

The old technology in the grid presented a lot of downsides—chiefly, that most operations required time-consuming human labor. For example, even though home and business locations had long been equipped with meters to monitor power usage, individuals known as *meter readers* had to visit meters on a monthly basis to gather the consumption quantities used to calculate customers' bills. Similarly, workers had to manually test lines for proper voltage and inspect equipment of all types for potential defects. Power producers (utilities) and grid operators had to plan for anticipated peaks in usage and attempt to balance load delivery accordingly, and small failures could lead to larger outages called *brownouts*. In the case of smaller, more local power outages, the utilities relied on customers to phone in outage reports and potential causes, such as downed trees across power lines. Various inefficiencies in the transmission grid also led to leakage, or the loss of some of the power between the production site and the customer using the power. In the age of instant performance metrics and immediate two-way communications, with loads of computers and other devices relying on the grid to deliver power consistently, the old grid began seeming "not yet smart."

All these problems resulted from the fact that the old grid technology worked as a one-way system. Power flowed from the utility to the customer over transmission lines, but nothing flowed back. While enhancements to increase grid efficiencies were made between the 1960s and 1980s, in the early 1990s, operators began to build automation into parts of the grid—for example, enabling local substations to manage electricity loads automatically. Throughout the 1990s, clean air legislation produced a more serious push for cleaner energy sources, as well as cleaner vehicles driven all or in part by electricity. The electric industry itself began developing better standards for interoperability, automation, and two-way communication across the grid. By the late 1990s, the term *Smart Grid* was being used to describe the new direction for the electric power grid.

So, what exactly does the term mean? **Smart Grid** refers to the technology being added to the electric grid to bring it into the twenty-first century, including computer, communication, automation, and sensing technologies. The Smart Grid allows for two-way communication and computer-based monitoring and automation of other activities. Much like devices in a regular computer network, devices attached to the Smart Grid can communicate to the utility's network operations center (NOC). Smart Grid devices include sensors such as power meters, voltage sensors, and fault detectors to gather data, as well as digital communication capabilities for sending the data to the NOC or another location. (Older devices may still use analog communications.)

Smart Grid technology delivers these benefits:

- **More efficient electric power production and transmission.** When fully implemented, the Smart Grid will be able to manage loads better, calling for more power production when needed and directing power to the areas of highest demand. Automation enables this to occur with lower operations costs, potentially resulting in lower power costs. Plus, updating or replacing aged and obsolete parts of the grid will provide a more efficient energy infrastructure overall.

- **Faster recovery from outages.** Smart Grid technology can detect and isolate outages, and reroute power around an outage where possible. Outage reporting from the grid means that utilities can deploy repair crews more rapidly.

 Activity 13.1.1

Video
The Smart Grid and Smart Meters

- **Increased security.** The ongoing upgrades to the grid will make it more durable in the event of a natural disaster or terrorist attack. Plus, the Smart Grid can reroute power to emergency services first in the case of an event-related outage.
- **Improved ability to integrate renewable energy systems.** Renewable energy generation systems vary in scale from small residential customer production to utility-sized installations in deserts. Because some types (wind, solar) also typically vary quite a bit in the amount of power they produce throughout each day, Smart Grid technology helps ensure their uneven power loads enter the grid without causing other problems.
- **More information and control for consumers.** The Smart Grid can work with the **smart meter**: a device that tracks electricity usage at a residential or commer-

cial customer site and sends the meter reading (often over a secure wireless connection via low radio frequency) to the energy supplier for billing and other purposes (see Figure 13.2). The utility also can turn service on and off remotely, saving travel and labor time. Depending on the utility and the type of smart meter installed, the consumer may be able to see usage details via an in-home display or online, though not all services may be offered immediately after installation. Some utilities partner with a service such as MyUsage.com to give customers an online location for accessing power consumption information. By 2012, more than 43 million smart meters had been installed for residential, commercial, and industrial electric users in the United States.

Figure 13.2

A Smart Meter

The OpenWay CENTRON smart meter, produced by Itron, can calculate detailed usage and other data and then transmit that data to an electric utility via two-way radio frequency wireless communication.

Hotspot

From Smart Meter to Free Wi-Fi

Because the electric utility serving a given area needs to deploy a secure wireless network to collect smart meter data, the utility also could decide to make access to that network available for other purposes. For example, the utility could allow the local government or its employees to access the network using mobile devices to cut down on the costs of mobile phone data.

In 2013, Silicon Valley Power (SVP) became the first US utility to take the concept one step further, offering free Wi-Fi to everyone throughout the city of Santa Clara,

California, for low-bandwidth services, such as email and basic browsing. (The network doesn't support high-bandwidth activities, such as streaming audio and video and interactive gaming.) The network features two channels: a highly encrypted channel to transmit meter data and an unencrypted channel for the free Wi-Fi data. The public network also takes advantage of the wireless infrastructure in the city, which it purchased from an older wireless service called *MetroFi*. More than 3,000 people took advantage of the service during its first week alone.

Note that in addition to the electric industry, other utilities also employ smart technologies to improve delivery and service. For example, some water and natural gas providers also use smart meters to enhance service and reduce expenses.

Smart Medical Systems and Devices

Prior chapters in this book touched on the fact that information systems technology stands poised to be part of big changes in how medical providers gather, store, and share patient medical information. For example, doctors and other healthcare professionals will be able to access patient records from a single source, and take advantage of online data to help with diagnosis and treatment. The use of computers, tablets, and communications technology in healthcare is sometimes referred to as **eHealth**.

Newer devices and systems take this concept a step further. Smart medical devices with built-in communications capabilities will be able to monitor a patient's vital signs and other metrics in a healthcare facility or in his own home. These devices include sensors that touch the skin, gathering data and automatically transmitting that data to the healthcare provider. This **mHealth** practice will employ these medical devices, along with connected mobile (smartphone) apps and software, to enhance patient monitoring and healthcare. The smart medical devices will include various types of sensors continuously collecting data about everything from blood oxygen and glucose content to blood pressure. The devices connect wirelessly (via Bluetooth or Wi-Fi) or via USB to a mobile device or PC to transmit the collected data.

For example, patients with chronic respiratory diseases—such as chronic obstructive pulmonary disease (COPD), congestive heart failure (CHF), and asthma—can use a wireless finger

Tech Career Explorer

Getting Hands-On as an Engineer or IT Pro

Technology development and convergence lead to quite a bit of overlap between career disciplines, including IT and other forms of engineering. For example, while a computer engineer might design a new type of ultrabook, another specialist, such as an engineering technologist, might be involved with testing the ultrabook's ability to withstand mechanical shocks. To learn more about careers that require an applied approach to technical skills, complete this exercise.

Practical TECH

Smart Meter Verification

Smart meters should be more accurate than the meters they replace. However, all meters need calibration and verification. If you suspect that a newly installed smart meter may not be properly calibrated, you can start by checking that the value for the electricity, gas, or water calculated by the meter actually matches what the meter reports to the utility company. To do so, look at your last bill and determine the first and last days of the next full billing cycle. On the first day of the billing cycle, go to the meter (usually outdoors, unless the utility company also provided an indoor monitoring device), and write down the number shown on the meter. On the last day of the billing cycle, do the same, and then subtract the first value from the second to find the total amount of the utility consumed. When your next bill arrives, compare the amount billed versus what you calculated from your meter readings to make sure the values match. After you report any discrepancy, the utility company can use its own diagnostics and calibration tools to double-check the meter function. (Note that this same method can be used to check traditional meters.)

In some cases, a utility company may allow customers to monitor and double-check usage via a third-party, in-home display (IHD). For example, PG&E enables customers to purchase a third-party display such as the Aztech Energy Information Display, available for around $50 from the manufacturer. This particular IHD uses the ZigBee Smart Energy standard, so any smart meter it communicates with must be ZigBee capable, as well.

pulse oximeter like the one shown in Figure 13.3 to monitor blood oxygen level and pulse. A patient can check her levels while at home or on the go, and then use the device's built-in Bluetooth to send data to a mobile device or PC, sharing it with her physician from there. Having this technology enables the patient to maintain a normal lifestyle, while still providing adequate monitoring information to her healthcare professional. Other current and future examples of medical monitoring devices that communicate wirelessly or connect with mobile devices for sharing data with medical professionals include heart rhythm and rate monitors, blood glucose monitors, wireless blood pressure monitors, body fat meters, and even shirts with heart rate sensors woven in the fabric.

Beyond such small, external monitoring devices, other types of smart medical devices in use and in development both within and outside of healthcare facilities include:

- Implantable sensors that perform tasks such as heart rate monitoring, blood glucose monitoring, and medication delivery
- Robots that monitor patients and even perform surgery
- Smart beds and bar coding for home healthcare
- Smartphone add-on devices and companion apps for performing diagnostics in remote areas, such as for eye exams and ultrasounds
- Orthopedic surgeon Christopher Kaeding, MD, used Google Glass to stream live video of a surgery from Ohio State University's Wexner Medical Center
- Other smart hospital equipment, such as digital stethoscopes (see Figure 13.4), tumor-tracking and radiation delivery systems (such as Calypso), and radio frequency identification (RFID) tools

Each year, the number of health- and fitness-tracking devices sold to consumers and professionals continues to increase, and tens of millions of Bluetooth-equipped devices are included among them. As might be expected, for some types of these devices to work together, new standards and approaches have been developed. (The level of security and privacy called for with regard to medical information in part drives the need for new standards.) For example, many health- and fitness-tracking devices use the **Bluetooth Health Device Profile (HDP)** standard developed for medical device data transmission.

In 2013, the firm research2guidance estimated that the mHealth market would grow to $26 billion worldwide by 2017, and noted that about 97,000 mobile health apps were

Figure 13.3

A Wireless Finger Pulse Oximeter

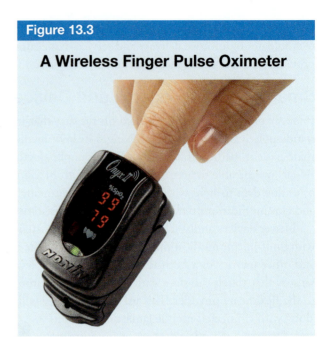

Nonin Medical's Onyx II 9560 finger pulse oximeter with Bluetooth wireless technology monitors blood oxygen saturation levels and pulse and then sends the data via Bluetooth to the patient's smartphone, tablet, or PC.

Figure 13.4

A Digital Stethoscope

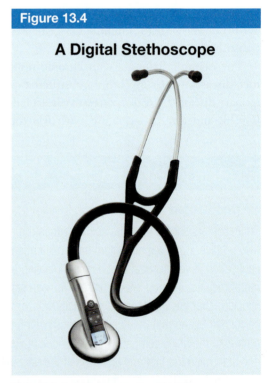

This digital stethoscope, the 3M Littmann Electronic Stethoscope Model 3200, provides sound noise reduction and recording and transmits recorded sounds via Bluetooth for later evaluation. The software included with the stethoscope also enables visualization of the recorded sound.

already in use. Some smart devices are supported by multiple apps. For example, the Zephyr HxM BT wireless fitness heart rate monitor can be used with dozens of apps, including Runtastic and Sports Tracker. Using a specific app works great for tracking specific health or fitness information, but usually doesn't capture enough detail or handle data consistently enough for overall medical monitoring.

Other systems address the need for a more comprehensive approach to smart medical technology. For example, consumers can take advantage of the free HealthVault service from Microsoft. Figure 13.5 provides a snapshot of some of what HealthVault lets users do. Not only can you upload health information to your account (including X-rays and other images), but you can also collect records for emergencies and other situations (such as when you need to provide a child's medical records to school or for a sports team) and review your overall health picture. In addition, you can share your HealthVault information securely with your physician or other healthcare provider. HealthVault also works with numerous compatible apps and smart devices, including the wireless oximeter shown in Figure 13.3. So, for example, once you have uploaded the latest data from the oximeter to HealthVault, you can share it with the appropriate doctor, other medical staff person, or other trusted people. Some labs, pharmacies, hospitals, and clinics also will transmit lab results and other records to a patient's HealthVault account.

Other organizations are working to create more comprehensive ecosystems for the use of smart medical technologies in hospitals and beyond. For example, Qualcomm Life has developed the 2net and the HealthyCircles platforms to help integrate smart medical devices using wireless cellular technology with the systems used by healthcare service companies (which manage specific diseases, such as diabetes) and healthcare providers. Similarly, the Continua Health Alliance aims to create an ecosystem where smart medical and fitness devices work together with other health and fitness services in the areas of health and wellness, chronic disease management, and independent aging. The Continua Health Alliance doesn't create new standards; instead, it creates

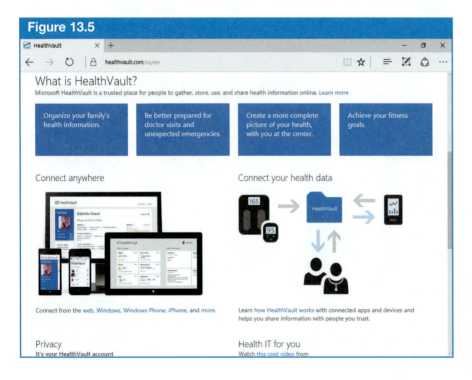

Figure 13.5

You can use HealthVault from Microsoft to track health and fitness information in a central online location and then share the information with your healthcare practitioners.

design guidelines that help to address gaps in existing interoperability standards. It operates a certification program, and products meeting certification are granted the right to display a certification logo to help consumers identify them.

Smart Technology in Transportation

Like the power consumption and healthcare industries, the transportation industry provides a ripe arena for new tech developments. As you learned in Chapter 1, modern cars include numerous sensors, as well as software and computing technology. These capabilities provide car owners with some useful features, such as greater monitoring for problems in vehicle operation. However, vehicles represent just one segment of the transportation industry.

In the trucking industry, for example, hundreds of thousands of trucks consume tens of billions of gallons of fuel and move nearly 70 percent of the freight tonnage and most shipments of consumer products in the United States. Like a regular auto-mobile, a truck driven at higher speeds consumes more fuel (not to mention being a safety issue), so trucking companies may install electronic engine controls to limit drivers' speeds. Reducing truck speed from 75 mph to 65 mph can improve fuel use by 27 percent. Today's trucks are equipped with sensors, GPS, and other technology that gather data for real-time analysis, to provide further feedback to drivers about how they can alter their driving behaviors to conserve fuel, save time, and drive more safely.

GE and AT&T have partnered to add wireless technology to a variety of transportation and other devices, including jet engines, locomotives (trains), turbines, and medical devices. The jet and train engines can communicate data via the cloud, providing remote tracking, monitoring, operation, and optimization of these machines. GE has also developed a software platform called *Predix* to provide a standard interface for connecting with these intelligent machines and using analytics to

Activity 13.1.2

Article
Computer Engineering

Practical TECH

Know Your Limits

Law enforcement officers have long used Breathalyzer test devices to check the blood alcohol levels of drivers suspected of driving after indulging in too many drinks. Technology now gives you tools for testing and estimating your own blood alcohol level before you get behind the wheel of a car or other vehicle. For example, the Breathometer device connects to your smartphone. Connect the device, blow into it, and the free companion app provides a blood alcohol concentration result and relative level of intoxication. If needed, you can press a button to call a cab service for a safe ride home. Similar technology may one day be built into all new vehicles.

Cutting Edge

Autonomous Cars

For many of us, driving has become a necessary evil, getting us to and from our jobs, household errands, and other events. But the downsides can add up. Traffic jams. Expensive fuel. Accidents. All of these involve human expense and human error. In 2010, Google started a project to address the downsides of driving: the Self-Driving Car Project. The prototypes of the self-driving or autonomous cars use sensors, computing, and software to drive the cars in place of a steering wheel, accelerator pedal,

and brake pedal. Major auto companies have followed suit in developing self-driving vehicles, and assuming that these vehicles become legal to use in more states and that consumers truly want self-driving cars, we may see them on the roads by 2020.

To see a video of Google's self-driving car prototype, go to http://CUT6.emcp.net/SelfDrivingCar. As you watch the video, think about whether you would be comfortable traveling in this vehicle.

manage these assets. This type of setup helps reduce downtime by increasing the ability to predict needed maintenance, provide fuel savings and other efficiencies, and increase transportation reliability.

13.2 Printing and Displaying in 3-D

In the last few years, technological developments have accelerated surprisingly in certain parts of the computing industry, such as printing and displaying. Objects in the world occupy three dimensions: height, width, and depth. Until fairly recently, computer printers and displays (monitors) could depict images only in two dimensions: height and width. They simulated the third dimension via color changes and shading, much as an artist painting an apple uses shading to create the illusion of depth and dimension, simulating the apple's rounded shape.

3-D Printing

3-D printing has emerged as a practical technology. **3-D printing (3-DP)** or **additive manufacturing** refers to the ability to use printer-like technology to output three-dimensional objects using one of a variety of materials. Various 3-D printing methods have been in development since the 1980s. The first 3-D printer was created in 1984 by Chuck Hull of 3D Systems Corp. Predictably, the early 3-D printers were expensive and therefore not very widely used. However, over time, the processes and machines have evolved and become more mainstream, with entry-level 3-D printers priced at $500 or so, ranging up to $10,000 to $20,000-plus for professional-grade machines. 3-D printing can be used for rapid prototyping, mass customization, and a variety of hobbyist applications.

 Recheck 13.1

Recheck your understanding of the concepts covered by this objective.

 Precheck 13.2

Check your understanding of the concepts covered by this objective.

 **Activity 13.2.1**

Article
Uses for 3-D Printing

Just as a 2-D printer prints from a 2-D image (such as a JPEG or TIFF), a 3-D printer creates its output based on a 3-D image file (or 3-D model). Many of the programs used to produce 3-D files are CAD or CAD-like programs. An early patent pertaining to 3-D printing called the process *stereolithography*; hence, one of the most widely used 3-D file formats for 3-D printers uses the **.stl file name extension**. Software for creating 3-D models for printing ranges from the free, online 3DTin (by Lagoa) and the FreeCAD and Google SketchUp programs to commercial products such as AutoCAD (by Autodesk), Geomagic (by 3D Systems), SolidWorks 3D CAD programs (by SolidWorks), and ZBrush (by Pixologic).

After you create a 3-D file, you can send it to the printer. A 3-D printer includes robotic elements. As it lays down the material to create the 3-D object (usually by applying many thin layers), the platform or table where the object rests moves to control where the printer deposits the material. (In other words, the "print head" doesn't move as in an inkjet printer, only the "paper" moves.) The table also automatically lowers as the 3-D object becomes taller. You may see the movement directions referred to as the x, y, and z dimensions. Figure 13.6 illustrates the overall process for 3-D printing. In some cases, the object may require a bit of postprocessing, such as smoothing the surface or removing excess material. Each layer in a 3-D printed object can be as tiny as 100 microns, so it can take a little time to build an object—several hours to several days, but this may be much faster than it takes to build a unique item with other manufacturing processes, such as injection molding.

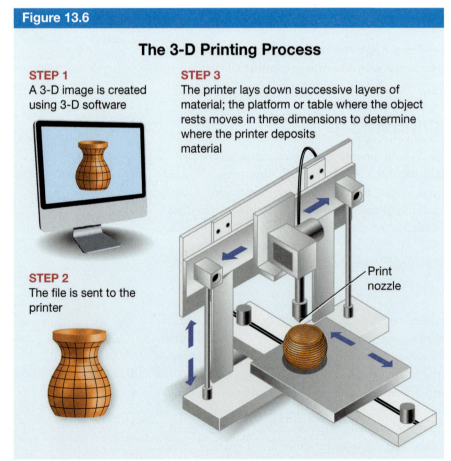

Figure 13.6

The 3-D Printing Process

STEP 1
A 3-D image is created using 3-D software

STEP 2
The file is sent to the printer

STEP 3
The printer lays down successive layers of material; the platform or table where the object rests moves in three dimensions to determine where the printer deposits material

Print nozzle

Most 3-D printers create an object by depositing many layers of material.

 **Activity 13.2.2**

Practice
The Steps for 3-D Printing

Different 3-D printers use different methods to deposit the material, and in some cases, the desired type of material for the object also determines what type of printer and method should be used. Table 13.1 describes various materials and methods for depositing the material in 3-D printing.

A variety of manufacturers offer 3-D printers. High-end industrial 3-D printers used for processes like rapid prototyping are made by companies such as Stratasys. Manufacturers of home- and hobbyist-level 3-D printers include MakerBot Industries and Ultimaker. 3D Systems offers a range of 3-D printers for production, professional, and personal use. You also can learn how to make your own 3-D printer at http://CUT6.emcp.net/RepRap3DPrinter. Home and hobbyist users can use 3-D printers to make decorative items and to make replacement parts and other useful items for the home. If you can't afford a 3-D printer, online 3-D printing services such as Shapeways and Ponoko can print your object and ship it to you.

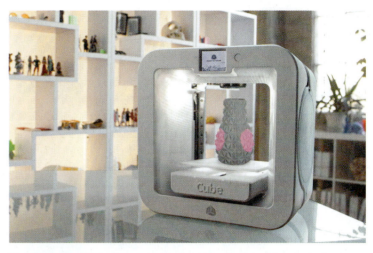

The Cube, by 3D Systems, is a 3-D printer designed for use in the home by anyone over the age of 8. Like most 3-D printers, it creates an object by depositing many layers of material—in this case, plastic. You can use the Cube to create unique, colorful items using your own designs.

Table 13.1 3-D Printing Methods and Materials

Method	Example Materials	Description
Extrusion or fused deposition modeling (FDM)	Plastics, metal (metal wire), edible materials (such as chocolate), modeling and precious metal clays	Material is applied via an extrusion nozzle; in some cases, the material starts out as a plastic or metal wire and is fed to the extrusion nozzle and melted for application. Patented in the late 1980s.
Granular or powder, also called *stereolithography* *(SLS)*	Thermoplastics, metal and titanium alloys, metal powders, ceramic powders, and plaster	The printer adds a layer of granules and fuses it to the previously applied layer. Invented in 1986.
Laminated	Paper, metal foils, thin plastic film	The printer cuts, applies, and fuses layers of the material.
Light polymer	Photopolymer (light-sensitive plastic)	The printer exposes specific areas of photopolymer stored in a vat to harden it in small increments, and then drains off the excess. Another method sprays the photopolymer and then light hardens it.

Hands On

Making a 3-D Design

You can use any of a number of free tools to create 3-D images and models. For example, you can sign up for a free account with Tinkercad or download the free Google SketchUp app. Or if you want to go directly to work, you can use 3DTin. This online tool is free as long as you share your designs via Creative Commons. 3DTin can save to the widely used STL and OBJ file formats. Follow the steps in this resource to try creating a 3-D file with 3DTin.

3-D Display

Science fiction TV shows and movies have long incorporated holograms as a futuristic way to project images. For example, in the original *Star Wars* movie, the robot R2-D2 projects a 3-D distress message in the form of a hologram of Princess Leia saying, "Help me, Obi-Wan Kenobi." In the decades since the release of that movie, holograms have moved from fiction to fact.

Early efforts to create 3-D effects for viewers (so that 2-D images appear to have depth as in the real world) involved special movie-filming techniques. The audience wore special glasses with one red lens and one blue lens to get the effect of depth beyond the plane of the screen or monsters and more leaping off the screen. 3-D TVs provide a more modern take on the technology, but still require the viewer to wear special (and not cheap) glasses to see the 3-D effect.

A hologram projects from a screen as a full 3-D image.

Now, the 3-D technology built into some display screens can provide a 3-D effect without requiring the viewer to wear special glasses. The Nintendo 3-DS portable gaming system, for example, includes a stereoscopic display that creates the 3-D effect. The user can drag a slider on the device to adjust the 3-D depth, and the device includes two lenses on the front for taking photos with the 3-D camera. Amazon's Fire smartphone also features a 3-D display, which uses multiple low-power cameras along with the software to create a 3-D effect.

Holograms take basic 3-D display effects a step further. Generally created by splitting laser light, a **hologram** appears as a full 3-D image, either still or in motion. The hologram may appear to float, or may be projected so it appears positioned on a surface. By late 2015, we should see hologram technology being built into the displays of some smartphones and tablets. Ostendo, a California company, has developed tiny 5,000 pixel per inch (ppi) projectors capable of creating holographic images. Six of the projectors can layer light to create the floating image. The microchip that makes this possible—the **Quantum Photonic Imager (QPI)**—contains micro LEDs, which makes it possible to layer light to create floating hologram images. The chip can control the color, brightness, and angle of each tiny light beam.

Tech Ethics

Projecting Real People

In May 2014, the Billboard Music Awards presented a holograph of deceased performer Michael Jackson dancing along with a group of live dancers. The team that put together the performance took six months to tweak the video and animation used for the holograph and prepare compatible choreography. The cost of the brief production reportedly was multiple millions of dollars. Hologram USA and Musion Das Hologram sued to block the display, claiming that their hologram technology was infringed, but a judge ruled against them. Similar technology was used to create a Tupac Shakur hologram at the 2012 Coachella Valley Music and Arts Festival.

Celebrities and others have enough concerns about privacy and use of their likenesses. What are the ethical implications of creating 3-D digital images and holograms of living and dead persons? If a hologram includes simulated content, who controls that aspect of the image? What other concerns do you envision arising from future use of this technology?

Otoy, a cloud graphics company, offers its Octane Render as standalone software or plug-ins for other software. Octane Render enables fast 3-D rendering for still images and video. Otoy also has introduced the world's first portable 360-degree holographic video capture system. Those captures can then be published as interactive videos viewable on some mobile devices and virtual reality headsets.

13.3 Pursuing Innovation through Special Project Labs

You might think that technology companies emphasize **research & development (R&D)**: the process of creating and commercializing new technologies and products for new markets. While most tech companies do have substantial R&D budgets, the need to conform to business factors such as limited budgets and sales targets can leave some product developers feeling stifled and less than creative.

To work around organizational constraints, some companies create a **skunkworks** operation, which is a more loosely organized team allowed to pursue extreme innovation—often operating not only outside the corporate rulebook but also in a separate location away from a main corporate campus. Lockheed Martin created its Skunk Works project during World War II, leading to the origin of the term. Hewlett-Packard and Apple, notably, have employed skunkworks teams, including the team that developed the original Macintosh computer.

A **special projects lab** is the modern take on a skunkworks operation. Typically larger and a bit more formal than a skunkworks, a special project lab occupies the forefront of R&D efforts for such companies as Alphabet Inc. (parent of Google and other divisions) and Facebook.

X

The self-driving car you read about in the section "Smart Technology in Transportation," on page 582, as well as Google Glass (an augmented reality head-mounted display), are examples of technologies emerging from the **X** (formerly Google X) lab division of Alphabet. Figure 13.7 shows a smart contact lens originally developed at X and now graduated for further development by Verily, Alphabet's life sciences division. It was designed to help people with diabetes monitor their blood glucose levels via

Recheck 13.2
Recheck your understanding of the concepts covered by this objective.

Precheck 13.3
Check your understanding of the concepts covered by this objective.

Figure 13.7

A Smart Contact Lens

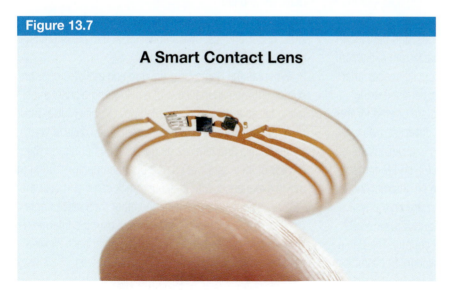

This smart contact lens will help diabetics monitor blood glucose levels.

a tiny monitoring sensor and a wireless chip. This lens may eventually include LED warning lights to alert the wearer about unsafe blood glucose levels. X's Project Loon has been working on a plan for using hot air balloons to provide Internet service to everyone, starting with people in remote areas.

X generally operates with a great deal of secrecy from a location off the main Alphabet campus. However, media such as *Re/code* and *Business Insider* frequently report news about X projects.

Other Labs

Other organizations may have a general special projects lab like X, or they may establish a more limited projects lab to tackle a particular goal. For example, in 2014, Facebook's CEO, Mark Zuckerberg, announced that the company's Connectivity Lab was working with Internet.org to use satellites and solar-powered high-altitude drones to bring Internet connections to areas lacking them—a goal very similar to that of X's Loon Project. Facebook also has a general research division investigating topics such as artificial intelligence.

Tech Career Explorer

Seeking a Job with Google

Many employers in the IT space follow quite rigorous hiring practices, but Google has the reputation of being one of the toughest. Its HR department uses various types of problem-solving questions to screen applicants before they can even move on to the interviewing process. To explore Google's hiring practices, complete this exercise.

Hotspot

Back to the Fifties

Drive-in movies were all the rage in the 1950s. The fresh air, the stars above, and Americans' infatuation with the automobile made the drive-in the place to be on a Saturday night. The first drive-in movie theater opened in 1933, and by 1958, more than 5,000 were operating across the United States. Then the lights started to dim on drive-ins. Daylight savings time was introduced in 1966, delaying show times too late for many families. The advent of air conditioning chased more viewers indoors, and the introduction of the VCR and cable TV gave drive-in theaters the final kick in the pants. Today, fewer than 500 drive-ins are left.

But nostalgia, high theater ticket prices, and new technology may bring the drive-in theater back from extinction. Renegade movie buffs are taking over public spaces after dark and offering the outdoor cinema experience using everyday digital equipment. The movies are offered for free, shown at ever-changing locations, and advertised via word of mouth and website. All that's needed is a DVD player or laptop with a DVD drive, a digital projector, an FM transmitter, and a large wall to show the film on. Instructions for converting an iPod to a radio transmitter are on the web.

The first guerilla drive-in began in Santa Cruz in 2002 but soon spawned copycats across the country. The Santa Cruz guerilla website, which gives detailed instructions

to fellow drive-in aficionados, claims that finding a dark spot in today's ubiquitously lit world is the hardest part. The site also reminds wannabes without large car batteries to bring

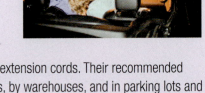

yards and yards of extension cords. Their recommended sites: under bridges, by warehouses, and in parking lots and even fields (bring a sheet).

Whereas the Santa Cruz drive-in and affiliates offer an outdoor movie experience with a pillow and blanket substituting for an automobile, the MobMov (Mobile Movie) movement emphasizes the car component. As in days of yore, lovers cuddle and families gather for togetherness in the privacy of their cars, yet as part of a community sharing the movie experience, with the soundtrack coming in over the FM car radio. Like flashmobs and other mob movements, word of MobMov showtimes is spread over the Internet. The shows occur in random locations, and after each movie, everyone disappears as quickly as they arrived.

Joining the rush to push technological limits, Microsoft's Research division announced its own Special Projects Group in 2014. Rather than focus on pushing the limits of software and other computing technology specifically, this group planned to take the lead on "disruptive" next-generation technologies—those intended to benefit both the creating company and society. The Microsoft Research (MSR) division has already developed applications for see-through 3-D display technology.

With three powerful "horses" and more running in the special project lab race, we will certainly see many ground-breaking developments in the next decade or two.

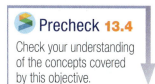

Recheck 13.3
Recheck your understanding of the concepts covered by this objective.

13.4 Pushing the Limits with Artificial Intelligence

Precheck 13.4
Check your understanding of the concepts covered by this objective.

In the nineteenth century, American writer Edgar Allan Poe exposed an elaborate hoax: a supposed chess-playing machine that had a small man concealed within it. Poe was outraged by the idea that a machine could exhibit a "spiritual" quality like intelligence and confidently predicted that no real chess-playing machine would ever be built. But time proved Poe wrong. In the summer of 1997, a supercomputer built by IBM and named Deep Blue defeated the world champion chess player Garry Kasparov. Chess programs good enough to beat the average player are today available for use on personal computers.

Are today's chess-playing programs and the machines on which they run intelligent? Can any machine properly be called "intelligent"?

These are deep and hotly debated questions. Over half a century ago, the brilliant English mathematician Alan Turing proposed a procedure for answering such questions. Turing called his procedure the *Imitation Game*, but today it's widely known as the *Turing Test*. Here's what Turing suggested: Imagine two rooms, one containing a computer and one containing a human being. Outside these rooms sits a person who asks questions (perhaps by typing them at a keyboard) that are answered by the computer and by the human being. The questioner attempts to determine which respondent is a person and which is a machine. If the questioner can't tell the difference, the Turing Test states, then the computer must be considered intelligent. So far, no computer has passed this test—not even in our age of supercomputers and sophisticated programs. Futurists predict, however, that by 2030, computers will be able to meet the Turing standard.

The **artificial intelligence (AI)** computing field has fueled the continual effort to create faster and more powerful machines. The goal of AI is to develop computers that can perform functions normally reserved for humans: thinking, talking, seeing, feeling, walking, and learning from their mistakes.

AI Technology Trends

Current AI development trends toward limited, focused applications. Rather than attempting to perform the broad range of tasks humans can perform, modern AI systems focus on simulating specialized human functions. Instead of focusing on replacing human capabilities, those in the AI field

Tech Ethics

Is It OK to Turn Decision Making Over to Machines?

From *2001: A Space Odyssey* to the *Terminator* and *Matrix* movie series, the science fiction movie industry has provided many examples of computers taking over, with fearful results for humans. Both the *Terminator* and and *Matrix* series predicted that intelligent machines would turn on humans, with much of the planet devastated by machine-human war. In the film *Ex Machina*, an AI robot kills her creator and traps a friendly programmer when she escapes to enter human society. Can you identify any real-world instances of computer intelligence being beneficial, such as the ability for the Siri feature in iPhones or Cortana in Windows 10 to provide information in response to questions? Are automation and other forms of computerized decision making and activity beneficial for humans, or things to be concerned about?

Figure 13.8

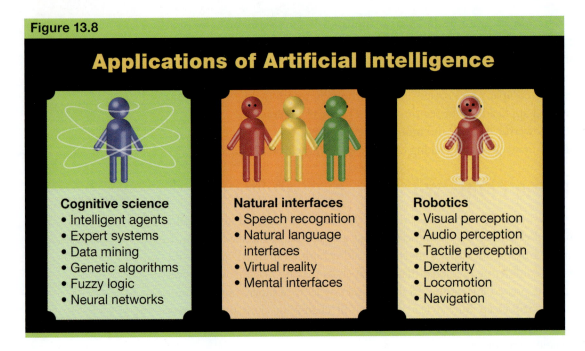

Applications of Artificial Intelligence

Cognitive science
- Intelligent agents
- Expert systems
- Data mining
- Genetic algorithms
- Fuzzy logic
- Neural networks

Natural interfaces
- Speech recognition
- Natural language interfaces
- Virtual reality
- Mental interfaces

Robotics
- Visual perception
- Audio perception
- Tactile perception
- Dexterity
- Locomotion
- Navigation

work on technologies and tools for augmenting human capabilities. Figure 13.8 illustrates the three primary areas of artificial intelligence applications: cognitive science, natural interfaces, and robotics.

Cognitive Science Applications

Cognitive science is the study and simulation of the human mind, and is the area most commonly thought of when considering AI. Based on biology, neurology, psychology, and other disciplines, it focuses on researching how the human brain thinks and learns. Major types of applications in this area are intelligent agents, expert systems, data mining, genetic algorithms, fuzzy logic, neural networks, and machine learning.

Intelligent Agents The use of an **intelligent agent** (sometimes called a *software robot*, or *bot*) is increasing in popularity. This technology provides an intuitive assistant (agent) that can utilize knowledge based on past experience and predictions of likely future behavior. The intelligent agent can then use that knowledge to assist computer users.

Agents have the general goal of reducing a difficult task to a few simple mouse clicks that can be completed quickly. The best-known agents are the wizards found in Microsoft Office products. They aid users by advising them of the different options available for performing tasks, and by taking them step by step through the process.

Expert Systems Another common and easy-to-understand AI application is the expert system. As you learned in Chapter 10, an expert system attempts to embody human expertise in a particular field, such as law or medicine. Because the expert system might encompass the knowledge of an entire group of experts, the software theoretically "knows" more than any single luminary about a specific topic. Most expert systems work by questioning the user and then drawing a conclusion from the information provided. If the computer is given enough information, it can sometimes offer several possible solutions to a problem. Since an expert system can be easily copied and distributed, the knowledge it possesses can be made widely available.

Recognized authorities in a specific field of study develop expert systems with the help of a **knowledge engineer**: a programmer who specializes in building knowledge bases, each consisting of a set of rules that the computer will try to prove or disprove by asking a battery of questions. An **inference engine** enables the expert system to draw deductions from the rules in the knowledge base in response to user input.

Data Mining   Data mining, which is discussed in detail in Chapter 12, is considered a relatively new application of artificial intelligence. Recall that the core idea of data mining is to find new patterns in the masses of data stored in corporate databases and other large collections of data, such as Facebook posts. When viewed as a mountain of market research that has already been gathered and paid for, a large database has untapped value. Rather than going out and paying for a survey to see if a new product might sell to a given customer demographic, why not sort through the existing data to see how those customers reacted to similar products in the past?

Bank of America (BofA) and other large financial institutions, for example, use data mining to provide more carefully targeted marketing and pricing of financial products, such as home loans. By sifting through masses of existing data concerning customer-purchasing patterns, a bank can determine with good accuracy whether a new offering will succeed or fail. What's more, a bank can use the system to generate winning combinations for a given demographic, with the added benefit of knowing exactly whom to sell the financial products to, reducing the marketing costs as well as increasing the sales rate.

Genetic Algorithms   Using a **genetic algorithm** to solve design problems represents a new application of an old process. The idea is to apply a Darwinian (survival-of-the-fittest) method to problem solving. This technology uses a computer to create thousands or even millions of slightly varied designs, and then tests and selects the best of them. This ensures, for example, the best solution to the curvature of a jetliner wing, the structure of a walking robot, and almost any other design task.

The best of these programs have evolved to another generation, where more random variations (called **mutations**) are made. For further enhancement, this selection process uses a **crossover**, which means the most successful mutations are mixed to produce a new generation of "offspring."

For example, in the case of designing a walking robot, the system might start out with a very simple design—perhaps only three connected blocks with the ability to flex the connections. Applying thousands of slight variations to this structure will produce different results, but some will be better than others. The most successful designs will be chosen for new mutations, producing crossovers by mixing together the traits of

Cutting Edge

Sensors, Sensors, Sensors

The growing use of sensors, chips, and RFID to gather and transmit information continues to be a technology trend. In a world that will soon have billions of sensors, massive computing intelligence will be required to make sense of all the data. The effort pays off, because all this data and sensor information can be used to make everyday life more productive and safe. For example, after the I-35W St. Anthony Falls Bridge in Minneapolis collapsed due to maintenance issues, resulting in the death of 13 people, efforts were made to enhance the safety and efficiency of the bridge during rebuilding. The new bridge features more than 300 sensors that monitor corrosion, stress, and bridge movement. They also monitor weather conditions and trigger an anti-icing system when needed. The resulting data, monitored by engineers, supplements visual inspections for improved maintenance and safety.

The design for a walking robot is an example of an applied genetic algorithm.

the "survivors." With each new generation of robots, only the best walkers will survive. After several generations, robots resembling crabs, worms, and insects will begin to appear. Developers have been able to use this approach to quickly simulate thousands of years of evolution, saving countless hours of failed design effort.

Interestingly, the use of a genetic algorithm frequently produces solutions to problems that programmers hadn't anticipated. This technology is now being applied to business problems as an aid in business model decision making. New business plans can be devised through trial-and-error investment modeling.

Fuzzy Logic   The oddly named fuzzy logic branch of AI attempts to model human reasoning by allowing for approximations and incomplete input data. Instead of demanding precise yes/no or numerical information, a **fuzzy logic system** allows users to input "fuzzy" data. The terminology the system uses is deliberately vague: *very probable, somewhat decreased, reasonable,* or *very slight.* This vagueness is an attempt to simulate real-world conditions, where precise answers are hard to come by. A fuzzy logic system attempts to work more naturally with the user by piecing together an answer in a manner similar to what a traditional expert system does. Fuzzy logic SQL database queries seem significantly more human than traditional queries, as illustrated in Table 13.2.

Table 13.2 Comparison of Traditional SQL Query and the Equivalent Fuzzy Logic Query

Traditional SQL	Fuzzy Logic SQL
Select * From Customer Where Customer.PurchaseTotal > $100,000 and Customer.Collections = False and Customer.Profit >= $10,000	Select * From Customer Where PurchaseTotal is high to very high and Collections are reasonable and Profits are good to very high

Neural Networks A **neural network** simulates the physical workings of the human mind, and presents the ultimate attempt to model human intelligence. While the human brain has in excess of 100 trillion neural connections, a computer-based neural simulation is much smaller. Today's largest neural network systems are composed of 11 billion or more neural connections. They operate in much the same way as a human brain. A neural network generally starts off with only an input source, some form of output, and a goal. The system will learn by trial and error how a desired output affects the input. For example, consider calculating how much pressure should be applied to brakes to stop a car. The input is the pressure on the brake, the output is the deceleration rate of the vehicle, and the goal is to stop the car. Using this test and feedback system allows the neural network to learn how to stop a car.

One benefit of neural networks is their simplicity; most have very few options once they are set up. The most important option is the "gain," which controls the change rate of the firing threshold of the neurons. This in turn controls how quickly the system will learn or unlearn something.

Machine Learning The term **machine learning** refers to an AI system that can learn from data. For example, the IBM Watson supercomputer uses machine learning to improve its performance in games of *Jeopardy!* played against humans. A system using machine learning learns via representation, or evaluating similar instances that occur in known data. It then applies that learned information to make generalizations when confronted with new data. In other words, a machine "learns" by taking what it identifies in prior data and applying that information to future data.

Natural Interface Applications

Another major area of artificial intelligence has the goal of creating more of a **natural interface** between humans and machines. Currently, computer users are restricted, in most instances, to using a mouse, keyboard, or touchscreen for input. For output, they must gaze at a fairly static, two-dimensional screen. Speakers output sound, and a printer outputs hard copy. The user interface consists of typing, pointing, clicking, and tapping. Improving speech recognition and natural language technologies promise to change that soon.

Speech Recognition One of the most immediately applicable interface improvements comes in the area of speech recognition. Rather than typing information into a PC or tapping the screen of a mobile device, users can direct the computer with voice commands. Having a computer that can take dictation and perform requested actions is a real step forward in convenience and potential.

Speech recognition technology developed rather slowly at first, mainly because the typical PC didn't have the necessary speed and capacity until recently. Microsoft Windows contains speech recognition capabilities, and requires a microphone, sound card, and speedy system (measured in gigahertz, GHz) to operate.

The Siri voice recognition system, introduced in the iPhone 4s, enables the user to ask search questions and request that Siri complete tasks. For example, you can ask Siri to "Set an alarm for 6 a.m.," and the phone will do so. A Siri-enabled iPhone also enables the user to dictate text messages and other types of content, rather than inputting it via touchscreen. More and more PCs and devices include speech and voice recognition technologies of all types. Many in-car control systems also include voice recognition for such tasks as using the navigation system, using the entertainment system, and making hands-free calls via a smartphone connected via Bluetooth.

Natural Language Interfaces It would certainly be helpful if computers were able to communicate using spoken English or Japanese, or any of the hundreds of other languages currently in use around the world. It's almost certain that in the not too distant future, computers will be able to read, write, speak, and understand many human languages. Language translators already exist, and they are getting better all the time. For example, Facebook can translate posts from one language to another on demand. Programmers are also looking forward to a human language–computer interface. With a better interface, programmers will be able to describe what they want using natural (human) language, rather than writing programs in the highly structured, restrictive, and rather alien programming languages in use today.

Cutting Edge

I'll Take AI for $1,000

In a controversial match in 1997, Deep Blue beat chess champion Garry Kasparov. What was Deep Blue? An IBM-designed supercomputer. Deep Blue sparked worldwide attention and discussion about the capabilities of artificial intelligence (AI). That computer was eventually dismantled, but IBM's research in AI continued and it developed Watson: the game-playing supercomputer designed to play and win *Jeopardy!* against humans. In 2011, Watson took on and beat two of the most successful players in the history of the TV game show.

Watson employs natural language–processing techniques to better understand the nuances of human speech. Traditionally, getting computers to understand human language required manually manipulating the speech to make it comprehensible to the computer's algorithms. Watson, however, processes and responds to information more like a human does and even learns as it goes. As described by former IBM CEO Samuel J. Palmisano, "The essence of making decisions is recognizing patterns in vast amounts of data, sorting through choices and options, and responding quickly and accurately."

When Watson receives a *Jeopardy!*-style question, it breaks the information in the question into smaller parts and searches its databases for answers, which it then pieces back together to form a response. While searching databases is a relatively easy function for a computer, the programming challenge is in getting the computer to understand exactly what to search for. As you may recall,

Jeopardy!'s cleverly worded questions often contain double entendres, analogies, puns, and other tricky language.

Watson's success in besting its *Jeopardy!* competitors encouraged IBM to explore meaningful uses for the supercomputer's capabilities. Now, IBM enables organizations in the healthcare, finance, and retail fields—as well as governments and researchers—to take advantage of Watson's capabilities. For example, Memorial Sloan Kettering Cancer Center has a project to use Watson to help with cancer treatment planning. Not only is Watson being trained to accept and interpret physicians' notes and dictation so it can find gaps in the information gathered about a patient, but it is also "learning" to compare the patient's data with a vast amount of previous data about other patients to suggest treatment options. This and other projects using Watson could make a dramatic impact on daunting human problems.

A **natural language interface** is an area of AI that's broader in scope than simple speech recognition. The goal is to have a machine that can read a set of news articles on any topic, and *understand* what it has read. Ideally, the machine will be able to write its own report summarizing what it's learned. In **natural language processing (NLP)**, a person might interact with a computer by either speaking or typing sentences. One type of intelligent agent that uses AI is a **chatbot** or chatterbot. This type of computer program simulates intelligent conversation with the user via either spoken or typed inputs and responses (see Figure 13.9).

Virtual Reality

The term *virtual reality (VR)* describes the concept of creating a realistic world within a computer. Massively multiplayer online (MMO) games, which have thousands of interacting players, are growing a great deal in popularity. In these games, people take on personas and move about virtual landscapes, adventuring and chatting with other players. People become friends, are "virtually" married, and in a sense have entire virtual lives in a game world.

The quality of a virtual reality system is characterized in terms of its **immersiveness**, which measures how real the simulated world feels, and how well it can make users accept it as their own and forget about reality. With each passing year, systems are able to provide increasing levels of immersiveness. Called by some the "ultimate in escapism," VR is becoming increasingly common—and increasingly real. For example, the Oculus Rift virtual reality headset by Oculus VR (now owned by Facebook)

Hands On

Using Natural Language with a Chatbot

Some of today's chatbots let you chat for fun and games. Others serve in online help and technical support roles. For example, the Toshiba France customer support website chatbot Yoko responds immediately to user questions 24 hours a day—in French, of course. Follow the steps in this resource to chat with a little guy named Elbot.

Activity 13.4.1

Article
Haptics

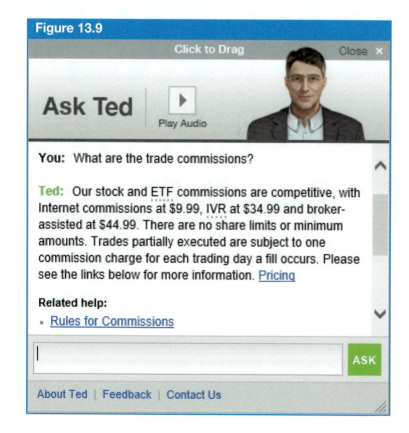

Figure 13.9

Click to Drag   **Close** ✕

Ask Ted   ▶
Play Audio

You: What are the trade commissions?

Ted: Our stock and ETF commissions are competitive, with Internet commissions at $9.99, IVR at $34.99 and broker-assisted at $44.99. There are no share limits or minimum amounts. Trades partially executed are subject to one commission charge for each trading day a fill occurs. Please see the links below for more information. Pricing

Related help:
- Rules for Commissions

[   ]   **ASK**

About Ted | Feedback | Contact Us

The Ted chatbot on the TD Ameritrade website can provide written and audio feedback in response to basic questions that you type in using regular, natural sentences.

features its own tracking technology, so that when you move your head, the virtual world you see looks natural. This system overcomes the latency—or lag in the displayed image versus, in this case, how quickly the wearer's head turns. The stereoscopic headset gives each eye a separate yet parallel image, much like our eyes function normally. Video game developers are working to create or adapt content for the Rift, and future possibilities include using it to view other types of enhanced video content.

Mental Interfaces Some interfaces take things a bit further than VR, and they don't even require the user to click a mouse, speak a word, or tap a finger. A **mental interface** uses sensors mounted around the skull to read the different types of waves or power spectrums the brain gives off, also called *electroencephalogram (EEG)* activity. Thinking of the color blue might be used to move a mouse pointer to the right, or thinking of the number 7 might move it to the left. The computer measures brain activity and interprets it as a command, eliminating the need to physically manipulate the mouse to move the screen pointer. This technology has obvious applications for assisting people with disabilities, and military researchers are using it to produce a superior form of interface for pilots.

Another company, NeuroSky, has developed portable EEG biosensors that translate brain activity for interacting with education and entertainment programs for adults and kids. Its products use brainwave algorithms to digitize analog electrical brainwaves, and then amplify and process those brain signals into device input. For example, its MindWave Mobile device, which is compatible with a number of other portable devices, includes a headset, an ear clip, and a sensor arm with an EEG electrode that rests on the forehead. You can purchase the device bundled with a number of apps such as an archery game, brainwave visualizer, meditation journal, and tutorial.

A virtual reality system is often evaluated by its immersiveness, or the realness of the simulated environment.

This headset from NeuroSky reads brainwave activity, digitizes it, and uses it to work with compatible apps such as a brainwave visualizer.

Robots as Androids

The science of **robotics**—creating machines capable of independent movement and action—has a place in robotic factories. Such factories are becoming increasingly common, especially in heavy manufacturing, where tolerance of repetitive movements, great strength, and untiring precision are more important than flexibility. Robots are especially useful in hazardous work, such as defusing bombs and handling radioactive materials. They also excel in constructing tiny components, such as those found inside notebook computers, which are often too small for humans to assemble.

Some people think of a robot as it is portrayed in science fiction, which generally depicts it as an **android**, or simulated human. Real robots don't look human at all, and judged by human standards, they also aren't very intelligent. The task of creating a humanlike body has proved incredibly difficult. Many technological advances in visual perception, audio perception, tactile perception, dexterity, locomotion, and navigation need to occur before robots that look and act like human beings could "live" and work among us.

 **Activity 13.4.2**

Article
Drone Revolution

Visual Perception **Visual perception** is an area of great complexity. A large percentage of the human brain is dedicated to processing data coming from the eyes. As our most powerful sense, sight is the primary means through which most of us understand the world around us.

A single camera isn't good enough to simulate an eye. Two cameras are needed to provide **stereoscopic vision**, which allows perception of depth and movement. Even with two cameras, visual perception also involves *understanding* what the cameras are seeing. Processing the image is the most difficult part. For a robot to move through a room full of furniture, it must build a mental map of that room, complete with obstacles. The robot must judge the sizes of objects and the distances between them before it can figure out how to move around them.

Building a mental map of a room is just the tip of the iceberg in visual perception. How will a computer learn to recognize a single human face among thousands of faces, or recognize an emotional state portrayed on a human face? How will a robot read road signs that are flashing by a moving vehicle?

Although considerable work must still be done to solve all these problems, rapid strides are being made in many areas. For instance, in Las Vegas, computers analyze the faces of

Robots are particularly useful in heavy manufacturing environments requiring repetitive movements, great strength, and untiring precision.

patrons as they enter casinos and attempt to match their faces with those of known cheaters. Increasingly, airports are adopting computerized facial recognition (CFR) systems to protect against terrorism. And recently, X organized 1,000 computers with 16,000 computing cores into an AI system, and then let the system evaluate 10 million YouTube video stills to learn how to identify cat faces in the images.

Audio Perception **Audio perception** is less complex than visual perception, but no less important. People respond to audible cues about their surroundings and the people they are with without even thinking about them. Listeners can determine someone's emotional state just by hearing the person's voice. A car starting up when someone crosses the street prompts the walker to glance in that direction to check for danger.

Identifying a single voice and interpreting what's being said amid accompanying background noise is among the most important tasks for human beings—and the most difficult. Imagine the confusion of a computer program trying to do this in a noisy classroom, where several students and an instructor are all talking at once. Which set of sounds will it listen to? How will it pick out the correct voice to obey? Programmers and technology still have a long way to go before computers will be able to handle problems like this—problems that are easily handled by humans, even when they are only a few years old.

Cutting Edge

"We Can Rebuild Him, We Have the Technology"

If you've ever heard the intro for an episode of the popular mid-1970s TV series *The Six Million Dollar Man* (clips are available on YouTube), you'll recognize the title of this Cutting Edge as a quote from that narrative. The series followed Steve Austin, an astronaut who suffered catastrophic injuries during an experimental aircraft crash. His handlers rebuilt him with bionic implants for his right arm, legs, and left eye. His bionics enabled him to run at 60 mph, lift heavy equipment, and zoom his sight 20 times or use infrared vision. For this reason, fans often called the series and the character "The Bionic Man." Steve Austin's subsequent exploits as a secret agent for the OSI (Office of Scientific Intelligence) made the series popular, even with viewers who weren't normally sci-fi buffs.

Science fiction aside, for nearly all of human history, some people have needed prosthetic limbs. For centuries, limb replacements usually consisted of crude wooden replicas. Early prosthetics changes involved minor improvements, such as split-hook grips and the SACH (Solid Ankle, Cushion Heel) foot from the 1950s, which offered greater stability. Improvements also included mechanical articulated joints, and changes in socket designs. Some limbs began to offer control via cables attached to muscles elsewhere on the body. Eventually, electrodes attached to existing muscles could use the electrical signals from the muscle to power the limb. Another version of this approach—targeted muscle reinnervation (TMR)—requires surgery to move severed nerves to muscles elsewhere that can then control the limb via their electrical signals.

Still, the limbs themselves needed more development, especially in replicating complex joint and muscle activity or the biomechanics of walking or using your arm. In the 1990s, the first lower limbs with microprocessor controlled knees became available. This advancement ushered in the era of robotic or bionic replacement limbs. These limbs include more than just articulation and control technology. Modern bionic limbs have actuators (motors) and energy sources, as well as embedded computers (processors) and sensors. This means the limbs can not only produce the muscle power needed to result in a real-world walking gait or hand grip, but also adjust stiffness as needed to respond to varying conditions.

In addition to making improvements in limb function and power, researchers continue to work on improving the user's control of the artificial limb. Researchers continue to explore building in true neural interfaces, so the user can use mind rather than muscle to control the limb.

Many recent war veterans and survivors of the Boston Marathon bombing in 2013 have been fitted with this sort of bionic limb technology. And the advances go beyond that. Other researchers have developed an exoskeleton or "wearable robot" than can help some paralyzed persons walk. Just think: in only about 40 years, robotics has evolved far enough to transform bionics from a pop culture sci-fi fantasy to a reality helping people achieve a better quality of life after a difficult loss.

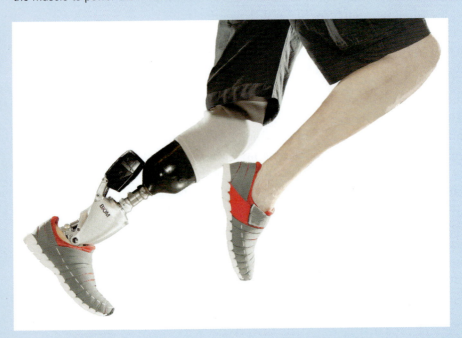

The commercially available BiOM Ankle System includes embedded computers and sensors. BiOM calls itself a Personal Bionics company.

Tactile Perception **Tactile perception**, or touch, is another critical sense. A robot can be built with any level of strength, since it's made of steel and motors. How does a robot capable of lifting a car pick up an egg in the dark without dropping it or crushing it? The answer is by having a sense of touch. The robot must not only be able to feel an object, but also be able to sense how much pressure it's applying to the object. With this feedback, it can properly judge how hard to squeeze. Tactile perception is a very difficult area, and it may prove that simulating the human hand is even more difficult than simulating the human mind.

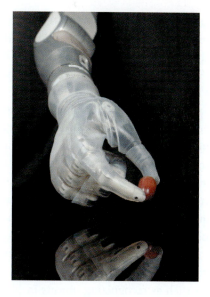

To pick up a delicate object like a grape without crushing it, a robotic hand must be equipped with tactile perception—that is, the ability to both feel the object and sense how much pressure it is applying to the object.

Related to the sense of touch is the skill of **dexterity**, or hand-eye coordination. The challenge is to create a robot that can perform small actions, such as soldering tiny joints and placing a chip at the precise spot in a circuit board, within half a millimeter.

Locomotion **Locomotion** includes broad movements, such as walking. Getting a robot to move around isn't easy. This area of science presents challenges, as locomotion requires maintaining balance within an endlessly changing set of variables. How does the program adjust for walking up a hill or down a set of stairs? What if the wind is blowing hard or a foot slips?

Currently, most mobile robots work with wheels or treads, which limits their mobility in some circumstances, but makes them much easier to control. However, newer robots, such as Raptor (by the Korea Advanced Institute of Science and Technology, or KAIST) and WildCat (by Boston Dynamics, now owned by X), running robots travel quickly on multiple legs in a motion that simulates an animal's stride.

Navigation Related to perception, **navigation** deals with the science of moving a mobile robot through an environment. Navigation isn't an isolated area of AI; it must work closely with a visual system or some other kind of perception system. Sonar, radar, mechanical "feelers," and other perception systems have been tried in experiments.

A robot can also plot a course to a location using an internal map created by a navigational perception system. If the course is blocked or too difficult, the robot must be smart enough to backtrack so that it can try another route.

 Recheck 13.4

Recheck your understanding of the concepts covered by this objective.

13.5 Moving Forward with Quantum Computing and More

 Precheck 13.5

Check your understanding of the concepts covered by this objective.

The technology march continues, as researchers seek new approaches and new materials to tackle ever more complex problems in business and society. This last section previews technologies you will hear more about in the coming years.

Quantum Computing

Quantum computing represents the next wave of computing technology beyond supercomputers. Rather than being based on binary on/off states, like a prior digital computer, a **quantum computer** operates based on many superpositions of states. Rather than evaluating on/off bits, a quantum computer evaluates **qubits** (short for *quantum bits*), which can represent on/off as well as a number of other probable superpositions of those states. A quantum computer manipulates qubit states via quantum logic gates, as dictated by a quantum algorithm (or pattern for the gates).

Because some level of probability factors into how a quantum computer operates, it can only provide a solution within known probabilities, as opposed to an absolute correct or incorrect solution. In other words, while a digital computer based on binary operation provides yes/no outcomes by nature, a quantum computer provides for many more possibilities in between.

According to D-Wave Systems, a maker of commercial quantum computing hardware and software, quantum computing has applications for the most complex problems being tackled today. For example, D-Wave's systems can be used to simulate protein folding to better understand biological challenges and aid in drug development. Quantum computing can also be used for advanced machine learning, and to automate complex tasks such as recognizing objects in photos to tag them for an archive or cataloging news articles by title.

Operating a quantum computer presents some challenges. For example, a D-Wave system must run at cold temperatures (near absolute zero). According to the company's website, the latest system is "cooled to 150x colder than interstellar space." In addition, it operates in a vacuum and uses magnetic shield protection.

In late 2013, Google launched its Quantum Computing Artificial Intelligence Lab (QuAIL), using D-Wave equipment and technical assistance from NASA. The Google-NASA partnership hopes to use its quantum computer to solve complex problems relating to space flight and optimization challenges, such as air traffic control.

Activity 13.5.1

Article
Shor's Algorithm

Quantum computers use qubit processors, like this 512-qubit chip shown in a D-Wave system. D-Wave quantum computers require cold operating temperatures, as well as a vacuum and magnetic shielding.

New Approaches to Computer Architecture

In addition to quantum computing, other new approaches to computer design may lead to significant increases in computing capabilities:

- **More cores.** Beyond today's top-end CPUs with 6 or 8 cores, researchers are exploring processor designs including 36 cores, each with its own router. Such processors will function as a "network on a chip," eliminating the bottleneck of having a single bus to transmit calculated data from the various cores.

- **The Machine, by HP.** This new concept for computing takes its name from the fact that it encompasses being a server, workstation, PC, tablet, and phone. It will use specialized processor cores that transmit data via photonics, rather than wires. It will also include a new type of resistor called a *memristor*, capable of retaining data even without power. The machine will be superfast and much more energy efficient than current computing technologies.

- **Neurosynaptic computing.** **Neurosynaptic computing** (also called *cognitive computing*) aims to mimic the functioning of the human brain via greater interconnectivity among memory, processors, and communications. IBM Research has developed new neurosynaptic chips, along with a programming language capable of exploiting the chip capabilities. The language includes a library of corelets addressing particular functions. While not yet released, neurosynaptic chips will nearly approach the speed and power efficiency of the human brain. IBM plans to invest up to $3 billion in quantum and neurosynaptic computing.

- **Hybrid memory cube.** This developing RAM technology uses 70 percent less energy and moves data up to 15 times faster than current DDR3 DRAM technology. A hybrid memory cube layers vertical stacks of dynamic RAM on a logic (control) layer. Through-silicon-via (TSV) interconnects provide the communications links between the layers.

Activity 13.5.2

Article
**Keeping Up
with New Tech
through Certification**

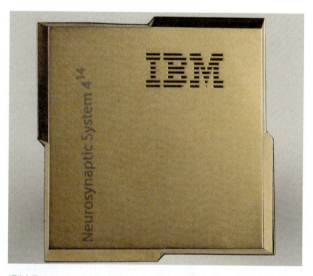

IBM Research has developed neurosynaptic chips, which will nearly approach the speed and power efficiency of the human brain.

Cutting Edge

Quantum Cryptography

A security technology called *quantum cryptography* has yet to be placed in wide use due to technical challenges. (The current method requires a dark fiber or private fiber connection and is limited to a distance of 100 km.) This technology requires fiber-optic transmission of the encryption key. The photons of data transmitted over fiber optic may have multiple states, including polarity—the direction in which the photons vibrate. The companion decryption key with "entangled" matches for each photon only works if the decryption key has not been "disturbed" by someone trying to intercept or eavesdrop on it. This is because according to theory, any eavesdropping will change the state of paired photons in the decryption key, causing the two keys not to match. Japanese researchers have proposed an alternative method of sending a phase-modulated photon signal that is split into two signals with a random delay at the receiving end. The split signals then can be superimposed and decoded as photons. The recipient can ask the sender to confirm the pulse numbers. Research in this field continues.

New Technology Materials

Sometimes, the materials involved in creating new technologies can drive innovations as much as the designs themselves. Many exciting materials await us on the technology horizon:

- **Nanotechnology.** Creating material at the atomic or molecular level, the concern or activity of nanotechnology, means we will have the ability to create increasingly smaller devices and components over time. In the future, it may be possible to create processors using carbon **nanotubes**, or nanoscale tubes—in this case, made of carbon molecules. More compact processors could operate much faster and conserve power. Carbon nanotube processors in a supercomputer such as Watson, for example, could consume 1,000 times less power.

- **Graphene. Graphene** is essentially a sheet of graphite that's one atom thick. It's harder than a diamond and can conduct electricity 1,000 times better than copper, which is commonly used in computer wiring. While graphene has just recently been isolated as a substance, its possible future applications include making more dense and fast integrated circuits, and reinforcing plastics while also enabling them to conduct electricity.

- **Liquidmetal and sapphire glass.** Liquidmetal is really an amorphous metal alloy, also known as a *bulk metallic glass (BMG)*. Unlike other metals, which have a regular crystalline atomic structure (leading to the possibility of fractures and weaknesses), Liquidmetal's amorphous (irregular) structure eliminates grains and other weaknesses. And unlike other metals, which must be milled, Liquidmetal can be injection molded into a variety of complex shapes. Sapphire glass isn't glass at all, but is instead sapphire mineral "grown" in a furnace in a block called a *boule* that can then be sliced using a diamond saw or laser. If a saw is used it must be a diamond saw because diamond is the only material harder than sapphire. Sapphire glass is an incredibly hard and scratch-resistant material. Sapphire glass may therefore be instrumental in creating more compact mobile devices. The iPhone 5s, 6, and 6 Plus models use sapphire glass on features such as the Touch ID home button, and two Apple Watch models will have sapphire display and sensor covers.

Self-healing materials are made of a fiber composite substance that can remix and repolymerize, thus healing surface scratches.

- **Self-healing materials.** These materials go beyond being scratchproof. They can crack, but when the type of fiber composite substance they are composed of breaks, it breaks apart further, so some of its compounds can remix and repolymerize, thus healing the material. Some smartphones, such as the LG G Flex, already feature a coating of this self-healing material, so any scratches to the case quickly fix themselves.

Recheck 13.5

Recheck your understanding of the concepts covered by this objective.

Chapter Summary

An interactive **Chapter Summary**, **Study Notes**, and a **Slide Presentation** with audio are available from the links menu on this page in your ebook.

13.1 Making Old Tech New

Convergence occurs when two technologies come together to make something new. Computing and communications technologies have been converging with the technologies from other industries to make old tech new. For example, in the electric power industry, the **Smart Grid** involves using computing and communications technologies to upgrade and replace aging parts of the power transmission grid, resulting in new capabilities (such as the ability to reroute power around outages). **Smart meters** also enable two-way communications with customer sites to enhance monitoring and provide more data to customers. In the medical field, smart medical devices use sensors to gather data from contact with the patient's skin. Many can communicate data wirelessly to a PC or the cloud.

The term **mHealth** refers to the use of various mobile devices to enhance patient monitoring and healthcare. Some of these devices also work directly with platforms such as Microsoft's HealthVault and hospital-scale ecosystems. Other smart medical devices include implantable sensors, digital stethoscopes, and surgical robots. Finally, in the transportation industry, sensors, computing, and communications are being used to optimize fuel consumption and increase safety and reliability. Now, even jet engines and locomotive engines may use such technology.

13.2 Printing and Displaying in 3-D

3-D printing (3-DP) or **additive manufacturing** refers to the ability to use printer-like technology to output three-dimensional objects using any of a variety of materials. The user sends a 3-D design file to the printer, which deposits layers of material on a moveable platform or table to build the object. Many 3-D printers accept files using the **.stl file name extension**. 3-D printers use a variety of methods to deposit the material, including extrusion, granular, laminated, and light polymer. Materials for 3-D printing include plastics, metal, precious metal clays, and more. Generally created

by splitting laser light, a **hologram** appears as a 3-D image, either still or motion. Technology such as the **Quantum Photonic Imager (QPI)** microchip, which has micro LEDs, will enable handheld and other devices to display holograms.

13.3 Pursuing Innovation through Special Project Labs

Research & development (R&D) involves the process of creating and commercializing new technologies and products for new markets. A **skunkworks** team operates outside the normal rules that can constrain R&D, so the team can pursue extreme innovations. **Special project labs** are modern skunkworks operations. **X**, the Alphabet special projects lab, has been developing a self-driving car and a blood glucose-monitoring contact lens. Facebook and Microsoft have also established special projects labs.

13.4 Pushing the Limits with Artificial Intelligence

Artificial intelligence (AI) is a field of computer science that focuses on creating machines that think, or that can at least perform tasks traditionally associated only with human beings. There are three major branches of artificial intelligence, each with different goals: cognitive science, natural interface, and robotics.

Cognitive science focuses on imitating human thought and learning. AI systems that play chess, for example, fall into this category. An **intelligent agent** provides a helping hand when learning applications or performing complicated steps. A **genetic algorithm** uses an evolutionary process to design a physical object. A **fuzzy logic system** (more popular overseas than in the United States) allows making inferences from less than complete data. A **neural network** straightforwardly attempts to model the physical behavior of the human brain. **Machine learning** comprises an AI system that can learn from data.

A major area of AI application involves the creation of a more **natural interface** between human and machine. Speech recognition trades in the mouse and keyboard for a microphone and speakers, allowing the user to talk to the machine directly. The quality of a virtual reality system is characterized in terms of its **immersiveness**, which measures how real the simulated world feels, and how well it can make users accept it as their own and forget about reality. A **mental interface** is experimental, and actually allows a user to control a computer through thought alone.

Robotics involves the creation of computers that can move and act autonomously. Robotics is perhaps the most difficult area of AI, as it requires the combination of software and physics working in harmony. Getting a computer to understand what it sees (**visual perception**) and hears (**audio perception**) to interpret what's going on in the world around it involves very advanced fields of research.

In general, it's much easier to program a computer to play chess than it is to teach it **locomotion** tricks (such as walking on two legs).

13.5 Moving Forward with Quantum Computing and More

A **quantum computer** operates based on many superpositions of states. Rather than function according to on/off bits, a quantum computer evaluates **qubits** (quantum bits), which can represent on/off as well as a number of other probable superpositions of those states. Emerging technologies include CPUs with more cores, computing technology that uses photonics rather than wires, and **neurosynaptic computing**. New materials, such as **nanotubes** and graphene, also may lead to leaps in computing capabilities.

Key Terms

Numbers indicate the pages where terms are first cited with their full definition in the chapter. An alphabetized list of key terms with definitions is included in the end-of-book glossary.

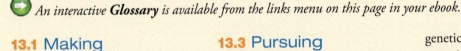 *An interactive **Glossary** is available from the links menu on this page in your ebook.*

Chapter Exercises

Complete the following exercises to assess your understanding of the material covered in this chapter.

 Interactive **Flash Cards** *and an interactive* **Game** *are available from the links menu on this page in your ebook.*

 Go to your SNAP Assignments page to complete the Terms Check, Knowledge Check, Key Principles, and Tech Illustrated exercises.

Terms Check: Matching

Match each term with its definition.

a. additive manufacturing
b. X
c. mHealth
d. quantum computer
e. android
f. convergence
g. Smart Grid
h. hologram
i. machine learning
j. neural network

__ 1. A special projects lab.
__ 2. A 3-D image created by splitting laser light.
__ 3. Describes a process where an AI system learns from data.
__ 4. A simulated human.
__ 5. Simulates the physical workings of the human mind.
__ 6. Device representing the next wave of computing technology beyond supercomputers.
__ 7. Refers to the use of various mobile devices to enhance patient monitoring and healthcare.
__ 8. Refers to the technology being added to the electric grid to bring it into the twenty-first century.
__ 9. Occurs when different technologies and industries merge to form a newer, better product or process.
__ 10. The use of printer-like technology to output 3-D objects.

Knowledge Check: Multiple Choice

Choose the best answer for each question.

1. Which of the following is *not* a benefit of the Smart Grid?
   a. less consumer control
   b. faster recovery from outages
   c. increased security
   d. more efficient electric power production and transmission

2. Which file name extension represents a 3-D file format?
   a. .jpg
   b. .gif
   c. .stl
   d. .tiff

3. Which of the following is *not* a primary area of artificial intelligence?
    a. cognitive science
    b. natural interfaces
    c. quantum cryptography
    d. robotics

4. Which technology uses a computer to create thousands, even millions, of slightly varied designs, and then tests and selects the best of them?
    a. data mining
    b. fuzzy logic
    c. genetic algorithm
    d. robotic engineering

5. Which technology attempts to model human reasoning by allowing for approximations and incomplete input data?
    a. data mining
    b. fuzzy logic
    c. genetic algorithm
    d. robotic engineering

6. Which technology will allow a computer to read a news article and then write a report summarizing it?
    a. fuzzy logic system
    b. natural language interface
    c. neural network
    d. speech recognition

7. Which describes the concept of creating a realistic world within the computer?
    a. fuzzy logic system
    b. inference engine
    c. neural network
    d. virtual reality

8. To develop a human-like robot with a sense of touch, technological advancement have to occur in what area?
    a. locomotion
    b. navigation
    c. tactile perception
    d. visual perception

9. Which material would create processors that are faster and conserve power?
    a. carbon nanotubes
    b. graphene
    c. Liquidmetal
    d. sapphire glass

10. Which material would create mobile device parts that are incredibly hard and scratch resistant?
    a. carbon nanotubes
    b. graphene
    c. Liquidmetal
    d. sapphire glass

Key Principles: Completion

Complete each statement with the appropriate word or phrase.

1. A _____ is the modern take on a skunkworks operation.

2. The goal of artificial intelligence is to develop computers that can perform functions normally reserved for _____.

3. _____ science is the study and simulation of the human mind.

4. The quality of a virtual reality system is characterized in terms of its _____.

5. For a robot to simulate human eyes, two cameras are needed to give the robot _____ vision.

6. A programmer who specializes in building knowledge bases, each of which consists of a set of rules that the computer will try to prove or disprove by asking a battery of questions, is called a _____.

7. _____ uses voice commands to direct a computer or device.

8. Hand–eye coordination is referred to as the skill of _____.

9. A quantum computer evaluates _____.

10. _____ computing aims to mimic the functioning of the human brain.

Tech Illustrated: Figure Labeling

Fill in the blanks with the correct labels.

1. 3-D printing methods and materials

Method	Example Materials	Description
a. _____	Plastics, metal (metal wire), edible materials (such as chocolate), modeling and precious metal clays	Material is applied via an extrusion nozzle; in some cases, the material starts out as a plastic or metal wire and is fed to the extrusion nozzle and melted for application. Patented in the late 1980s.
b. _____	Thermoplastics, metal and titanium alloys, metal powders, ceramic powders, and plaster	The printer adds a layer of granules and fuses it to the previously applied layer. Invented in 1986.
c. _____	Paper, metal foils, thin plastic film	The printer cuts, applies, and fuses layers of the material.
d. _____	Photopolymer (light-sensitive plastic)	The printer exposes specific areas of photopolymer stored in a vat to harden it in small increments, and then drains off the excess. Another method sprays the photopolymer and then light hardens it.

2. Three primary areas of artificial intelligence
   For each area of artificial intelligence, list two examples.

Cognitive science

a. _____

b. _____

Natural interfaces

c. _____

d. _____

Robotics

e. _____

f. _____

Tech to Come: Brainstorming New Uses

In groups or individually, contemplate the following questions and develop as many answers as you can.

1. Animals learn behaviors by getting positive reinforcement and rewards, such as dog treats. Some researchers are using animals as models to build machine-learning algorithms. The researchers are hoping robots and devices such as smartphones can learn in a similar manner. How might this technology improve the capabilities of a smartphone? What repetitive tasks might it eliminate, saving the smartphone user from having to perform them over and over again?

2. This chapter discusses different methods and materials that can be used in 3-D printing. Researchers around the world are experimenting with the potential of this technology. For example, in China and Holland, entire houses have been built with 3-D printing, and in England, the first 3-D hamburger was printed. Think about the potential of this technology, and list possible future applications for it. How will consumers benefit from 3-D printing technology?

Tech Literacy: Internet Research and Writing

Conduct Internet research to find the information described, and then develop appropriate written responses based on your research. Be sure to document your sources using the MLA format. (See Chapter 1, Tech Literacy: Internet Research and Writing, page 38, to review MLA style guidelines.)

1. Research the Smart Grid further. What impacts might it have on your life? On a larger scale, use statistics to indicate the impact the Smart Grid could have on the United States and its environment.

2. Healthcare is a field where technology has had significant effects on day-to-day operations. Document how technological developments affect day-to-day operations. How have these developments affected operating costs and employees?

3. Technology has impacted the field of transportation in several positive ways, including improving safety, reducing harmful environmental effects, and improving travel times. Research and summarize how technology has impacted the field of transportation. Include statistics in your report.

4. A lot of exciting developments are centered around 3-D display technology. Research 3-D display technology, and describe products and technology options currently on the market as well as products in development. Include visuals and product prices in your report.

5. This chapter discussed artificial intelligence technology trends. Research breakthroughs in artificial intelligence and describe at least three recent breakthroughs. Reflect on the impact the breakthrough technology will have.

Tech Issues: Team Problem-Solving

In groups, develop possible solutions to the issues presented.

1. Quantum computers are projected to be the next wave of computing technology beyond supercomputers. However, issues and challenges are associated with operating these computers. Research the issues and challenges associated with quantum computers, and then discuss possible solutions. When do you predict this technology will be available?

2. This chapter discusses new materials, such as graphene and Liquidmetal, that will be used in computers and devices of the future. There is a strong consumer demand for new technology, but what will happen to all the old technology? How should old technology, some of which is still usable, be recycled or disposed of?

Tech Timeline: Predicting Next Steps

Artificial intelligence and multimedia are two evolving technologies that will continue to change the way we work with computers. A major area of advancement that both applications affect is the nature of the computer interface. To date, multimedia has played a bigger role in interface changes than has AI, but AI will be an even bigger player in the near future. Add to the timeline below, which lists developments in multimedia and artificial intelligence, some predictions for the future.

1984 Apple introduces the MacIntosh computer with a graphic user interface (GUI) and a mouse.

1990 Microsoft releases Windows 3.0, and this significantly increases the use of a mouse as opposed to a keyboard to select commands.

1993 The World Wide Web brings multimedia to every Internet-connected PC.

1995 The US Marine Corps requests a modification of the popular computer game *Doom* for military training purposes.

1997 IBM's Deep Blue supercomputer beats chess champion Garry Kasparov.

2001 Microsoft releases early speech recognition technology in its Office products.

2002 The US Transportation Security Administration (TSA) tests facial recognition software at airports to identify potential terrorists.

2003 Chess master Garry Kasparov plays a game against IBM's Deep Junior computer that ends in a tie.

2005 A Japanese student is arrested for developing "bots" that beat up online gaming characters and steal their goods.

2006 A robotic lizard pet named Pleo is released; it interacts with its environment through touch, motion, sight, and sound.

2009 Using a robotically controlled tactile sensing device, doctors can detect cancer tissue more accurately and conduct examinations and surgery less invasively.

2009 In a *Jeopardy!* challenge, IBM's Watson computer defeats its human opponents.

2011 Apple introduces a smartphone app called *Siri* that uses natural language to answer questions, make recommendations, and perform actions.

2014 Microsoft develops Project Adam, a new system for machine learning and artificial intelligence that's able to identify different breeds of dogs.

2016 The National Highway Traffic Safety Administration says that the artificial intelligence system developed for the Google Self-Driving Car Project will be interpreted as a driver by federal regulations.

Ethical Dilemmas: Group Discussion and Debate

As a class or within an assigned group, discuss the following ethical dilemma.

In 2013, an estimated 1.2 million robots were working worldwide. Many of these robots have replaced humans in performing jobs. As technology progresses, what will the workforce of the future look like? Research jobs that are predicted to be replaced by robots and then discuss these questions:

- What does the use of robots mean for the workforce of the future?

- Do companies have a responsibility to retrain workers for different jobs if they are being replaced by robots?
- Would you trust a robot with tasks such as filling your prescription or driving you to an appointment?
- Are some tasks better suited to robots than humans?

Acronyms and Abbreviations

Acronym or Abbreviation	Meaning	Page
1000BaseT	1,000 Mbps twisted-pair cable	270
3-DP	3-D printing	583
3G	3rd generation	250
4G	4th generation	250
4GL	fourth-generation language	496
AAC	Advanced Audio Coding	223
AC	alternating current	55
ACH	automated clearinghouse	479
AI	artificial intelligence	589
ALU	arithmetic logic unit	62
app	application	138
ASCII	American Standard Code for Information Interchange	54
ASP	Active Server Pages	518
AUP	acceptable use policy	414
B2B	business-to-business	452
B2C	business-to-consumer	453
BASIC	Beginner's All-purpose Symbolic Instruction Code	513
BD	Blu-ray disc	124
BdaaS	Big data as a Service	565
BI	business intelligence	437
BIOS	basic input/output system	94
bit	binary digit	53
bot	robot	590
BSOD	Blue Screen of Death	347
CAD	computer-aided design	161
CAM	computer-aided manufacturing	437
CASE	computer-aided software engineering	510
Cat5	category 5	245
CBT	computer-based training	158
CCD	charge-coupled device	47
CD	compact disc	124
CDA	CD audio	163
CFR	computerized facial recognition	384
CGI	computer-generated imagery	161
CIM	computer-integrated manufacturing	438
CIPA	Children's Internet Protection Act	413
COBOL	COmmon Business-Oriented Language	512

Acronym or Abbreviation	Meaning	Page
COM	communications; commercial; Component Object Model	60; 199; 514
COPPA	Children's Online Privacy Protection Act	398
CPU	central processing unit	61
CRM	customer relationship management	438
CRT	cathode ray tube	69
CSMA/CD	carrier sense multiple access with collision detection	261
CSP	cloud service provider	289
CSS	cascading style sheets	202
DAS	direct-attached storage	126
DBA	database administrator	557
DBMS	database management system	148
DC	direct current	55
DDR	double data rate	67
DHTML	Dynamic HTML	516
DIMM	dual inline memory module	67
distro	distribution	105
DM	direct message	217
DMCA	Digital Millennium Copyright Act	230
DoS	denial of service	369
dpi	dots per inch	48
DRAM	dynamic RAM	66
DRM	digital rights management	409
DSL	digital subscriber line	193
DSS	decision support system	435
DVD	digital versatile disc	124
DVI	digital visual interface	59
ebook	electronic book	224
e-commerce	electronic commerce	452
EDI	electronic data interchange	478
EDP	electronic data processing	435
EEG	electroencephalogram	596
EEPROM	electrically erasable programmable ROM	68
EFT	electronic funds transfer	469
EIS	executive information system	437
email	electronic mail	169
EMI	electromagnetic interference	245

Acronym or Abbreviation	Meaning	Page
EPOS	electronic point of sale	431
EPROM	erasable programmable ROM	68
ERP	enterprise resource planning	440
eSATA	external Serial ATA	58
ESD	electrostatic discharge	337
e-signature	electronic signature	480
ESRB	Entertainment Software Ratings Board	168
e-tailer	electronic retailer	453
EULA	End User License Agreement	141
FAT	file allocation table	120
fax	facsimile	79
FEDI	financial electronic data interchange	479
FLAC	Free Lossless Audio Codec	223
FORTRAN	FORmula TRANslator	513
FTP	File Transfer Protocol	220
Gbps	gigabit per second	191
GIGO	garbage in, garbage out	7
GPS	global positioning system	52
GPU	graphics processing unit	72
GUI	graphical user interface	99
GUID	global universal identification	396
HaaS	Hardware as a Service	565
HDD	hard disk drive	119
HDMI	High-definition multimedia interface	59
HDP	Bluetooth Health Device Profile	580
HTML	Hypertext Markup Language	202
HTTP	Hypertext Transfer Protocol	269
HTTPS	Hypertext Transfer Protocol Secure	386
Hz	hertz	72
IaaS	Infrastructure as a Service	316
IANA	Internet Assigned Numbers Authority	270
IEEE	Institute of Electrical and Electronics Engineers	247
IM	instant messaging	216
IMAP	Internet Message Access Protocol	269
IP	Internet Protocol	198
IP	Internet Protocol	270
IrDA	Infrared Data Association	253
IS	information system	430
ISP	Internet service provider	189
IT	information technology	3

Acronym or Abbreviation	Meaning	Page
IXP	Internet exchange point	189
JIT	just-in-time	477
JSP	JavaServer Pages	518
JVM	Java virtual machine	514
Kbps	kilobit per second	191
K-slot	Kensington security slot	333
LAN	local area network	256
LCD	liquid crystal display	70
lm	lumen	73
LMS	learning management system	188
LPT	line printer	60
Mac	Macintosh	104
MAC	media access control	267
MAN	metropolitan area network	257
Mbps	megabit per second	191
m-commerce	mobile commerce	452
MFD	multifunction device	79
MFT	master file table	120
MIDI	Musical Instrument Digital Interface	163
MIS	management information system	435
MOOC	massive open online course	227
MOV	metal oxide variable	332
MP3	Moving Pictures Expert Group Layer III	223
MPEG	Moving Picture Experts Group	223
NAS	network-attached storage	126
NAT	network address translation	270
net	Internet; network	10; 229
NIC	network interface card	267
NLP	natural language processing	595
NSP	network service provider	189
NTFS	New Technology File System	120
OCR	optical character recognition	48
OIS	office information system	434
OLAP	online analytical processing	437
OLE	object linking and embedding	152
OLTP	online transactional processing	556
OOP	object-oriented programming	504
OS	operating system	94
OSI	Open Systems Interconnection	268
P2P	peer-to-peer	221
PaaS	Platform as a Service	316

Acronym or Abbreviation	Meaning	Page
PAN	personal area network	255
PATA	parallel ATA	121
PC	personal computer	28
PCIe	Peripheral Component Interconnect Express	57
Perl	Practical extraction and report language	515
PHP	PHP: Hypertext Preprocessor	518
piezo	piezoelectric	76
PIM	personal information management	153
PM	private message	217
PMPO	peak momentary performance output	74
POP	point of presence	189
POP3	Post Office Protocol 3	269
POS	point of sale	431
POST	power-on self-test	98
ppm	pages per minute	76
QA	quality assurance	493
QBE	Query by Example	543
QPI	Quantum Photonic Imager	586
QR	quick response	473
qubit	quantum bit	600
R&D	research & development	587
RAD	rapid application development	504
RAID	redundant array of inexpensive disks	127
RAM	random access memory	17
RAM	random-access memory	65
RFID	radio frequency identification	434
RFP	request for proposal	443
RJ	registered jack	59
RMS	root mean squared	74
ROM	read-only memory	65
RPG	Report Program Generator	513
RSA	Rivest, Shamir, and Adleman	386
SaaS	Software as a Service	315
SAN	storage area network	126
SATA	serial ATA	121
SCM	supply chain management	476
SDLC	system development life cycle; software development life cycle	442; 492
SDR	single data rate	67
SDRAM	synchronous dynamic RAM	67

Acronym or Abbreviation	Meaning	Page
S-HTTP	Secure HTTP	387
SMBs	small and midsize businesses	296
SMTP	Simple Mail Transfer Protocol	269
SOC	system-on-chip	107
SOP	standard operating procedure	435
SQC	statistical quality control	438
SQL	Structured Query Language	542
SRAM	static RAM	66
SSD	solid-state drive	115
SSHD	solid-state hard drive	121
SSI	server-side include	518
SSL	Secure Sockets Layer	386
STL	stereolithography	584
STP	shielded twisted-pair	245
T line	telephone line	246
TCP	Transmission Control Protocol	270
TCP/IP	Transmission Control Protocol / Internet Protocol	270
TLD	top-level domain	198
TLS	Transport Layer Security	386
TOS	trusted operating system	480
UPC	universal product code	48
UPS	uninterruptible power supply	332
URL	uniform resource locator	198
USB	universal serial bus	58
UTP	unshielded twisted-pair	245
VaaS	Visualization as a Service	566
VAN	value-added network	190
VB	Visual Basic	513
VGA	video graphics adapter	59
VoIP	Voice over Internet Protocol	221
VPN	virtual private network	257
VR	virtual reality	226
WAN	wide area network	257
web	World Wide Web	187
WIPO	World Intellectual Property Organization	406
WMA	Windows Media Audio	223
WMV	Windows Media Video	223
WYSIWYG	what you see is what you get	165
XHTML	eXtensible HTML	517
XML	eXtensible Markup Language	203

Glossary and Index

Image Credits

Chapter 1

Page 1 © Creativa/Shutterstock.com; *2* Courtesy of Whirlpool Corporation (left), © Zeljkodan/Shutterstock.com (right); *4* Used with permission from Belkin, International, Inc.; *5* Used with permission from Intel Corporation (top), © Bettmann/Corbis (bottom); *7* © iStock.com/Cristi Matei; *8* © iStock.com/JackF (top), Courtesy of the National Human Genome Research Institute (bottom); *9* Courtesy of Sandisk Corporation; *11* Reproduced with permission from Yahoo. ©2014Yahoo. YAHOO! and the YAHOO! logo are registered trademarks of Yahoo.; *12* Google and the Google logo are registered trademarks of Google Inc., used with permission; *17* Courtesy of ASUSTek Computers Inc.; *18* © tele52/Shutterstock.com, © Popcic/Shutterstock.com, © Nata-Lia/Shutterstock.com, © AlinaMD/Shutterstock.com (top), © iStock.com/greg801 (bottom); *19* © dny3d/Shutterstock.com (top), Used with permission from Microsoft (bottom); *20* Courtesy of Apple Inc. (top, bottom); *23* Courtesy of Spectrum Brands Holdings, Inc., Courtesy of Whirlpool Corporation, Used with permission from Belkin, International, Inc., Courtesy of iSmart Alarm, Inc., Courtesy of Honeywell International, Inc., Courtesy of TCP International Holdings, Courtesy of Garageio (top to bottom); *24* Used with permission from Apple Inc.; *25* Used with permission from Vandrico Solutions; *26* © TATSIANAMA/Shutterstock.com; *28* © Oleksiy Mark/Shutterstock.com; *29* © iStock.com/MichaelDeLeon; *30* © Can Stock Photo Inc./AndreyPopov (top), © iStock.com/GodfriedEdelman (bottom); *31* Courtesy of International Business Machines Corporation. Jon Simon/Feature Photo Service for IBM; *32* Courtesy of Oak Ridge National Laboratory, U.S. Department of Energy.

Chapter 2

41 © asharkyu/Shutterstock.com; *44* Used with permission from Microsoft (top), © Pressmaster/Shutterstock.com (bottom); *45* © ivelly/Shutterstock.com (right), © Mau Horng/Shutterstock.com (top), © Olga Popova/Shutterstock.com (bottom); *46* © goldyg/Shutterstock.com (left), © Valeriy Lebedev/Shutterstock.com (right); *48* © Mile Atanasov/Shutterstock.com (top), © mrkob/Shutterstock.com (bottom); *50* © Oleksiy Mark/Shutterstock.com (left), © Portfolio/Shutterstock.com (center), © Volodymyr Krasyuk/Shutterstock.com (right), © Maridav / Shutterstock (bottom); *51* © wavebreakmedia/Shutterstock.com (top), © chungking/Shutterstock.com (bottom); *52* © Maxx-Studio/Shutterstock.com; *56* Courtesy of ASUSTek Computers, Inc.; *57* Courtesy of PCMCIA/Expresscard and the Rabbit symbol are trademarks of PCMCIA (top), © ASUSTek Computers (left), © Bastiaan va den Berg/Creative Commons Wikipedia (right); *58* © tatajantra/Shutterstock.com (top), © Dragana Gerasimoski/Shutterstock.com; *60* © John Kasawa/Shutterstock.com; *61* © jelome/Shutterstock.com; *65* © Andrea Danti/Shutterstock.com; *67* © Julio Embun/Shutterstock.com; *68* © Jianghaistudio/Shutterstock.com; *70* © pryzmat/Shutterstock.com (left), © cobalt88/Shutterstock.com (right); *72* © Olena Zaskochenko/Shutterstock.com; *73* Used with permission from Microsoft; *74* QiLux/Shutterstock.com; *75* © Dja65/Shutterstock.com; *76* © photosync/Shutterstock.com; *77* © Tomislav Pinter/Shutterstock.com; *78* © Piotr Adamowicz/Shutterstock.com; *79* © Singkham/Shutterstock.com; *80* © Hewlett-Packard Company (top), © Newell Rubbermaid Inc. (middle), Courtesy of Apple Inc. (bottom); *81* © Creativa/Shutterstock.com; *88* Courtesy of ASUSTek Computers, Inc. (bottom).

Chapter 3

93 © Watchara Rojjanasain/123RF; *94* © Syda Productions/Shutterstock.com; *98* Used with permission from Microsoft; *99* Used with permission from Microsoft; *100* Used with permission from Microsoft; *101* Courtesy of Apple Inc.; *102* Used with permission from Microsoft; *103* Used with permission from Microsoft; *104* iMac®, iTunes®, and iPhoto® are registered trademarks of Apple Inc.; *105* Used with permission from the Linux Foundation; *106* Google and the Google logo are registered trademarks of Google Inc., used with permission; *107* iPad®, Facetime®, and iTunes® are registered trademarks of Apple Inc. (top), Google and the Google logo are registered trademarks of Google Inc., used with permission (bottom); *108* Used with permission from Microsoft (top), Courtesy of International Business Machines Corporation (bottom); *109* Courtesy of Symantec Corporation; *116* Used with permission from Microsoft (top, bottom); *117* Used with permission from Microsoft; *122* Used with permission from Microsoft; *126* © Can Stock Photo Inc./Scanrail (top), © Can Stock Photo Inc./Vlucadp (bottom).

Chapter 4

137 © Alexander Kirch/123RF; *140* Used with permission from Microsoft (left, right); *144* Used with permission from Microsoft; *145* Used with permission from Microsoft; *146* Adobe product screenshot reprinted with permission from Adobe Systems Incorporated; *147* Used with permission from Microsoft; *149* Used with permission from Microsoft (top, bottom); *150* © Peter Bernik/Shutterstock.com; *151* Used with permission from Microsoft; *153* Used with permission

Chapter 5

Chapter 6

Chapter 7

Chapter 8